North Carolina Illustrated, 1524–1984

H. G. Jones

North Carolina Illustrated
1524–1984

The University of North Carolina Press

Chapel Hill / London

Copyright © 1983 The North Caroliniana Society

All rights reserved

Set in Galliard by G & S Typesetters and the

University of North Carolina Press

Designed by Richard Hendel, Laura Dunne,

and Melissa Polier

Manufactured in the United States of America by

Kingsport Press

Library of Congress Cataloging in Publication Data
Jones, H. G. (Houston Gwynne), 1924–
   North Carolina illustrated, 1524–1984.

   Includes index.
   1. North Carolina—History—Pictorial works.
2. North Carolina—Description and travel—Views.
I. Title.
F255.J77 1983 975.6 83-6958
ISBN 0-8078-1567-5

In memory of
Christopher Crittenden (1902–1969)
David Leroy Corbitt (1895–1967)
Elizabeth Wall Wilborn (1917–1974)
C. Frederick W. Coker (1933–1983)
and in honor of
the members of the staffs of the
State Department of Archives
and History (1956–1974) and the
North Carolina Collection (1974–1984)
who shared my mission to preserve,
promote, and teach the history
of our state

Contents

Preface

The visual record of North Carolina lurks in places near and faraway, some of it unseen, some of it unrecognized, much of it seen and recognized by a few historians but never reproduced for the education and enjoyment of my fellow citizens at Kill Quick, Locust Hill, and Rabbit Shuffle. I have had these Caswell County neighbors in mind during the past eleven years as I viewed hundreds of thousands of illustrations depicting the 460-year documented history of my state. This book is for them.

A career in North Caroliniana has convinced me that a state, like an individual, develops over the centuries a unique character—a sort of collective soul—that can be seen, felt, and understood by its citizens. To be a North Carolinian is not simply to live in North Carolina; it is to *feel* like a North Carolinian—one who is conscious of the struggles of many generations against the twin obstacles of humble beginnings and modest resources. To a taunt that the state lags in a particular measurement, a North Carolinian is likely to respond, "You're right, but we are working on it." This absence of defensiveness is a trait ingrained in North Carolinians who appeal for fairness: "Judge us not so much on where we are as on how far we have traveled to get here."

This collective soul, of course, is not static. Historians from Hugh Williamson to William Powell have narratively captured much of the changing character of North Carolina, and pictorial works on several institutions and localities have given graphic dress to their words. Yet why is it that until now no one has undertaken an illustrated volume covering the entire sweep of North Carolina history? I will answer that question presently.

In one sense, *North Carolina Illustrated, 1524–1984* had its beginning more than a decade ago when I was engaged by another publisher to prepare a different type of pictorial history. That project was jettisoned in the sea of coffee-table picture books that accompanied the commemoration of the bicentennial of the American Revolution, but I recognized then that the job had to be completed. In another sense, the germ of this book

was that day nearly a half century ago when a youngster from a tenant farm, riding in a 1926 Dodge and carrying the bloody severed head of a dog, peered through the window and saw the stately capitol of North Carolina—the symbol of my native state. Even the dreaded confirmation by the State Board of Health that the dog was indeed infected by rabies failed to obliterate from my mind the drama of that first sighting of the domed building on Union Square. During each of the next twenty-one days I watched and listened in horror as my father—we were too poor to hire a doctor—injected into my older brother's swollen belly a monstrous vial of fluid designed to counteract the otherwise fatal effect of the mad dog's bite. Somehow, I could not bring myself to regret that forced trip to Raleigh. Nor could I anticipate that years later the "Old Gray Lady" would come to have an even more intimate meaning for me—that the state capitol would be framed by the window of my office in the Department of Archives and History and that I would persuade a governor and legislature to provide funds for the restoration of the structure so that other youngsters might be inspired by it.

My hunt for the hidden visual record of North Carolina has been in some respects an odyssey. The search started among the hundreds of thousands of photographs and negatives in the State Archives, then branched out to repositories and private collections in North Carolina and other states. Upon taking charge of the North Carolina Collection in 1974, I began leafing through thousands of books and pamphlets, long runs of newspapers and journals, and rich clipping files. Xerographic copies and photographic prints accumulated by inches, then feet. Through friends and finding aids, I searched foreign sources, and it is with some pride that I call attention to illustrations made in, obtained from, or otherwise related to Australia, Bermuda, Canada, China, East Germany, England, France, Iran, Italy, Japan, Scotland, Spain, Switzerland, and the Vatican—and one from space. Included are handwriting by Verrazzano and Annie Oakley, drawings by O. Henry and Dwight Eisenhower, paintings by John Trumbull and Charles Willson Peale, photographs by Mathew Brady and the Wright brothers, a map by Kosciuszko, and illustrative materials by hundreds of lesser-known persons.

This is not a book of portraits of famous men; there are enough of those. Nor is it a book of lovely pictures, for history is seldom pretty, and North Carolina has never been a mecca for artists and photographers. Still, the state's bountiful pictorial record has been only meagerly utilized, for historians have tended to reproduce over and over a tiny portion of the available illustrative documentation. In each painful round of eliminations (from 10,000 to 1,600, then to 1,200, and finally to 1,158), I have had several aims in what I retained: first, to portray North Carolina's past in its great variety; second, to use period illustrations where possible; third, to introduce into the literature many pictures that have previously appeared not at all or only in publications of limited distribution; fourth, to compensate partially for state histories written in the "great men" tradition; and, finally, to key the illustrations and captions to ten interpretive essays tracing the development of the distinctive behavior of North Carolinians that exemplifies the state's collective character. (In the process, I have identified and eliminated several images that have been attributed mistakenly to North Carolina in widely disseminated publications.) Colleagues questioning why I did not include their favorite scenes may have the answer for the cost of lunch—or perhaps a cup of coffee. At the same time I can explain why in chapter 10 I did not follow my own advice as set forth in my essay in *Writing North Carolina History*, edited by Jeffrey J. Crow and Larry E. Tise.

Help came from many sources: Queen Elizabeth II allowed me to reproduce two of her original Catesby prints; Anthony Quinton, president of Trinity College, Oxford, personally brought the Hariot picture to the United States; Toni Seiler, director of the Garst Museum in Ohio, lent an autographed picture of Annie Oakley; Irving Wallace of Los Angeles dug into his archives and furnished the fascinating photograph of the original Siamese twins and seventeen of their twenty-one children; Frances Griffin of Old Salem guided me through the complicated permissions required from several repositories, including one behind the Iron Curtain; Eric P. Newman of St. Louis shared a number of his colonial money bills, heretofore unpublished in North Carolina; Samuel M.

Holton of Chapel Hill, Zeb R. Denny of Roanoke Rapids, and others dug into family possessions to locate rare pictures of North Carolinians who should not be forgotten; Charlesanna Fox of Randolph and officials of other county historical societies helped track down interesting scenes; Janet Seapker of the New Hanover County Museum, William J. Moore of the Greensboro Historical Museum, and officials of other historical agencies, like Mattie Russell and William E. King at Duke and Carolyn A. Wallace and Richard A. Shrader of the Southern Historical Collection, opened their rich holdings; heads of other state historical organizations, such as James C. Kelly of Tennessee and Louis L. Tucker of Massachusetts, cooperated fully; the splendid holdings of the Library of Congress and of the National Archives were opened to me by Annette Melville and Jim Trimble, respectively; newspaper librarians Barbara Semonche of the *Durham Herald-Sun*, Fran Kelly of the *Charlotte Observer*, Robbin Hyde of the *News and Observer*, R. L. Beall of the *Greensboro Daily News*, and Lucile Kearn of the *Asheville Citizen-Times* supplied modern photographs; and famed Tar Heel photographers like Hugh Morton, Bruce Roberts, Ken Cooke, and Bill East generously provided prints.

In all, about two hundred repositories and individuals furnished pictures that survived repeated cullings and are reproduced in *North Carolina Illustrated, 1524–1984*; their help is usually credited in the captions. Several persons, however, must be recognized for their very special roles in the making of the book. First, there is David Wilborn Zehmer, who a decade ago reviewed thousands of photographs in the State Archives and furnished a selection of copies, many of which survived successive screenings. Second, there are Jesse R. Lankford, Jr., iconographic archivist, who has brought order out of the huge and valuable photographic collection in the State Archives, and photographer Walton W. Haywood and his associates, who provided hundreds of prints during the busiest season of the year. Other members of the Archives and History staff who provided assistance include Robert J. Cain, Jerry C. Cashion, Stephen Massengill, George Stevenson, Keith Strawn, and Robert M. Topkins. Then there are Jerry W. Cotten, photographic archivist, and photographer L. C. Scarborough, who performed similar services in the North Carolina Collection. Linda B. Lloyd typed the drafts and final manuscript; Robert G. Anthony, Jr., read and commented on the text and helped with the proofreading; and all members of the staff of the North Carolina Collection aided in ways that only they and the curator can appreciate. Finally, William S. Powell generously provided sound advice throughout the project.

Now, back to the question of why no similar book has yet appeared. The answer is simple: Such a project would have been doomed except with the backing of the enormous resources of the two historical agencies that I have headed. Years of twelve-hour days were but a beginning. There were hundreds of repositories and collections to be searched (either in person, through colleagues, or through finding aids); more than ten thousand xerographic copies to be obtained and evaluated; hundreds of letters to be written and a myriad of permission forms (all seemingly different) to be filled out; innumerable telephone calls to be made pleading for assistance; and the ordering of and paying for nearly two thousand prints. At every stage a complicated control system tying together the text, captions, credits, conditions, and prints suggested the plight of a juggler with five balls in the air.

The copies alone cost many thousands of dollars, for, though some prints were loaned and others were furnished without charge, most required laboratory copying, and one-time rights for reproduction of wire services photographs cost up to seventy-five dollars each. A special obstacle resulted from the relatively new copyright law, which has frightened repositories into a virtual nightmare of red tape (and often special permission fees). Some museums declined to furnish prints until the current owner of an illustration could be traced down and his or her written permission obtained. A pictorial volume utilizing photographs from around the world, therefore, is beyond the time and financial means of individual historians, and

this one has been accomplished only because the by-products—illustrations for the study files of the North Carolina Collection and additions of negatives and prints to its photographic files—have justified the cost. Still, the project has been immensely rewarding for the compiler-author, and I am particularly proud that it was conducted the North Carolina way—that is, without a cent of federal or foundation grant money and with no thought of reward except the satisfaction of accomplishing a job that no one else would undertake without the promise of remuneration. Any royalties emanating from the sale of the book will go to the North Caroliniana Society, Inc., which helps support the North Carolina Collection. My one regret is that the time required in the project made it advisable for me to leave the American Quadricentennial Corporation and America's Four Hundredth Anniversary Committee, both of which I organized and chaired for three years.

Readers are informed that photographs published in *North Carolina Illustrated, 1524–1984* may be reproduced *only* with the permission of the individual or institution identified by the credit line in the captions. My desire to use only illustrations contemporaneous with the subject was thwarted from time to time; the caption usually indicates when only a later picture was available.

This is, without apology, H. G. Jones's North Carolina, but I hope that others will recognize in the following pages *their* North Carolina, a state whose collective character—despite occasional aberrations—is epitomized in the motto *Esse Quam Videri*, to be rather than to seem.

H. G. Jones
Chapel Hill
1 September 1983

North Carolina Illustrated, 1524–1984

1. "A New Land," 1524–1590

1-1 *. . . there appeared a new land which had never been seen before by any man, either ancient or modern. At first it appeared to be rather low-lying; having approached to within a quarter of a league, we realized that it was inhabited, for huge fires had been built on the seashore.*

1-2 Whether or not in fact the "new land" had been seen by another European, this account of Giovanni da Verrazzano appears to be the earliest written description of North Carolina.

1-3 Sailing in *La Dauphine* with a crew of about fifty men, the Florentine in the service of the king of France arrived off Cape Fear about 1 March 1524. After scouting southward for a harbor, Verrazzano anchored off the cape, sent a boat ashore, and observed the natives, who were reluctant at first to approach the strangely dressed white men. The captain described these native Carolinians as follows:

They go completely naked except that around their loins they wear skins of small animals like martens, with a narrow belt of grass around the body, to which they tie various tails of other animals which hang down to the knees; the rest of the body is bare, and so is the head. Some of them wear garlands of birds' feathers. They are dark in color, not unlike the Ethiopians, with thick black hair, not very long, tied back behind the head like a small tail. As for the physique of these men they are well proportioned, of medium height, a little taller than we are. They have broad chests, strong arms, and the legs and other parts of the body are well composed. There is nothing else, except that they tend to be rather broad in the face: but not all, for we saw many with angular faces. They have big black eyes, and an attentive and open look. They are not very strong, but they have a sharp cunning, and are agile and swift runners.*

Leaving Cape Fear, the explorers followed the irregular coast northeastward, observing the flora and fauna and the kindness of the natives. Not far from Hatteras, Verrazzano committed an error in judgment that would plague mapmakers for dec-

ades. There, at a place he called Annunciata, he recorded, "We could see the eastern sea from the ship, halfway between the west and north. This is doubtless the one which goes around the tip of India, China, and Cathay." The map drawn by his 1-4 brother Girolamo five years later showed Annunciata (or, as he immodestly renamed it, "Verazanio") as a narrow waist separating the Atlantic from the Sea of Verrazzano, an error repeated by Robert de Bailly and other cartographers. 1-5

Two years after Verrazzano returned to France, 1-6 the Cape Fear region attracted a hoard of some 500 Spaniards who, under the leadership of Lucas Vasquez de Ayllon, sought to establish a colony on 1-7 "Rio Jordan"—believed to be the Cape Fear River. For an unknown period the settlers clung tenaciously to their plans, but they were tormented with malaria, hunger, and bad weather. Ayllon himself succumbed, and the survivors trekked southward. Only about 150 survived; they were eventually evacuated to Santo Domingo, from which they had started.

Another Spaniard, Hernando de Soto, pene- 1-8 trated North Carolina by land in 1540, passing through the southwestern mountains. His search for gold was unsuccessful, but the myth endured that the precious metal was to be found in the Ap- 1-9 palachians. Other Spaniards, including Pedro de Coronas, Juan Pardo, Hernando Boyano, and Angel de Villafañe, passed through North Carolina, but no lasting influence resulted from their brief visits.

Of the four great powers whose vessels sailed the waters of the New World in the sixteenth century, England was the last to undertake colonization. In 1578, however, Queen Elizabeth issued to Sir 1-10 Humphrey Gilbert a charter authorizing the dis- 1-11 covery and settlement of "remote heathen and barbarous lands, Countries, and territories, not actually possessed of any Christian prince or people." Gilbert was "swallowed up of the sea" before he

*These two translations are by Susan Tarrow in Lawrence C. Wroth, *The Voyages of Giovanni da Verrazzano 1524–1528* (New Haven: Yale University Press, 1970), pp. 133 (for the first quotation) and 134 (for the second).

could carry out his plans. Still, his exploits, and those of previous explorers as publicized in Richard Hakluyt's *Divers voyages touching the discoverie of America*, stimulated great interest among the English, and in 1584 the queen issued a new charter to Gilbert's half-brother, Walter Raleigh.

The young native of Devonshire, already one of the queen's favorite courtiers, was authorized to establish colonies whose inhabitants would "have and enjoy all the privileges of free Denizens and persons native of England." Within five weeks Raleigh had dispatched two vessels, under captains Philip Amadas and Arthur Barlowe, to America. After scouting the outer banks, the expedition slipped through an inlet north of Hatteras, made contact with hospitable natives, and spent several weeks exploring the coast and islands.

When Amadas and Barlowe returned to England, they carried with them two intelligent natives, Manteo and Wanchese, and glowing reports of the "sweet, fruitful and wholesome land" where lived a people "most gentle, loving and faithfull, void of all guile and treason." There, they boasted, "the earth bringeth foorth all things in aboundance, as in the first creation, without toile or labour."

Englishmen were elated, and bountiful financial support enabled Raleigh to outfit their country's first genuine colonization expedition to "Virginia," as the new land was christened in honor of the Virgin Queen. Knighted and given the title of lord and governor of Virginia, Raleigh sought to lead the expedition himself, but Elizabeth refused him permission (he never came to North America). Instead, his kinsman Sir Richard Grenville was placed in charge of the seven ships, including the queen's own *Tiger*, which sailed from Plymouth in April 1585. Aboard were several hundred men, including John White, an artist; Thomas Hariot, a mathematician and scientist; Ralph Lane, a soldier; and Thomas Cavendish, "high marshal" of the expedition, who returned to England on his ship, the *Elizabeth*.

In late June the expedition reached the outer banks, explored the Pamlico Sound area, and in the following weeks established on Roanoke Island a colony of 108 men under Lane's military command. Wattle and bark buildings were hastily thrown up, an earthen Fort Raleigh was constructed, and liaisons were established with the natives. Many of the colony's supplies had been spoiled when the *Tiger* ran aground, and it was, of course, too late in the summer for the Englishmen

to hope for a full crop. Consequently, they were dependent upon the remaining supplies brought with them and foodstuffs provided by the natives. The latter source had already been jeopardized when, in retribution for the disappearance of a silver cup at a village near Lake Mattamuskeet, the English had meted out their form of justice: "We burnt, and spoyled their corne, and Towne, all the people being fledde." News of this behavior was bound to reach the Indians at Roanoke Island.

The colonists lasted through the winter and spring, but their deteriorating relationship with the natives in the spring and their failure to receive new supplies from England prepared them to accept a ride home when in June 1586 Sir Francis Drake stopped by Roanoke Island on his return from an attack upon the Spanish in the West Indies and Florida. Had they held out a few more days, they could have welcomed a ship laden with the desperately needed supplies. Still, the first colonists had not failed altogether, for they had explored as far as the Chesapeake Bay, and John White had busied himself in drawing dozens of revealing pictures of a race of people virtually unknown to England.

Grenville also arrived at Roanoke Island a few weeks later and found the site deserted. To maintain England's claim to the new land, he left fifteen of his own men at Fort Raleigh, then returned home.

Undeterred by the failure of the first colonization attempt, in 1587 Raleigh launched a more ambitious expedition under the governorship of John White. This was a civilian colony, including seventeen women and nine children, well financed and highly publicized. Its destination was the Chesapeake Bay, where the fleet could avoid the treacherous, shifting sands of the outer banks and could anchor in deep, sheltered waters. On their way, however, they stopped at Roanoke Island to pick up the men that Grenville had left the year earlier.

White and forty of his best men loaded into one of the smaller boats for the trip into Roanoke Island. No sooner were they on board, however, than Simon Fernandez called out the alarming command to his sailors that the colonists were not to be brought back to the boat. He was setting the colony ashore here, rather than in the Chesapeake, so that he could get on with a privateering expedition. Governor White had little choice but to bring his settlers ashore and repair the houses at Fort

Raleigh and build new ones. Even more disturbing, the fifteen men left by Grenville the previous year were nowhere to be found, and damage to the houses suggested that they had been overwhelmed by the natives.

Again, much of the growing season had passed, and the change of plans made it necessary for a vessel to return to England for additional supplies. It was with great reluctance that Governor White agreed to sail back to England only a short time after his daughter Eleanor Dare gave birth to a child christened Virginia, the first English child born in the New World.

There he found the country busily engaged in preparations for battle with Spain, and it was only with considerable difficulty that he put to sea in April 1588 with two vessels loaded with supplies for his American colony. To the governor's astonishment, the captains of both ships turned to piracy on the high seas; then they were in turn overtaken by French privateers, who seized the supplies intended for America. White returned empty-handed to an England even more desperate before the Spanish alarm. Nearly every seaworthy vessel was needed in battle, and even the defeat of the Spanish Armada failed to reassure Elizabeth and her countrymen. All the efforts of White and Raleigh to undertake another relief expedition failed for nearly two years, and not until 1590, three years after White left his family and friends at Roanoke Island, was he able to set sail for Roanoke.

It was late August when White finally approached Fort Raleigh. He later wrote, "We let fall our Grapnel neere the shore, & sounded with a trumpet a Call, & afterwardes many familiar English tunes of Songs, and called to them friendly; but we had no answere."

There was no one to answer—a dreaded fact revealed when White found the fort and houses abandoned, chests broken open, and a tree carved with the word "CROATOAN." The absence of the previously agreed upon sign of distress (a cross) reassured him, for he assumed that the colonists had departed for Croatoan (probably modern Ocracoke Island) to accept the protection of friendly natives. Wrote White, "This [plundering of the fort and houses] could be no other but the deed of the savages, our enemies at Dasamonguepeuc, who had watched the departure of our men to Croatoan, and as soon as they were departed, digged by every place where they suspected anything to be buried; but although it much grieved me to see such spoil of goods, yet on the other side I greatly joyed that I had safely found a certain token of their safe being at Croatoan, which is the place where Manteo was born, and the savages of the island our friends."

John White was never able to learn whether his supposition was correct, for a storm arose and damaged his ships. So fierce was the storm—probably a hurricane—that the relief expedition had to put to sea. Despite bits of evidence and a plethora of theory, the "Lost Colony" remains lost to history nearly four centuries after White sailed away, fully expecting to return the following spring for a reunion with his daughter and granddaughter.

Whatever the fate of the men, women, and children of the Roanoke colonies, they contributed significantly to the world's knowledge of and interest in the North American continent. For the English the failure was temporary; when within two decades they established their first permanent colony at Jamestown, the lessons of Roanoke Island had been well learned.

1-1
The earliest written description (1524) of the "new land" now encompassed in North Carolina. (By permission of Pierpont Morgan Library, New York.)

1-2
Giovanni da Verrazzano (ca. 1485–ca. 1528), a Florentine navigator, sailed westward in 1524 and described the Cape Fear region in a letter to King Francis I of France. (By permission of Pierpont Morgan Library, New York, and Il Sindaco, Comuni di Greve in Chianti, Italy.)

1-3
A sailing vessel pictured on his brother's map in 1529 may have represented the *Dauphine* on which Giovanni da Verrazzano explored the Carolina coast five years earlier. (Courtesy North Carolina Collection, Library, University of North Carolina, Chapel Hill; original in Vatican Library, Rome.)

GIOVANNI DI PIER ANDREA DI — BERNARDO DA VERRAZZANO
PATRIZIO FIOR. GRAN CAPIT. — COMANDANTE IN MARE PER
IL RÈ CRISTIANISSIMO — FRANCESCO PRIMO,
E DISCOPRITORE — DELLA NUOVA FRANCIA.
nato circa il MCDLXXXV. morto nel MDXXV.
Dedicato al merito sing.re dell' Ill.mo e Rev.mo Sig.re Lodovico da Verrazzano
Patrizio, e Canonico Fiorentino Agnato del Med.o
Preso dal Quadro Originale in Tela esistente presso la sud.a Nobil Famiglia
G. Zocchi del. F. Allegrini inci: 1767

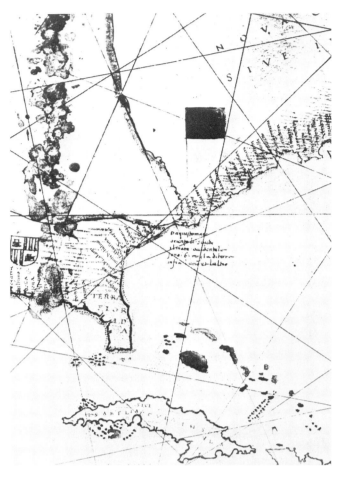

1-4
Portion of Girolamo da Verrazzano's map of 1529 showing the narrow waist at "Verazanio"—the present outer banks of North Carolina—separating the Atlantic Ocean from "el mare orientale." (Courtesy North Carolina Collection; original in Vatican Library, Rome.)

1-5
The Robert de Bailly copper globe, 1530, also shows Verrazzano's mistaken belief that the two oceans almost merged at the outer banks. (By permission of Pierpont Morgan Library, New York.)

1-6
Historian Samuel Eliot Morison believed that the present location of Kitty Hawk was the place described by Verrazzano as Arcadia, and he reproduced this landscape from the Miller I Atlas as representing that area. Most American historians and geographers, however, place Arcadia considerably farther up the coast. (By permission of Bibliothèque Nationale, Paris.)

1-7
The Juan Vespucci map of 1526, the first map of the Carolina coast after Verrazzano's exploration, names the newly discovered country "Ayllon" in honor of the

leader of an unsuccessful Spanish colonization attempt in the Cape Fear region. (By permission of Hispanic Society of America, New York.)

1-10
A contemporary painting of Sir Humphrey Gilbert hangs in Compton Castle, so familiar to his half-brother, Walter Raleigh, who followed him

into the field of exploration. (Courtesy National Trust for Places of Historic Interest or Natural Beauty, owner of Compton Castle.)

1-8
The Spaniard Hernando de Soto led an expedition through the southwestern mountains of North Carolina in 1540. (By permission of Hispanic Society of America, New York.)

1-9
Evidence is lacking that the Spaniards found gold in the Appalachians, but the drawing by Jacques Le Moyne engraved by Theodor de Bry in

titled "Mode of collecting gold in streams from the Apalatcy Mountains" was engraved by Theodor de Bry in

part 2 of his *America* (1591). (Courtesy North Carolina Collection.)

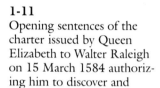

1-11
Opening sentences of the charter issued by Queen Elizabeth to Walter Raleigh on 15 March 1584 authorizing him to discover and profit from lands not already occupied by Christians. (Courtesy North Carolina Division of Archives and History, Raleigh, hereinafter cited as NCDA&H; original in Public Record Office, London.)

1-12
Sir Walter Raleigh and his nine-year-old son, Wat, in 1602. Wat was killed during Raleigh's second expedition to Guiana, less than a year before his father was beheaded. (By permission of National Portrait Gallery, London.)

1-13
In a contemporary drawing by William Camden, Sir Walter Raleigh is shown as captain of the guard in the funeral cortege of Queen Elizabeth in 1603. (By permission of British Library, London.)

1-14
The fact that Raleigh never came to North America did not prevent Chowan County from depicting him on its seal in 1772. He can be seen on the shore with his shield and liberty pole. The inscription reads, "Sir Walter Raleigh landed in America A.D. 1584." A ship and gabled buildings may be seen at right. (Courtesy NCDA&H.)

1-16
Raleigh's seal as lord and governor of Virginia carried the motto "Amore et Virtute." It was executed in the spring of 1584/5, about the time he was knighted. (Courtesy North Carolina Collection.)

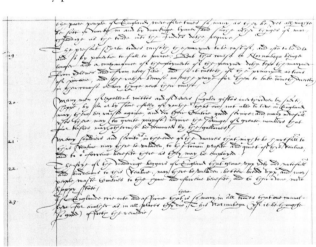

1-15
At Raleigh's request, Richard Hakluyt prepared in 1584 *A particular discourse concerning the greate necessitie and manifolde comodyties that are like to growe on this Realme of England by the Westerne discoueries lately attempted. . . .* A portion of the final page in chapter 20 suggests that the new land would offer a haven for the underprivileged. (By permission of Rare Books and Manuscripts Division, New York Public Library, Astor, Lenox, and Tilden Foundations, New York.)

1-17
When Raleigh again was denied the opportunity of coming to America, the 1585 expedition was commanded by Sir Richard Grenville, shown in a portrait dated 1571. (By permission of National Portrait Gallery, London.)

1-18

The *Teager*, shown on a portion of the Smerwick Map of 1580, is believed to have been the flagship *Tiger* of the 1585 voyage. (By permission of Public Record Office, London.)

1-19

The Roanoke voyages originated in the Devon port of Plymouth, pictured on a portion of a map of the southern coast of England dated ca. 1536. (By permission of British Library, London.)

1-20

Thomas Hariot (1560–1621), mathematician and astronomer, was a member of the Ralph Lane colony of 1585–86. Two years after his return to England he published his *Briefe and True Report of the New Found Land of Virginia*. Not all scholars agree that this is a portrait of Hariot. (By permission of President and Fellows of Trinity College, Oxford.)

1-21

Thomas Cavendish, captain of the *Elizabeth* in the 1585 expedition, is one of the few Roanoke voyagers for whom a portrait remains. (Courtesy Newberry Library, Chicago; by permission of the Marquess of Bath, Longleat House, Warminster, Wiltshire.)

1-22
The earliest known map of Raleigh's "Virginia" was probably drawn in 1585 by John White or Thomas Hariot. Roanoke Island is identified as "ye Kings Ile." Secoton and Pomeiock, both of which the Englishmen visited, are shown on the mainland. (By permission of British Museum, London.)

1-23
Theodor de Bry's engraving of a lost drawing by John White showed a palisaded Fort Raleigh on Roanoke Island and the neighboring Indian village of Dasamonguepeuc on the mainland. (By permission of British Museum, London.)

1-27
A wrought-iron ax, recovered from the site of Fort Raleigh in 1862, is one of a few extant artifacts believed to be associated with the Roanoke colonies. Many years in the possession of historian Stephen B. Weeks, the ax is now owned by the North Carolina Collection. (Courtesy North Carolina Collection.)

1-24 and 1-25
The relative accuracy of a portion of John White's watercolor map of the coast of North Carolina is revealed by the photograph (right) taken from the Apollo 9 spacecraft in 1969. (Left, by permission of British Museum, London; right, courtesy National Aeronautics and Space Administration, Washington.)

1-28
Sir Francis Drake, who seven years earlier had claimed California for the British, provided transportation for Ralph Lane and his colonists from Roanoke Island to England in 1586. (By permission of National Portrait Gallery, London.)

1-26
Fort Raleigh, reconstructed by archaeologists after World War II, appears at left in this air view of a portion of Fort Raleigh National Historic Site. At right is the Waterside Theatre, where Paul Green's *The Lost Colony* is performed each summer. (Courtesy National Park Service.)

The Watercolor Drawings of John White

Among the lasting contributions of Sir Walter Raleigh's colonization attempts were the watercolor drawings of John White, most of which were prepared, or at least sketched, during his year as a colonist in the Ralph Lane expedition, 1585–86.

When the 1585 expedition arrived at Wococon—an island comprising a portion of present-day Ocracoke and Portsmouth islands—White, Grenville, Lane, Hariot, and several others went to the mainland of modern-day Hyde and Beaufort counties. They visited at least three native villages, including Pomeiock, near the east end of Lake Mattamuskeet, and Secoton (or Secota), perhaps near the modern town of Aurora. There and elsewhere White made drawings, later refined and colored, of the villages and their inhabitants, thus furnishing to the world of both his and our day a fascinating visual description of the sixteenth-century Algonquians. (Unless credited to Theodor de Bry, who embellished, engraved, and published a large selection of the drawings in 1590, the reproductions here are of the original drawings, © 1964 The Trustees of the British Museum.)

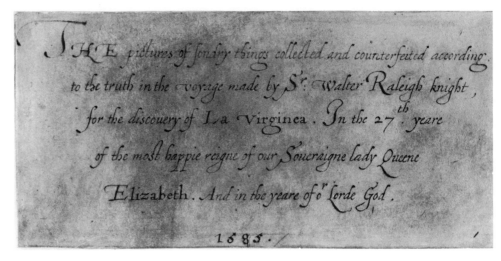

1-29
Autograph title—presumed to be in White's own hand— of his original drawings.

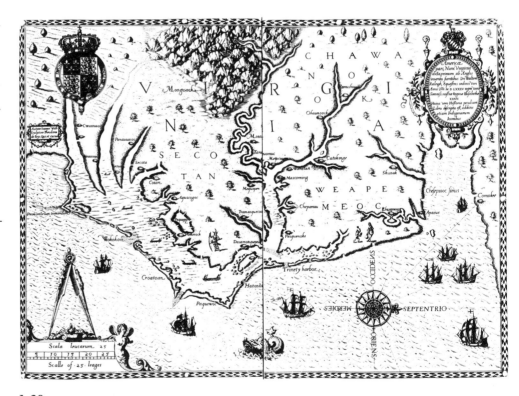

1-30
Theodor de Bry's engraving of White's map of "Virginia," from Cape Lookout to Chesapeake Bay, locating Secota (Secoton), Pomeiock, and Roanoke Island.

1-31
The palisaded village of
Pomeiock, near modern Lake
Mattamuskeet, showing
houses built from bent poles
covered by bark or rush mat-
ting. Sleeping platforms are
visible inside.

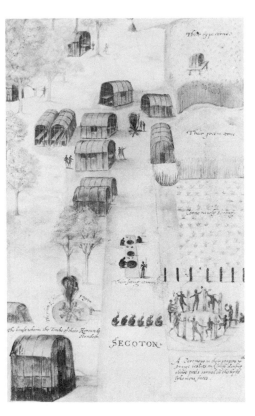

1-32
The wife and daughter of the
chief "herowan" of Pom-
eiock. The woman carries a
large gourd and wears a deerskin skirt; the child carries an
English doll and wears a
moss pad.

1-33
An old Indian man of
Pomeiock, dressed in deerskin "with the hair on and
lyned with other furred
skinnes."

1-34 and 1-35
To White's original drawing
of Secoton (top), de Bry's
engraving (bottom) added
patches of tobacco, pump-
kins, and sunflowers. Unlike
Pomeiock, Secoton was an
open village, but the construction of its houses was
similar.

1-36
Indians dancing around a circle of posts with tops carved as human heads. Hariot wrote of their ritual dances, "They dance singe, and use the strangest gestures that they can possiblye devise."

1-39
Indians singing around a fire to the accompaniment of gourd or pumpkin rattlers.

Hariot assumed this to be a thanksgiving ceremony.

1-37
An Indian charnel house in which the defleshed bodies of the chiefs were guarded by "Kywash," an idol who "mumbleth his prayers nighte and day, and hath charges of the corpses."

1-38
"The manner of their fishing"—perhaps a composite view with the fire in the boat representing night fishing. Various specimens of marine life are shown in the water, with a fish weir in background.

1-41
Indian conjuror with a bird fastened to the side of his head which has been shaved except for the crest. "They be verye familiar with devils of whom they enquier what their enemys doe, or other suche thinges."

1-40
De Bry's engraving of White's lost drawing of In-   dians making canoes from a tree.

1-42
Title page of Theodor de Bry's *America*, published in four languages in 1590 and featuring Hariot's report and White's drawings, some of which are engraved around the pediment and columns.

2. The English Return, 1607–1689

Twenty years after Sir Walter Raleigh failed to plant a colony near the Chesapeake Bay, another group—the Virginia Company—succeeded in establishing the first permanent English colony in the New World. From the beginning, the leaders of the Jamestown settlement sought to locate the survivors of the Roanoke voyages, and in 1608 they sent Michael Sicklemore and a small party "to search for the lost company of Sir Walter Rawley." Sicklemore returned with a report that he "found little hope and less certainetie" of the survival of the Roanoke group. A roughly drawn map of 1608, based on Indian reports of dubious reliance, gave hints that several of the Roanoke survivors might be living at native settlements called Ocamahawan and Pakerakinick. There were other rumors and other searches, but John Smith wrote that "nothing could they learne but they were all dead." Despite theories to the contrary, no convincing evidence has been turned up to dispute Smith's assumption that there were no survivors.

The new settlers, nevertheless, maintained an interest in "Ould Virginia," as Smith called the area explored by the Roanoke colonists, and other expeditions were sent out. In 1622, for instance, John Pory, former secretary of the Virginia colony, traveled to the Chowan River area, where he found "a very fruitful and pleasant Countrey, full of Rivers, wherein are two harvests in one yeere." His reports—of rich corn lands, thriving silk-grass (from which the Indians made thread and string), and pine trees "which will serve well for Masts for Shipping, and for pitch and tarre"—helped stimulate continuing interest in the area around Albemarle Sound.

In 1629, King Charles I granted to his attorney general, Sir Robert Heath, a vast tract extending from near the present northern boundary of Florida to the southern shore of Albemarle Sound, an area named Carolana in the king's honor. The new proprietor was given broad powers to settle and govern the province, though the king's authority was to be respected by the requirement that Heath keep in the colony a twenty-ounce gold crown for use in case Charles chose to visit.

Heath developed ambitious plans "to lead thither a Colony of men, large and plentiful, professing the true religion, sedulously and industriously applying themselves to the culture of the said lands and to merchandizing," and he negotiated with a group of French Protestants who were interested in establishing themselves in America. The leader, the Baron de Sancé, went so far as to draw plans for protective fortifications in the colony. The privy council, however, took a dim view of introducing foreign Protestants into America, and in 1632 commanded Heath to admit only communicants of the Church of England.

The following year, Edward Kingswell was appointed governor of Carolana. He sailed with a small group aboard Peter Andrews's ship, the *Mayflower*, but instead of landing his passengers in Carolana, Andrews transported them to Jamestown, thus frustrating another attempt to settle Carolana. Heath soon transferred his title to Henry Frederick Howard, Lord Maltravers, who obtained a royal warrant to "stamp farthing tokens of copper with a distinction of brass" for use in the colony. Maltravers appointed Captain William Hawley, then living in Maryland, as his lieutenant general of Carolana, and in 1640 the Virginia council gave Hawley approval for his proposal to solicit settlers for the Carolana grant. No evidence has been found to indicate that he was successful.

Shortly after the execution of Charles I in 1649, a London newspaper reported that "there is a Gentleman going over Governour into Carolana in America, and many Gentlemen of quality and their families with him." The article described the opportunities in the colony in glowing terms and claimed that "conditions shall be given to Adventurers, Planters, and Servants; which shall be as good, if not better, than have been given to other Plantations." Promotional tracts, such as William Bullock's *Virginia Impartially examined* (1649), Edward Williams's *Virgo Triumphans: Or, Virginia . . . The fertile Carolana, and no lesse excellent Isle of Roanoak . . .* (1650), and Edward Bland's *The Discovery of New Britainne* (1651), continued to stimulate interest in the settlement of Carolana,

2-8 sometimes still referred to as "Ould Virginia" and "Rawliana."

Roger Green, a Virginia minister, was given a grant in Carolana in 1653 "next to those persons who have had a former grant in reward of his charge, hazard and trouble of first discoverie, and encouragement of others for seating those southern parts of Virginia," but he apparently failed to occupy it. Francis Yeardley, son of a former Virginia governor, developed a friendship with the Indian chief at Roanoke and purchased lands in Carolana, less than forty miles south of his own plantation near the James River. It was Yeardley

2-9 who sent Robert Bodnam, a carpenter, to the mouths of the Roanoke and Chowan rivers in 1655 to build a two-room, twenty-by-twenty-foot

2-10 house for Nathaniel Batts, "a young man, a trader for beavers." If this house was the first permanent residence built by an English settler in Carolana, it was not to be the only one for long, for adventuresome hunters, trappers, traders, and explorers became increasingly familiar with the territory north and west of the body of water later named the Albemarle Sound.

The proprietary grants having been neglected, Virginians looked upon the area as simply a frontier of their own colony, and by the time of the ascension to the throne of Charles II in 1660 a small number of Englishmen had established themselves in the region. Among them was John Harvey, to whom in that year were willed goods and livestock described as "at the Southward in the Custody of the aforesd Harvey." The earliest known recorded deed of land in the Albemarle was

2-11 from Kiscutanewh, "Kinge of Yausapin," 24 September 1660, to Nathaniel Batts for a tract on the southwest side of Pasquotank River. The chief had earlier sold this land to men by the name of Willoughby and Mason, but they had failed to pay him for it. A deed from King Kilcocanen to George Durant in 1662 refers to adjoining land already held by Samuel Pricklove. Other early settlers in the Albemarle included Richard Sanderson, Samuel Davis, Robert Lawrence, George Catchmaid, Thomas Jarvis, John Jenkins, and Dr. Thomas Relfe. In fact, by 1662 the number of settlers in the region was sufficient for Governor Berkeley of Virginia to commission Samuel Stephens as commander of the "Southern Plantation," with power to appoint a sheriff.

The Albemarle was not the only area in Carolana that was attracting settlers in the early 1660s. In 1662 the "Committee for Cape Faire at Boston" sent William Hilton and his ship *Adventure* to explore the Charles (now Cape Fear) River. A longboat reached perhaps fifty miles up the Cape Fear, and in his report the captain described an "abundance of vast meddows, besides upland fields, yt renders ye Contry fit to be calld a Land for Catle, whereby they yt dwell there, may enjoy ye freedom from yt toyle in other plantacons, where they are necessitated to provide hay." The natives were timid and courteous; mosquitoes were few; trees, fruits, and wildlife were plentiful; and Indian corn stalks, as big as a man's wrist, reached a height of twelve feet. "We wish all Englishmen, yt know how to improve and use a plentifull Contry and condicon, not to delay to posses it," concluded the report.

This was enough to induce the New England committee early in 1663 to send out a colony of unknown size, together with swine and cattle. The ill-fated colony remains a mystery; according to one report, the livestock was indeed put ashore, but the New Englanders themselves chose to leave the area "without so much as sitting down." Some of them sought to sail to "Roano[ack] where the   2-12 English doe Inhabite," but all probably returned to Massachusetts. They left behind their livestock, a contemptuous note, and many legends, including that of an imaginary "James Forte."   2-13

The restoration of the English monarchy in 1660 left Charles II with heavy debts to those who had engineered his ascension to the throne, and on 24 March 1663, he rewarded eight of his leading supporters with a charter for a vast slice of North   2-17 America from the thirty-first to the thirty-sixth parallels from the Atlantic to the South Seas (essentially the same lands previously granted to Sir Robert Heath in 1629). Over this province of Carolina, as the name was now confirmed in honor of Charles II, the Lords Proprietors were given   2-14 broad feudal powers similar to those formerly exer-   2-15 cised by the bishop of the county palatine of Durham in England. These included full authority to establish offices and commission officials, to establish courts, to levy taxes, to grant land, to confer titles of nobility, and even to recruit an army and wage war. There were, however, limits to their power: Laws were to be enacted "with the advice, assent, and approbation of the Freemen of the said Province, or of the greater part of them, or of their Delegates or Deputies." Settlers were to have "all liberties, Franchises, and Privileges of this our

Kingdom of England," and the proprietors were authorized to grant "Indulgences and Dispensations" to settlers who "in their Judgments, and for Conscience sake" could not conform to the theology and ritual of the established Church of England.

2-16

At first one of the proprietors, Sir William Berkeley, governor of Virginia, was delegated to exercise governmental authority over the Carolina settlers, but in October 1664, William Drummond was appointed governor of Albemarle, with Peter Carteret as his assistant. In addition, a council of six men was appointed to join with the freemen or their delegates "to make good and wholesome lawes."

2-19

When it became known that a portion of the Albemarle settlement extended above the thirty-sixth parallel, a new charter was issued in 1665, extending the northern line by half a degree and the southern boundary by two degrees, thus impinging upon both Virginia and Spanish Florida. In the spring of 1665 the first assembly of freemen convened under a tree in Pasquotank Precinct. The province of Carolina was at last a reality.

2-18

The king's gift to the Lords Proprietors constituted a broad swath of land that today includes all or part of seventeen states and Mexico. In this territory were a few hundred white settlers along the Albemarle Sound and the rivers emptying into it; several groups of Indians already known to the English; and an unknown population of natives reaching to the "South Seas."

The New Englanders who had departed Cape Fear that very year had left a hastily written note attached to a post, "the Contents whereof tended not only to the disparagement of the Land . . . but also to the great discouragement of all those that should hereafter come into these parts to settle." The note, however, did not deter William Hilton, whose glowing report two years earlier had led to the ill-fated New England venture. In 1663 he was in the employ of a group of citizens of the island of Barbados. The following year he wrote his *Relation*, and he purchased for his employers "the River and land of Cape-Fair" from the Indians. Encouraged by Hilton's report, John Vassall led a group of Barbadians to the Cape Fear, where they established Charles Town near the later site of Brunswick Town on the west bank. First under Vassall and then under the governorship of Sir John Yeamans, the colony grew until an estimated eight hundred settlers dotted the banks for as much as fifty miles upstream.

2-20

All was not as well as Robert Horne's *Brief Description* implied in 1666, however, for Vassall's pleas for assistance from the Lords Proprietors went unheeded. The whites soon wore out their welcome by enslaving Indian children, and the settlers probably found the soil productive only through intensive cultivation, to which they were unaccustomed. Furthermore, an expedition of Robert Sandford, secretary of the newly designated Clarendon County, returned with reports of a much more desirable location at the mouth of the Ashley River to the south. Dissatisfaction spread rapidly, and by 1667 the whites had abandoned the Cape Fear, leaving behind their buildings and familiar names (such as Stag Park and Rocky Point) to remind future adventurers of their failure. The natives along the Cape Fear were relatively undisturbed for the remainder of the century.

2-21
2-22

The Albemarle settlement was more fortunate, but while its survival was not threatened, its early decades were filled with confusion, even anarchy. Most of its residents had chosen the untamed frontier over the more rapidly developing communities along the James River; others had arrived on shallow-draft vessels from New England, a few even directly from England. Once in Albemarle, they were virtually marooned, their isolation broken only by newly arrived Virginians seeking land to call their own, by occasional adventuresome merchantmen who dared to negotiate the shifting sand bars in the sound, or by infrequent visitors.

With hand implements the settlers felled trees, built cabins, cleared land, and cultivated crops. Guns provided them meat and protection. Horses were few, and while oxen were trained for simple chores, human labor performed most of the tasks. Clothing, household furniture, farm implements, and canoes were commonly made by hand. Basic foods—corn, wheat, and pork—were grown on each farm. A variety of wildlife yielded furs and skins, and pine trees provided logs for cabins, wood for fires, and naval products.

2-23

Subsistence farming, of course, was not what the Lords Proprietors had in mind for their colony. They viewed themselves as a sort of board of directors of a huge land company. The headright system offered land grants of varying sizes, but ownership was not absolute: the settlers were obligated to pay annual quitrents in specie. Controversies over the amount and method of payment of quitrents strained relations between the proprietors and the settlers for several decades.

The Lords Proprietors were interested in large-scale operations. Perhaps for example as well as profit, in 1665 four of the proprietors put Assistant Governor Peter Carteret in charge of a winery and livestock and grain operation on Colleton (now Colington) Island. Carteret inhabited a twenty-foot-square cabin and managed a ten-foot-square "hogg howse." At Powell's Point he later built an eighty-by-twenty-foot hog house, but it was destroyed by one of the frequent storms that lashed the area. For seven years Carteret and his tenants struggled to grow grapes, make wine, raise cattle and swine, and hunt whales, but at the end of that time the entire operation was worth only about half the amount that the speculators had put into it. Only the whaling operation, which yielded 195 barrels of whale oil in four years, lightened the loss. If an enterprise sponsored by half of the Lords Proprietors and managed by the governor (Carteret had succeeded Samuel Stephens in 1670) fared so poorly, the fortunes of the other struggling farmers must have been pitiful indeed.

The settlers did not have to look far to find what they believed to be one of the largest contributors to their problems. The Concessions and Agreement of 1665 and the Great Deed of Grant of 1668—both salutary in their pronouncements—were soon revealed to be empty promises. But worse was to come, for in 1669, in anticipation of the future settlement of the Port Royal–Ashley River areas to the south, the proprietors promulgated the Fundamental Constitutions of Carolina, penned by John Locke. This "Grand Model," which was also applicable to Albemarle, sought to impose a feudal economic, social, and political structure, complete with ranks of nobility carrying large tracts of land and special privileges. Freemen would continue to elect delegates to a "Parliament," but real power would be exercised by the proprietors, the nobility, and the "Grand Council."

Although proclaimed "sacred and unalterable," the several editions of the Fundamental Constitutions were never fully implemented in Albemarle; the effort to apply their unrealistic provisions, however, caused increasing estrangement between the residents and the proprietors. The assembly passed several acts for the relief of the colony, including one to protect settlers for five years from suits for debts incurred outside Albemarle, and in 1672 the Grand Council sent Governor Carteret to London with instructions to seek more liberal treatment of the colony.

Governor Carteret neither returned to the colony nor gained concessions for the settlers. Indeed, conditions and relations deteriorated, and the residents were emboldened to take affairs into their own hands when they could get no relief from the English navigation acts and the Virginia embargo on tobacco grown in Albemarle. George Durant and John Culpeper led a revolt that deposed and imprisoned Governor Thomas Miller in 1677. "Culpeper's Rebellion" reflected the struggle between the supporters of the Lords Proprietors and an "antiproprietary" faction; it also revealed the virtual anarchy that prevailed in Albemarle during its first three decades.

To quiet the controversy, one of the proprietors—Seth Sothel, who had recently purchased Edward Hyde's share—was appointed governor. Following his capture at sea and imprisonment by pirates, Sothel finally reached Albemarle in 1683. During the next six years he so thoroughly mismanaged the governorship that he was convicted by the assembly of thirteen offenses and banished from the colony.

Oddly enough, during the period of factional struggles, the proprietors put forth their most strenuous efforts to attract new settlers to Carolina. In 1682 alone, at least four promotional publications were issued, all flattering to the colony. Each, however, gave little space to Albemarle, emphasizing instead the attractiveness of the Ashley River settlement, thus demonstrating where the real interests of the proprietors lay.

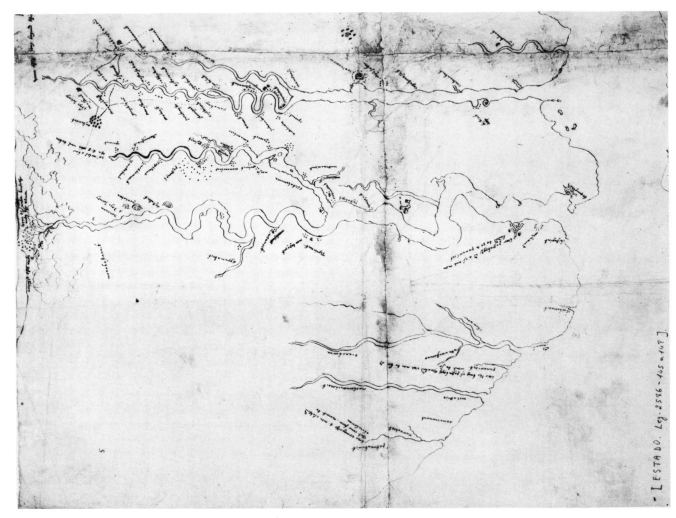

2-1
The Zuñiga map of 1608 referred to "4 men clothed that came from roonock to Ocamahawan," but repeated searches by early Virginians produced no proof of survivors from the colonies sent to Roanoke Island. (Courtesy North Carolina Collection; original in Archivo General de Simancas, Valladolid, Spain.)

2-2
Sir Robert Heath sought to colonize "Carolana" with French Protestants. (By permission of Master and Fellows of St. John's College, Cambridge.)

2-3
Heath engaged the Baron de Sancé to draw specifications for fortifications to protect the proposed colony in Carolana. (Courtesy NCDA&H; original in Public Record Office, London.)

Aprill 1632

Instructions (by way of Indenture) betwixt his Matie and Sr Robert Heath Knt. Chiefe Justice of our Court of Comon Pleas to bee observed in the plantation of Carolana:

That noe Strangers borne Subiects to any Prince or State out of our obeysance shalbe willingly entertained into the said plantation unlesse it be by our speciall direction and Comandment.

That none shalbe willingly admitted or entertayned into this plantation wch shall not bee of the Protestant Religion.

That none whosoever shalbe admitted to inhabite there who shall not submitt and conforme themselves to the discipline of the Church of England.

And wee doe hereby declare that all former Instructions heretofore given by us touching this plantation shalbee voyd and that these only shall stand in force according to our Lres patente.

Dated the 20th day of October in the fift yeare of his Maties Raigne.

Dated the 20th of this Month.

Copia Vera.

Phi: Warwicke

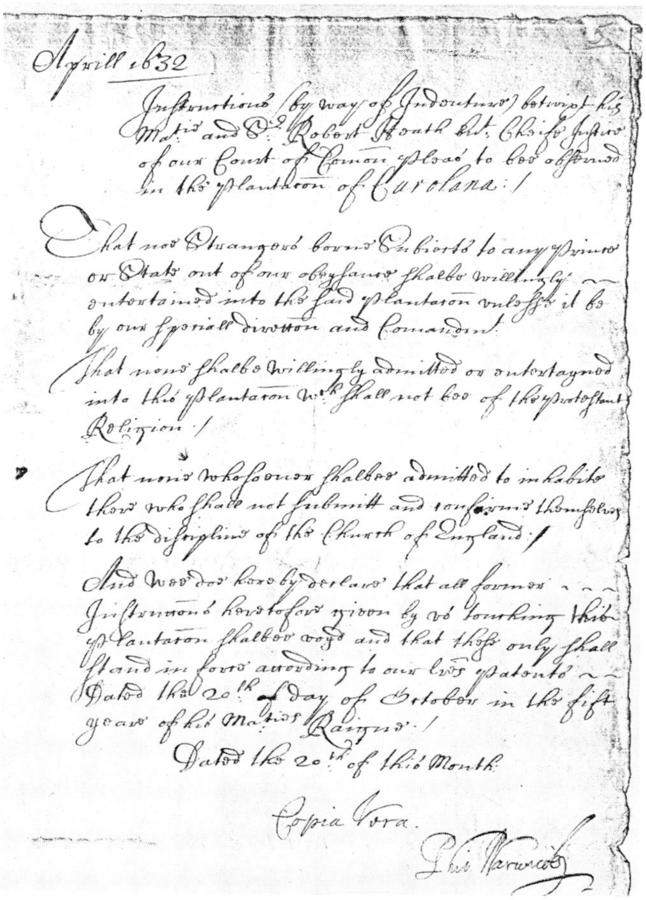

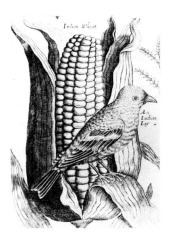

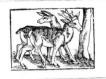

2-4

Heath's ambitious plans came to naught when the privy council ordered that "none whosoever shall be admitted to inhabit there who shall not submitt and conform themselves to the discipline of the Church of England." (Courtesy North Carolina Collection.)

VIRGO TRIUMPHANS:

OR,

VIRGINIA

richly and truly valued; more especially the South part thereof: *viz.*

The fertile CAROLANA, and no lesse excellent Isle of ROANOAK, of Latitude from 31 to 37 Degr. relating the meanes of raising infinite profits to the Adventurers and Planters:

Humbly presented as the Auspice of a beginning Yeare, To the Parliament of ENGLAND, And Councell of STATE.

By EDVVARD WILLIAMS, Gent.

LONDON, Printed by *Thomas Harper*, for *John Stephenson*, and are to be sold at his Shop on Ludgate-Hill, at the Signe of the Sunne, 1650.

2-6

Edward Williams in 1650 described "the beauties of a long neglected Virgin the incomparable Roanoke, and the adjacent excellencies of Carolana, a Country whom God and Nature has indulged with blessings incommunicable to any other Region." (Courtesy North Carolina Collection.)

2-7

A sketch of a blue jay and an ear of maize (mislabeled wheat) provided the frontispiece for Edward Bland's promotional pamphlet *The Discovery of New Britainne* in 1651. Authorized by the Virginia assembly "to discover and seate to the Southward in any convenient place," Bland apparently failed in his venture. (By permission of New-York Historical Society, New York.)

At the intreaty of a well-willer, the following lines are inserted.

There is a Gentleman going over Governour into Carolana *in* America, *and many Gentlemen of quality and their families with him.*

THis place is of a temperate Climate, not so hot as *Barbado's* nor so cold as *Virginia*; the Winter much like our *March* here in *England*. The Northern latitude begins where *Virginia* ends, at 37, neer Cape *Henry*, and takes in six degrees Southerly; no bounds to the East and West, but the Seas. At Point *Comfort*, neer Cape *Henry*, you enter into a fair Navigable River, called *James* River, about two leagues over: on both sides that River, are the chiefe Plantations in *Virginia*, and their chief Town *James* Town. On the South side of this River, are two Rivers, *Elisabeth*, and *Nansamond*, which convey you into *Carolana*; so that this River is a Haven to both Colonies. This *Carolana*, besides the temperature of the Climate, hath many Native Commodities to feed and cloath the body: Deer in abundance, bigger and better meat then ours in *England*, having two young ones at a time; their skins good cloathing, being better dressed by the *Indians* then ours: Elkes of a large size, admirable meat, having three young at a time; their Hides make good Buffe: besides Hares and Conies, and many other that are good meat: Beasts of prey, that are profitable for their Furres, as Bevers, Otters, Foxes, Martins, Minches, and Musk-Cats, their Cods better sented then those of *East-India*, and more lasting: Fowle of all sorts, Partridges and wild Turkies 100 in a flock, some of the Turkies weighing 40 pound. Fish there are in great abundance, of all sorts. In the

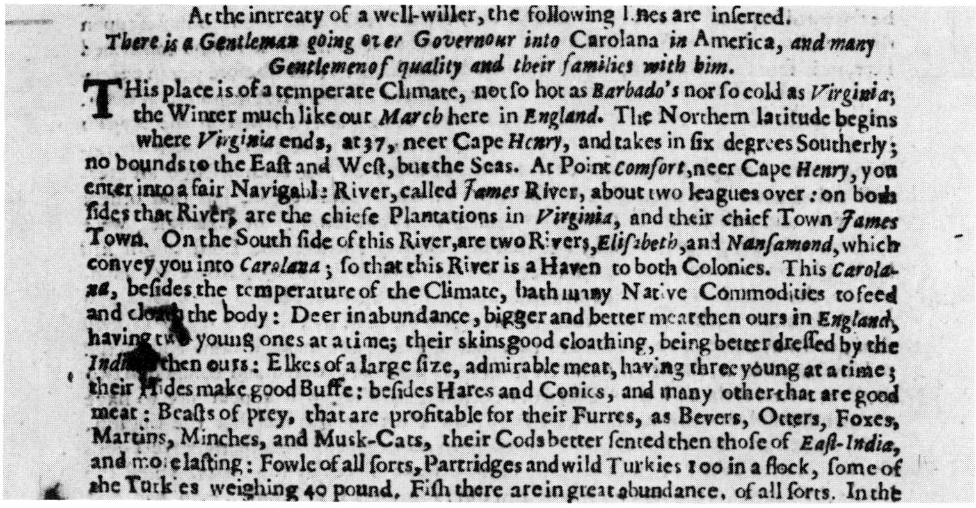

2-5

The Moderate Intelligencer of London, 26 April–2 May 1649, gave an enticing description of Carolana and reported that many families were preparing to settle there. (Courtesy North Carolina Collection.)

2-8
John Farrer's map of 1651 gave three names to North Carolina: Carolana, Ould Virginia, and Rawliana. In the Albemarle Sound appear the words "Rolli passd." The Pacific Ocean laps at the western slopes of the Appalachian mountains. (By permission of I. N. Phelps Stokes Collection, New York Public Library, Astor, Lenox, and Tilden Foundations, New York.)

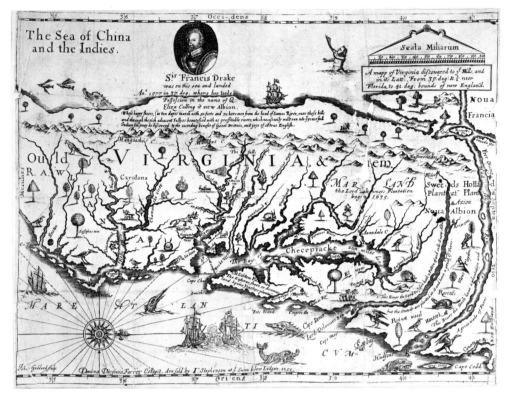

2-9
The lawsuit of Robert Bodnam sought payment for "going twice to the Southward and staying there 5 Monthes" to build a house (containing a lodging chamber, buttery, and chimney) for "Batts to live in and trad with the Indians." (Courtesy North Carolina Collection; original in Norfolk County Deed Book C, pp. 180–81, in office of clerk, Lower Norfolk County, Virginia.)

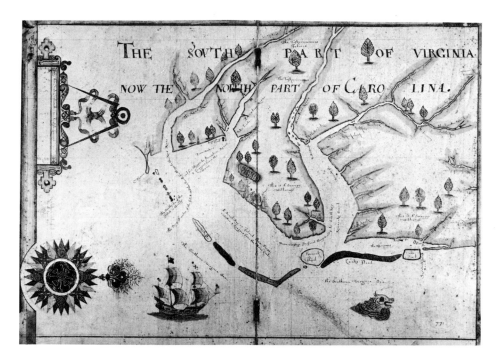

2-10
The house built for Nathaniel Batts is the only one shown on the Nicholas Comberford map of 1657. It stands at the confluence of the Roanoke and Chowan rivers (labeled Morattico and Choan on the map). (By permission of Rare Books and Manuscripts Division, New York Public Library, Astor, Lenox, and Tilden Foundations, New York.)

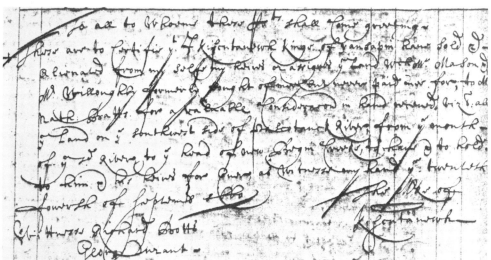

2-11
In 1660, Kiscutanewh, king of the Yausapin (Yeopim) Indians, sold Nathaniel Batts "all ye Land on ye southwest side of Pascotanck River, from ye mouth of ye s^d River to ye head of new Begin Creeke." (Courtesy North Carolina Collection; original in Norfolk County Deed Book D, p. 293, in office of clerk, Lower Norfolk County, Virginia.)

2-12
A deposition taken by the deputy governor of Massachusetts reveals that some of the New Englanders at "Cape Fayr" in 1663 wished to be transported to Roanoke Island. (Courtesy North Carolina Collection.)

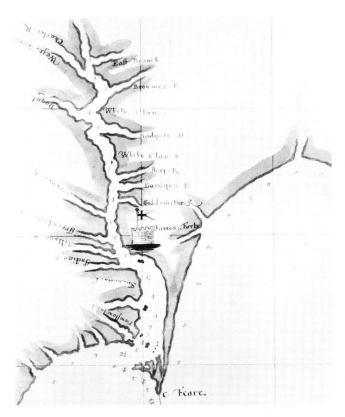

2-13
A map from the Blathwayt Atlas, apparently copied from the Nicholas Shapley map drawn following the first William Hilton voyage in 1662, pictures an imaginary (or perhaps planned) "James Forte" near the present site of Wilmington. (By permission of John Carter Brown Library, Brown University, Providence.)

2-14 (above right)
One of the eight Lords Proprietors of Carolina, George Monck, Duke of Albemarle, gave his name to the sound into which the Roanoke and Chowan rivers flow. (Courtesy NCDA&H.)

2-15 (center right)
Heirs of Sir George Carteret, one of the eight original proprietors, held on to his share when in 1728 the crown repurchased seven-eighths of the Carolina grant, thus forming the Granville District (Granville having become a Carteret title in the intervening years). (Courtesy NCDA&H.)

2-16 (lower right)
Sir William Berkeley (pictured here), governor of Virginia and also one of the eight proprietors of Carolina, initially was given authority over the new province. In 1664, however, Albemarle was granted a separate governor, William Drummond. (Courtesy NCDA&H.)

2-17
The Carolina Charter of 24 March 1663 conveyed to eight supporters of King Charles II an immense strip of real estate in America. The first letter of his name framed an ink portrait of the monarch. This is the first of four sheets of the vellum document, which is displayed in the North Carolina Division of Archives and History. (Courtesy NCDA&H.)

2-18
In 1672, Richard Blome dedicated his new map of Carolina to the Lords Proprietors and prominently displayed their coats of arms. (Courtesy North Carolina Collection.)

2-19
Seven of the eight proprietors signed the document appointing Peter Carteret as councillor and assistant governor of the county of Albemarle in 1664. (Courtesy NCDA&H.)

2-20
A Relation of a Discovery lately made on the Coast of Florida, by William Hilton (1664), described the Cape Fear country, including the cattle left behind by the departed New England colony. (Courtesy North Carolina Collection.)

nerally two or three, Sand and Oaze. We viewed the Cape-land, and judged it to be little worth, the Woods of it shrubby and low, the Land sandy and barren; in some places Grass and Rushes, and in other places nothing but clear sand : a place fitter to starve Cattel in our judgement, then to keep them alive; yet the *Indians,* as we understand, keep the *English* Cattle down there, and suffer them not to go off the said Cape, as we suppose, because the Countrey-*Indians* shall have no part with them, and as we think, are fallen out about them, who shall have the greatest share. They brought aboard our Ship very good and fat Beef several times, which they could afford very reasonable; also fat and very large Swine, good cheap penny-worths : but they may thank their friends of *New-England,* who brought their Hogs to so fair a Market. Some of the *Indians* brought very good Salt aboard us, and made signes, pointing to both sides of the Rivers mouth, that there was great store thereabouts. We saw up the River several good places for the setting up of Corn or Saw-mills. In that time as our businesse called us up and down the River and Branches, we kill'd of wild-fowl, four Swans, ten Geese, twenty nine Cranes, ten Turkies, forty Duck and Mallard, three dozen of Parrakeeto's, and six or seven dozen of other small Fowls, as Curlues and Plovers, &c.   Where-

[9]

Such as are here tormented with much care how to get worth to gain a Livelyhood, or that with their labour can hardly get a comfortable subsistance, shall do well to go to this place, where any man what-ever, that is but willing to take moderate pains, may be assured of a most comfortable subsistance, and be in a way to raise his fortunes far beyond what he could ever hope for in *England*. Let no man be troubled at the thoughts of being a Servant for 4 or 5 year, for I can assure you, that many men give mony with their children to serve 7 years, to take more pains and fare nothing so well as the Servants in this Plantation will do. Then it is to be considered, that so soon as he is out of his time, he hath Land, and Tools, and Clothes given him, and is in a way of advancement. Therefore all Artificers, as *Carpenters*, *Wheel-rights*, *Joyners*, *Coopers*, *Bricklayers*, *Smiths*, or diligent Husbandmen and Labourers, that are willing to advance their fortunes, and live in a most pleasant healthful and fruitful Country, where Artificers are of high esteem, and used with all Civility and Courtesie imaginable, may take notice, that

There is an opportunity offers now by the *Virginia* Fleet, from whence *Cape Feare* is but 3 or 4 days sail, and then a small Stock carried to *Virginia* will purchase provisions at a far easier rate than to carry them from hence; also the freight of the said Provisions will be saved, and be more fresh, and there wanteth not conveyance from *Virginia* thither.

If any Maid or single Woman have a desire to go over, they will think themselves in the Golden Age, when

2-23
One enterprising Englishman in 1682 offered to come to Carolina and "raise Trees up by the Roots quite out of the Earth." (Courtesy North Carolina Collection.)

2-21
Robert Horne's promotional pamphlet *A Brief Description of the Province of Carolina . . . and More perticularly of a New-Plantation begun by the English at Cape-Feare* (1666) proclaimed bright opportunities for women. The last sentence on the page reproduced here continued, "when Men paid a Dowry for their Wives; for if they be but Civil, and under 50 years of Age, some honest Man or other, will purchase them for their Wives." (Courtesy North Carolina Collection.)

2-22
Horne's booklet also reproduced a map showing a chapel at Charles Town (near the later town of Brunswick) and names given to sites up the Charles (Cape Fear) River. (Courtesy North Carolina Collection.)

May it please yor Lordshipp=

I have given yor a true & perfect acompt by which I doe plainly
demonstrate to yor Lordshipp the reasons wherefore I could nott make
those returnes & profitts yor Lordshipp did Expect which proably
in time if suplyed & well manidged may answer yor Lordshipps
Expectations but if Neglected soone ruined yor Lordshipp
may plainly apperceive that my Industrie Labour & paines have
Nott in the Least beene wanting and that it hath pleased God
of his providence to Inflict Such a Generall calamitie
upon the inhabitans of these contreys that for Severall
yeares they have Nott Injoyed the fruitts of their Labours
which causes them Generally to growne under the burtyn
of poverty & many times famine thus my Lord I have
given yor Lordshipp as plaine a demonstration as
my weak capacity hath Enabled mee humbly humbly
craving pardon for my proxility & to Subscribe my-
selfe

December ye 3 1674

Yor Lordshipps Most humble Servant

Carteret

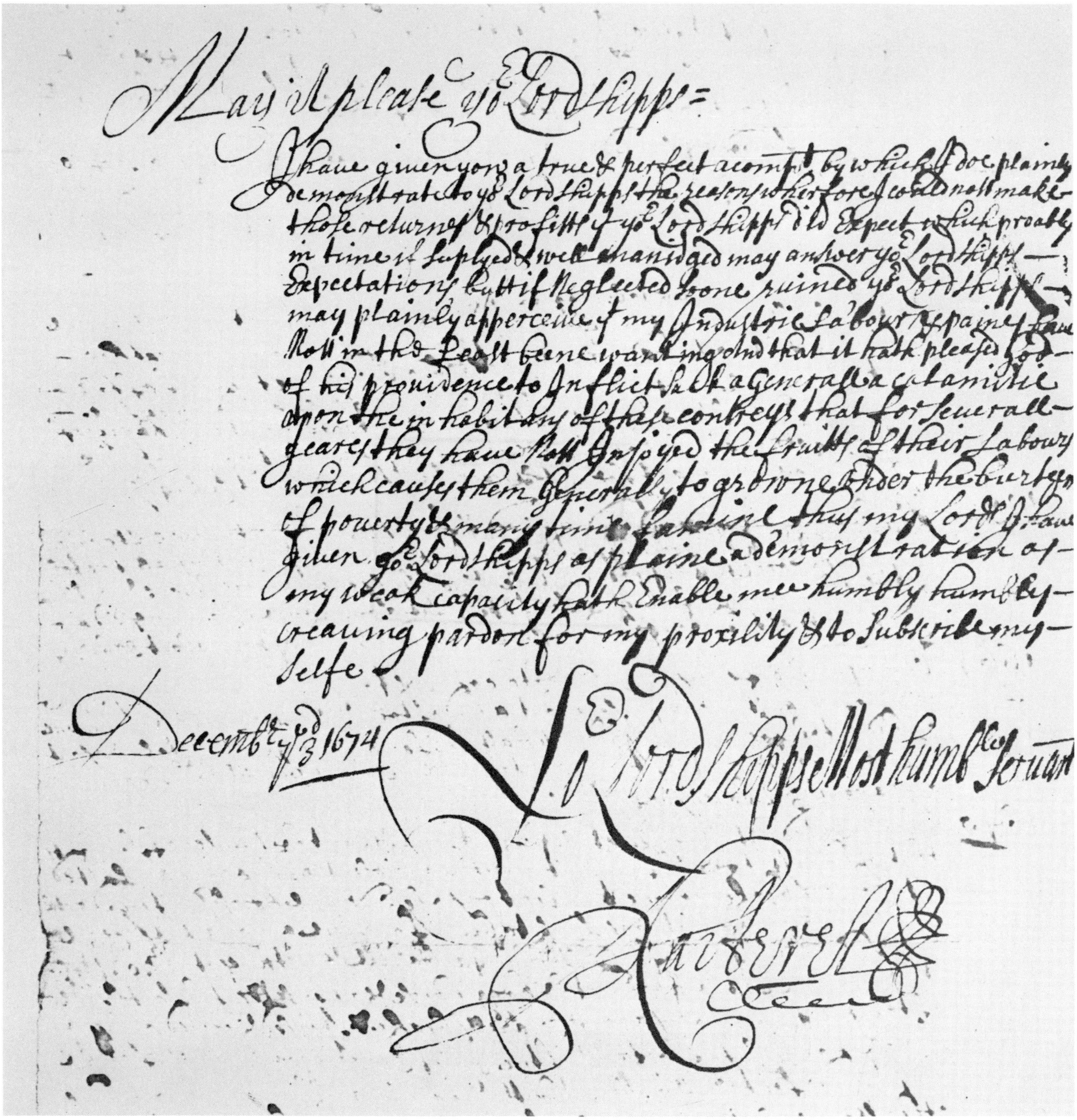

2-24

After seven years managing an unsuccessful farming operation, Governor Peter Carteret complained in 1674, "It hath pleased God of his providence to Inflict Such a Generall calamitie upon the inhabitans of these countreys that for Severall yeares they have Nott Injoyed the fruitts of their Labours which causes them Generally to growne under the burtyn of poverty & many times famine." (Courtesy NCDA&H.)

2-25
John Locke (1632–1704),
English philosopher, has
been credited with formula-
ting the Fundamental Constitutions of Carolina. This
portrait by M. Dahl was
painted about 1696. (By permission of National Portrait
Gallery, London.)

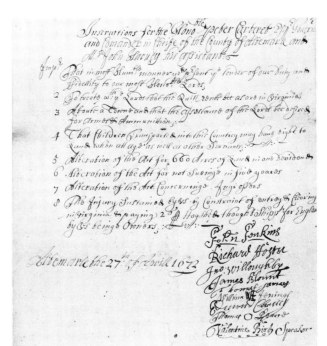

2-26
First issued in 1669, the Fundamental Constitutions
(or "Grand Model") went
through several editions (including this one issued in
1682), but never succeeded
in imposing a feudal system
upon the colony. (Courtesy
NCDA&H; original in Public
Record Office, London.)

2-27
Governor Carteret was sent
to England in 1672 to seek
from the Lords Proprietors
more liberal treatment of the
colony, including quitrents
similar to those in Virginia
and a provision for head-
rights for children transported into the colony.
(Courtesy NCDA&H.)

durſt not lie down on the Ground, for my Cloaths were wet to my Skin. I had eaten little or no-thing that Day, neither had I any thing to re-freſh me but the Lord. In the Morning I re-turn'd to ſeek my two Companions, and found them lying by a great Fire of Wood : I told them how I had far'd ; he that ſhould have been the Guide, would have perſwaded me, that we were gone paſt the Place where we intended ; but my Mind drew to the Path which I had found the Night before : So I led the Way, and that Path brought us to the Place where we in-tended, viz. Henry Phillips's Houſe by Albemarle River.

Henry Phil-lips by Albe-marle-River

He and his Wife had been convinc'd of the Truth in New-England, and came there to live, who having not ſeen a Friend for ſeven Years before, they wept for Joy to ſee us ; yet it being on a Firſt Day Morning when we got there, al-though I was weary and faint, and my Cloaths all wet, I deſired them to ſend to the People there-away to come to a Meeting about the middle of the Day, and I would lie down upon a Bed, and if I ſlept too long, that they ſhould awake me. Now about the Hour appointed many People came, but they had little or no Religion, for they came and ſate down in the Meeting ſmoking their Pipes ; but in a little time the Lord's Teſtimony aroſe in the Authori-ty of his Power, and their Hearts being reach'd with it, ſeveral of them were tender'd and re-ceived the Teſtimony. After Meeting they de-ſir'd me to ſtay with them, and let them have more Meetings.

One

This was the firſt Houſe we came to in Carolina : And here we left our Horſes, which were over-wearied with Travel. From hence we went down the Creek in a Canooe to Macocomocock-River, and came to a Man's Houſe, whoſe Name was Hugh Smith ; where the People of the World came in to ſee us (for there were no Friends in that part of the Country :) and many of them did receive us gladly. Amongſt others that came to us, there was one Nathaniel Batts, who (we heard) had been Governour of Ronoack : He went by the Name of Captain Batts, and had been a Rude, Deſperate Man. He asked me about a Woman in Cumberland, who, he ſaid he was told, had been healed by our Prayers, and Laying on of Hands, after ſhe had been long ſick, and given over by the Phyſicians ; and he deſired to know the certainty of it. I told him, We did not glory in ſuch things ; but many ſuch things had been done by the Power of Chriſt.

Not far from hence we had a Meeting among the World's People, and they were taken with the Truth ; bleſſed be the Lord. Then paſ-ſing down the River Maratick in a Canooe, we went down the Bay Connie-oak ; and came to a Captain's Houſe, who was loving to us, and lent us his Boat (for we were much wetted in the Canooe ; the Water flaſhing in upon us.) With this Boat we went on to the Go-vernour's Houſe : but the Water in ſome places was ſo ſhallow, that the Boat being loaden, could not Swim ; ſo that we were fain to put off our Shooes and Stockings, and wade through the Water a pretty way. The Governour, with his Wife, received us lovingly : but there was at his Houſe a Doctor, who would needs Diſpute with us. And truly, his Oppoſing us was of good Service, giving Occaſion for the Opening of many things to the People, concerning the Light and Spirit of God, which he denied to be in Every one ; and affirmed, that it was not in the Indians. Whereupon I called an Indian to us, and asked him, ' Whether or no, when he did lie, or do wrong to any one, ' there was not ſomething in him, that did reprove him for it ? And he ſaid, There was ſuch a thing in him, that did ſo reprove him ; and he was aſhamed, when he had done wrong, or ſpoken wrong. So we ſhamed the Doctor before the Governour and the People ; inſomuch, that the poor Man run out ſo far, that at length he would not own the Scrip-tures. We tarried at the Governour's that Night : and next Morning he very courteouſly walked with us himſelf about two Miles through the Woods, to a place, whither he had ſent our Boat about to meet us. Where taking our Leave of him, we entred our Boat again, and went that Day about Thirty Miles to one Joſeph Scot's, who was one of the Repreſentatives of the Country. And there we had a Meeting, and many People were at it : a ſound, precious Meeting it was, and the People were tender ; and much deſired after Meetings. Wherefore we went to another Houſe about four miles further, and there we had another Meeting ; to which the Governour's Secretary came, who was Chief Secretary of the Province, and had (it ſeems) been for-merly Convinced.

2-28

In 1672, an English Quaker, William Edmundson, nego-tiated the treacherous route from Virginia to the Al-bemarle, "it being all Wilder-ness, and no English Inhabi-tants or Pad-Ways, but some mark'd Trees to Guide Peo-ple." Here he describes a ser-vice in the home of Henry Phillips, who had previously lived in New England. (Courtesy North Carolina Collection; reprinted from William Edmundson, *A Jour-nal* . . . [London, 1715], p. 59.)

2-29

Another Quaker, George Fox, wrote about his travels to the Albemarle in 1672 (without, apparently, meeting Edmundson). According to Governor Henderson Walker, Fox "by strange infatuations, did infuse the Quakers' prin-ciples into some small num-ber of the people; which did and hath continued to grow ever since very numerous." (Courtesy Rare Book Collec-tion, Library, University of North Carolina at Chapel Hill; reprinted from George Fox, *A Journal or Historical Account* . . . [London, 1694], p. 376.)

2-30
Thomas Miller, collector of customs in the Albemarle, complained in a petition in 1680 that the "Rebells" then in control of the government continued to persecute their opponents "by heavy fines, imprisonm^t, Banishm^t, loss of Eares, &c." (Courtesy NCDA&H; original in Public Record Office, London.)

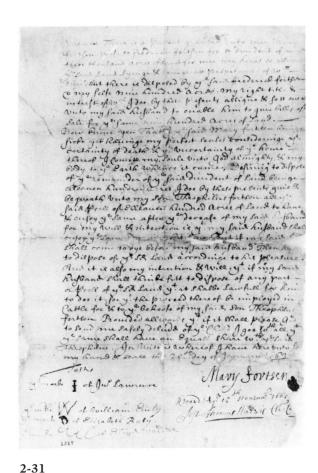

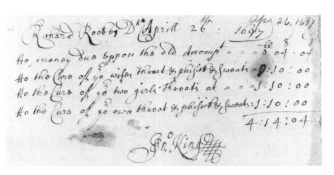

2-32
John King, presumably a physician of sorts, billed Richard Rookes for "the Cure" of sore throats. His treatment included medicines and sweating. (Courtesy NCDA&H.)

2-31
The earliest will on record in North Carolina is that of Mary Fortsen, who boldly affixed her signature 25 January 1663, hoping that God would see her "safely delivered of ye child I goe wth." She died two years later. (Courtesy NCDA&H.)

2-33 and 2-34
In an attempt to increase mediums of exchange in Carolina, the Lords Proprietors coined a copper halfpenny, commonly called the "Elephant Token," the elephant being an unofficial symbol for the province. (By permission of Frank Lawrence Stevens, Falls Church, Virginia.)

3. The Waning of the Proprietorship, 1689–1728

3-1 The appointment in 1689 of Philip Ludwell as governor of "that part of our Province of Carolina that lyes north and east of Cape feare" marked the beginning of more settled government in the Albemarle. Two years later Ludwell was elevated to the governorship of the entire Carolina colony with headquarters in Charleston, and a deputy governor was placed in the Albemarle. This arrangement continued until about 1712, when the colony was officially divided into North and South Carolina, each with its own governor.

Under provisions of the Fundamental Constitutions, the governor, council, and assembly (plus, at times, deputies of the proprietors) sat as a unicameral legislative body, though this procedure was not always followed in practice. After 1691, however, the governor and council met as an upper house while the assembly formed the lower house. Freemen twenty-one years of age who had been in the colony for a year and had paid the year's levy were permitted to vote for assemblymen. Negroes, mulattoes, mustees, Indians, and white men "not made free" were, of course, disfranchised. Despite the power of the proprietors to disallow legislative acts, representative government had taken an important step forward.

During this time, despite proposals for settle-
3-2 ments and public buildings, the government continued to meet in private homes or taverns. One of the favorite places was George Durant's house in Perquimans Precinct, and by 1677 stocks and a pillory had been erected there. At that time the records of Albemarle County were housed in the home of a deputy, Timothy Biggs, and the governor kept his papers and great seal in a box hidden in a tobacco hogshead. Even as late as 1689 the log prison in which Governor Sothel was incarcerated apparently was the only public building in Albemarle County. In the 1690s, however, the assembly ordered plans for a sixty-by-twenty-foot court-
3-3 house, and by 1701 there was a "Gran Court House for the Precinct of Piquimons." Mysteriously, no further reference to this building has been found, and the county may have been without another public structure until 1718 when the

council met at the "Court House in Chowan." Four years later Edenton—the new name for "ye Towne on Queen Annes Creek"—was designated the first fixed capital of North Carolina. In the intervening years public meetings had occurred wherever there was room. In 1708, for instance, innkeeper John Pettiver provided lodging for twenty-four men and four servants, along with a revealing assortment of food and drink: a barrel of strong drink, seven gallons of rum, fifty pounds of sugar, two castrated rams, and £5 worth of "beafe and porke and jowles."

The charter of 1663 characterized the Lords Proprietors as men "excited with a laudable and pious zeal for the propagation of the Christian Faith," but they did little to demonstrate that zeal. Seventeenth-century Albemarle was without priest or altar, and it was less a demonstration of Christian charity than a desire to attract settlers that led the proprietors to tolerate dissenters. Following the visits of William Edmundson and George Fox, the Quakers constituted the only formal religious orga- 3-4 nization in Albemarle, for their simple faith required no church or priest. Probably the majority of the settlers acknowledged no religion, but in addition to the Quakers and Anglicans, who vied for dominance, there were some Presbyterians and independents.

It was not until 1701 that the first Anglican missionary, Daniel Brett, arrived in the colony under sponsorship of the recently formed Society for the 3-5 Propagation of the Gospel in Foreign Parts. He brought along three libraries—layman's and paro- 3-6 chial libraries for "St. Thomas Parish in Pamplico" 3-7 and a second layman's collection for an unidentified location (almost certainly Chowan) in "Albemarle Settlement." Deputy Governor Henderson Walker, an avid Anglican, charged the Reverend Mr. Brett with behavior "so ill as to give the Dissenters so much occasion to charge us with him." Still, Walker persuaded the assembly to pass the Vestry Act of 1701 formally establishing the Church of England, laying out parishes, and levy- 3-8 ing a poll tax for its support. St. Paul's Parish in 3-9 Chowan was organized on 15 December, followed 3-10 soon by others. In 1709, William Gordon wrote from Perquimans, "Here is a compact little church, built with more care and expense, and better contrived than that in Chowan; it continues yet unfinished."

Even more galling to the Quakers was legislation passed two years later that denied them the right of affirmation, and for eight years the colony was embroiled in a civil struggle culminating in the "Cary Rebellion." Thomas Cary, who had succeeded Deputy Governor Robert Daniel, was removed in 1706 as a result of Quaker complaints, but he was returned to office with their support two years later. Cary's strange alliance with the non-Anglicans led the proprietors in 1711 to replace him with Edward Hyde. Armed resistance by the Cary forces was overcome, and Hyde assumed the governorship of a divided people weakened by years of internal strife.

Meanwhile, settlers had taken up lands along the Pamlico River to the south, and a few travelers had even ventured into the backcountry. Of the latter, the most influential was John Lawson, a newly arrived Englishman hired by the proprietors to conduct a reconnaissance survey. From Charleston he and several companions made their way up the Wateree River, crossing the imaginary line between North Carolina and South Carolina around Waxhaw in January 1701. For another month Lawson made his way from one Indian camp to another on an irregular route to Occoneechee Town (near present-day Hillsborough), then turned eastward, finally reaching Richard Smith's home on Pamlico River, where Lawson soon purchased land. His book *A New Voyage to Carolina; Containing the Exact Description and Natural History of That Country* . . . , in which he described the land, natives, animals, and wildlife of the interior, was published eight years later in London. Considering his contributions to North Carolina, Lawson was probably the most important settler during the proprietary period, even though he spent only ten years in the colony. His was the first book devoted mainly to North Carolina, and he helped establish the first two towns (Bath and New Bern), served as surveyor general and as a promoter of immigration, and furnished specimens of plant life to English naturalists.

The growth of settlements along the Pamlico led the proprietors in 1696 to create Bath County. The population was augmented about 1705 by a contingent of French Huguenots from Virginia, who

became, in Lawson's words, "good Neighbours amongst us." Within a year the colony's first incorporated town, Bath, was laid off on land partially owned by Lawson, and at about the same time the new county was divided into three precincts— Wickham (Hyde), Pamtecough (Beaufort), and Archdale (Craven).

Shortly after the turn of the century, Carolina began attracting other settlers from the European continent. While in England for the publication of his book, Lawson negotiated with a Swiss land company, led by Baron Christoph von Graffenried, which purchased from the Lords Proprietors 17,500 acres at the junction of the Neuse and Trent rivers. Lawson personally led the first group (which consisted more of English and Germans than Swiss settlers), and Graffenried later brought more Palatines. By the end of 1710 the colony's second town, New Bern, had been laid out.

The Graffenried colony arrived during the civil strife associated with the Cary Rebellion and at a time when the Indians were smarting under continued encroachment and the occasional enslavement of their women and children by the whites. Lawson himself wrote of the Indians, "They are really better to us than we have been to them." Surprisingly, there had been few major attacks upon the whites during the previous half century, but the appearance of about four hundred new European settlers at New Bern united the Tuscaroras and several smaller tribes. In September 1711, while boating up the Neuse River, Lawson, Graffenried, and the latter's black servant were captured and taken to the Indian town of Catechna, where their fate was placed before a council meeting. Lawson was executed. Graffenried and his servant were spared, but King Hancock revealed an awful secret to them: The Indians planned a surprise attack upon the white residents throughout the colony.

At daybreak on 22 September 1711, an estimated five hundred Tuscaroras and their allies began their assault, moving from farm to farm in Bath County, killing, looting, and burning. Governor Hyde called upon Virginia and South Carolina for assistance, and the latter responded, sending Colonel John Barnwell and a small number of white officers and about five hundred friendly Indians, mostly Yamassees, who marched to the Neuse River. This force assaulted the Tuscaroras as mercilessly as the Indians had treated the white settlers, and after months of indecisive fighting, a peace was agreed upon.

After Barnwell returned to South Carolina, the Tuscaroras accused the whites of violating the agreement, and they resumed the war in the summer of 1712. Again South Carolina responded to the plea for aid, this time sending Colonel James Moore with a group of white officers and about a thousand friendly Indians. Finally, on 25 March 1713, at Fort Nohoroco on Contentnea Creek, the Tuscaroras were routed with losses described as "Prisoners 392, Scolps 192, out of ye sd. fort—and att least 200 kill'd and Burnt in ye fort—and 166 kill'd and taken out of ye fort." The power of the eastern Indians was broken forever, and the Tuscaroras were soon herded onto a reservation. Eventually most of them left North Carolina.

Ironically, the Cary Rebellion and the Tuscarora War had a salutary effect on North Carolina, as the colony was now officially called. The sufferings of the residents and the removal of any serious threat from the Indians resulted in a more united population. Acting Governor Thomas Pollock said that the events had extinguished "the fire of difference and division among the people." That was an overstatement, but the colony did experience better times in the following decades. Just after the war, another town—Beaufort—was laid out, and in 1722 Edenton was the designated capital of the colony. This, however, soon appeared incongruous, for by the mid-1720s settlers, emboldened by the removal of the Indian menace, were rapidly occupying lands as far south as the Cape Fear River, which had remained virtually untouched by the whites since 1667. About 1725 the town of Brunswick on the lower Cape Fear was established, and five years later Edward Moseley estimated—perhaps excessively—the number of tithables in the area at one thousand. Bertie and Carteret precincts were created in 1722, New Hanover and Tyrrell seven years later.

Colonial life in the first quarter of the new century became more regularized. Frequent quarrels over land boundaries encouraged owners periodically to "procession" their property (that is, walk off the boundaries, re-marking the lines), but land records at the precinct level were better kept. Tobacco continued to be the chief item of export, though subsistence farming remained common. Furniture, too, was frequently made at home, and

a few substantial residences began to appear. Along the coast, whaling occupied some courageous sailors. A few public buildings were constructed for governmental functions, though taverns or ordinaries appeared to be the most common places for public meetings.

The assembly in 1715 reviewed the laws of the previous half century and purged those no longer in force. Because there was no printing press, the laws were laboriously copied by hand, bound in leather, and furnished to each precinct. The combination of better facilities, improved recordkeeping, revised laws, and an able if controversial chief justice, Christopher Gale, promoted more equitable administration of justice.

Still, all was not quiet in the years following the Tuscarora War. The opposition of the colonists to the English trade laws encouraged some of them to evade payment of the duties. This attitude, coupled with the physical protection provided by the strip of islands and sandbars constituting the outer banks, explained the attractiveness of the coast of North Carolina to visiting pirates, such as Edward Teach (or Thatch), better known as Blackbeard. Teach, Stede Bonnet, and even female pirates such as Anne Bonney and Mary Read were tolerated if not welcomed by the residents of the coast, and Teach married and moved for a time in respectable circles at Bath. There is strong evidence to suggest that Governor Charles Eden's secretary, Tobias Knight, and perhaps the governor himself, was associated with Blackbeard, and both Virginia and South Carolina accused the government of North Carolina of protecting the pirates. Unchallenged by local residents, Blackbeard was finally killed by a seaborne expedition of Virginians in 1718 at Ocracoke, and his head was hung from the bowsprit. The "golden age of piracy" ended a few years later.

After six decades, the original Lords Proprietors were all dead, and their successors chafed under the absence of profit from their holdings. The English government had become increasingly dubious of the merits of continued private ownership of the growing colonies of North Carolina and South Carolina, and in 1729 the crown repurchased seven of the eight proprietary shares for £17,500. The Carteret heirs held onto their eighth share of the land, but lost their civil jurisdiction. Henceforth, North Carolina would be a royal colony.

3-1

Philip Ludwell served as governor of Albemarle, 1689–91, and of the entire province of Carolina until 1694. (Courtesy North Carolina Collection.)

3-2

The Lords Proprietors in January 1670 pledged "wth ye first money we shall receive of our quitt rents fines or forfeitures to Erect a State house . . . , prison & a Church." The promise went unfulfilled. Six years later the proprietors ordered the establishment of three towns—one on Roanoke Island "wch wee will have bee the chiefe towne and the place for ye Councell & Assembly to meete," one at the mouth of Little River, and a third at the confluence of Salmon Creek and Morratock (Roanoke) River. The instructions came to naught. (Courtesy NCDA&H.)

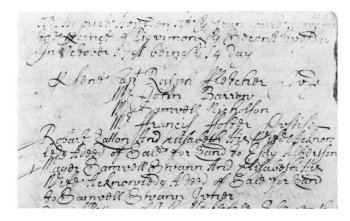

3-3

In 1701 the Perquimans Precinct Court of Pleas and Quarter Sessions met in "ye Gran Court House," perhaps the first meeting place constructed with public funds. The court served as the administrative body of the precinct. (Courtesy NCDA&H.)

3-4

Minutes of the yearly meeting (1704) of North Carolina Quakers, the province's most numerous religious body during the first seventy-five years. (Courtesy Friends Historical Collection, Guilford College.)

3-7
One of the books in the parochial library brought by the SPG missionary, Daniel Brett, to St. Thomas Parish, Bath, in 1701. (Courtesy North Carolina Collection.)

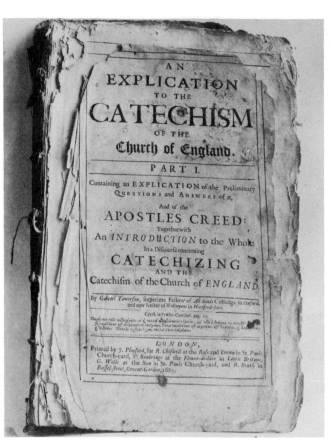

3-5
Seal of the Society for the Propagation of the Gospel in Foreign Parts, which in 1701 sent the first Anglican clergyman, Daniel Brett, to North Carolina. (Courtesy NCDA&H.)

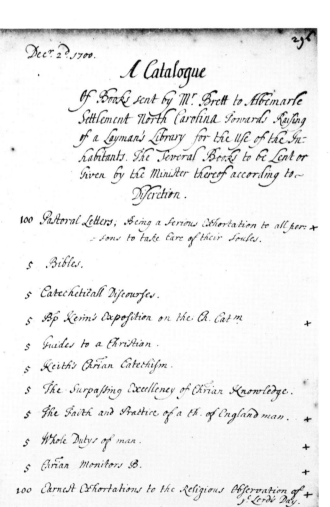

3-6
First page of the catalog of one of the two laymen's libraries sent to North Carolina by the SPG in 1701.

One went to Bath, the other almost certainly to Edenton. (Courtesy North Carolina Collection.)

3-8
A page from St. Paul's vestry book, Edenton, 4 April 1703, refers to the purchase of weights and measures for

Chowan Precinct, an indication of the close relationship of church and government. (Courtesy NCDA&H.)

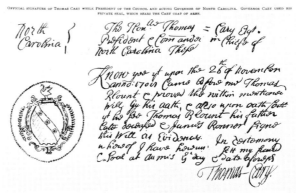

3-9
St. Paul's communion plate, a paten and chalice, was probably made by Alexander Kerr of Williamsburg. It was a gift of Edward Moseley in 1725 and is still owned by the church. (Courtesy NCDA&H.)

3-12
A certification by Thomas Cary, 26 November 1708, is one of the few documents surviving from his two troublesome administrations as governor. (Courtesy North Carolina Collection; reprinted from *North Carolina Day Program*, 1904.)

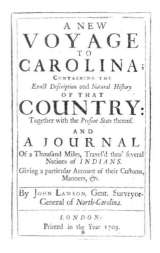

3-10
The Reverend John Blacknall (ca. 1690–1749) served as rector of St. Paul's Church at Edenton in 1725–26. He left the colony after being indicted for performing the marriage of a white man and a mulatto woman (Courtesy Frick Art Reference Library, New York.)

3-11
Robert Daniel, deputy governor 1703–5, invoked English law to exclude from the assembly Quakers who refused to swear any oath, including one of allegiance to Queen Anne. The Quakers then joined with other dissenters to bring about Daniel's suspension. (Courtesy North Carolina Collection.)

3-13
Edward Hyde was governor when the Tuscaroras attacked the white settlements along the Neuse and Pamlico rivers. He died in a yellow fever epidemic in 1712. This recently rediscovered portrait has been heavily retouched. (Courtesy NCDA&H.)

3-14
John Lawson's *A New Voyage to Carolina . . .*, the first book chiefly devoted to North Carolina, was published in London in 1709. Twenty-eight years later Dr. John Brickell drew heavily on Lawson's account for his *Natural History of North-Carolina*. (Courtesy North Carolina Collection.)

3-15
Lawson's *New Voyage* carried fanciful sketches of "Beasts of Carolina" including, from top to bottom, buffalo, terrapin, king snake, opossum, panther or wildcat attacking a deer, rattlesnake, raccoon, and bear. (Courtesy North Carolina Collection.)

3-16
In an essay, *A Description of North-Carolina*, published a year earlier, Lawson described the early settlement of the province, noting that "the Ruins of a Fort are to be seen at this day" on Roanoke Island. (Courtesy of North Carolina Collection.)

> 62 A DESCRIPTION
>
> *First Colony of Carolina.* The first Discovery and Settlement of this Country was by the Procurement of Sir *Walter Raleigh*, in Conjunction with some publick-spirited Gentlemen of that Age, under the Protection of Queen *Elizabeth*; for which Reason it was then named *Virginia*, being begun on that Part called *Ronoak*-Island, where the Ruins of a Fort are to be seen at this day, as well as some old *English* Coins which have been lately found; and a Brafs-Gun, a Powder-Horn, and one small Quarter deck-Gun, made of Iron Staves, and hoop'd with the same Metal; which Method of making Guns might very probably be made use of in those Days, for the Convenience of Infant-Colonies.
>
> *Hatteras Indians.* A farther Confirmation of this we have from the *Hatteras Indians*, who either then lived on *Ronoak*-Island, or much frequented it. These tell us, that several of their Ancestors were white People, and could talk in a Book, as we do; the Truth of which is confirm'd by gray Eyes being found frequently amongst these *Indians*, and no others. They value themselves extremely for their Affinity to the *English*, and are ready to do them all friendly Offices. It is probable, that this Settlement miscarry'd for want of timely Supplies from *England*; or thro' the Treachery of the Natives, for we may reasonably suppose that the *English* were forced to cohabit with them, for Relief and Conversation; and that in procefs of Time, they conform'd themselves to the Manners of their *Indian* Relations. And thus we fee, how apt Humane Nature is to degenerate.
>
> *Sir Walter Raleigh's Ship.* I cannot forbear inserting here, a pleasant Story that passes for an uncontested Truth amongst the Inhabitants of this Place; which is, that the Ship which brought the first Colonies, does often appear amongst them, under Sail, in a gallant Posture, which they call Sir *Walter Raleigh*'s Ship; And the truth of this has been affirm'd to me, by Men of the beft Credit in the Country.
>
> *Second Settlement of North-Carolina.* A second Settlement of this Country was made about fifty Years ago, in that part we now call *Albemarl*-County, and chiefly in *Chuwon* Precinct, by several substantial Planters, from *Virginia*, and other Plantations; Who finding mild Winters, and a fertile Soil, beyond Expectation, producing every thing that was planted, to a prodigious Increafe; their Cattle, Horses, Sheep, and Swine, breeding
> very

3-17
Baron Christoph von Graffenried, a Swiss nobleman, founded New Bern in 1710. The town was named for Bern, Switzerland. (Courtesy NCDA&H.)

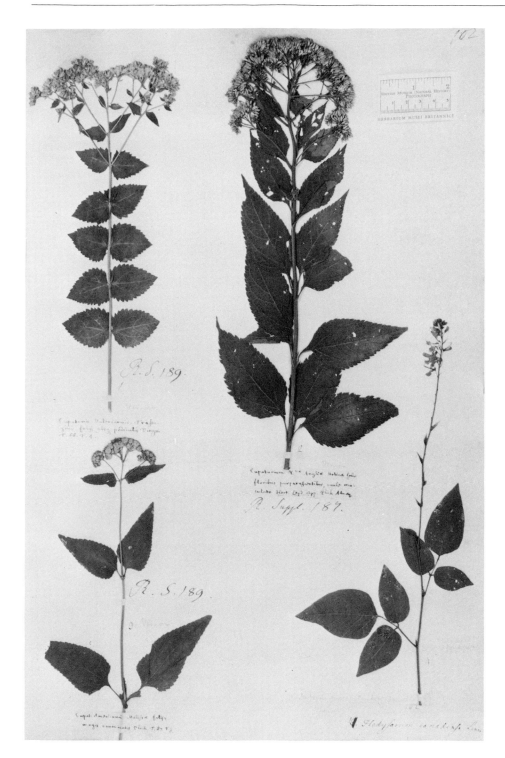

3-18
Several varieties of plants, including these specimens still preserved in the British Museum, were sent from North Carolina by Lawson to James Petiver in England in 1710. (By permission of British Museum [Natural History], London.)

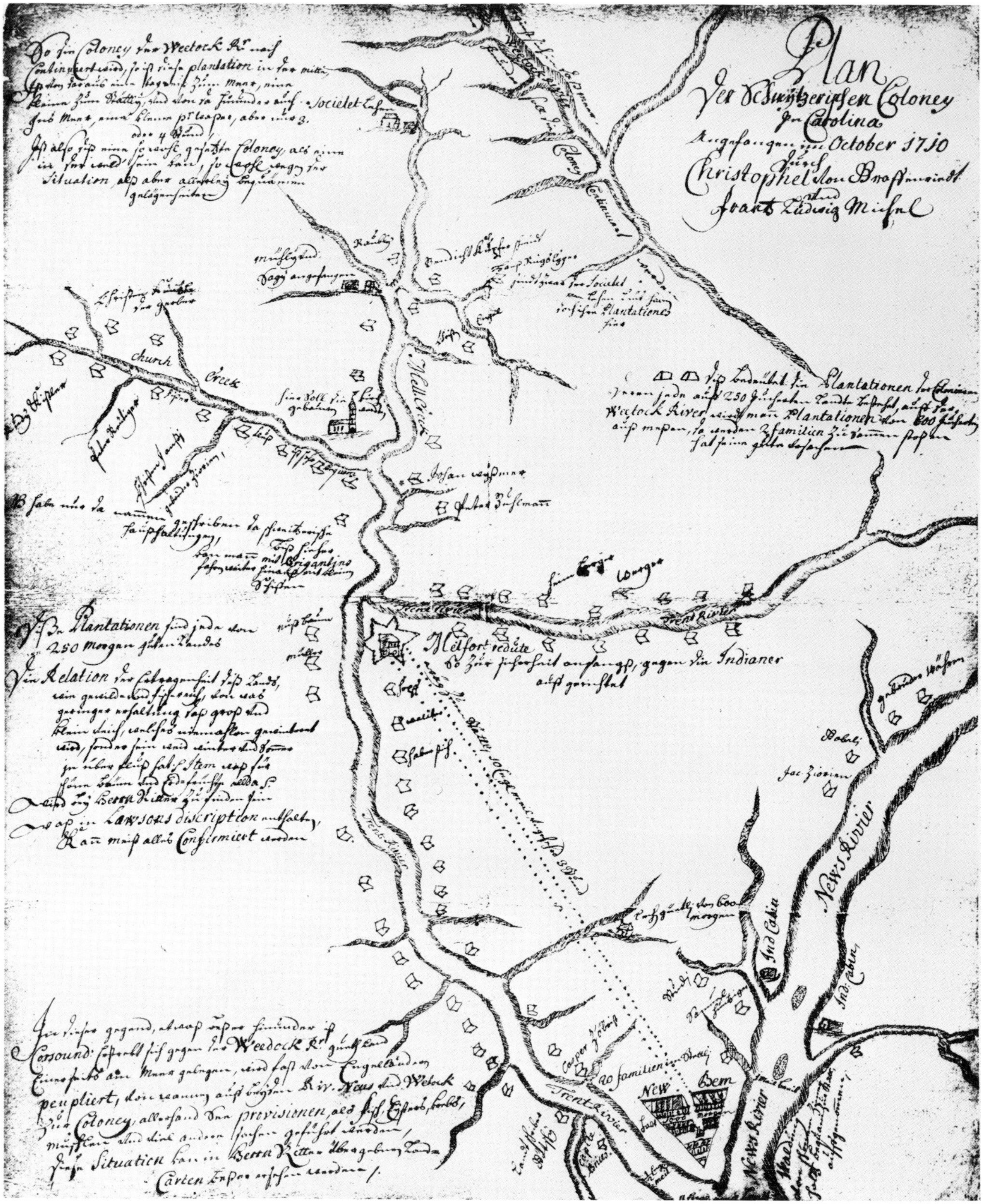

3-19

The plan for the town of New Bern, drawn in 1710, revealed Graffenried's am-bitious proposals along the Neuse and Trent rivers. (Courtesy North Carolina Collection; reprinted from *Neujahrsblatt herausgegeben vom Historischen Verein des Kantons Bern fur 1897* [Bern, 1896].)

3-20
Franz Ludwig Michel, associated with Graffenried in the founding of New Bern, visited America earlier and made a watercolor drawing of three Algonquian (or possibly Powhatan) Indians. This contemporary copy was made by his brother, John Louis Michel. (By permission of Burgerbibliothek, Bern.)

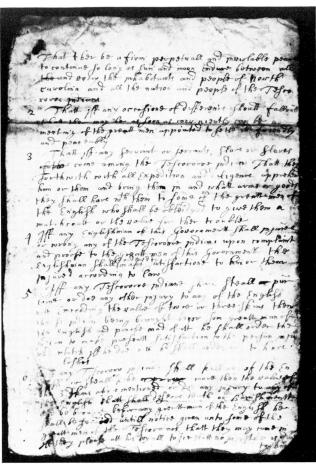

3-22
The first page of an undated draft treaty between "the inhabitants and people of North Carolina and all the nation and people of the Tuscarora Indians" reflected characteristic condescension of the English toward the natives. (Courtesy Southern Historical Collection, Library, University of North Carolina, Chapel Hill, Cupola House Papers [microfilm].)

3-21
This drawing of an Indian hunting a deer or elk appeared on a deerskin map drawn by an "Indian Cacique" and copied in 1724 for presentation to the governor of South Carolina. (Courtesy North Carolina Collection.)

3-23
The capture of John Lawson, Baron von Graffenried, and their black companion was depicted in this nineteenth-century drawing, which appeared in Lambert Lilly [pseudonym for Francis Lister Hawks], *The Early History of the Southern States* . . . (Philadelphia, 1832), p. 125. (Courtesy North Carolina Collection.)

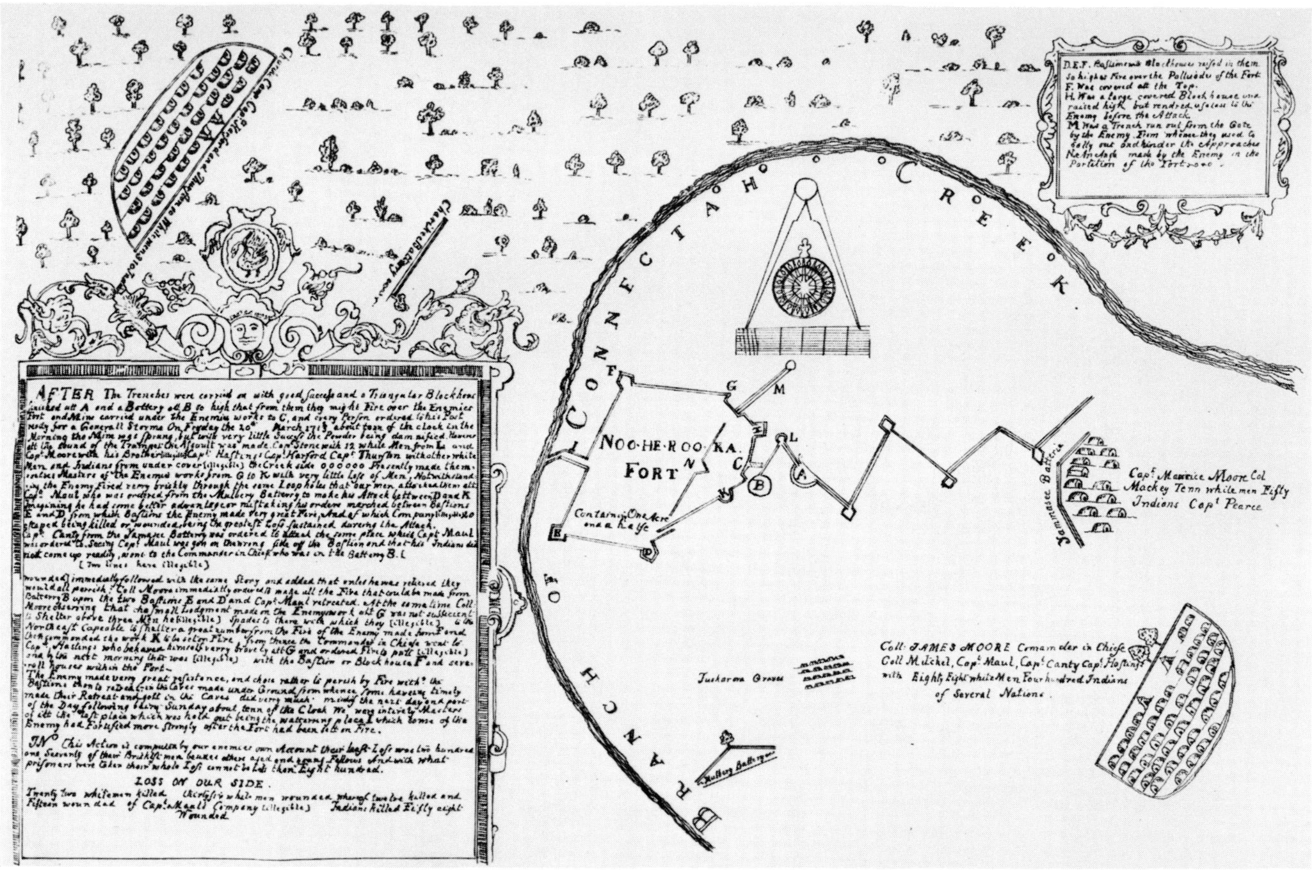

3-24
The Tuscaroras were crushed at the battle of Fort Nohoroco in 1713. The tribe was never again a threat to the whites. (Courtesy North Carolina Collection; original in South Carolina Historical Society, Charleston.)

These are to Certifie That Mr William Charlton hath been eight days in the Country Service as interpreter for the laying out of the Tuscororoes Lands as witness my hand this 27 of June 1722.
Tho Pollock
To captn John Worley: to satisfy him
Recd of Capt Jno Worley the above Contents
Wm Charlton

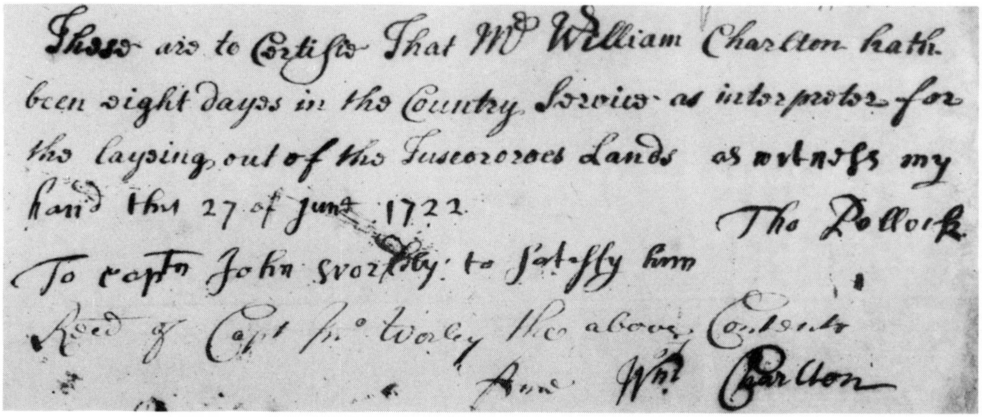

3-25
A reservation for the Tuscaroras was surveyed in 1722 in Bertie County, but even there they were not safe from land-hungry whites. William Charlton of Chowan County was engaged as an interpreter during the survey. (Courtesy NCDA&H.)

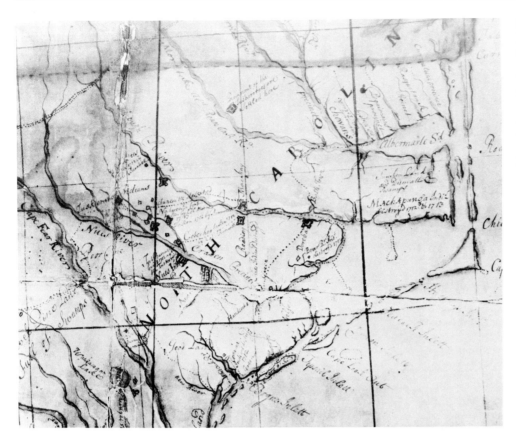

3-26
John Barnwell's map of southeastern North America, 1722, reveals the results of white campaigns against the natives. Among the notations are "Coranine Indians destroy^{d} 1712" and "Machapunga Indi^{s} Destroy^{d} 1712 & 1713." (Courtesy North Carolina Collection.)

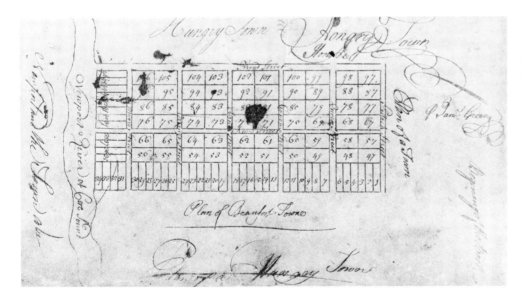

3-27
Beaufort, laid out in 1713, was labeled by a scribbler as "Hongry Town" on this recorded plat. (Courtesy NCDA&H.)

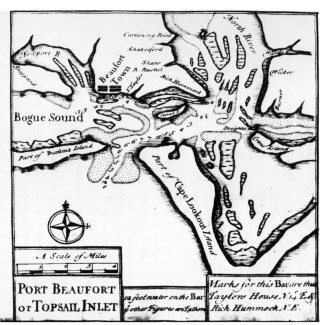

3-28

Edward Moseley's map of 1733 showed Beaufort and Brunswick as important towns. Each served as a port, but the terms "Port Beaufort" and "Port Brunswick" included other landings along nearby rivers. (Courtesy East Carolina Manuscript Collection, Library, East Carolina University, Greenville.)

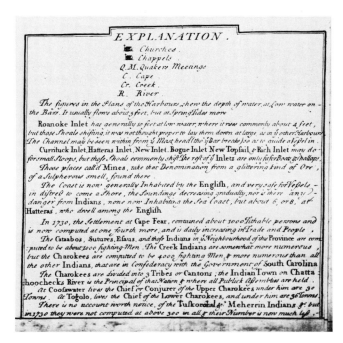

3-29

Moseley included on his map a useful description of the colony, even his estimate of the strength of the Indian groups. (Courtesy East Carolina Manuscript Collection, Greenville.)

3-30

Simple furniture, such as this child's armchair, ca. 1725, was made in the colony, but until after the middle of the century finer pieces usually were purchased elsewhere. (Courtesy Museum of Early Southern Decorative Arts, Winston-Salem.)

3-31
Styles lagged behind those in England, but the William and Mary style had reached North Carolina when this stretcher table was made by a turner in the first quarter of the eighteenth century. (Courtesy Museum of Early Southern Decorative Arts, Winston-Salem.)

3-33
In 1725, Samuel Chadwick of Carteret Precinct was licensed "with three boats to fish for Whale or other Royall fish" on condition that he pay the governor 10 percent of the "oyle and bone [baleen]." (Courtesy NCDA&H.)

3-32
Perhaps the grandest structure in the colony at the time was the "Cupola House," built in Edenton about 1725. This is a recent view of the restored building. (Courtesy NCDA&H.)

3-34
More reminiscent of houses in Virginia than in North Carolina, the Newbold-White House in Perquimans County—possibly dating from the seventeenth century—has been restored to its probable earlier appearance. (Courtesy NCDA&H.)

3-35
A whaling scene appeared near Core Banks on Edward Moseley's map of 1733. Here five men in a boat, with no weapon but a harpoon, confront a leviathan. (Courtesy East Carolina Manuscript Collection, Greenville.)

3-37
Christopher Gale served, with minor interruption, as chief justice of North Carolina from 1712 to 1731. This portrait is attributed to Henrietta Johnston. (Courtesy NCDA&H.)

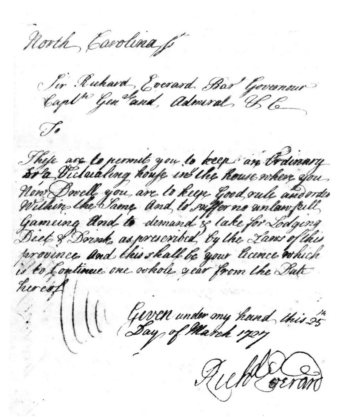

3-36
Governor Richard Everard in 1727 signed a blank license for the operation of "an Ordinary or a Victualing house" on condition that good rule and order be kept. No "unlawfull gameing" was to be permitted. (Courtesy NCDA&H.)

3-38
Edward Teach, or Thatch ("Blackbeard"), was North Carolina's most famous pirate, operating out of Bath and Ocracoke. This sketch appeared in Captain Charles Johnson's *A General History of the Pyrates* only seven years after Blackbeard was beheaded during hand-to-hand fighting off Ocracoke in 1718. (Courtesy North Carolina Collection.)

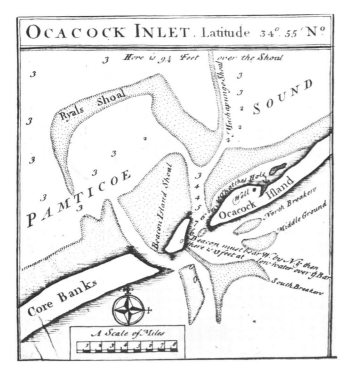

3-39

Moseley's map commemorated the legendary Blackbeard with the label "Thatches Hole." Also noted is a well reputed to have held the pirate's treasure. (Courtesy East Carolina Manuscript Collection, Greenville.)

3-41

The obverse of the seal of the Lords Proprietors pictures an Indian couple with two naked children. The reverse side contains coats of arms of the individual proprietors. (Courtesy NCDA&H.)

Rhode-Island, February 20. On the 12th Currant arrived here John Jackson from Piscataqua for Connecticut, and Humphry Johnston in a Sloop from North Carolina, bound to Amboy who sailed the next Day, and informs that Governour Spotswood of Virginia fitted out two Sloops, well mann'd with Fifty pickt Men of his Majesty's Men of War lying there, and small Arms, but no great Guns, under the Command of Lieutenant Robert Maynard of his Majesty's Ship Pearl, in pursuit of that Notorious and Arch Pirate Capt. Teach, who made his Escape from Virginia, when some of his Men were taken there; which Pirate Lieutenant Maynard came up with at North Carolina, and when they came in hearing of each other, Teach called to Lieutenant Maynard and told him he was for King GEORGE, desiring him to hoist out his Boat and come aboard, Maynard reply'ed that he designed to come aboard with his Sloop assoon as he could, and Teach understanding his design, told him that if he would let him alone, he would not meddle with him; Maynard answered that it was him he wanted, and that he would have him dead or alive, else it should cost him his life; whereupon Teach called for a Glass of Wine, and swore Damnation to himself, if he either took or gave Quarters: Then Lieut Maynard told his Men, that now they knew what they had to trust to, and could not escape the Pirates hands if they had a mind; but must either fight and kill or be killed: Teach begun and fired several Great Guns at Maynard's Sloop, which did but little damage, but Maynard rowing nearer Teach's Sloop of Ten Guns, Teach fired some small Guns, loaded with Swan shot, spick Nails and pieces of old Iron, in upon Maynard; which killed six of his Men, and wounded ten; upon which Lieutenant Maynard, ordered all the rest of his Men to go down in the Hould, himself, Abraham Demelt of New-York, and a third at the Helm stayed above Deck, Teach seeing so few on the Deck, said to his Men, the Rogues were all killed except two or three, and he would go on board and kill them himself, so drawing nearer, went on board, took hold of the fore sheet and made fast the Sloops; Maynard and Teach themselves two begun the Fight with their Swords, Maynard making a thrust, the point of his Sword went against Teach's Gartridge-Box, and bended it to the Hilt, Teach broke the Guard of it, and wounded Maynard's Fingers, but did not disable him, whereupon he Jumpt back, threw away his Sword, and fired his Pistol, which wounded Teach. Demelt struck in between them with his Sword and cut Teach's Face pretty much; in the Interim both Companies ingaged in Maynard's Sloop, one of Maynard's Men being a Highlander, ingaged Teach with his broad Sword, who gave Teach a cut on the Neck, Teach saying, well done Lad; the Highlander reply'd, if it be not well done, I'll do it better, with that he gave him a second stroke, which cut off his Head, laying it flat on his Shoulder, Teach's Men being about 20, and three or four Blacks, were all killed in the Ingagement, excepting two carried to Virginia: Teach's body was thrown overboard, and his Head put on the top of the Bowsprit.

3-40

The 23 February–2 March 1719 issue of the *Boston News-Letter* vividly described the fate of Blackbeard: "Teach's body was thrown overboard, and his Head put on the top of the Bowsprit." (Courtesy Connecticut Historical Society, Hartford.)

4. A Royal Colony, 1728–1775

4-6 The transition from a proprietary to a royal colony proceeded fairly quietly for the two years during which Sir Richard Everard, initially appointed by the Lords Proprietors, continued in office; when
4-1 news arrived in 1731 that George Burrington had been appointed to succeed him, the independent-minded leaders of North Carolina had reason to be pleased. After all, Burrington had sided with the "popular party" against the proprietors in several important controversies during his earlier gubernatorial term. Surprisingly, however, Burrington arrived with a stern determination to enforce the crown's plan to make the officials of the colony independent of the elected assembly. Previous commissions were declared void; new officers were to be appointed by the crown; the governor and council were to set fees for public officers; and quitrents thereafter were to be paid in money acceptable in England. The reaction of the assembly was one of defiance: in three sessions, it failed to pass a single bill proposed by Burrington.

After three years of stalemate between the governor and the assembly, the crown in 1734 replaced
4-2 Burrington with Gabriel Johnston, a Scot, who would serve longer than any other governor in the history of North Carolina. The strong-willed colonists met their match in Johnston, who struck a bargain with the assembly: He would confirm title to lands illegally settled after the Lords Proprietors closed their land office on condition that the assembly pass an act directing the preparation of a quitrent roll. The governor's firmness and fairness
4-3 resulted in a begrudging payment of the quitrents by some—though by no means all—residents; and he might have succeeded in placing the colony on a firm financial base if complications had not arisen
4-4 from the laying off of Earl Granville's one-eighth
4-5 share of the original Carolina grant. As a settlement with Granville, a wide swath of North Carolina, reaching from the Atlantic westward and containing some twenty-six thousand square miles of the most populated and productive lands of the province, was surveyed after 1743. This vast territory, extending sixty miles southward from the Virginia border to a line running approximately

from Bath westward, henceforth was called the Granville District. Though Granville set up his own land office and issued grants and sought to collect rents independent of the royal government, his officers were continually embroiled in controversy with the residents. The crown, which retained governmental jurisdiction over the district, was thus deprived of the rents from the most valuable portion of the colony. Despite the efforts of Johnston and his successors, the remainder of the colonial period passed without the compilation of an accurate rent roll or the systematic collection of the rents.

Even as the seal of George II replaced that of the Lords Proprietors, marked changes were appearing in the population of the frontiers of North Carolina, particularly in the region of the Cape Fear River. On the assumption that lands south and
4-7 west of the river belonged to South Carolina, Maurice Moore established the town of Brunswick in the 1720s, and soon other South Carolinians joined him. Quickly, Governor Burrington and some influential Albemarle planters, including Edward Moseley and Samuel Swann, obtained land along the river. Others came by sea, and in 1733 New Carthage—later known as New Liverpool, Newton, and finally Wilmington—was laid out at the junction of the two branches of the Cape Fear. By that time the population of the entire colony was perhaps forty thousand, one-sixth black.

The growth of the colony, however, had hardly
4-8 begun. The trickle of Scots, which started in 1732 when James Innes obtained a grant near present-day Lake Waccamaw, became a stream a decade later. Governor Johnston, himself a Scot, encouraged immigration, and the new precinct of Bladen (1734) took on a distinctly Scottish flavor. Shortly
4-9 after mid-century two towns—Cross Creek and Campbellton (combined during the Revolution to form Fayetteville)—served as the heart of an area where Gaelic remained a familiar language through 4-10 the century.

Expansion, moreover, was not limited to the Cape Fear region. Migration from three directions increased the population of the backcountry, and other precincts—henceforth designated counties—were formed by mid-century: Onslow, Edgecombe, Northampton, Granville, Johnston, Anson, and Duplin.

By the early 1730s, land along some of the western streams had also been granted to speculators. Following his exploration of the region during the survey of the colony line, William Byrd of Virginia acquired twenty thousand acres on the Dan near present-day Eden, where, he wrote, "a colony of one thousand families might, with the help of moderate industry, pass their time very happily." Less than fifty miles southeastward, Sir Richard Everard, Jr., and Governor George Burrington were among the prominent Carolinians who staked 4-11 out lands along the Saxapahaw River at "Stanford" (present-day Hawfields), astride the Indian Trading Path. The mention of previous owners and "Brick-house Branch" suggests even earlier settlement by whites. Less than two decades later speculators obtained permission of Lord Granville for a grant of two million acres "on the Branches of Missisippi [*sic*] River."

The most dramatic influx was from the north, 4-12 particularly from Pennsylvania via the Great Wagon Road, the name given to a series of heavily used trails through the Shenandoah Valley of Virginia to the Carolina Piedmont. As early as the 1730s Ulster Scots—that is, Scots who had lived for a time in northern Ireland—began making their way southward from Pennsylvania, and their numbers increased in the following decades. Descendants of German families used the same route to locate good lands in the Piedmont, particularly along the Yadkin River. One group came as a larger "family." Anxious to find a place where they could establish a communal civil and church government, the Unitas Fratrum (United Brethren, more popularly called Moravians) in 1752 sent Bishop August 4-13 Gottlieb Spangenberg to Lord Granville's district, where he acquired a tract of about one hundred 4-14 thousand acres, which they called Wachovia. They 4-15 established Bethabara and in 1766 built the first 4-16 house in Salem, destined to be their principal 4-17 town, an oasis on the frontier where industry and 4-18 culture exceeded that of any other part of the 4-19 colony.

The immigration of Scots, particularly those who came from Ulster and were mislabeled "Scotch-4-20 Irish," increased after Arthur Dobbs, himself a native of Ulster, became governor of the colony in 1754. Although their imprint was most notable on

the agricultural Piedmont, the Scots settled throughout the province and took with them their Presbyterian heritage of hard work and thrift. The few Irish residents—most of whom settled in the 4-21 east—appear to have carried a less complimentary stereotype. Though other nationalities, such as French and Swiss, were represented in the colonial population, their influence was not marked.

Among the towns that followed westward settlement were Hillsborough (originally Corbinton, then Childsburgh), Halifax, and Salisbury. By the end of the Dobbs administration, North Carolina's 4-23 estimated population of 130,000 was scattered as far as the Blue Ridge.

Throughout the previous history of the colony, both the northern and southern boundaries were in dispute. A joint party surveyed the Virginia line in 1728, an experience memorialized by William Byrd of Virginia in prose and maps. The South 4-22 Carolina line was not as easily settled, and disputes continued long after the initial survey of 1737.

In the decades of the 1740s and 1750s the British Empire was almost continually embroiled in struggles with Spain or France, or both. During the "Spanish Alarm," privateers brazenly raided coastal communities and held Beaufort for several 4-24 days in 1747 before being driven off by the county militia led by Thomas Lovick. In September of the following year another Spanish force landed and plundered the town of Brunswick before being re- 4-25 pulsed by local militiamen under leadership of Wil- 4-26 liam Dry. 4-27

A greater threat to the colony came with the French and Indian War (or, more properly, the Seven Years' War). Fort Johnston, constructed several years earlier, stood sentinel on the coast, but the main danger to North Carolina was along its western frontier. There Hugh Waddell directed the 4-28 construction of Fort Dobbs, a log structure on 4-29 Fourth Creek. Attacks upon and by Indians re- 4-30 sulted in numerous casualties along the frontier, 4-31 and hundreds of North Carolinians joined other colonists to help bring about the cessation of hostilities in 1763. The Cherokees had already sued for peace after attacks from British regulars and South Carolina troops under command of James Grant in 1761.

As settlement spread through the colony, the location of the seat of government at Edenton became an inconvenience to western and southern residents. Governor Johnston proposed that the capital be fixed at New Bern or Wilmington, but the predominance of Albemarle delegates in the assembly (each of the older counties had five or three delegates, while the newer ones had only two each) stood in his way. So in 1746 the governor called for the legislature to meet at Wilmington. This session, boycotted by the Albemarle representatives, picked New Bern as the capital and equalized representation from the various counties.

The delegates from the Albemarle region, however, continued their boycott for eight years, sent agents to London to plead their case before the Board of Trade, and eventually succeeded in having the laws disallowed. In 1758, Governor Dobbs persuaded the assembly to fix the capital at Tower Hill, near the present city of Kinston, but at subsequent sessions the assembly changed its mind and the plan came to naught.

In the 17–24 August 1764 issue of his *North-Carolina Magazine*, James Davis warned that the governor was intent upon having the capital established at Wilmington. He asked, "Can you *Contentedly*, see the Province in this *Discontented* State? Can you see the PUBLIC RECORDS *Carted* from Place to Place, and your Properties and Estates trusted to the Mercy of a Shower of Rain, and at the Discretion of a *Cart-Driver*? Forbid it Heaven! O Tempora!"

The fixing of a permanent seat of government would have to await a new administration. Government, therefore, remained peripatetic, meeting in borrowed buildings in several villages. There were, in fact, few substantial public buildings in the entire colony. Jurors and sheriffs complained of the condition of the jails, and county and colonial officials rankled under poor facilities for their records. The most ambitious public building yet undertaken was the Chowan County Courthouse, constructed in 1767.

Inland travel was arduous. The earliest roads simply evolved from repeated use of trails. Later, laws were passed for the licensing and setting of rates of ferry-keepers; and property owners were required to contribute a specified number of days of labor per year to the building and upkeep of roads and streets. Those who defaulted on the obligation were fined. Marshy areas were particularly troublesome and sometimes required the construction of "corduroy" roads with logs laid upon runners at 90-degree angles. The speed of travel varied with the terrain; in 1736 a juror expended a day to ride twenty-five miles to Edenton.

Communication was slow and unpredictable. Although messages were usually conveyed from plantation to plantation, the province had no official postal service until 1738 when William Parks obtained a commission for a monthly mail service from Williamsburg to Edenton and return. Dr. Abraham Blacknall was appointed "Post-Master of Carolina"—not a very burdensome job at the time. The following year Edenton was connected with Charleston by a monthly mail stage, which also ran through Wilmington. This first postal route appears to have been discontinued in a few years, for in 1755 Dobbs reported that "there is no Established Post thro this Province." On the governor's recommendation, the assembly contracted with James David, the printer, to convey by messenger all public letters, expresses, and dispatches every fifteen days between Suffolk, Virginia, and Wilmington. By 1774, there was a north-south weekly post through the colony.

The economy of colonial North Carolina depended heavily upon the fruits of the soil. In 1721 the Board of Trade reported to the crown that the natural produce of the colony was rice, pitch, tar, turpentine, buck skins, hides, corn, beef, pork, soap, myrtle wax candles, masts, cedar boards, staves, shingles, and hoop poles. But, the report added, the soil was thought capable of producing grapes, indigo, potash, hemp, and flax. Forty years later, Governor Dobbs wrote, "The natural produce and Staple Commodities of this Province, for the Manufactures are none; Consist of Naval Stores Mast yards Plank and Ship Timber, Tar pitch and Turpentine Lumber of all Kinds, furs and peltry Beef pork Hides, and some tanned Leather—Indian Corn pease Rice and of late flour Hemp flax and flax seed, Tobacco Bees and Myrtle wax and some Indigo: We export little or no bullion or Sterling the whole Trade being carried on by paper Currency." He complained that the commodity inspectors, chosen not by the crown but by the county courts, did not always properly carry out their responsibilities and that fraud was widespread in the export trade.

North Carolina had four "ports"—Roanoke, Bath, Beaufort, and Brunswick. A "port" included not just a town but also the landings in the region around it; the port of Brunswick, therefore, included Wilmington and the docks up the Cape Fear River. Through these regional ports in 1768 went more than 127,000 barrels of naval stores, nearly half through Brunswick; 3,100,000 board feet of sawn lumber, most of it through Brunswick; and 6,000,000 shingles and 1,700,000

Margin notes: 4-32, 4-33, 4-47, 4-48, 4-34, 4-35, 4-36, 4-37 staves, mostly through Roanoke. Three years later exports included more than 1,700,000 pounds of tobacco (better than half of it to Scotland alone), nearly 175,000 bushels of Indian corn, and 629 barrels of rice.

4-39 Imports naturally consisted of goods and produce not native to the colony, such as rum, sugar, medicine, fancy clothing, and all types of manufactured products. A common term in early advertisements was "sundry British Goods." Merchants eagerly awaited the arrival of supply ships and, following the establishment of newspapers, proudly announced their stock to the public. Vessels trading with North Carolina ranged from tiny sloops

4-38 to ships of one hundred tons or more, but the shallow channels leading to most docks deterred the larger vessels that traded directly with Charleston and the Chesapeake landings. Not all of those that plied the coast reached their destinations; residents of the outer banks were especially fortunate when a supply-laden vessel foundered on the coast.

In 1775 the London magazine *American Husbandry* commented on "two great circumstances which give the farmers of North Carolina such a superiority over those of most other colonies": plenty of land and vast herds of animals requiring no fencing. The common care for cattle and hogs, the journal said, was "to let them run loose in the woods all day, and bring them up at night by the

4-40 sound of a horn." Owners identified their own livestock by means of marks or brands registered in the county records. Farmers often sowed newly cleared ground for several years in Indian corn, followed by peas and beans for a year, and then wheat for two or three years. When the fertility appeared exhausted, they cleared additional woodlands, leaving the old fields to "spontaneous growth."

With their livestock and crops, most North Carolinians produced sufficient food for themselves and their domestic animals. Virtually every country

4-41 district had its gristmill, where grain was ground
4-46 into flour or meal. Meats were preserved by smoking, salting, or drying. Skins and homespun cloth provided materials for clothing and cover, and plentiful wood gave fuel for cooking and warmth.

Many North Carolinians, of course, were not
4-42 farmers. Armand J. deRosset, a Swiss-educated Frenchman who settled in Wilmington about 1735, was possibly the first professionally trained physician in the colony. A note in the *Virginia Gazette* referred to a Samuel Ormes as "Surgeon and Apothecary" in Edenton in 1752, and among other physicians who took up residence in the

colony was Alexander Gaston, a native of Ireland, 4-43 who was executed in New Bern by the British during the Revolution.

Attorneys and merchants were more numerous. John Dawson moved from Virginia to Bertie County, married a daughter of Governor Gabriel Johnston, and became a member of Governor Dobbs's council. James Murray, a native of Scot- 4-44 land, settled in Wilmington in 1736 and developed a flourishing mercantile business, built up Point Repose Plantation on the river, and served in a variety of offices ranging from justice of the peace to president of the governor's council. By 1765 he had moved to Boston, where he sided with the British during the Revolution; his North Carolina property was subsequently confiscated. Other occupations represented included bakers, barbers, ferry keepers, tavern keepers, and shipbuilders. 4-45

Neither clamshell beads (called Roanoke)—the 4-49 aboriginal currency of the area—nor barter satisfied the need for a universally accepted medium of exchange in colonial North Carolina. There was little English money in the colony, so handwritten bills of credit were issued by the assembly in 1712 to help pay for the war against the Tusca- 4-50 roras. Other emissions followed, and in 1734 printed notes were issued to replace the much-counterfeited manuscript notes. In 1748, during the period of the Spanish depredations along the coast, the colony emitted indented bills of credit, including two thousand three-pound notes depicting a Union Jack flying over Fort Johnston, then 4-51 under construction. The new notes were proclaimed by the assembly to be legal tender at the rate of four shillings in the new notes to three shillings sterling. This "proclamation money," nonetheless, failed to hold its value. Meanwhile, William Borden, a New Englander who in 1732 4-52 settled in Carteret County and established a shipyard, not only wrote a treatise on North Carolina money problems but also issued his own due bills, which became known locally as "Borden's Scrip." Specie—that is, coins—was exceptionally scarce in the colony, and the Spanish milled dollar, for which the American dollar was later named, was eagerly sought after.

The instability of paper money had troubling effects upon many aspects of colonial life. Farmers who sought to pay their quitrents in produce frequently came into conflict with treasurers like Thomas Barker over the rated value of the com- 4-53 modities. Merchants experienced difficulty paying for their imported goods, and property owners encountered problems when dealing with out-of-colony buyers.

Only among a small portion of families was North Carolina's society equal to that of tidewater Virginia or South Carolina. The relative isolation of the province allowed for less distinct social classes, though each community did produce—or feign—an aristocracy of sorts. Planters with good manners tended to mix socially with the first families of the towns, and fancy balls were a favorite form of entertainment. John Brickell, an Edenton physician, wrote in the 1730s, "Dancing they are all fond of, especially when they can get a Fiddle, or Bag-pipe; at this they will continue Hours together, nay, so attach'd are they to this darling Amusement, that if they can't procure Musick, they will sing for themselves." Card playing, too, was a socially acceptable pastime, along with a variety of indoor games. Nearly every substantial town was supplied with a racetrack, and horse racing was a popular sport enjoyed by all classes. Hunting, fishing, cockfighting, and hand-to-hand competition were common.

4-54

Drunkenness was not unusual. Wrote Brickell, "I have frequently seen them [the "meaner sort"] come to the Towns, and there remain Drinking Rum, Punch, and other Liquors for Eight or Ten Days successively, and after they have committed this Excess, will not drink any Spirituous Liquor, 'till such time as they take the next Frolick, as they call it, which is generally in two or three Months." Funerals, for which a repast was usually provided, were sometimes invaded by neighbors more interested in the food and drink than in mourning the dead.

Because of isolation and relative poverty, residents of North Carolina tended to dress less imitatively of the English than their counterparts in Virginia. While wigs and fancy clothing were not uncommon for special occasions, Governor Burrington wrote that "there is no difference to be perceived in Dress and Carriage, between the Justices, Constables and Planters that come to a Court, nor between the Officers and Private men, at a Muster which Parity is in no other Country but this." The crudeness of the physical surroundings of both towns and rural areas undoubtedly inhibited excessive expenditures for the latest fashions.

4-55

Brickell wrote of North Carolinians: "Their Houses are built after two different Ways; *viz.* the most substantial Planters generally use Brick, and Lime, which is made of Oyster-shells, for there are no Stones to be found proper for that purpose, but near the Mountains; the meaner sort erect with Timber, the outside with Clap-Boards, the Roofs of both Sorts of Houses are made with Shingles, and they generally have Sash Windows, and affect large and decent Rooms with good Closets." But Brickell's observations reflect circumstances around Edenton, where he lived for a time, and they fail to convey the modesty of the homes of most Carolinians. More common than the substantial homes of the coastal region were the humble dwellings of the frontier, with few windows or closets. Brickell's characterization of domestic pieces as being "imported here commonly from England" also is misleading, for some of the fine furniture and many of the sturdy but less stylistic pieces were made in the colony.

4-56
4-57
4-58

4-59

4-60
4-61
4-62

"I believe this is the only Metropolis in the Christian or Mahometan World, where there is neither Church, Chappel, Mosque, Synagogue, or any other Place of Public Worship of any Sect or Religion whatsoever." Thus wrote Virginian William Byrd about Edenton in 1729. Ten years later, Governor Gabriel Johnston termed as "scandalous" the presence in the colony of only two places (presumably Bath and Edenton) where divine services were regularly performed. These and other statements concerning religion in North Carolina, taken out of context, have done the colony an injustice. Byrd became noted for his exaggerations, and Governor Johnston was referring only to Anglican parishes with a minister. Moseley's Map of 1733 located fourteen places of worship (chapels and Quaker and Baptist meetinghouses) in rural areas, and several others were known to exist. Still, there were few ordained ministers during the first half of the century except for missionaries, most of whom spent only a short while in the colony.

From the early years of settlement the Quakers in the Albemarle constituted the most numerous religious group, but their scruples concerning certain practices of the civil government lessened their influence upon the royal colony. The established church, therefore, exercised greater power than its limited membership would suggest. Its beginnings in the colony had been humble; its first church—St. Paul's in Edenton—was described in 1711 as having neither floor nor seats, and it was said that "all the Hoggs and Cattle flee thither for shade in the Summer and Warmth in the Winter." A brick structure, a part of which survives, was begun in 1736, only two years after the start of construction on St. Thomas, the oldest church building still standing in North Carolina. Later Anglican churches included Christ Church in New Bern, built about 1750; St. John's in Williamsboro, ca. 1757; and St. Phillip's in Brunswick, begun 1758. Because of the official relationship between the government and the established church, vestries were elected and received public support; in turn they assumed limited responsibility in caring for the unfortunate, particularly public poor relief.

George Whitefield, a spellbinding Calvinist, visited Carolina several times between 1739 and 1765, the time of great population growth in the Carolina Piedmont, and his sermons drew large crowds. The dissenting denominations, however, needed little outside stimulation, for they brought their religion with them. The Scots—both Highlanders and Ulstermen—were usually Presbyterian, and wherever they settled, churches soon followed. German immigrants were often Lutheran, Reformed, or Moravian. Baptists, who had a church in the Albemarle by 1728 and who by 1758 were strong enough to organize the Sandy Creek Association in the Piedmont, and Methodists, who remained unorganized during the colonial period, came from several national backgrounds. These evangelical groups, plus the Quakers, who established New Garden Meeting House in 1751, increased in importance in the fast-growing areas of the backcountry. Because of the vast number of dissenters, colonial officials had little choice but to condone independent worship, and Moravian and Presbyterian clergymen were even allowed to perform marriages.

The Masons constituted the strongest fraternal organization in the colonial period. A lodge was organized at New Bern at least as early as 1755, at Halifax by 1764, and at Edenton before the Revolution. Joseph Montfort of Halifax served as the provincial grand master for America.

Education fared even more poorly than religion in eighteenth-century North Carolina. Several citizens left wills instructing the education of their children without explaining how. In 1697, Alexander Lillington willed that "my Children be brought up in Learning, as conveniently as can bee." John Baptista Ashe in 1731 requested that a son be trained in law and another in merchandise and that a daughter be taught to "write and read, & some feminine accomplishments which may render her agreable." Three years later Edward Salter's will expressed the desire that his son should "have a thorough education to make him a compleat merchant,

let the expense be what it will"; and in 1745, Edward Moseley referred to the best education possible "from the Common Masters in this Province."

The first teacher yet identified in the colony was Charles Griffin, an Anglican lay reader who in 1705 opened a school on Symons Creek in Pasquotank Precinct. His school was soon taken over by James Adams, an Anglican missionary, and Griffin opened another one in Chowan Precinct. In 1736, Governor Johnston lamented that the legislature had "never yet taken the least Care to erect One School, which deserves the Name, in this wide extended Country." Undoubtedly there were family tutors in the colony, and there may have been other private schools in the east. Certainly the Moravians had teachers at Bethabara as early as 1756, and four years later James Tate, a Presbyterian, opened a classical school at Wilmington. At almost the same time the Presbyterians established Crowfield Academy in Mecklenburg County, and in 1767 David Caldwell opened what much later was called the "log college" in Guilford County. But it was left to James Reed, an Anglican missionary, to build the first "public" school in the colony. By subscription he opened a small school in New Bern with Thomas Thomlinson, another Englishman, as teacher. In 1766 the academy was chartered and subsidized by public funds.

The only "college" established in the colonial period was Queen's College at Charlotte (no relation to the modern college by that name). Its legislative charter in 1771 authorized the "publick seminary" to grant the degrees of bachelor and master of arts, and its rules and ordinances were to "correspond and be as near as may be agreeable to the Laws and Customs of the Universities of Oxford and Cambridge or those of the Colleges in America." This Presbyterian-oriented college, to be subsidized by a six-pence-per-gallon tax on alcoholic beverages "brought into and disposed of in Mecklenburg County," operated for several years as "Queen's Museum" despite the disallowance of its charter by the crown.

North Carolina was virtually a literary wasteland for the first century of its settlement. By far the most important book about the colony was John Lawson's history (see chapter 3), and it furnished much of the data for John Brickell's *The Natural History of North-Carolina. . .* , published in Dublin in 1737. Brickell did elaborate and improve upon Lawson's observations, but even so his book portrays less the reality than a romanticization of life in the colony. It featured some rather amateurish

4-79 illustrations of wildlife, some species of which have since become extinct. Far superior representations of wildlife were provided by Mark Catesby, whose splendid work *The Natural History of Carolina,*
4-80 *Florida, and the Bahama Islands* was published in
4-81 two volumes in 1731 and 1743, and by William
4-82 Bartram, whose *Travels Through North and South Carolina . . .* was published nearly two decades after he gave up his operation of a store at Ashwood in Bladen County.

There being no printing press in the colony, the laws were distributed to each county in manuscript. Except for a partial printing in Williams-
4-83 burg of the proceedings of the assembly in 1740, it was not until James Davis established the first printing press at New Bern in 1749 that a journal of the legislative body was published, the first book printed in North Carolina. He followed this two years later with the publication of *A Collection of All the Public Acts of Assembly. . . .* At last the laws of the province were available for widespread distribution.

Perhaps equally important, in 1751 Davis launched the colony's first newspaper, the weekly
4-84 *No^{th}-Carolina Gazette,* which he published for eight years. In 1764 he founded the *North-Carolina Magazine; or, Universal Intelligencer,* but four years later he reinstated the *Gazette,* which continued until the Revolution. The only printer in the colony, Davis published in 1753 Clement Hall's *Collection of Many Christian Experiences. . . ,* the first nongovernmental book printed in the province. Competition arrived in 1764 when Andrew Steuart of Philadelphia moved a press to Wilmington and published his own *North-Carolina Gazette* for three years. Following Steuart's drowning in
4-85 1769, Adam Boyd, formerly of Pennsylvania, acquired his press and published the *Cape-Fear Mercury* until 1775. Thus during the period from 1749 until the Revolution the colony had, at one time or another, two presses, three printers, and five newspapers (three of them Davis's).

Colonial North Carolina played only a minor role in fiction. The earliest recognized use of the word *Carolina* in fiction occurred in "The Fortunate Shipwreck, or a Description of New Athens . . . ," published in London in 1720, and the province provided the setting for *The Life . . . of Mr. Cleveland. . . ,* published in London fourteen years later. Thomas Godfrey, a Philadelphian who lived briefly at Masonborough near Wilming-
4-86 ton, wrote *Prince of Parthia,* the first drama written

by a native of the thirteen colonies and produced on the professional stage.

The sparseness of literary activity within North Carolina did not signify an absence of reading materials. In addition to books sent to the colony by Anglican officials, some residents acquired books and subscribed to journals and newspapers from outside. For instance, from its beginning in 1735, the *Virginia Gazette*—at times in two different versions published simultaneously—carried occasional news on North Carolina, and many North Carolinians read it avidly. A number of respectable private libraries existed, including those of Edward Moseley and James Hasell. Samuel Johnston acquired the books formerly belonging to governors Charles Eden and Gabriel Johnston, and some of these, plus nineteenth-century additions, have been preserved at Hayes Plantation at Edenton.

Not all North Carolinians shared equally in the freedom generally afforded under the colonial government. Children, particularly orphans and those   4-87 whose parents could not care for them, often were apprenticed, males until the age of twenty-one. In 1695, William, the son of Timothy Pead, was bound to Thomas Harvey "untill he be at the Age of twenty one yeares and the said Tho. Harvey to teach him to read." In Rowan County in 1764, Thomas Kelly, a seven-year-old orphan, was bound to John Bullin "to Learn the Art & Mistery of a Cooper"; Bullin was required to teach the boy to read and write and, at the termination of his apprenticeship, to furnish him "a Suit of Cloaths & Set of working tools Suitable for his trade & likewise £10 or in lieu thereof a horse, Saddle and Bridle of the Value of £10."

Some Europeans bound themselves for a term of years in payment for passage to America, and upon occasion persons convicted of offenses were sent to the colony as indentured servants in lieu of more   4-88 severe punishment in England. Occasionally, free   4-89 Negroes were indentured. The laws required that "Christian servants" be given "freedom dues" upon the expiration of their terms, and some of them subsequently became substantial citizens.

The institution of slavery had been recognized in the Concessions and Agreements of 1665, and as early as 1680 settlers were applying for fifty-acre "headrights" for importing blacks. An absence of   4-90 religious objections to slavery was indicated in   4-91 1716 when the Anglican missionary John Urmston requested funds with which "to buy me 3 or 4 Negroes in Guinea," adding that "there is no living without servants[.] [T]here are none to be hired of any colour and none of the black kind to be sold good for anything under 50 or 60 pounds." In 1733, Governor Burrington wrote, "It is hoped some Merchants in England will speedily furnish this Colony with Negroes, to increase the Produce and its Trade to England."

4-95
4-92
4-93
4-94
The importation of slaves did increase in subsequent decades, and newspapers were peppered with advertisements for the capture and return of runaway slaves and notices of the jailing of blacks pending claim and payment of jail charges by their owners. These and other notices reveal much about the laws governing slavery and the treatment, dress, and personal characteristics of the enslaved. Miscegenation was indicated by frequent use of the terms mulatto, yellow, and light-skinned. The official records are equally revealing. William Bartram's will mentioned "1 Mouth peice to put on Negros" and "1 pair Iron hoppels for Negros." An act of 1741 authorized the leasing of jailed blacks, but only on condition that "an iron Collar to be put on the Neck of such Negro or Runaway, with the Letters P.G. [Public Gaol] stamped thereon."

Blacks accused of crimes were tried not by regular juries but by a special tribunal of justices of the peace and four slaveholding freeholders, and punishment was swift and severe, including hobbling,
4-96 branding, whipping, castration, cropping of ears,
4-97 nailing ears to a post, and a variety of methods of execution. The tribunal also fixed the amount of recompense from public funds to the slaveowners, for a master was not held responsible for damages done by his slaves. Runaways could be declared outlaws with a reward to anyone who "may kill or destroy the said Negroes, or either of them, by such Means as he or they may think fit."

Slaveowning, however, was never as widespread in colonial North Carolina as it was in Virginia and South Carolina. For instance, it is estimated that in 1755 only 44 percent of the households in New Hanover and just 9 percent of those in Orange County owned any slaves at all, and in the latter county there were just four households (out of 724) with more than five slaves each. Still, the institution of slavery was firmly embedded in the society and economy.

The laws permitted the emancipation of slaves
4-98 for faithful service only with approval of the county court, but free Negroes did not enjoy full citizenship. Although the statutes directed that a manumitted black leave the province within six months, the provision was not rigidly enforced, and perhaps

as many as a thousand free persons of color lived in North Carolina in the late colonial period. Most of them became farmers or held menial jobs, but some became skilled artisans such as coopers, carpenters, and wheelwrights. The offspring of a master and a slave woman was more likely to be emancipated, often by will.

Slavery was not limited to Africans, for Indians too were sometimes held in bondage. Among the headrights claimed by John Bently in 1694 was one for the importation of "an Indian Boy," and John Aderne's will in 1707 mentioned "all ye Negro, Indian, Molato Slaves I am now in actual possession of." Following the Tuscarora War, northern newspapers advertised Indian children for sale. Other eastern Indians were only a little more fortu- 4-101 nate, for they were driven off their lands and became strangers in their homeland.

Following their defeat in 1712, the surviving Tuscaroras were forced to accept a reservation of 4-100 about thirty thousand acres on the Roanoke River in present-day Bertie County, but even there they were not safe from encroachment by whites. By 1766, their names had been anglicized ("Billy" was a favored given name), and upon their petition, the legislature allowed some of the Tuscarora lands to be leased and the income applied to the cost of moving more than 150 of their number to the colony of New York. The surviving 100 or so described their plight in a petition to Governor Tryon: "We are by Education and Custom, unable to acquire a Livelihood otherwise than by Hunting; and as Ill natured Persons frequently take away and break our Guns, and even whip us for Pursuing game on their Land, We beg of your Excellency to appoint Commissioners as heretofore to hear our complaints, and redress our grievances." They apologized for the smallness of their gift of deerskins, "for we are mostly old men, unable to hunt, our young men having gone to the Northward with the Northern Chief, Tragaweha."

By that time most of the names of the Indian groups listed on Edward Moseley's thirty-year-old map were little more than memories: Hatteras, Poteskite, Yawpim, Nansemond, Chowan, Acconeeche. In 1761, Governor Dobbs estimated that there were only about twenty fighting men each representing the Saponas and Meherrins, and just seven or eight among the Mattamuskeets. Thus within half a century white settlers had effectively wiped out, driven off, or extinguished the identity of most of the natives of the east.

In the western Piedmont, the Catawbas num- 4-99

bered about three hundred fighting men, but they too were forced into a reservation just over the boundary in South Carolina. The Cherokees in the mountains posed a more formidable problem. Noting in 1758 that the Cherokees had allied themselves with the French against the British, Governor Dobbs chastened the colonists for "their visible Neglect of the original native Inhabitants, by neither attempting to civilize, nor convert them to our holy Religion," and proclaimed a day of fasting and prayer for victory in the war with the French and Indians.

Two years later, Colonel James Grant led British and South Carolina forces to victory over the Cher-

okees near present-day Franklin, and the parties signed a peace treaty in 1761. The king issued a proclamation prohibiting white settlement of lands beyond the crest of the mountains, but it was not until 1767 that Governor Tryon himself participated in a survey of the Indian boundary and proclaimed that whites who crossed the line would "not only expose their Families and Effects to the Depredations of the Indians, but also deprive themselves of the Protection of this Government." In the turmoil of the next few years, whites conveniently ignored the proclamation. "Manifest destiny" was already a part of the European settlement of North Carolina.

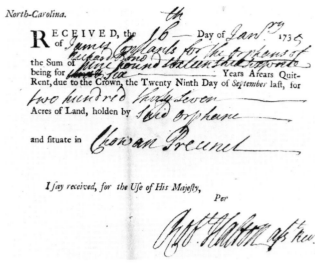

4-3
A receipt for the payment of six years' overdue quitrent on 237 acres of land owned by the orphans of Richard Bond in Chowan Precinct. (Courtesy NCDA&H.)

4-1
Governor George Burrington in 1732 showed uncharacteristic charity in dropping his charges against a Mr. Jeffries for "Speaking agt. me." (Courtesy NCDA&H.)

4-2
Armorial bookplate from Governor Gabriel Johnston's personal copy of George Stanhope's *A Paraphrase and Comment Upon the Epistles and Gospels* . . . (London, 1726). (Courtesy North Carolina Collection.)

4-4
Earl Granville retained title to the northern portion of North Carolina, but the crown exercised civil jurisdiction over the area. (Courtesy North Carolina Collection.)

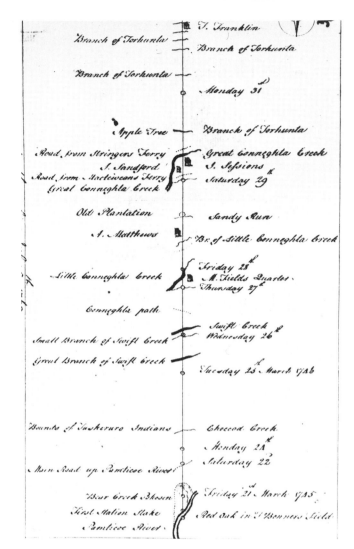

4-5

The southern boundary of Earl Granville's district ran westward from the vicinity of Bath on the Pamlico River (bottom). In this drawing the survey extends westward past Great Contentnea Creek in present-day Greene County (top). (Courtesy North Carolina Collection.)

4-6

The obverse of the seal deputed by George II for North Carolina from 1730 to 1737 pictured an outline of the coast, a sailing vessel, the monarch, and two figures holding a liberty pole and a cornucopia. The reverse carried the familiar royal seal. (Courtesy Royal Mint, London.)

4-7

Hugh Meredith visited the lower Cape Fear and published in two issues of the *Pennsylvania Gazette* a description of the area. This detail is from the 29 April–6 May 1731 issue. (Courtesy Historical Society of Pennsylvania, Philadelphia.)

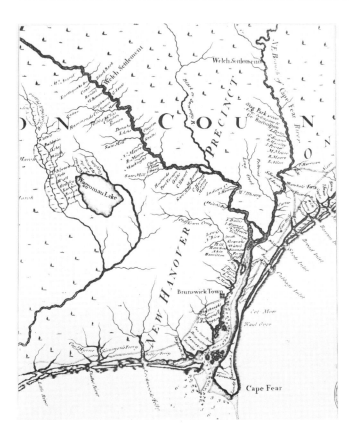

4-8
The names of many plantation owners along the two branches of the Cape Fear River appeared on Edward Moseley's map of 1733. Moseley also recorded a Welsh settlement on each branch of the river. (Courtesy East Carolina Manuscript Collection, Greenville.)

4-9
Cross Creek—later merged with Campbellton to form Fayetteville—received its name, according to tradition, because two streams appeared to cross. It was the central town for Scots along the northwest prong of the Cape Fear River. The map was drawn by Claude J. Sauthier in 1770. (Courtesy NCDA&H.)

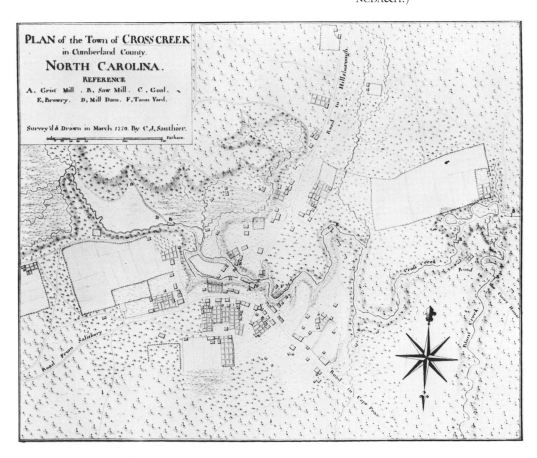

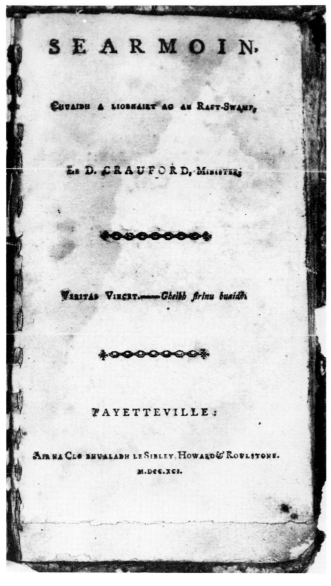

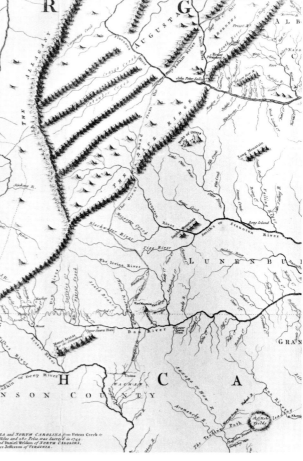

4-12

The Great Wagon Road, which brought thousands of settlers from Pennsylvania to the Carolina Piedmont in the 1750s, is traced on "A Map of the Most Inhabited Part of Virginia," by Joshua Fry and Peter Jefferson. (By permission of John Carter Brown Library, Brown University, Providence.)

4-10

Sermons were still preached in Gaelic at Raft Swamp when this one was printed in 1791. (Courtesy North Carolina Collection.)

4-11

An advertisement in Parks's *Virginia Gazette*, 10–17 February 1737/8, announced the availability of lands at "Stanford" (now Hawfields) formerly owned by prominent colonial officials. (Courtesy North Carolina Collection.)

4-13

Bishop August Gottlieb Spangenberg was the leader of Moravian settlers who established Wachovia as the most highly developed community in the colony. (Courtesy Old Salem Restoration, Winston-Salem.)

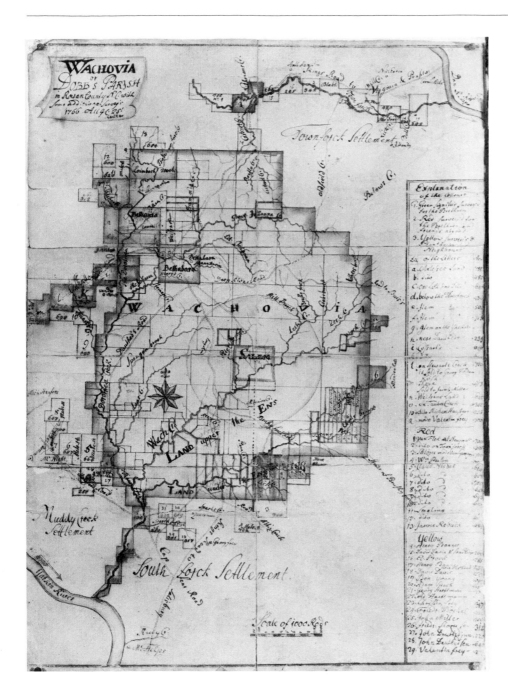

4-14
A map of Wachovia, 1766 (with some additional surveys), shows the several Moravian settlements, the chief of which were Salem, Bethabara, and Bethania. The "King's Road to Virginia & Pensilv:" leads through the Town Fork Settlement at top and continues toward Salisbury at bottom. (Courtesy Moravian Archives, Winston-Salem.)

4-15
The Moravians, as industrious as they were religious, built this large mill at Bethabara. (By permission of Moravian Archives, Bethlehem, Pa.; original in Archiv der Brüder-Unität, Herrnhut, DDR.)

4-16
Bethabara, the first of the Moravian settlements in Wachovia, was a flourishing community when this map was drawn by C. G. Reuter in 1766, the same year in which Salem was established. (Courtesy Moravian Archives, Winston-Salem.)

4-17
A log house, built in 1766 for workmen who constructed five more substantial houses for the brethren in the new community of Salem, stood until 1907. (Courtesy Moravian Archives, Winston-Salem.)

4-18
Floor plan for Salem's officially designated "First House," one of the five original residences, of which only the Fourth House remains. This "First House," however, has now been reconstructed. (By permission of Moravian Archives, Bethlehem, Pa.; original in Archiv der Brüder-Unität, Herrnhut, DDR.)

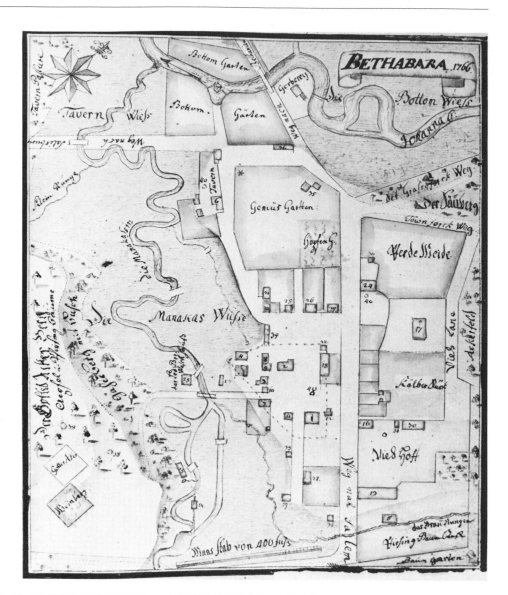

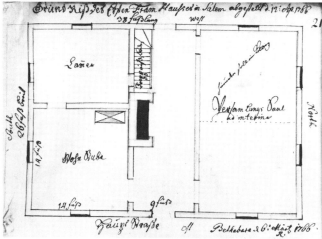

4-19
North Carolina's first "fire engine": Salem's eighteenth-century portable firefighting pump and leather water buckets. (Courtesy Old Salem Restoration, Winston-Salem.)

4-20
Arthur Dobbs was governor of North Carolina from 1754 to 1765, a period of unprecedented migration into the Piedmont. (Courtesy William S. Powell, Chapel Hill.)

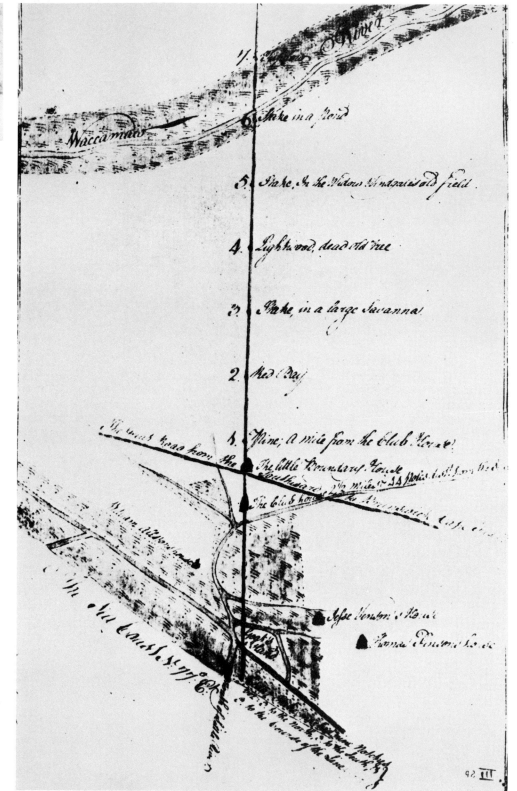

4-21
William Williams, Jr., in his advertisement in the 21–28 September 1764 issue of the *North-Carolina Magazine*, contemptuously described James Gibbon as "an Irishman," the alleged thief of Williams's horse. (Courtesy North Carolina Collection.)

4-22
The boundary between North Carolina and South Carolina started in New Hanover (now Brunswick) County and crossed the "Great Road from the Southward to Brunswick Cape Fear" near a tavern called the Little Boundary House. (Courtesy North Carolina Collection; original in Public Record Office.)

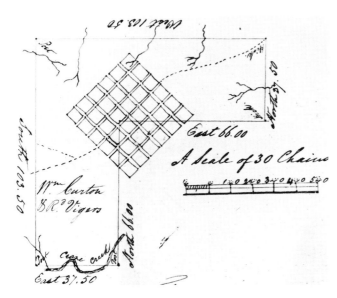

4-23
James Carter's plat for the town of Salisbury, established in 1755. (Courtesy NCDA&H.)

4-24
Colonel Thomas Lovick (1680–1759), collector of the Port of Beaufort and leader of the militia that drove out the Spanish invaders in 1747. (Courtesy North Carolina Collection.)

4-25
Bottle seal of William Dry, collector of the Port of Brunswick, who helped repel a Spanish attack on the town in 1748. (Courtesy NCDA&H.)

Mr. *John Swann* informed the House, That there was a Miſtake in the Sum given him out of the Public Cheſt, by this Aſſembly the laſt Seſſion, to pay the Expence of the Expedition at the Invaſion of the *Spaniards* at *Cape-Fear*, of Ninety Pounds, Proclamation Money, over and above the Sum ordered to be paid to the ſeveral Perſons on the ſaid Expedition; which ſaid Sum is now paid by the ſaid *John Swann* into this House, and lodged in the Hands of the Commiſſioners for Stamping and Emitting the Sum of Twenty One Thouſand Three Hundred and Fifty Pounds, Proclamation Money, and by them ordered to be depoſited in the Cheſt with other Public Monies.

4-26
The lower house of the assembly in 1749 was still straightening out the costs of the Spanish attacks on Brunswick. (Courtesy North Carolina Collection.)

4-27
One of the Spanish ships attacking Brunswick was disabled, and from it the local residents saved a painting of Christ, *Ecce Homo*, which now hangs in St. James Episcopal Church in Wilmington. (Courtesy North Carolina Collection.)

4-28
Hugh Waddell (1734–73) superintended the construction of Fort Dobbs near present-day Statesville and served as an officer during the French and Indian War and the Regulator suppression. (Courtesy NCDA&H.)

4-29
Hugh Waddell's silver-chased pistols were carried during the French and Indian War. (Courtesy NCDA&H.)

4-30
Aventon Felps sent out a scouting troop "on an Alarm of Indians being seen on the Frontiers of Rowan County" in 1759. (Courtesy NCDA&H.)

4-31
Richard King's tombstone in Thyatira churchyard in Rowan County recorded that he was "kild by Indians Feby. 6, 1760," at age 19. (Courtesy North Carolina Collection.)

4-32
Sheriff Henry Dedon of Pasquotank County protested against the "insufficiency" of the jail in 1756. (Courtesy NCDA&H.)

4-34
The minutes of the Wilmington town commissioners in 1753 recorded fines levied upon "defaulters"—citizens who failed to perform the specified number of days' work on the streets. (Courtesy NCDA&H.)

4-33
A primitive depiction of the Chowan County Courthouse on a late eighteenth-century transfer-printed creamware jug, probably Liverpool, that was owned by William Blair of Edenton. (Courtesy Museum of Early Southern Decorative Arts, Winston-Salem.)

4-35
William Parks, in his *Virginia Gazette* of 28 April–5 May 1738, announced that he would begin a monthly stage to deliver the mail (and presumably passengers) to and from Edenton. This was the first regular postal service in North Carolina. (Courtesy North Carolina Collection.)

4-36
Hugh Finlay, inspector of
post roads for the colonies,
visited Wilmington in 1774
and made this drawing of the
town. (Courtesy NCDA&H.)

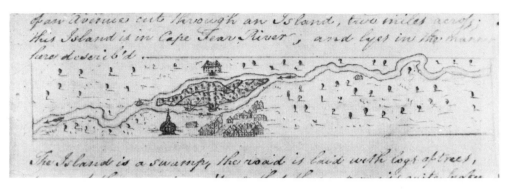

4-37
Exports on the sloop *Betsy
and Nancy* from Beaufort to
New Castle on Delaware in
1761 included naval stores,
wax, tallow, leather, and deerskins. (Courtesy NCDA&H.)

4-38
This 1766 painting of the
schooner *Baltic* in the Middle
Ground off Oak Island at the
mouth of the Cape Fear
River has been called "the
earliest known contemporary
view of a Salem [Massachu-
setts] vessel." (By permission
of the Peabody Museum of
Salem, Massachusetts.)

Entered in Port-*Beaufort*, from the 1st of *October* 1763, to the 1st of October 1764, the following Vessels, *viz.*

2 Ships, | 72 Sloops,
1 Snow, | 43 Schooners,
9 Brigs. |
| In all 127

Imported in the said District, between the 1st of *October* 1763, and 1st of *October* 1764.

320 Hhds. Rum, | 352 Barrels Flour,
318 Do Molasses, | 1072 Do of Bread,
342 Bar. brown Sugar, | 28000 lbs. of Iron,
18160 lbs. Loaf Do | 179 Slaves,
40 Casks of Wine, | 2479 lbs. of Cheese,
913 Barrels Cyder, | 96 Barrels of Beer,
10865 Bushels Salt, | 1600 lbs. of Flax,

Exclusive of *European* Goods, Coffee, Tea, *&c.*

Exported from the said District, between the 1st of *October* 1763, and 1st of *October* 1764.

30403 Barrels of Tar, | 619 Barrels Rozin,
3303 Do Turpentine, | 1279 Do Spirits Turp.
3721 Do Pitch, | 47000 Feet Scantling,
4731 Do Pork, | 87560 Do Boards,
495 Do Beef, | 11305 lbs. Deer Skins,
32805 Bushels Corn, | 1800 Furr Skins,
3556 Do Peese, | 29 Barrels M Wax,
253161 Staves, | 19 Do Bees Wax,
122150 Do Shingles, | 190 Do Rice,
19900 lbs. of Tallow, | 199731 Pieces Heading,
404 Hides, | 160 Barrels Flour,
18732 lbs. tann'd Lea. | 107 Do Hogs Fat,

Exclusive of Live Stock, *&c.*

PRICE CURRENT in NEWBERN.

Tar, 9 s. to 10, | Jamaica Spirit, 7 s.
Pitch, 12 s. 6 d. | N. E. Rum, 2 s. 6 d.
Turpentine, 11 s. | Melasses, 1 s. 8 d.
Flour, 16 s. | Loaf Sugar, 1 s. 4 d.
Corn, 2 s. 6 d. | Muscovado do. 45 s. to
Pease, 3 s. | 50 s.
Rice, 13 s. 4 d. | White-oak Hhd. Staves,
Tallow, 7 d. | 4 l.
Bees Wax, 1 s. 8 d. | Pipe do. 6 l.
Deer Skins, 1 s. 8 d. | Barrel do. 35 s.
Do. dress, 3 s. 4 d. | Saw Mill Lumber, 66 s. 8d
West-India Rum, 4 s. | Tann'd Leather, 1 s.

4-39
Imports to and exports from Beaufort and current prices in New Bern were published in the 28 September–5 October 1764 issue of James Davis's *North-Carolina Magazine.* (Courtesy North Carolina Collection.)

4-40
Lacking a fence law, farmers adopted marks and brands for their livestock. This is a page from the Edgecombe County stock mark book for 1738–39. (Courtesy NCDA&H.)

4-41
Yates Mill in Wake County, built in the eighteenth century but probably later enlarged, was representative of the gristmills required throughout the colony to grind corn, wheat, and other grains. This photograph was made in 1970. (Courtesy NCDA&H.)

4-42
Armand J. deRosset
(1695–1770), a native of
France, practiced medicine in
Wilmington after about
1735. (Courtesy North Carolina Collection; reprinted,
with permission, from Dorothy Long [editor], *Medicine
in North Carolina* [Raleigh,
1972], volume 1.)

4-43
Alexander Gaston, an Irish
immigrant to New Bern, was
a practicing physician and
pharmacist. The father of
William Gaston, noted jurist,
Dr. Gaston was killed by the
Tories during the Revolu-
tion. (Courtesy Frick Art
Reference Library, New
York, with permission of
Chalmers G. Davidson.)

4-45
A shipyard was operated on
the lands of Sir Nathaniel
Duckenfield in 1767 when
William Churton prepared
this survey. It was located
near the site of the house
built for Nathaniel Batts
more than a century earlier.
(Courtesy NCDA&H.)

4-44
Margaret Bush-Brown's portrait of James Murray, after
an original by John Singleton
Copley. Murray was one of
the colony's most prosperous
residents and a longtime
member of the council.
(Courtesy North Carolina
Collection; reprinted from
Nina Moore Tiffany [editor],
*Letters of James Murray, Loyal-
ist* [Boston, 1901].)

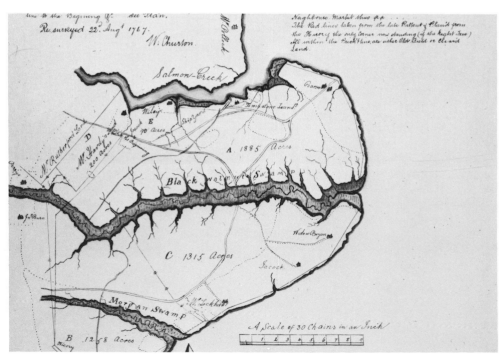

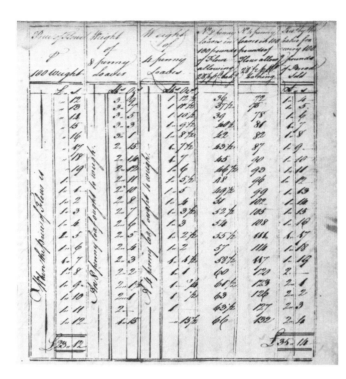

4-46

The Wilmington town commissioners in 1768 strictly regulated the making and selling of bread. This table calculated the allowable price per loaf based on the weight of the loaf and the price of flour. (Courtesy NCDA&H.)

4-48

The Tyrrell County Court of Pleas and Quarter Sessions in 1771 established fees for bed and board furnished by ordinaries, differentiating between the quality of libations. (Courtesy NCDA&H.)

TO be Sold, by Charles Evans, *Ferry-keeper on* Tar River, 15 *Miles from* Speere's Ferry *on* Roanoke River, *in* North-Carolina, *at Ten Pounds* Virginia Currency *per Hundred, Two Thousand Acres of very good Land, being Purchase Land, granted in the Proprietor's Time, at Six Pence per Hundred Quit-Rents, for ever: And in the Banks thereof is a Copper Mine, twice tried in England. It runs 5 Miles on the River, is very commodious for Trade, with two Cyprus Swamps thereon, full of vast large Cyprus, and near adjoining to a Desart, called the* Canctar; *which is suppos'd to be* 10 *Miles wide, and* 30 *Miles long; and when fenced to the Desart at each End, you may keep* 1000 *Head of Cattle, without any Feeding, for* 1000 *Years, being full of vast high Reeds, and there is brave hunting the Bear.*

Charles Evans.

4-47

Ferry-keeper Charles Evans, who advertised land in Parks's *Virginia Gazette* of 16–23 February 1738/9, undoubtedly exaggerated its potential. (Courtesy North Carolina Collection.)

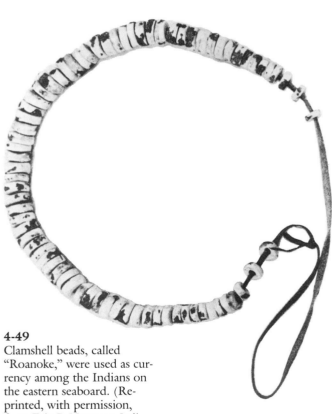

4-49

Clamshell beads, called "Roanoke," were used as currency among the Indians on the eastern seaboard. (Reprinted, with permission, from Eric P. Newman [editor], *Studies in Money in Early America* [New York, 1976].)

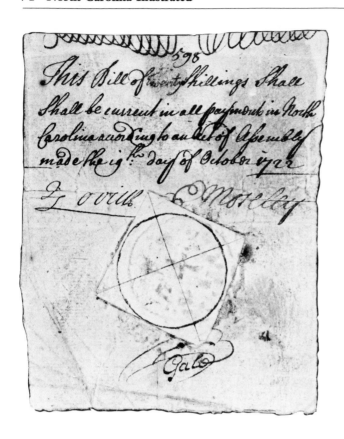

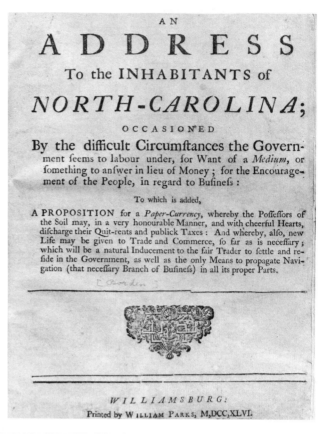

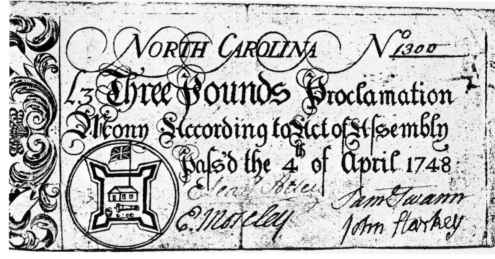

4-50
Although manuscript notes of credit were issued as early as 1712, the earliest surviving one appears to be an issue of 1722. (Courtesy American Antiquarian Society, Worcester.)

4-51
The £3 notes issued in 1748 pictured the plan of a fort, probably Fort Johnston, construction of which began that year near the mouth of the Cape Fear River. (Courtesy Eric P. Newman Numismatic Education Society, St. Louis.)

4-52 (top right)
William Borden moved from New England to North Carolina and in 1746 published a booklet proposing a new system of paper currency. (Courtesy Massachusetts Historical Society, Boston.)

4-53
This portrait of Thomas Barker, treasurer of the northern district, is attributed to Sir Joshua Reynolds. (Courtesy North Carolina Collection.)

4-54
A handsome silver tankard, with a ladle shaped to resemble a jockey's cap, was awarded to Thomas Barker in April 1754 when his horse Sparrow (depicted on the tankard) won a race at Pembroke near Edenton. The mementos descended through the family of the sister of Barker's second wife, Penelope. (Courtesy George D. Nan, Richmond, Va.)

4-55
On a visit to North Carolina just prior to the Revolution, Janet Schaw described fashions in Wilmington, where silk shoes were inappropriate for the streets. (Courtesy North Carolina Collection.)

4-56
The eighteenth-century Palmer-Marsh house in Bath, shown here in the 1920s after alterations but before restoration, featured a massive end chimney. Early officials conducted their affairs from the house. (Courtesy NCDA&H.)

4-57
The German influence is evident in the Michael Braun house, built in 1766 in Rowan County. The building was restored after this photograph was taken in the 1920s by Bayard Wootten. (Courtesy North Carolina Collection.)

4-58
The paneling removed from the Cupola House (built ca. 1725), Edenton, is now exhibited in the Brooklyn Museum of Fine Arts. The original house, now restored, contains copies of the paneling. (Courtesy Brooklyn Museum of Fine Arts, Brooklyn.)

4-59
Log houses, like Robert Cleveland's in Wilkes County (shown here with a twentieth-century roof), were common in the backcountry in the late eighteenth and early nineteenth centuries. (Courtesy NCDA&H.)

4-60
By the middle of the century, a small amount of fine furniture was being produced in North Carolina, including this Chippendale-style arm-chair, made at Edenton. (Courtesy Museum of Early Southern Decorative Arts, Winston-Salem.)

4-61
This walnut cellaret with yellow pine as a secondary wood was made in northeastern North Carolina. It was used for the storage of alcoholic beverages. (Courtesy Museum of Early Southern Decorative Arts, Winston-Salem.)

4-62
The Piedmont Room in the Museum of Early Southern Decorative Arts in Old Salem features simple backcountry furniture, such as this walnut stretcher table probably made in Rowan County after 1770. (Courtesy Museum of Early Southern Decorative Arts, Winston-Salem.)

4-64
Christ Church, built in New Bern about 1750, was pictured on Jonathan Price's map of New Bern in 1822, a year or so before the building burned. (Courtesy North Carolina Collection.)

4-63
The oldest church building in North Carolina, St. Thomas at Bath, has undergone decorative alterations over the years, as can be seen in this photograph made in the 1920s before restoration. (Courtesy North Carolina Collection.)

4-65
The barrel vault of St. John's Church, built at Williamsboro (now Vance County) about 1757, was exposed during the modern restoration of this, the oldest frame church in the state. (Courtesy NCDA&H.)

4-67
An eighteenth-century elevation of "Cupola for Edenton Church" remains a mystery. It may have suggested the design of the cupola on the Chowan County Courthouse. (Courtesy Southern Historical Collection, John Hawks Papers.)

4-66
This depiction of New Bern's Christ Church appeared on 40-shilling notes in 1754. (Courtesy Eric P. Newman Numismatic Education Society, St. Louis.)

4-68
The *North-Carolina Magazine* of 13–20 July 1764 reminded readers that freeholders who failed to vote for vestrymen could be fined. The school built by the commissioners was the first to receive support from taxes. (Courtesy North Carolina Collection.)

4-69
Minutes of the vestry of St. Paul's Church, Edenton, for 5 July 1755 recorded several cases of assistance to the poor. (Courtesy Southern Historical Collection, St. Paul's Episcopal Church Parish Records [microfilm].)

4-70
In 1754 the Quakers organized New Garden Meeting in what is now Guilford County. The original small meeting house was replaced in 1791 by a commodious structure, shown here in a drawing by John Collins in 1869, only seven years before it was dismantled. (Courtesy Friends Historical Collection, Guilford College.)

NEWBERN, December 14.

Since our laft, feveral Veffels arrived here from the Northward, particularly a Sloop from Maryland with 57 Paffengers, chiefly Families, who are come to fettle in the Province.

Laft Night arrived here a Quaker Preacher, and his Wife, and this Day they both preached here to a numerous Audience. The Doctrines which they chiefly handled, were Original Sin, and the Neceffity of Regeneration; moral Reflections on the Luxuries, Pomps and Vanities of the World, and a particular Caution to the young Ladies againft Drefs, and other juvenile Pleafures and Diverfions; concluded with a fuitable Prayer, to deprecate God's Judgments on a finful World; and that he would be mercifully pleafed to diffufe his holy Spirit among the People. It may not be amifs to take Notice, that the Caution and Advice to the Ladies, was delivered by the Preacher's Wife, who feem'd to have a more than common Influence of the holy Spirit; as her Doctrine was delivered with great emphatic Energy and Elocution.

Advertifements.

NOTICE is hereby given, That on Thurfday the 3d Day of January next, will be rented, to the higheft Bidder, for one Year, the PEWS of the Church in *Newbern*; agreeable to an Order of the VESTRY of *Chrift-Church* Parifh for that Purpofe.

Jacob Blount, } Church-
and
James Davis. } wardens.

4-71
The *North-Carolina Magazine* of 30 November–7 December 1764 reported that a Quaker "preacher" and his wife delivered sermons in New Bern; and Christ Church offered to rent its pews to the highest bidders. (Courtesy North Carolina Collection.)

4-72
This was one of four Bow China punch bowls ordered by the Halifax Masonic lodge in 1767. Other items ordered included three dozen punch cups and six dozen wine glasses. (Courtesy Museum of Early Southern Decorative Arts, Winston-Salem; original in Collection of Royal White Hart Lodge, Halifax.)

4-73
A Masonic master's mahogany and walnut armchair was made for the Edenton lodge by Benjamin Bucktrout of Williamsburg between 1766 and 1778. (Courtesy Museum of Early Southern Decorative Arts, Winston-Salem; original in Collection of Unanimity Lodge Number 7, Edenton.)

4-74
In his will in 1731, John Baptista Ashe instructed that his daughter "not be kept ignorant as to what appertains to a good house wife in the management of household af-[fairs]." (Courtesy NCDA&H.)

4-75
Governor Gabriel Johnston, in a message printed in Parks's *Virginia Gazette* of 8–15 October 1736, called the assembly's failure to establish a school "one of our greatest Misfortunes." (Courtesy North Carolina Collection.)

4-76
On Charles Pettigrew's commission as "Master of the Publick School in Edenton" in 1773, Governor Josiah Martin's scribe misspelled the teacher's name as "Pettigrove." (Courtesy Southern Historical Collection, Pettigrew Family Papers.)

4-77
W. J. Williams's pastel (1785) of the Reverend Charles Pettigrew (1743–1807), teacher, first Protestant Episcopal bishop-elect of North Carolina, and trustee of the state university. (Courtesy Frick Art Reference Library, New York.)

4-78
Receipt for tuition of Josiah Alexander in Queen's Museum in Charlotte ca. 1775 included a calculation of the currency exchange rate. (Courtesy North Carolina Collection.)

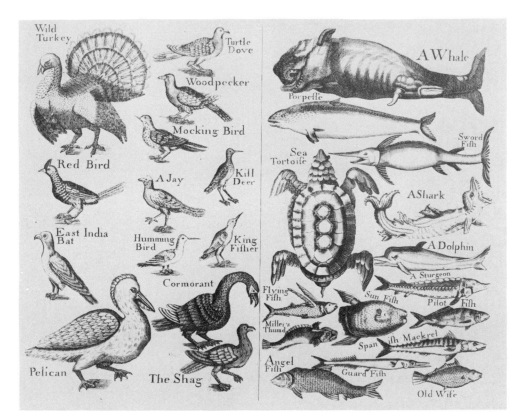

4-79
Two (of four) pages of drawings of wildlife in John Brickell's *The Natural History of North-Carolina*, published in Dublin in 1737. The other pages contained drawings of such animals as the buffalo, tiger, and bear. (Courtesy North Carolina Collection.)

4-80
Mark Catesby's original painting of the "only one of the Parrot kind in Carolina" is preserved in the Royal Library, Windsor Castle. The bird is now extinct. (Reproduced by gracious permission of Her Majesty Queen Elizabeth II.)

A
True and Faithful
NARRATIVE
Of the Proceedings
OF THE
House of Burgesses
of North-Carolina,

Met in Assembly for the said Province at New-bern, Feburary 5th 1739.

On the Articles of Complaint exhibited before them against the Honourable *William Smith*, Esq; Chief Justice of the said Province, for high Crimes and Misdemeanors done and committed by the said *William Smith* in the execution of his Office.

Published for the Justification of the Gentlemen Members of that House, who voted the said Articles sufficiently proved for the said Chief Justice to be charged therewith.

Addressed to the Freeholders of *North-Carolina.*

Pro. xxix. 2. *When the Righteous are in Authority the People rejoyce, but when the Wicked beareth Rule the People mourn.*

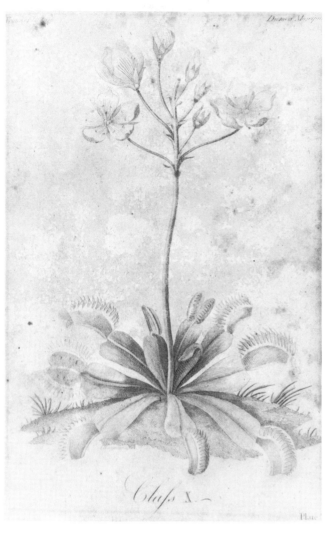

4-81
Buffalo, like this one painted by Catesby about 1724, roamed through Carolina before being exterminated by Indians and whites. (Courtesy Royal Library, Windsor Castle; reproduced by gracious permission of Her Majesty Queen Elizabeth II.)

4-83
Legislators seeking to impeach Chief Justice William Smith in 1740 arranged for the printing in Williamsburg of a portion of the proceedings. The printer was unaware that, unlike Virginia, North Carolina did not call its lower house the "House of Burgesses." (Courtesy Massachusetts Historical Society, Boston.)

4-82
William Bartram, who for several years ran a store at Ashwood in Bladen County, drew this tipitiwichet, or Venus flytrap, an insectivorous plant of the sundew family, native to southeastern North Carolina. (Courtesy North Carolina Collection; reprinted from Benjamin Smith Barton, *Elements of Botany* . . . [Philadelphia, 3rd edition, 1827], volume 2.)

4-84 (facing page)
Front page of the earliest extant issue (15 November 1751) of James Davis's newspaper, the *No^{th}-Carolina Gazette*, published at New Bern. (Courtesy NCDA&H.)

December 13, 1751.

NorthCAROLINA GAZETTE.

I have the freshest Advices, Foreign and Domestic.

All Persons may be supplied with this PAPER, at *Four Shillings*, Proclamation Money, *per* Quarter, by JAMES DAVIS, at the Printing-Office in *Newbern*; where all Manner of Printing-Work, and Book-Binding, is done reasonably. ADVERTISEMENTS of a moderate Length, are inserted for *Three Shillings* the first Week, and *Two Shillings* for every Week after.

The TEMPLE of HYMEN. A VISION.

A Few Days ago I had an Account of the Marriage of a Friend. When Occurrences of this Nature make an Impression upon the Mind, it is insensibly betrayed into little Animadversions upon them. This was my Case in an extraordinary Manner; for having mused some time on this Incident, I fell into an easy Slumber, when Fancy resumed the Subject, and sally'd out in the following Excursion.

I thought I was in an Instant placed on the Boundaries of a spacious Plain; in the Center of which was presented to the Eye a large Temple consecrated to *Hymen*, the God of Marriage. At a small Distance from me I observed a giddy Crowd of both Sexes, who were making towards the Building, in order to celebrate the Ceremony of the God. There was shuffled in among them, a Dæmon, whose Form was so peculiar, and whose Sway with the Multitude so universal, that I shall here give my Reader a particular Description of him: It seems the Name of this Fury was *Lust*; in the upper Part of his Body, he carried the Likeness of a human Shape; from the Middle downwards he wore the Resemblance of a Goat, his Eyes were turgid and sparkling, and inflamed, his Complexion was very irregular, attended with the most sudden Transitions from a sanguine Red to a livid Paleness, and a Tremor frequently seiz'd every Member.—Close followed him *Distaste*, with a sickly Countenance and supercilious Eye; and *Remorse*, with his Hat flapped over his Face, and a Worm gnawing his Vitals. I was shocked at these monstrous Appearances, and the more so, to observe how readily my Fellow-Creatures gave into the impious Suggestions of the Dæmon. But my Surprize was somewhat abated on a nearer Approach; for I took notice that his Breath was of such a malignant Nature, that all those who rashly advanced within its Influence, were presently intoxicated, and deprived of their Reason.

I was in such a Consternation at this Discovery, that I hesitated for a while, whether I should enter into Conversation with the blithe Adventurers formerly mentioned. In the midst of my Suspence there came towards us a grave old Gentleman of a steddy and composed Aspect, whose Name was *Deliberation*. He was one of the principal Agents belonging to the Temple, and so high in the God's Esteem, that *Hymen* was very rarely known to give his Benediction at the Conclusion of the Ceremony to any Couple who were ushered into his Presence, by this venerable Officer. Upon his joining the Company (to the Majority of which I found he was a perfect Stranger) there was expressed an universal Uneasiness and Discontent; and many of them industriously avoided all Conversation with him. But it was very remarkable that all those, who thus imprudently turned their Backs on this valuable Monitor, in their Return from the Temple, were seized by one or both of the melancholy Attendants of the Fury.

At my Entrance into the Building, I observed the Deity marching at a small Distance towards it.—The first in the Procession was *Love*, in the Form of a *Cupid*, who was continually practising a thousand little Arts and Graces, to draw upon him the Smiles of the God; and by the tender Regards which *Hymen* cast upon the Child, I found he was a very great Favourite.

The God followed next, holding in his Hand a flaming Torch; which shone the brighter the longer it burn'd; he approach'd its Supper by *Virtue*, a Lady of the most engaging Form that I had ever beheld. She was cloathed in a white refulgent Garment, and her Head was encirled with Glory.

The next Attendant was *Beauty*, arrayed in the most gorgeous Apparel, and full of herself, even to Distraction. She was handed along by *Youth*, a gay Stripling, wearing a Chaplet of Flowers on his Head, and Wings on his Shoulders.

Then appeared *Wealth* in the Figure of an old Man, meanly attired; his Eyes were the Eyes of a Hawk, and his Fingers curved and pointed inwards, like the Talons of a Raven; He was noisy, impudent, and presuming.

The Retinue was closed by *Fancy*, ever varying her Features and Dress; and what was very extraordinary, methought she charm'd in all.

The Deity immediately after his Entrance into the Temple, ascended his Throne; and sat with his Head gently reclin'd on *Virtue*'s Bosom. *Love*, and *Beauty*, took their Station on the Right Hand; and on the Left, were disposed *Wealth* and *Fancy*.

The God quickly proceeded to the Celebration of the Nuptial Rites; but there was such a confused Sound of Sighs and Laughter, that I could not give the Atttention which was requisite, in order to present my Reader with the several Circumstances that occurred; only I took Notice, that many of the Matches were so very unequal, that the God yoked them with Reluctance, and but half consented to his own Institution.

After the Ceremony was over, Silence was proclaimed in Court; for *Hymen* was determined to decide a Contest, which had been of long standing, between the Personages that attended the Alter. Upon this Declaration, the whole Multitude divided, and according to the particular Impulses of their Passions, took the Party of the several Competitors. The Young had ranked themselves on the right Hand of the Throne, while others of more advanced Years, had posted themselves behind the Disputants on the Left.

Love began with entering his Complaint against *Wealth*; setting forth, that his Antagonist had seduced such large Numbers to his Sentiments; that as to himself, his Interest very visibly declined every Day, to the great Prejudice of that State, wherein the Gods had design'd him the Preheminence. While he was pursuing his Arguments with great Warmth, *Poverty* stepp'd forth from amidst the Crowd, and stared the young Plaintiff full in the Face; who was so frighten'd at his sorrowful Countenance, that he fluttered his Pinions in order for Flight. When *Wealth* rising up addressed the Judge, with shewing the Necessity of his Presence, to make the Married State as replete with Happiness, as it was originally intended by its Institution; together with many other Arguments, which, if they had been delivered with the same Modesty as Force, could not have failed of creating a Multitude of Converts to his Side. This his Speech was followed with a Thunder of Applause from the Company behind. Upon which Incident the old Man began to triumph, and to renforce his Discourse when, through the Violence of his Emotions, his Garment flew open, and betrayed to View, *Cares* in the Form of *Vultures*, hanging at his Breast. Hereupon *Love* stood up, and would fain have reassumed his Cause. But *Hymen*, who well knew that the Presence of both was of the utmost Importance in the Performance of his Institution, and

4-85
Adam Boyd (1738–1803) published the *Cape-Fear Mercury* in Wilmington and planned (but apparently failed) to establish a paper titled the *Salisbury Rider*. In 1783 Boyd was one of the organizers of the Society of the Cincinnati in the state. (Courtesy North Carolina Collection.)

4-87
Less than a year after his son was apprenticed to John Cleland, Moses Wellwood accused the silversmith of mistreating the boy. (Courtesy NCDA&H.)

4-86
The *Pennsylvania Journal* of 23 April 1767 announced the first performance of a drama written by a North American: *Prince of Parthia*, by Thomas Godfrey, a Pennsylvanian who finished the tragedy in blank verse while working as a factor at Masonborough near Wilmington in 1759. He died near Wilmington in 1763. (Courtesy North Carolina Collection.)

4-88
A certificate dated 1736 attested that Benjamin Grove, a barber and wigmaker of Sussex, was free of obligation in England and willing to serve a four-year term as indentured servant in North Carolina. (Courtesy NCDA&H; original in Corporation of London Record Office, London.)

4-89
In the *Cape-Fear Mercury* for 22 September 1773, George Barnes, "at the sign of the Harp & Crown in Wilmington," offered a reward for the return of a red-headed Irish indentured servant woman with an interesting wardrobe. (Courtesy North Carolina Collection.)

4-90
Henry White earned a headright of fifty acres of land in 1680 for importing "a Negro woman named Jane." (Courtesy NCDA&H.)

4-91
Perhaps the earliest illustration of a black person in North Carolina was Franz Ludwig Michel's drawing of Baron von Graffenried's slave during their trial by the Tuscaroras in 1711. The third figure is that of John Lawson, who was killed by the Indians. (By permission of Burgerbibliothek, Bern.)

4-92 (left)
Mary Wilson's advertisement in Parks's *Virginia Gazette* for 9–16 May 1745 refers to "Ozenbrig" (Oznabrig) clothing, a coarse material named for the German town which made it an international trade item. It was sometimes called "Negro cloth." (Courtesy North Carolina Collection.)

4-93 (right)
Advertisements such as these two in the 13 March 1752 issue of *Noth-Carolina Gazette* indicated that some slaves were literate and that some were branded. (Courtesy North Carolina Collection.)

4-94
The institution of slavery would have been even more cruel but for persons like Robert Williams, who evaded the law to protect two runaways in Carteret County in 1773. (Courtesy North Carolina Collection; reprinted from *North-Carolina Gazette* [New Bern], 7 January 1774.)

4-95
Richard Bradley advertised "some breeding wenches" in the *Cape-Fear Mercury*, supplement 50 [17 November 1770?]. (Courtesy North Carolina Collection.)

4-96
In 1775, Richard, a slave owned by Joseph Jones of Pasquotank County, received forty lashes on his bare back; then his right ear was nailed to a post and, after an unspecified period, cut off. (Courtesy NCDA&H.)

4-97
Onslow County clerk William Gray sought payment in 1764 for handling the paperwork involving Joe, who was castrated, and Simon, who was hanged. (Courtesy NCDA&H.)

TAKEN up and committed to Goal at *Beaufort* in *Carteret* County, Two new Negroes, they came in a Canoe to *Bogue* Sound, but where from we cannot understand. By some Accident, or Act of Humanity, they got out of Goal, of a cold Evening (almost starved even in the fore part of the Night, and must have inevitably perished before Morning) and Strayed to the Subscriber's Kitchen, who wishes the proper Owner had them, but cannot send them any more into Confinement to starve and freeze to Death according to Law : For the Great Law-Giver *Moses*, had in Command, that we should do no Murder.
·ROBERT WILLIAMS.
Hamlet, Carteret County,
Nov. 22. 1773.

To be SOLD, by the subscriber cheap for cash or produce ;
RUM, sugar, oznabrigs, checks, salt, linnens, broad-cloth, blue and white negro cloth, &c. &c.——ALSO, will be exposed for sale on the 30th instant, eight or ten negroes, all used to country work ; amongst which are two coopers and some breeding wenches ; the terms will be known at the time of sale........All persons indebted to me by bond note or book-debt that has been due four months or upwards, are desired to settle the same, or they may depend their accounts, &c. will be put into the hands of an Attorney, if not paid within two months from this date.
RICHARD BRADLEY.
tbcuf. *Wilmington*, Nov. 15.

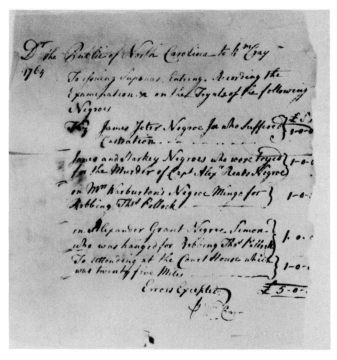

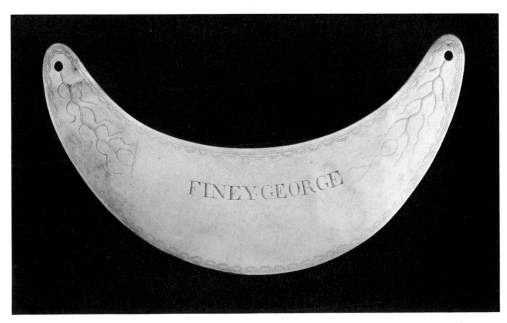

4-98
Thomas Long of Perquimans
County in 1754 provided in
his will that his "Negro fellow Welcome at paying the
sum of Fifteen Pounds Virginia Currancy may be set
free." (Courtesy NCDA&H.)

4-99
A silver gorget, made by
Thomas W. Machen of New
Bern for Finey George, a
Catawba Indian, was worn as
a badge of rank. It was found
in an Indian grave near
Charlotte. (Courtesy Mu-
seum of Early Southern
Decorative Arts, Winston-
Salem.)

4-100
By the time this petition was signed about 1766, most Tuscarora names had been anglicized. (Courtesy Southern Historical Collection.)

4-101 (top right)
Sheriff Thomas Kearny of Edgecombe County received payment in 1751 for executing two Negroes and for sending "a Sapponey Indian" to jail in Edenton on suspicion of murder. (Courtesy NCDA&H.)

4-102
In 1730, Sir Alexander Cuming took a group of Cherokee chieftains to London, where they were introduced to English society. In this engraving by Isaac Basire after a painting by Markham, young Attakullakulla or Ukwanneequa (Little Carpenter) appears second from right. The English subsequently benefited from his friendship. (Courtesy Smithsonian Institution National Anthropological Archives.)

4-103
Francis Parson's painting of Cunne Shote, a friendly Cherokee leader who was taken to London in 1762. (Courtesy Smithsonian Institution, National Anthropological Archives; original in Thomas Gilcrease Institute, Tulsa.)

4-104
The Moravians at Bethabara constructed a palisade around their central buildings for protection from Indians who occasionally approached the settlement. (By permission of Moravian Archives, Bethlehem; original in Archiv der Brüder-Unität, Herrnhut, DDR.)

4-105
Governor Arthur Dobbs proclaimed 7 June 1758 as a day of fasting and supplication for God to "vanquish and overcome our insatiable and inveterate Enemies." (Courtesy NCDA&H.)

NORTH-CAROLINA,

By his Excellency ARTHUR DOBBS, Esq; Captain-General, and Governor in Chief, in and over his Majesty's said Province.

A PROCLAMATION.

WHEREAS the Enormity of our Sins, the Neglect of the Divine Service and Worship of God, and from our gross Sensualities and Immoralities, God Almighty has been pleased to correct Britain and these Colonies, by a heavy and dangerous War, by which we are in imminent Danger of losing the invaluable Blessing of our holy Religion, Liberties and Possessions: And whereas he has justly corrected these Colonies, by raising a Spirit in our Indian Neighbours, to invade, massacre, and make Prisoners, the British Inhabitants of these Colonies, upon their visible Neglect of the original native Inhabitants, by neither attempting to civilize, nor convert them to our holy Religion, and therefore God Almighty has left us, more immediately to be punished by them, at the Instigation of our cruel and inveterate Enemies the French, who, from their Principles, endeavour to extirpate the Protestant Religion wherever they have Power; and have not only in these Provinces, but in Europe, formed a formidable Popish League, to extirpate and ruin the Protestant Interest of Europe: And whereas it appears, that after a short Correction of the Protestants in Germany, God Almighty has most wonderfully manifested himself in Defence of the Protestant Cause in Germany, and has apparently headed their Armies, by inspiring them with an invincible Courage, and conducting their Councils, and at the same Time dispiriting their Popish Enemies, and turning all their Councils into Foolishness, so that it manifestly appears that God will not desert the holy Protestant Religion, provided we, with humble Hearts, sincerely repent of our gross Sensualities and Immoralities, and our shameful Neglect of his Divine Service and Worship, and serve him and his Christ with our whole Hearts, and not with only a Lip-Service, and external Worship.

Let us therefore, with sincere Hearts, fall down before him, and supplicate him, through the Merits and Satisfaction of his dear Son Christ Jesus, our only Mediator and Redeemer, to forgive us our Sins, upon our sincere Resolution of Amendment; and that he will avert those Judgments hanging over us, accept of the Punishments already poured out upon us, and leave us no longer to be corrected by our Enemies, but that he will restore us to his Favour, go out and lead our Armies, Fleets and Councils, and inspire us with Courage to defend our holy Religion, and Civil Liberties; and to return him the utmost Praise for manifesting himself so eminently in Defence of the Protestant Interest, and Civil Liberties of Europe; with a lively Hope and Faith, that if we repent and amend, that he will also manifest himself as the God and Protector of the Protestant Cause, and Liberties of Britain and these Colonies, and implore a Blessing on his Majesty's Arms and Councils.

As therefore a Day of public Fasting and Humiliation is, at this critical Time, most highly necessary, I have, by the Advice of his Majesty's honourable Council, thought fit to issue this my Proclamation, and do hereby appoint Wednesday the Seventh of June next, to be kept holy by all Ranks of People within this Province, as a Day of Fasting and Supplication; and also to give Thanks to Almighty God, and our blessed Saviour Christ Jesus, for having hitherto preserved this Province in Peace, in the Midst of surrounding impending Dangers, and on Account of the Manifestation of his Providence, so remarkable in protecting the Protestant Interest, and Civil Liberties of Europe, from the united Popish Powers; hoping also that he will declare himself the Protector of the Protestant Interest in America, lead our Armies and Councils, and give a Blessing to the Arms of his most gracious Majesty by Sea and Land; and that he may support our religious and civil Liberties, and may vanquish and overcome our insatiable and inveterate Enemies.

I therefore strictly command and require, that Public Service be had in all Churches and Chappels within this Province, and that it be kept holy, from all manual Labour, and that this Proclamation be publickly read, either on that Day, or some convenient Sunday before it, to give Notice to all Persons within this Province, to pay a Regard and Obedience to it.

GIVEN under my Hand and the Seal of the said Province, at Newbern, the Twenty-ninth Day of April, in the Thirty-First Year of his Majesty's Reign, and in the Year of our Lord, One Thousand Seven Hundred and Fifty-eight.

By his Excellency's Command,
Richard Fenner, Dep. Sec.

ARTHUR DOBBS.

GOD Save the KING.

4-106
Governor William Tryon in 1767 issued a proclamation prohibiting interference with the Indians living west of a partition line that he ordered run. His order was soon ignored. (Courtesy North Carolina Collection.)

NORTH-CAROLINA.

By His Excellency William Tryon, Esquire,

Captain-General, Governor, and Commander in Chief, in and over the said Province, and Vice-Admiral of the same:

A PROCLAMAITON:

WHEREAS a PARTITION-LINE has been run, between the Western-Frontiers of this Province and the Cherokee Hunting-Grounds, beginning at Reedy-River, where the South-Carolina and Cherokee Dividing-Line terminates, running a North Course to Tryon-Mountain, of the Blue-Ridge of Mountains, supposed to be Sixty Miles from the said River, and from the Top of Tryon-Mountain, aforesaid, beginning at the marked Trees thereon, a direct Line to Chiswell's Mines, which said Line is established and confirmed as a Deviding-Line between the Cherokee Indians and this Province (until his Majesty's Pleasure be farther known thereon) by an Instrument of Writing, executed between the Commissioners appointed for this Province, and the Cherokee Chiefs, on the Thirteenth Day of June last past.

I HAVE THEREFORE thought fit, by and with the Advice and Consent of his Majesty's Council, to issue this Proclamation, strictly requiring all Persons settled within the Indian Lands, to remove from thence by the First Day of January next; and that no Person on any Pretence whatsoever may disturb the said Indians, in the quiet and peaceable Possession of the Lands to the Westward of the aforesaid Line, or presume to Hunt thereon, or any other Way or Means to give them Cause of Uneasiness: And all Persons, who, regardless of their own Interest, and disobedient to his Majesty's Command, shall neglect to remove from off the Indian Lands as required, or shall at any Time hereafter settle thereon, will not only expose their Families and Effects to the Depredations of the Indians, but also deprive themselves of the Protection of this Government.

AND as no Land will be granted within one Mile of the aforesaid Line, the Surveyor-General, or his Deputies, are forbid making any Surveys or Returns of Surveys into the Secretary's Office, within one Mile of the said Dividing-Line. Any of the Inhabitants of this Province who desire to Trade with the said Indians are required to take out a Licence from the Governor or Commander in Chief for the Time being, and subject themselves to such general Regulations as may be required by the Superintendant of Indian Affairs.

AND as the Peace and Security of the Western Frontiers of this Province greatly depend upon cultivating the Harmony and Friendship that at present subsists between the several Nations of the Indians and the Inhabitants thereof, I recommend that all Indians, who may have Business within the Settlements, may be received in the most friendly and amicable Manner, and assisted with any Necessaries agreeable to Humanity and Hospitality; as all Injuries and Violences offered them will be prosecuted with the utmost Rigour of the Law: The Indians having promised a kind and friendly Treatment to all white Persons that may have occasion to go into their Nations.

GIVEN under my Hand, and the Great Seal of the Province, at Brunswick, the Sixteenth Day of July, 1767, and in the Seventh Year of His Majesty's Reign. WILLIAM TRYON.

By His Excellency's Command,
BENJAMIN HERON, Sec'ry.

(GOD SAVE THE KING.)

5. Rebellion, Revolution, and Independence, 1765–1783

Like his predecessors, Arthur Dobbs found the governorship of North Carolina more frustrating and less rewarding than the royal appointment implied. The French and Indian War occupied most of his term; he was thwarted in efforts to establish the capital at Tower Hill; and he repeatedly ran afoul of the recalcitrance of the Carolinians. Furthermore, the aging governor's marriage to a fifteen-year-old girl made him the subject of much gossip. To relieve him, the crown in 1764 sent a lieutenant governor—a dashing young former army officer, William Tryon. His arrival in the colony rekindled competition for the location of the capital.

The lieutenant governor felt a "thunderbolt" when Governor Dobbs announced plans to delay his departure from office until spring when the weather would be more favorable for sailing. "This was no flattering Intelligence to me," the eager young appointee wrote; however, he promised to behave toward the governor "with the respect that is due to his Character, Age and Infirmities."

In December, chafing under the delay in his succession to the governorship, Tryon began a tour of the eastern counties. At New Bern on Christmas Eve he was met eight miles from town "by a great Number of Gentlemen, who accompanied him to Lodgings prepared for his Reception; where he was immediately saluted with 19 Guns from the Artillery.—In the Evening the town was handsomely illuminated, Bonfires were lighted, and plenty of Liquor given to the Populace." Two nights later, Tryon and his socialite wife, the former Margaret Wake, were guests at an elegant ball in the courthouse. Returning to the Cape Fear after traveling as far as the Virginia border, the lieutenant governor spent the winter in an awkward role, but on 28 March, Governor Dobbs died. Tryon took office as governor and by June had moved his family into Russellborough, Dobbs's former home, which was renamed Bellfont.

Even as Tryon took the oath of office, the spirit of independence characteristic of early Carolinians was asserting itself in contrasting, even conflicting, ways. During his tenure eastern leaders rose in opposition to many English colonial policies, while backcountrymen rebelled against governmental practices condoned by those same leaders.

For decades, the colonists had suffered no serious consequences from evading unpopular English policies. After the French and Indian War, however, Parliament passed a number of acts designed to tighten control over the colonies and to require them to assist in payment of debts incurred by England in their defense. Opposition to the new laws was expressed by James Davis in his *North-Carolina Magazine* of 20–27 July 1764: "Countrymen, shall we be idle, when the general Alarm to Industry is sounded? No, let the Maids trim their Spinning Wheels, the Wives clean their Knitting-Needles, and the Husbands look to their Flocks and Herds, and encourage the Scheemers to erect Fulling-Mills, and we shall presently have little Use for the Merchants." The Stamp Act of 1765 precipitated a series of confrontations that might have resulted in bloodshed under a royal governor less diplomatic than Tryon.

Opposition became general, and on 19 October 1765, hundreds of citizens from the Lower Cape Fear gathered in Wilmington for a massive demonstration. Rumors of the impending arrival of a ship carrying the hated stamps led to the organization of the Sons of Liberty; further demonstrations resulted in the resignation of William Houston as stamp officer and a dangerous confrontation with Governor Tryon. When HMS *Diligence* arrived, the colonists prevented the crew from unloading the stamps, an action that led to the governor's suspension of all courts. For several months government was virtually at a standstill.

Danger of open rebellion was heightened in February 1766 when British officials seized two ships whose clearance papers had not been stamped. Nearly a thousand men marched on Brunswick to force the release of the ships and the suspension of the Stamp Act. Led by Cornelius Harnett, the citizen-army forced William Pennington, the comptroller of customs, who had taken refuge in the governor's home, to swear not to enforce the Stamp Act.

American resistance resulted in the repeal of the Stamp Act, but Parliament responded to the colonists' theories of taxation by passing the Declaratory Act of 1766, which reiterated parliamentary rights. Within another year Parliament adopted the Townshend Act, imposing duties on wine, tea, paper, glass, and lead. The purpose of this act—to pay salaries of royal officials in America—threatened the tradition under which the lower house of the assembly held the power of the purse; in an address to the king, the house pronounced that "free men cannot legally be taxed but by themselves or their representatives."

When late in 1769 the house took up for consideration a nonimportation agreement proposed by Virginia, Tryon dissolved it. Not to be outdone, Speaker John Harvey immediately reconvened sixty-four of the sixty-seven "late representatives of the people," who adopted a "nonimportation association," pledging not to import slaves, wine, or enumerated British goods after 1 January. Even though Parliament repealed the Townshend Act early in 1770, the Wilmington Sons of Liberty in June appointed a committee to enforce the nonimportation policy and to cooperate with the other colonies in resistance to policies deemed by Americans to be illegal. Thus the decade ended amidst a widening disagreement over the rights of the colonies to manage their internal affairs.

"Whereas that great Good may come of this Great designed Evil, the Stamp Law, while the Sons of Liberty withstand the Lords of Parliament, in Behalf of true Liberty, Let not Officers under them carry on unjust Oppression in our own Province. . . ." Thus began a paper presented to public officials of Orange County only a few months after the Stamp Act crisis. The paper proposed a meeting of citizens and officers to determine "whether the free men of this Country labor under any abuses of power or not." The refusal of county officers to appear at the meeting reflected the growing distrust between the country people and those who served them in public office.

"Abuses" were real enough for the struggling farmers of the backcountry. Land problems were aggravated by the practices of Lord Granville's agents; taxes and quitrents were burdensome; money was so scarce that purchases were commonly by barter; militia musters and road work required nearly a month of the working year of each able-bodied man; and the west was grossly underrepresented in the assembly (the western counties, with about half the colony's population in 1766, were represented in the assembly by only seventeen delegates; the eastern counties sent sixty-one).

More than any other cause, however, antagonism toward local public officials fueled the resistance of the backcountrymen that would culminate in the Battle of Alamance in 1771. Except for the elected delegates to the lower house of the assembly, all county officers were appointed, usually by the governor upon nomination by the assembly. Thus the citizens had no direct voice in the selection of justices of the peace, who constituted the court of pleas and quarter sessions—both the administrative and minor judicial body of the county—or of the judge, sheriff, clerk, register, or colonel of the militia. These appointed officials were characterized as the "courthouse ring"—a tightly knit little group often made even smaller by multiple officeholding. Since few local citizens studied law, county seats offered attractive prospects for non-native attorneys; Edmund Fanning, for example, a New Yorker, practiced law in Hillsborough and held the offices of assemblyman, register, judge of the superior court, and colonel of the militia. 5-8

Tax collection was an odious task at best, but citizens accused some sheriffs of conspiring with other members of the courthouse ring to foreclose on properties for the nonpayment of taxes in order to auction them off for piddling sums without giving the owners reasonable time to raise the levies. Even more abusive in the eyes of the farmers was the fee system, by which lawyers, judges, sheriffs, clerks, and registers made their salaries by collecting a fee for each of their actions. Complaints of extortionate fees were not new, but their number seemed to multiply in the 1760s. 5-9

Instances of strong citizen expression of their grievances likewise were not new. In Halifax County in 1759 and in Mecklenburg County in 1765, for example, land controversies led to physical action by small numbers of citizens. In the latter case, the clerk of court of Rowan County, John Frohock, while surveying lands for himself and his associate, Henry Eustace McCulloh, was attacked by squatters and "got one damnable wipe across the Nose and Mouth." A fellow surveyor, Abraham Alexander, was "striped from the nape of his neck to the Waistband of his Breeches, like a draft-Board; poor Jimmy Alexander had very near had daylight let into his skull:—a *pack of Unmannerly Sons of Bitches* as Abraham called them."

Only a month later in Granville County a schoolmaster named George Sims issued his "Nutbush Address," in which he complained of excessive taxes and rents, extortionate fees, and fraud in the accounting for public funds. Still, he wrote, "it is not our Form or Mode of Government, nor yet the Body of our Laws that we are quarreling with, but with the Malpractices of the Officers of our County Court, and the Abuses that we suffer by those that are impowered to manage our publick Affairs."

Officers sought to ignore or label seditious the "advertisements" issued by complaining citizens of Orange County in 1766. Within a year news of new taxes—a poll tax and a levy on imported liquors for the purpose of constructing a luxurious "palace" in New Bern for the governor—increased unrest in the backcountry. Westerners were little hurt by the import tax, but the poll (that is, head) tax was particularly burdensome to poor men, who paid the same amount as the wealthy. Furthermore, the farmers vociferously objected to paying any sort of tax to provide a mansion for the governor. "Not one man in twenty of the four most populous counties [Anson, Orange, Mecklenburg, and Rowan] will ever see this famous house when built," wrote one Mecklenburg citizen.

Tryon's Palace was built at a cost of about fifteen thousand pounds, but it served to divide rather than unify North Carolinians. This divisiveness helps explain the short life of the building as the seat of government, for perhaps more than any other tangible factor it symbolized the insensitivity of eastern officials to the grievances of the backcountry farmers. Early in 1768 these men resumed their "advertisements" and formed themselves into an "association" for "regulating publick Grievances & abuses of Power." They pledged to pay no taxes or fees other than those allowed by law. Finally, on 4 April, the "Mob," as they were called initially, gave themselves the title "Regulators" and demanded that the two most recent sheriffs and the vestrymen meet with their representatives to inspect the public accounts. This request was probably not unreasonable; Governor Tryon himself had written the previous year that "the Sheriffs have embezzled more than one-half of the public money ordered to be raised and collected by them."

To the extent of issuing a warning to officials and lawyers concerning their conduct, Governor Tryon responded to the Regulator petitions. In addition, he led an armed force through the backcountry, arriving at Hillsborough in September 1768 for the trials of Fanning, indicted for taking excessive fees, and Hermon Husband, the Quaker leader of the Regulators, who was charged with "inciting the populace to rebellion." A large body of Regulators—estimated variously between 800 and 3,700—camped outside the town almost in sight of the colonial militia under Tryon's command. A clash of arms was perhaps averted by the court's verdicts of guilty for Fanning and not guilty for Husband. The register, however, was fined only one penny and court costs.

Popular support of the Regulators was indicated in 1769 when they elected their candidates to the legislature in the counties of Anson, Granville, Halifax, and Orange. Among the new representatives was Husband, who presented a petition to the legislative body complaining of conditions in the backcountry.

Another crisis occurred at the superior court session in Hillsborough in September 1770. Judge Richard Henderson presided; the docket listed a number of cases for and against the Regulators. A large group of Regulators broke up the court and dragged Fanning out into the street, whipped him, and vandalized his house. They then beat up other attorneys and drove the judge out of town. The following day the intruders held a mock court and scrawled insulting "verdicts" in the court docket.

Virtual anarchy prevailed in Orange County. Governor Tryon issued a proclamation requiring an investigation into the riot, and the ensuing session of the assembly expelled Hermon Husband and—amid rumors that the Regulators might march on New Bern—passed the "Act for Preventing Tumultous and Riotous Assemblies" (called by the Regulators the "Bloody Act"), which outlawed persons who resisted arrest or interfered with the government's efforts to subdue the insurgents. The Regulators responded by threatening court officials and declaring Fanning an outlaw to be killed on sight. This contempt for authority forced Tryon's hand, and in the spring of 1771 he again mobilized the militiamen and led them westward.

Meanwhile, Regulators were gathering their own forces from the western counties. Without a real leader, the armed citizens camped at Great Alamance Creek in western Orange (now Alamance) County. Tryon marched his militia to the same vicinity. Both sides spent a tense day and night. On 16 May the Regulators sent a message offering to confer with the governor in an effort to satisfy their grievances. Tryon curtly refused to meet with the rebel leaders unless their men put down their arms and dispersed. Emboldened by their superior numbers (about two thousand, compared to fewer than fifteen hundred militiamen), the Regulators called the governor's bluff. It was their mistake, for Tryon ordered his troops to attack, and within two hours the militia routed the untrained and leaderless protesters. Fewer than two hundred men on both sides were killed or wounded. One captured rebel was executed as an example, and six others were later convicted and hanged for treason. The governor offered to pardon most of the insurgents who submitted to authority, and nearly sixty-five hundred citizens subsequently received the king's pardon.

The Battle of Alamance was not, as some romanticists have called it, the "first battle of the American Revolution"; it was, instead, a crushing defeat of backcountry farmers by their fellow citizens. Perhaps, in the final analysis, the issue was not home rule but rather who would rule at home. The victors were the same men who had rebelled against a parliamentary law five years before and who in five more years would rebel against the entire British government. Squarely between those two instances of armed resistance of their own, they boasted "Pax reddita [Peace restored] May 1771" to celebrate their triumph over their fellow citizens, many of whom subsequently moved westward where government had not been firmly established.

After the suppression of the Regulators, Tryon returned to the palace to which history has given his name; but he was there only a short while before going to his newly appointed post as governor of New York. He was soon joined by a new private secretary, Edmund Fanning, the antagonist of the Regulators.

The suppression of civil disorder in the backcountry enabled provincial leaders to focus attention on policy disagreements between themselves and the English government. In 1770 the American boycott of British manufactures had influenced Parliament to repeal all of the Townshend taxes except that on tea, the symbolism of which continued to gall the colonists. Consequently, when Josiah Martin replaced Tryon as governor in 1771, there was no honeymoon, for the assembly scrutinized every move by royal officials for signs of new encroachments upon the rights of the colonies. Following the lead of Virginia, North Carolinians established a Committee of Correspon-

dence; henceforth, a network of committees in the various colonies coordinated information about parliamentary actions affecting America.

In 1773 the distrust between Martin and the assembly intensified when the crown disallowed a new court act because it contained the traditional provision of attachment of property owned by absentee landlords—mostly British merchants. Lacking statutory provision for a superior court, Martin, without legislative sanction, set up courts of oyer and terminer. When he sought an appropriation for his new courts, however, the assembly rebuffed him, and for three years the colony was without a tribunal for the trial of major civil cases.

Meanwhile, Parliament was again stirring the wrath of the colonists. It gave the British East India Company exclusive right to sell tea in America, an act that threatened the very livelihood of New England merchants. No previous action had so solidified the colonists as did the Boston Port Bill and the other "Coercive Acts," which Parliament passed in response to the Boston Tea Party in December 1773 and other demonstrations of opposition. The closing of the port of Boston was viewed as an attack upon all the colonies, and the Committees of Correspondence whipped up anti-British sentiment from New Hampshire to Georgia. North Carolina joined in the protest by sending the *Penelope*, loaded with supplies, to assist the beleaguered Bostonians.

Virginia and Massachusetts issued a call for a "Continental Congress" to devise mutual strategy in opposing the "Intolerable Acts." When Governor Martin sought to avert the election of delegates to the congress by refusing to call a meeting of the assembly, a mass meeting of citizens in Wilmington proposed a "provincial congress independent of the governor," and in the next few weeks several counties and towns adopted resolutions deploring British policies and naming delegates to the extralegal congress. Notwithstanding Governor Martin's issuance of a proclamation calling on all citizens to "forbear to attend any such illegal meetings," seventy-one delegates from thirty counties and four boroughs met on 25 August 1774, within a few blocks of the governor's house in New Bern. This First Provincial Congress—one of the earliest popularly elected colonywide assemblies of Americans to meet in defiance of the crown—adopted a ringing statement professing loyalty to George III but vigorously denying the power of Parliament to tax the colonies. The congress also endorsed an economic boycott of British goods, recommended establishment of committees of safety in each county, authorized John Harvey (the presiding officer) to call additional congresses, and elected Richard Caswell, Joseph Hewes, and William Hooper delegates to the First Continental Congress in Philadelphia the following month. Americans thus committed themselves to mutual defense, and within a year trade between the colonies and England was dramatically reduced.

5-26
5-27
5-28
5-29
Men were not alone in demonstrating their support for the American cause. At Edenton on 25 October 1774, four dozen women from at least five counties met under the leadership of Penelope Barker and signed a resolution supporting the "several particular resolves" of the First Provincial Congress. The "Edenton Tea Party," an early demonstration of political activity by women, was but one of many public expressions of concern by the womenfolk of North Carolina during the period of the Revolution.

5-23
5-25
5-30
Harvey called for a second congress to meet in New Bern on 3 April 1775. Martin again issued a condemnatory proclamation; he also sought to upstage the congress by calling the assembly into session on 4 April. The strategy failed, however, for the composition of the congress and the assembly was almost identical, Harvey presided over both, and both endorsed nonimportation and nonconsumption of British goods and reelected Caswell, Hewes, and Hooper to the Continental Congress. Angrily, Martin dissolved the legislature—the last assembly to meet in North Carolina under royal auspices.

Meanwhile, in Massachusetts words gave way to action when local minutemen clashed with British soldiers at Lexington and Concord. The arrival of news of the Massachusetts skirmishes further emboldened North Carolinians. At New Bern members of the local committee carted off cannons from the palace grounds and indignantly protested when Governor Martin removed others to prevent

5-31
their capture. On 31 May the Charlotte committee adopted a set of resolves declaring void all commissions granted by the king and urging citizens to elect military officers with powers derived from the people, not the English government. Forwarding the text to London, Martin wrote that the Mecklenburg Resolves "surpass[ed] all the horrid and treasonable publications that the inflammatory spirits of the Continent have yet produced." On 1 June the Rowan committee resolved that "by the

Constitution of our Government we are a free People, not subject to be taxed by any power but that of the happy Constitution which limits both Sovereignty and Allegiance."

5-32
5-33
Governor Martin, who had already taken the precaution of sending his family to New York, fled the palace and took up residence at Fort Johnston at the mouth of the Cape Fear. Hearing of Whig designs against the fort, Martin slipped aboard the British ship *Cruizer* in the river just before armed Americans captured and burned the fort. North Carolina thus became the first colony to drive out its chief executive. Persons who communicated with the governor were to be "deemed Enemies to the Liberties of *America*, and dealt with accordingly," and citizens neglecting to sign the articles of association were to have their firearms confiscated. Governmental authority was transferred to the Provincial Congress and the committees of safety.

5-34
Still, when the Third Provincial Congress met at Hillsborough on 20 August, the 184 delegates from every county and borough took an oath of allegiance to King George III. Parliament was the culprit: "Neither Parliament, nor any Member or Constituent Branch thereof" had power to tax Americans, the delegates declared. Preparing for defense, the congress established a Committee of Secrecy to procure arms and ammunition; declared that all citizens were bound by the decisions of the Continental and Provincial congresses; devised a complex governmental structure to replace royal authority; and directed the raising of two regiments for the Continental Line, with James Moore and Robert Howe as colonels. Six battalions of minutemen were also authorized. The congress also directed the collection of back taxes, issued $125,000 in bills of credit, and levied a poll tax. The Hillsborough congress had put North Carolina on a war footing, and before the end of the year troops from the colony had faced British forces near Norfolk and the "Scovellites" (a Tory group) in South Carolina.

5-50
The ease with which the Provincial Congress moved the colony toward armed resistance was deceptive, for war sentiment was by no means unanimous. In fact, few North Carolinians really believed that war was likely; most believed that firm resistance would cause Parliament to back down. The population was divided; the Patriots (or Whigs) felt strongly enough to fight the mother country if their grievances were not redressed; the Loyalists (or Tories) preferred British rule to that

5-35 of the colonial leaders; and a large element without title was uninformed about, unconcerned with, afraid of, or neutral toward the issues that excited the Provincial Congress.

Governor Martin, still aboard the ship at Cape Fear, firmly believed that a great majority of the people would rally to the king's standard, and in January 1776 he issued a proclamation asking them to do just that. This exhortation was coupled with a complex military strategy designed to regain his control over the colony. He proposed, through his agents, to raise an army of several thousand from among the former Regulators, still resentful over their defeat by soldiers under command of the eastern leaders; the Scots Highlanders of the Upper Cape Fear, who in accepting land from the crown had pledged their allegiance; and other citizens who for varying reasons remained—or could be persuaded to become—loyal to Britain. The combined force would march to the Cape Fear, where they would be met by a major British naval and land force. This exhibition of strength, Martin thought, would quell resistance in North Carolina.

This grand scheme did not remain secret to the Whigs, who mobilized the militia and called out the two regiments of the Continental Line to prevent the Tories from reaching Wilmington. As a force of about 1,600 Highlanders under the com-
5-36 mand of Donald MacDonald marched southeastward from Cross Creek, the colonials awaited them at a bridge across Widow Moore's Creek northwest of Wilmington. Planks of the bridge were loosened and the log sleepers were greased with soap and tallow. As the Scots began crossing the bridge, they were raked by gunfire. Within a few minutes at least 30 of them were killed and 850 captured. Among the latter was Allan MacDonald, husband
5-37 of Flora, famed for protecting Prince Charles Ed-
5-38 ward Stuart in 1746. The Whigs lost 1 man killed and 1 wounded.

The overwhelming Whig victory at Moore's Creek Bridge thwarted Martin's scheme to reestablish his governorship, and it emboldened provincial leaders to think more seriously about independence from Great Britain, rather than simply seek concessions. It also made a deep impression upon the British, and North Carolina was virtually free of redcoats for the first four years of the war that followed.

The Fourth Provincial Congress met at Halifax in April. Samuel Johnston, the presiding officer, accurately characterized the mood there when he wrote that "all our people here are up for indepen-

dence." Reconciliation was no longer the goal. Whereas previous congresses had blamed the troubles on Parliament, the new congress took up "the usurpations and violences attempted and committed by the King and Parliament." On 12 April all eighty-three delegates present (sixty-five elected delegates were absent) voted for a resolution which read in part, "The Delegates for this Colony in the 5-39 Continental Congress be impowered to concur with the Delegates of the other Colonies in declaring Independency, and forming foreign Alliances, reserving to this Colony the Sole and Exclusive right of forming a Constitution and Laws for this Colony."

Thus North Carolina became the first colony specifically to authorize (but not direct) its delegates to join an independence movement. Virginia went a step further in May and instructed its representatives to "move for independence," and on 4 July 1776, the Continental Congress approved the final draft of the Declaration of Independence to which North Carolina's delegates—Joseph Hewes, 5-40 William Hooper, and John Penn—later affixed 5-41 their signatures. A copy of the document reached 5-42 Halifax on 22 July, and three days later the Council 5-43 of Safety absolved North Carolinians from "all Al- 5-45 legiance to the British Crown." On 1 August, Cornelius Harnett publicly read the declaration for the first time at a rally in Halifax.

The new state was without a constitution, and in elections in the fall for delegates to a Fifth Provincial Congress the harmony that had marked the independence movement was shattered by bitter debates over the nature of the new government. Conservatives like Samuel Johnston and William 5-44 Hooper advocated a strong executive, an independent judiciary, and property qualifications for voting and holding office. Others, like Willie Jones and Thomas Person, supported a "simple democracy" with a weak executive, a dominant legislature, and frequent elections. Johnston, who failed to win a seat, wrote acrimoniously, "Everyone who has the least pretensions to be a gentleman is borne down *per ignobile vulgus*—a set of men without reading, experience, or principles to govern them." Actually, the factions were fairly well divided in the congress, and Richard Caswell, a moderate, was elected president.

The constitution adopted in December was a 5-46 bundle of compromises. A liberal declaration of 5-47 rights and the provision for three branches of gov- 5-48 ernment with a strong bicameral legislature pleased the radicals; high qualifications for holding office and voting and the appointment of judges for life (subject to good behavior) pleased the conservatives. The governor, elected annually by joint ballot of the senate and house of commons, was given little more authority than "to sign a receipt for his own salary," quipped William Hooper. There was no provision for amendment.

5-49 Caswell, respected by both factions, was elected governor and took office in January 1777. At New Bern he was greeted with "a handsome collation" at Mrs. Edward Wrenford's tavern and salutes from the vessels in the harbor. Three months later the first General Assembly of the independent state convened in New Bern. Its first order of business was the raising and provisioning of a large number of soldiers. In the next five years North Carolina 5-51 furnished ten regiments to the Continental Line— 5-52 about seven thousand men in all—plus perhaps ten 5-53 thousand militiamen. Except for the suppression of 5-54 5-55 the Cherokees by militiamen under General Grif- 5-56 fith Rutherford in 1776, North Carolina was the 5-57 scene of little warfare for four years. Troops from the state, however, fought alongside fellow Americans elsewhere—in the defense of Charleston; with General George Washington at far-off places like Brandywine, Germantown, and Monmouth; in bloody battles both north and south. Even a small state navy was built and privateers were commissioned; in return, the English conducted raids upon North Carolina's exposed coastline.

5-59 Inflation, high taxes, shortages of goods, and 5-60 loyalty were continuing problems. With its treasury 5-61 empty, the state—like the Continental Congress— 5-62 printed more and more paper money, backed by 5-63 little more than a promise to pay. Inflation so re- 5-64 duced the value of money that at one time twenty 5-65 thousand pounds in paper money was worth only 5-66 about twenty-five pounds in specie. Various tax 5-67 5-68 levies, including taxes in kind (that is, in goods), 5-69 became almost confiscatory. Manpower was required not only for the armed forces but also for new industries made necessary by the curtailment of imports. The exportation of salt, corn, peas, flour, pork, bacon, and beef—except for the use of troops—was prohibited, and many other commodities were in short supply. Loyalty was severely tested; desertions were widespread; citizens sus- 5-58 pected of British sympathies were forced to take an oath of allegiance or be banished; and the property of persons convicted of aiding and comforting the enemy was subject to confiscation.

North Carolina again became a battleground late in 1780. Following the capture of Charleston, British forces under Lord Charles Cornwallis swept northwestward and at Camden in August inflicted 5-70 a demoralizing defeat upon the Americans. The following month, Cornwallis marched across the 5-71 border into North Carolina just as Governor Abner Nash asked for creation of a board of war to substitute for the Council of State, whose members had neglected their duties. With the general was Josiah Martin, the last royal governor, who declared that North Carolina was "rescued, saved, redeemed and restored" to his governorship. As in 1775, Martin was over-optimistic, for Cornwallis found Charlotte a hornet's nest of Patriot opposition, and about thirty miles westward on 7 October his subordinate Colonel Patrick Ferguson was trapped and killed, along with more than a hundred of his men, by mountain militiamen atop a ridge called King's Mountain near the border be- 5-72 tween the two states. The rude reception given him 5-73 in the Mecklenburg area sent Cornwallis back into 5-74 South Carolina, where he prepared for a campaign to subjugate North Carolina.

He did not move fast enough, for in December 1780 Nathanael Greene assumed command of 5-75 American forces in the South, and the earl had 5-76 found his match. Initially, Greene had only about twenty-three hundred men, mostly untrained militia, and he knew that his forces were not equal to the seasoned British soldiers. Nevertheless, in the next three months he conducted a masterful retreat through the Carolina Piedmont, rested and trained his troops and enlisted others north of the Dan in Virginia, and then recrossed the river and picked the site for a major battle. The place was Guilford 5-77 Courthouse, and there on 15 March 1781 he took 5-78 his stand. When the fighting stopped, the British 5-79 held the field, but their army was so weakened that 5-80 Cornwallis chose not to pursue the Americans. 5-81 Commenting that "I never saw such fighting since God made me," he recognized his victory as hollow. Horace Walpole put it in this way: "Lord Cornwallis has conquered his troops out of shoes and provisions, and himself out of troops."

Greene, with reinforcements and provisions, marched back to South Carolina, leaving most of the Piedmont under Patriot control. Cornwallis's march to Wilmington caused the chaotic state gov- 5-82 ernment to anticipate a British attack upon New Bern, so the public records were loaded on wagons 5-83 and sent off on a circuitous route to the transmontane area. Governor Nash fled to Tarborough, and other state officials sought their own places of safety. Meanwhile, Cornwallis marched northward to Yorktown and surrender.

The war was not yet over in North Carolina, though, as the people of Hillsborough learned in September 1781. An impudent young Tory, David Fanning, with about a thousand Tories, captured the town, killed or wounded three dozen Patriots, and captured about two hundred others, including Governor Thomas Burke. The humiliation was deepened when Fanning paraded his distinguished quarry to Wilmington. Burke soon broke his parole and resumed his gubernatorial role. Fanning's Tories continued to terrorize some rural areas of the Piedmont until May of the following year.

5-84

5-1
On the back of this portrait are the words "Govr. Wm. Tryon of No. Carolina— J[ohn] Wollaston, pinxt. New York—Anno D. 1767." It is not known whether Tryon visited New York in 1767. (Courtesy NCDA&H.)

NEWBERN, August 10, 1764.

We hear from Cape Fear, that a Lieutenant-Governor of this Province is appointed at Home, one Col. *Tryon*, an Officer in the Guards; and that he is expected out immediately. 'Tis also said, that his Excellency the Governor goes home in March next. The good People of Wilmington, ever intent on the Good of the Province, and always foremost in every Scheme for its Welfare and internal Quietude, immediately upon this News, engaged a large House in Wilmington for the Reception and Accommodation of the Governor on his Arrival in the Province, upon a Certainty that he will settle among them there. But the People of Newbern, having, for their Disobedience, drank largely of the Cup of Affliction, and intirely depending on the Goodness of their Cause, have engaged a large genteel House in Newbern, for the Governor's Residence; upon a Supposition he will settle rather in the Centre of the Province, than at Cape-Fear, a Place within Fifty Miles of the South Boundary of a Province almost 300 Miles wide, and the Passage to it gloomy and dismal, through hot parching Sands, enliven'd now and then with a few Wire Grass Ridges, and Ponds of stagnant Water: And where, on your Arrival, not as Dr. *Watts* says,

> *Sweet Fields, beyond the swelling Flood,*
> *Stand drest in living Green;*
> *So to the Jews old Canaan stood,*
> *While Jordan roll'd between;*

But as the Passage, so the Entrance, dismal;— a Turkey 15s. a Fowl 2s. 8d. a Goose 10s. Butter 2s. 8d. and so *pro Rata* for every Thing else.—— Terrible Horribility!

†§† The great Length of the Act of Parliament, has prevented our inserting any News this Week, which we hope our Readers will excuse.

In the Evening, there was a very elegant BALL, in the Great Ball-Room in the Court house, where were present his Honour the Governor, and his Lady, the Mayor, Mr. Recorder, and near 100 Gentlemen and Ladies.——About Ten in the Evening the Company withdrew to the Long Room over the Ball-Room, where was spread a very elegant Collation: After Supper, the Gentlemen and Ladies returned to the Ball-Room, and concluded the Evening with all imaginable Agreeableness and Satisfaction. The Courthouse was beautifully illuminated the whole Evening.

On *Thursday*, being the Feast of St. *John* the Baptist, the Members of the Ancient and Honourable Society of FREE and ACCEPTED MASONS, belonging to the LODGE in this Town, met at their Lodge-Room; and after going thro' the necessary Business of the Day, retired to the Long Room in the Courthouse, to dine, where was served up an elegant Dinner; the Lieutenant-Governor honoured them with his Company; where also dined many other Gentlemen: The usual and proper Healths were drank; and at drinking the KING and the CRAFT the Artillery fired 3. 3. 3.

5-2
An article in the 3–10 August 1764 issue of *North-Carolina Magazine* expressed editor James Davis's fear that the new governor might take up residence in Wilmington. (Courtesy North Carolina Collection.)

5-3
Newly arrived William Tryon and his wife visited New Bern on a tour of the colony. The *North-Carolina Magazine* of 21–28 December 1764 described their entertainment. (Courtesy North Carolina Collection.)

5-4
A sample of the stamps that led to the Stamp Act crisis in North Carolina. (Courtesy NCDA&H.)

5-5
Maurice Moore (d. 1777), a native of the lower Cape Fear, rushed into print a pamphlet, *The Justice and Policy of Taxing the American Colonies in Great-Britain, Considered*, in which he joined other colonial theoreticians in denouncing "taxation without representation." (Courtesy NCDA&H.)

5-6
Andrew Steuart, in a special continuation of his *North-Carolina Gazette* (Wilmington) of 20 November 1765, described the confrontation at Brunswick over the Stamp Act. (Courtesy NCDA&H.)

5-7
Cornelius Harnett (1723–81), who helped arouse defiance of the Stamp Act, lived at Maynard (later called Hilton), shown here before its demolition about 1904. It overlooked the northeast branch of the Cape Fear at Wilmington. (Courtesy North Carolina Collection.)

5-8
Edmund Fanning (1737–1818), a New York lawyer, moved to Orange County and held multiple offices. Much of the wrath of the Regulators was directed toward him. Thomas Goddard painted the miniature. (Courtesy Frick Art Reference Library, New York, with permission of Captain William C. Wickham.)

5-9
A legislative act of 1748 fixed fees for the office of county registers, but Fanning and others were accused of violating the law by making excessive charges. (Courtesy NCDA&H.)

" A poor Man is fuppofed to have given his Judgment Bond for Five Pounds ; and this Bond is by his Creditor thrown into Court.———The Clerk of the County has to enter it on the Dock-et, and iffue Execution, the Work of one long Mi-nute, for which the poor Man has to pay him the trifling Sum of Forty-one Shillings and Five-pence. ———The Clerk, in Confideration he is a poor Man, takes it out in Work, at Eighteen-pence a Day.———The poor Man works fome more than Twenty-feven Days to pay for this one Minute's Writing.

" Well, the poor Man refleſts thus,———At this Rate, when fhall I get to Labour for my Family ? I have a Wife and Parcel of fmall Children fuffer-ing at Home, and here I have loſt a whole Month, and I don't know for what ; for my Merchant is as far from being paid yet as ever.———However, I will go Home now, and try and do what I can. ———Stay, Neighbour, you have not half done yet,———there is a D———d Lawyer's Mouth to ſtop yet ;———for you impowered him to confefs that you owed this Five Pounds, and you have Thirty Shillings to pay him for that, or go and work nineteen Days more ; and then you muſt work as long to pay the Sheriff for his Trouble ; and then you may go home and fee your Horfes and Cows fold, and, all your perfonal Eſtate, for one Tenth Part of the Value, to pay off your Mer-chant. And laſtly, if the Debt is fo great, that all your perfonal Eſtate will not do to raife the Money, which is not to be had,———then goes your Lands the fame way to fatisfy thefe curfed hungry Caterpillars, that will eat out the very Bowels of our Common-wealth, if they are not pulled down from their Neſts in a very fhort time.——— And what Need, I fay, to urge a Reformation. ———If thefe Things were abfolutely according
                                                        to

5-10
A portion of George Sims's "Nutbush Address," 1765, described the multiple fee system that plagued residents of the backcountry. (Cour-tesy North Carolina Col-lection; reprinted from [Hermon Husband], *An Im-partial Relation of the First Rise and Cause of the Recent Differences in Publick Affairs* . . . [1770].)

5-11
The first printed use of the word *Regulators* appeared in the preface to Paper No. 6 in 1768. The initials refer to Pe-ter Craven and John Low. (Courtesy North Carolina Collection; reprinted from [Husband], *An Impartial Relation. . . .*)

5-12
A counterfeit $5 bill issued in 1775 bore the outline of Tryon's "Palace," the gover-nor's sumptuous residence in New Bern. The Regulators claimed that no more than 5 percent of the people of the backcountry would ever see the building. (Courtesy NCDA&H.)

" AT a General Meeting, of the * Regulators, held *April* the 4th, 1768, it was agreed to fend P———— C———— and J——— L———, to requeſt the two late Sheriffs and our Veſtry-men, to meet twelve Men that we fhall choofe on the Teufday after next Court, to Produce to them a Copy of the Liſt of Taxables for each Year, and a Liſt of the Number and Names of of the Infolvents returned each Year, with an Ac-count how the Money was applied, to whom paid, and to what Ufes, both Veſtry-men and Sheriffs, and to requeſt our Reprefentatives to confer with them in our Behalf, and fhew us Law for the cu-ſtomary Fees that has been taken for Deeds, In-dentures, Adminiſtrations, &c. If the Time ap-pointed don't fuit them, let them appoint another more fuitable."

Before thefe two Men had Time to perform this Meſſage, the Officers, either to try or exaf-perate the now enraged Populace, took, by way of Diſtrefs, a Mare, Saddle and Bridle, for one Levy,———and they immediately rofe to the Num-ber of Sixty or Seventy, and refcued the Mare,— and fired a few Guns at the Roof of Colonel *Fan-ning*'s Houfe, to fignify they blam'd him for all this Abufe.

The Paper No. 6. was then delivered to the eſtablifhed Miniſter of the County, who under-took to try to accommodate the Matter ; who, accordingly, returned with an Anfwer from the Officers, and that they had appointed the 11th Day of *May* for a Settlement.
                                                        The

* *This new Name, inſtead of Mob, was necef-fary, according to the Nature of the Bufinefs of the Day of altering the Articles.*

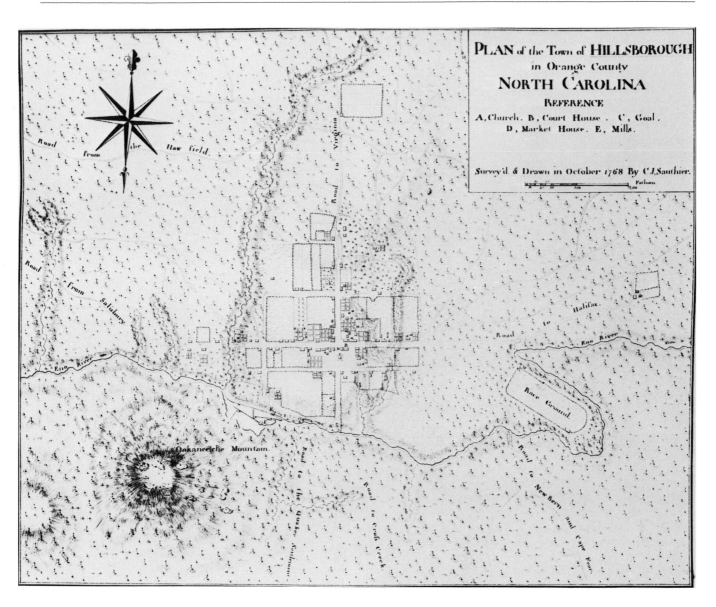

PLAN of the Town of HILLSBOROUGH
in Orange County
NORTH CAROLINA
REFERENCE
A, Church. B, Court House. C, Goal.
D, Market House. E, Mills.

Survey'd & Drawn in October 1768 By C.J.Sauthier.

5-13
On Claude J. Sauthier's map of Hillsborough, 1768, the courthouse—the scene of high drama during the Regulator movement—is identified as "B" near the center of the town. (Courtesy NCDA&H.)

An Impartial
RELATION
OF THE
First Rise and Cause
OF THE
RECENT DIFFERENCES,
IN
PUBLICK AFFAIRS,

In the Province of North-Carolina; and of the past Tumults and Riots that lately happened in that Province.

Containing most of the true and genuine Copies of Letters, Messages and Remonstrances, between the Parties contending:— By which any impartial Man may easily and see the true Ground and Reasons of faction that universally reigns all over Province in a more or less Degree.

Printed for the Compiler, 1770.

5-14
Hermon Husband (1724–95) earned the name of historian of the Regulator movement by publishing *An Impartial Relation.* . . . (By permission of John Carter Brown Library, Brown University, Providence.)

5-15
Purdie and Dixon's *Virginia Gazette* of 25 October 1770 carried a long but biased description of the violence in Hillsborough the month before. (Courtesy North Carolina Collection.)

5-16
The right-hand column of the Trial, Reference, and Appearance Docket for September 1770 contains sarcastic entries made by the Regulators who broke up the court session in Hillsborough. (Courtesy NCDA&H.)

5-17 (facing page)
A manuscript map of the backcountry by an unidentified mapmaker about 1770 shows the area in which the Regulators were most active. (Courtesy William L. Clements Library, University of Michigan, Ann Arbor.)

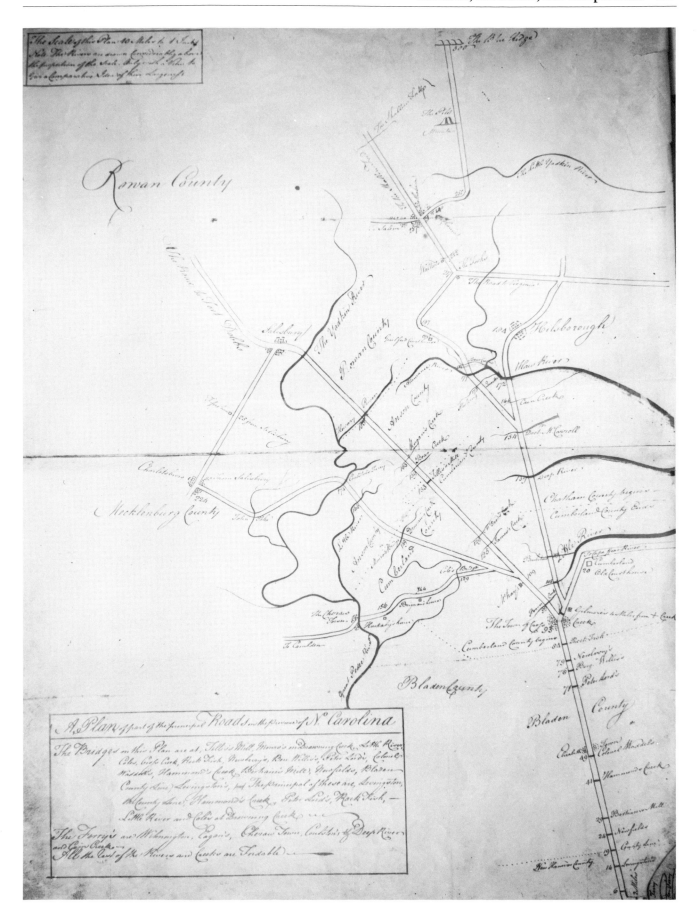

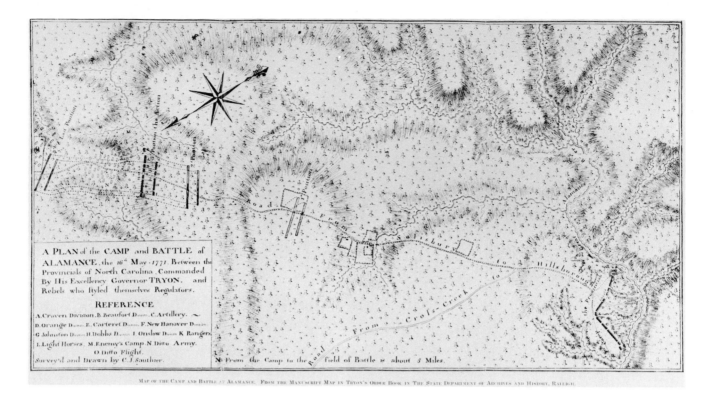

MAP OF THE CAMP AND BATTLE AT ALAMANCE. FROM THE MANUSCRIPT MAP IN TRYON'S ORDER BOOK IN THE STATE DEPARTMENT OF ARCHIVES AND HISTORY, RALEIGH.

5-18
Cartographer Claude J. Sauthier, superintendent of military stores during Governor Tryon's expedition against the Regulators, prepared a map of the Battle of Alamance, 16 May 1771. (Courtesy NCDA&H.)

5-19
A proclamation by Tryon the day after the battle extended the time for pardoning participants of the Regulator movement, outlaws and prisoners excepted. (Courtesy NCDA&H.)

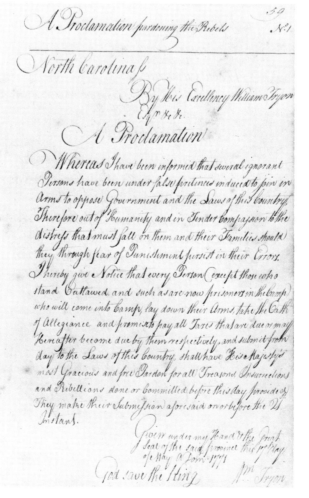

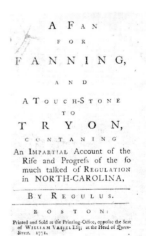

5-20
Edmund Fanning followed Governor Tryon to his new post in New York and became his private secretary; their names were indelibly linked in a pro-Regulator pamphlet, *A Fan for Fanning, and a Touch-Stone to Tryon,* probably written by Hermon Husband. (By permission of Rare Books and Manuscripts Division, New York Public Library, Astor, Lenox, and Tilden Foundations, New York.)

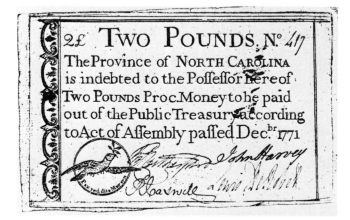

5-21
£2 notes issued in December 1771 pictured a dove carrying an olive branch and the words "Pax reddita [peace restored] May 1771." (Courtesy Eric P. Newman Numismatic Education Society, St. Louis.)

5-22
John Malcolm, aide-de-camp to Tryon at the Battle of Alamance, moved to Boston, where he became the target of Patriots who in 1774 tarred and feathered him. He sent a box of his dried skin, tar, and feathers to London and received a £200 pension from the government. (Engraving by and after F. Godefroy, 1783; courtesy Anne S. K. Brown Military Collection, Brown University Library, Providence.)

5-23
North Carolinians rallied to the aid of Bostonians, whose port had been closed by an act of Parliament, and early in 1775 sent a shipload of supplies to the beleaguered city. (Courtesy NCDA&H.)

ADVERTISEMENT.

NEWBERN, *January* 27, 1775.

PUBLIC Notice is hereby given, that Mr. *John Green* and Mr. *John Wright Stanly*, Merchants in *Newbern*, have agreed with, and are appointed by, the Committee of *Craven* County, to receive the Subscriptions which is now, or may hereafter be raised in the said County, for the Relief of the distressed Inhabitants of *Boston*, and to ship the same to the Port of *Salem* as soon as the several Subscriptions are received. Proper Stores are provided by the said Gentlemen for the Reception of Corn, Pease, Pork, and such Articles as the Subscribers may choose to pay their Subscriptions in.

Those Gentlemen therefore who have taken in Subscriptions, either in Money or Effects, are desired to direct the same to be paid or delivered to the above named Mess. *Green* and *Stanly*, on or before the Middle of *March* next; and to send, as soon as possible, an Account of the Subscriptions which are or may be taken, by which they may be governed in receiving.

R. COGDELL, Chairman.

5-25
On her visit to Brunswick, Janet Schaw was the guest of Richard Quince who, she wrote, was "deeply engaged in the new System of Politics"—that is, opposition to parliamentary restrictions. Bills of exchange, such as this one drawn by Quince, were common among merchants. (Courtesy Southern Historical Collection.)

5-24
Governor Josiah Martin's proclamation of 13 August 1774 condemned the "inflammatory, disloyal and indecent" expressions of the local meetings and forbade citizens to attend the Provincial Congress. (Courtesy NCDA&H.)

5-26
According to tradition, Penelope Craven Barker (1728–96), second wife of Thomas Barker, organized the "Edenton Tea Party" of 25 October 1774. (Courtesy North Carolina Collection.)

Extract of a letter from North Carolina, Oct. 27.

" The Provincial Deputies of North Carolina having refolved *not* to drink any more *tea*, nor wear any more Britifh cloth, &c. many ladies of this Province have determined to give a memorable proof of their patriotifm, and have accordingly entered into the following honourable and fpirited affociation. I fend it to you, to fhew your fair countrywomen, how zealoufly and faithfully American ladies follow the laudable example of their hufbands, and what oppofition your Minifters may expect to receive from a people thus firmly united againft them :

" *Edenton, North Carolina, Oct. 25, 1774.*

" As we cannot be indifferent on any occafion that appears nearly to affect the peace and happinefs of our country, and as it has been thought neceffary, for the public good, to enter into feveral particular refolves by a meeting of Members deputed from the whole Province, it is a duty which we owe, not only to our near and dear connections who have concurred in them, but to ourfelves who are effentially interefted in their welfare, to do every thing as far as lies in our power to teftify our fincere adherence to the fame ; and we do therefore accordingly fubfcribe this paper, as a witnefs of our fixed intention and folemn determination to do fo.

Abagail Charlton	Mary Blount
F. Johnftone	Elizabeth Creacy
Margaret Cathcart	Elizabeth Patterfon
Anne Johnftone	Jane Wellwood
Margaret Pearfon	Mary Woolard
Penelope Dawfon	Sarah Beafley
Jean Blair	Sufannah Vail
Grace Clayton	Elizabeth Vail
Frances Hall	Elizabeth Vail
Mary Jones	Mary Creacy
Anne Hall	Mary Creacy
Rebecca Bondfield	Ruth Benbury
Sarah Littlejohn	Sarah Howcott
Penelope Barker	Sarah Hofkins
Elizabeth P. Ormond	Mary Littledle
M. Payne	Sarah Valentine
Elizabeth Johnfton	Elizabeth Cricket
Mary Bonner	Elizabeth Green
Lydia Bonner	Mary Ramfay
Sarah Howe	Anne Horniblow
Lydia Bennet	Mary Hunter
Marion Wells	Trefia Cunningham
Anne Anderfon	Elizabeth Roberts
Sarah Mathews	Elizabeth Roberts
Anne Haughton	Elizabeth Roberts."
Elizabeth Beafly	

A SOCIETY of PATRIOTIC LADIES, AT EDENTON in NORTH CAROLINA.
Plate V.

A SOCIETY of PATRIOTIC LADYS. AT EDENTON NORTH CAROLINA.
Plate V.

5-27
The *Morning Chronicle and London Advertiser*, 16 January 1775, quoted from a "letter" from North Carolina which reported that a group of women in Edenton had entered into "an honourable and spirited association" to support the resolves of the Provincial Congress. Several of the names on the resolution are listed more than once. (Courtesy NCDA&H.)

5-28 and 5-29
A caricature of the "Edenton Tea Party"—probably by Philip Dawe—was issued in London in 1775 (top). A century later, patriots "cleaned up" the illustration and issued a new one more acceptable to Victorian tastes (bottom). (Courtesy North Carolina Collection.)

5-30
Broadsides issued by the local safety committees whipped up support for the American cause. Richard Cogdell's name was conspicuous in the orders of the New Bern committee. (Courtesy NCDA&H.)

5-31
The "Mecklenburg Resolves," adopted by a committee in Charlotte on 31 May 1775, were published in the 13 June 1775 issue of the *South-Carolina Gazette* (Charleston). (Courtesy Charleston Library Society, Charleston.)

In COMMITTEE, NEWBERN, *August* 5, 1775.

FROM the late Conduct of Governor *Martin* at Fort *Johnston*, and Intelligence since received by this Committee, it appears he intends erecting the King's Standard, and commencing Hostilities against the People of this Province. It is therefore *Resolved*, That no Person or Persons whatsoever have any Correspondence with him, either by personal Communication or Letter, on Pain of being deemed Enemies to the Liberties of *America*, and dealt with accordingly. And that no Person or Persons presume to remove him or themselves from hence to *Core Sound*, or any other Part of the Province where the Governor resides, without Leave of this Committee, as he or they will not be suffered to return here.

By Order,

R. COGDELL, Chairman.

NEWBERN August 14.
COMMITTEE CHAMBER.

Whereas all those who have not subscribed the articles of association, have sufficiently testified to the public, that they are enemies to the liberties of America; and as the principles of self-preservation makes it absolutely necessary that they should be deprived of their arms, therefore it is Ordered, that the Captains of the several companies in this county and town require of all such suspected persons, as well their fire arms, as swords, cutlasses, &c. and all gunpowder, lead, and other military stores; and that the said several captains be impowered to give receipts for all such guns, &c. and deliver them out to such persons of his or their company, not having arms &c. as may be willing to serve in the American cause.

By Order,
R. COGDELL, Chairman.
A true copy from the minutes.
J. SITGREAVES, Secretary.

5-32 (top)
A broadside issued by the New Bern committee on 5 August 1775 warned citizens not to communicate with the royal governor. (Courtesy NCDA&H; original in Public Record Office, London.)

5-33 (above)
In its issue of 1 September 1775, the *Cape-Fear Mercury* printed a resolution of the New Bern safety committee ordering the confiscation of arms from citizens who had not signed the articles of association. (Courtesy North Carolina Collection.)

5-34
Robert Howe, commander of one of the regiments of the Continental Line, was North Carolina's highest ranking officer—a major general in command of the troops in the South until his removal following the fall of Savannah. (Courtesy Southern Historical Collection, Preston Davie Collection.)

5-35
Many citizens, including the Moravians who promised to remain "quiet people," sought to avoid involvement in the disputes separating the Americans and the British. (Courtesy Moravian Archives, Winston-Salem.)

5-37
The Scot heroine Flora Mac-Donald, shown here in a 1747 portrait by Richard Wilson, used her prestige among the Highlanders to rally them to the support of the royal government. Two years after her husband was captured at Moore's Creek, she sailed for the Isle of Skye. (By permission of the Scottish National Portrait Gallery, Edinburgh.)

5-38
During a tour of the state about 1850, Benson Lossing made a drawing of the silver crescent worn on the hat of Alexander Lillington, a hero of the battle at Moore's Creek Bridge. (Courtesy North Carolina Collection; reprinted from Lossing, *Pictorial Field-Book of the Revolution* [New York, 1851–52], volume 2.)

5-36
Prior to the battle at Moore's Creek, Donald MacDonald, commander of the Highlanders, called upon Patriot forces to lay down their arms. (Courtesy NCDA&H.)

[Handwritten manuscript text:]

principles, have procured no Mitigation of the aforesaid Wrongs and usurpations, and no hopes remain of obtaining redress by those Means alone which have been hitherto tried, Your Committee are of Opinion that the house should enter into the following Resolve, to wit

Resolved that the Delegates for this Colony in the Continental Congress be impowered to concur with the Delegates of the other Colonies in declaring Independency, and forming foreign Alliances, reserving to this Colony the Sole and Exclusive right of forming a Constitution and Laws for this Colony, and of appointing Delegates from time to time (under the direction of a general Representation thereof) to meet the Delegates of the other Colonies for such purposes as shall be hereafter pointed out

The Congress taking the same into Consideration unanimously concurred therewith

5-43
A detail from John Trumbull's painting of the signers of the declaration shows William Hooper (left) and Joseph Hewes. John Penn was not included in this painting, which hangs in the capitol rotunda in Washington. (Courtesy Library of Congress.)

5-39
This paragraph from the resolutions adopted by the Provincial Congress at Halifax on 12 April 1776 constituted the first formal action of a colony authorizing (but not directing) its delegates to "concur" in a declaration of independence. (Courtesy NCDA&H.)

5-44
Samuel Johnston (1733–1816), a prime mover for independence, was defeated for reelection to the Provincial Congress in the fall of 1776. Factional politics were already at work. Elected first president of the Continental Congress after adoption of the Articles of Confederation, Johnston declined to serve. (Courtesy North Carolina Collection.)

5-40, 5-41, and 5-42
Portraits of North Carolina's three signers of the Declaration of Independence: (above left) Joseph Hewes, by Charles Willson Peale; (above right) John Penn, attributed to Charles Willson Peale; and (right) William Hooper, by James Reid Lambdin. (Courtesy, respectively, United States Naval Academy, Annapolis; R. W. Norton Art Gallery, Shreveport, Louisiana; and Independence National Historical Park Collection, Philadelphia.)

Monday July 22d 1776

Met according to Adjournment.

The Continental Congress having on the fourth day of July last declared the thirteen United Colonies free and independant States.

Resolved That the Committees of the respective Towns and Counties in this Colony on receiving the said Declaration, do cause the same to be proclaim:ed in the most public Manner, in Order that the good People of this Colony may be fully informed thereof.

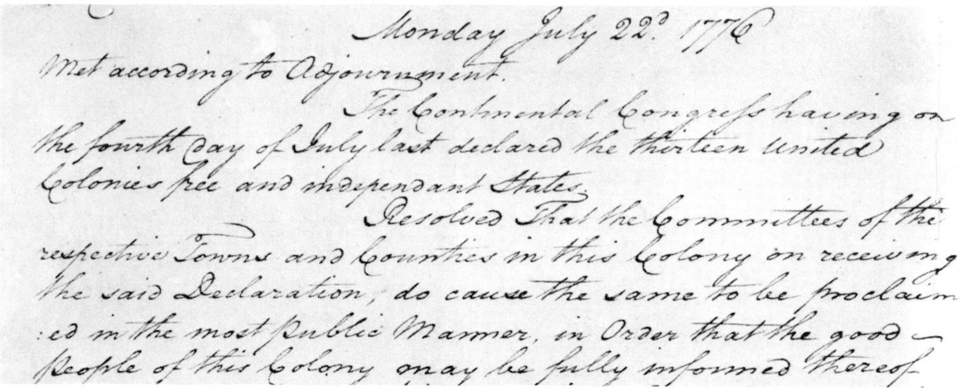

5-45
A resolution of the Provincial Congress on 22 July 1776 ordered the Declaration of Independence to be "proclaimed in the most public manner" in the towns and counties. (Courtesy NCDA&H.)

Dear Sir The Subject, on which you was pleased to request my Sentiments, is of infinite Importance to Mankind. Politicks is the Science of human Happiness – and the Felicity of Societies depends entirely on the Constitutions of Government under which they live. –

That famous Couplet of a very great Poet,
For Forms of Government let Fools contest
That is best administered, is best" Shews him to have been less attentive to the political and civil Part of History, than the poetical, – He must have read and Studied for fanciful Images, not Social Institutions, because the Rectitude of Administration depends upon the Forms; Some Species of Governments being always well administered, others never.

If you can determine, what Form of Government, will produce the greatest Quantity of human Happiness, you will at once decide which is the best, this being the only Criterion. – if you determine what the Dignity of human Nature, and the Happiness of Mankind consists in, you will decide what it is that produces the greatest Quantity of Happiness. – Divines, Moralists, Philosophers, and Men of Pleasure all agree that it consists in Virtue. – If there is a Form of Government, therefore, whose Principle or Foundation, is Virtue, will not all those kinds of Men acknowledge, it to be better calculated to promote the general Happiness, than another, the Principle of which is Fear, or even Honour.

I hold the Principle of Honour, Sacred – but am not ashamed to confess myself so much of a Grecian, or Roman, if not of a Christian as to think the Principle of Virtue of higher Rank in the Scale of moral Excellence than Honour. indeed Honour is but a Part, a very Small Part of Virtue. – As to Fear, it is so base and brutal a Passion, that it dont deserve the Name of a Principle, and I think no Gentleman of this Age and Country will think it a Foundation of Government proper for Americans. –

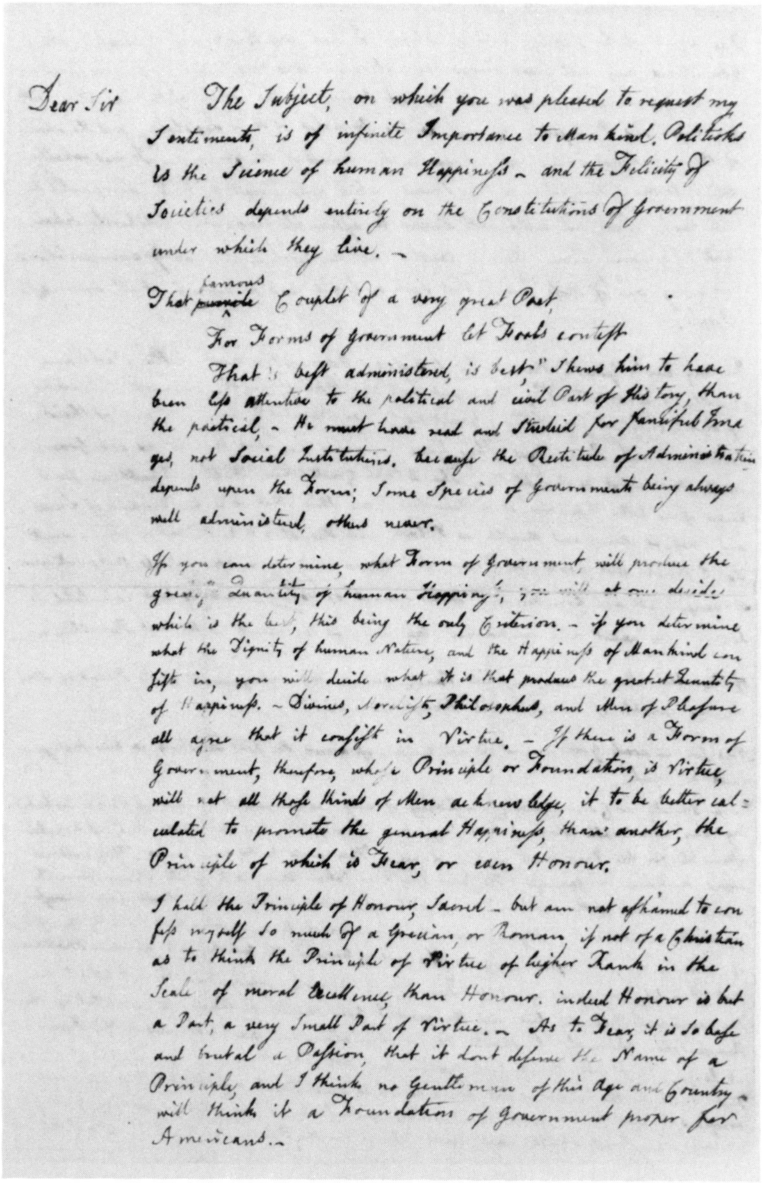

5-46
This is the opening page of John Adams's "Thoughts on Government," written for North Carolina's delegates to the Continental Congress and brought to the colony by William Hooper in 1776. This work influenced constitution-drafters in several colonies. (Courtesy NCDA&H.)

THE
CONSTITUTION,
OR
FORM OF GOVERNMENT,

AGREED TO, AND RESOLVED UPON,

BY THE

REPRESENTATIVES of the FREEMEN

OF THE

STATE

OF

NORTH-CAROLINA,

ELECTED and CHOSEN for that particular PURPOSE,

IN CONGRESS ASSEMBLED, AT HALIFAX,

The Eighteenth Day of December, in the Year of our LORD
One Thousand Seven Hundred and Seventy-Six.

PHILADELPHIA:
PRINTED BY F. BAILEY, IN MARKET-STREET.
M.DCC.LXXIX.

5-47
The Constitution adopted at Halifax in December 1776 was printed three years later and was widely distributed. (Courtesy North Carolina Collection.)

5-48
According to tradition, the constitution of 1776 was drafted by a committee meeting in the "Constitution House," pictured here before its restoration. (Courtesy North Carolina Collection.)

5-49
Richard Caswell (1729–89) served as the first governor of the independent state. This is reputed to be his portrait. (Courtesy NCDA&H.)

5-50
The coat of a North Carolinian who served with the British "Royal Provincials" during the Revolution. (Courtesy Provincial Archives of Nova Scotia, Halifax.)

5-51
John Massey, a soldier in the North Carolina Continental Line, drew this sketch in 1778. (Courtesy NCDA&H.)

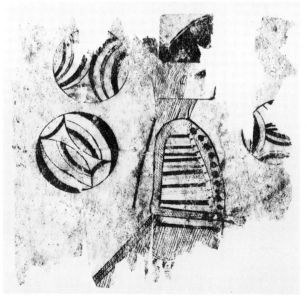

ADVERTISEMENTS.

NEWBERN, *August* 4, 1777.

WANTED immediately for the celebrated and well known Brig of War, STURDY BEGGAR, under Command of *James Campbell*, Efq; now fitting out at this Place for a fhort Cruize againft the Enemies of the Thirteen United States, a few good Seamen and Marines. The *Sturdy Beggar* is allowed to be the handfomeft Veffel ever built in *America*, is compleatly furnifhed with all Kinds of warlike Stores, Ammunition, &c. is remarkable for faft failing, having never chafed a Veffel but fhe foon came up with.

For the Encouragement of fuch Seamen as may choofe to enter on Board faid Veffel, TWENTY DOLLARS Bounty will be given. Such Seamen and Marines are requefted to repair to faid Veffel immediately, that fhe may be got to Sea in Time for the grand *Jamaica* Fleet, of the Sailing and Route of which there is the moft undoubted Intelligence received.

N. B. Prize Mafters, alfo petty Officers, are wanting.

5-52
In its issue of 8 August 1777 the *North-Carolina Gazette* (New Bern) carried an advertisement for men for "a short Cruize against the Enemies of the Thirteen United States." (Courtesy North Carolina Collection.)

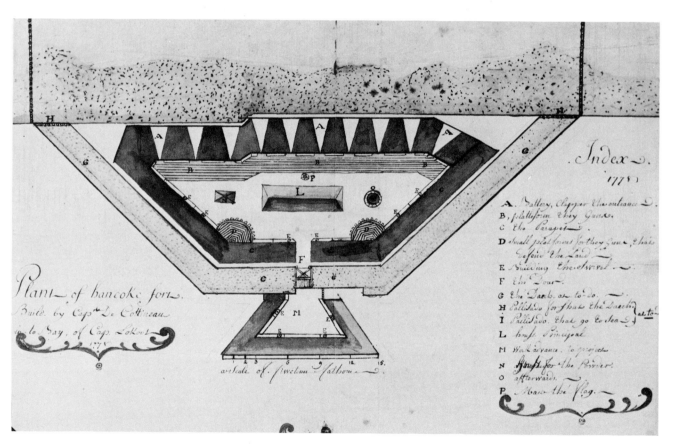

5-53
Fort Hancock at Cape Lookout was built in 1778 by Frenchmen from the frigate *Ferdinand*, commanded by Captain De Cottineau (spelled de Gatinau in the newspaper). (Courtesy New Hanover County Museum, W. G. Thomas Scrapbook.)

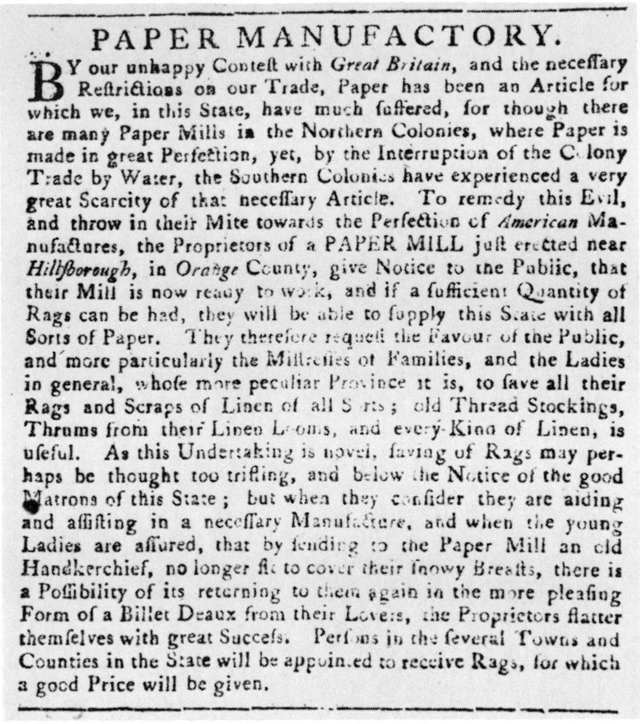

PAPER MANUFACTORY.

BY our unhappy Conteſt with *Great Britain*, and the neceſſary Reſtrictions on our Trade, Paper has been an Article for which we, in this State, have much ſuffered, for though there are many Paper Mills in the Northern Colonies, where Paper is made in great Perfection, yet, by the Interruption of the Colony Trade by Water, the Southern Colonies have experienced a very great Scarcity of that neceſſary Article. To remedy this Evil, and throw in their Mite towards the Perfection of *American* Manufactures, the Proprietors of a PAPER MILL juſt erected near *Hillſborough*, in *Orange* County, give Notice to the Public, that their Mill is now ready to work, and if a ſufficient Quantity of Rags can be had, they will be able to ſupply this State with all Sorts of Paper. They therefore requeſt the Favour of the Public, and more particularly the Miſtreſſes of Families, and the Ladies in general, whoſe more peculiar Province it is, to ſave all their Rags and Scraps of Linen of all Sorts; old Thread Stockings, Thrums from their Linen Looms, and every Kind of Linen, is uſeful. As this Undertaking is novel, ſaving of Rags may perhaps be thought too trifling, and below the Notice of the good Matrons of this State; but when they conſider they are aiding and aſſiſting in a neceſſary Manufacture, and when the young Ladies are aſſured, that by ſending to the Paper Mill an old Handkerchief, no longer fit to cover their ſnowy Breaſts, there is a Poſſibility of its returning to them again in the more pleaſing Form of a Billet Deaux from their Lovers, the Proprietors flatter themſelves with great Succeſs. Perſons in the ſeveral Towns and Counties in the State will be appointed to receive Rags, for which a good Price will be given.

5-54
Announcement of the first paper mill in the state was made in the *North-Carolina Gazette* (New Bern) on 28 November 1777. Subsequent issues carried advertisements for rags for conversion into paper. (Courtesy North Carolina Collection.)

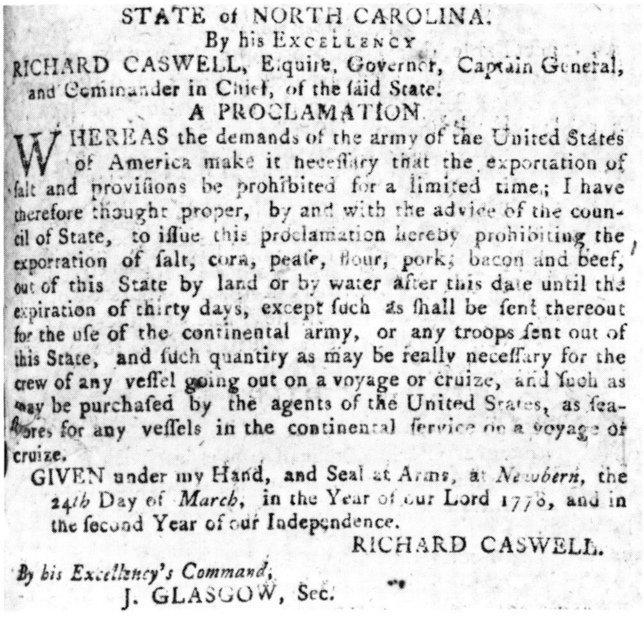

STATE of NORTH CAROLINA.
By his EXCELLENCY
RICHARD CASWELL, Eſquire, Governor, Captain General, and Commander in Chief, of the ſaid State.
A PROCLAMATION.

WHEREAS the demands of the army of the United States of America make it neceſſary that the exportation of ſalt and proviſions be prohibited for a limited time; I have therefore thought proper, by and with the advice of the council of State, to iſſue this proclamation hereby prohibiting the exportation of ſalt, corn, peaſe, flour, pork, bacon and beef, out of this State by land or by water after this date until the expiration of thirty days, except ſuch as ſhall be ſent thereout for the uſe of the continental army, or any troops ſent out of this State, and ſuch quantity as may be really neceſſary for the crew of any veſſel going out on a voyage or cruize, and ſuch as may be purchaſed by the agents of the United States, as ſeaſtores for any veſſels in the continental ſervice on a voyage or cruize.

GIVEN under my Hand, and Seal at Arms, at *Newbern*, the *24th* Day of *March*, in the Year of our Lord 1778, and in the ſecond Year of our Independence.
RICHARD CASWELL.
By his Excellency's Command,
J. GLASGOW, Sec.

5-55
Governor Caswell issued a proclamation in 1778 prohibiting the exportation of salt, corn, peas, flour, pork, bacon, and beef. (Courtesy North Carolina Collection; reprinted from *North-Carolina Gazette* [New Bern], 6 March 1778.)

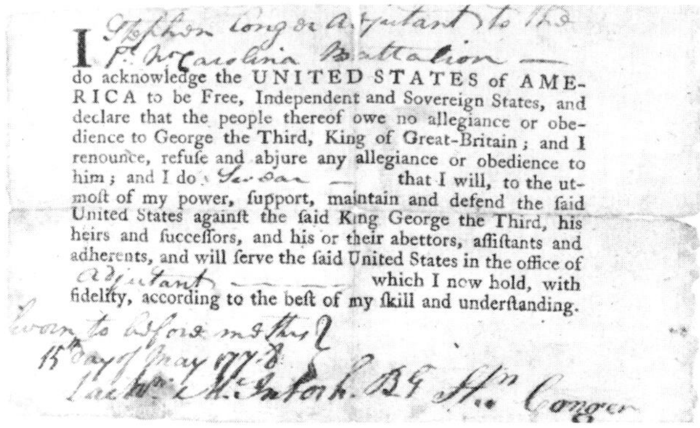

I Stephen Conger Adjutant to the 1st N Carolina Battalion do acknowledge the UNITED STATES of AMERICA to be Free, Independent and Sovereign States, and declare that the people thereof owe no allegiance or obedience to George the Third, King of Great-Britain; and I renounce, refuſe and abjure any allegiance or obedience to him; and I do Swear that I will, to the utmoſt of my power, ſupport, maintain and defend the ſaid United States againſt the ſaid King George the Third, his heirs and ſucceſſors, and his or their abettors, aſſiſtants and adherents, and will ſerve the ſaid United States in the office of Adjutant which I now hold, with fidelity, according to the beſt of my ſkill and underſtanding.

Sworn to before me this 15 Day of May 1778
Lachn McIntosh B.G. Stn Conger

5-56
An oath of allegiance to the United States was required of all civil and military officers. This one was signed by Stephen Conger, adjutant in the First North Carolina Continental Battalion, on 15 May 1778. (Courtesy NCDA&H.)

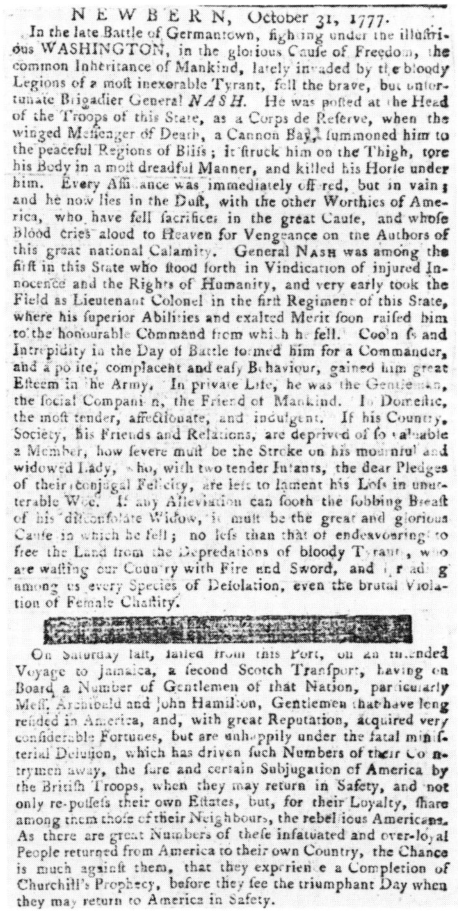

NEWBERN, October 31, 1777.

In the late Battle of Germantown, fighting under the illuſtrious WASHINGTON, in the glorious Cauſe of Freedom, the common Inheritance of Mankind, lately invaded by the bloody Legions of a moſt inexorable Tyrant, fell the brave, but unfortunate Brigadier General *NASH*. He was poſted at the Head of the Troops of this State, as a Corps de Reſerve, when the winged Meſſenger of Death, a Cannon Ball, ſummoned him to the peaceful Regions of Bliſs; it ſtruck him on the Thigh, tore his Body in a moſt dreadful Manner, and killed his Horſe under him. Every Aſſiſtance was immediately offered, but in vain; and he now lies in the Duſt, with the other Worthies of America, who have fell ſacrifices in the great Cauſe, and whoſe Blood cries aloud to Heaven for Vengeance on the Authors of this great national Calamity. General NASH was among the firſt in this State who ſtood forth in Vindication of injured Innocence and the Rights of Humanity, and very early took the Field as Lieutenant Colonel in the firſt Regiment of this State, where his ſuperior Abilities and exalted Merit ſoon raiſed him to the honourable Command from which he fell. Coolneſs and Intrepidity in the Day of Battle formed him for a Commander, and a polite, complacent and eaſy Behaviour, gained him great Eſteem in the Army. In private Life, he was the Gentleman, the ſocial Companion, the Friend of Mankind. In Domeſtic, the moſt tender, affectionate, and indulgent. If his Country, Society, his Friends and Relations, are deprived of ſo valuable a Member, how ſevere muſt be the Stroke on his mournful and widowed Lady, who, with two tender Infants, the dear Pledges of their conjugal Felicity, are left to lament his Loſs in unutterable Woe. If any Alleviation can ſooth the ſobbing Breaſt of his diſconſolate Widow, it muſt be the great and glorious Cauſe in which he fell; no leſs than that of endeavouring to free the Land from the Depredations of bloody Tyrants, who are waſting our Country with Fire and Sword, and ſpreading among us every Species of Deſolation, even the brutal Violation of Female Chaſtity.

On Saturday laſt, ſailed from this Port, on an intended Voyage to Jamaica, a ſecond Scotch Tranſport, having on Board a Number of Gentlemen of that Nation, particularly Meſſ. Archibald and John Hamilton, Gentlemen that have long reſided in America, and, with great Reputation, acquired very conſiderable Fortunes, but are unhappily under the fatal miniſterial Deluſion, which has driven ſuch Numbers of their Countrymen away, the ſure and certain Subjugation of America by the Britiſh Troops, when they may return in Safety, and not only re-poſſeſs their own Eſtates, but, for their Loyalty, ſhare among them thoſe of their Neighbours, the rebellious Americans. As there are great Numbers of theſe infatuated and over-loyal People returned from America to their own Country, the Chance is much againſt them, that they experience a Completion of Churchill's Prophecy, before they ſee the triumphant Day when they may return to America in Safety.

5-57
Hundreds of Tories, especially Scots, returned to their homeland rather than oppose the crown. This report appeared in the *North-Carolina Gazette* (New Bern) on 31 October 1777, along with an account of the death of Brigadier General Francis Nash. (Courtesy North Carolina Collection.)

5-58

Among the Loyalists who emigrated was Martin Howard, formerly the chief justice of the colony, who in 1775 had become "an obscure man in the woods" on his plantation, Richmond, on the Neuse River. (Courtesy Museum of Fine Arts, Boston.)

James Davis's *North-Carolina Gazette* (New Bern) captured the flavor of life in North Carolina in 1775 and 1778 (when the paper ceased publication). (All Courtesy North Carolina Collection.)

The Subscriber's HORSE
TELEMACHUS

WILL stand the ensuing Season at *Pembroke*, four Miles above *Newbern*, on *Trent River*, and will cover at the low Rate of Three Pounds the Season, payable if the Party chooses it in Corn, at 15 s. a Barrel. He puts up with this easy Mode of Payment with a View to encourage the Gentlemen Farmers of this Part of the Province the more readily to enter spiritedly on this very profitable and public spirited Business of breeding good Horses, as their Neighbours of *Halifax, Virginia*, and other Places, have done before them. *Telemachus* is of a most beautiful Colour, 15 Hands high, finely formed, and rising five Years old. He was got by the celebrated Horse *Jolly Roger*, whose Sire was an *Arabian* of the highest Character in *England*; his Dam was the famous *Bonny June*, an imported Mare of the *Godolphin* Family, whose Performances on the Turf are well known in *Virginia*: So that tho' this Horse cannot boast of having drawn his first Breath in the much favoured Island of *Great Britain*, yet it is hoped his Pretensions (next to *Bajazet*, who he does not pretend to rival) will be thought to stand very fair in the Calendar of Fame. An excellent Pasture for Mares, and good Care will be taken of them, though at the Owner's Risk.

March 14, 1775.   A. NASH.

5-59

7 April 1775.

To all to whom these Presents may come.

KNOW YE, that whereas I *Mary M'Gehe*, Wife of *Joseph M'Gehe*, of the County of *Bute*, in the Province of *North-Carolina*, being dissatisfied with my said Husband, and having eloped from his Bed for upwards of eight Months past; in which Time I have been gotten with Child by another Man, other than my said Husband, with which I acknowledge to be now pregnant, and being fully determined not to live with him more during my Life, nor at any Time hereafter to cohabit with him the said *Joseph M'Gehe*; and, in Consideration of the said *Joseph M'Gehe* delivering into my Possession, for my Use, one Hundred and Twenty Pounds Value in Effects, Part of his Estate, which I hereby acknowledge to have received, and am therewith fully satisfied, in full of the rateable Part of his Estate; and in Consequence said Estate being so delivered, I do hereby covenant and agree with him the said *Joseph M'Gehe*, that I never will at any Time hereafter, directly or indirectly, presume to depend on him as my Husband; nor will I ever hereafter ask, demand, look to, or receive from him the said *Joseph*, any further Monies, Goods, Wares, Chattles or Estate, of any Kind whatsoever, but from this Day forward look on myself as divorced from him, and no longer his Wife, nor dependant on him in any Manner or Form whatsoever, for any further Livelihood or Sustenance of any Kind. And the said *Joseph*, on his Part, doth acknowledge and agree, that the the said *Mary*, may and shall have the full Use and Occupation of the above-mentioned Effects, without any Hinderance or Molestation of any Kind by him, or any Person claiming by, from, or under him, but that she shall or may use, sell, and dispose of the said Effects as absolutely, to all Intents and Purposes, as she could or might do if she was his Wife, nor had never been married. And I do further agree, that I will never hereafter claim the said *Mary* as my Wife, but that she may from this Day forward be at large, and at Liberty to go to any Place or Part of the World she pleases, or any Choice; without Hinderance or Molestation. And further, the true Intent and Meaning of these Presents are, that we the said *Joseph* and *Mary*, have this Day most solemnly agreed before God and the World, to be no longer Man and Wife, but for ever hereafter be as if we had never been married, nor joined together as Man and Wife; but will live separate without Aid or Assistance of each other, from this Day forward to the End of our Lives. In Witness whereof, we have hereunto set our Hands and Seals, this 29th Day of *August*, 1769.

JOSEPH M'GEHE,
MARY M'GEHE.

Signed and acknowledged
in the Presence of
ROBERT GOODLOE,
THOMAS JACKSON.

5-60

7 April 1775.

ELOPED from the Brigantine *Friendship*, in *July*, 1774. two indented Servants, *viz.* GEORGE TAVERNOR, about 18 Years old, very slender, and pitted with the Small-Pox, and calls himself a Groom or Horse Jockey. EDWARD GILKS, about 23 Years old, a short hump'd Back Person with red Hair, and is by Trade a Currier or Leather Dresser. 'Tis supposed said Servants are working at or near *Newbern*. Also ran away in *August* last, a new Negro Fellow, by Name QUAMINO, about 4 Feet 10 Inches high, and about 30 Years of Age, has a Scar above his right Eye, his Teeth are filed, and is marked with his Country Marks; had on when he went away, a Collar about his Neck with two Prongs, marked G P, and an Iron on each Leg. Whoever delivers said white Servants and Negro to *Henry Young* in *Wilmington*, shall receive 6l. Proc. Money for the Whole, or 40s. for each, and reasonable Charges, or secures them in any Gaol so that they may be had again.
Wilmington, April 10, 1775.

5-61
5 May 1775.

GASPER BEAUFORT, from Philadelphia, gives this public notice, that on Monday next he proposes opening a school in this town, at the house of Widow Wosley, to teach the French tongue; to read, right, and speak it gramatically. Gentlemen and ladies that please to favour this undertaking may depend on his greatest care and assiduity. His price will be thirty shillings per month. He also proposes to attend any gentlemen or ladies at their own houses in the evening for the above purpose.

5-62
6 March 1778.

NEWBERN, *March 27.*
Mr. DAVIS,
I OBSERVED an advertisement in your last paper, that a person wanted a companion for the ensuing campaign: If a gentleman, and agreeable and handsome, as you say he is free and generous, I should like to be his companion for a campaign or longer, if he and I should prove agreeable to each other, upon further acquaintance. He must not expect a first rate beauty, but one as agreeable as most he will meet with, tolerable handsome, and not exceeding five and twenty. If the gentleman is serious in his proposal, he will be good enough to let me know in your next paper, which will very much oblige your constant reader,
BELINDA.
N. B. If the gentleman is agreeable, in every thing beside, I can excuse his generosity, as I have a fortune sufficient to supply me, and assist him if he should stand in need of my help.

5-63
27 March 1778.

THE subscriber, Doctor in Physick, and one of the first surgeons in the King of France's armies, gives the public notice of setting up in this town, to exercise the art of my profession, and offer my service to the ladies and gentlemen that will employ me; and further give notice that I possess the art of man midwife, I also undertake to cure all sorts of venereal distempers, ulcers, and ring worms. The poor people who may want assistance, I will attend *gratis*. I have to sell, by small or large quantity, rheubarb, bark, and flour of brimstone.
Edenton, July 28.   PAMBRUSE.

MR. JOSEPH BLYTH has opened school in the public school-house. And will teach Latin, English, Arithmetic, Geography, Geometry, Trigonometry, and several other of the most useful branches of the Mathematicks, according to the best and most approved methods. Gentlemen and ladies who favour him with their children may depend he will be diligent, and pay proper attention to their education.
Newbern, *July* 24.

ONE HUNDRED AND FIFTY DOLLARS REWARD.
STOLEN from on board the ship CORNELL, *One Thousand Dollars*, most of it in thirty dollar bills. Any person that will apprehend the thief or thieves concerned in the robbery, so that they may be brought to justice, and the money found, or any person concerned in the robbery, that will discover his accomplices, may depend upon having his crime concealed, and receive the above reward.
Newbern, July 16.   C. BIDDLE.

THIS is to inform the public, that GEO. HARRISON *intends opening a school on Monday next, opposite to Mrs. Dewey, where gentlemen and ladies may depend upon having their children carefully instructed in the English language, writing and cyphering. Also the French language taught.*   *Newbern, July 24.*

5-64
31 July 1778.

State of North Carolina, *Beaufort* County, ss.
To the sheriff, constables, and all other officers of the said county.
WHEREAS Sarah Blango Moore *(free negro) has this day made complaint to me, one of the justices for the county aforesaid, that she was last night robbed of two of her own children, by three men in disguise; one a boy about six years old named Ambrose, the other a girl named Rose, of the same age, they being twins; and that she hath just reason to suspect several idle and disorderly persons within your precincts to have taken the same.*
These are therefore in the name of the State to command you and each of you to search diligently within your respective Bailiwicks for the said robbers, and to make hue and cry after them from Town to Town, and from one county to another: And if you shall find the said robbers, that then you apprehend them and carry them before some justice of the peace where they shall be taken, there to be examined concerning the premises; herein fail not.
GIVEN under my hand and seal this 11th September, 1778.
THOMAS BONNER.

BOYLE ALDWORTH, *Limbner.*
JUST *arrived in this town, paints LIKENESSES on the following conditions, viz.*
Portraits for rings,   130
Do. for bracelets,   100 } Dollars.
Do. in crayons, as house ornaments from 1 to 2 feet, 75
N. B. Enquire for Mr. Aldworth *at Oliver's tavern.*
Newbern, *Sept.* 29.

5-65
9 October 1778.

ADVERTISEMENTS.

NEWBERN, August 21, 1778.

THE *subscriber takes this method of acquainting the public that* James Flett, *(taylor of this town) hath unjustly traduced the character of his lawful, prudent, and virtuous wife—And he further adds, that he will be accountable for any transgression said Flett can make evident against his wife.—Therefore he expects the public will consider said Flett an unjust and cruel man, if he cannot prove any reason for acting in so vile a manner.*

Methinks I hear Mrs. Flett express herself thus,

> *If from truths sacred paths I've stray'd, Convince the world I do, If not the world with justice may, Transfer the same on you.*

JOHN HORNER HILL.

5-66

In response to a notice by James Flett that his wife, Katy, had "eloped from me" and that he would "not be answerable for any debts she may contract," John Horner Hill came to her defense with this advertisement, printed in the *North-Carolina Gazette* (New Bern), 21 August 1778. (Courtesy North Carolina Collection.)

NEWBERN, *July* 10. 1778.

ON Saturday last, the ever memorable FOURTH of July, the RISING STATES of America entered the THIRD year of their INDEPENDENCE, in spite of numerous fleets and armies; in spite of tomahawk and scalping knife; in spite of the numberless wicked and diabolical engines of cruelty and revenge, played off against us by the magnanimous and heroic, humane and merciful George the Third, the father of his people, and his wicked and abandoned soldiery. On this day, the bright morning star of this western world arose in the east, and warned us to immerge from the slavish tyranny and servile dependence on a venal and corrupt court, and assume to ourselves a name among nations; a name terrible to tyrants, and wrote in indelible characters by the Almighty as a refuge from persecution. This day was observed here with every possible mark and demonstration of joy and reverence; tripple salutes were fired from the batteries in town, and on board the ship Cornell, and the privateer brig BELLONA, belonging to this port, the gentlemen of the town met, where many toasts suitable to the importance of the day were drank, and the evening happily concluded.

By several accounts from head quarters, it seems to be well authenticated, that the British troops have evacuated Philadelphia, and that our army are in possession of it.

5-67

Just two years after the signing of the Declaration of Independence, a celebration of the anniversary was reported in the *North-Carolina Gazette* (New Bern) for 10 July 1778. (Courtesy North Carolina Collection.)

5-68

The newspapers of the day carried no portraits, but manuscript records of the revolutionary era occasionally were decorated with pen drawings such as this one. (Courtesy NCDA&H.)

5-69
In the Nash County records for the period 1779–85 appears a drawing whose meaning is left to the reader. The legends read "Capt. Clinch" and "G—d damn him let me come at him." Joseph T. Clinch was an officer in the Nash County militia. (Courtesy NCDA&H.)

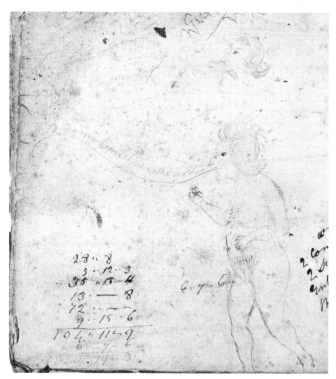

5-70
In the Battle of Camden, North Carolinians fought each other: American forces are shown at top, British and Tory forces at bottom. (With permission of the Duke of Northumberland, Alnwick Castle.)

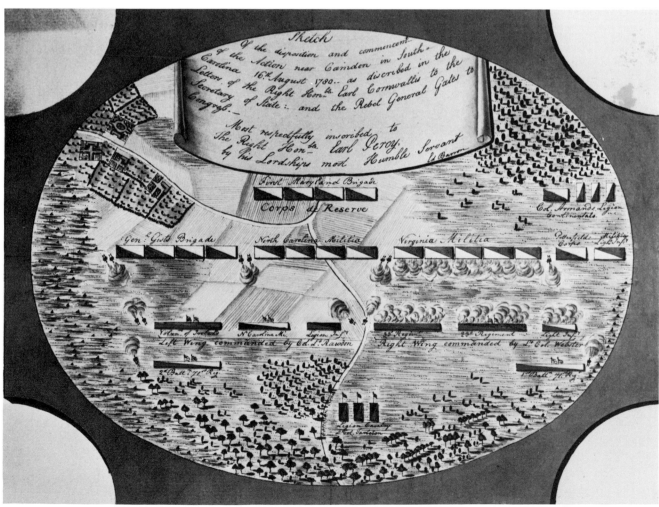

NORTH-CAROLINA.

By the Right Honourable

CHARLES Earl CORNWALLIS,

Lieutenant-General of His Majesty's Forces,

&c. &c. &c.

A PROCLAMATION.

WHEREAS the Enemies of His Majesty's Government continuing to practise every Artifice and Deceit to impose upon the Minds of the People, have, as industriously as falsely, propagated a Belief among the People of this Country, that the King's Army indiscriminately makes War, and commits Ravages upon the peaceable Inhabitants, and those who are in Arms and open Rebellion against His Majesty's Authority: I think it proper, in order to remove such false and injurious Impressions, and to restore as much Peace and Quiet to the Country as may be possible, during the Operations of War, hereby to assure the People at large, that all those who come into the Posts of His Majesty's Army under my Command, and faithfully deliver up their Arms, and give a Military Parole to remain thenceforth peaceably at Home, doing no Offence against His Majesty's Government, will be protected in their Persons and Properties, and be paid a just and fair Price in Gold or Silver, for whatever they may furnish for the Use of the King's Army; it being His Majesty's most gracious Wish and Intention rather to reclaim His deluded Subjects to a Sense of their Duty, and Obedience to the Laws, by Justice and Mercy, than by the Force and Terror of His Arms.

GIVEN _under my Hand and Seal at Head-Quarters in_ CHARLOTTE-TOWN, _this Twenty-seventh Day of September, One Thousand Seven Hundred and Eighty, and in the Twentieth Year of His Majesty's Reign._

CORNWALLIS.

By His Lordship's Command,
J. MONEY, Aid-de-Camp.

GOD SAVE THE KING.

CHARLESTOWN: Printed at WELLS's OFFICE, No. 71, Tradd-street.

5-71

When he arrived in Charlotte, Lord Cornwallis issued a call for the Patriots of the area to submit. The broadside was printed in Charleston. (Courtesy William L. Clements Library, University of Michigan, Ann Arbor.)

5-72

In 1781 the General Assembly ordered that "an elegant mounted sword" be given to every senior officer who had participated in the Patriot victory at Kings Mountain in the previous year. This one was presented to John Sevier. (Courtesy Tennessee State Museum, Nashville.)

5-73

The "plunder" taken at Kings Mountain was divided among the victors. In this document, William Cash certifies that he has sold his part to William Lenoir. (Courtesy Southern Historical Collection, Lenoir Family Papers.)

5-74
Shaken by the Tory defeat at
Kings Mountain, Cornwallis
led his troops from Charlotte
(*A* on the map) back into
South Carolina. (Courtesy
Cornell University Library,
Ithaca.)

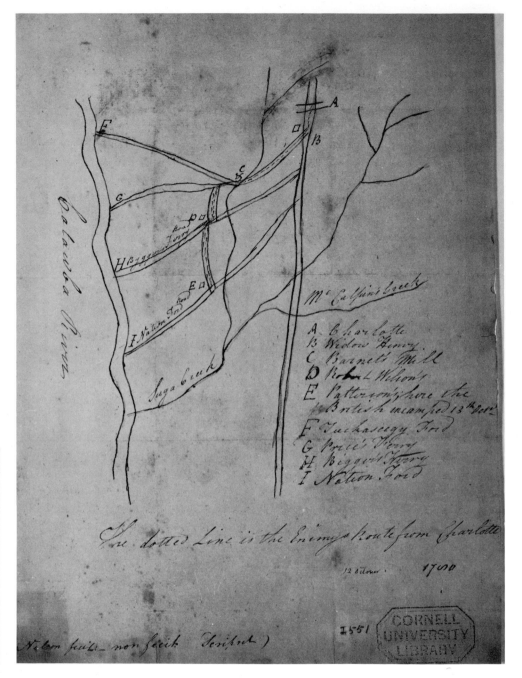

5-75
According to legend, this inscription on the back of a
portrait of George III was
made by General Greene at
Salisbury when a tavern
keeper, Elizabeth Maxwell
Steele, handed him her life's
savings for use in the war
against the British. (Courtesy
North Carolina Collection.)

5-76 (facing page)
Nathanael Greene (1742–86)
of Rhode Island succeeded
Horatio Gates in command
of the American forces in the
South in December 1780.
(By permission of the Metro-
politan Museum of Art, New
York, Bequest of Charles Al-
len Munn.)

5-77
General Greene, thinking that Cornwallis might march to Halifax, sent Colonel Tadeusz Kosciuszko to inspect defenses of the town on the Roanoke. The Polish engineer drew this map and concluded that the town could not be defended from the south. (By permission of Henry E. Huntington Library, San Marino, California.)

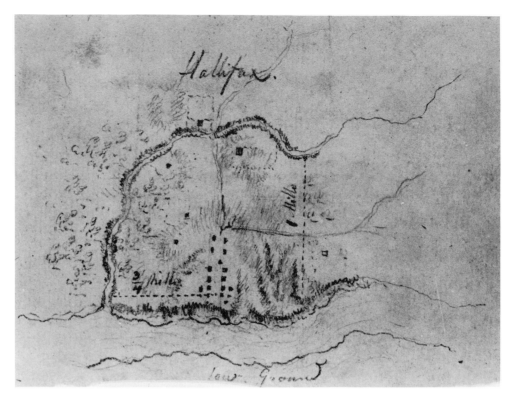

5-78
Inaccurate in several details, this engraving, ca. 1810, claims to show the British attacking the Americans across an open field near Guilford Courthouse. (By permission of Anne S. K. Brown Military Collection, Brown University Library, Providence.)

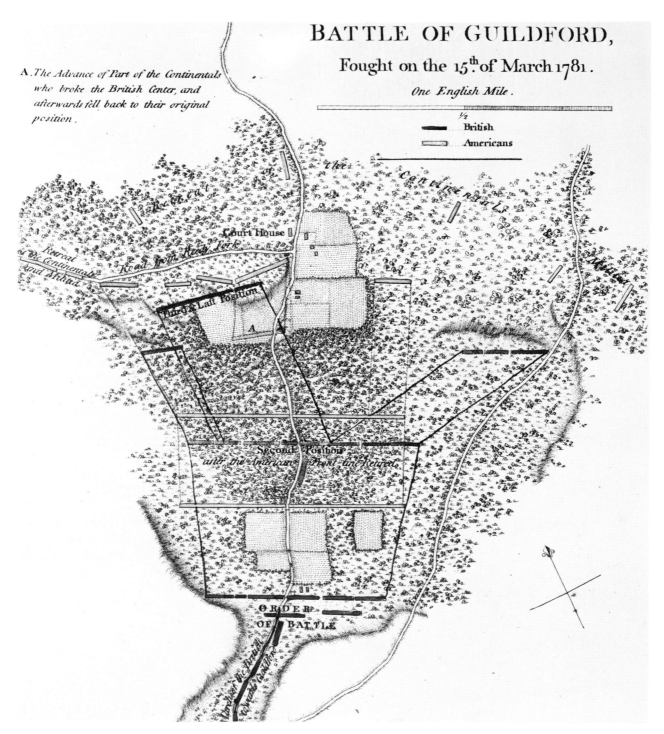

BATTLE OF GUILDFORD,
Fought on the 15th of March 1781.

One English Mile.

British
Americans

A. The Advance of Part of the Continentals who broke the British Center, and afterwards fell back to their original position.

5-79
A map of the Battle of Guilford Courthouse was published in Lieutenant-Colonel [Banastre] Tarleton, *A History of the Campaigns of* *1780 and 1781* . . . (London, 1787). The Americans retreated to the upper left. (Courtesy North Carolina Collection.)

5-80
A North Carolina militia drum and sticks, reputedly used by Luther W. Clark during the Battle of Guilford Courthouse on 15 March 1781. (Courtesy Guilford Courthouse National Military Park, Greensboro.)

5-81
Major Joseph Winston (1746–1814) led military units at Moore's Creek, Kings Mountain, and Guilford Courthouse; later he served in Congress, and the town of Winston was named for him. (Courtesy Guilford Courthouse National Military Park, Greensboro.)

5-82
A 1781 map of Wilmington under British occupation shows the galleys *Comet*, *Dependence*, and *Adder* in the Cape Fear River. Cornelius Harnett's home is on the northeast branch of the Cape Fear at far left, and British fortifications are seen at right center. (Courtesy NCDA&H.)

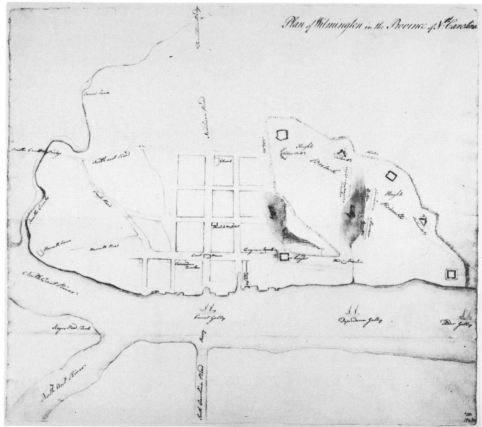

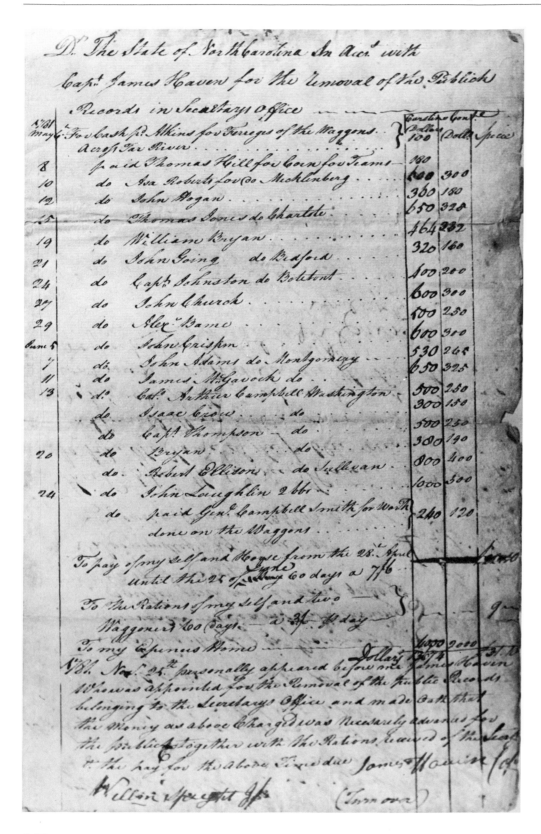

5-83
Captain James Haven was responsible for evacuating the state's public records as the British approached New Bern in 1781. Wagons carried the records into Virginia, thence across the mountains to Sullivan County (now Tennessee). (Courtesy NCDA&H.)

5-84
This delicate, patriotic drawing made in 1781 appears in
Martha Ryan's cipher book.
The names of the ships are,
left to right, *Property*, *Continental Congress*, *Freedom*, *Liberty*, *American*, and *Union*.
Inside the boxed "L" are
these lines: "Let's all unite /
and freely fight / For Liberty
& Right." (Courtesy Southern Historical Collection.)

6. A State in the American Union, 1783–1835

6-1
6-7
6-8
6-9
6-2
6-3
Alexander Martin was elected governor in 1782 of a state still torn by the emotions of a civil war, for the victorious Whigs exhibited little charity toward their neighbors suspected of having given aid or comfort to the British. Furthermore, independence—formally proclaimed the following year by the Treaty of Paris—was not accompanied by the dramatic economic and social progress that some citizens had expected. Frederick William Marschall of Salem wrote, "This country is in the condition of a patient convalescing from a fever, who begins to be conscious of his weakness and still needs medicine and care. The land itself, the people of property, commerce, public and private credit, the currency in circulation all are laid waste and ruined."

6-4
6-5
6-6
During the war the scarcity and devaluation of money forced the government to pay soldiers and civilian suppliers with paper promises—vouchers or certificates acceptable in payment of taxes but of dubious value for commercial exchange. Some veterans of the army waited for years for compensation, but the military land warrants for acreage in the transmontane region partially eased the conscience of the people, who felt a deep obligation to their liberators.

The unsettled condition of state government was matched by that of the new central government, which had been established when Maryland ratified the Articles of Confederation in 1781. North Carolina had ratified the articles in 1778, but throughout the formal existence of the shaky confederation the state's delegation showed little enthusiasm for it. Several of the North Carolinians elected to the confederation congress refused to go northward, and most of the others served short, undistinguished terms. The severely limited powers of the congress, the absence of a federal judiciary, and the ineffectiveness of the committeelike executive branch reflected the provincial sentiment of the postwar period, but even some North Carolinians soon recognized that confederation government by thirteen virtually autonomous states aggravated American problems.

Even so, when the congress issued a call for a constitutional convention to meet in Philadelphia in 1787, the General Assembly only reluctantly chose delegates—William R. Davie and Richard
6-10
6-12
6-11
Dobbs Spaight, representing conservatives favorable to a stronger central government; Willie Jones, a vocal opponent of centralization; and Richard Caswell and Alexander Martin, moderates on the subject. Caswell was ill, and Jones declined to serve; they were replaced by William Blount and Hugh Williamson, thus strengthening the conservative complexion of the delegation. All five had served in the Revolution, four were substantial slaveholders and landowners, and one (Williamson) was a physician and merchant. The delegation, therefore, was not representative of the state's population, and only Williamson exercised much influence in the convention.

The document submitted to the states for ratification evoked spirited debate among North Carolinians. Conservatives like Davie, James Iredell, and Samuel Johnston strongly supported ratification and assumed the designation of Federalists; nevertheless, while advocating a stronger federal government, they publicly stressed the constitution's provisions for checks and balances, popular representation, and amendment. Leading opponents of ratification were Jones, Thomas Person, and Timothy Bloodworth—former radicals who accepted the new designation of Antifederalists. They charged that individual as well as state rights would be trampled by a government with little direct citizen participation. Others, like William Lenoir, favored ratification only if the constitution included amendments to remove some of the fears of the Antifederalists.
6-13

6-14
In a vituperative campaign, the Antifederalists won most of the seats in the convention that met in 1788 in Hillsborough, defeating even Caswell, William Hooper, and some other well-known former officeholders. It was something of a surprise, therefore, that the convention did not formally reject the constitution but rather adopted a motion (by a vote of 184 to 83) proposing that "previous to the ratification of the Constitution" by North Carolina there should be called a second federal

convention to adopt a bill of rights and a number of amendments designed to protect "the great Principles of civil and religious Liberty, and the unalienable rights of the People." Despite North Carolina's delay, the necessary nine states ratified the Constitution and the new government was inaugurated. Thus for a year North Carolina was a sovereign state outside the new Union. 6-15

At their own expense the Federalists had hired a stenographer to record the debates at Hillsborough, and these notes were transcribed and published in the newspapers. This foresight resulted in a more intelligent public discussion of the issues during the campaign for delegates to a new convention in 1789. By then the status of North Carolina and Rhode Island as foreign countries subject to tariffs and other barriers, the submission of the Bill of Rights to the states, and the conciliatory attitude of both President Washington and the Congress led many former opponents of ratification to reconsider. Accordingly, Federalists won a surprising majority, and at the convention in Fayetteville the Constitution was ratified by a vote of 195 to 77. North Carolina thus became the twelfth state to join the Union. 6-16

Samuel Johnston resigned the governorship to join Benjamin Hawkins as the state's first United States senators; he was succeeded by former governor Alexander Martin. Both senators were Federalists, and the congressional delegation (John Baptista Ashe, Timothy Bloodworth, John Sevier, John Steele, and Hugh Williamson) was fairly well divided on federal-state issues. President Washington appointed James Iredell to the Supreme Court and later named John Steele comptroller of the Treasury. 6-17 6-18 6-19 6-20 6-21

The president was enthusiastically received on his tour of North Carolina in 1791, and he remained above the political factionalism that soon developed between advocates of a strong central government (led by Secretary of the Treasury Alexander Hamilton) and those (like Secretary of State Thomas Jefferson) who insisted that the federal government had only such powers as were specifically granted it by the Constitution. Despite the early strength of the Federalists, the Jeffersonian faction soon became dominant in North Carolina. By the turn of the century these "Republicans," exemplified by Warren County's Nathaniel Macon, who entered the House of Representatives in 1791 and transferred to the Senate in 1815, were in firm control. 6-22 6-23

In international sentiments also most North Car-olinians were out of step with the Federalists, who tended to favor Great Britain in her continuing conflicts with France. Although the War of 1812 was not universally popular, the appearance of British forces at Ocracoke and Portsmouth prompted a unified response, and the state furnished thousands of men. 6-24 6-25 6-26 6-27 6-28 6-29

Interest in military activities was continued through the Order of the Cincinnati, composed of former officers of the Revolution and their direct descendants; quarterly musters of the militia; special corps of troops in the various towns; construction of defenses along the coast; and the launching of the USS *North Carolina* in 1820. 6-32 6-33

The second victory over Great Britain brought little change to North Carolina. The views of Macon still were representative of those of his fellow citizens, but there were a few spokesmen for a more active state government. The most eloquent advocate of progressive public programs was Archibald Debow Murphey, a native of Caswell County representing Orange in the General Assembly during and immediately after the War of 1812. His characterization of the masses as "lazy, sickly, poor, dirty and ignorant" was less an insult than a commentary that government was not meeting the needs of the public. In a series of reports to the legislature he advocated programs of public education, internal improvements, and constitutional reform. 6-30 6-31 6-34 6-35

Except for the establishment of the Board of Internal Improvements, the chartering of a few companies to open rivers and canals, and the establishment in 1825 of the State Literary Board, little progress was made during Murphey's lifetime in implementing his proposals. So fervently did he believe in his own ideas, however, that he borrowed money to invest in internal improvements projects, only to be committed to jail for debt.

The stagnancy of economic and cultural conditions in the early statehood period was relieved somewhat by the appearance on the national scene of several additional North Carolinians. President James Madison's wife, the former Dolley Paine of Guilford County, cut a broad swath in social circles. Both supporters and opponents of Andrew Jackson in North Carolina were confident that he was born on the northern side of the border with South Carolina, and the state acquired its first cabinet member when in 1829 President Jackson appointed former governor John Branch as secretary of the navy. 6-36 6-37 6-38 6-39

Politics was a serious and sometimes deadly interest in the early years of statehood. Though soon outlawed in the state, dueling was still practiced with virtual impunity. For instance, John Stanly and Samuel Price Carson, both congressmen, killed their political opponents, yet both were reelected by the voters, and both eventually had counties named for them. John Clary, convicted of sexual assault on his stepdaughter, was elected to the house of commons, where a resolution was introduced to "free itself from the contamination of grossly impure and unworthy characters." He resigned, went back to Perquimans County, and received an even larger majority in the ensuing election. Upon his return to Raleigh, he was expelled because "he hath been guilty of a crime so enormous as renders it unfit that he should be permitted to continue a member," but his civic standing in his home county was undiminished. Such behavior, of course, was the exception, rather than the rule.

White settlement reached the Blue Ridge by the 1760s and before the end of the decade crossed the mountains. The creation in 1772 of the Watauga Association has been called the first experiment in self-government west of the Appalachians. Meanwhile, Richard Henderson of Granville County sent a young Rowan County hunter named Daniel Boone over the mountains to investigate opportunities for other white settlements. Encouraged by Boone's reports, Henderson in 1774 organized the Louisa Company—the name was changed the next year to Transylvania Company—which through the Treaty of Sycamore Shoals in 1775 acquired a huge tract in present-day Kentucky and Tennessee from the Indians. Boone supervised the cutting of the Wilderness Road and the founding of Transylvania, which Henderson envisioned as the fourteenth colony.

The grand scheme collapsed when Virginia refused to recognize the company's claims in its western territory. Henderson did succeed, however, in establishing a colony on the Cumberland River in the North Carolina portion of the tract under the leadership of James and Charlotte Robertson. In 1780, at the site of present-day Nashville, Tennessee, Henderson drafted and the settlers signed the Cumberland Compact. Three years later the territory was organized into a county named Davidson. Nearer the mountains three counties had been established—Washington, Sullivan, and Greene. Thus the transmontane country was inhab-

ited by a modest number of North Carolinians who shared both the advantages and disadvantages of living a great distance from the state capital.

The Continental Congress proposed that states possessing western lands cede them to the central government for the common good. North Carolina's General Assembly complied in 1784 on condition that the state retain title to sufficient lands for its war veterans, that neither the land nor population be assessed to North Carolina in the settlement of the federal debt, and that the offer be accepted within one year. News of the cession was especially welcome to many residents of Washington, Sullivan, and Greene counties, who sought to organize themselves into an independent state. They adopted a constitution, proclaimed the State of Franklin, and elected John Sevier governor.

The General Assembly, however, repealed the cession act, and Governor Martin issued a manifesto warning the over-mountain citizens not to be "led away with the pageantry of a mock government, the shadow without the substance, which always dazzles weak minds." In deference to North Carolina's objections, the Continental Congress refused to recognize Franklin. Residents of the Tennessee counties officially remained citizens of North Carolina until 1789, when the General Assembly finally ceded the western lands to the United States. Seven years later Tennessee was admitted as a state. Except for minor adjustments, the borders of North Carolina were fixed for all time.

As settlement moved westward, efforts were renewed for moving the state capital to a more central place. Because of the vulnerability of New Bern during the war, government had become peripatetic, and Tryon's Palace became only an occasional meeting place for the legislature. It was used for a variety of purposes, and in a 1798 fire all but the stable wing burned. Meanwhile, Wake County was the compromise choice for the new capital, and the Hillsborough convention of 1788 authorized the legislature to select a site within ten miles of Isaac Hunter's tavern. Four years passed before the site commission chose a portion of Joel Lane's plantation for the new seat of government. William Christmas laid out the new city of Raleigh and lots were sold to help pay for the construction of a cheap state house, which was still unfinished when the General Assembly convened in it late in 1794.

Several years after a roof fire in 1816 threatened the State House, the building was renovated and heightened to three floors by William Nichols. A cupola provided lighting for an extravagant piece of art for so poor a state, but Antonio Canova's controversial marble statue of toga-clad George Washington was the pride of governmental officials. A bill to provide funds for placing the statue on wheels was defeated, however, and the heavy sculpture was a casualty of the fire in 1831 that destroyed the entire building. Fortunately, the flimsy shell of the building had long before led the governor, secretary of state, and treasurer to move their offices into outbuildings, and few records were lost in the fire. Governor Stokes told the legislators, "Such were the defects of the Construction of the old Walls erected in 1794, that it is very probable, that a part of the building would have fallen in a few years, and perhaps caused the death of many of the assembled Representatives." Work was started a year or so later on a new capitol.

Returns from the first federal census in 1790 placed North Carolina fourth in population among the states behind only Virginia, Pennsylvania, and (if the district of Maine is included) Massachusetts. Rowan, with almost double the white population of any eastern county, was most populous; in fact, six of the ten counties with more than ten thousand population each were in the Piedmont and west. The white population, though still overwhelmingly Anglo-Saxon, was becoming more heterogeneous, for while there remained concentrations in the Cape Fear of Highland Scots and in the Piedmont of Ulster Scots and Germans, there were few closed communities, and mobility and intermarriage increased. Even Moravians occasionally moved from Wachovia, and some non-Moravians were admitted into the community.

Slavery, not surprisingly, was lightest in the Piedmont and west where farming, still the most prevalent means of livelihood, was largely a family undertaking. For blacks the Revolution changed little. More than 105,000 (about 25 percent) of the residents were of African descent, and all but 4,975 of them were in bondage. As chattels, slaves were bought, sold, worked, punished, and furnished shelter and sustenance much as an owner would care for a work horse. The law, of course, differentiated between enslaved humans and other chattels, but a master's authority over his slave was seldom curtailed. Nor were the lives of the "free persons of colour" without great peril, for they carried no physical mark to distinguish them from blacks in bondage.

Although many slaves ran away from their masters, conspiracies to win freedom by violence were infrequent. Consequently, there was little agitation of the slavery issue in North Carolina until abolition groups became active, and the Nat Turner rebellion in 1831 in Virginia, just a few miles north of Northampton County, sent a chill through the state. False reports of the burning of Wilmington and of armies of rebellious slaves in Duplin, Bladen, and Sampson counties "murdering and burning all before them" caused a panic in the Cape Fear valley.

The official response to increased concern over slavery was the passage of stringent laws further limiting the privileges of bonded people. These laws prohibited the teaching of slaves to read and write and outlawed preaching by blacks. Furthermore, slaves were forbidden to play "at any game of cards, dice, nine-pins, or any game of hazard or chance, for any money, liquor or any kind of property." The authority of an owner to emancipate his slave was limited, and an emancipated black was required to leave the state within ninety days and never to return. The laws further authorized county courts to establish patrol committees in each captain's district "to visit the negro houses . . . as often as may be necessary, to inflict a punishment not exceeding fifteen lashes on all slaves they may find off their owner's plantation without a proper permit or pass," adding that if the slave behaved insolently, "they may inflict further punishment for his misconduct, not exceeding thirty-nine lashes." Ironically, the same session authorized by special act the immigration of Aquilla Wilson, the new wife of Thomas Day, a mulatto cabinetmaker, who settled in Milton, and exempted her from the "pains, penalties, or liabilities" of the law prohibiting the entry of free persons of color into the state. Thomas and Aquilla, the act pronounced, were "of good and exemplary reputation and behavior." Finally, the legislature abolished the penalty of severing ears except in cases of perjury in a trial for a capital offense.

This increased repression of blacks made it more difficult for any to repeat the achievements of earlier freedmen, such as Henry Evans, a shoemaker who turned to preaching and established the first Methodist church in Fayetteville; William Meredith, who established a Methodist church in Wilmington which had a membership of 704 blacks and 48 whites in 1812; Louis Sheridan, a prominent Elizabethtown merchant; and John Chavis (or Chaves), a freeborn native of Oxford, who served in a Virginia regiment during the Revolution, attended Washington Academy and possibly Princeton University, and in 1801 became a missionary among his people for the Presbyterian church. By 1808, Chavis had established in Raleigh a prestigious school to which prominent whites sent their children. When some patrons objected to the biracial character of the student body, Chavis divided his classes and taught whites during the day and blacks at night; and when he appealed for exemption from the 1831 legislative act prohibiting preaching by blacks, the church advised him to "acquiesce in the decision of the legislature . . . until God in his Providence shall open to him the path of duty."

White servants—persons bound for a period of years—occupied a status between slavery and freedom. Orphans and children of the poor or unfit were apprenticed (usually to age eighteen for girls and twenty-one for boys) on condition that the master furnish their livelihood along with training for a trade—shoemaker, tailor, seamstress, blacksmith, carpenter, wheelwright, and so forth. The apprenticeship system, while sometimes harsh, did provide care and training for thousands of youngsters.

Lawbreaking, of course, deprived convicted persons of their freedom and sometimes of their lives, for in 1817 twenty-eight crimes were punishable by death. Even failure or inability to pay one's debts was a crime punishable by imprisonment, and nonpayment of taxes led to the sale of property by the county sheriff.

For a state so heavily dependent upon a farming economy (there were only six towns with more than one thousand population as late as 1820), it was remarkable that North Carolina produced no genuine "money" crop. Although tobacco was grown in quantity in the tier of counties along the Virginia border and cotton was becoming more common in a few counties, subsistence farming was a way of life throughout the state. Tools were crude, fertilizer was virtually unknown, and transportation of goods was slow and expensive. Grains, vegetables, fruits, cattle, and hogs were grown on nearly every farm, thus providing at least a portion of the foodstuffs needed for home use and exchange.

Spinning equipment was familiar in homes (by 1814 there were an estimated forty thousand looms in the state, producing seven million yards of cloth), and homespun clothing was commonplace, though ready-made items were available for those who could afford them. By the end of the eighteenth century primitive factories were being established, but the first financially successful cotton spinning mill appears to have been established by Michael Schenck near Lincolnton during the War of 1812; it produced cotton cloth, batting, candlewicks, carpet chain, and rope. Joel Battle's Edgecombe Manufacturing Company was chartered in 1829, and others followed. Some additional domestic items also were being made in North Carolina, including furniture.

Iron furnaces in Lincoln County turned out cannon balls during the War of 1812 and civilian goods thereafter, and several metals were produced in limited quantities. Metalsmiths worked in a number of communities, but the Moravians consistently made the highest quality products.

One metal brought national attention to North Carolina: gold. The first documented discovery of the precious metal within the present limits of the United States occurred in 1799 when Conrad, the son of John Reed, a former Hessian soldier who deserted and settled in present-day Cabarrus County, picked out of Little Meadow Creek a heavy, metallic-looking rock. The curious object was used as a doorstop in the Reed cabin until its content was finally recognized as gold. This revelation set off feverish digging in the community. When additional nuggets were found, gold fever spread, and discoveries were made in other parts of the state, notably Burke County. Until 1829 (at which time there were about fifty gold-producing operations) all of the native gold coined by the United States Mint came from North Carolina, the "Golden State."

Christopher Bechtler, Sr., a German watchmaker and jeweler, settled in Rutherfordton, and in 1831 he began stamping gold coins. Bechtler and his son and nephew operated the nation's most successful private mint. Over the next two decades they would stamp about three million dollars in gold coins. The need for circulating specie was still so great that a branch of the United States Mint was established in Charlotte and operated until the Civil War. Even so, most of North Carolina's gold was diverted to uses other than coinage.

The 14 December 1827 issue of the *Raleigh Register* reported a meeting in Pittsborough "for the purpose of enquiry and information with respect to the lately proposed Rail Road from Newbern to the mountains, through the central parts of the State." More than a decade would pass, however, before the first steam train would operate in North Carolina.

6-101
6-102
6-103
6-104
6-105
6-106
6-107
6-108
6-109
6-110
6-111
rafts continued to be the major means of transportation. Stage lines operated through the state on roads and streets maintained erratically at best. Acceptable accommodations were available in most towns, but country ordinaries were often spartan, crowded, and noisy. Boat travel was limited chiefly to the larger streams and canals below the fall line, and the Blount family operated out of Cape Lookout one of the few seagoing fleets based in the state. Imported goods naturally were priced higher in North Carolina than in states with better port facilities.

6-112
Leisure time activities varied with class and region. Pets were universally enjoyed, and children found amusement in traditional games and toys.
6-113
6-114
For rural people, trips to town were treats, whether for business or pleasure. Hunting and horse racing were popular sports; in 1796, Allen Jones Davie
6-115
6-116
6-117
called the Roanoke Valley "the race-horse region of America." The famous horse Sir Archie was valued at eighty thousand dollars when the estate of William Amis was settled. Cockfighting too attracted followers. For those inclined toward liquid refreshments and conviviality, there were taverns in the towns—three in Halifax alone in the 1790s, one of them with a billiard table. But there were more
6-118
genteel activities for the ladies. Ornamental sewing occupied leisure hours for many women, but from time to time dancing masters brought their skills to the state and as early as 1792 the town of Halifax
6-119
6-120
6-121
6-123
sported an Irish hairdresser. Tea parties and other types of get-togethers provided opportunities for the sexes to mix socially, and traveling companies furnished dramatic and musical entertainment.

Reading for information and for pleasure was limited to that segment of the population that could read and had access to printed materials. Despite widespread illiteracy, the number of newspapers published in the state increased dramatically in the early federal period, and two of them—the *Fayetteville Observer*, founded in 1816, and the *Free Press*, which started in Halifax in 1824, moved to Tarborough, and eventually became the *Tarborough Southerner*—are still being published. The most influential papers included the *Raleigh Register*, begun by Joseph Gales in 1799; the *Western Carolinian*, started in Salisbury in 1820; and, near the
6-122
end of the period, John Christian Blum's *Weekly Gleaner*, established in Salem in 1829.

North Carolina remained a virtual wasteland
6-124
with respect to the production of literary works and other creative enterprises. The state received

little notice from outside writers, and it produced no book or pamphlet that attracted national attention. The sparse literary output was almost exclusively of local or regional interest. Literate North Carolinians had to seek reading materials from beyond their state's borders. Music, too, was for the few, as was art.
6-125
6-126
6-127

6-128
6-129
North Carolina developed no unique architectural form; most of its buildings were simple and practical with a minimum of ornamentation. Homes were predominantly of log or unpainted weatherboard construction; roofs were typically of wooden shingles. Contemporary references to "mansion house" and "plantation" are often misleading because the words in earlier times were synonymous with dwelling house and farm, respectively, but some town and country estates compared favorably with those in Virginia and South Carolina.
6-130
6-131
6-132
6-133
6-134
6-135

The constitution of 1776 provided that "a School or Schools shall be established by the Legislature for the convenient Instruction of Youth, with such Salaries to the Masters paid by the Public, as may enable them to instruct at low Prices; and all useful Learning shall be duly encouraged and promoted in one or more Universities." The General Assembly chartered the University of North Carolina thirteen years later; a promontory near New Hope Chapel in Orange County was chosen for the campus; and in 1795, Hinton James
6-136
6-137
6-138
enrolled in the first state university to open its doors. The university remained the only institution of higher learning in the state until the 1830s. As the General Assembly provided little in the way of appropriations, the university struggled along mainly on receipts from escheats and the sale of lots, gifts from individual citizens and organizations, and tuition income.

The legislature was even less attentive to the instruction of children. To be sure, there were many advocates of public education: every governor from 1802 on urged legislative action, but scores of bills failed to pass "for the want of sufficient funds." Archibald D. Murphey associated the absence of a system of public education with the state's economic and cultural backwardness, but his exhortations resulted in little more than the establishment in 1825 of the State Literary Fund, which, when it reached a sufficient size, was to be allocated to the creation of common schools. The fund, however, was so mismanaged that it contributed almost nothing to education for fifteen years.

The low rate of literacy was described in 1811 by

Jeremiah Battle who estimated that in his county of Edgecombe "about two thirds of the [white] people generally 'can read': & one half of the males 'write' their names; but no more than one third of the women can write." Still, during public debate over a bill for the education of poor children, a citizen asked the *Raleigh Register*, "Would it not redound as much to young persons, and to the honour of the State, if they should pass their days in the cotton patch, or at the plow, or in the cornfield, instead of being mewed up in a school house, where they are earning nothing?" He concluded, "Gentlemen, I hope you do not conceive it at all necessary, that *everybody* should be able to read, write and cipher." The bill died in committee because, said the unfavorable report, it would have required "a proportional imposition of taxes upon the people which at this period they would but little sustain and to which they would never submit without a murmur."

Thus throughout the early federal period education in North Carolina was left to private academies, seminaries, and "old field" schools. At David Caldwell's school near Greensboro and at similar schools supported by tuition and gifts and patronized by the children of families of financial means, most of the early leaders of North Carolina received their only formal education. A majority of the children of the state prior to 1835, however, never sat in the presence of a teacher, and few of them ever saw a doctor.

Organized religion, too, languished in the post-revolutionary years. Having taken an oath of allegiance to the crown, the Anglican clergy generally remained loyal to England, and the church was thus compromised in the eyes of most North Carolinians. The constitution of 1776 disestablished the church, and not until 1817 was the new Episcopal diocese formally reorganized. As late as 1830 there were only eleven ministers and thirty-one congregations of Episcopalians in the state. Quakers and Moravians, officially pacifist during the

war, escaped a similar taint of disloyalty because of their hospitable treatment of wounded Americans. The Lutherans and Reformed denominations failed to show substantial increases in membership partially because of language barriers created as English gradually replaced German among the young people.

On the other hand, there was growth among the Methodists and Baptists, who were caught up in the evangelical fervor of the Great Revival after 1800. Visits by bishops Francis Asbury and Thomas Coke led in 1785 to the first general Methodist conference, and the new denomination spread slowly through the backcountry. Baptists, though almost continually embroiled in theological controversies among themselves, increased in membership and schism. Presbyterians, somewhat tainted by the disaffection of Highland Scots during the war, showed new vigor among Ulster Scots and their neighbors. While sectarianism was rampant among religionists, interdenominational work was not unknown. Church membership, which is estimated to have numbered no more than one of every thirty citizens in 1790, probably had not greatly surpassed that ratio by 1835.

Roman Catholics and non-Christians were legally barred from public office by the constitution, but the voters sometimes ignored the ban. William Gaston, a twenty-two-year-old Catholic lawyer, was elected to the state senate from Craven County in 1800 and seated without fanfare. Seven years later he was New Bern's borough representative in the house of commons. At a historic session in 1808, Gaston, a Catholic, and Jacob Henry, a Jew from Carteret County, took their seats, and three weeks later Gaston was unanimously elected speaker of the body. Gaston served again in both houses, represented his district in Congress, and in 1833— still technically barred because of his religion—was elected an associate justice of the North Carolina Supreme Court, the body charged with interpreting the constitution and legislative acts.

6-1
Alexander Martin (1740–1807), here in his military uniform, served as governor in 1782–84 and 1789–92 and as a member of the Constitutional Convention in

Philadelphia in 1787 and of the United States Senate from 1793 to 1799. First a Federalist, he became a Jeffersonian while in the Senate. (Courtesy NCDA&H.)

6-3
Samuel Marshall of New Hanover County left with British forces in 1781 and lost his property, but it eventually was returned to his heirs. (Courtesy North Carolina Collection.)

6-2
Sales of Loyalist lands were reported in this 1787 record of the Edenton District's commissioner of confiscated property. Hardy Murfree, the clerk of court, purchased two of the tracts listed on this page. (Courtesy NCDA&H.)

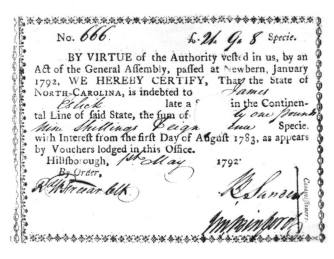

6-4
Due bill issued to James Eslick for Revolutionary service in the Continental Line. The hole in the document represented cancellation upon payment. (Courtesy NCDA&H.)

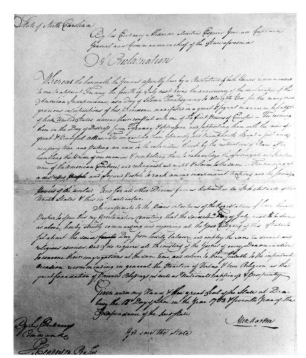

6-7
In 1783, Governor Martin proclaimed 4 July as a day of thanksgiving "to Almighty God for the many most gracious interpositions of his providence manifested in a great & signal manner in behalf of these United States. . . ." (Courtesy Moravian Archives, Winston-Salem.)

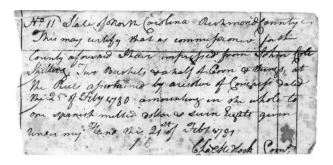

6-5
Voucher receipting for the wartime impressment of corn from John Cole of Richmond County. The value was given in Spanish milled dollars. (Courtesy NCDA&H.)

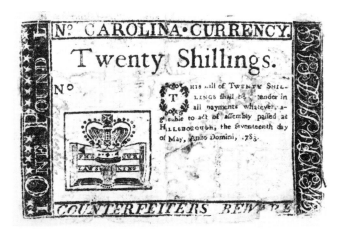

6-6
The optimistic slogan, "The laws our king," was printed on a crown decorating twenty-shilling notes issued by North Carolina in 1783. (Courtesy NCDA&H.)

6-8
The Moravians at Salem performed a "freudenpsalm" for their official thanksgiving ceremony on 4 July 1783. (Courtesy Moravian Archives, Winston-Salem.)

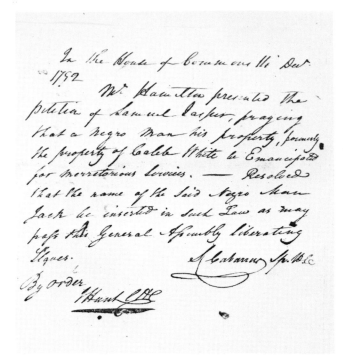

6-11
Willie Jones (1741–1801) was a leading spokesman for the "common people," though he himself was a prosperous and influential planter and businessman. Horse racing was his favorite sport. (Courtesy NCDA&H.)

6-9
Slave Jack White won his freedom for helping take over the British vessel that had captured him and his white fellow crewmen. (Courtesy NCDA&H.)

6-13
William Lenoir (1751–1839), revolutionary officer, was a moderating influence in the debate over the ratification of the Constitution. (Courtesy North Carolina Collection.)

6-12
Three North Carolinians in the Continental Congress are pictured in this detail from John Trumbull's painting of the resignation of George Washington on 23 December 1783: in foreground, left to right, Richard Dobbs Spaight (1758–1802) and Benjamin Hawkins (1754–1816); and standing, second from right, Hugh Williamson (1735–1819). Williamson was the state's most influential delegate; Spaight later served as governor and died in a duel; and Hawkins became a United States senator and Indian agent. (By permission of Yale University Art Gallery, New Haven.)

6-10
William R. Davie (1756–1820) was a skillful military officer during the Revolution, then served in the Constitutional Convention in Philadelphia and as governor (1798–99). He is regarded as the "father" of the University of North Carolina. The portrait is attributed to Eliza Lezinka Mirbel. (Courtesy Independence National Historical Park, Philadelphia.)

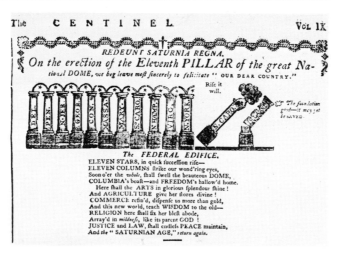

6-16
The federal constitution was
ratified in the "state house" in
Fayetteville, shown at left in
an engraving from a drawing
made by a passerby, M. Horace Say, who gave it to General Lafayette in 1814. The
painting hung in the general's
bedchamber in France as a
memento of the town named
for him. (Courtesy North
Carolina Collection.)

6-17
James Iredell (1751–99),
Samuel Johnston's brother-
in-law, in a chalk-on-paper
drawing by Saint-Memin.

Iredell served as a justice on
the United States Supreme
Court. (Courtesy NCDA&H.)

6-18
James Iredell's wife, Han-
na(h), in a painting at-
tributed to Jacob Marling, a

Raleigh artist. (Courtesy
NCDA&H.)

6-19
Hannah Johnston Iredell wore this gown to a reception in Philadelphia in honor of President Washington. She was a sister of Samuel Johnston. The petticoat and fichu are of twentieth-century materials. (Courtesy NCDA&H.)

6-20
John Steele (1764–1815), appointed comptroller of the Treasury by President Washington, in a watercolor on ivory by James Peale, 1797. (Courtesy Frick Art Reference Library, New York.)

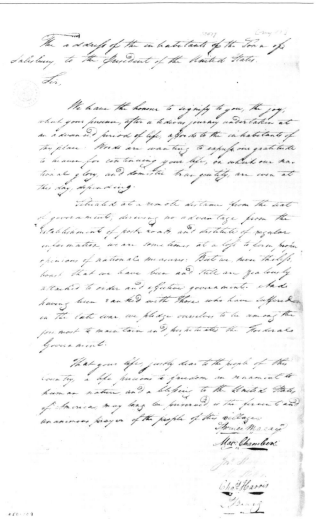

6-21
In their address to President Washington upon his visit on 30 May 1791, residents of Salisbury pledged their loyalty, though "situated at a remote distance from the seat of government, deriving no advantage from the establishment of post-roads, and destitute of regular information," they were sometimes at a loss to form proper opinions of national measures. (Courtesy Library of Congress.)

From the State Gazette of North-Carolina.

To the Voters and Electors of the district of Albemarle.

My Countrymen,

I OFFER my best abilities to represent and serve you, as your Delegate in the next General Congress, to be held at the city of Philadelphia. I shall not advert to my long and personal duties in the service of my country. This is intended, only, as a notification of my intention.—To solicit, or make interest, I shall not.—To solicit, on my part, would be a mean and low acknowledgment of unworthiness—to promise, on your part (without caution) disgraceful: It would be a forfeiture of the fidelity and allegiance you owe your country. Let an *ingenious* and an *ingenuous* comparison direct your choice.

If I possess a greater degree of learning, legal, governmental and political knowledge, than those who may be my competitors; and can walk the floor of Congress in the apt stile and character of the American Gentleman, I have a *right* without *solicitation* to demand your suffrages—*without which*, should they be lavished on me, you will disgrace yourselves—abuse the trust reposed in you—forfeit the allegiance you owe your country, by violating that binding sacrament you made with the first vital breath you drew—sink into contempt, and merit not liberty nor protection, but to be degraded in to slaves indeed!

Let honour, decorum and truth, in this generous contest, be attended to—be censure, reproach and calumny flung at a far distance

On whom the choice may fall, is tale untold; whoever he may be, may his manners and deportment be graceful, and his labours redound to the honour, interest and happiness of the empire, is the pure wish of, Gentlemen, your sincere friend and advocate of liberty.

WILLIAM CUMMING.

Edenton, Jan. 12, 1793.

6-22
William Cumming, a congressional candidate, in a letter published in the *North-Carolina Journal* (Halifax), 6 February 1793, suggested that he could "walk the floor of Congress in the apt stile and character of the American Gentleman." (Courtesy North Carolina Collection.)

6-23
Nathaniel Macon (1758–1837) was North Carolina's most influential member of Congress for more than three decades. He served successively as speaker of the House of Representatives and president pro tempore of the Senate during his thirty-seven years in Washington. (Courtesy Library of Congress.)

ACROSTIC.

Addressed to WILLIE JONES, Esq.

B rave warrior, boast of patriot France,
U nfurl her flag on Mantua's walls;
O 'er every obstacle, advance
N or cease till every tyrant falls.
A like for skill and worth admir'd,
P itying woes, you must deplore;
A nd by humanity inspir'd,
R ejoicing worlds to peace restore.
T ouch'd by thy generous deeds shall fame.
E nrich her annals with thy brilliant name.

AN. ADMIRER.

6-24
Pro-French sentiment in North Carolina was illustrated by an acrostic in the *North-Carolina Journal* (Halifax), 22 January 1798. Almost exactly five years earlier the same paper reported a convivial celebration in Gilmour's Tavern following victories of the French armies. (Courtesy North Carolina Collection.)

Warrenton, July 5.

☞ This day being celebrated here for the Anniversary of American Independence, an Oration was delivered at the Court-house by Doctor P. C. POPE, in a masterly style of eloquence. The Doctor commenced with an appropriate expression of the principles of American Patriotism. He proceeded with a short view of the nature and events of the Revolution. He drew a lively picture of the constitutional and practical ambition and perfidy of the British Government. He brought down the history of her injustice to the present time, depicting in very impressive, but correct strains, the injuries which produced the present war; invoked the Spirit of Liberty, still glowing in the American heart, to resist, with manly perseverance, the barbarous conduct pursued by the enemy, introducing, as a last proof, their dark enormities at Hampton. He concluded with an exhortation to the guardians of the rising generation, to instil into their minds the sentiments of virtue and liberty, that these sentiments might "grow with their growth, and strengthen with their strength." The Declaration of Independence was read by Wm. Miller, Esq. A Dinner was prepared by Mr. Terrell, and suitable toasts were drank as usual.

6-25
Anti-British emotions were stirred by the annual commemorations of the signing of the Declaration of Independence, like the one reported in the *Raleigh Register*, 16 July 1813. (Courtesy NCDA&H.)

The Enemy on our Coast.—The first intelligence of the British fleet having entered Occacock Inlet, and of their having landed at Portsmouth and Shell Castle, which was received here on Saturday last, excited a glow of Patriotism which has seldom been equalled. The electric spark flew from man to man, and their words and actions exhibited but one sentiment. Being so far in the interior, and remote from the fear of invasion, the necessary articles of equipment were not in readiness. But all obstacles vanish before minds determined to act, and the same spirit which animated our citizens to volunteer their services, communicated itself to their female connections and friends; and being apprized that the business 'cried haste and speed must answer it,' they exerted themselves, and in less than 24 hours, Capt. Clarke's Volunteer Corps of Infantry were on the road completely equipped, accompanied by Major General Calvin Jones, with his aids Mr. Geo. Badger and Mr. Junius Sneed.

On Monday morning, Capt. Hunter's Troop of Cavalry, with Major T. Henderson, marched; accompanied by his Excellency the Commander in Chief, his aid Col B. Daniel and Adjutant-General R. Williams. And on Wednesday, the portion of Wake Militia, held in readiness, under the requisition of a law of Congress, also marched from this place, under the command of Col. A. Rogers and Major D. L. Barringer.

6-26
The 23 July 1813 issue of the *Raleigh Register* reported that the British had landed on North Carolina soil and that state troops were on their way to the coast. (Courtesy North Carolina Collection.)

6-27
A portion of a pay and receipt roll for the Gates County militia for service during the War of 1812. All of the officers and more than half of the privates were able to sign their names. (Courtesy NCDA&H.)

6-28
Otway Burns (1775–1848) of Beaufort bought and outfitted the *Snap Dragon*, then preyed upon British merchant shipping. A cannon from his ship rests on his tombstone at Beaufort. (Courtesy NCDA&H.)

6-29
North Carolina's most famous naval officer in the War of 1812 was Captain Johnston Blakeley (1781–1814) of the *Wasp*. After his ship was lost at sea, Congress authorized a medal in his honor. (Courtesy NCDA&H.)

6-30
In an 1840 lithograph, the Marquis de Lafayette is depicted viewing Canova's controversial statue of George Washington in the old State House rotunda. The general visited the state in 1825 and was warmly received. (Courtesy NCDA&H.)

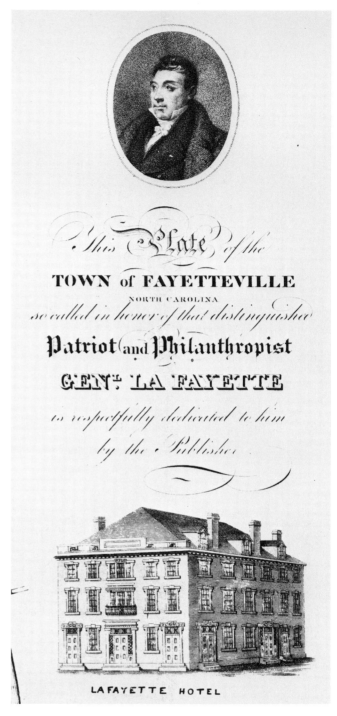

LAFAYETTE HOTEL

6-31
In Fayetteville, the general's namesake town, builders rushed to finish the Lafayette Hotel for his reception there, and John McRae drew a map for the occasion. (Courtesy North Carolina Collection.)

6-32
Neill McNair received this medallion from the Fayetteville Light Artillery in 1813 for superior marksmanship. (Courtesy Bill Shaw, Fayetteville.)

6-33
The 2,633-ton USS *North Carolina* was launched at Philadelphia in 1820 with Matthew Calbraith Perry as her first commanding officer. The ship served extensively in the Atlantic and the Mediterranean. This photograph was made during the Civil War while the vessel was serving as a receiving ship in the New York Navy Yard. She was the predecessor of two other vessels bearing the name of North Carolina. (Courtesy United States Naval Historical Center.)

6-35
This sketch, "Yadkin [River] from Flatswamp to Mountain Creek," accompanied a report by Joseph Caldwell and Elisha Mitchell to the Board of Internal Improvements, which was established at Murphey's insistence. (Courtesy NCDA&H.)

6-34
Archibald Debow Murphey (1777–1832), teacher, lawyer, legislator, and judge, was the state's most persistent spokesman for governmental sponsorship of education and internal improvements. (Courtesy NCDA&H.)

6-36
Portrait of North Carolina's Dolley Paine Todd Madison by Bass Otis, 1816. She was born near New Garden Meeting (now Guilford College). (By permission of New-York Historical Society, New York.)

6-38
The controversy over the birthplace of Andrew Jackson was settled in the minds of many North Carolinians who believed that he was born in this cabin in present-day Union County, North Carolina. (Courtesy Library of Congress; reprinted from William H. Milburn, *The Lance, Cross, and Canoe . . .* [New York, 1892].)

6-37
An 1844 lithograph of Andrew Jackson with the Hermitage in background. Born in the Waxhaw settlement near the border between the two Carolinas, Jackson practiced law in North Carolina before moving to Tennessee. (Courtesy NCDA&H.)

6-40
These pistols are believed to have been used in 1802 by John Stanly in his duel with Richard Dobbs Spaight, a former governor. Spaight was killed. (Courtesy Tryon Palace Restoration, New Bern.)

6-39
John Branch (1782–1863), governor from 1817 to 1820 and United States senator from 1823 to 1829, was Andrew Jackson's first secretary of the navy. He was later governor of the Territory of Florida. (Courtesy North Carolina Collection.)

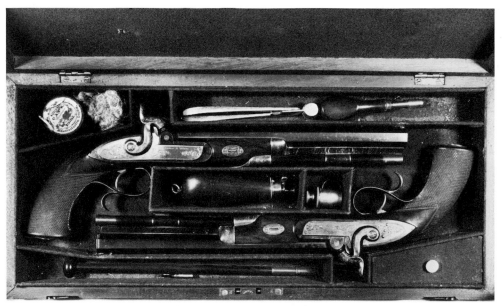

6-41
Samuel Price Carson (1798–1840), who killed his congressional opponent, Robert Brank Vance, in a duel in 1827, later helped establish the Republic of Texas and was its first secretary of state. (Courtesy NCDA&H.)

6-42
The career of Robert Potter (1800–1842) was only temporarily halted by a bizarre incident in which he castrated a minister and a youth the same Sunday; his Granville County constituents again elected him to the legislature, and later he participated in the formation of the Texas republic, was its secretary of the navy, and had a county named for him. (Courtesy NCDA&H.)

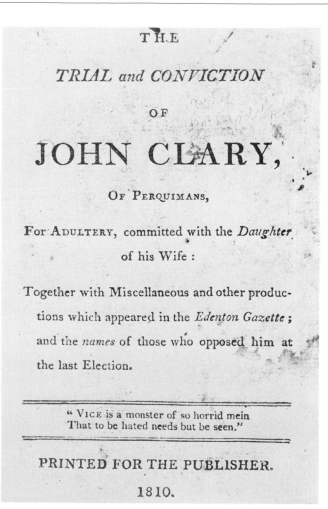

6-43
The opponents of John Clary printed a booklet describing his criminal conviction for sexual assault on his stepdaughter, but his neighbors twice elected him to the house of commons. (Courtesy North Carolina Collection.)

6-44
Richard Henderson (1735–85), the colonial judge whose home was burned by the Regulators in 1770, promoted settlement of the transmontane region. (Courtesy North Carolina Collection; reprinted, by permission, from James C. Kelly, *From Settlement to Statehood: A Pictorial History of Tennessee to 1796* [Nashville, 1977].)

6-45
Daniel Boone (1734–1820), then a resident of Rowan County, served as Henderson's scout, but their relationship was not always a harmonious one, as this writ indicates. (Courtesy North Carolina Collection.)

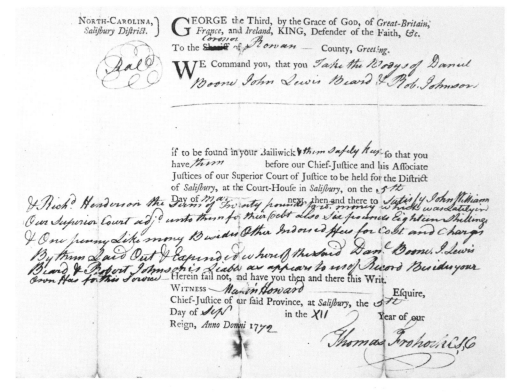

6-46
An advertisement in Dixon and Hunter's *Virginia Gazette*, 30 September 1775, predicted that Transylvania would "soon become a considerable Colony, and one of the most agreeable Countries in America." (Courtesy North Carolina Collection.)

6-47
James and Charlotte Reeves Robertson helped establish Nashborough on the Cumberland River. Charlotte, in a portrait painted many years later by Washington Bogart Cooper, epitomized the hardy women who helped tame the wilderness. (Courtesy Tennessee State Museum, Nashville.)

A COMPANY of Gentlemen of *North Carolina* having, for a large and valuable Confideration, purchafed from the Chiefs of the *Cherokee Indians*, by and with the Confent of the whole Nation, a confiderable Tract of their Lands, now called *Tranfylvania*, lying on the Rivers *Ohio, Cumberland*, and *Louifa*; and underftanding that many People are defirous of becoming Adventurers in that Part of the World, and wifh to know the Terms on which Lands in that Country may be had, they therefore hereby inform the Public, that any Perfon who will fettle on and inhabit the fame before the firft Day of *June* 1776, fhall have the Privilege of taking up and furveying for himfelf 500 Acres, and for each tithable Perfon he may carry with him and fettle there 250 Acres, on the Payment of 50s. Sterling *per* Hundred, fubject to an yearly Quitrent of 2s. like Money, to commence in the Year 1780. Such Perfons as are willing to become Purchafers may correfpond and treat with Mr. *William Johnston* in *Hillfborough*, and Col. *John Williams* of *Granville, North Carolina*, or Col. *Richard Henderfon* at *Boonfborough*, in *Tranfylvania*.——This Country lies on the fouth Side of the Rivers *Ohio* and *Louifa*, in a temperate and healthy Climate. It is in general well watered with Springs and Rivulets, and has feveral Rivers, up which Veffels of confiderable Burthen may come with Eafe. In different Places of it are a Number of Salt Springs, where the making of Salt has been tried with great Succefs, and where, with Certainty, any Quantity needed may be eafily and conveniently made. Large Tracts of the Land lie on Lime-ftone, and in feveral Places there is Abundance of Iron Ore. The Fertility of the Soil, and Goodnefs of the Range, almoft furpafs Belief; and it is at prefent well ftored with Buffalo, Elk, Deer, Bear, Beaver, &c. and the Rivers abound with Fifh of various Kinds. Vaft Crowds of people are daily flocking to it, and many Gentlemen of the firft Rank and Character have bargained for Lands in it; fo that there is a great Appearance of a rapid Settlement, and that it will foon become a confiderable Colony, and one of the moft agreeable Countries in *America*.   (6)

6-48
The first seal of Davidson County, established by North Carolina's General Assembly in 1783, is amusingly primitive. (Courtesy Tennessee State Museum, Nashville.)

6-49
The Cumberland Compact of 13 May 1780, drafted by Richard Henderson, provided a temporary government for the new colony near Fort Nashborough. (Courtesy Tennessee Historical Society, Nashville.)

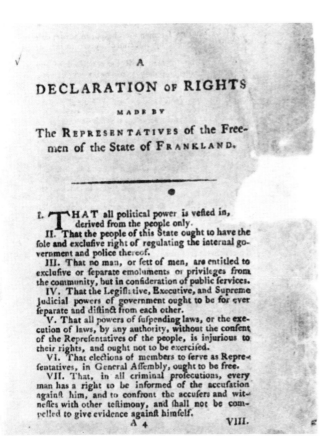

6-50
A declaration of rights served as the preamble to the constitution of the abortive State of Franklin (here spelled Frankland). (Courtesy Tennessee Historical Society, Nashville.)

6-51
John (Nolichucky Jack) Sevier, a hero of the Revolution, was governor of the short-lived State of Franklin. He later represented North Carolina in the first Congress. (Courtesy Tennessee State Museum, Nashville.)

6-53
A poem in the *North-Carolina Journal* (Halifax), 9 January 1793, referred to a "lofty *Dome* magnificently fair / Ascending from the top of *Union-Square*. . . ." (Courtesy North Carolina Collection.)

6-52
Governor Alexander Martin, in a stinging "manifesto" addressed to the "overmountain men," undermined public support of the State of Franklin. (Courtesy NCDA&H.)

For the North-Carolina Journal.

ON THE SEAT OF GOVERNMENT.

WHEN from dark chaos sprung this mighty frame,
  Of grandeur, glory 'midst the wide domain :
Where worlds unnumber'd thro' the boundless space,
Revolve with all the planetary race :
Where blazing comets thro' the vast expanse,
Their stated courses wheel in mystic dance :
Where flaming meteors bursting from the sky
With dreadful roar—and forked lightnings fly.
Primæval night, dark-brooding o'er the wild,
Then took its dreary flight and horror smil'd.
Up from the mighty void in wild extremes,
Emerged earth with all its pleasing scenes ;
Spangled with stars the shining fabrick stood,
Creation smil'd, and was pronounced good ;
And constellations bright in glory shone,
Amid the grandeur of the sacred dome.
  All nature spreading like the opening sky,
Presents its wonders to the fancied eye,
Of boundless seas that never ceafe to roll,
And earth's gay scenes, with clouds of fretted gold.
Behold the charming groves and fruitful fields,
Cloath'd with all that beaut'ous nature yields ;
There view the flow'ry plains and gliding rills,
Here smiling meads and gently rising hills.
  In awful pomp see potent cities rise,
And lofty temples tow'ring to the skies ;
Where once the humble shrub or hawthorn grew,
The aged oak, the cypress or the yew.
  With a prophetic eye, we now behold,
What some propitious hour may unfold.
A lofty *Dome* magnificently fair,
Ascending from the top of *Union-Square* ;
Where freeborn sons with patriotic zeal,
United shall promote the public weal ;
The common-weal inspiring ev'ry tongue,
In freedom's glorious cause by conquest won ;
Free, independent, gen'rous and brave,
That liberty support which nature gave ;
Each heart to heart unite, and hand to hand,
Unshaken, firm, in one harmonious band ;
While all to virtue's glorious summit aim,
Discord shall cease, and peace forever reign ;
See heav'n-born Liberty as she descends,
And o'er this western clime expands her wings ;
The sacred Goddess fire's her noble sons,
And ev'ry patriot soul with freedom burns :
Here Government shall her righteous sceptre sway,
Her virtuous sons with active voice obey ;
—Blessings dispense from her exhaustless store,
Till time on earth shall cease and be no more.
  A landscape fair thro'out this verdant *Seat*,
Will furnish here a calm and cool retreat ;
From noxious climes, and summer's sickliest rage,
For fading youth, and old decrepid age :
Each rising eminence to crown the scene,
Is mantled o'er with nature's cheerful green ;
Each vale with spreading vines or willows hung,
Oozes in cooling springs, or riv'lets run ;
Here rosy health sits blooming on the cheek,
Strength and activity together meet ;
Blessings peculiar to this gentle clime,
Wafted by balmy zephyrs unconfin'd.
No more shall Discord raise her standard here,
No more invectives foul pollute the air ;
But Unanimity resume the strain,
And justice, truth and peace forever reign.
Wake, December 20, 1792.

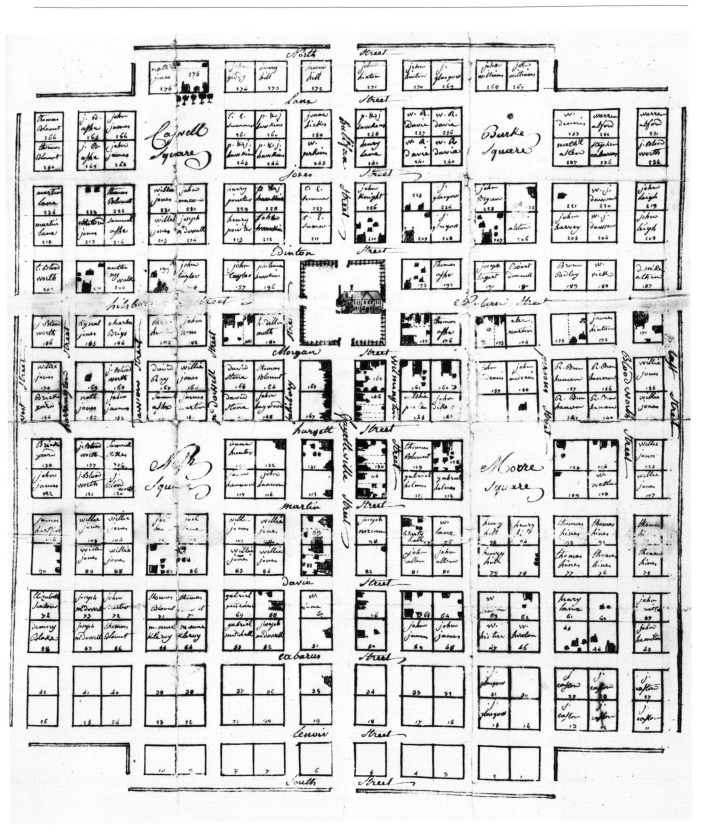

6-54

A manuscript map of 1797 pictured the new city of Raleigh with the State House and streets (named for the state's judicial districts) leading in four directions. The house purchased for the governor sits on the southwest corner of Hargett and Fayetteville streets. (Courtesy Southern Historical Collection.)

6-55
J. S. Glennie made a watercolor drawing of the original State House during a visit to Raleigh in 1811. (By permission of Princeton University Library, Andre de Coppet Collection.)

6-56
Jacob Marling, a Raleigh artist, painted this view of the enlarged State House in the late 1820s. Buildings on Fayetteville Street are seen in left background. (Courtesy North Carolina Collection.)

6-57
Hearing that the library was consumed in the fire that destroyed the State House in June 1831, former president James Madison donated his personal copy of John Lawson's *History of Carolina* to Governor Montfort Stokes. (Courtesy NCDA&H.)

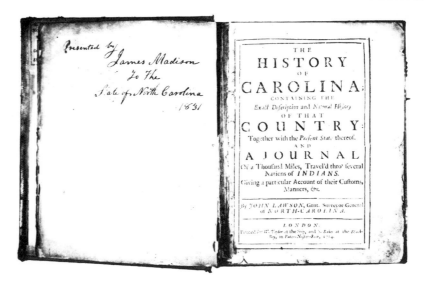

6-58
The population of the United States in 1790 was painted on this Liverpool pitcher. Most of the figures are approximately correct, but South Carolina (with 249,073 persons) was short-changed by the omission of a cipher. (Courtesy National Museum of American History, Smithsonian Institution.)

6-59
The geographical and racial character of the population in 1790 was published in *Nord-carolinische Kirchennachrichten* by Johann Caspar Velthusen, leader of a German missionary movement to aid in spreading Lutheranism in North Carolina. (Courtesy North Carolina Collection.)

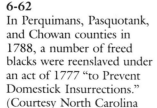

6-60
John Williams's advertisement in the *Raleigh Register*, 1 September 1808, described the scars and apparel of two runaways. (Courtesy NCDA&H.)

6-61
The Boyette slave house in Johnston County, shown here with a twentieth-century roof, is one of the few remaining stick chimney cabins in North Carolina. (Courtesy NCDA&H.)

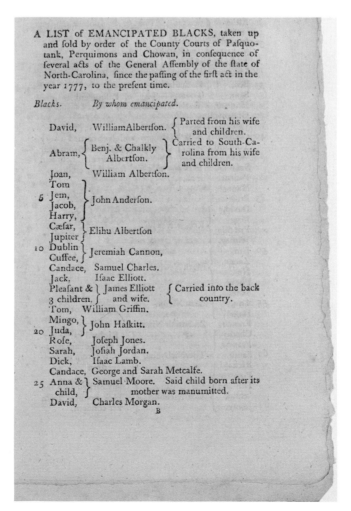

6-62
In Perquimans, Pasquotank, and Chowan counties in 1788, a number of freed blacks were reenslaved under an act of 1777 "to Prevent Domestick Insurrections." (Courtesy North Carolina Collection.)

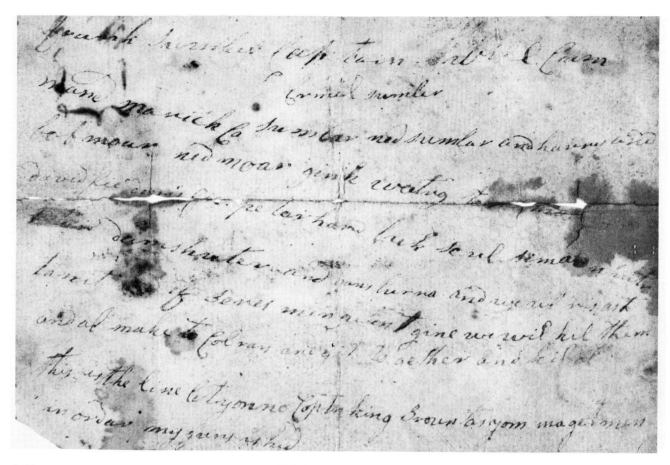

6-63
Sixteen blacks were executed
in 1802 when a planned slave
uprising near Colerain in
Bertie County was revealed
by this document, which was
found in Judy Raynor's
kitchen. The message appears
to read, beginning in the last
of the fifth line and going
through the seventh, ". . .
and we will rise tonight and
if Ben's men won't join we
will kill them and all make to
Colerain and get together
and kill all." (Courtesy
NCDA&H.)

> **Emigration to Liberia.**
>
> ——
>
> **NOTICE.**
>
> ——
>
> THE *MANAGERS of the AMERICAN CO-
> LONIZATION SOCIETY* give NOTICE,
> that they are ready to receive applications for the
> conveyance of free people of colour to the Colo-
> ny of Liberia.
>
> In all cases, the age, sex and profession of the
> Applicants must be mentioned.
>
> Application may be made in Baltimore to *Hon.
> Judge Brice, Charles Howard, John H. B. Latrobe,
> Esq. or Charles C. Harper, Esq.* Agents of the
> Society.   June 25.

6-64
The American Colonization
Society, in an advertisement
in the *Raleigh Register* (semi-
weekly edition) of 15 July
1828, offered to transport
blacks to Liberia. (Courtesy
NCDA&H.)

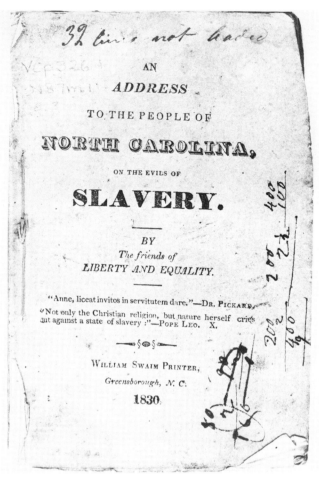

6-65
In 1830, William Swaim, grandfather of William Sydney Porter, printed the first important antislavery booklet in the state. (Courtesy North Carolina Collection.)

6-66
The *Raleigh Register* (semi-weekly edition) of 15 September 1835 reported the growing resistance to the antislavery movement. (Courtesy NCDA&H.)

ton; named several families that they intended to murder. Their object was to march by two routes to Wilmington, spreading destruction and murder on their way. At Wilmington they expected to have been reinforced by 2000 to supply themselves with arms and ammunition and then return.

Three of the ringleaders in Duplin have been taken and Dave and Jim executed. There are 23 Negroes in jail in Duplin county, all of them no doubt concerned in the conspiracy. Several have been whipped and some released. In Sampson 25 are in jail, all concerned directly or indirectly in the plot. The excitement among the people in Sampson is very great, and increasing; they take effectual measures to arrest all suspected persons. A very intelligent negro preacher named David, was put on his trial to day and clearly convicted by the testimony of another negro. The people were so much enraged, that they could scarcely be prevented from shooting him, on his passage from the Court House to the Jail. All the confessions made induce the belief that the conspirators were well organized, and their plans well understood in Duplin, Sampson, Wayne, New Hanover and Lenoir Counties. Nothing had transpired to arise even a suspicion that they extended into Cumberland or Bladen, except that Jim confesses that Nat, Col. Wright's negro (who had been missing since the discovery of the plot,) had gone into the neighborhood of Fayetteville to raise a company to join the conspirators.

D

6-67
Following the Nat Turner "rebellion" across the border in Virginia, Samuel Warner's *Authentic and Impartial Narrative . . .* was rushed into print, replete with exaggerations. (Courtesy North Carolina Collection.)

MEETING IN WILMINGTON.

We cheerfully copy the following Resolutions, as requested, which were adopted at a very numerous meeting of the citizens of Wilmington, in this State, held on the 22d ultimo. We should copy the whole proceedings, had we room.

"*Resolved,* That this meeting fully participates in the indignation and abhorrence which pervades the Southern country, against the reckless fanatics, enrolled as "*Anti-Slavery Societies.*"

"*Resolved,* as anarchy and extermination are the only results which reason and reflection can anticipate from their labors, their motives, like their acts, merit the reprobation of the wise and good."

"*Resolved,* That the conduct of our social relations and the uninterrupted continuance of our domestic policy are sacred, inviolable and CHARTERED RIGHTS, with which we will permit no interference, but maintain them as paramount obligations, against all aggression."

"*Resolved,* That the thanks of the country are due to the patriotic citizens of Charleston, for their prompt, manly and spirited resistance, to this unauthorized, daring and intrusive meddling with our peculiar institutions. That we fully concur with them in the Resolutions they have forwarded us;

6-68
When a booklet by David Walker, formerly a slave, reached Wilmington, Governor John Owen issued a letter urging that "every means which the existing laws of the State place within the reach of its citizens" be used to suppress the "inflammatory" pamphlet. (Courtesy NCDA&H.)

6-69
Receipt signed by Louis Sheridan, a free black, for furnishing ewers, pitchers, and chamberpots for the "Government House" in 1829. (Courtesy NCDA&H.)

6-70
A legislative act in 1831 made it illegal for anyone to teach a slave to read or write, "the use of figures excepted." (Courtesy NCDA&H.)

6-71
Patrols, like the one described here in Hertford County, were authorized by an act in 1831. (Courtesy North Carolina Collection.)

6-72
Testimonial concerning John Chavis's Revolutionary service in a Virginia regiment. Chavis, a free black, taught both white and black children in Raleigh. (Courtesy NCDA&H.)

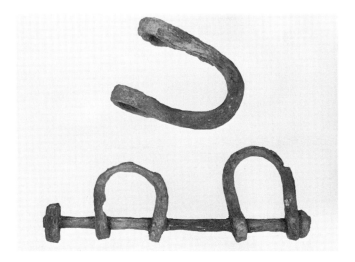

6-73
John Chavis's advertisement in the *Raleigh Register*, 25 August 1808, announced the segregation of his students by race. (Courtesy NCDA&H.)

6-75
The *Star* (Raleigh), 21 July 1820, reported that Anthony Metcalf, then in the Roxboro jail, had been married fifteen times before he was thirty-five years old. (Courtesy North Carolina Collection.)

6-74
Readers of the *Star* (Raleigh), 25 June 1824, could not have known that one of James Selby's runaway apprentices would grow up to be president of the United States. (Courtesy North Carolina Collection.)

6-76
This leg iron and handcuffs were excavated during the restoration of the old jail in Halifax. (Courtesy NCDA&H.)

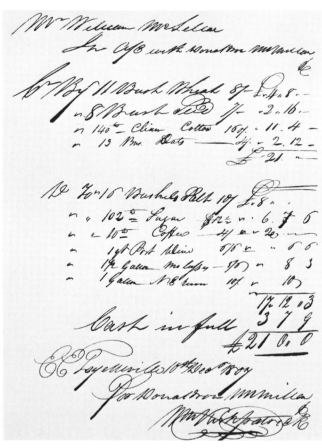

6-79
A bill of 10 December 1807, Fayetteville, describes the exchange of grain for imported foodstuffs. (Courtesy NCDA&H.)

6-77 and 6-78
Moravian farmers and their tools were painted in (top) Ludwig Gottfried von Redeken's "A View of Salem in North Carolina—1787" and (bottom) an unknown artist's "Salem from the North West," October 1832. (Courtesy Old Salem Restoration; by permission of Moravian Archives, Winston-Salem.)

6-80
A water-powered gristmill—an essential facility in every community—is shown on Christian Daniel Welfare's 1824 painting "Salem from the Southwest." (Courtesy Old Salem Restoration; by permission of Wachovia Historical Society.)

6-81
Few North Carolinians could afford a remarkable yarn reel with clock mechanism made by Johann Ludwig Eberhardt of Salem. (Courtesy Old Salem Restoration; by permission of Wachovia Historical Society.)

6-83
Isaac (1776–1858) and Elizabeth Boner (1778–1854), hatters, proudly sat about 1835 with two of their products for artist Daniel Welfare. (Courtesy Old Salem Restoration; by permission of Wachovia Historical Society.)

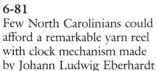

Mrs. A. C. Howard,

INFORMS the ladies of Edgecombe and vicinity, that she has opened, in the house immediately opposite the Bank in Tarborough, a handsome assortment of FANCY GOODS, suitable for fall and winter wear, which they are respectfully invited to call and examine —among them are—

Pattern silk, satin and velvet Bonnets, of the latest Northern fashions,
Leghorn Flats, assorted numbers,
Fine and coarse straw Bonnets,
Silks and satins, plain and figured,
Gros de Naples, different colors,
Black mode, velvet, and crape,
Florences, liece, gauze and sinchews,
Lutestring, satin and gauze ribands,
Superior bobinett caps and capes,
Curls, caps, and turbans,
Beaded and spangled wreaths, flowers and sprigs, new and elegant articles,
Black and white Ostrich feathers,
Feathered, velvet, and down flowers,
Bunches and wreaths of flowers,
Coral ear-drops and necklaces,
Fancy reticules, pin-cushions, &c.

The above articles were purchased this fall in the Northern cities, and will be sold on favorable terms.

Ladies' dresses, cloaks, pelisses, &c. made to order, in the latest and most approved fashions.

Leghorn and straw Bonnets bleached, dyed, or trimmed, at a short notice.
Tarborough, Oct. 30, 1828.

6-84
Like an increasing number of other women, Mrs. A. C. Howard entered the tailoring and retail clothing business, here advertised in the *Free Press* (Tarborough), 13 March 1829. (Courtesy North Carolina Collection.)

6-82
Mrs. Charles Gavin of Turkey made this bud and rose wreath quilt about 1820. (Courtesy NCDA&H.)

WILLIAM CAMP,
SADLER, HARNESS and CAP MAKER.

RESPECTFULLY informs the public, that he has on hand, and is making up at his manufactory in the city of Raleigh, Ladies and Gentlemen's Saddles of every description, on the most improved plan; a complete assortment of plated, polished and tinned, Portsmouth, halfguard, pelhamsharp and snaffle Bridles, with suitable furniture; Martingales with collars, plated Hooks, Slides, Buckles and Tips; Saddle-Bags, Valeices and Portmanteaus.

Coach and Chaise Harness in the newest taste, with the most fashionable furniture; Waggon Harness, &c. Horsemen's Caps, Holsters, Half Coverers, &c.

All which he will dispose of at the most reduced prices for cash or country produce.

He has also received from Philadelphia, a general assortment of Saddle and Harness Furniture and Ironmongery, which he will retail on reasonable terms.
November 13.   78

6-85
Through the *North-Carolina Journal* (Halifax), 20 November 1797, fashionable riding gear and habits were offered

for cash or "country produce." (Courtesy North Carolina Collection.)

SCHEME
OF THE
HALIFAX FACTORY LOTTERY,

FOR the purpose of raising 5000 dollars for the term of seven years, to enable CHRISTOPHER TAYLOR to establish an extensive FACTORY, for the purpose of carding, spinning, weaving, printing and dying of cotton, agreeable to an act of the last General Assembly.

	Doll.
6680 Tickets, at five dollars each, is	33,400
1 Prize of five thousand dollars, is	5000
1 Prize of one thousand dollars, is	1000
50 Prizes of one hundred dollars, is	5000
400 Prizes of twenty five dollars, is	10,000
500 Prizes of ten dollars, is	5000
1480 Prizes of five dollars is	7400
2412 Prizes.	33,400 dols.
4248 Blanks.	

The drawing of the above lottery will commence as soon as all the tickets are sold; the prizes to be paid in six weeks after the drawing is finished, upon the demand of the possessor of a fortunate ticket; which prizes shall be subject to a deduction of fifteen per cent. And if any such prize is not demanded within six months after the drawing is finished, the same shall be considered as relinquished for the benefit of the factory.

Tickets may be had of Mr. C. Taylor and the managers. WILLIE JONES, WILLIAM GILMOUR, BASSETT STITH, LUNSFORD LONG, THOMAS AMIS, } Managers.   48

6-87
A lottery to assist in the establishment of a textile factory in Halifax was announced in the *North-*

Carolina Journal (Halifax), 12 June 1797. (Courtesy North Carolina Collection.)

6-86
Elizabeth Dick Lindsay (1792–1845), wife of Andrew Lindsay, and her daughter, Mary Eliza Lindsay (later the wife of Wyatt F. Bowman), posed about 1825 for a painting that depicts high fashions in dress and

home furnishings in Guilford County. (Courtesy North Carolina Collection; reprinted, by permission, from Jo White Linn, *The Gray Family and Allied Lines* [Salisbury, 1976].)

6-88
Gottfried Aust (1722–88) is believed to have made in Wachovia this lead-glazed earthenware plate with slip

decoration. (Courtesy Old Salem Restoration.)

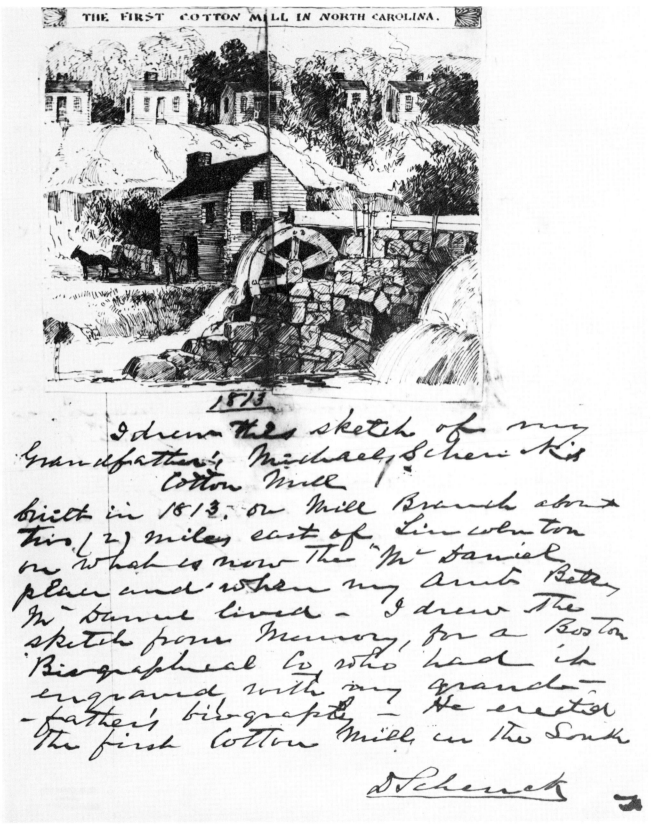

6-89
Michael Schenck, who built this mill in 1813 at Lincolnton, was joined three years later by Absalom Warlick in operating the first successful cotton mill in the state. (Courtesy North Carolina Collection.)

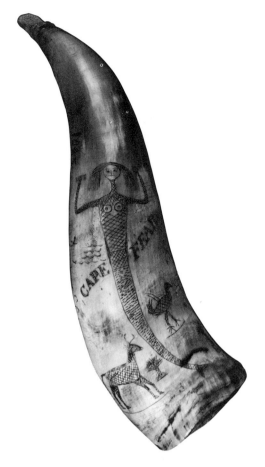

6-90

This powder horn, dated 18 March 1807, depicts a mermaid between the words "Cape" and "Fear," along with a comb, looking glass, and footed creatures. (Courtesy Museum of Early Southern Decorative Arts, Winston-Salem.)

6-91

A lead-glazed earthenware chamberpot, made by an unidentified North Carolina potter, was a useful item in early homes. (Courtesy Charles G. Zug III; by permission of Mr. and Mrs. William W. Ivey.)

Cabinet
FURNITURE.

THE Subscriber continues to make any article in his line, either of mahogany or walnut—also, plain and curled maple Bedsteads. Those who may please to favor him with their custom, may rely on having their furniture of good materials, in the modern style, and as faithfully executed as they can get from any of the northern cities. He has now on hand for sale:

One large mahogany Sideboard, with looking-glasses in the back board, four carved paws and columns in front.

One do. with a press on top of it for glass ware.

One mahogany Secretary and book case.

Two mahogany Bureaus, one with carved paws and columns, the other plain.

One mahogany Dressing-table, with carved pillar and claws.

A few pieces of walnut furniture.

ALSO, picture Glass, assorted sizes, from 10 by 12, to 25 by 35 inches.

Looking-glass plates, assorted, from $8\frac{1}{2}$ by $10\frac{1}{2}$, to 13 by 22 inches—those who have their looking-glasses broke and the frame good, can be furnished on moderate terms.

Copal Varnish, by the gallon or smaller measure.

Any of the above articles will be sold cheap for Cash.

Those indebted to the Subscriber, either by note or account, are particularly requested to settle the same between this and the first of May.

LEWIS BOND.

March 26th, 1829.

6-92

Fine furniture in mahogany, walnut, and maple was made by Lewis Bond, who advertised his stock in the *Free Press* (Tarborough), 3 April 1829. (Courtesy North Carolina Collection.)

6-93
John Swisegood (Swicegood) of the Abbotts Creek area of present-day Davidson County produced a wide assortment of furniture, including this walnut desk made for George Fultz in 1820. (Courtesy Museum of Early Southern Decorative Arts, Winston-Salem.)

6-94
Silver tobacco pipes, like this one that belonged to Abigail Sugars Jones of Warren County, were used occasion- ally after the Revolution. The silversmith is unknown. (Courtesy NCDA&H.)

6-96
One of North Carolina's most talented craftsmen was John Vogler of Salem, who turned out trigger lancets for bleeding humans or animals and a variety of other useful items. (Courtesy Old Salem Restoration.)

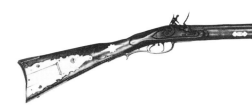

6-95
Longrifles—like this one made by "L M B" in Rowan County about 1815—were common for both hunting and protection. (Courtesy Museum of Early Southern Decorative Arts, Winston-Salem.)

6-97

The earliest known illustration of "People seeking for Gold in North Carolina" appeared in [Samuel Griswold Goodrich], *The First Book of History for Children and Youth*, published simul- taneously in Boston and Raleigh in 1833. By that time North Carolina was sometimes called "The Golden State." (Courtesy North Carolina Collection.)

NOTICE
TO GOLD MINERS & OTHERS.

C. BECHTLER, informs all interested in the gold mines and in assaying and bringing the gold of the mines into ingots or pieces of a standard value that he is now prepared to assay and stamp gold, to any amount, to a standard of 20 carats, making it into pieces of $2.50 and $5.00 value, at his establishment 3½ miles north of Rutherfordton, on the road leading from Rutherfordton to Jeanstown. The following are his prices:

For simply fluxing rough gold, ⅜ per cent.
For fluxing gold—to be stamped, ½ per cent.
For assaying gold, any quantity less than 3 lbs., $1.00
For stamping, 2½ per cent.
July 2, 1831. 20tf

6-99

In the *North Carolina Spectator and Western Advertiser* (Rutherfordton), 23 July 1831, Christopher Bechtler, newly arrived from Germany, announced the opening of what became the nation's most successful private mint. (Courtesy NCDA&H.)

Gold.—A new Gold Mine is discovered almost every week; and in fact, well nigh every day, in the county of Guilford.— These discoveries have produced considerable spirit and animation among our citizens. They have called many lazy lounging fellows, who once hung as a dead weight upon Society, into active & manly exertion. Many unfortunate men, who have long groaned under the iron hand of their unrelenting creditors, have by means of the gold digging interest, been enabled to square themselves with the world, and again place themselves in the ranks of independent men, bidding defiance to duns and constables. Tracts of land which have long gone begging at *three hundred dollars*, have recently been sold for *six thousand*. We like to *hear* these things, and we like to tell them. The rich treasure which our neighbors are digging from the bowels of the earth, will enable them to procure all the comforts and conveniences of life; and then we think it nothing but fair that they should reward us for our pains, by *subscribing to our Paper*. Greensboro' *Pat.*

6-98

An article in the *Greensborough Patriot* (here reprinted in the *Raleigh Register*'s semiweekly edition, 5 June 1829) described gold hunting activities in Guilford County. (Courtesy NCDA&H.)

6-100

Bechtler's coin press turned out gold coins like the one-dollar piece pictured here. Bechtler in fact minted the nation's first gold dollars. (Courtesy NCDA&H.)

6-101
In 1820–21, Joshua Shaw, an English landscape painter who settled in Philadelphia, combined with John Hill, an aquatintist, to produce *Picturesque Views of American Scenery*, the earliest series of aquatint views published in America. Among the twenty scenes was "View by Moonlight, near Fayetteville," of which this is a detail. (Courtesy Library of Congress.)

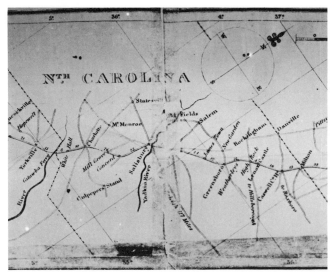

6-102
Map of the 1835 route through North Carolina of the South-Western Line of the United States Mail Coaches. (Courtesy North Carolina Collection.)

6-103
Advertisement of coach service from Morganton to Asheville in the *North Carolina Spectator and Western Advertiser* (Rutherfordton), 18 June 1831. (Courtesy NCDA&H.)

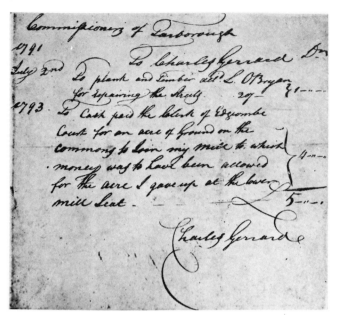

6-104
Planks were used to repair the streets of Tarborough as early as 1791. (Courtesy North Carolina Collection.)

6-105
The famed Horniblow's Tavern in Edenton was operated by Elizabeth Prichard Horniblow following her husband's death. (Courtesy Frick Art Reference Library, New York.)

EAGLE HOTEL,
AND STAGE-OFFICE,
RALEIGH, N. C.
CHARLES PARISH

INFORMS his Friends and the Public that his Tavern is now open for the reception of Travellers and Boarders in the new Three Story Brick-House, north of the State-House and fronting Union Square. The house is spacious, completely finished, and well furnished; and the Stables are equal to any. For a well supplied Table, (served from a neat and cleanly Kitchen,) luxuries of the Cellar, Rooms, Beds, Attendance, &c. &c. it is determined that this Tavern shall excel any in the Southern States.
Raleigh, July 1, 1812.

N. B. An ICE HOUSE and BATHING ROOMS will be constructed by the next Season.

. The Northern Stage arrives at this Tavern every other day to dinner.

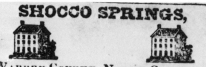

SHOCCO SPRINGS,

WARREN COUNTY. NORTH-CAROLINA.

ON the first day of June next, the houses at Shocco Springs, *nine* miles South of Warrenton and *three* miles from the Northern and Southern main Stage Roads, will be opened for the reception of Visitors. The great advantages of this watering place in most cases of disease and debility, have been so often tested by those who have attended it, that to such, it is only necessary to say, that all the buildings are in excellent repair and condition. The accommodations, in every respect, shall be such as my best efforts can effect, for comfort and convenience to all who may visit the place. To those who have not visited Shocco, it may be necesssary to say, that the buildings are sufficiently numerous, and conveniently arranged for the accommodation of a large assemblage. The private apartments will afford ample retirement to those who prefer it, and the public Halls are abundantly spacious to receive all who may desire company, and where music and dancing can be enjoyed by such as delight in it.

An arrangement will be made to have divine worship performed at the Spring on the Sabbath day, where such visitors as may choose, can attend preaching without inconvenience.

In addition to the valuable Medicinal qualities of the Shocco waters, it is located in a most healthy part of the county, surrounded by a polished society, where the invalid can be restored to health, in an agreeable circle.

My terms for board, &c. will be the same as last year, viz. $1 per day for each grown person; $22 50 per month, or $6 per week—Children and servants *half price.* For horses, $15 per month, or 60 cents per day.

ANN JOHNSON.

May 28, 1829.   78

The Fayetteville Observer, Cape Fear Recorder, Newbern Spectator, Halifax Minerva, Edenton Gazette, Tarboro' Free Press, Cheraw Spectator, Milledgeville Journal, Charleston Courier, Richmond Enquirer and Norfolk Herald will insert the above, *once a week* for *eight* weeks and forward their accounts to this Office for payment.

NOTICE.

THERE will be a BALL and PARTY furnished at Shocco Springs, on the evenings of the 1st and 2d of July.
Warren, May 28, 1829.

6-107
Shocco Springs in Warren County operated as a resort as early as the eighteenth century; here, in the *Raleigh Register* (semiweekly edition), 5 June 1829, owner Ann Johnson described accommodations. (Courtesy NCDA&H.)

6-106
The capital city's most famous hotel was the Eagle, facing Union Square, where the present Agriculture Building stands. "Bathing Rooms" had not been built when this advertisement appeared in 1812. (Courtesy North Carolina Collection.)

6-108
The Lake Drummond Hotel, on the Dismal Swamp Canal astride the North Carolina–Virginia border, was pictured in the *Norfolk and Portsmouth Herald*, 22 November 1830. (Courtesy Mariners Museum, Newport News, Virginia.)

6-109 and 6-110
Shell Castle and Harbor at Cape Lookout (left) and one of the Blount family's trans-Atlantic vessels, the *Tuley* (right), were pictured early in the nineteenth century on pottery pitchers of the Liverpool type. (Courtesy NCDA&H.)

Price Current,
At Tarboro', Petersburg & New-York.

APRIL 17.	per	Tar'o'		Pet'rg		NYo'k	
Bacon, - -	lb	6	7	6½	7	7	8
Beeswax, - -	-	20	25	25	30	23	24
Brandy, apple,	gal	45	50	30	45	36	40
Coffee, - -	lb	16	20	13	16	11	15
Corn, - - -	bul	30	35	40	45	50	53
Cotton, - -	lb	7½	8	7½	9	8¼	9½
Cotton Bagging,	-	20	25	20	25	19	21
Flour, supf. -	bbl	$6½	7	$8	8½	$7	8½
Lard, - -	lb	6	7	7	8	6	7
Molasses, - -	gal	40	50	35	40	27	32
Rum, New-Eng.	-	50	60	35	40	32	35
Sugar, brown, -	lb	11	13	9	12	8	11
Salt, loose,	bul	75	80	75	87	47	54
Wheat, - -	-	90	$1	$1¼	1½		
Whiskey, - -	gal	40	50	30	35	23	

North-Carolina Bank Notes.

At Petersburg, 2½ per cent. discount.
At New-York, 3 to 3½ do.

6-111
Comparative prices of commodities and the value of North Carolina bank notes were carried in the *Free Press* (Tarborough), 24 April 1829. (Courtesy North Carolina Collection.)

6-112
This portrait of John (1774–1833) and Ann (b. 1775) Stanly, children of John Wright Stanly, with their pet probably was painted in Philadelphia by Charles Willson Peale about 1782. (Courtesy Tryon Palace Restoration, New Bern.)

6-113
Visits to county seats—such as Warrenton, shown here in a painting by a Miss Somerville, ca. 1805, with the courthouse at left—provided diversions for farmers and their families. (Courtesy North Carolina Collection; by permission of Warren County Historical Society, Warrenton.)

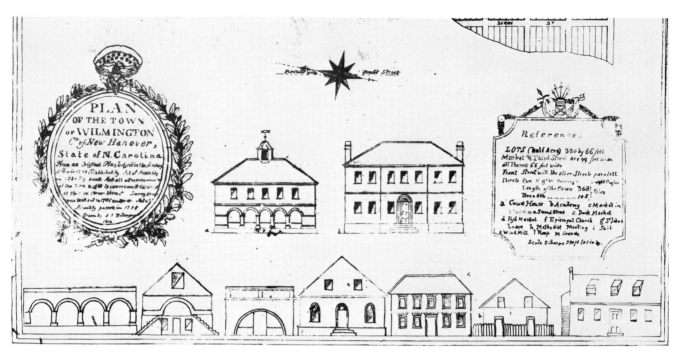

6-114
Public buildings of Wilmington were sketched on J. J. Belanger's map of 1810. The buildings at top are the courthouse (left) and the academy. At bottom are the central market, dock market, fish market, Episcopal Church, St. John's Lodge, Methodist Meetinghouse, and jail. (Courtesy NCDA&H.)

On Sabbath, the 15th day of October, 1797, there will be a Sermon preached in this town by a UNION MINISTER.

☞ The UNION MINISTER believes, that if all human inventions were laid aside, that it would be impossible that any more than one party could exist in the Christian church. He lovingly and kindly invites all the Lord's members to come and hear him. MOSES JENKINS.

UNION, RECONCILIATION, &c. &c. &c.

☞ THE HALIFAX RACES will commence on Thursday the 2d of November next. First day's purse, (for half the amount of the subscription) three mile heats; and third day's, (for the balance of the subscription) two mile heats. Weight for age, viz. three years old carrying 86lbs. four years old 100lbs. five years old 110lbs. six years old 120lbs. seven years old and upwards 130lbs.

On the intermediate day, the entrance money of the three days will be run for—mile heats, 100lbs. on each.

From the present state of the subscription, it is presumed that the above purses will be well worth contending for.

☞ THE Gentlemen subscribers to the HALIFAX RACES, are requested to pay the amount of their subscriptions at or before the 2d of November, to Mr. STITH, Mr. AMIS, or Mr. BARNES.

WILLIAMSTON RACES

WILL commence on Thursday, the 19th instant, free for any horse, mare or gelding. The first day, weight for age, two mile heats. The second day, 100lb. on each, two mile heats.

6-115
The *North-Carolina Journal* (Halifax), 9 October 1797, publicized two horse races and a Christian sermon. (Courtesy North Carolina Collection.)

The Celebrated Horse

SIR ARCHIE

Will stand the ensuing season at my stable, in Northampton county, North-Carolina, about 3 miles from the Court House, 9 miles from the town of Halifax, and 21 miles from Belfield, Va. He will cover mares at 75 dollars the season, payable on the 1st of January next, with one dollar to the groom in all cases. Such of Sir Archie's friends that live at a distance will send their notes with the mares, payable on the first of January; also feeding of the mares to be paid for when taken away. The season will commence on the first February, and terminate on the first of August.

Extensive fields of small grain and clover are sown for the benefit of mares, which may be left with the horse, with the addition of grain feeding, at 33 1-3 cents per day. Separate enclosures are provided for mares with colts. No pains will be spared in taking the best possible care of mares, &c. which may be left, but no responsibility for escapes or accidents.

☞ Sir Archie's blood, great size, performance on the turf, and celebrity as a foal getter, are sufficient recommendations.
JOHN D. AMIS.

February 13, 1827.

LAWRENCE & LEMAY, PRINTERS, RALEIGH.

6-116
Sir Archie, a fine racer and "foal getter," was the most famous horse ever to stand in North Carolina. (Courtesy Southern Historical Collection, Cameron Family Papers.)

6-117

The Jackson Jockey Club was one of the popular horse-racing organizations in northeastern North Carolina. Edmund Wilkins, who purchased this annual subscrip-

tion in 1833, owned the horse Omega. (Courtesy NCDA&H; original owned by Henry W. Lewis, Chapel Hill.)

6-119

Clocks made in Salisbury, plus "the newest and most approved style" of hairdressing by a "downright Hibernian," were advertised in the

North-Carolina Journal (Halifax), 26 September 1792. (Courtesy North Carolina Collection.)

6-118

Embroidery was a genteel pastime for women. Sarah Childress, future wife of James Knox Polk, made this piece while a student at Salem Female Academy in

1818. (Courtesy Ancestral Home of James K. Polk, Columbia, Tennessee; photograph by Orman Photo Shop.)

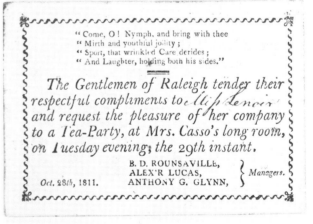

6-120

Martha (Patsy) Lenoir, daughter of General William Lenoir, received this invitation to a party at "Mrs. Casso's long room" in

Raleigh in 1811. (Courtesy Southern Historical Collection, Lenoir Family Papers.)

++++++++++++++++++++++++++++
BY AUTHORITY.

THIS EVENING, (May 21ſt)

At Mr. Barkſdale's Ball-Room, will be performed,

A Grand and Miſſcellaneous Entertainment of

ACTIVITY.

In Four Parts.

By JOHN W. ROBERTS.

Part Firſt

A variety of entertaining equipoiſes on the ſlackwire. Among many other ſurpriſing feats, he will ſtand on his head on the wire, on a quart bottle, with the wire in full ſwing.

Part Second.

A horn-pipe among a dozen of eggs, blindfolded.

Part Third.

Will be performed Harlequin's Maſquerade, or the Power of Magic. To which will be added a repreſentation in tranſpoſitions of the School for Scandal.

Part Fourth.

Will conclude with his ſurpriſing exertions on the ſlack cord.

Tickets may be had at Mr. Hartford's, at 6ſ each. No money taken at the door. To begin at half paſt 7.

6-121
Mrs. Barksdale's ballroom was the scene of a varied entertainment announced in the *North-Carolina Journal* (Halifax), 21 May 1794. (Courtesy North Carolina Collection.)

6-122
John Christian Blum purchased this 1810 Ramage printing press in Hillsborough and set up the first print shop in Salem. In 1829 he began publishing both the *Weekly Gleaner* and his popular *Blum's Farmers' and Planters' Almanac.* (Courtesy Old Salem Restoration; by permission of Wachovia Historical Society.)

RALEIGH THEATRE.

This Establishment opens on Monday, the 16th instant under the management of

MR. PRESTON.

The House, of late years, being so neglected as to render it almost unfit and uncomfortable for Ladies to enter, is now undergoing a thorough repair. And, instead of the cold stony (painted) Walls on the Proscenium and fronts of the Boxes, wh ch gave the looker-on a chill, will be found a soft warm painting of variegated colours, interm ngled with gold.

Over the Stage doors and Hollow wooden Windows, will hang a pair of fes ooned Curtain Drapery, neatly fitted up.

On the panel front of the Boxes will be seen figures of different shapes, tastefully painted by the young Artist of the Theatre, that would reflect credit on his great grandfather, with three times the experience.

And "last not feast," the Ladies' Boxes, are handsomely decorated, and the hitherto cold thick, clumsy benches, are transformed into beautiful crimson cushioned seats.

The broken Walls and Windows will have been repaired, and in short, the whole interior of the house is so altered as to make it almost unknown to the Theatre-going people of Raleigh.

By the opening, **Mr. Vincent** will have painted a new drop Curtain, and new Scenes, will follow. **Mr. Preston** has engaged an efficient, compact Stock Company from the different Northern Theatres, whose talents cannot be surpassed by any in the country. He has also a neat little Band, and he assures the public, that nothing shall be left undone that may add to the comfort and gratification of his Audience.

A strict Police will be employed to preserve order.

Hereafter will be given a List of the company.
Raleigh, Nov. 9, 1835. 52

The Old Lady's Addreſs:

I offer myſelf—but don't aſk for a vote,
For one that is aſk'd for, is not worth a groat;
Pray *ſend* me, my friends, but firſt give me the call,
For this *begging* in print, is not *aſking* at all.

Stick faſt to your oaths and your country ſo dear,
Then candidly me with thoſe fellows "compare,"
And if you're "*ingenious*," you'll find out at *once*,
That my rev'rend old hat ne'er cover'd a dunce.

My "learning" ſo deep, & my "knowledge" ſo ſound,
Compare with their bodies, ſo plump and ſo round;
And tho' much I don't *weigh*, put me inſide that door,
And, *almoſt* like a man, I will ſtrut "on the floor."

For my "aptneſs of ſtyle," and my "gentleman" air,
I *Command* you to ſend me, that C——ſs may ſtare,
And yet I can own with a *very good face*,
Should you "laviſh" on me, yourſelves you'll diſgrace.

"Let honour, decorum and truth," now prevail,
And malice and envy hung up by the tail,
And ſhould "tale untold" tell, that another's your choice,
To make his firſt ſpeech, I will lend him—*my voice.*

Whoever he be, may his merits be found,
Almoſt like my own, thro' the world to reſound,
His manners be graceful, deportment be free,
In ſhort, be in all things, a likeneſs of—ME.

I am yours to ſerve,

BETTY BORE.

Edenton, January 20.

6-123 (far left)
The Raleigh Theatre, according to the *Raleigh Register* (semiweekly edition), 17 November 1835, was grandly renovated, including a painted drop curtain. (Courtesy North Carolina Collection.)

6-124
The papers occasionally published poetry or other writings of local people. The *North-Carolina Journal* (Halifax), 6 February 1793, carried an "Old Lady's Address" in verse. (Courtesy North Carolina Collection.)

6-125
Hugh Williamson, the veteran statesman from Edenton, wrote the first history of North Carolina, published in 1812. (Courtesy Southern Historical Collection, John Haywood Papers.)

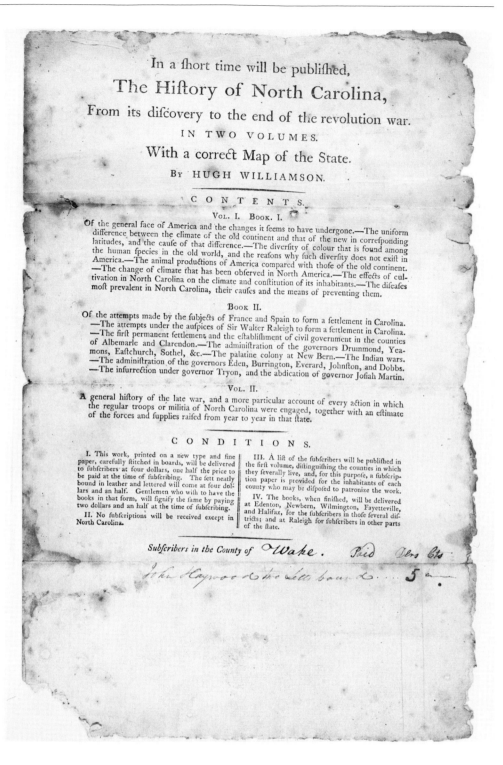

6-126
Francois-Xavier Martin (1762–1846), a French-born compiler of North Carolina laws while living in New Bern, moved to Louisiana, where he became attorney general and later chief justice. In 1829 he issued a two-volume cursory history of North Carolina. (Courtesy Louisiana State Museum, New Orleans.)

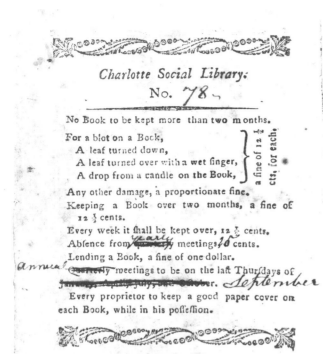

6-127
The Charlotte Social Library levied fines for turning a leaf with a wet finger and for failure to attend annual meetings. (Courtesy North Carolina Collection.)

6-128 (lower left)
Wilhelm Ludwig Benzien (1797–1832), shown here in a painting by Daniel Welfare, ca. 1830, was a popular music instructor in Salem. (Courtesy Old Salem Restoration, Winston-Salem.)

6-129
Subscription list for *Daniel's Selection*, published in Raleigh in 1812. No copy of the book is known to exist. (Courtesy North Carolina Collection.)

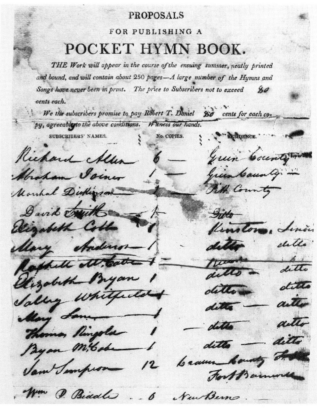

6-130
One of the few professional artists working in North Carolina in the early federal period was Jacob Marling (1774–1833), who painted this portrait of Mrs. John Mushro (Mary Elizabeth Jones) Roberts. In 1818, Marling opened the "North Carolina Museum" in Raleigh. (Courtesy Frick Art Reference Library, New York.)

6-131
This likeness of Archibald Henderson (1768–1822) is found in a Granville County record for 1788. Henderson was clerk of court in Granville before moving to Salisbury. He was a Federalist member of the Congress 1799–1803. (Courtesy NCDA&H.)

6-132
Charles Catton (1756–1819), an English painter who settled on a farm near the Hudson River in 1804, painted "Mill Dam at Fayette-Ville, No. Carolina." The scene is at Eccles Mill and Pond. The three-bay house at left center background is believed to have been the birthplace of Robert Donaldson, an early North Carolina promoter of the arts. (By permission of Print Collection, New York Public Library, Astor, Lenox, and Tilden Foundations, New York.)

6-135
Immigrant groups brought their own distinctive styles. German decorative treatment was evident in the John Stig- erwalt house, built in 1811 in Rowan County. (Courtesy North Carolina Collection.)

6-133
The Allen house was built near Snow Camp about the time of the Revolution and was representative of the substantial but plain homes of the Piedmont. It has been restored and relocated at the Alamance Battleground. (Courtesy NCDA&H.)

6-134
John Burgwyn, prosperous merchant of Wilmington and London, occupied "The Hermitage" on the north prong of Cape Fear River just prior to the Revolution. It burned in 1881. (Courtesy North Carolina Collection.)

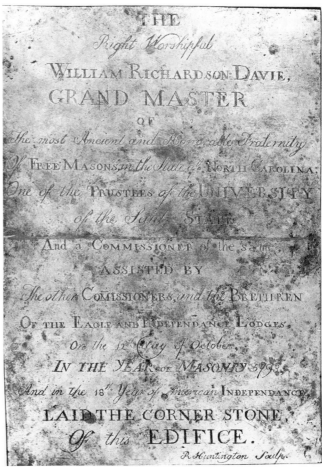

6-136
Roswell Huntington, a Connecticut silversmith who moved to Hillsborough, engraved the bronze plate commemorating the laying of the cornerstone for the university's first building (Old East) on 12 October 1793. (Courtesy North Carolina Collection.)

6-137
A student, John Pettigrew, made this drawing of East Building (now Old East) in 1797. (Courtesy Southern Historical Collection.)

6-138
A silhouette, cut from paper in 1814 by Frances Jones Hooper (wife of a professor, William Hooper), shows Main Building (now South) at right, Steward's Hall at left, and the bell tower in the center. (Courtesy Southern Historical Collection.)

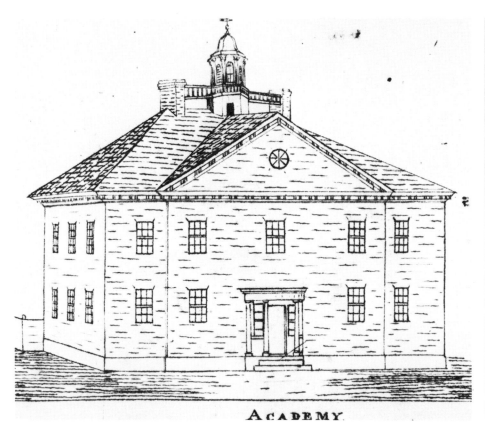

ACADEMY

6-139
New Bern Academy, drawn on Jonathan Price's map of New Bern, 1822, was one of the state's best schools. (Courtesy NCDA&H.)

6-140
The Raleigh Academy in 1808 issued scrip as a means of raising funds. (Courtesy American Antiquarian Society, Worcester.)

FEMALE EDUCATION
IN WARRENTON.

IN conformity to the wishes of some respectable Patrons in this place and its vicinity, I purpose to open an Institution for Female Improvement, on the first day of January next. The course of Instruction intended to be pursued, is the result of observation and some experience, and will be adapted to the varied dispositions and genius of my Pupils, not losing sight of systematic Arrangement and Progression. My object not merely to impart words and exhibit things; but chiefly to form the mind to the labour of thinking upon and understanding what is taught.— Whether my plan is judicious, a short experience will decide; and by the event I am content to be judged. The domestic arrangement for an emcient accommodation of my Scholars, will be an object of primary concern, and placed under the immediate inspection of Mrs. Mordecai—believing it to be no small part of Education bestowed on *Females*, to cultivate a *Taste* for neatness in their Persons and propriety of Manners: they will be placed under a superintendance calculated as much as possible to alleviate the solicitude of Parents.—In my Seminary will be taught the English Language grammatically, *Spelling*, Reading, Writing, Arithmetic, Composition, History, Geography and use of the Globes. The plain and ornamental branches of Needle Work—Drawing, Vocal and Instrumental Music, by an approved Master of distinguished talents and correct deportment.

TERMS—For Board, Washing, Lodging and Tuition (Drawing and Music excepted) $105 per annum. An additional charge will be made for necessary Books, Paper, Quills and Ink.

JACOB MORDECAI.
Warrenton, Aug. 18, 1808.

☞ Parents are requested to furnish a pair of sheets, a blanket, counterpane and hand-towels, which, without inconvenience to them, will render the accommodation of their daughters more easy and comfortable.

6-141
Jacob Mordecai operated the fashionable Mordecai Female Seminary in Warrenton. His advertisement appeared in the *Raleigh Register*, 1 September 1808. (Courtesy NCDA&H.)

Charlotte Male and Female Academy.

We, the subscribers, promise to pay the sums severally annexed to our names, for the purpose of erecting a Male and Female Academy in the Town of Charlotte, Mecklenburg county; which sums we promise to pay to the Trustees, in the following instalments, viz: One-fourth on the 1st of December next, and the balance in two annual payments, that is to say, one-half in December, 1824, the other half in December, 1825. Witness our hands, this 28th day of February, 1823.

N. B. It is agreed by the Trustees, that those who pay their subscriptions in advance shall have a discount of 10 per cent.

SUBSCRIBERS' NAMES.	SUMS SUBSCRIBED.

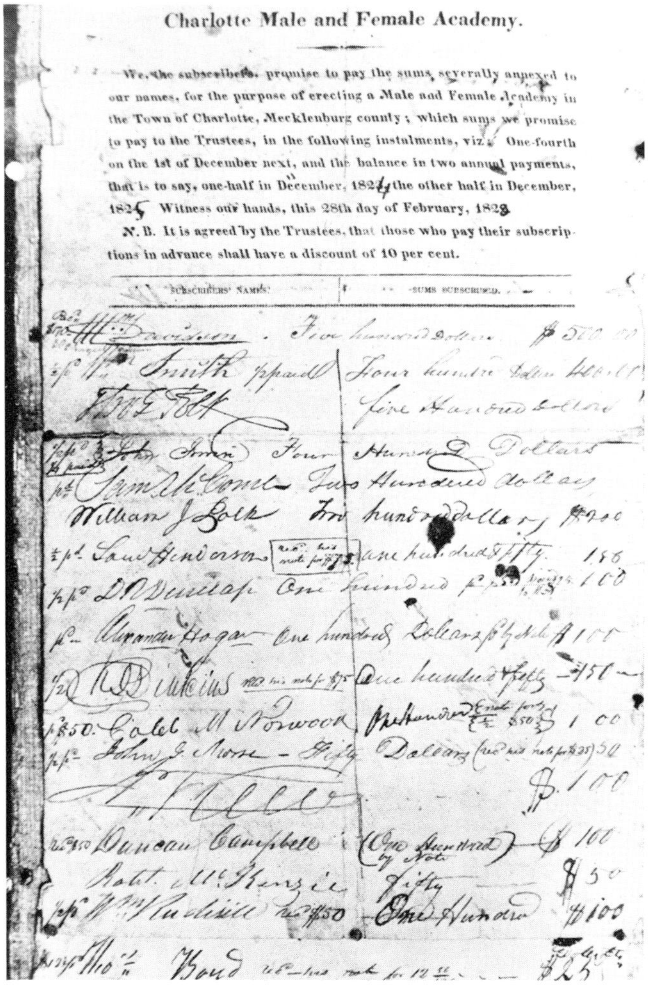

6-142
Subscription list for the construction of the Charlotte Male and Female Academy, 1823. (Courtesy North Carolina Collection; reprinted from Daniel A. Tompkins, *History of Mecklenburg County and the City of Charlotte* [Charlotte, 1903], volume 2.)

CIRCULAR.

Dearly Beloved,

THE Convention of the *Proteſtant Epiſcopal Church of America,* for the State of *North-Carolina,* at their Meeting held at Tarborough on the 21ſt day of November, 1793, *Reſolved,* That in conſideration of the great apparent decay of Virtue and vital Religion, every exertion was neceſſary to awaken and annimate the Zeal of thoſe Profeſsors of Chriſtianity, who call themſelves Members of the ſaid Church; have therefore thought proper to addreſs a Circular Letter to thoſe of the ſame perſuaſion in each County in the State, and requeſt you would convene at ſome public place, as the Church or Court-Houſe on an early day, thoſe of the Inhabitants who are deſirous of WORSHIPING GOD according to the Rules and Ceremonies as ſet forth in our *Book of Common Prayer*; and that order and good government may be reſtored, it is warmly recommended by the Convention to You, to ſelect from among yourſelves Perſons of good Morals and unexceptional Characters to act as a Veſtry, whoſe duty it ſhall be to procure a neighbouring Clergyman who has been regularly Ordained according to the form of the Proteſtant Epiſcopal Church, to Preach as often as convenient for the diſtance he may reſide at from you, and Adminiſter the Holy Ordinances at proper Times, but particularly the *Bleſſed Sacrament of the Lord's Supper,* at leaſt thrice every year, and on thoſe Sabbaths on which he cannot attend in conſequence of his other appointments, indiſpoſition or any other cauſe, that one of the Veſtry read the Service of the day, and ſome religious Diſcourſe to the People—By this means it appears probable the Members of our Church may again be collected, many of whom it is to be lamented, wander as ſheep without a Shepherd.

And may Almighty GOD in his mercy, bleſs your endeavours, that the happy purpoſe, the ſalvation of ſouls, for which we recommend theſe things to your practice, may be effected.

We commit you to the ſafe keeping and kind protection of our Heavenly Father, and ſhall always preſent our humble but fervent addreſſes to the Throne of Grace for your temporal proſperity and everlaſting happineſs.

With ſentiments of affection and charity, we are your Brethren in Our Lord and Saviour Jeſus Chriſt.

Signed in behalf of the Convention of the P. E. C. *for the State of* North-Carolina,

James L. Wilſon, Preſident.

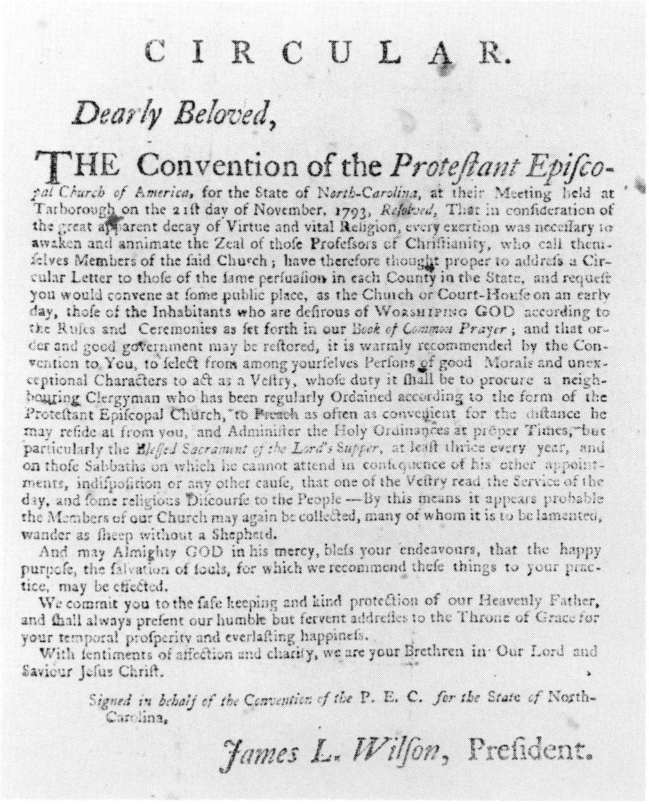

6-143
Despite efforts in the 1790s, the Episcopal church was not formally organized in North Carolina until 1817. (Courtesy NCDA&H.)

INOCULATION.

JONATHAN JACOCKS has a brick houſe, 30 feet ſquare, with three floors, ſituated on Walnut-Point, near Albemarle Sound, about two miles from his Ferry, which he will open on the 15th of May next, for the reception of ſuch perſons as are deſirous to have the SMALL-POX. The ſituation is pleaſant, a handſome proſpect, and quite retired.—The houſe will be continued open for this purpoſe until the 15th of Auguſt, if ſufficient encouragement is afforded.—Board and Lodging, with Attendance and Medicine, will be Ten Dollars for each white, or free perſon; and Six Dollars for each ſlave.—Accommodations for 50, or (with the addition of ſome out-houſes) 100 perſons, may be had.

Bertie county, April 28, 1798.

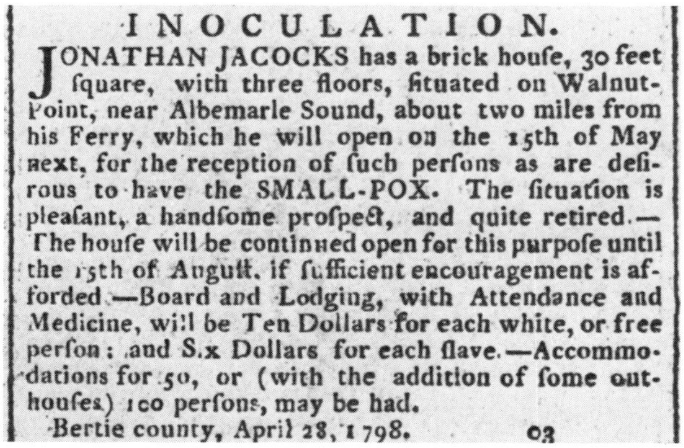

6-144
In 1798 on Walnut Point in Bertie County, Jonathan Jacocks opened a house where patients could recuperate from inoculation for smallpox. (Courtesy North Carolina Collection; reprinted from *North-Carolina Journal* [Halifax], 28 May 1798.)

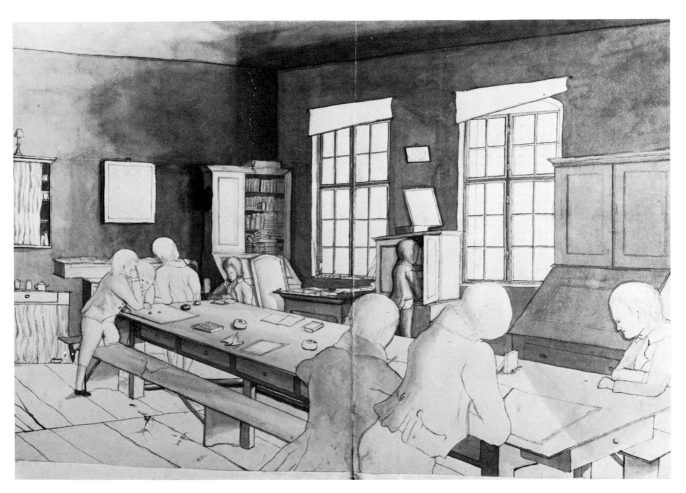

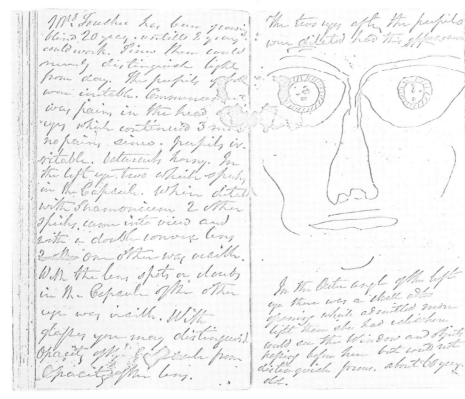

6-145
A Moravian boys' schoolroom, probably in Salem, was drawn by an unidentified artist about 1795. (Courtesy Old Salem Restoration; by permission of Moravian Archives, Winston-Salem.)

6-146
Calvin Jones (1775–1846), soldier and physician, in his journal in 1818 sketched eye ailments of a Mrs. Foushee. Jones served in the War of 1812 and later helped establish Wake Forest Institute. (Courtesy NCDA&H.)

6-147
The school (left) and Moravian meetinghouse at Friedland were built about the time of the Revolution. The community was settled by Moravians from Maine. (Courtesy Old Salem Restoration.)

6-148
German was still in common use in 1814 when Felix Gladfelter's tombstone was placed in the cemetery of Bethany Lutheran and German Reformed Church in present-day Davidson County. (Courtesy Museum of Early Southern Decorative Arts, Winston-Salem.)

6-149
William Hill (1773–1857), who until 1982 held the record for length of service as secretary of state, was converted to Methodism when Bishop Francis Asbury preached in the State House in Raleigh. (Courtesy North Carolina Collection.)

6-151
William Gaston (1778–1844), a Catholic, defied the constitutional ban and was repeatedly elected to office by his fellow citizens. This watercolor on ivory was painted by James Peale in 1796. (Courtesy Frick Art Reference Library, New York.)

6-150
Twelve-year-old Caroline Barge (later Mrs. D. A. Ray) in 1822 made this drawing of the first Presbyterian church building in Fayetteville. (Courtesy NCDA&H.)

Mr. Mills moved that the house do enter into the following resolution :

WHEREAS it is contrary to the freedom and independence of our happy and beloved government, that any person should be allowed to have a seat in this Assembly, or to watch over the rights of a free people, who is not constitutionally qualified for that purpose; it is therefore made known, that a certain Jacob Henry, a member of this house, denies the divine authority of the New Testament, and refused to take the oath prescribed by law for his qualification, in violation of the Constitution of this State. *Resolved.* That the said Jacob Henry is not entitled to a seat in this house, and that the same be vacated. The resolution being read, the house resolved that the consideration thereof be postponed until to-morrow.

6-152
Although William Gaston and Jacob Henry, Catholic and Jew, respectively, were allowed to serve in the House of Commons in 1808, a resolution was introduced on 5 December the following year seeking Henry's ouster. The next day the house concluded that "no proof had been adduced in support of the charges," and the constitutional ban against officeholding by Catholics and Jews was thus ignored. (Courtesy North Carolina Collection.)

7. Revival, Reform, and Reaction, 1835–1865

By the end of the third decade of the nineteenth century, North Carolina had acquired the unflattering sobriquet the "Rip Van Winkle State." This backwardness, however, was not altogether owing to drowsiness, for there was also outright resistance to change. The laissez-faire political philosophy of Nathaniel Macon was quite acceptable to many North Carolinians, who saw in the governmental activism proposed by progressives like Archibald D. Murphey a potential for an increased tax burden and an erosion of individual rights.

For the twenty years preceding 1835, the expenditure for the entire state government averaged only $132,000 per year, and most of that was spent on yearly sessions of the General Assembly and salaries of state officials. Even the taxes levied to provide these funds, however, were considered oppressive by people who depended upon subsistence farming for a living, for from 1815 to 1838 agriculture was almost continually in a state of depression. Many families thought they saw greener pastures elsewhere, and a growing stream of North Carolinians emigrated to such states as Tennessee, Georgia, Alabama, and Indiana. By 1840 North Carolina's population was increasing at only a miniscule rate, so great was the loss to emigration.

Dissatisfaction with economic and social conditions was most pronounced in the backcountry. There distances to markets were great, transportation was difficult and expensive, educational facilities were almost nonexistent, and slavery was not a consuming issue. Westerners, therefore, favored internal improvements, but a legislature controlled by easterners repeatedly thwarted their wishes.

The inequitable formula for legislative representation was based on the constitution of 1776, under which each county, regardless of its population, elected one senator and two representatives. As the population of the west increased, the legislature only begrudgingly created additional counties; by 1830 thirty-six eastern counties with only 41 percent of the population controlled 58 percent of the seats in the General Assembly. Furthermore, legislators were the only officials elected by vote of the people; the others—governor, council of state, judges, and justices of the county courts who controlled local government—were all chosen or confirmed by the General Assembly. In short, the policies of both state and local governments were dictated by a legislature generally unresponsive to the needs of the most populous region of the state. And, to make matters worse, the inequity was the product of a state constitution that provided no specific means of amendment.

The movement for constitutional reform was not new, but it became such a volatile issue early in the 1830s that talk of secession was heard in the west. By that time some easterners too saw the need for constitutional change. For instance, shocked by the Nat Turner rebellion and the intensification of the antislavery movement, some wanted to eliminate the voting rights of free blacks. There also was growing sentiment for reducing expenditures by limiting sessions of the legislature to alternate years, for allowing the people to elect the governor, and for removing the ban on officeholding by Catholics. Still, in a statewide referendum on the question, a convention was supported by a margin of fewer than 6,000 votes. Out of a total vote statewide of 49,244, only 3,611 easterners voted for a convention and just 2,701 westerners voted against it.

The Convention of 1835, presided over by the aging conservative Nathaniel Macon, managed to agree upon a slate of proposed amendments, but only with great difficulty. They were approved in another sectional vote, the east voting heavily in the negative.

The amendments barely met the minimum demands of the westerners. Representation in the house of commons was to be based on the principle of "federal population" and in the senate on the amount of taxes paid; the legislature henceforth was to meet biennially; the governor was to be chosen for two years by eligible voters; borough representation was abolished; and provision was made for future amendments. Liberalism, however, did not carry the day: Free blacks were denied suf-

7-1

7-3

frage, and despite an eloquent plea from William Gaston for removal of all religious qualifications for holding office, the only change adopted was the substitution of the word *Christian* for *Protestant*. Thus, while the amendments legitimized Catholic Gaston's service, the constitution proscribed voting by free blacks and officeholding by non-Christians.

Even though it produced only limited constitutional change, the Convention of 1835 marked a turning point in the history of North Carolina. It occurred while the new state capitol was under construction and as a two-party system was emerging; and the amendments, particularly the provision for a more democratic formula of representation, changed the tone of politics and encouraged participation by a larger voting population. The new Whig party, though stronger in the west, cut across sectional lines; the Democratic party, dominated by eastern planters, was also supported by some influential westerners.

As political party discipline increased, legislators began to cast their votes on the basis of issues rather than geography. The victorious Whigs adopted a program of governmental activism similar to that advocated by Murphey more than a decade earlier, and they inaugurated an era of unprecedented progress and reform that eventually forced the Democrats to abandon their negativism and to develop popular issues of their own. In the quarter-century following the convention, the state developed a system of common schools, built institutions to care for the physically and mentally handicapped, reformed laws, adopted less harsh penalties for criminal offenses, and assisted in the building of an extensive network of roads and railroads. Tragically, however, the humanitarian impulse of the era was restricted to whites. For blacks, there was only increased repression, and for many native Americans, there was exile from their own land.

The first statewide gubernatorial election, in 1836, stimulated widespread interest and a record-breaking turnout of more than sixty-three thousand. Both candidates—incumbent Richard Dobbs Spaight, Jr., and Edward B. Dudley—were easterners, but Whig Dudley favored the use of tax funds for internal improvements, which put him in agreement with most westerners. His margin of victory was slim, but two years later he won reelection by a landslide against former governor, senator, and federal cabinet officer John Branch. In that

same election the Whigs gained control of both houses of the General Assembly for the first time. They remained the strongest party until mid-century.

Ironically, the success of the Democratic administration of Andrew Jackson facilitated the acceptance of Whig policies in North Carolina. During his presidency the federal debt was paid off and surplus funds were allocated to the states. The Whig leadership invested most of North Carolina's share—nearly $1.5 million—in their programs to improve the state: about 40 percent was used to purchase bank stock, strengthening the state's banking system; a slightly lesser amount was used to purchase stock in railroads, providing capital desperately needed by the two railroads under construction; and a smaller portion was used to encourage other internal improvements, especially draining swamplands. Returns from these investments were applied to the Literary Fund.

Shortly after the demonstration of the first successful railroad in America, many in North Carolina became interested in the new mode of transportation. In 1827, Joseph Caldwell, president of the University of North Carolina, proposed the linking by rail of Beaufort in the east and Tennessee in the west. Public meetings along the proposed route discussed the issue and promoted the notion of state assistance for the project. The legislature authorized several private companies to sell stock, but offered no state aid.

In 1833, the Petersburg Railroad was extended about nine miles across the North Carolina border to Blakely (in Northampton County, across the Roanoke River from present-day Weldon), which became a stagecoach, wagon, and boat destination for connections to the north. The Wilmington and Raleigh Railroad (originally "Rail Road") Company, chartered in 1834, failed to elicit sufficient sales of stock in the capital city and consequently changed its proposed terminus from Raleigh to Weldon (its name was changed to the Wilmington and Weldon in 1854). Stung by this development, Piedmont promoters chartered the Raleigh and Gaston Company in 1835.

Both lines would provide connections with the Petersburg Railroad, but perceptive North Carolinians observed that these connections with the north failed to meet the needs for east-west transportation within the state. Nevertheless, when the two companies ran into financial difficulties, the General Assembly came to their aid by authorizing the purchase of stock by the state. Trains began running on both tracks in 1840, and in Raleigh a three-day celebration in June marked not only the completion of the Raleigh and Gaston Railroad but also the dedication of the proud new state capitol, which had cost the impoverished state more than a half million dollars.

7-7

State aid to railroads—at first favored by the Whigs and opposed by the Democrats—was an issue in all gubernatorial campaigns of the 1840s. The successful Whigs, John Motley Morehead (1841–45) and William A. Graham (1845–49), strongly advocated construction of lines east and west, to facilitate transportation within the state. Competition between supporters of different routes delayed the success of the plan until 1849 when, with the support of a few eastern Democrats and the deciding vote of Speaker Calvin Graves in the senate, the General Assembly approved a bill under which the state purchased two million dollars worth of stock in the North Carolina Railroad Company, to be built through Raleigh from Goldsboro to Charlotte. Segments of the road were opened earlier, and the full 223-mile length was in use in 1856. Meanwhile, the Atlantic and North Carolina Railroad was extending the line to the seaport of Beaufort, and by 1860 western connections had been made almost to Morganton, and construction was underway on several other lines. At last, the heartland of the state had been opened and, as one statesman put it, North Carolina had declared its economic independence.

7-11

7-12

7-13

Railroads, as important as they were, failed to meet all the needs of farmers; roads for animal-powered vehicles remained essential. Such roads traditionally had been the responsibility of land-owners, who were required by the county court to furnish "hands" for a number of days each year. A few private turnpike companies had been chartered, and private ferries operated under fees set by the county court. For a century or more logs or puncheons had been used to provide a surface in places where the soil was unstable, and in the 1840s the idea of connecting distant communities by plank roads was discussed. In the last year of the decade the General Assembly chartered the Fayetteville and Western Plank Road Company. When completed, this road stretched from the Cape Fear River to Bethania, the longest plank road in the world.

7-15

7-17

Subsequently, dozens of these companies were chartered, and six different plank roads radiated

7-16

from Fayetteville alone. "Farmers' railroads," these new all-weather transportation routes were called. Tolls varied, but the Fayetteville and Western charged a half cent per mile for a man on horseback, one cent for a one-horse vehicle, and four cents for a six-horse team. Plank roads brought considerable benefit to the state in the 1850s, but they were doomed to decay, and repair work was far more expensive than had been anticipated. Within a decade after they were built, most had been abandoned. Many of the roadbeds, however, continued in use as dirt roads.

Though transportation routes had been improved and lengthened, travel was still slow and tedious. Railroad cars were crude, and stagecoaches were bumpy and often crowded and smelly; furthermore, wagons and horseback remained the predominant modes of travel. John Hardy Steele, a Salisbury native who later served as governor of New Hampshire, described a trip from Henderson to Raleigh in 1838: "We were standing for more than half an hour on the damp ground half burning half freezing over a pine not fire waiting for Stages to get ready to carry us to Raleigh. . . . It was not much better when we took seats in the Coach which was to carry us onward. Both linings and quishions were thoroughly wet, there was no alternative this Coach or none. Fortunately one of the passengers had a Buffalow Robe which he spread on one of the seats."

7-14

7-18

7-19

Water transportation, too, was primitive. Frederick Law Olmsted wrote in the 1850s that at Gaston there were "long, narrow, canoe-like boats, of light draft, in which the produce of the country along the head waters of the Roanoke was brought to market. They were generally manned by three men each, who were sheltered at night under a hood of canvas, stretched upon poles, in the stern of the boat. The mouth of this hood opened upon a bed of clay, laid upon the boat's bottom, on which a fire was made, that would keep them warm, and cook their food."

Steamers on the Cape Fear offered more comfortable facilities. One early steamer, the *Cotton Plant*, made its maiden trip to Wilmington in 1826. It offered music, dancing, and other diversions. Along the seashore, and to a lesser extent in the interior, resort communities began to develop, providing competition for the famed "watering holes," such as Shocco Springs.

7-20

7-21

Not a single public school had resulted directly

7-22 from the Literary Fund since its establishment in 1825, but the Whigs had wisely chosen to assign to the fund dividends from the stock purchased by the state in banks and internal improvements companies. By 1839 the fund was worth about two million dollars; state assistance in the establishment of common schools awaited only the will of the legislature, since higher taxes would not be required at the state level.

7-23 That year the General Assembly passed a public school law that directed referendums in each county. If a majority of the voters of a county favored public schools, the county court was to lay out school districts, each with a school committee. Committees that furnished a structure and raised twenty dollars in local taxes could apply to the State Literary Fund for forty dollars. The total of sixty dollars was sufficient to hire a teacher for several months. Although seven counties—Columbus, Davidson, Edgecombe, Lincoln, Rowan, Wayne, and Yancey—initially voted against having schools, this modest piece of legislation provided the basis for the establishment of North Carolina's common school system. On 20 January 1840 the community of Williamsburg in Rockingham County opened the state's first publicly financed school. By 1850 more than one hundred thousand students were enrolled in nearly three thousand schools, most of them small and wretched but all providing a few months of free education for white children.

7-24 The state's role was strengthened significantly in 1853 when Calvin H. Wiley, an attorney and author, accepted the newly created position of superintendent of common schools. He wrote a text-
7-25 book, *The North-Carolina Reader*, founded the *North Carolina Journal of Education*, established institutes for teacher training, devised examinations and certification for teachers, served as an effective public relations agent for the cause of education, and until 1865 presided over the best state system of public education in the South. Still, the tardiness with which the government had assumed its role in education perpetuated the stereotype described by Frederick Law Olmsted in the mid-1850s: "North Carolina has a proverbial reputation for the ignorance and torpidity of her people; being, in this respect, at the head of the Slave States." Fully one-fourth of the white adults could not read and write in 1860.

The awakening of Rip Van Winkle was accompanied by modest progress in private education. While common schools after 1840 replaced many of the old field schools, families willing to pay tuition were still attracted by private schools with higher academic standards. According to the census of 1860, there were 434 academies and other private schools in North Carolina with a combined enrollment of 13,169 students.
7-26
7-27
7-28

7-30 The University of North Carolina remained the only institution of higher learning until the decade
7-31 of the 1830s. Still without regular appropriations from the legislature, the university was given new life by President Joseph Caldwell, whose involvement in progressive political issues brought public attention to the institution. Caldwell also brought to Chapel Hill a graduate of Yale, Elisha Mitchell, who introduced new instruction in mathematics and the sciences and explored the mountain later
7-29 named for him, on which he fell to his death. Under Caldwell's successor, former governor David Lowry Swain, the enrollment increased from 104 to 456 between 1835 and 1859.

Swain may have done more than any other antebellum citizen to stimulate interest in the state's history and literature. In 1844 he founded the first active state historical society and the *University of North Carolina Magazine*. He also collected books and manuscripts and collaborated with such au-
7-32 thors as John Hill Wheeler, whose fact-filled and error-prone history was published in 1851, and Francis Lister Hawks, an Episcopal clergyman who published two volumes later in the decade. Meanwhile, newspapers increased, as did the number of those reading them. By 1860 eight dailies and fifty-
7-33 six nondaily newspapers were being published in the state, and sensitivity to the state's cultural backwardness encouraged the establishment of a number of special-interest journals.
7-34

Four schools that grew into institutions of higher learning were opened during the 1830s—
7-35 Wake Forest Institute in Wake County by the Bap-
7-36 tists; New Garden Boarding School (Guilford College) in Guilford County by the Quakers;
7-37 Davidson College in Mecklenburg County by the Presbyterians; and Union Institute (Trinity College and, later, Duke University) in Randolph County by a Methodist minister, Brantley York. Of these, only New Garden initially admitted women,
7-38 but Salem Boarding School, founded in 1802 by the Moravians, had long provided excellent education for women. It was joined in 1838 by the
7-39 Methodists' Greensboro Female College and four years later by the Episcopalians' St. Mary's School in Raleigh. Other institutions were opened in sub-

sequent years, and the census of 1860 listed sixteen colleges in the state with 1,540 students, male and female. Thus, though the number of institutions was rather impressive, enrollment was low except at Chapel Hill.

Less than half the adult white population belonged to any church. Not unexpectedly, the evangelical sects associated with the backcountry revival movements were strongest: the Baptists were most numerous, with about 65,000 members, followed closely by the Methodists with about 61,000. Far 7-40 behind in numbers came the Presbyterians with 15,000. The Episcopalians counted only 3,036 communicants on the eve of the Civil War, but, true to their tradition, they still exercised an influence beyond their numerical strength.

Additional humanitarian reforms grew from Whig initiative. Care for the handicapped had long been a local matter, but state support was needed if adequate institutions were to be provided. The widespread belief that the deaf and dumb were uneducable was dramatically contested in 1843 when Governor Morehead invited William D. Cooke, the head of a Virginia school for the deaf, to demonstrate his pupils' learning ability before the General Assembly. The next year the legislature appropriated a small amount from the Literary Fund for experimental education, and in 1845 a school for 7-41 the deaf was opened in Raleigh under Cooke's superintendency. Funds for a new building were soon appropriated, and within a few years a department for the blind was added.

A nonresident also played an influential role in persuading the legislature to establish a state asylum for the mentally ill. Dorothea L. Dix of Massachusetts, a noted exponent of state hospitals, toured North Carolina and found scores of mentally ill persons receiving primitive treatment in dirty and crowded jails, in appalling county "poorhouses," and in squalid private homes. Her report, 7-42 submitted in 1848, shocked state legislators. With the assistance of Fayetteville's James C. Dobbin, whose terminally ill wife Dorothea Dix had befriended, proponents of a bill to establish an institution finally were successful, and construction 7-43 of the State Hospital for the Insane was begun.

Efforts toward appropriating state funds for the 7-50 care of prisoners, orphans, alcoholics, and the poor were unsuccessful, and counties retained responsibility for these unfortunates. The state's harsh penal code was relaxed somewhat, but there remained a dozen offenses that were punishable by hanging. Corporal punishment likewise was only

slightly lessened, though branding, mutilation, and use of the ducking stool, pillory, and stocks were applied less frequently against whites. After former governor Benjamin Smith—one of the university's most generous benefactors—died in prison while incarcerated for debt, public sentiment led to alteration of the law regarding debtors.

The rights of white women were enhanced by an act of 1848 which made it illegal for husbands to misuse real estate owned by the woman before their marriage, and the branding, whipping, and forcing of women to work in public were also outlawed. Notwithstanding, the husband retained control over almost every aspect of his wife's life, and voteless women exercised only minor political influence in a male-oriented society.

Pine trees yielded the raw material for North Carolina's largest industry. Perhaps two-thirds of the naval stores produced in the United States in 1860 came from North Carolina's 1,526 turpentine distilleries, which were mostly located along the Cape Fear in Bladen and New Hanover counties. Thousands of workers, mostly black, were en- 7-51 gaged in tapping the trees, operating the stills, and barreling and transporting the pine products to the banks of the river for shipment to Beaufort and Wilmington. Milling of grain was close behind 7-52 naval stores in value of production, with tobacco manufacturing—mostly in the counties along the Virginia border from Granville to Stokes—in third place. Fourth was lumber and saw milling.

Although the cotton textile industry had been introduced earlier, it still ranked only fifth among industries in 1860, employing 1,764 workers and producing a million dollars worth of goods. A majority of the thirty-nine textile factories were scattered through the Piedmont, where water was available as a source of power; among the best known were Edwin M. Holt's mill on Great Alamance Creek, which in 1853 introduced "Ala- 7-53 mance Plaids," the first colored cloth manufac- 7-54 tured in the South, and Henry Humphreys's 7-55 Mount Hecla Steam Cotton Mill in Greensboro.

Farmers in several sections of the state—particularly in Halifax, Guilford, Cabarrus, Mecklenburg, Montgomery, and Burke—spent portions of their time digging for gold, and a few operations were large enough to be called mines. The most spectacular development occurred in Rowan County at 7-56 Gold Hill, which became in the 1840s a genuine 7-57 gold-rush town with a thousand workers, includ- 7-58 ing Cornish miners imported to oversee the extrac- 7-59 tion of ore from the gold-bearing quartz veins far below the surface. North Carolina's gold industry faced competition following the discovery of the precious metal near Dahlonega in Georgia, but it was not eclipsed until the California gold rush of 1849. Iron ore was mined on a small scale in Lincoln, Stokes, and a few other counties, and coal was taken from the Deep River area of Chatham County.

The continued predominance of agriculture in the economy of the state was indicated by the census of 1860, which identified only twenty-five towns; Wilmington, with 9,552 inhabitants, was by far the largest, followed by New Bern with only 5,432. After the depression of 1837 agriculture experienced an era of relative prosperity. Tobacco production increased significantly in both quantity and quality, and cotton emerged as a money crop in a swath of counties. Grains, including rice in the lower Cape Fear, were produced in larger quantities, a considerable proportion for the market. Reflecting renewed enthusiasm for farming, the State Agricultural Society, organized in 1852, sponsored the first state agricultural fair the following year and issued publications to encourage farmers to adopt improved cultivation practices such as fertilizing, crop rotation, deep plowing, and contour plowing. Old ways die slowly, however, and improved methods of farming attracted the interest of only a small proportion of farmers.

The Piedmont continued to produce an impressive number of craftsmen; and teachers, attorneys, and physicians—often with only a modicum of professional schooling—located wherever their services were in sufficient demand. This often meant the county seats, where opportunities for those whose talents and interests included the legal, military, business, or social arts were plentiful. Itinerants often introduced new products and services. For instance, "Mr. Humphrey" came to Wilmington from New York early in 1846 and for a year offered "daguerreotype miniatures" in the town; six years later, however, Isaac Briggs advertised his "Daguerreian Gallery" in the Female Academy building in Salisbury and promised "superior likenesses, not commonly possessed by itinerant operators." Almost every demand initially met by itinerants became a home industry within a few years.

The antebellum period was characterized by an increasingly distinct stratification of society. Relative prosperity in agriculture produced a substantial number of wealthy planters, and they in turn contributed to the well-being of business and professional people. In 1860, heads of households owning twenty slaves or more numbered 4,065, and they, with a few prominent town dwellers, formed a class that aspired to aristocracy. Still, they made up only about 5 percent of the white population. A less pretentious class of property owners, both rural and urban, made up about a quarter of the white population, leaving in a third class fully two-thirds of the whites—small farmers, tenants, and laborers.

Almost three out of four North Carolina families owned no servants at all, and of the 34,658 slaveholding families, nearly three-fourths possessed fewer than ten. Furthermore, while 311 planters owned a thousand acres or more, 46,300 farmers owned fewer than a hundred acres each. Thus North Carolina, despite a concentration of slaveholders in the cotton- and tobacco-growing counties, had overall a low incidence of slavery. With the ascendance of the Democrats in the 1850s, however, the wealthy planters exercised political power far beyond their numbers.

Contrasts in standards of living between the social classes were naturally exhibited in homes, furnishings, dress, and diversions. Log structures, sturdy and easy to build, provided homes for a growing number of poor farmers; in fact, log construction reached its peak in the nineteenth century. But the demand for fashionable structures attracted a few architects whose plans, often copied by local builders, changed the architectural landscape of the state. By mid-century Victorian furnishings—their gaudiness reflective of the social veneer of the nouveau riche—had often replaced the more dignified styles of earlier periods.

Better times for whites did not translate into better times for other North Carolinians—Indians, free blacks, and Negro slaves.

From colonial days the story of the white man's relations with the Indians was a record of broken promises. As whites encroached upon Indian lands, new treaties were negotiated, and they too were soon violated. By the turn of the century North Carolina's Cherokees had been shoved into the southwest corner of the state along the Tuckasegee, Little Tennessee, and Hiwassee rivers. Their kinsmen lived nearby in Georgia, Alabama, and Tennessee, and when gold was discovered in north Georgia, whites respected no boundaries as they rushed in. Georgia led the efforts to force the Indians out of the mountains, and in 1835 one faction of the Cherokees signed the Treaty of New

Echota with the federal government, under which they gave up title to their lands east of the Mississippi in return for five million dollars and guarantees of good land in the Oklahoma territory. At that time there were 16,542 Cherokees, of whom 3,644 lived in North Carolina.

The treaty, however, was angrily repudiated by a large segment of the Cherokees, and it was enforced only after President Andrew Jackson sent in thousands of soldiers under command of General Winfield Scott. The removal to the Oklahoma territory—the "Trail of Tears," on which about one-fourth of the travelers died—did not end until 1839. A thousand or more Cherokees were determined not to leave their homeland; instead, they hid out in the mountains. Their leader, Tsali (Charley), was captured and executed for his part in an incident that resulted in the death of a soldier, but in view of the brutality so evident in the removal, his followers were allowed to repurchase tracts and remain in the state. The Eastern Band of Cherokee was later incorporated, and the Qualla Boundary—the Cherokee Indian Reservation—was recognized by both the federal and state governments.

North Carolina's 30,463 free persons of color in 1860 were hardly *free* or *persons* under the hardened laws of the antebellum decades. Their rights to preach, vote, and discuss issues with slaves were abrogated, and their freedom to travel or to avail themselves of the services of the courts was restricted severely. They carried passes to distinguish themselves from slaves, but because of widespread fear of counterfeited passes, the only safe freedmen were those in the presence of their acquaintances. Lacking food and shelter furnished by slaveowners, free blacks had to make their own way in competition with their brothers and sisters in bondage. Most of them occupied a sort of twilight zone between poor whites and even more unfortunate black slaves.

Nonetheless, nearly 12 percent of the free persons of color in 1860 possessed property, and a few owned slaves. Hundreds learned useful trades and skills; leading occupations, in numerical order, were common laborer, washerwoman, carpenter, spinner, seamstress, blacksmith, mason, painter, seaman, shoemaker, and cook. Twenty-four were classified as planters by white census takers. That free persons of color—particularly mulattoes—could in exceptional cases attain positions of prominence was illustrated by Thomas Day of Milton.

With his work force of adult whites, white apprentices, and slaves working side by side, he produced fashionable furniture and building interiors and became the state's leading cabinetmaker. Day and his wife Aquilla were full members of the Presbyterian church, and they sent a daughter to Salem Academy for music lessons.

There was hardly a twilight zone for slaves. Legally, they were persons only in the sense that they were humans; their bodies were given limited protection under the law, and their souls were of concern to religionists. In 1829, Chief Justice Thomas Ruffin ruled that under the law "the master is not liable to an indictment for battery committed upon a slave" because the power of the master "must be absolute to render the submission of the slave perfect." But, he added, "I must freely confess my sense of the harshness of this proposition; . . . and as a principle of moral right every person in his retirement must repudiate it." Some years later, in pronouncing the court's authority to try a master in exceptional circumstances, Justice William Gaston wrote that "where the punishment is barbarously immoderate . . . and denotes plainly that a master must have contemplated a fatal termination . . . he is guilty of murder."

A third of North Carolina's population of 992,622 in 1860 was held in bondage by 34,658 slaveowners, by far the largest proportion of whom lived in the "black belt" of the east. Buying, selling, renting, and bequeathing slaves were as common as transferring any other piece of property. Auction advertisements simply lumped Negroes along with grain, livestock, farming tools, and household furniture, and it is likely that slaves were sold at Sunday church services as well as at marketplace auctions. Prices of slaves fluctuated with the economy, but a rule of thumb was that a healthy black male in his prime was worth at least ten times the price of a horse.

Many owners showed their humanity by attempting to keep families together; others were bothered little when youths were torn from their mothers. Treatment of slaves differed from owner to owner, and perhaps the only valid generalization is to point to the ultimate indignity of the institution: the ownership of one human being by another.

Even among slaves there was status, both in their eyes and in those of the whites. Servants might be considered members of the family, and fortunate owners of blacks with talent prized them above almost any possession. A "good Nigger"—in the twentieth century a hated epithet—was a high compliment in the antebellum period—so high, in fact, that manumission by will or by purchase was not uncommon for faithful service.

7-96
7-97
Some slaves attained the respect of a wider audience. George Moses Horton, the property of James Horton of Chatham County, taught himself to read and write, then spent his spare time—sometimes rented from his master—on the campus of the university at Chapel Hill where he learned from and composed poetry for white students intrigued by this black bard. His poems, many of them published in book form, brought him fame but not freedom, for George's status as the "property" of James Horton was not terminated until general emancipation.

7-98
An equally remarkable slave was Omar ibn Said (Omeroh, Moreau), a Mohammedan from the Sudan, who was owned by Governor John Owen in Bladen County. Captured and sold into slavery, Omar was bought by a South Carolina planter who put him to work in the cotton fields. The African ran away, and was acquired by Owen, whose household was never the same again. Whether or not Omar was a prince as he claimed, he learned English, became a devout Christian, sent Bibles back to his people, and with his artistic touches made the Owen residence into a showplace. Offered his freedom and transportation back to the Sudan, Omar chose to remain with his master; he was buried in the family cemetery about 1858.

The institution of slavery was recognized by the Constitution, and although it had been abolished in the northern states and was under increasingly vocal attacks by abolitionists, slavery was not a major issue in the campaign of 1840. Electioneering tactics were introduced in that election, however, that would greatly enliven future presidential races. Each party held a statewide convention, nominated a gubernatorial candidate, endorsed the party's presidential nominee, and adopted a "platform." Boisterous electioneering tactics—torchlight parades, giant rallies, banners, and cartoons—whipped up enthusiasm, and debates between candidates often degenerated into personal attacks.

The Democrats attempted to justify the lackluster administration of Martin Van Buren, whom the
7-99
7-100
7-101
Whigs pictured as a silk-stockinged aristocrat. The Whigs, meanwhile, sought to portray their candidate, William Henry Harrison, as a plain, hard-

working Indian fighter and frontiersman. Never was a more ridiculous comparison made between candidates, but in the "Log Cabin Campaign," with the slogan "Tippecanoe and Tyler too," the Whigs carried North Carolina and the nation. When Harrison died in 1841, John Tyler of Virginia, rather than North Carolina's John Owen— 7-103 who had chaired the Whig national convention and declined the vice-presidential nomination— succeeded to the presidency.

Slavery obliquely entered the campaign of 1844 in the issue of the annexation of Texas. In their national convention, presided over by Caswell County's Romulus Mitchell Saunders, the Democrats strongly advocated annexation and nominated for president a native of Mecklenburg County, 7-102 James Knox Polk. Annexation was voted by Congress, but Mexico refused to recognize American 7-104 claims. War—"Mr. Polk's War," the Whigs called 7-105 it—broke out the following year. Hundreds of 7-106 North Carolinians rushed to volunteer for service, but relatively few of them saw action against the Mexicans.

The American victory, which resulted in the acquisition of Texas and a huge territory reaching to the Pacific, was tainted by the slavery issue, and henceforth the extension of slavery into the newly acquired lands would divide North and South. Although southern Whigs opposed the exclusion of slavery from the territories, they found themselves in a party divided at the national level, and in 1848 7-107 they won their last presidential and gubernatorial victories in North Carolina.

As abolitionist activity in the North increased, 7-108 public opinion in North Carolina grew less tolerant of antislavery sentiment. Especially noisome were "seditious" tracts published under the names of expatriates purporting to describe brutal treatment of 7-109 Negroes in the state. Equally aggravating were rumors of an "underground railroad," by which 7-110 runaway slaves were being spirited northward to freedom. Quakers in particular were suspected of 7-111 being involved, a suspicion that was confirmed when some members of the sect moved to Indiana and became more open in their activities.

Perhaps most disturbing to Southerners, though, was the passage in northern states of personal liberty laws to protect runaways and to facilitate the liberation of servants traveling with their masters. 7-112 By the mid-1850s North Carolina was no longer a place of free expression. Benjamin Sherwood Hedrick, a Rowan County native teaching chemistry at the University of North Carolina, was hounded from the state when he expressed his desire to vote for John C. Frémont, the Republican candidate for president, who was barred from the ballot in the state.

The following year another native of Rowan 7-113 (now Davie) County, Hinton Rowan Helper, published *The Impending Crisis of the South: How to Meet It*, which was a bitter attack upon slavery, the prime cause, he maintained, of the South's backwardness. His arguments were economic, not humanitarian, but the book created a sensation in the North, where it sold in great quantities, and in the 7-114 South, where it was outlawed. Daniel Worth, an aging minister of the Wesleyan Methodist Church, who had returned to his native state as a missionary, was convicted and sentenced for selling this "incendiary" book; he escaped possible flogging and imprisonment by fleeing the state and forfeiting his bond. Antislavery literature continued to infiltrate the state, however, and incidents such as 7-115 John Brown's raid in 1859 at Harper's Ferry, Virginia, seemed to confirm the growing belief among Southerners that they were no longer safe in the Union.

With the sectional split in the Whig party, the Democrats emerged as the avowed protectors of slavery. That issue alone, however, did not account for the successes of the Democratic party in North Carolina. Exiled from office for fourteen years, it was rejuvenated by a more youthful leadership which retained the loyalty of planters while picking up support among the less affluent. The key figure in this feat was William W. Holden, who had risen from an illegitimate birth to the editorship of the *North Carolina Standard*, the state's most powerful political voice.

The key issue—other than slavery—was "free suffrage," a misnomer for a proposal to remove the fifty-acre property requirement for voting for state senators. A constitutional amendment to allow adult male taxpayers to elect their senators was adopted in 1857, thus assuring loyalty to the Democratic party from many newly enfranchised voters. The Democrats also became less obstructive on such issues as internal improvements and education, and, beginning in 1850, they carried every gubernatorial and presidential campaign in North Carolina prior to the war; after 1853, they also controlled both houses of the General Assembly and the state's delegation in Congress.

In 1852 the vice-presidential candidates for both

political parties were natives of North Carolina— William Alexander Graham, a Whig from Orange County, and William Rufus de Vane King, a Democrat then living in Alabama. James Cochran Dobbin of Fayetteville became the fourth North Carolinian to serve as secretary of the navy (the others had been John Branch, George E. Badger, and William A. Graham), and Jacob Thompson, a native of Caswell County then living in Mississippi, was secretary of the interior under President James Buchanan.

7-116
7-118

Even so overriding an issue as slavery almost failed to sustain the Democrats as the decade grew to a close. Many North Carolinians were alarmed by the bellicose statements of disunionists. Secession as an abstract right of the states was generally accepted, but the prospect of its application was unpopular. The sentiments of most citizens of the state were probably more nearly represented by a young congressman from Buncombe County, Zebulon Baird Vance, who counseled settlement of the slavery issue within the Union. The Democrats had overplayed their hand, and some voters recoiled from extreme positions.

Another issue arose to threaten the Democrats: taxes. A slave between the ages of twelve and fifty, regardless of his or her value, was taxed as a poll rather than as property. In 1859 this amounted to only eighty cents—the same that a poor white man paid. Seeing an opportunity to win the votes from slaveless citizens, the Whigs proposed a constitutional amendment to tax slaves ad valorem (according to value). Even Holden, who had been denied the gubernatorial nomination by the eastern planters in 1858, favored the proposal, but out of loyalty to his party he supported the election (and subsequent reelection) of John W. Ellis. Ellis was reelected over the Whigs' John Pool, but by a slim margin.

7-117
7-120

7-119

Anxiety, rather than hysteria, characterized the mood of North Carolinians following the election of Abraham Lincoln in 1860. John C. Breckinridge, the "southern" candidate, won the state's electoral votes by a bare majority over John Bell and Stephen A. Douglas, avowed Unionists, but thousands of Breckinridge's supporters too were moderates, and his victory was less an endorsement of southern extremism than a rejection of abolitionism.

North Carolina was predominantly a state of poor, non-slaveholding farmers, most of whom found themselves in competition with, rather than beneficiaries of, slave labor. The slaveholders, however, exercised a disproportionate influence, and the vast majority of North Carolinians opposed federal interference in the institution of slavery. Nonetheless, they did not consider Lincoln's election justification for radical action by the South. Democratic editor William Holden expressed the popular sentiment four days after the election when he wrote that while the people disapproved of secession, they would "never permit Mr. Lincoln or his party to touch the institution of domestic slavery." He added, "For our part our motto is, Watch and Wait."

When the General Assembly met in December, the legislative chambers rang with debate over the impending secession of South Carolina. Governor Ellis and some legislators favored concerted action, but Bedford Brown, a devout Union Democrat, spoke for the majority: Even if the states of the Deep South should withdraw, he said, "by maintaining our position firmly in the Union, the border slave States and those adjacent may yet demand and receive terms to enable them to reconstruct the constitution."

Antisecession sentiment was dramatically expressed on 28 February 1861, when the electorate voted against calling a convention to discuss the crisis brought on by the formation of the Confederate States of America by seven seceded states. Simultaneously, in the election of delegates—now with no convention to attend—only thirty out of eighty-six counties favored secessionist candidates. Calling the attention of Governor Ellis and advocates of disunion to his earlier advice, Holden wrote, "The people have spoken, and you *must* watch and wait."

But the Unionist sentiment expressed in the referendum was deceptive, for while North Carolinians wanted to remain a part of the United States, they would not tolerate any military effort to coerce the seceded states back into the Union. Consequently, when—following the firing on Fort Sumter—President Lincoln called for two regiments of North Carolina troops to suppress the rebellion, Governor Ellis spoke for an aroused public opinion when he curtly replied, "You can get no troops from North Carolina."

The die was now cast, and the governor called the General Assembly into special session and began putting the state on a war footing. By the time a state convention met on 20 May, Virginia had

7-121
7-122
7-123

seceded and Tennessee had declared its independence preliminary to joining the Confederacy. Cut off from the Union, North Carolina had little choice but to adopt an ordinance of secession and ratify the provisional constitution of the Confederate States of America; neither of these actions was submitted to the people for a vote. Some citizens celebrated, but Senator Jonathan Worth of Randolph County wrote, "I think the South is committing suicide, but my lot is cast with the South and being unable to manage the ship, I intend to face the breakers manfully and go down with my companions." Worth would be called upon four years later to attempt to salvage the remains of the shipwreck.

7-124

Even before the convention acted, Confederate recruiters were at work in North Carolina, and troops from the state were already on their way to Virginia. Union army officers from North Carolina resigned and rushed home to take command of raw, hastily enlisted recruits who patriotically volunteered by the thousands. The federal arsenal at Fayetteville and military installations in the state were captured, along with equipment and supplies, and the United States Mint at Charlotte was turned over to the Confederate government. Church bells and scrap iron were melted down for the manufacture of cannons; cloth from the four dozen cotton and woolen mills of the state was sent to Raleigh to be made into uniforms; women sewed flags for their local military units and turned to making uniforms, medical kits, and other accoutrements of war.

7-125
7-126
7-127

7-131

A patriotic fervor swept over the state, and the superiority of southern soldiers appeared to be confirmed by the initial Confederate battle victory at Big Bethel in Virginia. Even the death of Henry Lawson Wyatt of Edgecombe County, the first Confederate to be killed in battle, seemed to contribute to the confidence of North Carolinians, whose men constituted about half of the southern troops at Big Bethel. The feverish pace of war preparations wore down Governor Ellis, however, and he died on 7 July and was succeeded by Henry Toole Clark.

7-130
7-128

7-129

The sobering reality of war fell upon North Carolina in August when federal forces landed at Cape Hatteras, overran the Confederates there, and soon gained control over the inlets to the Albemarle and Pamlico sounds. More than 250 outer banks residents took an oath of allegiance to the United States, and in November a convention at

7-132

Hatteras proclaimed an obscure Methodist minister, Marble Nash Taylor, provisional governor of North Carolina. Charles H. Foster was elected to Congress, though he was never allowed to take his seat.

The shock of enemy occupation of North Carolina soil had hardly worn off when, early in 1862, Union forces captured Roanoke Island and Elizabeth City and, far up the Chowan River, temporarily occupied and burned Winton. Not long afterward, Plymouth and Washington were seized.

7-133
7-134
7-135
7-136
7-137

Encouraged by these successes, federal land and naval forces in March attacked New Bern, drove out the Confederates, and distributed captured goods to the slaves. The following month, after intense preparations, including the use of heavy guns floated in on scows, Union troops took Fort Macon, thus securing the valuable coaling ports of Beaufort and Morehead City and leaving the Confederates with only one deep-water port in North Carolina.

7-138
7-139
7-140

The farcical Hatteras government was ignored by Lincoln, but following the capture of New Bern the president appointed Edward Stanly military governor of North Carolina. A former Whig congressman and member of a prominent New Bern family, Stanly had more recently practiced law in California, where he ran unsuccessfully for governor on the Republican ticket. He triumphantly returned to his native state with the avowed purpose of "leading the people back to the Union."

7-141

This intention, so promising in the summer of 1862, was thwarted by inept policies in Washington, the behavior of the invaders, the continued resistance of Confederate sympathizers, and Stanly's own image as a turncoat. Following promulgation of Lincoln's emancipation proclamation—which he angrily denounced—Stanly resigned in disgust in January 1863.

The federal occupation of a major portion of the coastal areas was as perilous for the remainder of the state as it was galling, for except for the port of Wilmington virtually all avenues of maritime commerce for North Carolina were cut off. Furthermore, the Federals posed a threat to the "Lifeline of the Confederacy"—the Wilmington and Weldon Railroad running supplies to Confederate armies in Virginia. The threat became a reality for a short time in December 1862, when Union forces drove back the Confederates at Kinston and destroyed the railroad bridge at Goldsboro before returning to New Bern.

7-142
7-143
7-156

North Carolinians complained bitterly that the Confederate government was stripping the state of its manpower to fight in other areas, thus leaving enemy troops virtually free to drive inland from the coast. Not until the spring of 1863 was a major offensive launched against the Federals at New Bern, and it failed. Thousands of square miles of North Carolina's fertile farm land, several of its important port towns, and a substantial number of its citizens remained under enemy control. Crops, livestock, and provisions were carted off by foraging troops and "Buffaloes," as Union sympathizers were called. The behavior of his occupying troops was condemned by military governor Stanly: "Thousands and thousands of dollars' worth of property were conveyed North. Libraries, pianos, carpets, mirrors, family portraits, everything in short, that could be removed, was stolen by men abusing . . . slaveholders and preaching liberty, justice and civilization." Even as enemy troops occupied the coastal area, thousands of North Carolinians in Confederate service died on distant battlefields—at places like Gettysburg, Vicksburg, Chickamauga.

The third year of the war was even worse in eastern North Carolina, but on two occasions hopes were temporarily raised. Finally convinced of the importance of recapturing New Bern, the Confederate high command authorized a major attack under the leadership of Major General George E. Pickett. In February 1864 one of three prongs of the drive reached within a mile of New Bern, but the other two failed to carry out their missions, and the expedition failed. This strategic city thus remained under Union occupation for the remainder of the war.

7-144
7-145

7-146
7-147
7-148
7-149
7-150
7-157

Another important offensive was taken against enemy-occupied Plymouth on the Roanoke River. There in April the CSS *Albemarle*, an unfinished ironclad built at Edwards Ferry far up the Roanoke River, assisted land forces in recapturing the town. For several months the *Albemarle* posed a substantial threat to federal occupation of the coast. Finally, in October, a young Union naval officer, William B. Cushing, ran a launch across a protective log boom and exploded a torpedo beneath the vessel. After the destruction of the *Albemarle*, the federal forces reoccupied Plymouth and Washington. At the end of 1864, except for the Cape Fear region, enemy forces still occupied most of the coastal area of North Carolina.

7-151

Conditions had been far from happy in the remainder of the state since the beginning of the war. Despite the enthusiasm raised by initial Confederate victories in Virginia and Maryland, morale gradually deteriorated, as more and more men were killed or wounded on far-off battlefields, the burdens of supporting vast armies became heavier, and prewar political wounds were reopened. Particularly annoying were policies of the Confederate government which, in the eyes of many North Carolinians, were contrary to the principles of states' rights for which the South had seceded. One sign of this dissatisfaction was the election of Zebulon Baird Vance to the governorship in 1862. The youthful colonel of the Twenty-sixth Regiment had been a Whig congressman and outspoken Unionist before the war; now as wartime governor he promised to "prosecute the war for liberty and independence to the bitter end"—not, however, without insisting upon the rights of the state within the Confederacy. He particularly opposed the central government over conscription, taxation in kind, impressment of property, and suspension of the writ of habeas corpus.

His task, however, was extraordinarily difficult, for as casualties, taxes, and controversies with the Confederate government mounted, disaffection grew, particularly in the mountains, where organized bands of deserters terrorized some communities. While most blacks remained loyal to the South, some slaves and free blacks in the occupied east were enlisted into the Union army. Confederate money deteriorated in value, state and Confederate taxes became oppressive, and the state issued notes and bonds to help finance the war. Still, reports of heroism on the battlefield gave slim hope to people on the home front.

Governor Vance's practice of feuding with the Confederates and fighting the Yankees failed to satisfy some North Carolinians who by 1863—particularly after the southern defeats at Gettysburg and Vicksburg—were in a mood to return to the Union, with or without the remainder of the South. The leader of the peace-at-any-cost faction was William Holden. In 1864 a number of antiwar conventions nominated Holden for governor on a Peace party ticket, but in the election Vance defeated him by a four-to-one margin.

Throughout the war one of Vance's most significant accomplishments was his conduct of commerce and trade. In addition to being the only state to clothe its own troops, North Carolina carried on direct negotiations for supplies and equipment from foreign countries, particularly England. State-owned ships joined with Confederate and foreign vessels in bringing into Wilmington supplies and equipment worth $65 million in gold.

Gradually, though, the blockade was tightened, and by the end of 1864, the Federals were ready to close the last major port still open to the Confederates. Following one unsuccessful attempt to capture Fort Fisher at the mouth of the Cape Fear River in December, Union forces in January overwhelmed the "Gibraltar of the South" and the following month took Wilmington.

In March, General William T. Sherman's forces entered North Carolina from the south, captured Fayetteville, and defeated General Joseph E. Johnston's troops at Bentonville. At Goldsboro Sherman's forces joined those driving from the east and began the march toward Raleigh. Meanwhile, General George Stoneman's Union cavalry invaded the state from Tennessee, destroying railroads and military stores as far east as Guilford County.

Stoneman's virtually unimpeded raids, General Robert E. Lee's surrender at Appomattox Court House, and Sherman's occupation of Raleigh on 13 April made further resistance by the Confederates hopeless. Johnston met Sherman at James Bennett's modest house near Durham's Station on 18 April and negotiated the surrender of the thirty-seven thousand southern troops. Sherman's terms, however, were so generous that they were rejected in Washington, and the two generals met again and signed a new agreement on 26 April, essentially ending the Civil War.

North Carolina, so reluctant to be forced out of the Union and into the Confederacy, contributed mightily to the lost cause. With one-ninth of the population of the South, the state furnished about one-sixth of the Confederate troops, a fourth of the Confederate dead, and far more than its proportionate share of provisions. Much of its territory was occupied by enemy troops during most of the war, and Wilmington was the last major Confederate port to fall. Yet, perhaps because of the traditional attachment of its people to the Union, the state was never fully trusted by Jefferson Davis and the leaders of the Confederacy. Not a single North Carolina officer was promoted to the rank of general, and only two—one of whom was never confirmed—served as lieutenant generals. And just as North Carolina troops were led by officers from other states, so the people were governed by officials from other states, for only two North Carolinians served in the Confederate cabinet, both for short times as attorney general. The loyalty of most North Carolinians to the cause of the Confederacy, however, was exemplified by Captain James Iredell Waddell, who at war's end refused to surrender the CSS *Shenandoah* to the victors and, instead, continued to fly the Confederate flag until November 1865, when he turned the vessel over to the British government.

7-181

The proscriptive denunciation contained in this article—whether it could or could not be enforced—never has been enforced. The question before us is one, not of practical convenience, but of fundamental principles. He who would sacrifice such principles to the passion or caprice or excitement of the moment, may be called a politician, but he is no statesman. We are now examining into the soundness of the foundation of our institutions. If we rest the fabric of the constitution upon the prejudices—unreasoning and mutable prejudices—we build upon the sand. But let us lay it on the broad and firm basis of natural right, equal justice and universal freedom—freedom of opinion—freedom, civil and religious—freedom, as approved by the wise, and sanctioned by the good—and then may we hope that it shall stand against the storms of faction, violence and injustice, for *then* we shall have founded it upon a ROCK.

———

NOTE.—The amendment proposed by the committee, substituting the word *Christian* for "Protestant," was decided by the following vote of the Convention, viz.

For the Amendment, ... 74
Against it, ... 51

Majority, ... 23

VOTE OF THE PEOPLE

ON THE

Question of Ratification or Rejection of the New Constitution.

	Ratification.	Rejection.		Ratification.	Rejection.
Anson,	815	44	Moore,	110	370
Ashe,	466	88	Macon,	502	19
Brunswick,	—	466	Montgomery,	538	103
Buncombe,	1322	22	Mecklenburg,	1097	67
Burke,	1359	1	Martin,	14	795
Beaufort,	90	639	New-Hanover,	54	365
Bladen,	6	564	Nash,	8	757
Bertie,	96	315	Northampton,	12	286
Craven,	131	270	Onslow,	97	357
Carteret,	32	332	Orange,	1031	246
Currituck,	22	115	Person,	180	287
Camden,	61	333	Pasquotank,	7	442
Caswell,	466	162	Pitt,	32	710
Chowan,	7	322	Perquimons,	10	431
Chatham,	556	200	Rowan,	1570	24
Cumberland,	331	439	Randolph,	426	163
Columbus,	3	391	Rockingham,	612	68
Cabarrus,	598	46	Robeson,	86	458
Duplin,	56	532	Richmond,	263	43
Davidson,	1034	33	Rutherford,	1557	2
Edgecomb,	29	1324	Sampson,	148	463
Franklin,	85	617	Surry,	1751	4
Guilford,	971	237	Stokes,	1061	71
Gates,	12	502	Tyrrell,	1	459
Granville,	433	308	Washington,	14	409
Greene,	9	423	Wilkes,	1757	8
Halifax,	239	441	Wake,	243	1124
Hertford,	7	376	Warren,	46	580
Hyde,	2	431	Wayne,	28	966
Haywood,	481	8	Yancy,	564	13
Iredell,	1194	18			
Jones,	22	239		26,771	21,606
Johnston,	73	776		21,606	
Lincoln,	1887	42			
Lenoir,	54	320	Majority,	5,165	

7-1 (left)
The State House had burned in 1831 and the "Governor's Palace" offered unsatisfactory surroundings, so the Convention of 1835 held most of its sessions in Raleigh's First Presbyterian Church. The supreme court utilized the session house (left). (Courtesy NCDA&H.)

7-2 (top right)
The vote by which the amendment was approved by the convention follows the concluding paragraph of William Gaston's address to the convention pleading for repeal of the ban on officeholding by non-Protestants. (Courtesy North Carolina Collection.)

7-3
The package of constitutional amendments was approved by a sectional vote—the east strongly opposed, the west heavily in favor. (Courtesy North Carolina Collection.)

7-4
Edward Bishop Dudley (1789–1855), a Whig from Wilmington, won the first statewide gubernatorial campaign in 1836 and was reelected two years later. (Courtesy North Carolina Collection.)

Railway to convey Granite. Limestone near Raleigh.

The State-House of North-Carolina, which (together with a large portion of the town) was destroyed by fire, is now in the course of being rebuilt, with the beautiful and excellent granite furnished by the neighboring quarries. This stone is as hard as is at all desirable, and will form so large a portion of the whole structure, that it may well be considered as imperishable. A Railway of 1¼ miles, was made from the quarry to the State House square, solely to bring the stone, and has yielded profitable dividends to the proprietors, and at the same time enabled the transportation of the stone to be effected at one third of the expense (as I heard) that it would otherwise have cost. This facility, also induces a much larger use of granite for the new houses which are erecting on Fayetteville street, and will ultimately cause the town of Raleigh to show more beauty than many others of thrice its wealth and population.

This little Rail Road has doubtless had much effect in promoting the present zeal for similar and more extensive works.— We are much more ready to be impressed by what we see, than what we hear, even if we hear truths demonstrated, and made undeniable ; and very many, who have come to the Seat of Government from every quarter of the State, have been first convinced of the advantages of railways by seeing the enormous masses of stone conveyed as fast and as easily as the empty car could be drawn on good common roads. Of the 2200 yards of the whole road, 1304 required excavation or embankment, the greatest depth being apparently four feet, and the greatest height eight, judging by my eye. The length of the places excavated and embanked, was counted by the sills. The total cost of the Railway, 2200 yards, including every material, and every source of expense, amounted to only $2,700, or $2,160 the mile. It is true that the sills are not of as large, nor of as good timber, as a work intended for permanent use would have required, and that the iron strips are not more than one-sixth of an inch in thickness. But if the timber and the iron had been such as was used on the Petersburg and Roanoke Railway, it would scarcely have made this cost $3,000 the mile ;

7-5
The railway for horse-drawn vehicles carrying granite from the quarry to Union Square for use in constructing the new state capitol was described in the *Raleigh Register* (weekly edition), 28 January 1834. (Courtesy North Carolina Collection.)

Rail Road Notice.
—:§:—

PASSENGERS going North, and especially those who desire to pass through Washington and Baltimore, or to visit the Virginia Springs, are respectfully informed, that a TRAIN OF CARS with the Mail and Passengers from Tarborough via Halifax, leave Blakely regularly three times a week, running thro' to Petersburg and Richmond in time for the Western

Line of Stages,

Through Lynchburg and Charlottesville and Staunton, and for the Daily Mail train of the Richmond and Fredericksburg Rail Road, arriving by this Line at Washington to dinner and in Baltimore by 8 o'clock in the evening.

Passengers who take the
Wilmington and Halifax Line,

Will find the route by the Petersburg Rail Road the most certain and agreeable and although the Mail Train of Cars, leave but three times a week, yet almost every day an Engine with a train by which Passengers can be conveyed; leaves Blakely and arrives at the junction with the Greensville and Roanoke Rail Road in good time to take the Daily Express Mail Line for the North, which connects at Petersburg with all the fast Northern Lines of Rail Road, steamboats or stages.

OFFICE PETERSBURG RAIL ROAD CO. }
14th Aug. 1837.   {

7-6
An advertisement in the *Free Press* (Tarborough), 2 September 1837, promoted stagecoach connections with the Petersburg Railroad in Northampton County. (Courtesy NCDA&H.)

7-7
David Paton, an architect from Scotland, completed the design and directed construction of the new state capitol. The building was dedicated in 1840 at the same time the completion of the railroad to Gaston was celebrated. This half of a stereograph, possibly made just prior to the Civil War, is believed to be the earliest extant photograph of the building. (Courtesy NCDA&H.)

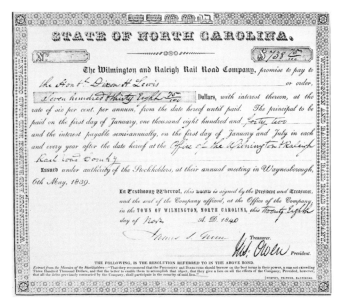

7-8
A promissory note from the Wilmington and Raleigh Railroad Company before Weldon was substituted for Raleigh as the road's northern terminus. (Courtesy NCDA&H.)

7-9
The locomotive *Romulus Saunders* ran on the Raleigh and Gaston Railroad in the 1850s. In this early photograph, Rufus H. Horton is in the cab, Dr. William J. Hawkins (president of the company) is on the running board, and Major W. W. Vass (treasurer) is leaning on the engine at front. In the foreground is the son of Rufe Smith (fireman), whose house is in background. (Courtesy NCDA&H.)

7-10
Tradition claims that this log cabin served as the station house of the Wilmington and Weldon Railroad at Halifax. (Courtesy NCDA&H.)

7-11
William Alexander Graham (1804–75), governor 1845–49, later secretary of the navy and in 1852 the unsuccessful Whig candidate for vice-president, posed during the last year of his life with his seven sons. Visible behind the neck of the son standing at left is a photographer's brace, used to steady subjects during the lengthy exposure period required in 1875. (Courtesy North Carolina Collection.)

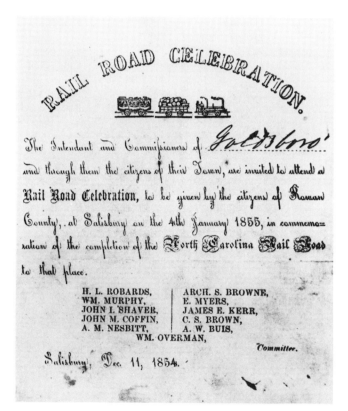

7-13
Completion of the North Carolina Railroad from Goldsboro to Salisbury was celebrated in 1855. (Courtesy NCDA&H.)

Letter from Gov. Swain.

CHAPEL HILL, July 13th, 1849.

To Governor Morehead, Chairman of the Executive Committee of the Salisbury Convention.

My DEAR SIR: I left here in the stage on the evening of the 10th ult., on a Southwestern tour, taking the Salisbury Convention in my way. I returned after an absence of 29 days on the 8th instant, having travelled about 1,550 miles—210 of which were along the stage route from Goldsborough to Charlotte, and 831 on the South Carolina and Georgia Railroad, viz: from Camden, South Carolina, to Dalton, Georgia, 424 miles; returning from Dalton, Georgia, to Charleston, S. C., 407 miles.

Along the line of our proposed Rail Road from Goldsborough to Charlotte, the stages run tri-weekly. If you reach Goldsborough precisely at the hour of departure, which is only possible, three times in the week, and meet with no delay from any cause, you may arrive in Charlotte in three days and a half, or 84 hours. Your expenses will be, stage-fare from Goldsborough to Raleigh $4 50—thence to Salisbury $10 50—to Charlotte $3—$18.

In tavern bills—dinner at Smithfield, 50 cents—a day's board in Raleigh $1 50—supper at Moring's 50—breakfast at Holt's 50—dinner at Greensborough 50, supper 50, (if you get any)—breakfast in Salisbury 50—dinner in Concord 50—$5.

Making the aggregate expense $23 for 210 miles stage travel, performed at the rate of less than 2½ miles an hour, at the average expense of about 11 cents per mile.

On the line of Rail Road referred to, I left Camden at 5 o'clock in the morning and arrived at Dalton at 7 the next evening, making 424 miles in 38 hours—returning, I left Dalton at 5 A. M., and the train arrived at Charleston the next day at 12 M., making 407 miles in 31 hours. I paid for fare going and returning $15—tavern bills and omnibus fare, going and returning $6,—making the aggregate expenses $21 for 831 miles rail road travel, at the rate of twelve miles an hour, at the average expense of 2½ cents per mile.

The result of the whole is simply this: You travel along the rout of the proposed Rail Road at a fifth of the speed, and at four times the expense, in approaching the capital of your own State, that is required to take a Georgian or South Carolinian to his capital, or to any of the great commercial markets of these States. This journey from Goldsborough to Charlotte cost me $23—the same distance in South Carolina and Georgia a fraction over $5. I paid a tax therefore on this single jaunt of about $18 for the omission of the government to provide a great highway for her citizens. I am not a very great traveller, but

7-12
In a letter to the *Raleigh Register* (semiweekly edition), 3 August 1849, former governor David L. Swain described the cost of a stagecoach trip from Goldsboro to Charlotte. In comparison, he traveled by railroad in South Carolina and Georgia at an average of twelve miles per hour and 2½ cents per mile. (Courtesy North Carolina Collection.)

7-14
The *North Carolina Whig* (Charlotte), 1 November 1859, carried an advertisement of Overman & Wilson picturing a fancy phaeton. (Courtesy North Carolina Collection.)

7-16
Dozens of plank roads, such as this one, were built in the 1850s, but most of them were abandoned because of the expense of upkeep. (Courtesy NCDA&H.)

To Toll Keepers

In the County of Cumberland:

You will take notice that at March Term, 1851, of our Court of Pleas and Quarter Sessions, it was ordered by the Court, that the tolls charged at the several Bridges and Ferries in Cumberland County shall not exceed the following, that is to say:

At Bridges and Ferries, over the Cape Fear river,
For all Wagons and Carriages drawn by 4 or more
horses,	50	cents.
Drawn by three horses,	40	"
" two "	30	"
" one "	20	"
Horse and rider,	10	"
Loose horses, each,	5	"
Persons on foot,	2	"
Cattle, hogs, sheep, &c.,	1	"

At all other Bridges and Ferries,
For all wagons or carriages drawn by 1, 2 or 3
horses,	10	cents.
Drawn by 4 or more horses,	15	"
Horse and Rider,	5	"

Extract from the Minutes.

J. McLAURIN, Clerk.

March 29, 1851.

7-15
A schedule of ferry and bridge tolls over the Cape Fear River in Cumberland County in 1851. (Courtesy North Carolina Collection.)

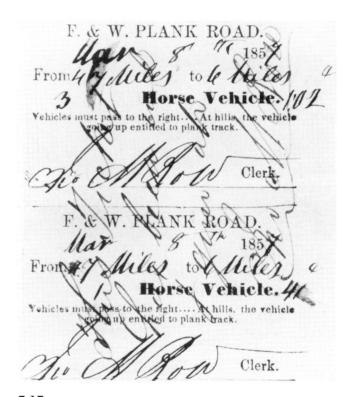

7-17
Toll tickets for the Fayetteville and Western Plank Road in 1857 cautioned, "At hills the vehicle going up entitled to plank track." (Courtesy NCDA&H.)

7-18
An illustration of farmers awaiting daybreak outside Fayetteville was published in Olmsted's *A Journey in the Seaboard Slave States* (1856).

He wrote, "Next morning I counted sixty of their great wagons in the main street of the little town." (Courtesy North Carolina Collection.)

7-19
Covered wagons were pictured along Market Street in Wilmington in the 1850s.

(Courtesy North Carolina Collection.)

7-20
Calvin H. Wiley's *North-Carolina Reader* (1851) carried an illustration of a steamer, presumably on the Cape Fear River. It may represent the *Cotton Plant*, launched in 1826. (Courtesy North Carolina Collection.)

NORTH CAROLINA SEA BATHING.
Nag's Head Hotel.

THIS extensive establishment, recently improved, will be opened for the reception of Visitors, superintended by the Junior Partner, A. J. BATEMAN, on the 1st day of July. The Hotel situated in view of the Ocean, presents a magnificent prospect. The great benefits resulting from Sea Bathing and the sea breeze, are becoming more known and appreciated daily. No place can be more healthy or possess a finer climate than Nag's Head. The Bathing is unsurpassed in the United States. We have engaged a good Band of Music, our Ball Room is very spacious and will be opened every evening. Active and efficient assistants have been engaged, and no exertions will be spared to render it in all respects an agreeable and interesting resort. A Rail Road will be completed early in July from the Hotel to the Ocean, that persons preferring a ride to walking may be accommodated.

The steamer Schultz will make a trip every Saturday from Franklin Depot, Va., to Nags' Head, commencing July 12th, immediately after the arrival of the Cars from Norfolk, and returning leave Nags' Head Sunday evening, at 5 o'clock. Passage from Franklin $3, Riddick's Wharf, Winton, &c., $2 50, Edenton to Nags' Head $2. Meals extra. The Schultz will make several Excursions to Nags' Head through the season, due notice of which will be given. The Packet schr. Sarah Porter, Capt. Walker, will make two trips from Edenton, (N. C.,) to Nag's Head each week through the season, leaving Edenton Tuesday and Friday, at 8 o'clock, A M. The Packet schr. A. Riddick, Capt. Dunbar, will make three trips each week through the season, from Elizabeth City, (N. C.,) to Nag's Head, leaving Elizabeth City immediately after the arrival of the Stage Coach from Norfolk, Va. Passage on each Packet $1, meals extra. Board per day at the Hotel $1 50. By the week at the rate of $1 25. By the two weeks at the rate of $1. By the month at the rate of 75 cents per day. Children and Servants half price. The patronage of the public is very respectfully solicited.

RIDDICK & BATEMAN.
June 11, 1851-38-2m.

7-21
An advertisement in the *North State Whig* (Washington), 11 June 1851, described the facilities of the

Nag's Head Hotel on the outer banks. A railroad was planned from the hotel to the beach. (Courtesy NCDA&H.)

7-22 (far left)
Senator Charles Applewhite
Hill (1784–1831), principal
of Franklin Academy at
Louisburg, was author of the
1825 law that established the
State Literary Fund. (Cour-
tesy NCDA&H.)

7-24
Calvin Henderson Wiley
(1819–87), as superinten-
dent of common schools
1853–65, built North Carolina's public school system
into the best in the South.
(Courtesy NCDA&H.)

7-23
Introducer of the common
school act of 1839 was Senator William Walton Cherry
(1806–45), a Bertie County
teacher and lawyer. (Courtesy
North Carolina Collection.)

INTRODUCTION.

THE design of this work is obvious.

It occurred to the author while anxiously revolving in his mind different plans for the resuscitation of his native state; and he still believes that the surest and speediest way to attain the object desired, is to imbue the minds of the rising generation with just ideas of the resources and desirableness of the country in which they live. This has been the first impulse of enlightened patriotism in all ages and countries; and if it be not profane to make such a reference in this connection, it may be stated that, as an example for our instruction, the first day's work of the Almighty, when he formed the heavens and the earth, was the creation of *light*.

We have needed light; generation after generation has grown up in ignorance of the capabilities and the actual advantages of their native state. Like the Israelites in Egypt, the North Carolinians have still entertained vague expectations of a good time coming; but these were hopes without fixed and tangible purposes, indulged without an effort to realize, and without any definite notions of the ways and means necessary to the deliverance of their state.

And, unfortunately, they have, in another respect, resembled the descendants of Jacob while in exile and in bondage; they have ever regarded their location as being not their permanent abiding-place, while their children and children's children have been carefully taught to look beyond the limits of North Carolina for wealth, happiness, and fame.

All this has been the result of ignorance; and it has caused a constant drain of enterprise and wealth from the state.

Not only has ignorance of her resources and her history prevailed in North Carolina, but her people have never been characterized by common feelings and sympathies; and, strange to say, the state has run a career of honour for more than a century and a half without producing a single bard, annalist, historian, or novelist, to call forth, embody, and fix on common objects the affections of the public.

7-25
Ignorance, said Wiley in the introduction to his *North-Carolina Reader* (1851), accounted for the "drain of enterprise and wealth from the state." (Courtesy North Carolina Collection.)

7-26
The term "old field schools" came from the rather common practice of locating small subscription schools in abandoned fields whose fertility had been exhausted by repeated use. This drawing, made by Benson J. Lossing across the line in South Carolina, was published in his *Pictorial Field-Book of the Revolution* (New York, 1852), volume 2. (Courtesy North Carolina Collection.)

7-27 (right)
Academies with higher academic standards remained in demand even after common schools were built. The Oxford Female Academy advertised in the *Raleigh Register* (semiweekly edition), 1 June 1841. (Courtesy NCDA&H.)

7-28 (far right)
Among the many antebellum schoolmasters was Peter Stewart Ney, believed by his constituents in Davie, Iredell, and Rowan counties to have been Napoleon's most brilliant general, Marshal Michel Ney, who according to the story, escaped execution in France in 1815 and made his way to the backcountry of North Carolina, where he taught at a succession of schools. His tombstone in the cemetery of Third Creek Presbyterian Church helped perpetuate the legend. Twentieth-century research by William Henry Hoyt indicates that Ney was a Scot who was naturalized in South Carolina in 1820. (Courtesy NCDA&H.)

Oxford Female Academy.

THE first Session in the above Institution, for the present year, will close with a public Examination on Thursday, the 10th, and the second Session will commence on Monday, the 28th day of June next.

This School is under the control and direction of the undersigned, who superintends its operations, and who is determined to spare no pains or expense to make it a Seminary of sound and thorough instruction in all the usual branches of useful and elegant learning, and deserving the full confidence and the liberal patronage of the friends of education. The Ladies to whom the business of imparting instruction in the Academy is chiefly confided, (Miss S. A. Nichols, with whom is associated Miss L. T. Jones, in the departments of Literature, Drawing and Painting, and Miss J. K. Watson in the department of Music,) have proved themselves eminently qualified for the parts assigned them, and have gained for the School a high and distinguished reputation in this community. Young Ladies who may be entrusted to the care of the undersigned, will find in his house another home, in which Teachers and Pupils live together as one family.

Terms by the Session of five months:

For Board,	$40 00
For tuition in Reading, Writing and Arithmetic,	7 50
Reading, Writing, Arithmetic, English Grammar, Composition and Geography,	10 00
All or any of the above, with Algebra, Geometry, Natural, Moral and Intellectual Philosophy, Chemistry, Botany, History, Logic, Rhetoric, Mineralogy and Geology.	12 50
Latin, Greek and French Languages, each.	10 00
Piano Forte,	20 00
Guitar,	15 00
Drawing and Painting,	10 00

Vocal music and Needle work taught without charge.
BENJ. SUMNER.
Oxford, N. C. 18th May, 1841.
REFERENCES.
Hon. R. B. Gilliam, Oxford. Hon. W. H. Battle, Raleigh. Hon. L. D. Henry, Fayetteville. David Outlaw, Esq. Windsor. A. Moore, Esq. Rev. S. Johnson, Edenton. T. F. Jones, Esq. Hertford. C. R. Kinney, Esq. Elizabeth City. C. G. Lamb, Esq. Camden. Col. J. McLeod, Smithfield. 43 3t

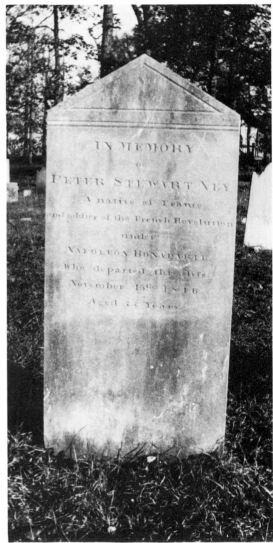

7-29
This lithograph, showing the falls from which Elisha Mitchell slipped to his death in 1857, was drawn by Oscar M. Lewis only six months after the event. The mountain—the highest in the eastern United States—was named for Mitchell. (Courtesy North Carolina Collection.)

7-30
The campus of the University of North Carolina in an 1861 lithograph by E. Valois. Left to right are New East, Old East, South Building, Old West, and New West. Almost hidden in the rear are Smith Hall (behind Old East) and Gerrard Hall (behind Old West). (Courtesy North Carolina Collection.)

7-31
Teaching schedule for the faculty of the University of North Carolina in 1844. "The President" was David L. Swain, former governor. Saturday was free of classes, but recitations began at 7:00 A.M. Tuesday through Friday. (Courtesy University Archives.)

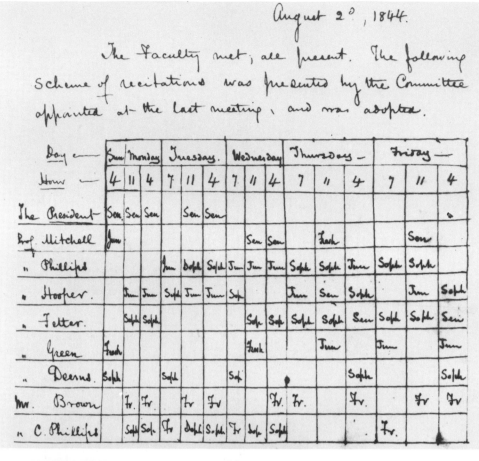

7-32
John Hill Wheeler (1806–82) of Hertford County, superintendent of the United States Branch Mint at Charlotte and state treasurer, published in 1851 a history of North Carolina so favorable to Democrats that the Whigs called it "The Democratic Stud Book." This portrait is attributed to Wheeler's wife, Ellen, or to her famous father, Thomas Sulley. (Courtesy Mint Museum of Art; by permission of Dr. Samuel J. Calvert, Fayetteville.)

7-33
The *Milton Chronicle* carried humorous letters from the "Fool Killer"—actually its editor, C. N. B. Evans, under the fictitious name of Jesse Holmes. (Courtesy NCDA&H; reprinted from *Milton Chronicle*, 10 March 1859.)

7-34

Shortly before his death, William Gaston (1778–1844), caught up in the patriotic fervor of the times, wrote "The Old North State," which was adopted as the state song in 1927. (Courtesy North Carolina Collection.)

Wake Forest Institute.

THE following is the general outline of the Plan of this Institution, adopted at the late sitting of the Board of Managers:

1. The name of the Institution is "The Wake Forest Institute."

2. The object of the Institute is to enable young Ministers to obtain an education on moderate terms, and to train up youth in general to a knowledge of Science and practical Agriculture.

3. Every pupil shall labor three hours a day, under the direction of an experienced and scientific farmer, subject to the control of the principal teacher, who is to be a Minister of the Gospel.

4. The total expenses of the Academic year shall not exceed $60, of which $25 are to be paid in advance, and an allowance shall be made to each student according to the value of his labor.

5. No pupil shall be admitted under 12 years of age.

6. Every pupil shall furnish himself with an axe and a hoe, a pair of sheets and a pair of towels.

7. There shall be one vacation in the year, from the middle of December to the first of February.

8. This Institute shall be open to the reception of all youth of good moral character, who will comply with the above regulations.

Arrangements are now making to carry into effect the objects of the Institute by the first of February.

All persons who wish to enter the Institute, are requested to make application by the 15th December, to the Rev. J. G. HALL, of Raleigh, (post paid).

The Board of Managers have limited the number of students to fifty for the first year.

All Editors of the State friendly to the Institute are requested to give the above an insertion in their papers.

JNO. ARMSTRONG, Cor. Sec.

7-35
Plans for the establishment of Wake Forest Institute were announced in the *Raleigh Register* (weekly edition), 12 October 1832. Each student was required to bring an axe and a hoe. (Courtesy North Carolina Collection.)

7-36
A needlework picture of New Garden Boarding School in 1841 by a student, Martha M. Hunt. (Courtesy Friends Historical Collection, Guilford College.)

7-37
Literary societies occupied an important role on early campuses. In a mural depicting Davidson College about 1850, the buildings of the two societies faced each other—Eumenean at left, Philanthropic at right. In the background are the chapel and three small dormitories. (Courtesy Chalmers G. Davidson, Davidson College.)

7-38
In one of the earliest campus group photographs in the state, students at the Salem Academy and College posed for a photographer in 1858. (Courtesy Salem College Alumnae Association, Winston-Salem.)

7-40
Watercolor of Oxford Presbyterian Church (erected 1830) drawn prior to 1847 by Mary Anderson Duty (later Mrs. James Davis) of Oxford. (Courtesy Edith Howell Wheeler and the Presbyterian Church of Oxford; by permission of Frank Holeman, Washington, D.C.)

7-39
A portion of the student body at Greensboro Female College was photographed in front of the Main Building prior to its destruction by fire in 1863. (Courtesy Greensboro College Alumnae Association, Greensboro.)

7-41
The *Deaf Mute* is believed to have been the first periodical published by a school for the deaf in America. The original building on Caswell Square is pictured in the oval. (Courtesy American Antiquarian Society, Worcester.)

You will not, Legislators of North Carolina—Senators and Representatives of a noble State, you will not forget amidst the heat of debate, the clash of opinion, and the strife for political supremacy ; you will not forget the majesty of your station, the dignity of that trust confided to you by the suffrages of your fellow-citizens.

It is not often that you are solicited to exercise your functions in behalf of the unfortunate. That you possess the power, and now the opportunity of exercising a gracious, benignant, and God-like influence upon the present and future destiny of hundreds, nay of thousands, who pine in want and misery, under privations and sufferings, wearily borne through heavy months and years—the light of whose reason is quenched, and whose judgment is as the stubble upon a waste field ; this it is believed is a sufficient argument to determine your decisions in favor of justice, and of humanity, and of unquestionable civil obligation.

As benefactors of the distressed whose mental darkness may, through your agency, be dispersed, how many blessings and prayers from grateful hearts will enrich you ! As your last hours shall be slowly numbered, and the review of life becomes more and more searching, amidst the shades of uncompromising memories, how beautiful will be the remembrance that of the many of this life's transactions, oftenest controlling transient and outward affairs, frequently conducting to disquieting results, and sometimes to those of doubtful good, you have aided to accomplish a work whose results of wide-diffused benefits are as sanctifying as they are permanent: blessing through all Time—consecrating through all Eternity !

Gentlemen, the sum of the plea of your Memorialist is embodied in the solicitation for an adequate appropriation for the construction of a Hospital for the remedial treatment of the Insane in the State of North Carolina.

Respectfully submitted,

D. L. DIX.

Raleigh, November, 1848.

7-42
Closing paragraphs of Dorothea Dix's memorial to the General Assembly in 1848. The hill just outside Raleigh on which the asylum was built was named for her father. (Courtesy North Carolina Collection.)

7-43
David Hunter Strother (Porte Crayon) made this drawing of the Asylum for the Insane on Dix Hill for *Harper's New Monthly Magazine* (July 1857). (Courtesy NCDA&H.)

7-44, 7-45, 7-46, and 7-47
Chang and Eng, attached twins from Siam, were brought to the United States for exhibition in circuses. Inseparably fastened at the breast, they married, respectively, Adelaide and Sarah Ann Yeates, took the surname Bunker, and settled first in Wilkes County and then in Surry. The brothers built homes a short distance apart, operated farms, shared nights with each wife on an alternating schedule, and fathered a total of twenty-one children (eighteen of whom are shown here about 1865, along with the twins, their wives, and "Aunt Grace," a slave woman given Eng and Sarah Ann [Sallie] as a wedding present). A plaster cast made following an autopsy by the College of Physicians of Philadelphia in 1874 indicated that separation would have been fatal. (Courtesy: poster, North Carolina Collection; Chang and Eng's wide chair and the plaster cast, Mütter Museum, Philadelphia; family portrait, Amy and Irving Wallace Photographic Archive, Los Angeles.)

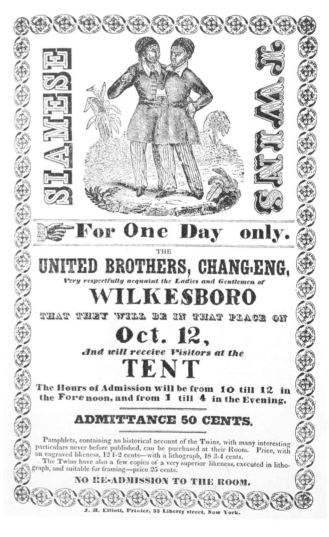

GREAT ATTRACTION!

THE CELEBRATED CAR-OLINA TWINS will be ex-hibited at Raleigh during the Agricultural Fair.

These Children have been pronounced by Physicians the most interesting specimen of Humanity ever seen or record-ed, and one which must command Universal At-tention. They were born in Columbus county, North Carolina, and are healthy, active, and for their age, unusually intelligent.

They are joined together at the back by the u-nion of the two spines in one, making the connec-tion much more intimate than that of the Siamese Twins.

Many Physicians have examined them, and all agree in their being the greatest curiosity ever seen or heard of,—some of their organs being in common, while others are perfectly distinct. It is often the case that one child is playful and ac-tive while the other is fast asleep.

Most visitors have expressed surprise to find them so "PERT" and "CUNNING," with such intel-ligent, happy faces, where they had not expected to see such interesting children.

Call at once if you would not miss the opportu-nity of seeing the greatest wonder of the Age, as you may "ne'er look upon their like again!"

Doors open from 9 o'clock A. M. till 12. M. for Ladies only; and from 2 P. M. till 4, for Gentle-men alone.

Admission 50 cts.

BROWER & SHELTON.

October 7th, 1853.   td—82

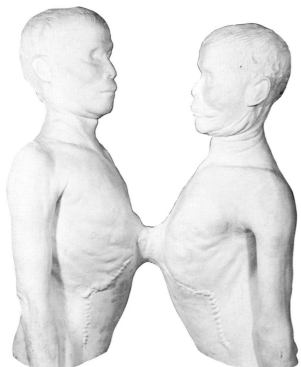

Double headed Girl

7-48 and 7-49

Even before the word *Siamese* became a common adjective to describe bodily attached twins, two daughters who shared part of a common spine were born to a slave woman in Columbus County. The *Raleigh Register* (semi-weekly edition) of 8 October 1853 announced the exhibi-tion of the "Celebrated Caro-lina Twins" at the state fair. Under the name "Millie-Christine"—they always spoke of themselves as one— they lived sixty-three years, traveled with circuses, and were buried in their native county. (Both courtesy North Carolina Collection; picture reprinted from William H. Pancoast, *The Carolina Twins* [No place, ca. 1871].)

Office of Grand Scribe,

RALEIGH, March 27, 1853.

WORTHY BROTHER: Below I give you the Quarterly P. W. and Exp. for the Quarter beginning April 1st, 1853, which you will communicate to the Division or Divisions under your jurisdiction, as soon as the Returns for the previous Quarter has been made out, the Per Centage due the Grand Division appropriated, and they have been or are ready to be forwarded to the Grand Scribe; AND NOT BEFORE.

QUARTERLY PASSWORD AND EXPLANATION,

P. W.—51, 38, 14, 51, 17.
Ex.—33, 10,—18, 33, 37, 17, 51, 35.

TRAVELING PASSWORD FROM OCT. 1, 1852, TO OCT. 1, 1853.

P. W.—17, 39, 15, 11.
Ex.—40, 39, 38—10, 14, 13, 13, 11, 10, 10.

7-50
The Sons of Temperance, founded in 1846 with a motto of love, purity, and fidelity, periodically revealed passwords to the members. The antialcohol group published a paper, *Spirit of the Age*. (Courtesy North Carolina Collection.)

7-51
Scraping rosin from pine trees was pictorially described by Porte Crayon in *Harper's New Monthly Magazine* for May 1857. (Courtesy North Carolina Collection.)

SCRAPING TURPENTINE.

7-52
Wilmington was a busy naval stores port. Here vast quantities of barreled turpentine await loading on sailing vessels in the river. (Courtesy NCDA&H.)

7-53
Letitia Harper Lindsay married Henry Humphreys, the original owner of Blandwood in Greensboro and proprietor of the Mount Hecla Cotton Mill. (Courtesy Mrs. Stephen W. Frontis, Greensboro.)

7-54
Scrip issued by Humphreys's mill in 1837 bore a drawing of the factory. (Courtesy Greensboro Historical Museum.)

7-56, 7-57, and 7-58
Porte Crayon visited Gold Hill in Rowan County and published in the August 1857 issue of *Harper's New Monthly Magazine* drawings and an account of the extensive gold operations there. Shown here are Cornish miners Mat Moyle and Nicky Trevethan deep in the mine, a kibble (an ore-bearing bucket) at the mouth of the bucket shaft, and rocking cradles operated by women. (Courtesy North Carolina Collection.)

AT MOUTH OF BUCKET SHAFT.

ROCKING CRADLES.

Rules and Regulations
To be observed by those living at the Salem Cotton Factory.

Article I.

§ 1. No family or individual need apply for employment, without at the same time furnishing a certificate from some of their most respectable and trustworthy neighbours, that they are of industrious habits and unexceptionable character.

§ 2. Families that are employed are considered as engaged for as long a time as they and the employer can agree, but are in no case to leave before they have given the employer one month's notice of their intention to do so.

§ 3. Single individuals are considered as engaged for as long a time as they and the employer can agree, but are in no case to leave before they have given the employer two weeks' notice of their intention to do so.

§ 4. Any one that wilfully or negligently injures any part of any building or of any machine, will be held accountable for such injury, and the damages deducted from his or her wages.

§ 5. The working hours in the mill will be from sun-rise until sun-set, from the 20th of March until the 20th of September; and the remaining six months of the year from sun-rise until half past seven, except on Saturday, when the machinery will stop at four o'clock.

Article II.

§ 1. Persons occupying the family apartments are considered as holding them from week to week, and shall furnish at least five competent hands to work in the factory.

§ 2. They are to take in as many boarders as they are requested to do by the main superintendent, and to furnish them with plain, wholesome and cleanly food.

§ 3. They are to keep their houses clean and orderly, and are to permit nothing to be done in the same contrary to the established rules of the place.

§ 4. They shall take every precaution to guard against fire. They shall not keep their ashes in wooden vessels, nor pour them out on the lot when warm. They shall not carry fire from one house to another in an open vessel, especially when there is any wind. They shall be careful not to let too much soot collect in the chimneys, but burn them out from time to time, during rainy weather.

§ 5. They shall not permit any of their boarders to leave the house at an unseasonable time, or do any thing that is not strictly according to the established rules.

§ 6. If the boarders in any manner misbehave, they shall never fail to remind them of their duty.

§ 7. If their admonitions to such boarders are not regarded, they shall inform the employer of the misconduct of such individuals; and if they fail to do this, they will be considered as encouraging such misconduct.

§ 8. They will be held accountable for any thing done in their families.

Article III.

§ 1. Individuals engaged to attend the different machinery, will repair to their posts punctually when the bell calls them to work, and are not to leave the same until the principal machinist stops the mill.

§ 2. During the working hours they are to act strictly according to the rules of the mill, and the directions given by the superintendents of the rooms in which they are employed.

§ 3. If they cannot attend from sickness or other cause, they are to acquaint the manager of the fact, and of the cause of absence.

§ 4. Unless called away by business, they are to remain at their boarding houses, and after nightfall especially, every one is expected to be at home.

§ 5. They are not to leave on a visit to any distance without informing the employer of their intention.

§ 6. Every one is expected carefully to avoid all that may tend to disturb the peace and harmony of the persons employed in this establishment.

§ 7. Every one is expected most strictly to observe the rules of order and morality, as otherwise his or her presence is no longer desirable.

7-55
In the 1840s the Salem Cotton Factory published strict rules and regulations for employees, who were required to work from sunrise to sunset during the spring and summer. (Courtesy Moravian Archives, Winston-Salem.)

7-59
The Charlotte Branch Mint, designed by William Strickland and built in the 1830s to provide coinage from North Carolina gold, is shown at about mid-century. The building was later moved and now houses the Mint Museum of Art. (Courtesy Daisy Wade Bridges, Charlotte.)

7-60
An advertisement of the sale of Frost's Ironworks in Stokes County in 1836 listed slaves along with land and grain. (Courtesy North Carolina Collection.)

LAND AND NEGROES FOR SALE!

Under an order of the late Court of Equity, held for the county of Stokes, I will sell on the first day of December next, at

FROST'S IRON-WORKS,

the following Tracts of Land, belonging to the heirs of James B. Frost, dec'd, to wit:

One called the HOMESTEAD TRACT, on Neetman's Creek, including the *Dwelling House, Tan-Yard, Grist Mill* and *Forge,* containing

183 Acres, more or less.

Also a Tract adjoining, containing **50** acres; another Tract of **75** acres. Also a Tract on Neetman's Creek, containing

100 Acres.

Also two Tracts on the north side of Dan river, one containing **25** and the other **70** acres, called the

IRON ORE BANK TRACTS.

At the same time and place, I will sell, as Executor of James B. Frost, A QUANTITY OF

Corn, Wheat, Rye and Oats.

The LANDS will be sold on a credit of one and two years, on bond and security with interest from the date. The terms of the Executor's sale will be made known on the day of sale.

Under the same decree, I will sell, at the

Court-House door in Germanton, on the 26th day of November (instant,)

SEVEN NEGROES,

consisting of Men, Women and Children. A credit of six months will be given, with note and security with interest from the date.

John H. Winston,
Commissioner.

Stokes County, N. C., Oct. 31, 1836.

Printed at the Chronicle office—Salem, N. C.

7-61
Farming the sea—fishing—provided a livelihood for whites and blacks in some communities near the coast. "Heading Herring," Porte Crayon captioned this drawing made at Belvidere Fishery on the Chowan River. It appeared in *Harper's New Monthly Magazine* in March 1857. (Courtesy NCDA&H.)

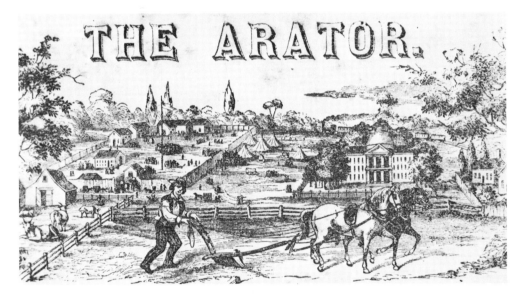

7-62
A romanticized farm scene decorated the front page of the *Arator*, May 1856, published in Raleigh. (Courtesy North Carolina Collection.)

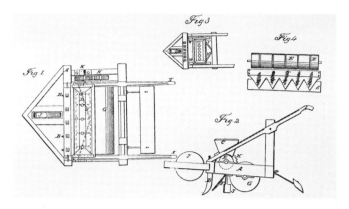

7-63
Among the many inventions of Richard J. Gatling, a native of Hertford County, was an improved seed planter, patented in 1844. (Courtesy National Archives, Washington.)

THE MARKETS.

Salisbury, June 17.

Apples, (dried) 50 @ $00; Bacon, 12 @ 15 ; Cotton, 6 @ 7 ; Cotton Yarn, 75 @ 00 ; Coffee 11 @ 12½ Corn, 75@00; Beeswax, 20@0 ; Butter 10 12½ ; Flour $4½ @ ; Feathers 28 ; Iron 3½ @4½; Linseed Oil 80 Molasses 35@40; Nails 4½@5; Oats 40@00; Irish Potatoes 125@ 00; Sweet do. 35 @ 40 ; Sugar, (brown) 7 @9 ; Do. Loaf. 00@ 12½ ; Salt, sack $2 75 ; Tallow 8 @9 Wheat 75@ $; Pork $6¼

FAYETTEVILLE, N. C.
June 10 —Beeswax 22 @ 23 : Bacon 12½ @ 13½ ; Cotton 8 @8¼ Corn 85 @95; Coffee 10½@11½ : Flour 475 @ : Feathers 32@35 : Flaxseed $100@000 Iron, Swedes, 5 @6 : do. English 3 @4 : Lard 13 @ 15 : Leather, sole, 20 23: Molasses 24@26: Nails, cut, 4½ 5: Oats, 50@ 60: Sugar, bro., 6 @ 9: do. loaf, 10 @ 11 : Salt, sack, 1 50 @ 1 60 : Tallow, 7 @8 : Wheat 85 $@ 90.

CHERAW, Jun 8.— Bacon per lb. 00 @ 12½ : Butter 20 @28 : Beeswax @ 20@21 : Coffee 12@ 15 : Cotton 8½@9½ : Corn $1 @ $112½ Eggs 12@15 : Flour 5½ @ $6 : Feathers 30 @35 : Iron 5@6½ : Lard 00@ 13: Leather (sole) 18 @ 22 : Molasses 35 @ 40 : do. Cuba 33 @ 37: Nails, cut, 6 @ 7 : Rice 4½ @ 5 ; Sugar, brown, 8 @ 10 : do. Loaf, 12½ @ 15 : Salt, Liverpool, 1 40 @ 1 50.

7-64
Market prices for commodities were published periodically by the newspapers. This list appeared in the *Carolina Watchman* (Salisbury), 17 June 1852. (Courtesy North Carolina Collection.)

7-65
William Little, who made this fine secretary with bookcase in Anson County, was one of the leading cabinetmakers in the Piedmont. (Courtesy Museum of Early Southern Decorative Arts, Winston-Salem.)

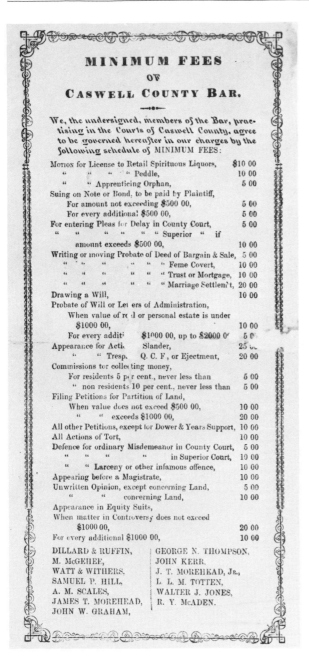

MINIMUM FEES
OF
CASWELL COUNTY BAR.

We, the undersigned, members of the Bar, practising in the Courts of Caswell County, agree to be governed hereafter in our charges by the following schedule of MINIMUM FEES:

Motion for License to Retail Spirituous Liquors,	$10 00
" " " Peddle,	10 00
" " Apprenticing Orphan,	5 00
Suing on Note or Bond, to be paid by Plaintiff,	
For amount not exceeding $500 00,	5 00
For every additional $500 00,	5 00
For entering Pleas for Delay in County Court,	5 00
" " " " " Superior " if	
amount exceeds $500 00,	10 00
Writing or moving Probate of Deed of Bargain & Sale,	5 00
" " " " " Feme Covert,	10 00
" " " " " Trust or Mortgage,	10 00
" " " " " Marriage Settlem't,	20 00
Drawing a Will,	10 00
Probate of Will or Letters of Administration,	
When value of real or personal estate is under	
$1000 00,	10 00
For every additi $1000 00, up to $2000 0'	5 0
Appearance for Acti Slander,	25 0
" " Tresp. Q. C. F, or Ejectment,	20 00
Commissions for collecting money,	
For residents 5 per cent., never less than	5 00
" non residents 10 per cent., never less than	5 00
Filing Petitions for Partition of Land,	
When value does not exceed $500 00,	10 00
" " exceeds $1000 00,	20 00
All other Petitions, except for Dower & Years Support,	10 00
All Actions of Tort,	10 00
Defence for ordinary Misdemeanor in County Court,	5 00
" " " " in Superior Court,	10 00
" " Larceny or other infamous offence,	10 00
Appearing before a Magistrate,	10 00
Unwritten Opinion, except concerning Land,	5 00
" " concerning Land,	10 00
Appearance in Equity Suits,	
When matter in Controversy does not exceed	
$1000 00,	20 00
For every additional $1000 00,	10 00

DILLARD & RUFFIN,	GEORGE N. THOMPSON,
M. McGEHEE,	JOHN KERR,
WATT & WITHERS,	J. T. MOREHEAD, Jr.,
SAMUEL P. HILL,	L. L. M. TOTTEN,
A. M. SCALES,	WALTER J. JONES,
JAMES T. MOREHEAD,	R. Y. McADEN.
JOHN W. GRAHAM,	

7-66
Members of the Caswell County bar published their minimum fees in the 1850s. (Courtesy North Carolina Collection.)

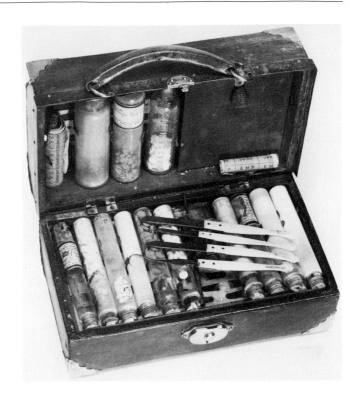

7-67
Dr. Wood Tucker Johnson (1802–62) carried this leather medical bag during his practice in Franklin County. (Courtesy Anthony of Wilson; by permission of the Country Doctor Museum, Bailey.)

DAGUERREOTYPE MINIATURES.

MR. HUMPHREY would respectfully announce to the citizens of Wilmington, that he purposes remaining in this place a short time, and of giving all an opportunity of procuring a correct likeness of themselves and friends in his superior style.

Having connection with three of the most successful Daguerreotype Rooms in the State of New York, he has advantages which but few artists can realize.

Portraits taken in a superior style, perfectly true to nature, of very fine tone, gilded and colored so that no climate will effect them in the least.

Daguerreotypes taken by the old process, gilded and colored so as to render them equal to those taken at the present day.

Portraits of sick or diseased persons taken at their residences if required.

Particular attention given to those wishing to engage in the business. Instruction with all the latest improvements, apparatus and stock, furnished on reasonable terms.

For further information inquire at his room, on Front street up stairs adjoining Dr. Ware's, directly opposite the Chronicle Office,

January 30, 1846.   20-tf

7-68 and 7-69

In 1846, only a few years after the daguerreotype was invented, a "Mr. Humphrey" set up a "room" in Wilmington and advertised his services to both the living and the dead. The earliest known outdoor photographic scene in North Carolina, probably made by Humphrey in mid-1846, may have been taken from his window. It shows St. James Episcopal Church and the John Burgwyn house. The foreground is unclear, but may picture a fire engine during a public ceremony. The daguerreotype was acquired by the Amon Carter Museum in 1981 along with a number of Mexican War scenes, a suggestion that Humphrey may have been the first war photographer. (Advertisement from *Wilmington Journal*, 25 December 1846, courtesy North Carolina Collection; daguerreotype by permission of Amon Carter Museum, Fort Worth.)

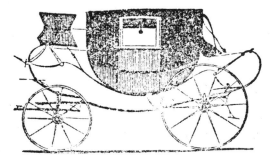

Encourage Home Manufactures.

Gardner & McKethan

HAVE lately made considerable improvement in their style of Work, and have now on hand a GENERAL ASSORTMENT, consisting of

Carriages, Barouches, Buggies, Gigs, Sulkeys, Wagons, &c.

Which for elegance of shape and finish, and durability, will compare with any made in the United States.

Persons wishing to buy, would do well to call and examine our Work, as we have determined to sell LOW for Cash, or approved Notes.

Having in our employ first rate Smiths, we are prepared to do any Iron work in the above line on moderate terms.

We warrant all our Work to be of good and faithful workmanship and materials, for one year

☞ REPAIRING faithfully executed, at short notice, and on reasonable terms.

FAYETTEVILLE, Feb. 9, 1846.

7-70
In the spirit of the times, Gardner & McKethan used the slogan "Encourage Home Manufactures" in an advertisement in the *Fayetteville Observer*, 27 April 1847. (Courtesy North Carolina Collection.)

7-72
William Joseph Griffin (1854–97) of Elizabeth City posed with his horse rocker for an unknown artist. (Courtesy North Carolina Collection.)

7-71
The life insurance industry in North Carolina had its beginning in the antebellum period. (Courtesy Rare Book Room, Duke University Library.)

NORTH CAROLINA
MUTUAL LIFE INSURANCE COMPANY.

FIRST ANNUAL REPORT, RALEIGH, JULY 1, 1850.

The following statement will show the operations of the Company, since its organization, on the 1st of April, 1849, to the 20th June, 1850, when the Books of the Company were closed.

		DISBURSEMENTS.		
Whole number of Policies issued,	615			
Whole number of Policies Cancelled and Expired,	5	A'mt paid Salaries, Commissions to Agents, Medical Examiner's fees, Printing, Ad'tising, Books, Blanks, Stationery, Postage, Office Rent, and Office Furniture,	6,613 15	
Whole number of Policies in force,	610			
Amount Insured in the above Policies,	937,236 00			
Amount Cancelled and Expired,	4,150 00	Amount paid Losses, by death	1,400 00	8,013 15
Total Liabilities,	$933,086 00	Nett proceeds.		$23,565 33
RECEIPTS.		**ASSETS.**		
		Cape Fear Bank Stock and Premium Notes,	14,262 82	
Nett Premiums Rec'd during the year,	31,417 49	Amount in hands of Treasurer,	8,519 83	
Interest Rec'd on Renewals, &c.	160 99 — 31,578 48	Amount in hands of Agents,	782 68	23,565 33

7-73 (right)
Porte Crayon attended a picnic and party in 1857 at Holtsburg Depot on the Yadkin River in Davidson County and made this drawing for *Harper's New Monthly Magazine*, August 1857. (Courtesy North Carolina Collection.)

7-74
Backcountry sports included butting, here pictured by Harden E. Taliaferro in his *Fisher's River Scenes and Characters* (1859). (Courtesy North Carolina Collection.)

7-75
A cockfight in eastern North Carolina was depicted by Porte Crayon in *Harper's New Monthly Magazine*, May 1857. (Courtesy North Carolina Collection.)

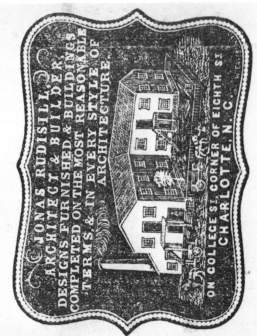

☞ **The Raleigh City Temperance Society,** will meet in the *METHODIST* E. CHURCH, on Friday evening next, (the 29th inst.) at 7½ o'clock.   D. H. HOLLAND, Sec'y.
June 27.   191-1t.

TO MR. GIDEON ALSTON,
OF CHATHAM COUNTY, N. C.

SIR: In looking over The North Carolina Standard of the 20th inst. I discover a challenge over your signature, headed "Chatham against Nash," in which you state that you are "authorized to take a bet of any a- " mount that may be offered, to fight a main of cocks, " at any place that may be agreed upon by the parties, " to be fought the ensuing spring," which challenge I ACCEPT, and do propose to meet you at Rolesville, in Wake county, N. C. on the last Wednesday in May next, the parties to show thirty one cocks each— fight four days and be governed by the rules as laid down in Turner's Cock Laws—which, if you think proper to accede to, you will signify through this or any other medium you may select, and then I will name the sum for which we shall fight, as that privilege was surrendered by you in your challenge.
I am, sir, very respectfully, &c.
NICHOLAS W. ARRINGTON,
near Hillliardston, Nash county,
North Carolina.
June 22nd, 1838.   191-3t.

HILLSBORO' FEMALE SEMINARY.
The Fall Session of this institution will commence July 19th. The Terms of Tuition (payable in advance) are, as heretofore,

Fourth or Lowest Class,	$12 50
Second and Third Class,	15 00
First or Highest Class,	17 00
Ornamental Needle Work,	5 00
Drawing and Painting,	12 00
Music, on Piano or Guitar,	25 00
French,	15 00

June 27.   191-3t

WOULD most respectfully announce to the Citizens of Charlotte and surrounding country, that he still continues the above business in Charlotte. Were he is prepared to furnish DOORS, BLINDS AND SASH, to the public on the most reasonable terms, and on the shortest notice.

Having a great many small claims for work done, scattered all over the country, he is determined to change his method of doing business *and hereafter will require*

CASH,

for all work done in his Machine Shop, before removal.
Dec. 7. 1858.   59—6m

7-76
Nicholas W. Arrington, in the *North Carolina Standard* (Raleigh) of 27 June 1838, accepted the challenge of Gideon Alston for a Nash versus Chatham cockfight at Rolesville under Turner's Cock Laws. (Courtesy North Carolina Collection.)

7-77
Frederick Law Olmsted pictured a log cabin with mud and stick chimney, located near Fayetteville, in his *A Journey in the Seaboard Slave States* (1856). (Courtesy North Carolina Collection.)

7-78
Jonas Rudisill, architect and builder, offered his services through the *North Carolina Whig* (Charlotte), 1 November 1859. (Courtesy North Carolina Collection.)

A CARD.

WM. PERCIVAL,
Architect and Civil Engineer,
Office Fayetteville Street,
Raleigh, N. C.
RESPECTFULLY offers his services to the public.

In the *Architectural* line will supply *Designs, Specifications* and *Superintendance* for *Churches* and *Public* and *Private Buildings.*

In the *Civil Engineering* Department will make surveys and locations for *Rail Roads, Canals,* &c. and Superintend their Construction. He will also attend to *Drainage* of *Farm Lands,* and all other branches connected with his Profession.

With an *Educational Training* and a thorough *Practical Experience* of more than sixteen years, he hopes to give satisfaction.

Respectfully he refers to those by whom he is engaged in this State.

Ex-Governor Bragg.
Building Committee, University, N. C.
Building Committee, Raleigh New Baptist Church
Building Committee, Yanceyville Court House.
m. S. Battle, Rocky Mount, Edgecombe County,
R. S. Tucker, Raleigh,
M. Boylan, do.
C. Harrison, do.
K. H. Lewis, Nash County,
Robert Norfleet, Tarboro'.

All letters on business promptly attended to.   March 12, 1859.

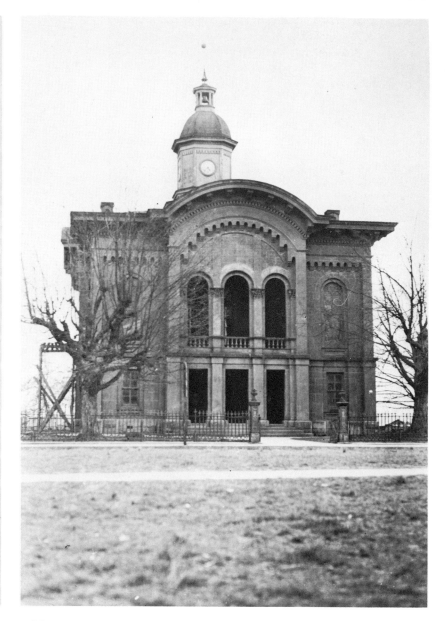

7-79
William Percival, who placed this advertisement in the *Tarborough Southerner* on 12 March 1859, was one of the best-known architects to practice in the state. (Courtesy NCDA&H.)

7-80
Among the buildings designed by Percival was the unique Caswell County Courthouse, completed about 1860 and shown here in a postwar photograph. (Courtesy North Carolina Collection.)

7-81
The library at Hayes Plantation, built about 1818 for James C. Johnston with the probable assistance of architect William Nichols, held the state's best private collection of books in the antebellum period. This photograph was made by Frances Benjamin Johnston. (Courtesy North Carolina Collection.)

7-82
Post-Civil War painting of Fort Defiance, the home built by William Lenoir in Happy Valley (Caldwell County) late in the eighteenth century. (Courtesy North Carolina Collection; reprinted from Thomas Felix Hickerson, *Happy Valley* [Chapel Hill, 1940].)

7-83
Among the unusual number of fine antebellum homes in Warren County was Montmorenci, whose stairway is shown prior to its dismantlement and transfer to the Winterthur Museum. (Courtesy Henry Francis du Pont Winterthur Museum, Winterthur Archives.)

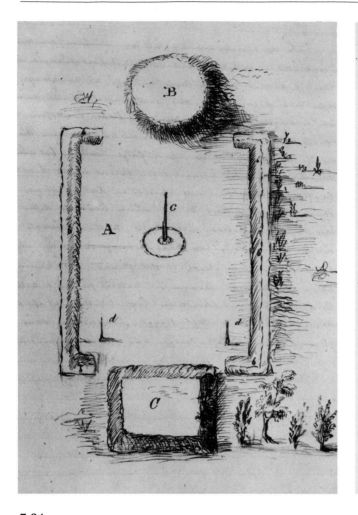

7-84
The game of chunky (chungke, chenco) was a favorite Indian sport. This yard was drawn by William Bartram in 1789. (Courtesy Historical Society of Pennsylvania, Bartram Papers, Philadelphia.)

7-85 (top right)
William Holland Thomas (1805–93), a white friend who was adopted by the Cherokees, prepared this list of Indians who helped capture Tsali (Charley); for their service, they were allowed to remain in the state. (Courtesy Manuscript Department, Duke University Library.)

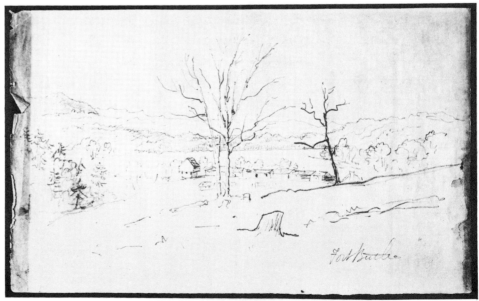

7-86
Fort Butler at Murphy was used by federal troops who sought to drive the Chero-kees out of the mountains in the 1830s. (Courtesy Jerry C. Cashion; original in National Archives, Washington.)

7-87
Junaluska (1776?–1858), the Cherokee who saved Andrew Jackson's life in the Battle of Horseshoe Bend, was repaid by being forced into exile. Homesick in the Oklahoma territory, he walked back to his beloved mountains and was buried near Robbinsville. If this is in fact a photograph of Junaluska, a photographer must have visited the remote mountain region no later than 1858. (Courtesy NCDA&H.)

63. If any free negro, or person of mixed blood, shall knowingly suffer any slave to play at any game of cards, dice, nine pins, or any game of chance, hazard, or skill, whether for money, liquor, or any kind of property, or not, in his house, or in the yard, field, or garden attached or belonging to his house, he shall be deemed guilty of a misdemeanor; and, on conviction, shall receive not exceeding thirty-nine lashes on his bare back.

64. If a free negro shall entertain any slave in his house, during Sunday, or in the night between sunset and sunrise, he shall forfeit and pay two dollars for every offence, for the use of the county in which the offence shall be committed.

65. No free negro shall hawk or peddle in any county, without first obtaining a license from the court of pleas and quarter-sessions of that county; which license shall be granted for but one year, and only when seven or more justices are present, and upon satisfactory evidence of the good character of the applicant. And if any free negro shall offend against this section, he shall be deemed guilty of a misdemeanor.

66. If any free negro shall wear or carry about his person, or keep in his house, any shot-gun, musket, rifle, pistol, sword, dagger, or bowie-knife, unless he shall have obtained a license therefor from the court of pleas and quarter-sessions of his county, within one year next preceding the time of the wearing, keeping, or carrying thereof, he shall be guilty of a misdemeanor.

67. If any free negro shall, directly or indirectly, sell or give to any person, bond or free, any spirituous liquor, he shall be deemed guilty of a misdemeanor.

68. Every slave or free person of color, who shall hereafter be convicted of any felony, for which no specific punishment is prescribed by statute, and which is now allowed the benefit of clergy, shall be imprisoned at the discretion of the court, not exceeding two years; and, in addition to such imprisonment, the court may sentence the convict to receive one or more public whippings, or to stand in the pillory, or (if a free negro) to pay a fine, regard being had to the circumstances of each case.

7-88
Excerpts from the code in effect in 1854 reveal that the word *free* had a severely limited meaning when it modified the word *Negro*. (Courtesy North Carolina Collection.)

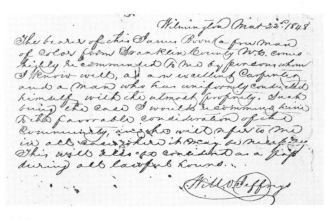

7-89
A pass for James Boon, a "free man of color," signed by William Jeffreys of Wilmington in 1848. (Courtesy NCDA&H.)

NOTIE.

THE subscriber wishes his friends to know
he has still a large assortment of fine

Cabinet Furniture,

on hand, ... varieties of the most Fashionable and durable mahogany, rosewood, and walnut house-hold

FURNITURE

used in the most fashionable Parlors, and also
among housekeepers of all circumstances.
French Sofas,
   Chairs,
      Bedsteads of all kinds,
         Bureaus with mirrors,
            Mahogany, Walnut, and Oak
               Extension Tables,
                  Ataydias of all kinds
are on hand. Persons wanting Furniture will
find it to their interest to call and examine. Money is greatly desired by the proprietor, and for
cash good bargains may be expected.
For all

BURIAL

purposes full and ready accommodation is ever
at hand to carry to any distance at very short
notice and with all necessary care and attention.
   We invite and solicit our customers to consult
their own interest, and we shall not lack support.   THO'S DAY.
Milnto, march 1858.   tf

7-90
Thomas Day, a free person of color, had been making furniture in Milton for more than thirty years when he placed this advertisement in the 21 May 1858 issue of the *Milton Chronicle*. (Courtesy NCDA&H.)

7-91
This sampler chest made by Thomas Day once belonged to Calvin H. Wiley and is now in the North Carolina Collection. (Courtesy Los Angeles County Museum of Art; printed in *Two Centuries of Black American Art* [Los Angeles, 1976].)

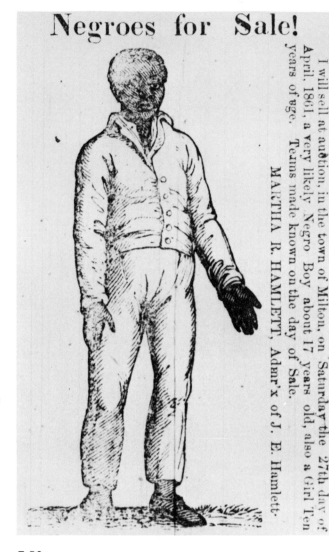

Negroes for Sale!

I will sell at auction, in the town of Milton, on Saturday the 27th day of April, 1861, a very likely Negro Boy about 17 years old, also a Girl Ten years of age. Terms made known on the day of Sale.

MARTHA R. HAMLETT, Adm'r'x of J. E. Hamlett.

7-92
The *Milton Chronicle* for 12 April 1861 advertised "a very likely Negro Boy about 17 years old" and a 10-year-old girl. (Courtesy NCDA&H.)

7-93
A mulatto woman named Julia and her two children brought James Hargrove $2,035 in Mecklenburg County in 1854. (Courtesy North Carolina Collection; reprinted from Daniel A. Tompkins, *History of Mecklenburg County and the City of Charlotte* [Charlotte, 1903], volume 1.)

NOTICE.

WAS committed to the Jail of Johnston County, on the 4th inst. a negro man, who says his name is JESSE and that he belongs to George Bell, of Georgia. Jesse appears to be about twenty-five years of age, black thin visage, about five feet high. I am induced to think that he belongs to the Raleigh rail road, as that appears to be the only thing that he knows any thing about. The owner is requested to come forward, prove property, pay charges and take him away.
A. BALLENGER, Sheriff.
Johnston County, July 6th 1838.   193-tf.

Saddle and Harness Maker Wanted.

A Good Saddle and Harness maker will find constant and profitable employment. Address to J. B. M'DADE, Chapel Hill, N. C.
July 11, 1838.   193-3t.

$20 REWARD. Runaway or Stolen, from the Subscriber, on the 27th of last month, a negro woman and two children; the woman is tall and black, and a few days before she went off, I burnt her with a hot iron on the left side of her face; I tried to make the letter M. and she kept a cloth over her head and face and a fly bonnet on her head, so as to cover the burn, she has a very wide vacancy between her upper fore teeth; her children are both boys; the oldest one is in his seventh year; he is a mulatto; he has blue eyes; the youngest is black; he is in his fifth year, he is cock'eyed, inclined, to be cross eyed. The woman's name is Bettey, commonly called Bet. The oldest boy's name is Burrel and the other ones name is Gray. The above reward of 20 dollars will be given to any person that will deliver the said negroes to me. It is probable they may attempt to pass as free.
MICAJAH RICKS.
Nash County, July 7th, 1838.   193-3t.

7-94
In the 18 July 1838 issue of the *North Carolina Standard* (Raleigh), Micajah Ricks described what apparently was an unsuccessful effort to brand a female slave on the cheek with the letter *M*. (Courtesy North Carolina Collection.)

7-95
Southerners were not the only Americans guilty of the stereotyping of blacks; *Harper's New Monthly Magazine* prior to the Civil War carried Porte Crayon's prose and drawings treating blacks as objects of amusement. Aunt Rose, who worked at the fisheries along the Chowan River, was pictured in the March 1857 issue. (Courtesy North Carolina Collection.)

George M. Horton. —This is the name of an extraordinary young slave, the property of Mr. James Horton, who lives in Chatham county, about half way between Chapel Hill and Pittsborough, who has astonished all who have witnessed his poetic talent. He is about 25 years of age, and of a mild and humble disposition and deportment. The following account of his beginning and progress in learning, was derived from himself and has been communicated to us by a friend, proverbial for his philanthropic feelings. He first learned the Alphabet, from hearing the school children rehearsing it. He then took the Spelling-book and became acquainted with form of the letters. Gratified with such employment, he was soon able to spell and read. At this period, some person gave him a copy of Westley's Hymns, with which he was delighted, spending most of his leisure hours in reading it, and while at work endeavoring to make verses in imitation of it. Finding himself at a loss, in properly constructing his verses, he studied Grammar and Prosody. Being very intimate with the Students of the University, who had discovered his extraordinary genius, he delighted to visit them, whenever a Sunday or holyday permitted. He received from them, a variety of Poetic Works, the reading of which constitutes his greatest pleasure.— They were in the habit of selecting topics upon which to exercise his poetic muse; the following Sunday he would return and have them transcribed. What is very astonishing, he has not only to make his verses, but retain them in memory, until he can meet with some one to copy them; and though he may have three or four sets of verses, upon different subjects, his memory is so retentive, that he has no difficulty in recounting them in turn, to his scribe. Where an abbreviation is necessary to preserve the metre, he will point it out. He has no pleasure in associating with any but those of intelligence, and is always most delighted, when he can get an amanuensis to transcribe his verses, & for this purpose, every Sunday, will walk 8 or 9 miles, to visit the Students of College. We insert in to-day's Register, one of his effusions, on the Evening and Morning, and shall select others from a number which have been sent us.

7-96 (left)
The discovery of George Moses Horton's literary talents was reported in the *Raleigh Register* (semiweekly edition), 18 July 1828. (Courtesy NCDA&H.)

7-97 (top)
One of George Moses Horton's acrostics, the first letter of each line combining to spell "Julia Shepard." His *The Hope of Liberty* (1829), the first book written by a southern black, made Horton North Carolina's first "professional" poet. He was taken to Philadelphia after the war by a federal soldier. (Courtesy Southern Historical Collection, Pettigrew Family Papers.)

7-98
Omar ibn Said, called Omeroh or Moreau, was a Mohammedan slave owned by Governor John Owen. He learned English and translated the Bible into his native language. (Courtesy North Carolina Collection.)

7-99
The banner of the Tippecanoe Club of Greensboro sought to contrast William Henry Harrison's "Republican simplicity" with Martin Van Buren's "Locofoco arrogance." (Courtesy NCDA&H.)

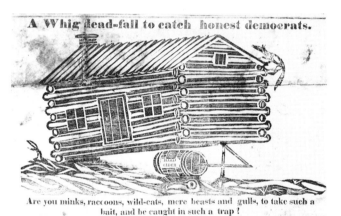

7-100
Van Buren supporters countered with a cartoon portraying Whig symbols—log cabin, hard cider, and a raccoon mascot—as tricks to catch "honest" Democrats. (Courtesy North Carolina Collection; reprinted from the *North Carolinian* [Fayetteville], 10 October 1840.)

7-102
Three natives of North Carolina are portrayed in this Whig political cartoon: Polk (Mecklenburg) is being held up by Thomas Hart Benton (Orange) and being prodded by Andrew Jackson (Union County). At left is John C. Calhoun, and at the top of the pole is Clay. (Courtesy Library of Congress.)

7-101
A Whig banner used in Yadkin County in the presidential campaign of 1840 carried on the reverse the slogan "The Hero and Farmer for us!" (Courtesy North Carolina Collection.)

7-103
John Owen (1787–1841), governor 1828–30, declined the Whig vice-presidential nomination in 1839 and thus forfeited the opportunity of succeeding to the presidency upon Harrison's death two years later. (Courtesy North Carolina Collection.)

7-104
When President Polk visited his alma mater at Chapel Hill in 1847, he was accommodated in an annex to the Eagle Hotel, specially built by proprietress Nancy Hilliard. (Courtesy North Carolina Collection.)

7-105
Louis D. Wilson, a senator from Edgecombe County, was colonel of the Twelfth Infantry in the Mexican War, but, like many other soldiers, he died from fever rather than from battle. Wilson County was named for him. (Courtesy NCDA&H.)

HEAD QUARTERS,
Salisbury, May 18, 1852.

THE Officers of the 3rd Regiment of Volunteers are hereby commanded to appear at the Court House in Salisbury, on the 2d day of July, at 10 o'clock, with side arms for Drill and Court Martial, and on the 3d, at 9 o'clock, with their respective Companies for Review and Inspection, with three rounds of cartridge.   By order of
C. S. BROWN, Col. Com'ant.
W. M. BARKER, Adj.   6w3

To the People
DEMOCRATS AND WHIGS!!

PUBLIC MEETINGS

WILL be held at the following times and places in the County of Rowan, to discuss the great and important questions that now agitate the country---that is to say :

At Christopher Lyrely's on Monday, 25th Sept.
" Jas. C. Roseman's on Wednesday, 27th "
" Gold Hill on Saturday, 30th September.
" Thomas Wood's on Friday, 13th October.
" Tobias Kesler's on Saturday, 14th   "

Never before, since the foundation of our Government, have the rights of the people of the SOUTHERN STATES been in greater danger ---the UNION itself is in peril. Let all those who value the Union---who love their own families, and their own firesides, rally to the rescue. Come up, hear, and judge for yourselves.

N. B.---Speakers of both political parties are invited, and, no doubt, will attend.

7-106
Militia drills remained popular in the state after the Mexican War. This notice appeared in the *Carolina*
Watchman (Salisbury), 17 June 1852. (Courtesy North Carolina Collection.)

7-107
Northern attempts to pass the Wilmot Proviso, which would have blocked the extension of slavery to the newly acquired territory, led
to bipartisan opposition in North Carolina in 1848. (Courtesy North Carolina Collection.)

7-108
Bedford Brown (1795–1870) of Caswell County served in the United States Senate from 1829 to 1840. A staunch unionist, he warned "fire eaters" both North and South that agitation of the slavery issue would lead to disunion. The picture was made by Matthew Brady. (Courtesy North Carolina Collection.)

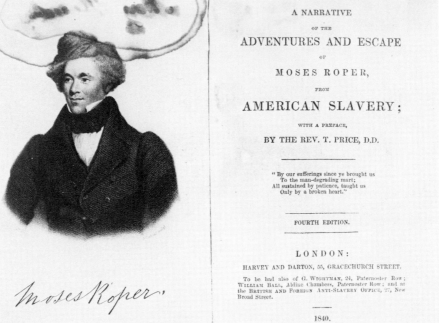

7-109
Moses Roper ran away from his owner in Caswell County, and in 1838 his story was published in London. The fourth edition of his narrative carried an unusual portrait of the former slave. (Courtesy North Carolina Collection.)

7-110
David Beard, owner of a hat shop in Guilford County, was on several occasions accused of providing sanctuary for runaway slaves by hiding them beneath animal skins. The photograph of the shop was made in 1873. (Courtesy Friends Historical Collection, Guilford College.)

7-111
In a letter written from Guilford County in 1852, Daniel Wilson described the temper of the people against members of the American Missionary Association. (Courtesy Fisk University, American Missionary Association Archives.)

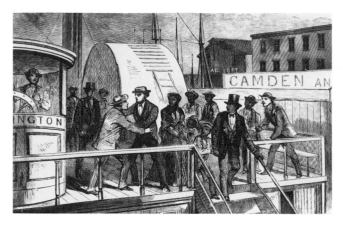

7-112

In an engraving made in Philadelphia, John Hill Wheeler, on his way to his post as minister to Nicaragua, is being restrained while his slaves, Jane Johnson and her children, are escorted to freedom by abolitionists. A court declined to return them to Wheeler. (Courtesy North Carolina Collection; reprinted from William Still, *The Underground Rail Road* [Philadelphia, 1872].)

TAXES!
TAXES! TAXES!

All persons who owe their Taxes for the year 1858, and preceeding years are requested to call at my office and settle by the first of August next, or meet me at the different precints at the time of listing and pay up or they will find their property at the *Court-House door for sale*, as no longer indulgence will be given.

P. F. WHITE, Sh'ff.

June 22d, 1859.

7-117

"No longer indulgence will be given," Sheriff P. F. White of Chowan County warned delinquent taxpayers in 1859. Loss of property for nonpayment of taxes was an annual threat. (Courtesy North Carolina Collection.)

7-113

Hinton Rowan Helper (1829–1909) was only twenty-eight years old when he published *The Impending Crisis. . .*, a flawed but powerful prowhite, antislavery book. After the war, Helper advocated the rounding up of blacks and placing them on reservations prior to their expulsion from the country. He committed suicide at the age of eighty. (Courtesy North Carolina Collection; reprinted from *Frank Leslie's Illustrated Newspaper*, 24 December 1859.)

7-114

Daniel Worth (1795–1862) organized the first antislavery society in Indiana. Back in his native North Carolina in 1860, he was convicted of violating the "David Walker law" of 1830 by distributing "incendiary" literature. While Worth was in jail awaiting trial, the *Daily Progress* (New Bern) asked, "Why not take him out and hang him?" (Courtesy North Carolina Collection.)

7-115

John Anthony Copeland, formerly of Raleigh, participated in John Brown's raid. Prior to being hanged at Harper's Ferry, Copeland was reported to have said, "I had rather die than be a slave." (Courtesy NCDA&H.)

7-116

William Rufus King (1786–1853), a native of Sampson County, was elected vice-president of the United States on the Democratic ticket in 1852. He was given the oath of office in Cuba, where he had gone for his health, but he died in Alabama before going to Washington to assume his duties. (Courtesy North Carolina Collection.)

7-118
James Cochran Dobbin
(1814–57), a Democrat
from Fayetteville, was influential in guiding through the
legislature a bill to establish a
state asylum for the insane.
He served as secretary of the
navy under President Franklin Pierce. The portrait was
painted by Eastman Johnson
in 1856. (Courtesy North
Carolina Collection.)

7-119
John W. Ellis (1820–61) of
Rowan County was elected
governor in 1858 and won
reelection two years later. He
died 7 July 1861 at Red Sulphur Springs, Virginia,
where he was seeking rest
from the strain brought on
by secession and war. (Courtesy NCDA&H.)

THE RACE BETWEEN LITTLE AD AND HIS MAMMA!

Pool. Farewell Ellis!—I must leave thee,—
　　My steed picks up his feet so well—
　　When out of sight,—don't let it, grieve thee,
　　But listen!—and, you'll hear my bell!
　　Say! where are all your *"Eastern speeches"?*
　　Where's the *"eggs"* these *"geese"* have laid?
　　Where, are now, these same, *"horse-leeches"?*
　　You mentioned, in that *"speech"* you made?

Ellis. Hold! Mister Pool!—stop! just a minute—
　　I want my *"tin-cup"* from Ad's tail!
　　Oh! now I wish there was "suthin" in it!
　　For, alas! my strength—begins to fail!

Little Darkie.—
　　Go it! Little Ad—I, bid you,
　　Hear de white-folks how dey shout!
　　De "little darkies" now am wid you,
　　Your "mudder" knows dat you are out!

Old Sow.—
　　Remember her, who gave you being!
　　And suckled you *so well* till now,
　　On! do not slight your mother!—seeing
　　That, sadness sits upon her brow!

Ad. Farewell "mater"!—thou dids't give me
　　Life, before your fortune's fell,
　　Farewell Ellis!—tho' 'twill grieve thee
　　Yet I bid you *both farewell!*

Tune—"The Old Sow's Tail."

Ellis. Toll the Bell mournfully, sadly and sorrowfully;
　　Running this race, is not "wisely nor well."

Pool. Strike the Bell cheerily, ring it out merily,
　　Echo shall catch it from Mountain and dell.

Ellis. Then, go it! old Porker, "desaving" old joker—
　　Show 'em such racers can *drive all before 'em.*

Pool. Dash! darling, dash away! spread out and
　　　　splash 'em,
　　Show 'em *the tail* of our Pig, Ad Valorem!

So spake the Twa Johnnies, astride their pig ponies,
　　Young Ad, and his Mother, to run for *the Cup;*
The Pig was in keeping; his Mother was weeping,
　　One tail was a beauty, the other *"druv up."*

"On! on! Ad Valorem," cried Johny, "before 'em"
　　"Hurra for Free Suffrage"! cried Johny, behind;
Young Ad was in glory; but sad is the story,
　　Free Suffrage was spavined, and broken in wind.

She was lame of a leg, and could scarce move a peg;
　　She limped and she blowed, and could only *but follow,*
When the Palace was won, by our Pasquotank John,
　　John Ellis was sprawled in the nearest *hog wollow.*

7-120
"Equality at the ballot box,
equality at the tax box," was
the slogan of the Whigs,
whose newspaper, the *Little
Ad* (Greensboro) on 23 June
1860 depicted Democratic
Governor John W. Ellis attempting to retrieve his tin
cup from the tail of a pig, the
Whig mascot. (Courtesy
NCDA&H.)

7-121
On 21 April 1861, following the firing on Fort Sumter by South Carolinians, Secretary of War Simon Cameron wired Ellis for two regiments of troops to help put down the secessionists. (Courtesy NCDA&H.)

7-122
The governor indignantly replied, "You can get no troops from North Carolina" for the purpose of "subjugating the States of the South." (Courtesy NCDA&H.)

STATE OF NORTH CAROLINA.

A PROCLAMATION,
BY JOHN W. ELLIS,
GOVERNOR OF NORTH CAROLINA

WHEREAS: By Proclamation of Abraham Lincoln, President of the United States, followed by a requisition of Simon Cameron, Secretary of War, I am informed that the said Abraham Lincoln has made a call for 75,000 men to be employed for the invasion of the peaceful homes of the South, and for the violent subversion of the liberties of a free people, constituting a large part of the whole population of the late United States: And, whereas, this high-handed act of tyrannical outrage is not only in violation of all constitutional law, in utter disregard of every sentiment of humanity and Christian civilization, and conceived in a spirit of aggression unparalleled by any act of recorded history, but is a direct step towards the subjugation of the whole South, and the conversion of a free Republic, inherited from our fathers, into a military despotism, to be established by worse than foreign enemies on the ruins of our once glorious Constitution of Equal Rights.

Now, therefore, I, JOHN W. ELLIS, Governor of the State of North-Carolina, for these extraordinary causes, do hereby issue this, my Proclamation, notifying and requesting the Senators and Members of the House of Commons of the General Assembly of North-Carolina, to meet in Special Session at the Capitol, in the City of Raleigh, on Wednesday the first day of May next. And I furthermore exhort all good citizens throughout the State to be mindful that their first allegiance is due to the Sovereignty which protects their homes and dearest interests, as their first service is due for the sacred defence of their hearths, and of the soil which holds the graves of our glorious dead.

United action in defence of the sovereignty of North-Carolina, and of the rights of the South, becomes now the duty of all.

Given under my hand, and attested by the Great Seal of the State. Done at the City of Raleigh, the 17th day of April, A. D., 1861, and in the eighty-fifth year of our Independence,

JOHN. W. ELLIS.

By the Governor,
GRAHAM DAVES, *Private Secretary.*

7-123
Ellis called President Lincoln's actions "tyrannical outrage" and summoned the legislature into special session. (Courtesy NCDA&H.)

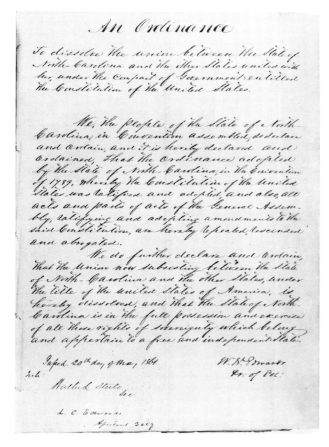

7-125
A Confederate recruiting poster was issued in Salisbury twelve days before North Carolina seceded. (Courtesy National Archives, Washington.)

7-124
The ordinance adopted in convention on 20 May 1861 did not include the word *secede*. Instead, it repealed, rescinded, and abrogated the ordinance of 1789 by which North Carolina had ratified the Constitution. (Courtesy NCDA&H.)

7-126
Eleven days after adoption of the ordinance of secession, eighteen-year-old Charles Stevens Powell of Johnston County enlisted as first sergeant in Company E, Fourteenth Regiment of Volunteers. He posed with an arsenal of weapons—a Colt revolving rifle with bayonet, an officer's sword, a Colt "Model 1855" revolver, and a bowie knife. (Courtesy William S. Powell, Chapel Hill.)

7-127
According to legend, women converted their gowns into the regimental flag for the Gaston Blues. Captured by the Federals, the flag was later returned to North Carolina. (Courtesy North Carolina Collection.)

7-128
Men and boys often formed local organizations to learn the rudiments of community protection. Early in the war faculty and students organized the Trinity Guards at the Methodist school in Randolph County. Braxton Craven, the school's principal and first commandant of the Salisbury Prison, stands in front center. (Courtesy Duke University Archives.)

7-129
Henry Lawson Wyatt (1842–61) of Edgecombe County lost his life in the fighting at Bethel, Virginia, on 10 June 1861; he was the first Confederate soldier to die in battle. (Courtesy NCDA&H.)

NORTH CAROLINA SHOE FACTORY.

THE SUBSCRIBERS ADOPT THIS METHOD of informing the public that they have established, and have now in operation in Raleigh, a manufactory of **WOODEN SHOES,** which they can confidently recommend as the cheapest shoes now manufactured, and also as an article which will prove valuable and lasting.—Their shoes are made of gum and poplar wood, and are lined, and finished off with leather tops and ears. These shoes are lighter than leather brogans of the same number. They are impervious to water, and, while they will last a *long* time, they will also keep the feet perfectly dry. They will be found very suitable for Railroad and field hands and also for sentinels and soldiers who are much exposed. The poplar shoes are very light, and can be easily worn by any one.

The subscribers have also in operation, at their establishment, a machine for making SHOE LASTS; and they are turning out large quantities of this article so indispensable to shoemakers, at fair prices.

They are selling their shoes at $1.75 per pair wholesale, and $2 retail. Terms, cash on delivery.

THEIM & FRAPS.

Raleigh, N. C., Dec. 31, 1861.   1—tf.
☞ Register copy.

7-130
Perhaps with a premonition that the war would impose unprecedented demands upon the people, Theim and Fraps advertised their new manufactory of wooden shoes in the 1 January 1862 issue of the *Semi-Weekly Standard* (Raleigh). (Courtesy Southern Historical Collection, Julius Leinbach Papers.)

7-131
Perhaps the most unusual soldier in the Civil War was Private Samuel Blalock who enlisted, along with "brother" William McKesson (Keith) Blalock, in Company F, Twenty-sixth North Carolina Troops, on 20 March 1862. The two tented and messed together, and both gave promise of becoming good soldiers. However, Keith exhibited an outbreak from poison sumac and was ordered discharged. Thereupon Private Sam divulged that "he" was in fact Keith's wife, Sarah Malinda Pritchard Blalock. Malinda is pictured long after the war

holding a photograph—possibly of herself in uniform. (Courtesy Southern Historical Collection.)

7-132
From his sketch made on the spot, Alfred Waud later painted the scene of the landing of Union troops at Cape Hatteras on 28 August 1861. Only fourteen weeks after the state seceded, federal troops occupied North Carolina soil. (Courtesy Franklin Delano Roosevelt Library, Hyde Park.)

7-133
Union soldiers celebrated their capture of Fort Bartow on Roanoke Island, 9 February 1862, with a pig-picking. (Courtesy NCDA&H; reprinted from *Pictorial War Record*, 22 July 1882.)

7-134
This drawing (made from an on-the-spot sketch by Lieutenant LeRony) shows the destruction of Fort Ocracoke on the Beacon Island at the entrance to Pamlico Sound in December 1861. In background, according to the legend, are Portsmouth Island and (at extreme left) the Ocracoke Island lighthouse. (Courtesy National Archives, Washington.)

7-135
Troops under General John Gray Foster captured Winton and burned the Hertford County Courthouse in 1862 before retreating down the Chowan River. The drawing was made by a New York soldier, Charles F. Johnson, from whose book, *The Long Roll* (East Aurora, N.Y., 1911), it is reprinted. (Courtesy North Carolina Collection.)

7-136
Artist Merrill G. Wheelock (1822–66), traveling with the Union army, made this watercolor of Plymouth in 1863. (Courtesy North Carolina Museum of Art, Raleigh.)

7-137
Wheelock also painted this view of Castle Island in the Pamlico River at "Little Washington." (Courtesy North Carolina Collection.)

7-138
Following the capture of New Bern by the Federals, *Frank Leslie's Illustrated Newspaper* of 14 June 1862 pictured the distribution of clothing to "contrabands" by the superintendent of the poor, Vincent Colyer. (Courtesy Library of Congress.)

7-139

The lowering of the Confederate flag following the capture of Fort Macon was depicted in *Frank Leslie's*

Illustrated Newspaper on 17 May 1862. (Courtesy North Carolina Collection.)

7-142

A federal soldier, Lieutenant J. E. McDougall, made this drawing of a four-gun battery on the railroad between New

Bern and Goldsboro on 14 July 1863. (Courtesy National Archives, Washington.)

7-140

Salt was an essential commodity for food preservation, and among the saltworks was this one at Morehead City which was pictured (after its

capture by the Federals) in the supplement to *Frank Leslie's Illustrated Newspaper*, 26 April 1862. (Courtesy North Carolina Collection.)

7-141

Edward Stanly (1808–72) was appointed military governor of occupied North Carolina by President Lincoln, and he triumphantly entered Washington in April 1862. Stanly had practiced law in

the Pamlico River town prior to his migration to California. (Courtesy North Carolina Collection; reprinted from *Harper's Weekly*, 19 July 1862.)

7-143

Zebulon Baird Vance (1830–94), right, is shown in William George Randall's 1897 painting of the three colonels of the Twenty-sixth North Carolina Regiment. His successors were Henry King (Harry) Burgwyn, Jr. (center), and John R. Lane (left). Vance was elected governor while commanding the troops. (Courtesy NCDA&H.)

7-144
New Bern was continually occupied by Union troops after its capture in the spring of 1862. In a lithograph issued in 1864, ships fill the Trent and Neuse rivers; Fort Totten is in center background. (Courtesy North Carolina Collection.)

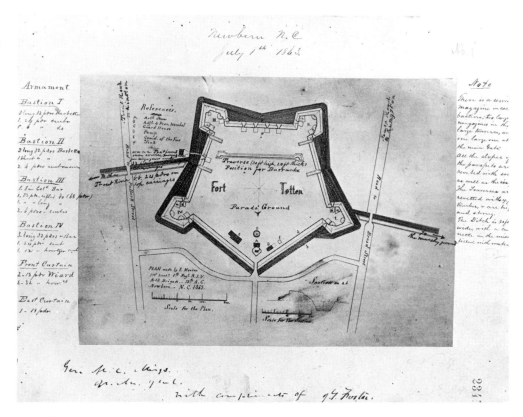

7-145
A detailed map of Fort Totten, just outside New Bern, was drawn by Lieutenant E. Meulen in 1863 and was sent by General John G. Foster to General M. C. Meigs. (Courtesy National Archives, Washington.)

The United States Army established in New Bern the Union Photograph Rooms. The photographer, O. J. Smith (and perhaps others), made a permanent visual record of the town under occupation. Five of Smith's pictures are reproduced here (all courtesy North Carolina Collection):

7-148
"School Ma'ams" outside their residence.

7-146
Foster General Hospital.

7-149
The Sanitary Commission and White Refugees Office.

7-147
Academy Green Hospital (New Bern Academy Building).

7-150
Bishop's Mill.

7-151
J. O. Davidson's drawing "The Steamship 'Sassacus' Ramming the Rebel Ram 'Albemarle'" was published in *Harper's Weekly* on 4 June 1864. A scrimshaw artist—perhaps a sailor aboard a Union ship—followed Da-

vidson's drawing for this scene on a whale's tooth. The ironclad *Albemarle*, constructed in Halifax County, survived the ramming by the *Sassacus* but was finally sunk in October. (Courtesy North Carolina Collection.)

7-153
Desertion was a major problem among the Confederate forces, particularly as the war dragged on. "Confederate deserters in the mountains of

North Carolina" was the title of this drawing reproduced in *Pictorial War Record*, 27 October 1883. (Courtesy NCDA&H.)

7-152
Edward Leinbach of Salem, a member of the Twenty-sixth Regimental Band, composed the march played by his band in the inauguration of Governor Vance. (Courtesy Harry H. Hall, Rome, Georgia; by permission of Moravian Music Foundation, Winston-Salem.)

7-154
Parker D. Robbins, a free black carpenter from Bertie County, joined the Union army and served as a sergeant-major. After the war he was elected to the constitutional convention of 1868 and served four years in the state house of representatives. (Courtesy NCDA&H.)

7-155
Some slaves accompanied their masters to the battlefield. Kinchin, the body servant of the "Boy Colonel," Harry Burgwyn, posed beside a tent with his horse Hawkeye. His master died a hero at Gettysburg, but Kinchin survived and for years vividly described wartime experiences. (Courtesy Archie K. Davis, Winston-Salem.)

7-157
Federal recruiters were at work too. At New Bern an appeal was issued for men to enlist in the Union navy. (Courtesy National Archives, Washington.)

7-158
Zebulon B. Vance was only thirty-two years old and had been governor less than four months when his portrait appeared on fifty-dollar notes issued by the state in January 1863. (Courtesy North Carolina Collection.)

7-156
A Federal raid on the Wilmington and Weldon Railroad bridge at Goldsboro in December 1862 brought an appeal for recruits to defend the "Lifeline of the Confederacy" from continued Union threats. (Courtesy North Carolina Collection.)

7-159
As the value of paper money dropped, Warren County began accepting farm produce and issued vouchers receivable only in payment of the next year's county taxes. (Courtesy North Carolina Collection; reprinted from Manly Wade Wellman, *The County of Warren* [Chapel Hill, 1959].)

7-160
Doctors abandoned their practices to care for the wounded. Pettigrew Hospital in Raleigh was the first Confederate military hospital in the state. It was organized by Dr. E. Burke Haywood, a Raleigh surgeon. (Courtesy NCDA&H.)

7-161
Colonel Isaac Erwin Avery died from wounds at Gettysburg, but not before he scrawled a note with the message, "Major Tell my Father I died with my face to the enemy." (Courtesy NCDA&H.)

7-162
Songs dedicated to military units were distributed by enterprising publishers. The Fourth North Carolina Regiment was commanded by Colonel Bryan Grimes in 1863. (Courtesy North Carolina Collection.)

7-163
Alexander Meinung sketched the scene of a battlefield divine service conducted for the Twenty-sixth North Carolina Regimental Band in August 1863. (Courtesy Southern Historical Collection, Julius Leinbach Papers.)

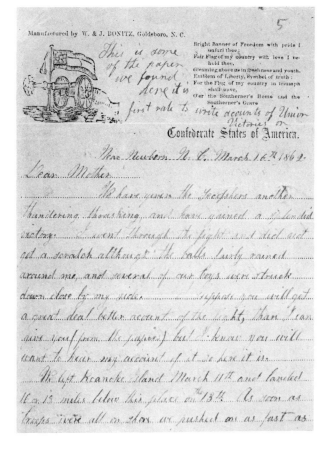

7-164
Near Petersburg one night in 1864, an enemy minié ball struck Charlie Transou's band book, which he was using as a pillow. He was unharmed. (Courtesy Harry H. Hall, Rome, Georgia; by permission of Moravian Music Foundation, Winston-Salem.)

7-165
Patriotic Confederate stationery manufactured by German immigrants to Goldsboro, William and Joseph Bonitz, was captured and used "to write accounts of Union Victories on" by George Washington Whitman, brother of Walt Whitman. (Courtesy Rare Book Room, Library, Duke University, Durham.)

7-166

Named for the governor, the blockade-runner *Ad-Vance* brought desperately needed equipment and supplies from England. This ship made eleven trips through the blockade before being captured in 1864. This water- color was painted in Ber- muda, ca. 1863, by Edward James and furnished to the American consul as a means of keeping him posted on southern vessels in the port. (Courtesy Bermuda National Trust, Hamilton.)

7-168 and 7-169

The *Modern Greece* ran aground near Fort Fisher in 1862. The recovery of her cargo a century later revealed that the vessel was loaded with war materiel sorely needed by the South. (Both courtesy NCDA&H.)

7-167

Confederate agent Rose O'Neal Greenhow sought to return to the Confederacy in September 1864 aboard the *Condor*. The ship ran aground while trying to evade the Union fleet near Fort Fisher, and the secret agent was drowned. When her body was washed upon the shore, her diary and this cipher code were recovered. (Courtesy NCDA&H.)

7-170

A drawing by J. M. Alden shows mound battery during the Union naval bombard- ment of Fort Fisher in Janu- ary 1865. (Courtesy North Carolina Collection.)

7-171

Following the bombardment, federal troops waded ashore and overwhelmed the defenders of the "Gibraltar of the South" on the evening of 15 January. Timothy H. O'Sullivan photographed a row of underground bunkers after the Confederates had capitulated. (Courtesy NCDA&H.)

7-172

In March 1865, General William T. Sherman's troops invaded North Carolina after marching from Georgia and South Carolina. In a postwar drawing, troops are advancing over a corduroy road. (Courtesy NCDA&H; reprinted from *Battles and Leaders of the Civil War* [New York, 1884–88], volume 4.)

7-173 and 7-174

Sherman's forces occupied Fayetteville in March. A soldier is said to have made these two drawings—one showing a skirmish near the Market House, the other depicting the arsenal buildings just before they were burned by Union troops. (Courtesy North Carolina Collection.)

7-175

The Union forces drove on to the community of Bentonville in Johnston County. There Confederates under General Joseph E. Johnston attacked, but in the largest battle ever fought on North Carolina soil, Johnston retreated on 21 March. This drawing is reprinted from George Ward Nichols, *The Story of the Great March* . . . (New York, 1865). (Courtesy NCDA&H.)

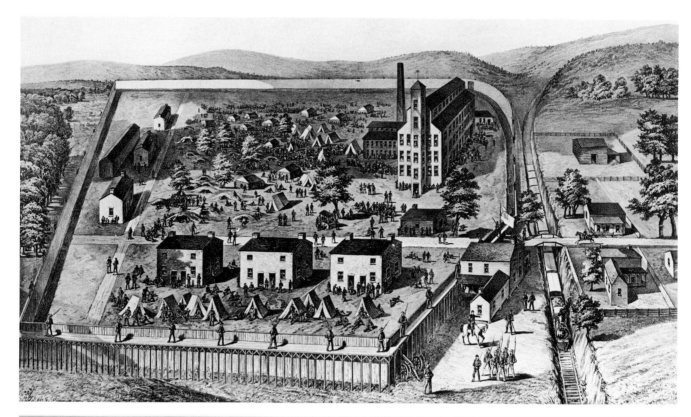

7-176 (top)
While the Federals were occupying much of the east, Union General George Stoneman's cavalry invaded North Carolina from the west, conducting raids in the northern Piedmont. At Salisbury a converted factory, which only a few weeks earlier had held thousands of captured Union troops, was destroyed by Stoneman's raiders in April. (Courtesy North Carolina Collection.)

7-177
A year or so earlier, an artist captured an idyllic scene as soldiers incarcerated in the Salisbury military prison played baseball on the grounds. This is one of the earliest illustrations of the game. (Author's collection.)

7-178
After joining federal forces marching from Wilmington, the combined Union army occupied Raleigh on 12 April. Six days later, Sherman and Johnston met at James Bennett's house near Durham's Station to discuss cessation of hostilities, and their meeting was commemorated by a drawing in Frank Leslie's newspaper. When their armistice agreement was repudiated in Washington, a new one was signed at Bennett's place on 26 April, effectively ending the war. (Courtesy NCDA&H.)

7-179
Union Lieutenant George C. Round established his signal station inside the crown atop the state capitol in Raleigh. When a messenger arrived with the report of the surrender of General Johnston's army, the lieutenant waited until dark and then fired colored rockets spelling P-E-A-C-E. (Courtesy NCDA&H; reprinted from *Twenty-seventh Annual Reunion of the Signal Corps U.S.A.* [Manassas, Virginia, 1902].)

7-180
Thousands of North Carolinians were authorized to return to their homes after giving their oath not to take up arms against the government of the United States. F. P. Cogdill was from Buncombe County. (Courtesy North Carolina Collection.)

7-181
The CSS *Shenandoah*, captained by James Iredell Waddell of North Carolina, was operating off the coast of Alaska when the armistice was signed. Unaware of developments, Waddell and his crew continued preying upon Union whalers until convinced in late summer that the South had indeed lost the war. Then, rather than surrender to the North, Iredell sailed the *Shenandoah* around the world and turned the vessel over to British officials in Liverpool. This is a page from the ship's log for 21 July 1865. (Courtesy NCDA&H.)

8. Reconstruction, Redemption, and Repression, 1865–1900

Two days after generals Sherman and Johnston signed their second armistice agreement at James Bennett's home near Durham, Governor Zebulon B. Vance issued a proclamation acknowledging the defeat of the Confederacy and pledging "to settle the government of the State, to restore the civil authority in her borders and to further the great ends of peace." Yet only seven months later, Vance confided to a young friend in Australia that he was seriously considering leaving the United States.

Vance's dejection in December 1865 was a measure of developments that had occurred during the intervening months. The antebellum Unionist, battlefield commander, and wartime governor had been deprived of the opportunity to help restore peace, for in May he had been arrested and imprisoned for two months in Washington. Paroled but not pardoned by President Andrew Johnson, Vance had returned to North Carolina to find his political adversary, the chameleonic William W. Holden, installed in the governor's chair and his state still occupied by federal troops.

Already hopes for a quick return to the Union had been dashed. President Johnson, himself a former tailor's apprentice from Raleigh, had intended to make the restoration of the Union as painless as possible, and thousands of North Carolina's white males had taken the oath of allegiance to the United States and elected delegates to a convention which in October repealed the ordinance of secession, abolished slavery, made provisions for elections the following month, and—over strenuous objections of many delegates—repudiated the state's war debt. Jonathan Worth, another antebellum Unionist, defeated Holden for the governorship, and a conciliatory General Assembly ratified the Thirteenth Amendment and elected Unionists William A. Graham and John Pool to the United States Senate. But when the senators-elect and the full delegation of Union congressmen arrived at the Capitol, they were barred from taking their seats on the grounds that the Congress, not the president, had authority to fix the conditions for the readmission of states.

The Congress was controlled by a faction of the Republican party called Radicals, some of whom genuinely favored full citizenship for the freedmen and others of whom were concerned with the creation of a Republican party in the South. Their influence had already been felt in North Carolina, especially through agents of the Freedmen's Bureau, a sort of legal aid society and welfare agency. These agents, together with some military men and other new arrivals from the North, were active in political discussions relating to the rights of blacks. Some advocated full civil rights, including voting.

A convention of freedmen held in Raleigh in October 1865, however, was temperate in its petition. Under the leadership of James Walker Hood, a recent arrival from Connecticut, and James H. Harris, a native who had been educated in Ohio, the more than one hundred blacks professed lasting friendship with whites and pleaded for fair treatment, educational opportunities, and repeal of oppressive laws. Significantly, they did not ask for the right to vote; however, the convention established the North Carolina State Equal Rights League, which, with Harris as its chairman, did demand full civil rights at a second freedmen's convention the next year.

It was the question of the place and rights of the freedmen in the postwar society that most concerned the Radicals on the one hand and Vance and white Southerners on the other. The difficulties of whites were staggering enough, for the war—a great leveler—had wiped out virtually all investments except real estate. But adjustments were enormously complicated for and by the other third of the population—former chattels, now fellow citizens. Removal of the yoke of slavery was done by the pen, but it was not automatically accompanied by the blessings of liberty. For the freedmen, there was the basic task of subsistence. The rumored "forty acres and a mule" was a cruel deception, and only a minority of blacks received direct material aid from the federal government. Some had deserted their owners during and immediately following the war; others faced expulsion or a choice of leaving or remaining with their former masters in a mutual effort to survive. Without property or money, the freedmen had only their labor to offer, and few whites could afford to hire them.

As the struggle intensified between the president and the Congress over reconstruction policies, legislatures of the South inadvertently aided the Radicals by passing laws that immensely increased the rights of blacks but which fell short of full civil rights. Called "black codes" by Radicals, these laws were interpreted as evidence that the unrepentant South was attempting to reenslave the Negroes. Southern legislatures also refused to ratify the Fourteenth Amendment. During the congressional campaign of 1866, northern Republicans successfully exploited the sectional prejudices generated by the war and won a two-thirds majority of both houses. Henceforth they could pass legislation over the president's veto and treat the southern states as "conquered provinces." The following March, a new reconstruction act reimposed military rule upon the South and directed that the army conduct a new registration of voters open to both black and white males. Excluded, however, were the approximately 10 percent of North Carolina's white males whose "political disabilities" had not been pardoned. No state could be readmitted to the Union until a convention had met and adopted a new state constitution extending universal manhood suffrage, the constitution had been approved in a referendum, and the legislature had met and ratified the Fourteenth Amendment.

Within two weeks after the passage of this act, the Republican party was formally organized in North Carolina. Its diverse composition included sincere Unionists who recognized that military occupation was at best a short-term solution; politicians who hoped to capitalize on the opportunity for reward from the party in control of the Congress; and blacks. Allied with the new party were the Union League, Heroes of America, some smaller societies, and many officers and agents of the military and Freedmen's Bureau. The opposition, called the Conservative party, was composed largely of prewar Democrats who viewed the admission of the freedmen to the ballot box as calamitous. Some of the Conservatives were no more racist than the opportunist faction of the Republican party, but the subject of race was one that often—perhaps usually—degenerated from rational discussion into emotionalism.

Extremists on both sides of the controversy helped create the climate for the Ku Klux Klan, a secret, hooded society that sought to counteract the influence of the Republicans' own secret societies. A basic difference between the Ku Klux Klan and its adversaries, however, was the Klan's willingness to go beyond intimidation and commit violence, even murder upon rare occasion, to accomplish its objectives.

Although the Klan had been organized in North Carolina shortly after the formation of the Republican party, it played little part in the campaign in 1867 when proconvention forces won by a nearly three-to-one margin. Since white registration outnumbered that of blacks by only 106,721 to 72,932, it was obvious that about half of the whites remained away from the polls. Consequently, there were only 13 Conservatives in the convention that met early in 1868. Of the 107 Republicans, 74 were native whites ("scalawags," the Klan called them), 18 were "foreign" whites ("carpetbaggers"), and only 15 were blacks. Among the last were Hood, Harris, and A. H. Galloway, who had been prominent in the freedmen's convention of 1865. Calvin Cowles, son-in-law of Holden, was elected president of the convention.

The constitution framed by the Convention of 1868 reflected the influence of newcomers to the state, such as Albion W. Tourgée, one of the most able politicians of the period. Among its provisions were universal manhood suffrage, abolition of property qualifications for voting and holding office, popular elections every four years of the governor and other high state officials, four months of public schools, a board of charities and public welfare, and replacement of the county court system with a township-county commission type of government. In a bitter referendum in which both the Klan and the Union League were active, the constitution was approved by a vote of 93,084 to 74,015. Holden, so often a bridesmaid but never an elected bride, finally achieved the governorship, defeating Conservative Thomas S. Ashe. The new General Assembly, heavily Republican, ratified the Fourteenth Amendment and chose John Pool and Joseph C. Abbott as United States senators. The seven men elected to Congress also were Republicans; they and the senators took their seats on 20 July 1868.

North Carolina, though still under military rule, was back in the Union. But never had the state been so bitterly divided, and the political atmosphere would remain highly charged for three more years. In control of all three branches of state government as well as the congressional delegation, the Republicans had an unexcelled opportunity to build upon the solid constitution by setting an example for responsible government. Indeed, they did pass progressive legislation—for example, revival of the public school system, reform of criminal and civil justice, establishment of a state penitentiary, reestablishment of the militia, general amnesty for citizens with political disabilities associated with the war, ratification of both the Fourteenth and Fifteenth amendments, and state assistance to railroads. But the party was shackled with liabilities: With his checkered past, Holden was intensely hated by a large segment of whites and not entirely trusted by many of his supporters; troops, even in their legitimate protection of the freedmen, were accused of excesses; the Union League, Freedmen's Bureau, and other politically oriented organizations and agencies inflamed passions; and a number of legislators, in their well-intentioned advocacy of railroad assistance, became involved in indiscretions with influence peddlers, such as Milton S. Littlefield and George W. Swepson.

The scandals involving fraud and bribery associated with legislative authorization for the state's purchase of railroad bonds were magnified by journalists sympathetic to the Conservative cause, especially Josiah Turner, Jr., editor of the *Sentinel* in Raleigh. The legislature, in which only twenty blacks served in 1868–69, was portrayed as a minstrel of ignorant Negroes and greedy carpetbaggers and scalawags. Vituperation reached an unprecedented level, and many respectable whites, likening conditions to civil war, either joined or allowed themselves to become apologists for the Ku Klux Klan, which in 1870 reached a membership of perhaps 40,000. As a sort of vigilante group, the Klan not only tried to keep the Negro in his "place" but also in some communities sought to enforce morals by bestowing its curious form of justice upon whites, including a few women. By publicizing the alleged "pillage and plunder" of the Republican legislature and the excesses of the Holden regime, the press indirectly gave credibility to the Klan, which appeared to many citizens to be the only organization resisting what they considered an oppressive, brutal, and corrupt state government.

It was the Klan that goaded Holden into the actions that led to his repudiation. The cross-burnings and cryptic warnings from the hooded order had given way to violence in scattered instances, but in 1870 physical attacks upon blacks and their friends became more common. In Ala-

mance County a black Union League official, Wyatt Outlaw, was murdered. A more brazen incident occurred in the Caswell County Courthouse when State Senator John W. Stephens, a close ally of Holden, was lured into a small room and murdered by members of the Klan while a political convention was in session in the courtroom. Outraged, Holden, acting under the Shoffner Act passed the previous year, placed the two counties under martial law.

The occupation of Alamance and Caswell by troops under command of Colonel George W. Kirk, the summary arrest of citizens by the soldiers, and the suspension of the writ of habeas corpus by Holden gave the fiery editor of the *Sentinel* additional fuel for his attacks. Calling Holden a "white-livered miscreant," Turner dared the governor to arrest him, and the challenge was accepted. This was another in a series of mistakes that led an increasing number of Republicans to view Holden as a liability to the party. Conservative attacks charged his party with corruption, doubling the state debt, increasing taxes, and violating the civil rights that it professed to hold sacred. Even Hinton Rowan Helper, whose book ten years earlier had been distributed by Republican campaigners, now spoke of the "incompetent and worthless State and Federal officials in power . . . pestiferous ulcers feeding upon the body politic."

With the intimidating support of the Klan and under the slogans "home rule" and "white supremacy," the Conservatives won a stunning victory in the legislative elections of 1870, and on 9 December Representative Frederick N. Strudwick of Orange introduced a resolution of impeachment against Governor Holden. The following March, after a trial marked by an observance of all legal proprieties but fired with emotion, the state senate convicted the governor of six counts relating to the "Kirk-Holden War" and ordered him removed from office. Holden thus became the only governor of North Carolina to be dismissed from office by impeachment. Lieutenant Governor Tod R. Caldwell, who succeeded to the governorship, wore his Republicanism thin, worked as best he could with a legislature controlled by the opposite party, and surprisingly won reelection the following year.

Even with Holden out of the picture, the Conservatives controlled only one branch of state government. Furthermore, the Congress passed several additional laws designed to protect the freedmen and to suppress civil disorders in the South. Late in 1871 federal soldiers were again sent into the state to assist federal authorities in arresting and trying a thousand or more persons accused of Ku Klux Klan activities. Of those convicted, the most prominent was Randolph Shotwell, a western editor whose mild manners camouflaged his influence among members of the Klan in the Rutherford County area. William L. Saunders, allegedly the head of the Klan, was never convicted, and his repeated response to questions from a congressional investigating committee, "I decline to answer," was later carved on his tombstone.

8-28   The election of 1872, while intensely fought, lacked the vitriol of campaigns involving Holden. Governor Caldwell, who had acted with restraint, defeated Augustus S. Merrimon by only a 1-percent margin. Conservatives retained a majority in the legislature, however, and elected Merrimon to the United States Senate when Vance declined—probably on the assumption that the Radicals in Washington would not allow him to take his seat. Many Conservatives refused to vote for the Democratic presidential candidate, Horace Greeley, an outspoken antislavery editor from New York who had been married in Warrenton, and President Grant carried the state handily. It was the last time until 1928 that the Republicans won a presidential campaign in North Carolina.

The Conservatives still chafed under the constitution of 1868, a symbol of Republicanism. Several amendments were approved by the legislative process, including the substitution of biennial for annual sessions of the General Assembly and the transfer of selection of university trustees from the State Board of Education to the legislature. But "redemption," in the eyes of the Conservatives, demanded more fundamental changes, and in 1875

8-29
8-30   the General Assembly issued a call for the election of delegates to a new constitutional convention. Republicans and some Conservatives feared that a convention would emasculate what was, prejudice aside, basically a good constitution; and the election results demonstrated how evenly divided

8-31   public opinion was: fifty-eight Republicans, fifty-eight Conservatives, and three independents were elected.

The death in August of William A. Graham deprived the Conservatives of a majority, but they were able to pass thirty amendments, some of them cosmetic but others of profound implications: marriages between whites and blacks were prohibited; separate schools were decreed for the two races;

several economy measures were adopted; secret political societies were outlawed; and, most significant of all, legislative appointment of justices of the peace replaced popular election. This transfer of the selection of justices to Raleigh had a single purpose: to prevent the election of Negroes to these offices in counties with heavy black populations. The amendments were approved by plebiscite. With the Conservatives firmly fixed with the image of the white man's party, the stage was set for one of the most exciting gubernatorial campaigns ever held in the state.

Words, not violence, characterized the "battle of   8-33
the giants" in 1876. The giants were Zeb Vance, the state's most widely known citizen with the possible exception of Holden, and the much-respected Thomas Settle, a Republican with a solid record. Both were able debaters, but Vance took advantage of the Republican debacle of 1870 and made much of the scandals that had occurred in President Grant's administration. The battle of words was also carried on in the press, and cartoons—particularly those by A. Weil for the Conservatives—appeared both in newspapers and on handbills. Something of a religious fervor permeated the campaign, both sides implying that it was the year of Armageddon. The results were unmistakable: Vance was elected governor, Democrat Samuel J. Tilden won the state's electoral votes, and the Conservatives retained control of the legislature and congressional delegation.

The Conservatives were so encouraged by this   8-34
success that they revived the designation of "Democrats." "Home rule" was restored not only in North Carolina but also throughout the South. The "tragic era" of Reconstruction was over, though its vestiges would continue to torment the state for decades, for both state and federal governments became less zealous in guarding the recently won rights of the freedmen. For more than a decade the Democrats saw blacks only as a problem; the Republicans courted their votes, but gave little more than lip service to their welfare.

In the remainder of the century, politics was not   8-35
an all-engrossing interest, but the state had suffered immensely from the conflict, and there was little sentiment for forgetting "The Waw." Young journalist Walter Hines Page alleged that the state's recovery was impeded by the ghosts of "the Confederate dead, religious orthodoxy, and Negro domination." He was right, for postwar society invented a mythical past, and many sought to resur-

8-36 rect it. Sectionalism was so strong that the state only reluctantly participated at Philadelphia in the Centennial Exposition, the planning commission of which was chaired by North Carolina native Joseph R. Hawley.

8-37 Confederate reunions kept the memories of the war alive; scores of monuments to Confederate veterans—usually facing north—were erected; and in 1889 the United Confederate Veterans was formed, followed five years later by the United Daughters of the Confederacy. Thousands of citizens streamed through the capitol in Raleigh to see the coffin containing the body of Confederate Pres-

8-38 ident Jefferson Davis when his remains were moved from New Orleans to Richmond for reburial in 1893. Reverence for the sacrifices of southern troops was expressed at nearly every public ceremony.

Still, there was the present to be concerned with, and the overriding interest of the people was in making a living. The recently established Raleigh *News and Observer*, founded in 1880, editorialized, "It is idle to talk of home independence as long as we go to the North for everything from a toothpick to a President." This commentary on the continued subservience of the South reflected the impatience of a people seeking to throw off the economic yoke imposed by agricultural and industrial backwardness. When the industrial revolution did move southward, it was more evolutionary than revolutionary.

During Reconstruction the attempt to revive the economy was the lonely task of natives, for little capital accompanied the outsiders who rushed to the South for economic, political, or humanitarian purposes. By 1870 the number of manufacturing establishments had almost reached the prewar level—nearly thirty-seven hundred—and the value of goods was considerably higher. Some additional growth was experienced in the 1870s, but it was not until the next decade that marked progress occurred. By then native-owned businesses had created a small coterie of industrialists who, in a favorable political atmosphere provided by the "Bourbon" Democrats, exuded genuine optimism for industry in the state. This optimism was infectious, and for the first time since the war northern investments, at first leerily and later enthusiastically, moved southward. The following table indicates the substantial industrial growth in the last two decades of the century:

	1880	1890	1900
Number of establishments	3,802	3,667	7,266
Number of workers	18,109	33,625	70,570
Capital invested in industry	$13 million	$32.5 million	$76.5 million
Value of manufactured goods	$20 million	$40 million	$94 million

While impressive, these statistics were misleading, for North Carolina was still a predominantly agricultural state and lagged far behind most of the northern states in manufacturing. In only two products did North Carolina show phenomenal progress: textiles and tobacco.

8-39 Emancipation weakened the plantation system
8-40 but did not reduce the state's production of agricultural products. In 1880, for example, the production of cotton was 389,598 bales, nearly triple that of prewar years. Watching cotton go northward for manufacture, imaginative North Carolinians proposed that the mills be brought nearer the cotton fields. Such a move would take advantage of the plentiful labor supply and eliminate the cost of transporting raw materials to—and finished products from—New England. Results were evident by 1880, when forty-nine mills produced $2.5 million

8-41 in goods. Most of these were small, family-owned,
8-42 water-powered enterprises that utilized the labor of
8-43 local whites. The gradual introduction of steam
8-44 power—from 16 percent in 1880 to 64 percent in 1900—freed the factories from the rivers and permitted their construction nearer the workers.

A successful factory often brought with it a mill village, sometimes with simple mill-owned houses available to the workers at low rent. By making families dependent upon the factories, owners found it easier to hire women and children at lower wages. By 1900 women comprised 34 percent of the cotton mill work force and earned an average annual wage of $157, compared to $216 for men; children represented 24 percent of the workers and earned an average of only $103. Together, 30,273 cotton mill workers produced goods valued at $28 million. Coarse yarns, warps, sheetings, and twilled goods gradually gave way to quality goods when better equipment was installed, often capitalized by northern investors in return for stock in the companies; finished goods, including hosiery, were manufactured by the turn of the century. The production of wool was about 800,000 pounds in 1870, when fifty-two establishments were making about $300,000 worth of goods. Legislation to encourage the growing of sheep met with only mediocre success.

8-45
8-46
8-47
8-51
The growing, sale, and manufacture of tobacco underwent extensive changes following the war. Heavy, dark leaf continued to be grown for chewing and as filler for cigars, but lemon-yellow tobacco—"bright leaf," cured by heat circulating through flues traversing the barn—quickly became a favorite for granulated or shredded smoking tobacco. Rolling crushed tobacco between thin paper had long been practiced by individual smokers, but after the war cigarettes were produced commercially by hand rollers, some of them Jewish immigrants. Not until 1881 did James A. Bonsack invent the first successful cigarette rolling machine which, by molding a continuous cigarette that was cut into individual lengths, initially outproduced forty-eight human rollers. From that point, tobacco manufacturing became a major industry in North Carolina. Meanwhile, the auction system, in which farmers sold their tobacco in large sky-lit warehouses with roving, chanting auctioneers, became a fixture in the trade.

Of the small tobacco factories plundered by occupation troops, that of J. R. Green at Durham's Station was the most fortunate, for the soldiers liked his tobacco so much that after the war they wrote back for more. Later W. T. Blackwell, Julian S. Carr, and John R. Day acquired Green's

8-48
company and introduced the Bull Durham brand, which created a sensation. Richard J. Reynolds of Winston, perhaps impressed by the popularity of the Durham bull, adopted a dromedary as the emblem of his new cigarette.

8-49
But it was Washington Duke and his sons who most dramatically revolutionized the industry. The elder Duke grew and flailed tobacco on his farm just outside Durham and then profitably peddled it around the country by wagon. In the early 1870s

8-50
the family moved their operation into the village and built a modern facility; a decade later they installed the Bonsack cigarette rolling machine. James B. Duke emerged as the shrewdest businessman among the sons; he launched a spectacular advertising campaign, acquired control of one competitor after another, and in 1890 organized the American Tobacco Company, which controlled the domestic trade and, after the turn of the century, gained world domination in the tobacco

8-52
industries. Once located in many communities, factories were gradually concentrated in Durham, Winston, and Reidsville.

The manufacture of furniture, formerly the province of a few craftsmen and their apprentices, expanded toward the end of the century. As early as 1881 the White family of Mebane began turning out spindles and soon expanded into the production of household conveniences. Farther west at High Point the first formal furniture company was organized in 1888. Twelve years later forty-four factories in the state employed two thousand workers who made $1.5 million worth of tables, chairs, bedsteads, washstands, sideboards, dressers, coffins, and other wood products. Most of these were cheaply made and designed for the home market. Fine, fashionable furniture usually was custom-made by local cabinetmakers or imported from other states. In 1893 there were fifty-seven carriage and thirty-two wagon factories, six hub and spoke factories, and twenty-four manufacturers of sashes, blinds, and doors.

Tar, pitch, and turpentine supported a substantial number of families, mostly blacks, in the pine belt. With a hack, the pine tree was opened and the rosin scraped, distilled, barreled, and carted off to ports for examination by inspectors of naval stores. Wilmington remained the chief port from which the pine products were shipped. Along the coast fishing remained a popular means of livelihood, and the Atlantic and North Carolina Railroad to Morehead City was given the nickname "Mullet Line." 8-53 8-54 8-55

Grains were grown throughout the state, and in 1870 there were 1,415 mills grinding products into flour, meal, and other foods. Ten years later 125,000 bushels of rice was grown in the Lower Cape Fear, but the production dwindled afterward. Nearly every farm grew livestock, and North Carolina ranked second in the nation in production of honey. 8-56 8-57 8-58 8-59 8-60 8-61

Gold mining did not regain its antebellum importance, but activity spread into additional sections of the state, including the southwestern counties. Among the more profitable operations was the Rudisill Mine under the town of Charlotte. At the famous Reed Gold Mine in Cabarrus County great excitement was stirred in 1896 when a seventeen-pound nugget was recovered only a short distance from the stream in which Conrad Reed nearly a hundred years earlier made the first documented discovery of gold in the present limits of the United States. This was the last large nugget found in North Carolina, and except for panning and sporadic reopenings of old mines, North Carolina's gold history was over. The branch mint at 8-63 8-62

Charlotte did not resume the minting of coins after the war. Gold Hill, however, did have a second life of sorts toward the end of the century when Thomas A. Edison sought to buy the mine property. It was eventually acquired by a slick-talking New Yorker named Walter George Newman, who reopened the shafts and mined for copper. After some initial success, the project failed, and Newman fled his creditors. Coal mining continued on a small scale along the Deep River in Chatham and Lee counties, and iron was mined near the Tennessee border.

Retail trade underwent dramatic change. While country stores provided many of the basic needs of farmers, court days and Saturday afternoons were favorite times for shopping in town, where more fashionable goods could be found. Retail trade remained largely in local hands, but there was a considerable influx of new merchants, including Jews. One of the South's leading twentieth-century chain stores originated in Monroe in 1888. Among the innovations of William Henry and John Montgomery Belk were marked goods and cash sales— no haggling over price and no credit books to be kept. In 1879, in nearby Charlotte, H. C. Butler opened a "five cents counter" and within three weeks sold four thousand items. He failed to publicize his innovation, however, and F. W. Woolworth won credit for starting the first five-and-ten-cent store in the country. Industrialists, especially those running textile mills, not infrequently established company stores that provided goods to workers on credit. Similarly, country stores extended credit through a lien on the farmer's crop. While "ontime" buying was a convenience—even a necessary evil—it was often accompanied by high charges that tended to keep the borrower in perpetual debt.

Optimism toward economic improvement was reflected in the state's participation in exhibitions in major cities, including Boston and New Orleans, and in the Columbian Exposition in Chicago. In 1884 North Carolina held its own exposition to show "the variety and magnificence of the products and resources" of the state. Tens of thousands of North Carolinians attended the month-long exhibition and saw displays of an infinite variety of agricultural and industrial products, livestock, minerals, and handicrafts. On a smaller scale, the annual state fair, sponsored by the North Carolina Agricultural Society, and local fairs and exhibitions increased awareness of the diversity of the state's resources. At the same time, their carnivallike atmosphere provided diversion and amusement for many people.

As was previously mentioned, steam power generated by coal largely replaced water-driven machinery in industry, but in the 1880s a more revolutionary power source was introduced for lighting and other purposes in the larger cities. Salem Mills utilized electricity for lighting as early as 1881, and Raleigh had street lights in 1885. Soon city streets were strung with lines providing lights and also power for railed streetcars, previously pulled by horses. Another landmark was reached in 1898 when the Fries Manufacturing and Power Company began supplying electricity for local industry from its hydroelectric plant at Idols Dam on the Yadkin River. Gas had already been introduced prior to the war.

The speed of communication was greatly accelerated by the introduction of the telephone and rural free delivery. In 1879, Bowling W. Starke, manager of the Raleigh office of Western Union Telegraph Company, strung a wire from his office to his home and carried on a two-way conversation. A month later at Wilmington, 125 miles away, the local Western Union manager picked up an instrument and heard the voice of Starke, who had attached instruments to the telegraph wire. Shortly afterward, Starke opened in his office the state's first telephone exchange, but it operated for only a short time. Finally in 1884, a successful telephone exchange was opened in Charlotte, followed soon by exchanges in other cities. Rural free delivery of the United States mail was inaugurated from China Grove in Rowan County in 1896, a favor to Representative John S. Henderson and Senator Marion Butler, strong supporters of the new service in the Congress.

While the postwar era brought no revolution in transportation, it did bring progress. The scandals surrounding railroad bonds authorized by the Republican legislature gave the Democrats an excuse for the withdrawal of state aid to railroads, but not before the bankrupt Western North Carolina Railroad was taken over by the state. The costly venture of pushing the line through the rugged mountains from Old Fort toward Asheville discouraged public ownership, and the line was sold in 1880 to investors who completed it to the Tennessee border two years later. The dream of a half century—to connect the coast with Tennessee by rail—had been achieved.

Already the North Carolina Railroad had been

leased to the Richmond and Danville which in 1894 was joined by the Western North Carolina to form the Southern Railway Company. Feverish building characterized the 1880s, when the mileage was more than doubled to three thousand miles. Many of the stopping points grew into stations, which in turn grew into settlements. Durham's Station was an example. Consolidation accelerated, and by the turn of the century most of the mileage was controlled by three giant companies—the Southern, dominating the Piedmont and west; the Seaboard Airline Railway, along the fall line; and the Atlantic Coast Line, in the coastal plain.

The labor tax, by which able-bodied men contributed about a half dozen days' labor on the roads each year, remained the standard means of building and maintaining roads and bridges in most counties. In the 1870s, however, some counties were authorized to assign convicts to road work. In addition, Mecklenburg, Forsyth, and Stokes were authorized to levy a property tax for roads, but only Mecklenburg took full advantage of the opportunity and in the 1890s built a number of model roads. Still, most roads and streets in North Carolina were rutty and bumpy, and stream crossings were usually by ferry or ford. Vehicles included carts, wagons, buggies, carriages, and a very few genuine stagecoaches.

For urban transportation, there were radical developments. Borrowing features of the railroad, several towns laid tracks and installed horse-drawn streetcars. Within a few years the arrival of electricity enabled them to convert to electric streetcars.

Wilmington maintained its status as the leading seaport. Fed by road, rail, and the Cape Fear River, the port city was especially active in the transshipment of cotton, naval stores, lumber, and grain. Morehead City, the terminus of the Atlantic and North Carolina Railroad, lagged far behind, and no other port in the state was prepared to handle deep-draft vessels. Small steamships plied the rivers of the east, notably the Cape Fear and Tar, carrying both freight and passengers from dozens of landings.

Though modest, the improvements in transportation nevertheless brought the rural areas into closer contact with the sparse but growing towns. Court days attracted people from miles around, and special events, including traveling exhibitions and performers, often drew large crowds. The arrival of a circus was a big event and was usually accompanied by a parade through town.

More and more citizens even visited their capital city and witnessed evidences of a growing state government. Until 1881 the entire bureaucracy of the state government was housed in the capitol, but in that year the National (formerly Eagle) Hotel facing Union Square was purchased to house the commissioner of agriculture and the State Museum (then largely a mineralogical, geological, and agricultural exhibit). Six years later a new building for the state supreme court was constructed beside the Agricultural Building. Thus additional space was made available for new agencies, including departments of agriculture and labor statistics.

The resort business also benefited from the additional mobility of the people. With the connection of the coast and the mountains by rail, both seacoast and mountain resorts drew increasing numbers of vacationers in the summer. Recreation, hunting, and sports helped to break down the isolation between regions.

Repudiation of the state's war debt and depreciation of state-owned railroad and bank stock virtually wiped out the Literary Fund, and the public school system was suspended in 1865. For the next four years almost the only schools operating were those administered by the Freedmen's Bureau and northern religious and philanthropic societies—about four hundred schools with an enrollment of twenty thousand blacks and a few whites. To carry out the new constitution's requirement for a uniform four-month school system, the General Assembly of 1869 appropriated $100,000 in state aid and authorized the counties to levy taxes sufficient to provide a separate school for each race in every township. This initial enthusiasm waned quickly, for the succeeding Republican legislature allocated only $38,000 in state aid.

The Conservatives, victorious in 1870, were less concerned with helping the schools than in getting rid of Samuel Stanford Ashley, a New England missionary who as the Republican superintendent of public instruction advocated mixed schools. Even after Ashley's forced resignation in 1871, the Conservatives would not rest until a constitutional amendment four years later mandated segregated schools. Still, with this bogey eliminated, the dominant tax-shy Democratic party remained apathetic about education and left the matter almost entirely to the local governments.

To be sure, a few forward steps were taken: For instance, the legislature of 1877 established a nor-

8-78
8-79
8-80
8-81
8-82
8-83
8-84
8-85
8-86
8-87
8-88
8-89
8-90
8-91
8-92

8-93
8-94
8-95
8-96
8-97
8-98
8-99
8-100
8-101
8-102
8-103
8-104
8-105
8-106

mal school for teachers of each race and authorized the larger towns to levy taxes for the establishment of graded schools, and within a few years Greensboro, Raleigh, Salisbury, Goldsboro, Durham, and Charlotte took advantage of the law. On the other hand, the Democratic-controlled supreme court in 1885 ruled that education was not a "necessary expense," despite its constitutional mandate, thus placing further constraints upon supporters of improved schools. These obstacles notwithstanding, about three-fourths of the counties supported one or more schools, and in 1880 nearly one-third of the school-age children of the state were attending one of 5,312 schools, whose property value averaged only ninety-five dollars each. There was only modest improvement in this situation in the next two decades, and the century ended with an illiteracy rate of 19.5 percent for whites and 47.6 percent for blacks. The figures for whites would have been worse had not private academies been available for those who could afford them. In education, "redemption" was not a blessing.

The University of North Carolina survived the war, but fell victim to partisan politics during Reconstruction. The effectiveness of David L. Swain, president since 1835, was compromised in the public eye when his daughter Eleanor married Smith D. Atkins, commanding general of the Union troops occupying Chapel Hill. That, along with internal problems and a decreasing enrollment, led to Swain's resignation in 1867.

The new constitution transferred control of the university to the State Board of Education, which declared the presidency and all faculty positions vacant, then filled them with Republicans. This blatant politicization of the university resulted in its closing in 1870. Five years later, Cornelia Phillips Spencer, one of the university's most persistent boosters, rang the school's bell signaling the passage of legislation enabling the reopening of classes that fall. Kemp P. Battle became president the following year and remained a familiar figure on the campus for more than forty years. Beginning in 1881, the university received a regular but small state appropriation.

Two additional state colleges for whites were established before the end of the century: North Carolina College of Agriculture and Mechanic Arts (now North Carolina State) in 1887 and the Normal and Industrial School (now the University of North Carolina at Greensboro) in 1891. More remarkable in view of the legislature's callousness toward elementary education was the establishment

of several colleges for blacks, including State Colored Normal (now Fayetteville State) in 1877, Elizabeth City Colored Normal (now Elizabeth City State) and Agricultural and Mechanical College for the Colored Race (now North Carolina Agricutural and Technical State) in 1891, and Slater Industrial (now Winston-Salem State) in 1892.

The first four private colleges organized after the war also were for blacks—Raleigh Institute (now Shaw), Scotia (now Barber-Scotia), Biddle Memorial (now Johnson C. Smith), and St. Augustine's. Significantly, all four benefited from northern philanthropy, and—like the four state colleges for blacks established during the period—all are still educating students. Several more private colleges for Negroes were chartered during the century, along with about two dozen for whites; in the beginning several of them constituted something less than institutions of higher learning. Nevertheless, North Carolina in 1900 offered proportionately better opportunities for higher education than it did for common schools.

Near Asheville in the 1890s George Washington Vanderbilt introduced a special type of education. Vanderbilt, a young man with a lot of money, bought up about fifty farms south of the town and established a baronial estate called Biltmore. The 250-room mansion, built in the style of a French chateau, was opened in 1895. It was designed by architect Robert Morris Hunt, and the grounds were landscaped by Frederick Law Olmsted, who also planned the English-style village in which workers on the estate lived, played, shopped, and went to church and school. Gifford Pinchot, a noted forester, supervised the cutting out of diseased trees, established a nursery with two million seedlings, and restored the forests. He was succeeded by Carl Alwin Schenck, a dynamic German who in 1898 opened in Biltmore Forest the first school of forestry in the United States. While few North Carolinians came into direct contact with these four leaders of their professions, their efforts introduced many to architecture, landscape architecture, and forestry.

North Carolina produced no literary figure of national prominence in the postwar era, though two—William Sydney Porter (O. Henry), a native of Guilford County, and Charles Waddell Chesnutt, who spent his formative years in Fayetteville—published their first works before the turn of the century and achieved recognition afterward. One carpetbagger, however, attracted considerable literary attention after he left the state. Albion W.

Tourgée, a member of the constitutional convention of 1868, judge of the superior court, and Republican politician, had fourteen years of experiences and observations from which to draw his scenes and characters for his novels, the most famous of which was *A Fool's Errand, by One of the Fools* (1879). Despite Tourgée's temperate view of Reconstruction—including criticism of the Radical Republicans for introducing Negro suffrage before adequate education had been provided—many southern whites were outraged by his books.

8-122 The most widely read native novelist was the prolific Frances Fisher Tiernan, who wrote under the name Christian Reid. The best-known native
8-123 poet of the era was Mary Bayard Devereux Clarke, who wrote two books of verse during the postwar period and contributed to newspapers and magazines many poems, some of which were collected in book form after her death. Edwin Wiley Fuller of Louisburg wrote one popular book of poetry, *An Angel in the Cloud*, and one of fiction, *Sea Gift*.

8-124 In nonfiction, Cornelia Phillips Spencer of Chapel Hill, one of the century's most confirmed "professional" North Carolinians, vividly described wartime conditions in *The Last Ninety Days of the War*. She also furnished a stream of articles—spiced with her Democratic bias—to current periodicals, and in 1883 she published *First Steps in North Carolina History*. In 1879, John Wheeler Moore of Hertford County wrote *School History of North Carolina*, which went through eight editions in ten years.

The most important work in history, however,
8-125 was performed by William Laurence Saunders, the crippled war veteran and alleged Klan director who became secretary of state in 1879. Recognizing the value of ancient manuscript records stored on Capitol Square, Saunders gathered them up and obtained legislative authorization to print the most important ones. He hired W. Noel Sainsbury of the Public Record Office in London to supervise copying of related documents there and arranged for copying of appropriate materials in a number of other repositories. Prior to his death in 1891, Saunders, though confined to a wheelchair, saw through to publication ten large volumes containing 10,982 printed pages of *The Colonial Records of North Carolina*, the most valuable series of historical documents ever published in the state. One of the persons who helped Saunders locate materials was young Stephen Beauregard Weeks, formerly of Pasquotank County, the first native of the state to acquire a doctorate in history (at the Johns Hop-

kins University) and the state's first professional historian. He later moved out of the state, but maintained his interest in history and accumulated the largest private library of North Caroliniana.

In art, music, and drama, North Carolina was almost a wasteland for three decades after the war; no North Carolinian achieved eminence in cultural accomplishments. A half century later, Archibald Henderson sought to look on the bright side: "If North Carolina has produced no painters, no sculptors, of eminence, at least she has shown, at intervals, some genuine appreciation of good painting, good architecture, and good sculpture." Perhaps William George Randall (1860–1905), a 8-126 native of Burke County, came closest to achieving national attention after establishing a studio in Washington, D.C. Most of the notable painting done in North Carolina, however, was by artists whose homes were elsewhere. William C. A. Frerichs (1829–1905), a native of the Netherlands who taught in Greensboro during the war years, painted scenes in the mountains; William Garl Browne, Jr., born in England, painted hundreds of portraits of prominent citizens during his travels through and temporary residence in the state; the Reverend Johannes Adam Simon Oertel, Bavarian-born, lived in Lenoir for several years and painted portraits and religious scenes; and William Aiken Walker (1838–1921), a Charlestonian, became a sort of summer artist-in-residence at Arden Park Lodge south of Asheville and recorded rural scenes, 8-127 especially blacks and their humble dwellings. 8-128

Music and drama also showed little progress 8-129 among North Carolinians, though the continued 8-130 popularity of traveling artists and the construction of "opera houses" in several towns indicated interest in and enjoyment of cultural performances. Low comedy, including black-face minstrelsy, catered to common tastes. A few local dramatic groups were organized, and in the 1890s women began forming groups to promote serious music.

The humanitarian urge to care for the ill and unfortunate was somewhat dulled by the anxieties of the times, but there was growing concern for the prevention of disease. Folk medicine prevailed among many families, and the medical schools established during the period—the University of 8-131 North Carolina in 1879, the North Carolina Medi- 8-132 cal College in Charlotte in 1887, and the Leonard Medical School for blacks in Raleigh in 1882— were described by a study commission as "thoroughly wretched" or as "half-schools." Not until toward the end of the century were adequate hospitals built, and then only in the more prosperous communities. A Davidson College professor, Henry Louis Smith, was credited with establishing the practical medical use of X-rays when his photographs of a thimble in a child's trachea enabled doctors to perform a lifesaving operation.

Outbreaks of typhoid and other types of fever increasingly focused attention upon sanitation and largely accounted for the establishment in 1877 of the State Board of Health, whose niggardly appropriation did not exceed two hundred dollars annually for eight years. In the larger towns central waterworks were installed by 1890, and fire departments were organized.

A growing population placed heavy demands upon the existing facilities for the handicapped, and a few additional institutions were provided, including a separate school for the black blind and deaf, a second school for white blind and deaf, and eastern and western asylums for the insane. A fortresslike Central Prison was completed in Raleigh about 1884, but most prisoners were still incarcerated and punished at the county level. In 1890 the new facility held 1,625 blacks and 408 whites. One factor that contributed to the prevalence of violent crime was the easy availability of alcohol, for liquors were distilled indiscriminately in the country and available at bars in town. The Friends of Temperance formed nearly three hundred chapters in the state, but a referendum in 1881 resulted in a more than three-to-one defeat for prohibition.

Ill will generated between the races during Reconstruction virtually ended mixed religious congregations, and the separation was not always voluntary. In Wilmington, for instance, Union general Schofield ordered the Methodists to select a minister satisfactory to the blacks. The churches were not immune to problems brought on by economic conditions, and for several years they suffered losses in both membership and property. In 1870 the relative strength of the major denominations, in number of congregations and missions, was Methodists, 1,193; Baptists, 986; Presbyterians, 204; Episcopalians, 77; Lutherans, 73; and Christians, 66. For the remainder of the century, however, there was substantial growth in membership of both black and white denominations, the Baptists making the largest numerical gain. By 1900 the Colored Baptist State Convention alone counted 1,200 churches and 140,000 members, and black Methodists were not far behind.

Though hindered by the "southern lady" stereotype, still subservient to husbands, and without suffrage, women threw aside some traditional taboos and took a more prominent role in society. Few, however, were as assertive as Abby House of Franklin County, who won the hearts of Confederate soldiers to whom she was nurse and cook on Virginia battlefields. After the war "Aunt" Abby became a privileged character in the Conservative party. In 1875 she barged into the party's convention, took a seat beside Paul C. Cameron, and was given the privilege of casting the vote of the absent Clay County delegation. Women continued to exercise influence on educational issues, and they often formed auxiliaries to all-male organizations, thus at least indirectly influencing political decisions. Teaching was a thoroughly honorable task for a woman, and an increasing number of businesses—particularly millinery stores—hired or were operated by women.

It was in the professions, however, that more precedents were broken, especially in medicine, and even in law. After years of self-study, Tabitha Ann Holton of Guilford County asked for admission to the bar in 1878. William H. Battle protested that no southern lady should be permitted to "sully her sweetness by breathing the pestiferous air of the court room," and when she passed the examination and became the only woman licensed by the bar of a southern state, the Greensboro *North State* sighed, "What next?" Despite these and other instances of liberation, most women remained prisoners of centuries of tradition, bound to housekeeping chores and caring for their families.

The Cherokee Indians who successfully resisted exile to the West a generation earlier lived quietly in the southwestern counties, chiefly Swain and Jackson. Like white mountaineers, they were tied to the rocky soil from which they eked out a living. About four hundred of the men joined the Thomas Legion, a regiment commanded by their white friend William H. Thomas, and for years they proudly commemorated their service to the Confederacy. In the postwar era, land acquired on their behalf by Thomas was incorporated into Qualla Boundary, and eventually the federal government extended protection, but little assistance. By contract with the government, Quakers established schools there in 1881, and missionaries of other Protestant denominations competed for the souls of the natives.

Eight years later the Eastern Band of Cherokee Indians was incorporated by the state, and in 1894 litigation between the Cherokees and many creditors and claimants to their lands was finally settled. At last the Indians were secure from eviction from the land of their fathers. Their plight, however, was precarious, for most of them possessed little but a log cabin, a few household items and crude tools, and—if fortunate—some free-roaming livestock. Still, the 1,376 hardy souls of the 1900 census were proud of the sacrifice of Tsali, and, citizens of the United States but not of the state, they were generally accorded the civil rights of other mountain residents. That tolerance changed during the vicious campaign of 1900, when white Democrats barred them from voting in the referendum on the proposed constitutional amendment to require a literacy test for registration. That affront was not to be forgotten easily.

Most of the descendants of the Tuscarora and other decimated tribes of the east gradually lost their identity. Some passed as whites; most were classified as free persons of color in the antebellum era. Along the Lumber River in Robeson County lived a large pocket of families with Indian features who first achieved statewide attention during the Civil War. Dissension developed, and two of them were executed by the Home Guard for alleged theft. In retaliation, Henry Berry Lowry, the son of one of the victims, organized a sort of guerrilla band and operated from the protection of the swamps. Lawless deeds were accompanied by humanitarian acts toward their own people, and the

8-156 "Lowry Gang" became folk heroes. Their evasion of the authorities added intrigue to their Robin Hood characterization, and their exploits were romantically exaggerated in booklets and magazine articles. Not until 1872 was the band defeated; and even then nobody came forward to collect the large reward offered for the capture of the leader, whose fate remained a mystery.

In the following decade, Hamilton C. McMillan, a white newspaperman from Red Springs, became convinced that the Lumber River people were descendants of the lost colonists of Roanoke, who, he concluded, had been befriended by and had intermarried with the Croatan Indians. In 1885, as a member of the house of representatives, he obtained passage of a bill recognizing the group as Croatans and providing for separate schools for them. Two years later he shepherded bills through the legislature to outlaw marriages between Croatans and blacks and to establish a Croatan Normal School. Finally, McMillan published a booklet, *Sir Walter Raleigh's Lost Colony*, in which

he introduced circumstantial evidence to support his case. Having since gone through several name changes, the Croatans are now called Lumbees.

Just six decades after a state law forbade the teaching of slaves to read and write, scores of Afro-Americans held positions as government officials, teachers, preachers, writers, and editors, and a few were preparing to enter other licensed professions. To admit that a considerable number of these new leaders were born free or of white fathers—or that they received unusual publicity because of their minority status—does not diminish their achievements; it is likely that no race of people ever advanced so far so quickly. Not even the removal of voting rights and the enactment of segregationist policies after the collapse of fusion hegemony in the 1890s could erase the accomplishments of the last third of the nineteenth century, for blacks now had a past to prove their ability to adapt to a new society.

A roster of black leaders in the postwar era would certainly include—in addition to those mentioned elsewhere in this chapter—John C. Dancy, who was born a slave in Tarboro in 1857, attended Howard University, returned to his hometown and worked as an office boy on the *Southerner*, and then published his own *North Carolina Sentinel*. Twice elected register of deeds of Edgecombe County, Dancy was for many years secretary of the state Republican convention, and for two years under President Benjamin Harrison he served as collector of customs at Wilmington—the highest-paid position held by a black in the state. As editor of the *Star of Zion* and the *Quarterly Review* of the AME Zion Church, he traveled extensively and earned a reputation as an orator. Later Dancy was recorder of deeds for the District of Columbia.

George L. Mabson, brother of William Patrick Mabson and believed to have been the first black to be licensed to practice law in North Carolina, was elected from New Hanover County to the house of representatives in 1870. The first black to pass the examination of the Board of Medical Examiners was Lawson Andrew Scruggs, born a slave in Virginia in 1857. After graduating from Shaw's Leonard Medical School, he taught there and at St. Augustine's, then organized the Old North State Medical, Dental, and Pharmaceutical Association. He was state correspondent of the *National Baptist* and in 1892 published a book, *Women of Distinction: Remarkable in Works and Invincible in Character*. William Harvey Quick was born of slave par-

8-158
8-159
8-160

8-157

ents in Richmond County in 1856, attended Shaw, read law, and was admitted to the bar in 1884. Cheated out of the election by Democratic officials when he ran for the state house of representatives, Quick in 1890 published *Negro Stars in All Ages of the World*. David Bryant Fulton, a native of Wilmington, moved northward and adopted the pen name "Jack Thorne," under which he published in 1892 *Recollections of a Sleeping Car Porter*. Eight years later he wrote a touching fictionalized version of the "Wilmington Massacre" in *Hanover; or, The Persecution of the Lowly*. . . .

Thomas Parker was reported to have baptized four thousand persons as pastor of churches in the Kenansville Baptist Association, of which he was moderator for thirty years. Calvin S. Brown graduated from Shaw, edited the *Baptist Pilot*, and was principal of Waters Normal Institute at Winton. R. H. W. Leak, editor of *National Outlook*, gained attention as a leading Methodist clergyman and Republican politician. Charles N. Hunter was editor of *Progressive Educator* and *Journal of Industry*, founder of the Berry O'Kelly School near Raleigh, and convener of the 1879 Colored Industrial Fair which exhibited to large crowds physical evidence of progress among blacks.

8-161 Probably the best-known black lawyer in North Carolina was Edward A. Johnson of Raleigh, a graduate of and teacher at Shaw, founder of the Pickford Sanitarium for consumptive Negroes, city alderman, and an active Republican. In 1890 he published *A School History of the Negro Race in America*, which went through repeated editions and was used as a textbook in black schools. Subsequently he published *History of Negro Soldiers in the Spanish American War* (1899) and *Light Ahead for the Negro* (1904). Richard Burton Fitzgerald of Durham was a prominent brick manufacturer in the 1890s and lived in "one of the handsomest residences in Durham."

The Coleman Manufacturing Company was the most ambitious business undertaking of North Carolina blacks in the nineteenth century. Warren Clay Coleman was born in 1849 in Cabarrus County to Roxanna Coleman, a slave, and Rufus Clay Barringer, a white who was then serving in the house of commons and who later became a Confederate general. Under the laws of the day and despite the prominence of his father, the child was given the mother's status as a slave. After emancipation he was bound to William M. Coleman, attorney general in the Holden administration.

Upon his release the young man entered busi-

ness as a collector of rags, bones, and junk; with his father's financial help, he soon established a barber shop and candy store. Thrifty with his money, Coleman invested in real estate and emerged the wealthiest nonwhite in North Carolina. As president of the all-black North Carolina Industrial Association, he became acquainted with industrialists and conceived the idea of a cotton mill employing blacks. Both black and white investors, including the Dukes of Durham, chipped in funds, and the Coleman Manufacturing Company was incorporated in 1897. Officers of the new company were Richard Burton Fitzgerald, president; Edward A. Johnson, vice-president; and Coleman, secretary-treasurer. John C. Dancy was a member of the board of directors.

8-162

The following year the cornerstone was placed for a building which, when completed, housed 7,000 spindles and 150 looms. The unique business was widely publicized. Within two years the plant employed sixty black workers, who turned out good yarn, but the entire textile industry was forced to resort to "short time" because of drops in sales, and layoffs became common. In midst of these economic problems, Warren Coleman died at the age of fifty-four, and, without his vision and attention, the company's financial situation worsened, and it was eventually sold by Benjamin N. Duke, holder of two deeds of trust. Thus the plant passed to white ownership and now is operated as Plant Number 9 of the Cannon Mills Company. Even in failure, though, the Coleman experiment proved that with adequate backing and proper management a business with black workers could compete in a textile industry dominated by whites.

8-163

One of the state's most illustrious natives made her mark in the nation's capital. Anna Julia Haywood Cooper, born in Raleigh in 1859 of a black mother and white father, earned a master's degree from Oberlin University and taught at St. Augustine's before moving northward. In 1890 she became woman's editor of *The Southland*, founded by Joseph Charles Price, the first president of Livingstone College. Two years later she published a collection of essays, *A Voice from the South: By a Black Woman of the South*, in which she pleaded for racial and sexual equality. In the next century she founded her own "university"—Freylinghuysen—in her home. She lived until 1964, reaching the age of 105.

8-164

Even a partial roll call of leaders of the race too easily obscures the fact that most blacks, like most whites, were ill-educated and tied to the soil with seemingly little hope of rising above bare subsistence. A vast majority of blacks and whites never got their names in print, even at death. Fortunately, the likenesses of a few of them were recorded by artists and photographers, including Mary Lyde Hicks Williams, a white artist of Duplin County, who painted a series of romantic views of blacks; and a New Englander, John H. Tarbell, who operated a studio for several years in Asheville and became photographically interested in the "characteristics of the negroes." Tarbell made a specialty of portraying blacks in their occupations "as well as in endeavoring to represent pictorially the humorous aspect of their nature." The work of Williams and Tarbell, like that of many others, tended to perpetuate stereotypes; yet they helped document a race of people who in a third of a century progressed from slavery to participation in self-government. Sadly, the road to full citizenship was still strewn with obstacles.

In control of the legislature from 1870 and of the executive branch after 1876, the Democratic party failed to provide the progressive leadership needed to heal the wounds of Reconstruction and achieve the benefits of recovery. In fact, modest gains in industry and transportation were exaggerated, while agricultural stagnation and other problems were virtually ignored. Viewing business as the hope of the New South, the Democratic-controlled General Assembly passed legislation favorable to industry and gave little but lip service to proponents of laws to protect workers from exploitation. In short, the "Bourbon" Democrats struck up an alliance with moneyed interests, which in turn financed the party and dispensed railroad passes and other favors. Farmers, who were almost continually in a state of economic depression, were kept in line by the ghost of Reconstruction, which the Democrats paraded at each election. The issue of white supremacy kept the governorship in the hands of the Bourbons until 1896, but the Republican party, which drew its strength from federal patronage and the votes of blacks, remained a formidable opposition. In 1880, for example, the Republicans lost the governorship by only about six thousand votes.

Tens of thousands of freedmen offered an unprecedented source of cheap labor in the postwar years, yet few whites were able to hire them except through the system of sharecropping. Furthermore, many whites distrusted the reliability of the recently emancipated blacks as a labor force. Con-

sequently, the state launched a campaign to attract white immigrants—especially those with capital to invest. Simultaneously, a stream of native whites and blacks left the state, the former to find cheap land in the West, the latter to search for the promised land in the North or Midwest. Still, the vast majority of members of both races remained in North Carolina, where more than 90 percent of them were tied to agriculture, an increasing number of them as tenants. In the thirty years after 1870, tenancy rose to 41 percent, the number of farms tripled, and the average acreage decreased from 316 to 101. The farmers were caught in a vicious circle: As prices of their products fell, they planted larger crops; and the resulting flooding of the market further depressed prices. For instance, while the production of raw cotton tripled by the end of the century, its market price dropped from twenty-five cents to only five cents per pound. Falling behind each year, the farmers often bought their supplies "on time," and the merchants not only levied high carrying charges but also took a lien on the crop, putting additional pressures on the debtors to devote more acreage to money crops. Thus, instead of becoming more self-sufficient by growing foodstuffs and other domestic needs, the farmers were driven to greater and greater dependence upon tobacco or cotton.

Some farmers sought to find answers to their problems by organizing. By 1875 there were perhaps fifteen thousand members of the Patrons of Husbandry—better known as the Grange—but the organization was never really influential in politics or economics. Meanwhile farmers became increasingly restless, for while their income dropped and their expenses increased, they saw industry expanding, railroads extending their lines, lending institutions thriving, and politicians boasting of progress. Despite the fact that white farmers furnished by far the largest number of Democratic votes, their party answered their pleas by raising the specter of Negro rule.

A turning point came in 1886 with the establishment of a weekly agricultural newspaper, the *Progressive Farmer*. The editor, Leonidas Lafayette Polk (1837–92), the first commissioner of agriculture (1877–80), organized the North Carolina Farmers' Association in 1887, which soon joined the National Farmers' Alliance. Within three years the state alliance counted ninety thousand members in 2,147 local chapters, and Polk had been elected to the presidency of the national alliance.

Initially the alliance was a self-help organization,

8-165
8-166
8-167
8-168
8-169
8-170
8-171
8-172
8-173
8-174
8-175

providing information on improved farming and housekeeping methods and establishing a cooperative business agency that bought and sold products in large quantities and passed the benefits on to members. But the opportunity for nearly a hundred thousand organized farmers to become involved in politics was too tempting, for, after all, only through legislative action could their grievances be corrected: discriminatory taxes and transportation costs, industrial collusion, high interest rates, high tariffs, and poor schools. Consequently, the alliancemen exerted their influence in the legislative elections of 1890 and, to the consternation of conservative party leaders, elected enough sympathetic members to control the General Assembly. Among the progressive acts passed by the "farmers' legislature" were the appropriation of additional funds for public schools, creation of two additional colleges for blacks and one for white women, and establishment of a railroad commission empowered to reduce transportation rates and to eliminate discrimination against small shippers.

Alliancemen, however, recognized that their problems were nationwide in scope, and action at the federal level was needed to lower tariffs, control interstate rate discrimination, and resume the free coinage of silver to provide a greater money supply. Consequently, Polk helped organize the People's party, better known as the Populists. In North Carolina this action split the state alliance almost in half; conservatives like Sydenham B. Alexander and Elias Carr refused to bolt from the Democratic party. Polk was almost assured the Populists' presidential nomination in 1892, but he died before the convention.

At the state level the party's leadership fell to Marion Butler of Sampson County, who broadened the platform in an effort to attract industrial workers. Many farmers, however, refused to desert the Democrats, and the Populists placed a poor third. Elias Carr, a former alliance leader, was [8-177] elected governor, but perceptive politicians were impressed by the fact that the combined votes of the losing candidates surpassed that of the victor.

That signal was ignored by the Democratic-controlled legislature of 1893, which, instead of seeking reconciliation, deliberately insulted the Populists. Seething under this mistreatment, Butler's forces turned to the Republicans and in the congressional and legislative elections of 1894 in many counties supported a single "fusion" ticket on which both parties were represented. The result was catastrophic for the Democrats: The fusionists

elected seven of nine congressmen and a majority of both houses of the legislature, which proceeded to elect Republican Jeter C. Pritchard and Populist [8-178] Marion Butler to the United States Senate. More- [8-179] over, the General Assembly of 1895 was the most constructive since Reconstruction: It returned local control to the voters of the counties, adopted a six-per-cent interest ceiling, reformed election procedures, increased taxes and appropriations for education, and granted charters to several eastern towns.

The marriage of convenience inevitably led to disputes between the Republicans and Populists, and in 1896 they could not agree upon a gubernatorial ticket. The split, however, did not benefit the Democrats, for in the largest vote ever cast in North Carolina to that time, enough blacks and Populists voted for the Republican candidate to elect Daniel L. Russell of New Hanover County. For the first time since 1870 the Democrats controlled neither the governorship nor the legislature, and they held only one of nine congressional seats. But again victory brought dissension, and the new legislature only partially satisfied the Populists.

The return of control of local government to popular vote resulted in more Negro officeholders in eastern counties, and several towns were governed by blacks. Shorn of political offices, the Democrats launched a racist campaign even surpassing that of 1870 by raising high the flag of white supremacy, and through the press—particularly through Josephus Daniels's weekly *North Carolinian* and his daily *News and Observer*— [8-182] charged the Republicans and Populists with corruption, extravagance, incompetence, and the imposition of Negro rule. If Furnifold M. Simmons served as the political strategist for the Democrats, Josephus Daniels was its mouthpiece, and Norman E. Jennett, a Sampson County youth on [8-176] Daniels's staff, became its artist; he drew scores of cartoons depicting blacks in local offices, blacks in the legislature, and blacks influencing Governor [8-180] Russell.

Even the Spanish-American War—in which a member of Daniels's family, Worth Bagley, was [8-181] killed and James H. Young, a black Republican editor, was appointed commander of the all-black Third Regiment—failed to restrain the barrage of horror stories circulated by the Democratic press. Wherever blacks won local seats—as in New Bern, Greenville, and Wilmington—published reports twisted incidents between the races into atrocities against whites.

Then on 18 August 1898, Alexander Manly, mulatto editor of the *Daily Record* at Wilmington, responded to Democratic charges that fusion rule had encouraged advances of black men upon white women. Manly wrote that "women of that [white] race are not any more particular in the matter of clandestine meetings with colored men than the white men with colored women." This "vile and inflammatory" editorial outraged whites across the state, and mounted, unmasked Klan-like groups called the Red Shirts operated in the southeast. Wearing flaming red shirts, members boldly proclaimed their mission, and fear gripped both races in the east. The Democrats vowed to overturn "Negro rule" by whatever force was necessary, including the "protecting" of the ballot box from blacks. They succeeded. Democrats swept to a majority in both houses of the General Assembly and six of the nine congressional seats. The fusionists, however, still held both Senate seats and thus controlled federal patronage in the state. In Raleigh, Daniels printed a likeness of a rooster letting out a lusty victory crow.

Not content with their statewide victory, the Democrats in Wilmington heaped revenge upon Alexander Manly, destroying his newspaper plant and running him and a number of black leaders out of town. Several blacks were killed, and still others jailed on a charge of "instigation of a riot."

While reasserting legislative control over local government and repealing several accomplishments of the fusionists, the new General Assembly nevertheless expanded the powers of the railroad commission (and changed its name to corporation commission) and adopted additional legislation of merit. Its chief interest, however, was in disfranchising the Negro, thus "solving" the race problem. In a campaign that greatly exaggerated the extent of Negro officeholding (only 4 blacks had been elected to the Congress, only 101 to the state house of representatives, and only 26 to the state senate), the legislature passed and placed before the voters a constitutional amendment so

transparent that few sought to deny its purpose. Under the proposal, existing registration books were to be retired and every citizen wishing to register to vote was required to read and write a section of the constitution—that is, everyone except a person, or his descendant, who was registered to vote on or before 1 January 1867. The registrar, of course, could be as liberal or as strict as he chose in judging the applicant's eligibility.

The patent unfairness of the proposed amendment, with its "grandfather clause," was hardly balanced by an otherwise liberal Democratic platform and the proposal of the gubernatorial candidate, Charles Brantley Aycock, for an educational renaissance that would prepare both whites and blacks to pass the literacy test in future years. Deserted by many of their former Populist allies, the Republicans helplessly maintained that the proposed amendment violated the federal Constitution and that it would disfranchise many illiterate whites in addition to a hundred thousand blacks.

The Democrats, in control of the election machinery, announced that the amendment had been approved by a margin of more than 53,000 votes, but returns from several counties suggested fraud. In New Hanover and Scotland, where the Red Shirts were particularly active, the reported margins for ratification were 2,967 to 2 and 1,803 to 7, respectively; and in Halifax, where fewer than 2,000 had voted for the Democratic candidate for governor four years earlier, the returns showed 6,280 votes for ratification, only 899 against. Not surprisingly, the strongest opposition came from the mountain counties, though Chatham, Moore, and Orange in the Piedmont also voted against the amendment.

Regardless of the tactics used to carry the referendum, the Democrats were now firmly in control of the state. Deprived of the Negro vote, the Republicans were no longer a serious threat, and Democratic hegemony would continue for decades. Soon a generation of progress by the Negro race would be virtually erased from memory.

8-185
8-183
8-184
8-186
8-187
8-188
8-189
8-190
8-191

8-3
The ambition of William Woods Holden (1818–92) was finally achieved when President Johnson appointed him provisional governor of North Carolina in 1865. That fall, however, he was defeated by Jonathan Worth. He was elected to the governorship in 1868, only to be impeached and removed from office three years later. (Courtesy NCDA&H.)

8-1
In a letter to John Evans Brown, a former resident of Asheville then in Australia, Governor Vance revealed his temptation to "leave the U.S. forever." The undated letter appears to have been written in December 1865. (Courtesy NCDA&H, W. Vance Brown Collection.)

8-4
Jonathan Worth (1802–69), a former legislator from Randolph County and state treasurer during and immediately after the war, defeated Holden and Alfred Dockery, successively, in the first two postwar elections for the governorship and served until he was removed by the military government in 1868. (Courtesy North Carolina Collection.)

8-2
Andrew Johnson, president of the United States 1865–69, was born in Raleigh 29 December 1808. Originally located to the rear of Peter Casso's tavern near Union Square, the house is pictured here in the 1890s at its second location, East Cabarrus Street. (Courtesy North Carolina Collection.)

8-5 (right)
Just prior to the meeting of the official state convention in October 1865, the Convention of the Freedmen of North Carolina met in Raleigh and adopted a polite but insistent address to the whites. (Courtesy North Carolina Collection; reprinted from *Convention of the Freedmen of North Carolina, Sept. 29–October 3, 1865* [Raleigh, 1865].)

8-6 (below)
The Freedmen's Bureau in North Carolina was the subject of an investigation in 1866 by Union generals James Scott Fullerton and James B. Steedman, shown here (in a sketch in *Harper's Weekly* of 9 June 1866) meeting with the freedmen in the chapel at the Trent River settlement, later called James City, across the river from New Bern. (Courtesy NCDA&H.)

Our first and engrossing concern in our new relation is, how we may provide shelter and an honorable subsistence for ourselves and families. You will say work; but without your just and considerate aid, how shall we secure adequate compensation for our labor? If the friendly relations which we so much desire shall prevail, must there not be mutual co-operation? As our longer degradation cannot add to your comfort, make us more obedient as servants, or more useful as citizens, will you not aid us by wise and just legislation to elevate ourselves?

We desire education for our children, that they may be made useful in all the relations of life. We most earnestly desire to have the disabilities under which we formerly labored removed, and to have all the oppressive laws which make unjust descriminations on account of race or color wiped from the statutes of the State. We invoke your protection for the sanctity of our family relations. Is this asking too much? We most respectfully and earnestly pray that some provision may be made for the care of the great number of orphan children and the helpless and infirm, who, by the new order of affairs, will be thrown upon the world without protection. Also that you will favor, by some timely and wise measures, the re-union of families which have long been broken up by war or by the operations of slavery.

Though associated with many memories of suffering, as well as of enjoyment, we have always loved our homes, and dreaded, as the worst of evils, a forcible separation from them. Now that freedom and a new career are before us, we love this land and people more than ever before. Here we have toiled and suffered; our parents, wives and children are buried here; and in this land we will remain unless forcibly driven away.

Finally, praying for such encouragement to our industry as the proper regulation of the hours of labor and the providing of the means of protection against rapacious and cruel employes, and for the collection of just claims, we commit our cause into your hands, invoking heavens choicest blessings upon your deliberations and upon the State.

J. H. HARRIS, Chairman.
JOHN R. GOOD,
GEO. A. RUE,
ISHAM SWETT,
J. RANDOLPH, Jr., Committee.

8-7 (right)
General Daniel E. Sickles, the first commander of the Second Military District under the "conquered province" plan adopted by Congress in 1867, was more conciliatory than his successor, General E. R. S. Canby. (Courtesy NCDA&H.)

8-8 (far right)
Albion W. Tourgée, a carpetbagger from Ohio then living in Greensboro, established a weekly paper, the *Red String*, as the official organ of the secret Unionist society, the Heroes of America. (Courtesy Southern Historical Collection, Frederick Stafford Papers.)

THE RED STRING:
THE OFFICIAL ORGAN
OF THE H. O. A.
LETTER to the MEMBERS of the ORDER:

BRETHREN:—It having been decided fit and proper, that this order should have an official organ in this jurisdiction, a contract has been concluded with the *Union Publishing Company*, at Greensboro, N. C., for publishing a small weekly paper to be entitled **The Red String.**

The terms of subscription have been put at the lowest possible rates, in order to put it within the reach of all, viz:

One Copy, One year,   75 cts.
Ten Copies, to one address,   60 cts. each.
Twenty Copies, do.   50 do.

☞ *Payment invariably in advance. No subscriptions for less than one year will be received.*

The first number of THE RED STRING will be published as soon as 800 subscribers have been received.

All officers of the H. O. A. are hereby constituted agents for the RED STRING, and are requested to give earnest and immediate attention to secure its circulation. And it is expected that every member will give it his cordial support. An earnest and united action among union men is now essential, and this offers, in our judgment, the best means for securing that end. It will be devoted to the political questions of the day and the interests of the Order. No declaration of principles is necessary, as the political faith of the Order is well known to friend and foe.

☞ Subscriptions, communications, &c., to be addressed to the UNION PUBLISHING Co., *Greensboro, N. C.*

By order of the Grand Council.
G. U. S. L., H. O. A.

The subscription books are now opened at this office, and persons desiring the first number of the "RED STRING," should address us immediately.

Union Publishing Co.
GREENSBORO, N. C.

March 14, 1867.

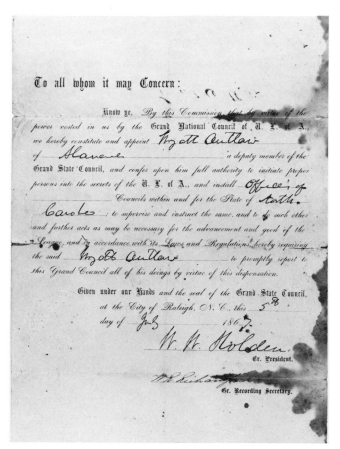

8-11
Under military rule, registration books were opened to the freedmen as well as whites. *Harper's Weekly*, 28 September 1867, depicted "an actual scene in the little mountain town of Asheville, North Carolina, but it will as well apply to all parts of the South." (Courtesy North Carolina Collection.)

8-9
William Woods Holden, who took the lead in organizing the Republican party in North Carolina in March 1867, was also president of the Union League. This document appointing Wyatt Outlaw to the state council mentions the "secrets" of the society. Outlaw, an Alamance County black, was murdered in 1870 by the Ku Klux Klan. (Courtesy NCDA&H.)

8-10
Judge William B. Rodman, presiding over Pitt County Superior Court in August 1867, drew a sketch of Joseph Grimes, the first black ever summoned for jury duty in North Carolina. (Courtesy North Carolina Collection; reprinted from Henry T. King, *Sketches of Pitt County* [Raleigh, 1911].)

8-12
John Adams Hyman (1840–91), born a slave in Warren County, was one of fifteen blacks in the constitutional convention of 1868. He served in the state senate for the next six years and in 1875 was elected to a term in the United States House of Representatives. (Courtesy North Carolina Collection.)

8-13
William B. Rodman, Victor C. Barringer, and Albion W. Tourgée (left to right) served as code commissioners in 1868. Barringer had represented Cabarrus County in the senate at the outbreak of war and in 1869 declined appointment as attorney general. Rodman was a supreme court justice in 1868–69, and Tourgée a judge of the superior court in 1868–74. Both Rodman and Tourgée were delegates to the 1868 convention, and the latter also served in the constitutional convention of 1875. (Courtesy North Carolina Collection.)

8-14
Among the signatures on the last page of the constitution of 1868 was that of Parker D. Robbins, a North Carolina black who had served in the Union army and who represented Bertie County in the convention and in the house of representatives. (Courtesy NCDA&H.)

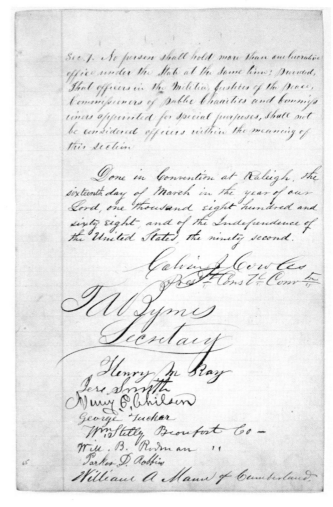

8-15
More than a century after Fred F. French, a delegate from Bladen County, signed the constitution of 1868, his quill pen and note were found in Maine and returned to North Carolina's Department of Archives and History. (Courtesy NCDA&H.)

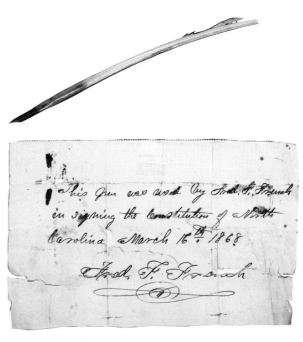

8-19
A banner used by the Ku Klux Klan. The motto translated is "What has been believed always, everywhere, and by everyone." (Courtesy North Carolina Collection.)

8-16
Cartoons in the *Greensboro Patriot* of 24 September 1868 applied the term "Carpet-Bagger" to Albion W. Tourgée (left) and "Scalawag" to William F. Henderson (right). The two Republicans were rivals for the congressional nomination. The drawing at left was stolen from a prewar issue of the *Little Ad* (see above, 7-120). (Courtesy NCDA&H.)

8-17
One of the electors on the national Republican ticket, which featured a cotton press, was Abraham H. Galloway, black, one of the leaders of the convention of freedmen in 1865, a member of the convention in 1868, and a senator from New Hanover County until 1870. (Courtesy North Carolina Collection.)

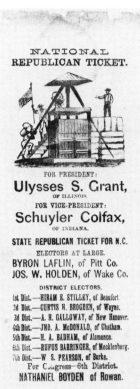

8-18
Cryptic warning from the Ku Klux Klan to Ben Turner of Northampton County. (Courtesy North Carolina Collection.)

8-20
Captain Albion Howe of the Fourth Artillery, United States Army, was sent to Shelby in 1871 to help suppress the Klan. There he acquired this KKK uniform and took it northward. (Courtesy Buffalo and Erie County Historical Society, Buffalo.)

8-21 and 8-22
John W. Stephens, elected to the senate from Caswell County in 1868 and afterward a close friend of Holden, was bound and stabbed to death by members of the Klan in the Caswell County Courthouse. At right is one of the three revolvers taken from Stephens. (Courtesy Gordon Plumblee, Burlington.)

8-23
George W. Reid, chairman of the Republicans in Randolph County, sought support of all who were "opposed to Whipping, Maiming and Hanging men, without Judge or Jury." Reid represented Randolph in the house of representatives in 1872–74. (Courtesy North Carolina Collection.)

8-24 (far right)
Fearless Josiah Turner, Jr., published a stinging challenge to Governor Holden in the 3 August 1870 issue of the *Sentinel*. Holden's acceptance of the challenge helped bring about his own impeachment and removal from office in March 1871. (Courtesy North Carolina Collection.)

NOTICE!

A Meeting of the citizens of Randolph County will take place at

ASHBORO,

ON

SATURDAY, JULY THE 2ND, 1870,

for the purpose of nominating Candidates to represent the people in the next Legislature, and to nominate County officers.

All, are invited to attend, who are opposed to Whipping, Maiming and Hanging men, without Judge or Jury, who are opposed to what is known as *Ku-Klux Democracy*.

By order of the County Executive Committee.

G. W. REID,

June 1st, 1870.   *Chairman.*

THE SENTINEL.

JOSIAH TURNER, Jr., EDITOR

WEDNESDAY, AUGUST 3, 1870.

CONSERVATIVE CANDIDATES FOR CONGRESS.

FOR THE 41ST CONGRESS.
HON. R. B. GILLIAM
OF GRANVILLE.

FOR THE 42D CONGRESS.
HON. S. H. ROGERS
OF WAKE.

FOR ATTORNEY GENERAL
HON. WM. M. SHIPP
OF MECKLENBURG.

COUNTY CANDIDATES.
For the Senate :
HON. DANIEL G. FOWLE OF WAKE.
JOSEPH J. DAVIS, ESQ., OF FRANKLIN.
For the House of Representatives :
DR. J B. DUNN,   J Q. DECARTERET,
C. F. DOWD.   B Y. ROGERS.
For County Commissioners :
G. W. NORWOOD,   B. W. JUSTICE.
D. B. HOLLAND,   S M. UTLEY.
PETERSON DUNN.
For Sheriff :   For Coroner :
W. H. HIGH,   KEARNY UPCHURCH,
For Treasurer :   For Surveyor :
W. S. TUCKER,   FENDALL BEVERS,
For Register of Deeds :
ISAAC H. ROGERS,

TO GOVERNOR HOLDEN.
HILLSBORO', August 3, 1870.
GOV. HOLDEN :—You say you will handle me in due time. You white-livered miscreant, do it now. You dared me to resist you, I dare you to arrest me. I am here to protect my family ; the jacobins of your club after shooting powder in the face of Mrs. Turner, threw a five pound rock in her window which struck near one of my children. Your ignorant jacobins are incited to this by your lying charges against me, that I am King of the Ku Klux. You villain, come and arrest a man, and order your secret clubs not to molest women and children. Yours with contempt and defiance—*habeas corpus* or no *habeas corpus*
JOSIAH TURNER, JR.

FACTS FOR THE PEOPLE

To Read, Ponder and Digest, if they can.

For the benefit of those who really desire information, and to show in proper light the Extravagance, Wastefulness, and utter disregard for the people's best interests, shown by the Radical party, we submit the following comparison of the expense of one year of Democratic rule, under Gov. Bragg in 1857 & '58 ; and one year ending Sept. 30th, 1869, under the Radical rule of William W. Holden :

	Expenditures 1857, '58.	Expenditures 1868, '69.
Adjutant General,	$ 200 00	$ 1965 56
Capitol Square,	1277 82	3687 73
Executive Department,	2550 00	7752 65
Treasury Department,	2750 00	6082 96
Keeper of Capitol,	266 00	1054 19
Auditor's Department,	1000 00	4010 54
Binding Laws,	1073 25	6596 96
Copying Laws,	348 50	1608 60
State Department,	800 00	3903 25
Public Printing,	5240 57	28,685 10
Judiciary,	28,163 15	54,130 50
General Assembly,	49,113 54	191,102 10
Fugitives from Justice,	572 75	6,834 00

Contingences for 1868, '69, $76,506 64

Among the expenditures for 1868, '69, may be found such items as these :—

D. D. Colgrove, one copy of " How to Make the Farm pay,"	$ 4 50	Douglass Bell, for Toilet Soap,	6 00
L. D. Wilkie, Holden's detective,	1042 90	Geo. W. Nason, jr., Drawer locks, Chairs and Water Coolers,	130 20
L. H. Mowers, " "	949 75	Phil. Thiem, 6 Baskets, 1 Corkscrew,	9 00
State Militia, (to outrage Jones County,)	1864 91	Half doz. ostrich feathers, water bucket and dipper,	16 75
Newbern Republican, for adv. duties S. C. C.,	250 00		
Newbern Times, printing Badges for Militia,	18 80		

OTHER FACTS FOR THE CITIZENS OF CRAVEN COUNTY ESPECIALLY.

The entire tax for this County levied for all purposes in 1867, under a Democratic State Government was $18,000. This, deducting the tax on Polls, was only 3-4 of one per cent on the assessed value of property.

The tax for this year, under Radical rule, will reach $47,000. Deduct the Poll tax and the tax levied on real and personal property as assessed, will reach 2 1-2 per cent.

Citizens of Craven, how like you this picture of increase in the short space of two years?

Again—It is a fact worthy of note, that the principal officials, County Commissioners, Legal Adviser of the Board, (R. F. Lehman, Esq., $500,) have all been paid dollar for dollar of their claims, while the jurors, witnesses, &c., have their tickets on hand, or have been subjected to a shave of seventy per cent. to get the money for them.

This is Radical justice—Radical love and care for the poor white and colored man, with a vengeance !

Next week we will show you other iniquities of the party in power.

Plan of the Contemplated Murder of John Campbell.

8-25
Democrats in Craven County in 1870 sought to exploit for political gain the increased cost of state and local government under Republican rule. (Courtesy Rare Book Room, Library, Duke University, Durham.)

8-26
The Klan was still active in Moore County in August 1871 when John Campbell, a Republican, was sentenced to be hanged by the hooded order. However, Captain Joseph G. Hester of the federal secret service led an attack which resulted in the release of Campbell and the capture of the Klansmen. This engraving is from a photograph made in Raleigh when the captives were forced to reenact the gruesome scene. (Courtesy Library of Congress.)

8-27
Frederick N. Strudwick of Orange, who introduced the bill of impeachment against Governor Holden the year before, received a letter dated 27 November 1871 which accused him of having been "at the murdering & hanging of four Negros" and closed with this drawing of a lynching and the words "death death death." (Courtesy Southern Historical Collection, William L. Saunders Papers.)

8-30
Cartoons were used extensively in the 1870s. In this one, which depicted whites being auctioned off by Republicans, the Conservatives appealed to westerners to "Help your Eastern Brethren by Voting for the Constitutional Amendments!" (Courtesy NCDA&H.)

White Men of North Carolina, Help your Eastern Brethren by Voting for the Constitutional Amendments!

8-28
John R. Bryant, a black from Halifax County, was elected to the house of representatives in 1870 and 1872 and to the senate in 1874 and 1876. (Courtesy NCDA&H.)

8-29
In the election of delegates to the constitutional convention of 1875, the parties were so evenly divided that William R. Cox, Conservative leader and future congressman, sent two urgent telegrams—one of which is shown here—to Senator W. Foster French of Robeson County. The other one read, "Robeson must give certificates to your candidates. State depends on it." The Conservative delegates from Robeson were seated. (Courtesy NCDA&H.)

8-31
John H. Smythe, black member of the constitutional convention of 1875 from New Hanover County, was minister to Liberia, 1878–85. (Courtesy North Carolina Collection.)

8-32 and 8-33
Albion W. Tourgée, one of the most capable carpetbaggers, was warned in 1870 that if he held another session of court, he might "share the fate of Jno. W. Stephens." Six years later when Tourgée left Greensboro for Raleigh to accept the position of federal pension agent, fourteen-year-old William Sydney Porter (afterward known as O. Henry) drew this view of his departure. The carpetbag is in full view. (Document courtesy North Carolina Collection; cartoon courtesy Greensboro Historical Museum.)

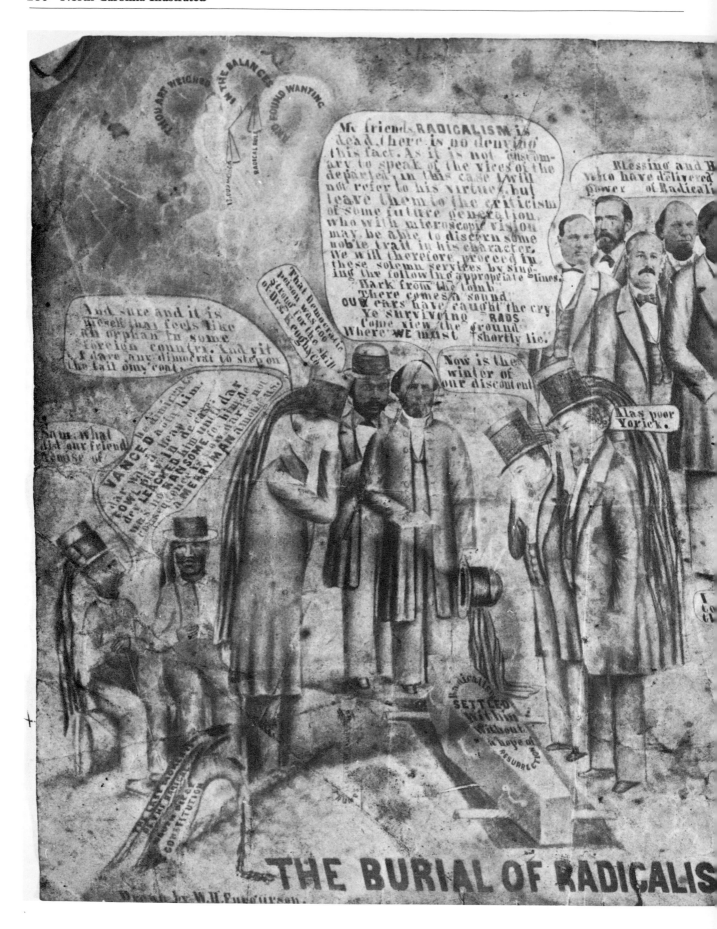

8-34

Willis Holt Furgurson was the artist for this celebration of the "redemption" of North Carolina by Zebulon B. Vance in 1876. Former governor Holden joins defeated Republicans around the coffin labeled "Radicalism SETTLED within without a hope of resurrection." Vance is accompanied by William R. Cox, Augustus S. Merrimon, Daniel G. Fowle, and Thomas J. Jarvis as "Carolina" blesses him; and Aunt Abby House throws up her hands and says, "Zeb, your setting Carolina free makes me feel like a gal again." At lower right Congressman John A. Hyman is labeled "A Surviveing Rad. on his last legs." Riding his back is Governor Brogden, who was elected to succeed Hyman in the Congress. (Courtesy North Carolina Collection.)

8-35
A year after the war ended, a family sat on the steps of "Purchase Patent," the William Duke house built about 1750 in Warren County. (Courtesy John Baxton Flowers III, Durham.)

8-37
On 4 July 1889, Brigadier General James M. Ray (standing with hat at left) opened his home in Buncombe County to veterans of the Sixtieth North Carolina Regiment. Remarkably, not a Confederate flag is in sight.

In an area where many residents were Unionist in sentiments, the general sought unity rather than dissension. Barrels on the upper porch were for catching rainwater for washing. (Courtesy Pack Memorial Library, Asheville.)

8-36
Johannes Adam Simon Oertel (1823–1909), a Bavarian-born artist and Episcopal clergyman in Lenoir, painted North Carolina's centennial banner, which was exhibited during the Centennial Exposition in Philadelphia. Inscriptions commemorate the battles of Moore's Creek, Kings Mountain, Ramsour's Mill, and Guilford Courthouse. (Courtesy North Carolina Collection.)

8-38
The coffin containing the remains of Confederate President Jefferson Davis, on its way from New Orleans to Richmond for reburial on 30 May 1893, was carried in a procession from the train station to the state capitol, where thousands of North Carolinians paid their last respects. (Courtesy NCDA&H.)

8-39
A Mecklenburg County couple, former slaves, lived in this cabin with mud-and-stick chimney and eked out a living growing a patch of cotton. The photograph dates from the 1890s. (Courtesy North Carolina Collection;

reprinted from Daniel A. Tompkins, *Cotton Mill, Commercial Features* [Charlotte, 1899].)

8-41
Local men in 1880 constructed a dam at Coleridge to provide water power for the Enterprise Manufacturing Company (cotton mill) which, beginning in 1882, hired about fifty workers who

produced Pocahontas and Battle Axe yarns and twines. (Courtesy Randolph County Historical Society.)

8-40
An engraving from a drawing by Edwin Forbes was published in *Harper's Weekly*, 12 May 1866. Captioned "Cotton Team in North Carolina," it pictures a cotton press and barn with lightning rod in the background and a two-wheeled cart loaded with cotton and pulled by an assortment of farm animals over a corduroy section of a rough road. (Courtesy Library of Congress.)

8-42
A primitive cotton knitting machine was designed for home use but was used in a small plant at Millboro, Randolph County, about 1890. (Courtesy Randolph County Historical Society.)

8-43

The documentation is remarkable for this photograph of a float of Arista Mills, Winston. It was made at 8:00 A.M., 4 July 1888, by ortho-graphic lens, number 2 diaphragm, Stanley plate, exposed three seconds. (Courtesy North Carolina Collection.)

8-45

Men, women, and children at work in the leaf department of Brown Bros. Tobacco Works in Winston in the 1890s. (Courtesy North Carolina Collection; reprinted from *Cotton States and International Exposition and South, Illustrated* [Atlanta, 1896].)

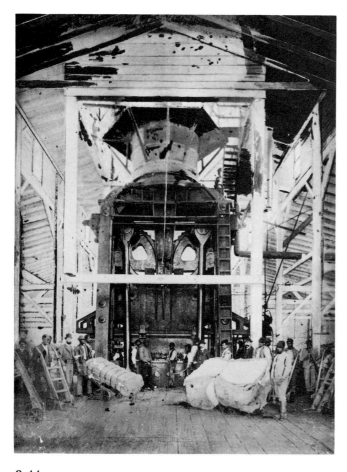

8-44

A giant cotton press in Wilmington, late nineteenth century. (Courtesy Library of Congress.)

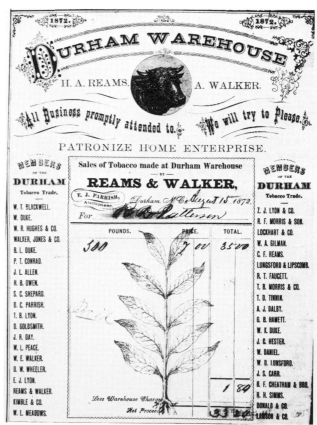

8-46

A "ticket" showing the sale of tobacco at seven dollars per hundred pounds in 1872. Nearly all of the Durham manufacturers were represented on the margins. (Courtesy Manuscript Department, Duke University Library.)

8-47
Wagons of farmers crowded the streets near a tobacco auction warehouse in Winston in the 1890s. (Courtesy Stephen Massengill, Raleigh.)

8-49
Washington Duke (1820–1905), shown here in front of his first tobacco production cabin at Durham, peddled his products from county to county. (Courtesy NCDA&H.)

8-48
The popularity of Blackwell's Durham bull spurred imitations. E. H. Pogue of Hillsboro advertised the "original and only genuine Sitting Bull" smoking tobacco, calling all other bulls "humbugs." (By permission of New-York Historical Society, New York.)

8-50
Duke and his sons moved their operation into the village of Durham, launched a dazzling advertising campaign, and revolutionized the industry. Shown here are the main factory (right) and Washington Duke's new home. (Courtesy North Carolina Collection; reprinted from *Art Work of Scenes in North Carolina* [Chicago, 1895].)

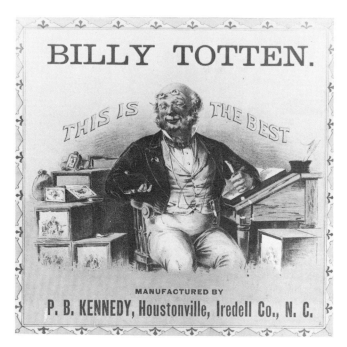

8-51
Small manufacturers of chewing tobacco, such as P. B. Kennedy of Iredell County, were ill-prepared to compete with the larger companies like Duke and Reynolds. (Courtesy Gary L. Freeze, Statesville.)

8-53
A turpentine still in Sampson County. (Courtesy North Carolina Collection; by permission of United States Forest Service.)

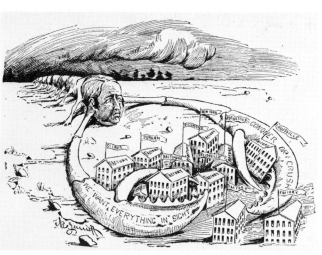

8-52
Norman E. Jennett drew this cartoon of James B. Duke grasping for control of the entire tobacco industry. Duke succeeded in gaining world domination, but his American Tobacco Company was ordered by the Supreme Court in 1911 to be broken up. (Courtesy Southern Historical Collection, Norman E. Jennett Papers.)

8-54
Steam seining for shad on Albemarle Sound near Edenton, 1884. One catch has been landed and the boats are preparing for another haul. (Courtesy North Carolina State Museum of Natural History.)

8-55

Women and boys making fishing nets on the outer banks about 1899. (Courtesy North Carolina Collection.)

8-58

Kapps Mill on Mitchell's River west of Dobson in Surry County around the turn of the century. With its nearby country store, the mill was a center of community activities. (Courtesy Surry County Historical Society.)

8-56

The Odell Grist Mill at Bynum, Chatham County, was typical of many located along streams in the nineteenth century. The miller's fee was often taken in shares of the milled product. The long covered bridge was dismantled in 1922. (Courtesy University of North Carolina Photo Lab, Chapel Hill.)

8-59

Black women planting rice with metal "gourds" about 1890 on the lower Cape Fear, probably at Orton Plantation in Brunswick County. (Courtesy New Hanover County Museum, Image Archive.)

8-57

On the J. G. Phillips farm in Avery County, power was provided an early threshing machine by means of a cable connected to a roundtable turned by mules. The man on the table prods the mules with a stick. (Courtesy University of North Carolina Photo Lab, Chapel Hill.)

8-60

Rice fields with the Orton mansion in the background, ca. 1890. Wooden rails provided tracks for vehicles. (Courtesy NCDA&H.)

8-61
An 1890s photograph made on the Charles S. Powell farm in Johnston County shows, from left to right in background, a hen house, shelter for a molasses pan, well sweep, old house used as a tobacco pack house, and smokehouse. The tree in right foreground appears to have been struck by lightning. (Courtesy William S. Powell, Chapel Hill.)

8-62
J. Wadsworth and R. M. Miller posed stiffly in 1882 for this picture at the Rudisil Gold Mine, which is now beneath the city of Charlotte. This was probably the most profitable gold mine in the state after the war. (Courtesy Bruce Roberts.)

8-63
In 1885 these miners ran gravel through a sluice near Dutton Island in western North Carolina. A dredge also operated in the stream, but it found little gold. (Courtesy Manuscript Department, Duke University Library.)

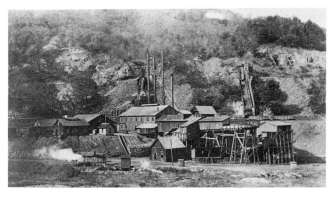

8-65
The Cranberry Iron Mine in Avery County furnished iron to the Confederacy and continued in operation until 1930. (Courtesy NCDA&H, Brimley Collection.)

8-64
Gold Hill, a boom town in the 1840s, was revived briefly in the late 1890s when it was reopened for the mining of copper. In the foreground are the operations of the Union Copper Company; in the background is the office building. (Courtesy Bruce Roberts.)

8-66
Women examine goods in a country store In this etching from a sketch by Mary L. Stone. It was published in *Harper's Weekly*, 20 April 1872. (Courtesy North Carolina Collection.)

8-67
Street scene in Goldsboro ca. 1890. The clock was a landmark for L. D. Giddens's shop, established prior to the Civil War. (Courtesy Wayne County Public Library, Goldsboro.)

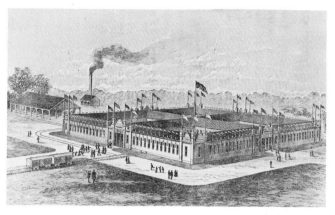

⇒SPOT CASH⇐

Wholesale Produce House,

W. A. POINDEXTER & CO., PROPRIETORS.

LOCK BOX 274,

Mt. Airy, N. C., NOV 1 1397 189

GENTS:

We beg to quote you as follows, F. O. B. here, subject to market changes:

Apples, extra fancy reds, per bushel,		-	-	$1.00
" fancy red,	"	"	-	-	.80
" good eating quality, "	"	-	-	.60
Irish Potatoes, per bushel,	-	-	-	-	.75
Onions, " "	-	-	-	-	1.00
Chestnuts, " "	-	-	-	-	2 00
Rye, per bushel,	-	-	-	-	.75
Cabbage, in crates, per 100 pounds,	-	-	-	1.00
Butter, per pound,	-	-	-	-	.20
Buckwheat Flour, per pound,	-	-	-	

Prices quoted strictly cash. Specify whether you desire goods shipped by freight or express, in barrels or crates. We ship only best selected stock and guarantee prompt attention. Send us your orders. We prefer to ship apples, potatoes and onions in crates.

Yours to please,

W. A. POINDEXTER & CO.

WRITE US FOR PRICES.

8-68
Price list for produce, 1897, in Mt. Airy. (Courtesy North Carolina Collection.)

8-69
For the North Carolina State Exposition of 1884, a square building, 336 feet on each side, with four inner courts, was constructed at a cost of $12,000 by the North Carolina Agricultural Society at the fairgrounds near the present site of Raleigh's Little Theatre. (Courtesy North Carolina Collection.)

8-70
At the state exposition of 1884 various counties proudly exhibited evidence of their industrial and agricultural progress. Tobacco dominated the Durham County display. (Courtesy NCDA&H; Brimley Collection.)

8-71
Like this one photographed at Beaufort in 1890, windmills still provided power for some purposes, particularly near the coast. (Courtesy NCDA&H.)

8-73
At Idols Dam on the Yadkin River, the Fries Manufacturing and Power Company introduced hydroelectric power to North Carolina industry in 1898. The company extended lines to Winston and Salem, thus becoming one of only three operations in the entire South engaged in the long-distance transmission of power—in this case, about thirteen miles. (Courtesy Bill East Collection, Winston-Salem.)

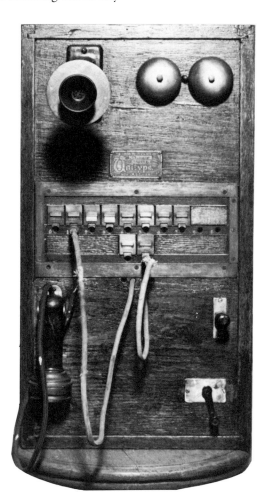

8-72
A painful prank was played by the operator of a wheeled generator of electricity in Raleigh in 1881. The operator stands on a box to prevent himself from being shocked inadvertently. (Courtesy North Carolina Collection.)

8-74
A small wall instrument was the entire telephone exchange for the village of Randleman in Randolph County around the turn of the century. (Courtesy Randolph County Historical Society.)

8-75
The first rural free delivery route established in the state was at China Grove in 1896. A few years later R. E. Ham-bright, the first rural carrier at Grover, posed with his postal vehicle. (Courtesy *Shelby Daily Star*.)

8-77
This photograph, made in 1884 when the Chester and Lenoir Railroad was opened to Lenoir, shows a crowd meeting Senator Zebulon B. Vance, the main speaker at the ceremonies. (Courtesy North Carolina Collection.)

8-78
A "complete road making outfit" in Mecklenburg County in the 1890s. Legislation permitted Mecklenburg to use convicts to build and keep up roads. (Courtesy North Carolina Collection; reprinted from Daniel A. Tompkins, *Cotton Mill, Commercial Features* [Charlotte, 1899].)

8-76
The tortuous climb of the Western North Carolina Railroad west of Old Fort was illustrated in this photograph made about 1881. In the Horseshoe Bend are a popular hotel and Andrews Geyser, named for Alexander Boyd Andrews, who oversaw the construction of the road. (Courtesy NCDA&H.)

8-79
These vehicles loaded with cotton are pictured traveling one of Mecklenburg's fine macadamized roads in 1898. (Courtesy NCDA&H, Brimley Collection.)

8-80
The treacherousness of crossing the French Broad River was illustrated in William Cullen Bryant's *Picturesque America* (1872). (Courtesy North Carolina Collection.)

8-81
Perhaps the best known manufacturer of wagons in North Carolina was J. I. Nissen of Winston. This was one of the early buildings of his wagon works. An unfinished Conestoga-style vehicle is seen at left. (Courtesy Bill East Collection, Winston-Salem.)

8-82
A one-horse sleigh—a rarity in North Carolina—appears in a photograph made on Fayetteville Street, Raleigh, during the deep snow in 1899. The state capitol is at the far end of the street. (Courtesy NCDA&H.)

8-83
The Gray family carriage is pictured in front of the post office in Greensboro in 1887, loaded with girls and local beaux. (Courtesy Mary Lewis Rucker Edmunds, Greensboro.)

8-84
N. B. Frost drew the sketch of a stagecoach "on the road to Asheville." It appeared in *Harper's New Monthly Magazine*, August 1880. (Courtesy North Carolina Collection.)

8-85

In an immensely instructive photograph, a loaded stagecoach stands in front of the Eagle Hotel in Asheville— probably about 1880, just before the arrival of the railroad. Visible is the large eagle on a pole to which is attached a telegraph sign, and at right is a barber's pole. This is one of the very few good photographs of a stagecoach in North Carolina. (Courtesy Pack Memorial Library, Asheville.)

8-86

Asheville, which put its service into operation in 1889, was one of the first towns in the South to operate electric streetcars. This picture was taken in the 1890s, after the construction of the village of Biltmore. (Courtesy Pack Memorial Library, Asheville.)

8-87

A drawing from the *Wilmington Messenger* of 22 March 1890 shows four ships being loaded by Alexander Sprunt & Son at the wharf of Champion Compress and Warehouse Company. From left to right, the vessels are the *George Davis*, *Roseville*, *Pensher*, and *Dalbeattie*. (Courtesy NCDA&H.)

8-88

A popular transport vessel on the lower Cape Fear around the end of the century was the *Wilmington*. (Courtesy North Carolina Collection.)

8-89

The Cape Hatteras Lighthouse was rebuilt in 1870 and has for more than a century warned seagoing vessels of the dangers near the cape. (Courtesy NCDA&H.)

8-90
John H. Tarbell, a New Englander who had a studio in Asheville at the turn of the century, took a photograph in 1897 which he titled "Waiting for Court to Open." Legal notices cover the bulletin boards, and blacks sit on the bench at right. (Courtesy Library of Congress.)

8-91
A crowd stands in front of the Mecklenburg County Courthouse in 1888. This building, which dated from 1836, was replaced by a third courthouse in 1897. (Courtesy NCDA&H.)

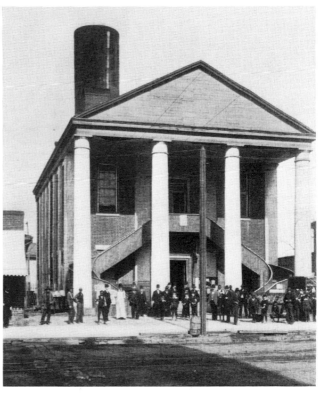

8-92
A tightrope artist attracted a large crowd to Market Street in Wilmington. Records indicate a visit in 1879 from a Professor Dare, who "walked backward and forward, played blind man's bluff on a straight line, . . . walked head downwards, and fairly danced at his giddy height." Dare contributed his "profits" to the poor, and the city fathers waived the twenty-dollar amusement tax. (Courtesy New Hanover County Museum, Hearn Collection.)

8-93
The governor's "palace" at the opposite end of Fayetteville Street from the capitol was left in ruins by the occupying troops during Reconstruction, and governors lived in private homes or in the Yarborough Hotel until 1893. (Courtesy NCDA&H.)

8-94
In 1894, F. S. Coburn drew this sketch of the new governor's mansion at 200 North Blount Street. It was published the following year in Julian Ralph, *Dixie; or, Southern Scenes and Sketches*. (Courtesy NCDA&H.)

8-95 (facing page)
A section of Drie's "Bird's Eye View of the City of Raleigh" (facing northeast) pictures buildings around Union Square in 1872. At the northwest corner of the square is the woodshed and public privy, and at the southwest corner is the arsenal. Number 13 is the First Presbyterian Church, 15 is the First Baptist Church, and 45 is the National (formerly Eagle) Hotel. Beyond the capitol is Christ Church (Episcopal), and to the right of it is the State Bank. Fayetteville Street dead-ends into Union Square at right center. (Author's collection.)

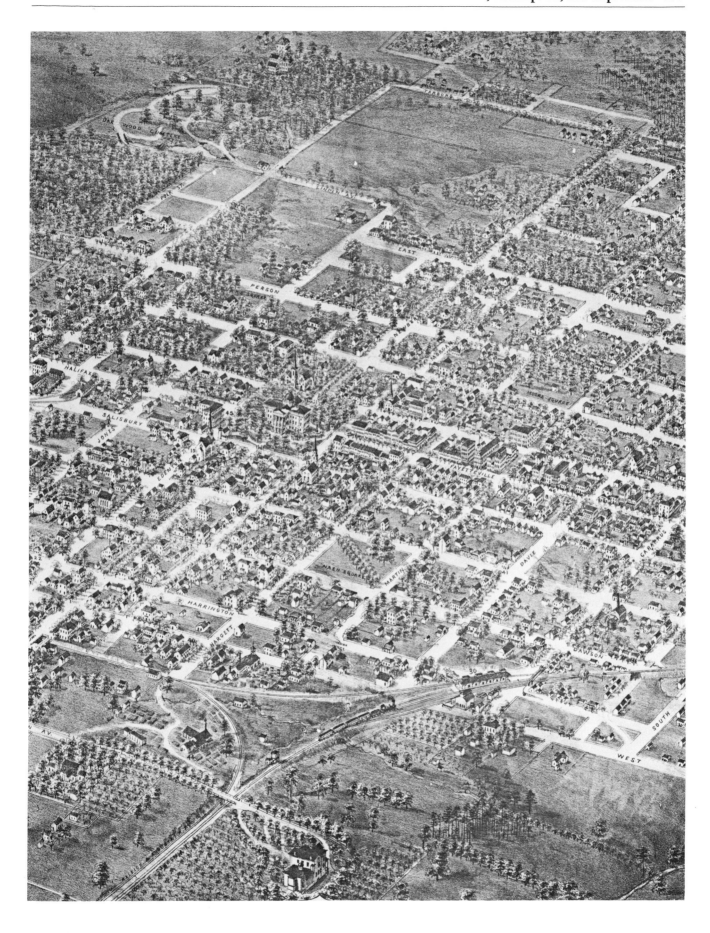

8-96
In the 1880s the state purchased the National Hotel (right) and built the new Supreme Court Building (left). The former was replaced by the present Agriculture Building and the latter is now called the Labor Building. (Courtesy North Carolina Collection.)

8-97
A popular resort in the mountains was Hot Springs in Madison County. This photograph was taken about 1890. (Courtesy North Carolina Collection.)

8-98
A new Atlantic Hotel replaced an earlier one at Morehead City in 1880. It became the showplace of the east. (Courtesy NCDA&H.)

8-101
A member of the Waynick family of Rockingham County is pictured during the Reconstruction period tap dancing to a banjo tune. (Courtesy NCDA&H.)

8-99 and 8-100
A group of men and women from Pennsylvania took a bumpy tour of western North Carolina and published a picture book of their journey, *Jolts and Scrambles; or "We Uns and Our Doin's"* (1884). At top their carriage is fording the Toe River; at bottom is the interior of the ladies' room at Hunter's, an overnight stop between Marion and Linville. (Courtesy North Carolina Collection.)

8-102
Norman E. Jennett made this drawing of President Grover Cleveland on a duck-hunting trip on Currituck Sound. At left is Pierce Hampton, a legislator from Currituck, and at right is Joseph Jefferson, noted actor. (Courtesy North Carolina Collection.)

8-105
An engraving in *Harper's Weekly*, 3 October 1868, over the caption "James's Plantation School, North Carolina." Joe A. Mobley suggests that this may have been one of the schools established in 1866 by Horace James at the Avon and Yankee Hall plantations in Pitt County. (Courtesy NCDA&H.)

8-103
Hunters at their camp at Hyde Park in 1892. Hyde Park was the scene of an unsuccessful attempt by W. H. Risley and a group of New York investors to establish a settlement in 1870. The ambitious project lost to the swampy soil of Hyde County. (Courtesy North Carolina Collection.)

8-106
Samuel Stanford Ashley (1819–87), a Congregational missionary from New England and a representative of the Freedmen's Bureau in establishing schools in the lower Cape Fear, helped write the educational clause of the new constitution. He was elected superintendent of public instruction in 1868 and revived the state's school system. He resigned and left the state in 1871 after the Conservatives cut appropriations for education. (Courtesy North Carolina Collection.)

8-104
The Edenton baseball team in 1895 won eight games and lost four. (Courtesy North Carolina Collection, Stuart Hill Scrapbooks.)

8-107
Several towns voted special taxes for public schools, but most communities provided only primitive facilities, such as the Rocky Branch School in Chatham County, which was attended in the 1890s by Clarence Poe, later editor of the *Progressive Farmer*. (Courtesy North Carolina Collection; original owned by Charles Aycock Poe, Raleigh.)

8-109
Tongues wagged when Eleanor Swain, daughter of the president of the University of North Carolina, married Smith D. Atkins, the commanding general of the federal troops occupying Chapel Hill at the end of the war. (Courtesy North Carolina Collection.)

8-110
A view of the University of North Carolina library (Smith Hall, now called Playmakers' Theater), probably taken in 1900 when the copy of the Venus de Milo was installed. (Courtesy North Carolina Collection.)

8-108
Private academies, such as the one at Trap Hill, continued to give basic education to students whose parents could afford the charges. (Courtesy North Carolina Collection.)

8-111
Two cadets study in their room at the Bingham School in Asheville about 1896. A fireplace provided heat; a kerosene lamp, light; and a bucket and dipper, water for drinking and washing. (Courtesy University of North Carolina Photo Lab, Chapel Hill.)

8-112
The State College of Agriculture and Mechanic Arts was photographed from the west around the turn of the century. Crops grow in the foreground, and sheep and cows graze along Hillsborough Street. (Courtesy NCDA&H, Brimley Collection.)

8-113
Two early buildings of the Agricultural and Mechanical College for the Colored Race (now Agricultural and Technical State University) as they appeared in the 1890s. (Courtesy North Carolina Collection; reprinted from *Art Work of Scenes in North Carolina* [Chicago, 1895].)

8-114
A woman (left) joins neatly dressed men for a posed photograph of the blacksmithing class at the Agricultural and Mechanical College for the Colored Race in Greensboro around the turn of the century. (Courtesy Library of Congress.)

8-115
Peter Weddick Moore (1858–1934) (center) stood in the early 1890s with his faculty of Elizabeth City Normal School (now Elizabeth City State University). (Courtesy North Carolina Collection; reprinted from Leonard R. Ballou, *Educational Architects* [Elizabeth City, 1978].)

8-116
St. Augustine's College in Raleigh was founded by Episcopalians for blacks in 1868. This photograph of the campus was probably taken around 1891, when Aaron Burtis Hunter (shown in street with his wife) became principal. (Courtesy NCDA&H.)

8-117
Livingstone College in Salisbury as it appeared in 1902. Founded in 1879, its first president was Joseph Charles Price, a popular minister of the AME Zion Church. (Courtesy North Carolina Collection; reprinted from *Evidences of Progress among the Colored Race* [Philadelphia, 1902].)

8-118
Julia Jones's report card from Greensboro College in 1880 includes the note "Her name has been entered on our Roll of Merit." (Courtesy Southern Historical Collection, Jones Family Papers.)

8-119
A spectacular view of the Biltmore mansion during its construction in the 1890s, made by Harry Shartle from below the garden house. (Courtesy Library of Congress.)

8-120
Carl Alwin Schenck (1868–1955), noted German forester, established the first forestry school in the United States while in the employ of George W. Vanderbilt. He stands in the rear center with his students. (Courtesy North Carolina Collection.)

8-121
Charles Waddell Chesnutt (1858–1932), a mulatto who could have passed as white, grew up in Fayetteville and taught at Fayetteville Normal School; his fame as a writer was earned after he moved northward. (Courtesy Cleveland Public Library.)

8-122
Frances Fisher Tiernan (1846–1920) wrote under the name Christian Reid to veil her identity and sex. She was the state's most prolific novelist of the era, and with the title of one of her books she coined a slogan for the mountain region: *The Land of the Sky* (1876). (Courtesy NCDA&H.)

8-123
Mary Bayard Devereux Clarke (1827–86), wife of Judge William J. Clarke, published the first anthology of North Carolina poetry before the war and continued to write poems until her death. The portrait is by William Garl Browne. (Courtesy North Carolina Collection.)

8-124
Cornelia Phillips Spencer (1825–1908) was one of the state's most outspoken women. She published two books and participated in the movement to reopen the University of North Carolina in 1875. (Courtesy North Carolina Collection.)

8-125
William Laurence Saunders (1835–91), cruelly wounded during the Civil War, was allegedly the chief strategist for the KKK in North Carolina, but he invoked the Fifth Amendment before a congressional committee, and his complicity was never proved. Later, as secretary of state, Saunders edited and saw through to publication the landmark ten-volume series *The Colonial Records of North Carolina*. (Courtesy Southern Historical Collection.)

8-126
Self portrait of William George Randall (1860–1905), 1894. The artist came from a poverty-stricken background in Burke County. (Courtesy North Carolina Collection.)

8-127
The Baxter N. Welch Pottery, Harper's Crossroads, Chatham County, as it looked about the turn of the century. The wagon holds raw clay; the kiln is at right; and finished churns and jugs are displayed at the front of the shop. (Courtesy Charles G. Zug III; by permission of Mr. and Mrs. Gails Welch, Bear Creek.)

8-129
A piece of sheet music, "Wearin' of the Grey," was published in Baltimore in 1866, written by "Tar Heel" —perhaps the earliest printed use of the nickname for North Carolinians. (Courtesy North Carolina Collection.)

8-128
Pitcher (1879) and jar and jug (third quarter of the nineteenth century), salt glazed stoneware, made in Randolph County. Most pottery produced in North Carolina was for utility, but artistic touches were sometimes added. (Courtesy Museum of Early Southern Decorative Arts, Winston-Salem.)

8-132
The second Twin-City Hospital, serving Winston and Salem, was opened in 1895 at a cost of $10,000. Mollie Spach, one of the first licensed nurses in the state, was superintendent. It was open only to whites until 1912. Physicians of the city took turns giving a month's service to the hospital. (Courtesy Bill East Collection, Winston-Salem.)

8-130
Jenny and Maude Spivey posed in Lee County with their "talking machine" and dolls. Manually wound phonographs provided home entertainment for families who could afford the machine and their discs or platters. (Courtesy North Carolina Collection.)

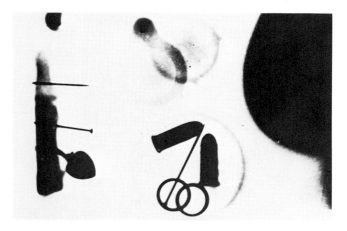

8-131
Richard W. Whitehead revived the medical school of the University of North Carolina in 1890, the year in which this photograph was made. Dr. Whitehead held this anatomy class in the woods to shield the cadaver from curious eyes. (Courtesy North Carolina Collection.)

8-133
Davidson College students sneaked into Professor Henry Louis Smith's physics laboratory and made this X-ray photograph in 1896. At left is a cadaver's finger with pendant ring and straight pins. Other items are a pocket magnifying glass, pillbox, and egg. Smith is credited with establishing the practical medical use of X-rays. (Courtesy Davidson College News Bureau.)

8-134
Citizens of Raleigh began obtaining water from their new water tank in 1887, when this picture was probably taken. The water tank was removed in 1924, and the granite-and-brick tower is now the headquarters of the North Carolina chapter of the American Institute of Architects. (Courtesy NCDA&H.)

8-136
Availability of running water greatly assisted fire departments. Pictured here by Will Wynne in 1890 is Raleigh's "championship" volunteer rescue steam fire engine company. (Courtesy NCDA&H.)

8-135
The perils of outdoor privies draining into wells were illustrated in Greensboro by young William Sydney Porter (later known as O. Henry). Many towns installed running-water systems in the 1880s, but few flush toilets were installed before the end of the century. (Courtesy North Carolina Collection.)

8-137
Central Prison in Raleigh was authorized by the legislature of 1869 and completed about 1883. In this early photograph, the water in the rock quarry reflects the turreted fortresslike structure. (Courtesy NCDA&H.)

8-138
Executions were carried out by public hangings, which sometimes drew thousands of spectators. This one occurred in Goldsboro, probably in the 1880s. (Courtesy Wayne County Public Library, Goldsboro.)

8-139
This gruesome triple lynching may have occurred in North Carolina, for the picture was found among others made by Arkansas (Can) Overby, itinerant photographer of Westfield near the Surry-Stokes county line. (Courtesy Baptist Historical Collection, Winston-Salem; original owned by Willis Overby, Walnut Cove.)

8-140
Two saloons and some of their patrons were photographed at the corner of Mangum and Peabody streets in Durham about 1883. A fence in the background advertises Blackwell's Durham tobacco. (Courtesy Manuscript Department, Duke University Library.)

8-141
Baptisms were popular occasions for denominations requiring total immersion, and crowds sometimes were worked into a frenzy of emotionalism. Here a black minister prepares to immerse a convert in a muddy stream in Wake County. (Courtesy NCDA&H.)

8-142
This view of the Society of Friends' Yearly Meeting House at Quaker Woods (High Point) was painted in 1887 by John Collins. (Courtesy Friends Historical Collection, Guilford College.)

8-143
As early as 1879 Christmas had been commercialized to include visits by Santa Claus. This advertisement appeared in the *Kinston Journal*, 25 December 1879. (Courtesy North Carolina Collection.)

HO ! FOR SALT RIVER.

The crazy, condemned, water-logged, leaky, unsafe and unreliable canal boat

KU KLUX

T. J. JARVIS,	Past Commander.
AH SIN MERRIMON,	1st Mate.
VIRTUOUS JIMMY LEACH,	2nd Mate.
DIRT EATING DORTCH,	3rd Mate.
WHITELINE GRAHAM,	Capt. of the Forecastle.
TWENTY D. ROBBINS,	Pilot.
JOSIAH TURNER, Jr.	} Engineers.
ABBY HOUSE.	
FRENCH O. DOPRAY,	Steward.
THEO. H. HILL.	Librarian and Poick.
JAW JAW LITCHFORD.	Purser.
GEO. H. SNOW,	Chief Cook.
THAT OTHER LEACH, M. D.,	Surgeon.
DEPUTY GOV. WARREN.	Chaplain.
WONDERFUL W. FLEMMING	} Pop Gunners.
FAB. H. BUSBEE,	
MONKEY W. MERRILL,	Spittoon Cleaner.
JOHN DeCONSEQUENTIAL,	Boot Black.
BEARDLESS BARRINGER.	Deck Swabber.
SIMON HAYES.	} Cabin Boys
PENITENTIARY WHITLOCK	

with a picked crew, who are warranted as unreliable as the boat, will leave the Sentinel office at midnight on Saturday the 12th of August, and each Saturday night thereafter, until the Conservative party are removed to the headwaters of Salt River.

8-144 (left)
The influence of Abby House upon the Conservatives was suggested by a card issued by the Republicans in 1876. She is paired with Josiah Turner, Jr., as the "engineers" of the party. "Aunt Abby" is also immortalized in Willis Holt Furgurson's drawing "The Burial of Radicalism" (8-34). (Courtesy North Carolina Collection.)

8-145
Susan Dimock of Washington, North Carolina, was refused admission to American medical schools, so she took her training in Zurich. She became one of the nation's first female licensed physicians and practiced in Boston, where she founded the first graduate school of nursing, before losing her life in a ship disaster. (Courtesy North Carolina Collection.)

8-146
Annie Lowrie Alexander (1864–1929) of Mecklenburg County graduated in 1884 from Woman's Medical College in Philadelphia, was licensed in Maryland, and in 1887 returned to Mecklenburg as the first woman to practice medicine in North Carolina. She is pictured here in the buggy used in making her rounds. (Courtesy *Charlotte Observer*.)

8-147
Mollie Spach, an 1889 graduate of St. Luke's Hospital, Bethlehem, Pennsylvania, was, with Adeline Orr, one of the first two licensed graduate nurses to practice in North Carolina. (Courtesy North Carolina Collection; reprinted from Mary Lewis Wyche, *The History of Nursing in North Carolina* [Chapel Hill, 1938].)

8-148
In 1878, after considerable hesitation, the state bar allowed Tabitha Ann Holton to take the bar examination, which she passed. She was then licensed to practice—the first woman lawyer in North Carolina. Her sponsor before the state bar was Albion W. Tourgée. (Courtesy North Carolina Collection; original owned by Samuel M. Holton, Chapel Hill.)

8-151
Members of the Brown family and their friends gathered for a quilting party in Rowan County in 1893. (Courtesy Roscoe Brown Fisher, Statesville.)

8-149
Although women had been permitted to attend the summer teachers' institute at Chapel Hill in 1879, it was nineteen years before Sallie Walker Stockard became the first woman to graduate from the university. (Courtesy North Carolina Collection.)

8-150
Rosa Lawrence and her son of the village of Goff near Brickhaven posed for this tintype in front of a wagon, probably the photographer's. (Courtesy North Carolina Collection; original owned by Ruby Rosser, Sanford.)

8-152
Cherokee medicine man Ayunini, or Swimmer, was photographed about 1888. Ayunini served as a historian for his people. (Courtesy Smithsonian Institution National Anthropological Archives.)

8-154
A Cherokee woman, Walini, was photographed by James Mooney in 1888. (Courtesy Smithsonian Institution National Anthropological Archives.)

8-153
Nimrod J. Smith (Tsaladihi) was principal chief of the Eastern Band of Cherokee Indians in 1886 when this photograph was made. (Courtesy Smithsonian Institution National Anthropological Archives.)

8-155
This photograph, made in 1888, shows Cherokees ready to begin a pregame dance. The lacrosse-like rackets were used in sports. (Courtesy Smithsonian Institution National Anthropological Archives.)

8-156
Cover of one of two romanticized booklets published about the Henry Berry Lowry Gang in 1872. (Courtesy North Carolina Collection.)

8-157
Lawson Andrew Scruggs, born a slave, graduated from Leonard Medical College. He was one of the first three Negroes licensed by the North Carolina Board of Medical Examiners (1886). (Courtesy North Carolina Collection.)

EXHIBITORS MAKING ENTRIES AT THE OFFICE OF THE SECRETARY.

8-158
The slave cabin in the Cameron quarters at Fishdam near Durham in which Morgan London Latta was born in 1853. He established Latta University in Raleigh in 1894 and operated it for a quarter of a century. (Courtesy North Carolina Collection; reprinted from Latta's *The History of My Life and Work* [Raleigh, 1903].)

8-160
Black men, women, and children entered exhibits in the Colored Industrial Fair in 1879. (Courtesy North Carolina Collection; reprinted from *Frank Leslie's Illustrated Newspaper*, 6 December 1879.)

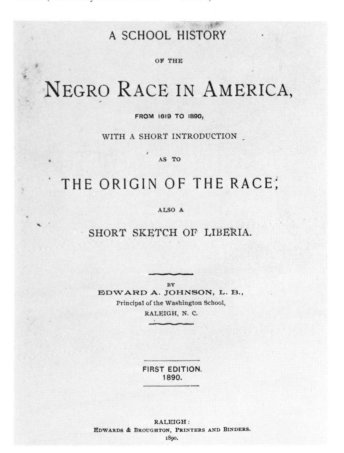

8-159
Augustus Shepard, formerly a slave, became a prominent Baptist minister. He was a founder of the Baptist Asylum (later the Colored Orphan Asylum) at Oxford and served as missionary and colporteur for the American Baptist Publication Society. (Courtesy North Carolina Collection; reprinted from J. A. Whitted, *Biographical Sketch of . . . Augustus Shepard* [Raleigh, 1912].)

8-161
Edward A. Johnson (1861–1944), author of the first Negro textbook in North Carolina, moved to New York after disfranchisement of the blacks and became the first member of his race to win a seat in the New York state legislature—in 1917, forty-nine years after freedmen first served as legislators in North Carolina. (Courtesy North Carolina Collection.)

8-162
This photograph of the board of directors of the Coleman Manufacturing Company of Concord was exhibited at the Exposition Universal in Paris in 1900. The founder and secretary-treasurer, Warren Clay Coleman, sits at right, and the vice-president, Edward A. Johnson of Raleigh, stands at left. Another identified member of the board is John C. Dancy, standing second from right. The man seated in center may be Richard Burton Fitzgerald of Durham, president of the company. (Courtesy Library of Congress.)

8-163
Exhibited at the Exposition Universal, a photograph of the Coleman building was labeled the "only Negro cotton mill in the United States." It measured 80 by 120 feet and was valued, including machinery, at $66,000. (Courtesy Library of Congress.)

8-166
John H. Tarbell, the New Englander who worked for several years in Asheville, photographed a black woman and her children around a wooden washtub. (Courtesy Library of Congress.)

8-164
Anna Julia Haywood Cooper, a native of Raleigh, is shown in her Frelinghuysen University office in Washington early in the twentieth century. The picture was taken by Addison Scurlock, a native of Fayetteville, who was one of the nation's best-known black photographers. (By permission of Scurlock Studio, Washington.)

8-167
Five generations of blacks were represented in this picture, taken in 1895 on the R. H. Ricks farm near Rocky Mount. The oldest couple is Ben and Harriet Speight. (Courtesy North Carolina Collection; by permission of Mr. and Mrs. Thomas B. Battle, Rocky Mount.)

8-168
Newlyweds Johnny Goss and his wife posed for a photographer in Durham in 1887. (Courtesy *Durham Morning Herald*; original owned by PhotoCarolina.)

8-165
A romanticized portrait of a former slave, smoking Duke's Mixture tobacco, painted by Mary Lyde Hicks Williams of Duplin County. (Courtesy NCDA&H.)

8-171
Henry Plummer Cheatham (1857–1935) became the state's third black congressman, 1889–93. Formerly he was register of deeds of Vance County and subsequently recorder of deeds of the District of Columbia and superintendent of the North Carolina Colored Orphanage at Oxford. (Courtesy NCDA&H.)

8-169
An election scene in Swain County in 1884. Heavy Democratic majorities were listed in Swain until that year, but by 1900 the county had become Republican, partly because of resentment over the imposition of the literacy test. (Courtesy North Carolina Collection.)

8-170
James E. O'Hara (1844–1905), member of the constitutional convention of 1875 from Halifax County, was the state's only black congressman in the period 1883–87. (Courtesy Eric Anderson.)

8-172
Beginning in 1879, many blacks left the state, particularly for the Midwest. Democrats blamed the emigration on a concerted effort to stock the midwestern states with Republicans, now that the South had been regained by the Democrats. The engraving of North Carolina blacks awaiting a train appeared in *Frank Leslie's Illustrated Newspaper*, 15 February 1890. (Courtesy NCDA&H.)

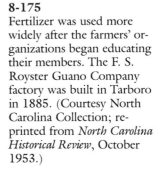

8-175
Fertilizer was used more widely after the farmers' organizations began educating their members. The F. S. Royster Guano Company factory was built in Tarboro in 1885. (Courtesy North Carolina Collection; reprinted from *North Carolina Historical Review*, October 1953.)

8-173
Leonidas Lafayette Polk (1837–92) was the state's first commissioner of agriculture. He founded the *Progressive Farmer* in 1886 and the following year moved it to Raleigh, where he helped organize the Farmers' State Alliance. As head of the National Farmers' Alliance and Industrial Union, he would probably have been the presidential candidate of the People's party had he not died before the convention in 1892. (Courtesy NCDA&H; reprinted from *Arena*, April 1892.)

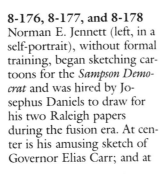

8-176, 8-177, and 8-178
Norman E. Jennett (left, in a self-portrait), without formal training, began sketching cartoons for the *Sampson Democrat* and was hired by Josephus Daniels to draw for his two Raleigh papers during the fusion era. At center is his amusing sketch of Governor Elias Carr; and at right, in one of his very first cartoons published in the *Sampson Democrat*, 25 October 1894, he depicted another Sampsonian, Marion Butler, trading the support of fellow alliancemen to J. J. Mott, Republican leader, for a promise of a seat in the United States Senate. Young Jennett's drawing was prophetic. (Courtesy North Carolina Collection.)

8-174
Advertisement from the *Progressive Farmer*, 21 May 1889, gives an example of the products sold by the alliance. (Courtesy NCDA&H.)

The Source of the Governor's Inspiration

8-179
Marion Butler (1863–1938), then a Democratic state senator, succeeded Polk as leader of the Populists in 1892 and agreed to a "fusion ticket" with the Republicans. The fusion legislature of 1895 elected him to the United States Senate, where he served for six years. Later he was an active Republican. (Courtesy NCDA&H.)

8-180 (top right)
In the 14 August 1898 issue of the *News and Observer*, Jennett showed Colonel James H. Young, commander of the all-black Third Regiment during the Spanish-American War, influencing Governor Daniel L. Russell. The squares in Russell's jacket contain Negro heads. (Courtesy North Carolina Collection.)

8-181
Ensign Worth Bagley of Raleigh was the only American naval officer killed in the Spanish-American War. He was Josephus Daniels's brother-in-law, so his death was given wide publicity, and a statue was erected on Union Square. (Courtesy NCDA&H.)

THIS HOUSE IS BUILT UPON A ROCK.

The Waves and Rain and Hail and Missiles of Fusion Orators are Hurled at It in Vain, Because it's Built Upon a Solid Foundation.

8-182
Josephus Daniels's *News and Observer*, with the largest circulation (about 8,000) of any paper in the state, was the acknowledged mouthpiece of the Democrats in their crusade against the fusionists. Its house, proclaimed this front-page drawing in the 9 October 1898 issue, was built upon a rock—the rock of white supremacy. (Courtesy North Carolina Collection.)

8-183
Some Populists adopted the racist tactics of the Democrats. *The Carolina Watchman* (Salisbury), for instance, in its 27 October 1898 supplement, showed the Democratic senate electing Negro magistrates. (Courtesy North Carolina Collection.)

A Democratic Legislature Electing 107 Negro Magistrates.

Sad and Disgraceful Scene in Alamance county, where "White Man's Party" Democrats work White Girls on Public Roads with Negroes.

8-184
A cartoon in the same issue of the *Carolina Watchman*'s supplement purported to show white women being forced to work on the roads with blacks (Courtesy North Carolina Collection.)

8-186
Alexander Manly, mulatto editor of the *Daily Record* in Wilmington, could have passed as white. One of his editorials was interpreted as questioning the innocence of white women, and he was forced to flee during the Wilmington race riots that followed the election. (Courtesy Southern Historical Collection, J. H. W. and Mary Bonitz Scrapbooks.)

8-185
The Red Shirts at Wilmington in 1898 threatened to "carry the election at any cost," and the Democrats did indeed "carry" the election. (Courtesy NCDA&H.)

8-187
Two days after the election, a mob of whites marched on the *Daily Record*'s plant at Seventh and Church streets and set it afire. Here firemen pose on the second floor of the smoldering building. (Courtesy North Carolina Collection.)

8-188
This is what was left of Alex Manly's printing press after the arson of his building by the white mob. (Courtesy North Carolina Collection.)

NORTH CAROLINA—Wake County.

John Hubbard, being duly sworn, deposes and says: That while working the public roads some days ago, he heard several negroes in Mark's Creek Township, Wake County, talking about the Constitutional Amendment, and one of the negroes, a preacher and neighbor of H. H. Knight, by the name of Offee Price. said they, referring to the white people, may pass the Amendment, but that they would have to fight, and that the right way to do them, the whites, would be to kill them from the cradle up.

JOHN HUBBARD,

Sworn and subscribed before me this the 29th day of June, 1900.

A. T. MIAL, J. P.

8-189
The specter of Negro rule was paraded again in 1900 in the campaign for popular endorsement of the constitutional amendment requiring a literacy test for registration. (Courtesy Library of Congress.)

Senator Butler at Morganton.

SENATOR BUTLER: Even if this Proposed Amendment were Constitutional, Which it is not, Yet this 11-year-old boy will be Disfranchised by it if he does not get an Education by the time he is Twenty-one Years old.

8-190
The Republicans—and the Populists who did not desert them—fought the proposed amendment on the ground that it would disfranchise illiterate whites. Here Senator Butler makes the point at Morganton. Democrats responded, however, that the "grandfather clause" would protect illiterate Democrats. (Courtesy North Carolina Collection.)

8-191
George Henry White (1852–1918), congressman from 1897 to 1901, was the last black man—north or south—to serve in the Congress for a quarter of a century. He is said to have remarked when it became clear that blacks would be disfranchised in 1900, "I cannot live in North Carolina and be a man." He moved to Philadelphia, where he engaged in law, banking, and real estate. (Courtesy North Carolina Collection; reprinted, by permission, from J. K. Rouse, *The Noble Experiment of Warren C. Coleman* [Charlotte, 1972].)

9. An Age of Paradoxes, 1900–1945

9-1 The public discussion of the suffrage amendment of 1900 revealed a spectrum of views supporting and opposing the amendment, but it is the shrill voice of racism that has been most often remembered. Among the voices of reason, however, was 9-2 that of Charles Brantley Aycock. The new governor was as liberal-minded toward the race issue as one could be and still win an election in North Carolina at the turn of the century; yet he too was a product of his time and spoke of the "God-given and hereditary superiority of the white man." What set Aycock apart from many whites was his insistence that the amendment was not a permanent bar against blacks but rather an opportunity and obligation for the state to provide schools to teach all children to read and write. Consequently, he vigorously opposed extremists who advocated a new amendment to eliminate the deadline for registration under provisions of the "grandfather clause." The purpose of the suffrage amendment, Aycock argued, was to remove ignorance, not people, from the ballot box, and the educational crusade conducted during his administration was aimed at reducing the widespread illiteracy among all races.

Since 1867 blacks had constituted a majority of registered Republicans in the South. Though they had shared only the crumbs of office, blacks counted the Republicans as their true friends. The shallowness of that friendship was painfully learned in 1902—just two years after the party of emancipation had so valiantly defended Negro suffrage— when the state Republican convention observed that Negroes had "passed out of the realm of politics." Local Republican committees closed their doors to blacks, and after a row over the seating of 9-3 delegates to the National Republican Convention 9-4 in 1908, Republican leaders wrote off the Negro vote in the South. Both major parties thereafter wore the label "lily white," for seldom could even educated blacks read, write, and interpret a section of the constitution to the satisfaction of white registrars.

The federal courts, although dominated by Republicans, seldom struck down discriminatory suffrage requirements and jim crow laws that made a mockery of the Fourteenth and Fifteenth amendments. With little hope of winning state and congressional offices, the Republican party in North Carolina became a patronage organization to help pass out the plums of office during Republican administrations in Washington. In the half century following 1902 (the effective date of the suffrage amendment) no Republican was elected to a high state office, none to the United States Senate, and only six (with a total of seven terms) to the Congress. Of the congressmen, all but two were from mountain counties where the legacy of unionism, neglect by the Democratic party, and resentment over the suffrage amendment led to strong Republican organizations. During the same fifty-year period the state voted Republican in a presidential election only once, in 1928 when religious bias replaced racial prejudice.

Freed from a preoccupation with blacks and Republicans, Democrats turned on themselves. There 9-5 was a portent in 1900 when Furnifold McLendel 9-6 Simmons, the brilliant and ruthless engineer of the downfall of the fusionists, defeated Julian Carr in a trial senatorial primary. The campaign was more personal than ideological, and its bitterness delayed for fifteen years the passage of a statewide primary law. Democratic state conventions, however, were scenes of internecine warfare between developing factions.

Simmons was the acknowledged leader of the "organization" or "machine," which supported conservative, probusiness policies, including tariffs and laissez-faire economics. The "insurgents," vaguely considered more progressive and sympathetic toward the problems of farmers and workers, agreed on little except opposition to the Simmons forces. Paradoxes abounded. For instance, insurgent Robert B. Glenn, who succeeded Aycock as governor, advocated allocating funds for schools in proportion to the amount of taxes collected from each race; yet his administration was characterized by significant advances in education. William W. Kitchin, another insurgent, was elected governor 9-7 in 1908, thus extending control of the capitol by the anti-Simmons faction.

All signs pointed to an epochal campaign for the United States Senate in 1912. Aycock, Kitchin, and Walter Clark—a supreme court justice whose liberalism marked him as a man ahead of his time— were candidates to unseat Simmons, and the public exhibited so much interest that the Democrats agreed to hold a primary. Aycock's sudden death lessened the drama, however, and Simmons then defeated both Kitchin and Clark by a surprising margin. Simmons's formal election by the General Assembly marked the end of an era; thereafter senators were elected by popular vote. Locke Craig won the governorship in 1912 in a campaign in which the third-party candidate, Progressive Iredell Meares, outpolled the regular Republican, Thomas Settle. Four years later, Thomas W. Bickett won the first gubernatorial primary and was elected in the fall.

9-8

In 1914 tne voters rejected ten proposed constitutional amendments, one of which would have substituted the words "War Between the States" for "insurrection or rebellion against the United States." The implication of that shocking repudiation needs further exploration.

After the election to the presidency of Woodrow Wilson—who had lived for a time in Wilmington and had attended Davidson College—North Carolinians in greater numbers than ever before or after held offices of great influence. Simmons was chairman of the Senate Finance Committee, and his colleague Lee S. Overman headed the Senate Rules Committee. In the House of Representatives, Edward W. Pou was the chairman of the Rules Committee; E. Yates Webb headed the Judiciary Committee; and Claude Kitchin was the Democratic leader. Major Wilson appointees included Josephus Daniels, secretary of the navy; David Houston, a native of North Carolina then living in Missouri, secretary of agriculture; and Walter Hines Page, ambassador to England. New positions of responsibility appeared to moderate the views of some of them; for instance, Simmons's high-tariff sentiments were softened, and he was coauthor of the Underwood-Simmons Tariff Act of 1913, which reduced duties an average of 30 percent and eliminated duties on some raw materials.

A plethora of membership organizations became active after 1890, some of the most influential of them to commemorate patriotism in past wars. The Society of the Cincinnati (organized in 1783), Daughters of the American Revolution, United Daughters of the Confederacy, and similar societies exercised influence far beyond their numbers, as

9-9

they counted among their members the social, political, and economic elites of the state. As war clouds gathered in Europe during Wilson's first administration, these organizations reminded North Carolinians of their past sacrifices.

9-10
9-11

Not all North Carolinians, however, favored the increasing assistance that the Wilson administration provided the Allied Powers (England, France, Russia, Italy, and several small nations) against the Central Powers (Germany, Austria-Hungary, Turkey, and Bulgaria). Adversaries on the issue included the ambassador to England and the Democratic leader in the House of Representatives, both North Carolinians.

9-12

The entry into the war by the United States ultimately was prompted by the Germans, whose submarine attacks led to the loss of American lives and property. Already young Americans had volunteered for service in Allied forces, and public sentiment had swung strongly toward England and France. Within weeks of the declaration of war in April 1917, North Carolinians were inducted into the armed forces, factories began converting to the production of war goods, and public policies were shifted to aid the war effort. By midsummer Camp Greene, a sprawling military training base of two thousand wood and canvas buildings capable of accommodating 50,000 men, was under construction at Charlotte; this was followed the next year by Camp Polk at Raleigh and Camp Bragg at Fayetteville. Yards at Wilmington, Morehead City, and Elizabeth City were converted to building vessels for ferrying men and supplies across the Atlantic.

9-13

9-14
9-15

9-16

9-17
9-18

In all, nearly 100,000 North Carolinians wore the American uniform, including over 20,000 blacks. Of the total, 2,375 died, 833 of them killed in action or from battle wounds. The state was heavily represented in the Thirtieth (Old Hickory) and Eighty-first (Wildcat) divisions, which were engaged in deadly fighting along the Hindenburg Line and in the Meuse-Argonne, respectively. Women, too, served—nearly two hundred nurses were in the armed forces, and at home thousands of women aided such organizations as the YWCA, YMCA, and Red Cross in providing services and supplies to the forces. Others performed such duties as planting victory gardens, canning fruit and vegetables, promoting economical use of scarce products, and preparing first-aid kits. Citizens invested millions in victory bonds and contributed several million dollars to the Red Cross and other humanitarian groups.

9-19

9-20
9-21

9-22 United States participation in World War I lasted only nineteen months, but it profoundly affected society. With the exception of the short, unspectacular Spanish-American War, it was the first opportunity for Northerners and Southerners to close ranks, and thousands of North Carolinians came into close association for the first time with men from other regions and different backgrounds. The war shrank the world immensely in the eyes of its participants and, more than any occurrence since the Civil War, stimulated a reassertion of an Ameri-

9-23 can nationality.

Just as the war was coming to an end, a catastrophic pandemic of Spanish influenza swept the world, leaving an estimated 20 million people dead. The disease, which often evolved into pneumonia, struck the strong and the weak, the young and the old, often leaving families without a healthy member to care for the others. Public meetings were canceled, assemblages of people prohibited, churches and schools closed, funerals made private, and hospitals and ambulances kept busy. By the end of 1918 the official death toll in North Carolina alone was 13,644, including Edward Kidder Graham, president of the University of North Carolina, and many lesser-known names, such as Eliza Riddick of Raleigh, who tenderly cared for sick students at the State College of Agriculture and Engineering until she herself succumbed.

The America of the postwar period was far different from the one that had entered the war in 1917. The divisions of Civil War and Reconstruction were partially bridged, and forty-eight united states emerged as a major world power. An exaggerated sense of patriotism expressed itself in a

9-24 wave of "Pure Americanism," which implied superiority of the nation's traditional values. The "American Way" was associated with the white race, Protestant religion, conforming behavior, and free enterprise. Conversely, there was fear of and resistance to foreigners, non-Protestants, organized labor, political "isms," and new ideas. Vigilante-type organizations again stalked the land, and Afro-Americans remained second-class citizens.

Paradoxically, an almost unbridled confidence pervaded political and economic policies, and pro-

9-25 gressive advances were made. Cameron Morrison, elected governor in 1920, crusaded for an extensive network of roads connecting the county seats and major towns, and, with the aid of a remarkably able and popular officer of the North Carolina Good Roads Association, Harriet Morehead Berry,

won approval of a $50 million bond issue that paid for construction of six thousand miles of improved roads. Morrison's administration also increased expenditures for public education, including extending the school term to six months, strengthening teacher certification requirements, establishing a salary schedule for teachers, consolidating small schools, and aiding counties in the construction of school buildings.

If Morrison earned the title of the "Good Roads Governor," his successor, Angus Wilton McLean of Robeson County, deserved that of the "Businessman's Governor," for he modernized the administration of state government by creating new agencies, abolishing old ones, and reallocating functions of others. His most significant accomplishments were the establishment of the Budget Bureau, which assisted the governor in preparing a more realistic balanced budget for presentation to the General Assembly, and the creation of study commissions whose findings and recommendations were of value when the Great Depression occurred.

9-28 In 1928 the nomination of Alfred Emanuel Smith for the presidency split the Democratic party. Big-city bred, a wet, and a Catholic, Smith was on all three counts unacceptable to many Southerners, including Senator Simmons, whose defection contributed to his own defeat by Josiah William Bailey two years later. Herbert Hoover became the first Republican to win the state's electoral votes since 1872; two Republicans—Charles Andrew Jonas and George Moore Pritchard—were elected to the Congress; and a larger than normal delegation of Republicans was sent to the legislature. Oliver Max Gardner, however, remained loyal to the party and won the governorship by a comfortable margin.

9-26
9-27 As Gardner took office, farm prices were dropping, industrial workers were restless, and the state's credit rating was precarious in light of the highest debt in history. Under these conditions, his program was only partially adopted. The legislature passed a workmen's compensation act (to be administered by the new Industrial Commission) and authorized the Australian (secret) ballot, but it refused to extend the school term to eight months. Gardner's troubles, moreover, were immensely aggravated by the October crash of the stock market, which signaled the beginning of the deepest economic depression ever suffered by the nation. Employment, wages, profits, and property values began dropping, followed quickly by a decrease in tax revenues.

The governor resisted the temptation to panic; instead of calling a special session of the legislature he commissioned the Brookings Institution to make a comprehensive study of state and local governments and to propose changes to improve efficiency. The institution's proposals were far-reaching, and not all of them were acceptable to Gardner. At his urging, however, the General Assembly of 1931 supported four fundamental changes in the operation of government: the state took over from the counties the responsibility for constructing and maintaining roads and for the operation of the six-month school term; a greater University of North Carolina was created by the consolidation of Woman's College at Greensboro, State College of Agriculture and Engineering at Raleigh, and the University of North Carolina at Chapel Hill; and the Local Government Commission was given supervision over the borrowing practices of county and municipal governments. The state left ad valorem taxes to the use of local governments, while corporation taxes were increased at the state level. Finally, economies were adopted, including the reduction of salaries of state employees and teachers.

These bold actions, however, failed to halt the economic downturn, and John Christoph Blucher Ehringhaus of Elizabeth City assumed the governorship in 1933 in the midst of the nation's worst economic crisis. Employment, wages, prices, and profits were at rock-bottom, and thousands of North Carolinians were delinquent in their taxes. State and local governments also were on the verge of bankruptcy; together they owed more than a half billion dollars.

A first order of business was a further slashing of expenditures, but the drama of the legislative session came in the battle between schools and taxes. Sentiment for lengthening the school term to eight months and for improving schools generally was hardly diminished by the deteriorating economic conditions; yet neither could be accomplished without higher taxes. After a marathon battle featuring an outpouring of public opinion both pro and con, the General Assembly passed a 3 percent sales tax on virtually all purchases except bread, flour, and meat. The tax was criticized as regressive, but it enabled the state to extend the term and to assume almost all of the costs of operating the public schools. Thereafter the counties furnished physical facilities, but the state provided funds for a minimum educational program in all units.

Franklin Delano Roosevelt, who had carried North Carolina and won the presidency on a platform of economy in government, shelved his rhetoric and launched the federal government on the radical economic course to which the term "New Deal" was applied. By exercising unprecedented powers granted him by the Congress, he moved boldly to restore confidence in the banking system, then pushed through the Congress a long list of costly programs, many of them overlapping, some of them unclear in objective, most of them designed to put money into the hands of the poor as quickly as possible, and all of them known by acronyms. The Federal Emergency Relief Administration (FERA), for instance, had relief as its main objective through a variety of productive jobs, make-work activities, and adult education classes. Nearly seventy-five thousand young North Carolinians—black and white—were enrolled in the Civilian Conservation Corps (CCC), given drab uniforms, sent to one of sixty-six camps in the state, provided subsistence and a small salary, and put to work encouraging farmers to plant leguminous crops, build strong fences, and control erosion by contour terracing of hillsides and constructing meadow strips. Among the legacies of the CCC was kudzu, an Asiatic vine imported to fight erosion but which showed some of the attributes of the mythical Jack's beanstalk. The National Youth Administration (NYA) employed thousands of high school and college youngsters in nearly 500 projects, many of them clerical in nature.

Of the dozens of such agencies, the ones that left the most tangible accomplishments in North Carolina were the three "works" programs—the Civil Works Administration (CWA), the Public Works Administration (PWA), and the Works Progress Administration (WPA). The WPA spent nearly $175 million in North Carolina and employed thousands in building roads, airfields, outdoor privies (63,311 of them in three years), hospitals, schools, and other permanent improvements. It also hired artists to decorate public buildings and paint pictures, musicians to teach and conduct concerts, actors to produce dramatic performances, and historians and clerical workers to inventory the records of public agencies. Under the WPA the Federal Writers Project conducted interviews, compiled folk tales, and published guides to institutions, cities, and states. In the first five years of the New Deal these and scores of other federally funded projects brought into the state nearly a half

9-29
9-30
9-35

9-31

9-32
9-33
9-34
9-36

9-37

billion dollars, although this was the lowest per capita allocation of all the states.

These New Deal programs were rife with politics, and whether they accounted for the improvement in the economy was a question of legitimate 9-38 debate. Nevertheless, conditions did improve, whether owing to the New Deal or to the stimulation of war-preparation policies, and by the outbreak of World War II the economy appeared to be in better condition than it had been prior to the Depression. Critics of the New Deal, of course, pointed to the high federal debt contracted under an administration first elected on a platform of economy in government.

With the defeat of Simmons and the death of Senator Overman in 1930 came the end of the machine that had heavily influenced North Caro-9-39 lina politics for a third of a century. A political machine exists when enough people think that it does, and the public perception was that the "Shelby Dynasty" succeeded to the title. At the heart of the new faction were Governor O. Max Gardner and his brother-in-law, Clyde Roark Hoey. In the gubernatorial primary of 1936, Hoey turned back a strong challenge from Ralph W. McDonald, a liberal candidate of pronounced New Deal leanings. Though conservative, Hoey worked well with the Roosevelt administration and maintained an unusually high popularity among the people. He was succeeded by Joseph Melville Broughton, a Raleigh attorney, who gained the largest majority ever given a gubernatorial candidate. Despite apprehension over breaking the two-term tradition, North Carolinians cast their electoral votes for Roosevelt over Wendell Willkie. Roosevelt also carried the state in 1944, at which time Hoey replaced United States Senator Robert Rice ("Our Bob") Reynolds, the flamboyant prewar isolationist who did not seek reelection after twelve years in office.

Previous industrialization was dwarfed by the growth of manufacturing in the twentieth century. The combination of labor, raw materials, climate, transportation, and electric power provided favorable conditions for a belated industrial revolution in the state. Within five decades North Carolina emerged as the South's leading industrial state and the nation's largest producer of cotton textiles, tobacco products, and wooden furniture. And though North Carolina had the nation's largest farm population after World War II, industry far

outstripped agriculture in total income. At the turn of the century the value of manufactured products ($95 million) was only slightly greater than that of agriculture ($90 million); by mid-century industrial production was $5 billion, about ten times the value of all farm products marketed.

Textile manufacturing made the most spectacular gains. In 1900 about 32,000 textile workers produced $30 million in goods; at mid-century a work force of 200,000 in more than 900 plants produced $2½ billion in goods. The state led the nation in underwear, hosiery, work clothes, towels, and damask. Factories dotted a crescent-shaped strip from Raleigh to Gastonia. The plants of brothers Moses and Ceasar Cone at Greensboro 9-40 grew into a textile empire; so did those of brothers John Wesley and Pleasant Henderson Hanes at Winston-Salem. Towns like Haw River grew up 9-41 around mills, and Kannapolis, owned and operated 9-42 by the Cannon family, grew into a large but unin- 9-43 corporated community.

Women and children continued to provide much of the labor early in the century, but the General Assembly passed an act in 1907 banning children under fourteen from working night shifts and prohibiting those under eighteen from working more than sixty-six hours per week. That even those weak provisions were violated was documented by Lewis Wickes Hine, who toured North Carolina 9-44 with his camera in 1908 and 1909 for the National 9-45 Child Labor Committee. 9-46 9-47

The individualism of native workers and the paternalism of industrialists made North Carolina a barren field for labor organizers. Following World War I, however, the United Textile Workers did enroll about thirty thousand employees, but several strikes failed and the union accomplished little. By 1929 low wages and dissatisfaction with working conditions had provided yeast for the emotionalism of the National Textile Workers Union, which was acknowledged to be under the influence of Communists. A small army of organizers sought to unionize Gastonia's Loray Mill, owned by northern capitalists. Workers chose sides, a majority shunning the "outside agitators" despite their need for higher wages and better conditions. Violence 9-48 erupted between the two sides, and Ella May Wig- 9-49 gins, a union sympathizer, and O. F. Aderholdt, 9-50 Gastonia's chief of police, were among those killed. Fred Beal and several fellow Communists were convicted of the second-degree murder of Aderholdt, but no one was convicted of assaults on the unionists. The strike failed, as did those in Marion and several other textile communities, and the violence associated with them bolstered antiunion sentiment. Even after passage during the New Deal of federal laws favorable to collective bargaining, organized labor made only modest gains in North Carolina, and at mid-century union membership was well under 10 percent of the industrial work force.

In the manufacture of tobacco, too, North Carolina maintained national leadership. From a value in 1900 of $16 million, tobacco products by mid-century had surpassed the $1 billion mark in yearly sales, still less than half the dollar value of textiles. Because of mechanization, the tobacco industry employed a much smaller work force in its factories, which were centered in Durham, Winston-Salem, and Reidsville. In one respect, however, tobacco was champion: it contributed a disproportionate share of federal taxes; at one time only New York paid more taxes into the treasury of the United States than did North Carolina. Cigarettes accounted for the major portion of tobacco sales, but World War I and the depression of the 1930s spurred a return to roll-your-own smoking tobacco. North Carolina's Camels, Lucky Strikes, and Chesterfields outsold other cigarette brands.

Furniture was the third industry in which North Carolina held national rank. From less than $2 million in 1900, the annual value of furniture products rose to $180 million in 1949. An increasing portion of this furniture was of high quality, and manufacturers acquired national and even international attention. In 1906, for instance, White Furniture Company of Mebane furnished a trainload of furniture for American buildings in the Canal Zone, and in World War II the company made fifty thousand double-decker bunks for the armed forces. Furniture manufacturers began organizing early in the century, and in 1921 the Southern Furniture Exposition Building opened in High Point. By 1944, 38 percent of the bedroom furniture and 40 percent of the dining room furniture sold in the United States were made within a 125-mile radius of High Point.

Other wood products recorded growth. Lumber companies brought huge tracts of timber, particularly in the east and west, and by mid-century the cutting of lumber was valued at about $170 million per year. The production of pulpwood and paper goods was only slightly less. The Champion Paper and Fiber Company built a plant at Canton in 1908; forty years later it employed more than

twenty-five hundred, owned nearly a quarter of a million acres, and contracted for wood from an additional five million acres. In 1906 the Halifax Paper Company at Roanoke Rapids manufactured the first kraft paper in the nation. Some naval stores continued to be produced in the pine belt, but on a much smaller scale.

Food products and chemicals were among the fastest-growing industries toward the middle of the century; their products in 1949 were valued at $293 million and $162 million, respectively. Some industries are not easily classified. For example, the Ecusta Paper Corporation in Transylvania County made most of the flax paper used in cigarettes; the Carolina Aluminum Company, established in Stanly County in 1915, was one of the country's largest producers of aluminum; and the Mount Airy Granite Quarry was among the largest open-face pits in the world. Finally, tourism, though hardly an industry in the traditional sense, surpassed the quarter-billion-dollar mark following World War II.

Except for the flurry of gold mining in the antebellum period, mining has never been a very widespread activity in North Carolina. The coal mines at Cumnock (formerly Egypt) along the Deep River in Lee County were drained and reopened, but they never recovered from a disastrous explosion that killed fifty-three miners in 1925. The Cranberry Iron Mine in Avery County produced two million tons of magnetite ore before closing in the 1930s, but the reopening of several gold mines during the Depression, including the Portis, Rudisil, and Howie, resulted only in dashed hopes. The state did, however, become a major producer of pegmatite minerals, furnishing all of the nation's primary kaolin and 70 percent of its mica.

Commercial fishing showed a decline, for at mid-century there were fewer commercial fishermen than fifty years earlier, and the production of food fish also was less. Conversely, the catch of menhaden, used for nonfood purposes, increased after World War I, and sport fishing became more popular.

In 1945 more than 125,000 North Carolinians were employed in retail stores whose sales ranged from automotive parts to zucchini. Supplying the retail stores were 4,000 wholesalers. These figures do not include service personnel, such as barbers, hairdressers, tailors, cobblers, mechanics, plumbers, and providers of the scores of other services to which the public had become accustomed.

Among the industries that started in North

Carolina but later moved from the state was a bottling firm in New Bern. In his pharmacy and soda shop in 1896 Caleb D. Bradham and his assistant, 9-66 R. F. Butler, concocted a tasty soft drink that his customers called "Brad's Drink." It became so popular that in 1902 Bradham formed the Pepsi-Cola Company, which soon had assets of over a million dollars. Economic conditions following World War I led to Bradham's bankruptcy, however, and the formula and trademark were taken out of the state.

Insurance emerged as an important business in the twentieth century. At Durham in 1898, John 9-67 Merrick and six associates organized the North Carolina Mutual and Provident Association. Success in its first dozen years was measured not only by the amount of insurance in force but also by the additional black-owned businesses that the company spawned, including a bank and a cotton mill. 9-68 Black leaders such as Booker T. Washington and W. E. B. DuBois agreed with the description given Durham by a black newspaper in Atlanta: "There is more grace, grit, and greenback among the Negroes in Durham and more harmony between the races than in any city in America."

9-69 In Greensboro the Pilot Life Insurance Company was formed in 1903, followed four years later by the Jefferson Standard; by mid-century the city had acquired the title "Hartford of the South" with nearly $2 billion worth of insurance in force. Among the other early insurance companies were Imperial Life (1905), Durham Life (1906), and Winston Mutual Life (1906). Total bank resources in the state rose from $32 million in 1900 to more than $2 billion in 1950; and building and loan associations grew in assets from $4 million to about $180 million.

A natural result of industrialization was the creation of a small wealthy class with social standing equal to that of the elite of other states. Almost without exception the state's wealthy families were 9-70 generously philanthropic. James B. Duke, for instance, gave millions to convert Trinity College into Duke University, then donated $40 million (with much more later) to establish the Duke Endowment for the support of educational institutions, hospitals, orphanages, and superannuated clergymen. If on a lesser scale, the Cones, Reynoldses, and other beneficiaries of the success of North Carolina industries were also noted for their good works and generosity. Some of these families were the objects of much attention and curiosity, and their well-publicized lifestyles contrasted

sharply with those of most of the workers in their plants. Significantly, however, labor problems were generally fewer in family owned and North Carolina–based industries than in factories with absentee ownership.

The first half of the century was characterized by a steady increase in the proportion of the state's inhabitants living in towns—from less than 10 percent in 1900 to over 30 percent in 1945—and a remarkable decrease in the proportion of North Carolinians earning their living from the soil. By the end of World War II more than a million North Carolinians lived in urban areas (that is, towns of more than 2,500 population). Another million or so lived in small towns or rural areas but made their livelihood in nonagricultural pursuits ("rural nonfarm"). That left about 1.5 million— men, women, and children—who could be classified as farmers.

A second feature of the period was an increase in farm tenancy, an increase in the number of farms, and a decrease in their size. By 1925 the average-sized farm had dropped to sixty-five acres; in the same year 45 percent of the farms were operated by tenants, two-thirds by black sharecroppers. This 9-71 worrisome trend began a slow reversal in the following decade.

A third feature was the dramatic increase in to- 9-72 bacco production. While the acreage devoted to 9-73 tobacco increased 350 percent between 1900 and 9-74 1945, the annual value of leaf crops jumped from 9-75 $8 million to $356 million. Inflation and higher 9-76 prices only partially accounted for the increase; im- 9-77 proved farming practices that led to higher produc- 9-78 tivity per acre also contributed. Fertilizer increased yields, and chemicals helped control disease and worms—and, later, pesky "suckers" that once had to be broken off by hand. Labor-saving devices removed some of the worst drudgery. For example, the stoop-and-peg method of setting plants was supplemented in the 1920s by the metal hand planter that permitted the setting of plants without stooping over; this implement also allowed planting in dry weather by squirting water around the roots. Still later, riding planters permitted the setting of two rows at once. By the 1930s, oil began replacing cordwood for the firing of flues in curing barns, eliminating hourly checks of temperature day and night. The genuine mechanical revolution in tobacco, though, awaited the postwar years.

Cotton cultivation reached its peak in the 1920s, 9-79 then steadily declined. The acreage planted in 1945 9-80 was only about 60 percent of that at the turn of the century, and its value was one-seventh that of the tobacco crop at the end of World War II. King Cotton was dethroned; it ranked below corn. Peanuts vaulted into fourth place in production with a $28-million crop in 1945. Fifth was the Irish potato crop ($15 million); sweet potatoes ($14 million) placed sixth. A relative newcomer to North Carolina agriculture, soybeans, brought in nearly $6 million. Other important crops included hay, fruits, berries, sorghum, and vegetables. Sales of cattle, poultry, eggs, and swine in 1940 totaled $94 million.

Agriculture was affected by changes in motive power. Hand harvesting of grain was replaced by reapers, threshers, and combines; tractors and bulldozers made possible deep-plowing and clearing of land; and mechanical pumps and piping enabled the irrigation of fields. Nowhere was the change more graphic than in the gradual substitution of motor power for animal power. In 1920 the census indicated the use of 256,569 mules and 171,436 horses. By mid-century the number of mules was about the same, but the number of horses in use as draft animals had been cut nearly in half; on the other hand, more than 50,000 tractors were in use on Tar Heel farms, along with 13,000 grain combines, 5,800 hay balers, 3,600 milking machines, and 1,900 corn pickers and field forage harvesters. Farming was on the verge of its own revolution.

Machinery, however, did not remove all drudgery from the farm. A typical farm family still arose before dawn, milked the cows, fed the livestock, performed other chores, had breakfast, and then went to the fields for a sweaty day cultivating or harvesting the crop until dusk, interrupted only for a noon-time "dinner" break and an occasional swig from a water jug. Men, women, and children, black and white, often worked side by side, their status measured by the order to which each had access to the water jug or bucket. There were additional chores before or after supper. Too tired to visit neighbors at night, some families were fortunate enough by the 1920s to own battery-operated radios, which could afford them short periods of relaxation. Except in the busiest of times, the farmer usually reserved Saturday afternoon for diversion—a trip to town, a visit at the country store, a community baseball match, a game of set-back, or simply a spell of sitting and rocking in the shade.

Chief among North Carolinians associated with the improvement of farm life was Clarence Poe. For half a century he was editor of the *Progressive Farmer*, the subscription to which was as little as

twenty-five cents a year. This magazine featured articles and practical suggestions for farmers and homemakers, but it was also a tireless advocate for better education, improved farming methods, and diversification. Poe encouraged 4-H Clubs, first organized in Hertford County in 1909; the establishment of the first agricultural experiment station in Granville County in 1914; the introduction of high school courses in agriculture, shop, and home economics; and the extension of agricultural and homemaking information and assistance by the State College of Agriculture and Engineering in Raleigh.

Individualism and the bitter memory of Farmers' Alliance politics obstructed advocates of the organization of farmers for mutual benefit. In 1913 the North Carolina Farmers' Union attained a membership of thirty-three thousand members in 1,783 local units, but it soon withered. The Tobacco Growers Cooperative Marketing Association was formed in 1920 to elevate prices by withholding tobacco from markets in times of low prices, but six years later it was declared bankrupt. The Grange, which had died out the previous century, was revived in 1929 with Clarence Poe as master, and membership reached seventy-five hundred in 1945. The North Carolina Farm Bureau Federation was more successful; organized in 1936, it had seventy-eight thousand members within twelve years.

Until the coming of the railroad early in the nineteenth century, the speed of land travel had changed little since the domestication of draft animals. Even for railed vehicles, speedy travel was limited to destinations served by the tracks. Few North Carolinians foresaw in 1900 that a spectacular revolution in transportation and communication was imminent.

Old ways were not made obsolete, however. Railroads continued to extend their tracks, attaining a total mileage of well over five thousand miles, and a fourth system—the Norfolk Southern—was developed to connect the Carolina Piedmont with the port of Norfolk, Virginia. In 1914 North Carolina was connected with Kentucky and the Ohio Valley by the Carolina, Clinchfield and Ohio, and dozens of small companies built lines between previously isolated towns. Railroad rates were increasingly regulated by the North Carolina Corporation Commission and the Interstate Commerce Commission.

Nor was animal-powered transportation replaced

9-98
9-99
9-100
9-101
immediately. Vehicles drawn by horses, mules, and oxen remained familiar sights for decades. The gasoline-powered automobile, however, introduced at the turn of the century, soon took over much of the long-distance travel. Although North Carolinians had little to do with the invention of the

9-102
9-103
automobile, several Tar Heels built their own machines, and other cars were assembled in the state. For instance, at Henderson, J. W. Corbitt between 1907 and 1915 built and marketed vehicles carrying his name; the Asheville Light Car Company manufactured the Asheville in 1914–15; and at Greensboro the manufacturer of the American Southern (1920–21) also produced the Vaughan (1921–23).

The largest automotive operation in the state was the Ford Motor Company's assembly plant which in the 1920s turned out as many as four hundred Model T's per day in Charlotte. Other companies produced bodies for motor vehicles—Hackney Brothers in Wilson, Thomas Built Buses

9-104
of High Point, and Jerome Bolick Sons at Conover, for example. Thomas also made trolley bodies, including New Orleans's "Desire," made

9-105
9-106
9-108
famous by Tennessee Williams. Thousands of garages and service stations sprang up to help keep motor vehicles on the road.

Most vehicles were private automobiles, but as early as 1909, Charlie Pruitt was operating a bus on the Leaksville-Spray-Draper run. Two years later Grove Park Inn at Asheville advertised "Two Packard Busses with French Buss bodies" to meet

9-107
all trains, and about 1918, P. B. Comer of Greensboro received an intercity bus franchise to operate a twice-a-day, nine-passenger touring car service between Greensboro and Asheboro.

9-109
The number of motor vehicles multiplied: 1910, 2,400; 1921, 150,000; 1950, more than 1,000,000. The movement for improved roads preceded the first automobile, however. In 1899, Frederick Law Olmsted, whose journal in the 1850s vividly described the sorry state of North Carolina's roadways, was instrumental in organizing the Good Roads Association of Asheville and Buncombe County. The local group connected Asheville and Biltmore with a macadam road that provided a model for other associations, which in 1902 formed a statewide organization. One of the most energetic promoters of improved roads was Harriet

9-110
9-111
Morehead Berry, a prime mover in the creation of a state highway commission in 1915, the participation of the state in the federal aid program the following year, and the passage of Governor Mor-

rison's $50 million bond issue in 1921. The Morrison bonds enabled the state to construct and maintain nearly six thousand miles of improved roads, mostly sand-clay but some macadam (crushed stone), and North Carolina boasted the

9-112
9-113
title "The Good Roads State."

Meanwhile events of worldwide significance were taking place on the sand dunes between the tiny Dare County settlements of Kitty Hawk and Kill Devil Hills on the outer banks. In 1900 the Wright brothers, Wilbur and Orville, brought

9-114
crates of materials from their bicycle shop in Dayton, Ohio, to Elizabeth City, and thence by boat to the banks. From these materials they constructed a kite-looking contraption with arched wings seventeen feet long and five feet wide. It was called a glider. Time and again during the next several weeks one of the brothers took a prone position in the middle of the lower wing while the other brother, together with William J. Tate, the postmaster, or his half-brother, Dan Tate, each

9-115
lifted an end and ran down the dune until the contraption glided into the air, sometimes to sail as much as 400 feet.

In each of the following three years, eager to take advantage of the favorable winds on the barren dunes, the Wrights returned to Kitty Hawk with an improved vehicle. In 1902 they reached 622 feet before the glider came to earth, and they were ready for an effort to make history. The new glider in 1903 was powered by a twelve-horsepower engine, and on 17 December, with Orville Wright at the controls, the *Flyer* propelled itself down the wooden track and into the air. It rose

9-116
about ten feet and fell to earth after a flight of only 120 feet and twelve seconds, but that was enough to earn it a page in history books—the first time that a heavier-than-air vehicle had been lofted by mechanical power. Three more flights were made that day: the final one by Wilbur lasted fifty-nine seconds and covered 852 feet. Then, as they were preparing to secure the flying machine, a savage gust of wind picked it up and sent it tumbling

9-117
9-118
9-119
9-120
across the sand, mangling it beyond repair.

Unpredictable winds, and treacherous shoals, took their toll of seagoing vessels along the coastline, which has long been known as the "Graveyard of the Atlantic." To the fury of nature were added the torpedoes of enemy submarines in two world

9-121
wars. And for all the state's intentions of establishing major port facilities, little progress was made prior to mid-century. The voters rejected a bond issue for improvement of the ports in 1924, and

only minimum development was undertaken at Morehead City and Wilmington. At its coast North Carolina remained a prisoner of nature.

In 1901–2 at the northwest end of Roanoke Island, almost within sight of the Wright brothers' efforts to conquer the sky for travel, another visitor from the North was conquering the sky for com- 9-122 munication. Reginald Aubrey Fessenden, a Canadian native who had worked for Thomas A. Edison, was experimenting with wireless telegraphy. Like the Wrights, he too was in a race with competing scientists. From a tower on the island, Fessenden exchanged coded messages with the national weather stations at Hatteras and Cape Henry. His object was to develop a device capable of receiving clear signals in code; he believed that such a receiver would also be capable of picking up intelligible voice communication. In 1902, after the Hatteras weather station had transmitted varying musical tones, he wrote exultantly that he had received them on Roanoke "with but 3 watts of energy, and they were very loud and plain. . . . The new receiver is a wonder!!!" Wireless telephony, and ultimately radio, awaited only additional refinements, and Marconi and others adopted the principles of Fessenden's system.

Nearly two decades passed, however, before North Carolina's first—and the nation's second— 9-123 station began broadcasting. Station 4XD—given the call letters WBT two years later—began beaming conversation and music from Charlotte in 1920, and soon other stations followed. Owning a radio became a sign of prestige, and the world was 9-124 shrunk by almost instantaneous communication. President Franklin D. Roosevelt made the radio a political instrument that was surpassed only by television which, though developed in the 1930s, did not come to North Carolina until the postwar period.

9-125 In 1900 there were only 10,932 telephones in 9-126 North Carolina, but the number ballooned to 123,000 by 1920 and more than 500,000 by midcentury. Some farm communities constructed their own lines in accordance with simple instructions published by Poe's *Progressive Farmer*. In 1910 a mile of line could be constructed for only fourteen dollars and a home could be wired and equipped with a hand-crank instrument for thirteen dollars. Still, only 5 percent of the farms of the state had telephones in 1945. Urban areas had more sophisticated systems, complete with bevies of female switchboard operators capable of connecting parties from across the country.

Rural free delivery was greatly expanded in the new century, and automobiles gradually replaced horse-drawn vehicles where road conditions permitted. Many communities, though, were still served by tiny post offices without delivery service, and in remote areas mail was sometimes carried by 9-127 foot. Air mail was introduced on a regular schedule in Greensboro in 1928.

Henry Fries's hydroelectric plant on the Yadkin River presaged a dramatic power revolution in the Piedmont. In 1904, foreseeing the potential of a new industry, James B. Duke established the Southern Public Utilities Company (later the Duke Power Company), which constructed a series of dams along the Catawba River; by 1927 it had grown into a $200 million enterprise. Other power 9-128 plants were constructed, and by 1935 only California, New York, and Oregon produced more current from waterpower. With the formation of the Rural Electrification Authority under the Roosevelt administration, transmission lines were extended to many rural areas, either by cooperatives or by private companies. The availability of electricity in rural areas not only resulted in improvements in home life—lights, radios, refrigerators, electric stoves, and so forth—but also permitted the dispersal of manufacturing. 9-129

If Governor Aycock needed any justification for his unprecedented educational crusade, the literacy test for suffrage gave him one. The constitutional amendment, he believed, obligated the state to provide an opportunity for all children, regardless of race, "to burgeon out" all that was within them. His administration, therefore, took on an evangelical fervor that enlisted allies from agriculture, industry, the professions, and the lay public. Educational rallies spread across the state, and the results during his term and those of his two successors were impressive: new schoolhouses were opened at a rate of almost one per day; the small black teacher-training institutes were consolidated into five colleges and three white teacher-training schools were given state support; about two hundred rural high schools with grades through eleven were opened; farm-life schools were established in several sections of the state; and state appropriations sought to help equalize schools in all counties. In 1913 a compulsory attendance law was 9-130 enforced, and a special statewide tax was levied to extend the school term to six months. Four years later a system of teacher certification was installed.

The educational renaissance was not without its

9-131 weaknesses. For example, most of the school buildings were primitive, as statistics from Wake County revealed: In July 1905 that county had ninety-six school buildings for whites, of which seventy-seven consisted of only one room, only three had cloakrooms, not one contained a "lunch cupboard," and most were in bad condition. Seven new one-room schoolhouses were ordered built at a cost of from $250 to $400 each. Wake, of course, was one of the wealthier counties; conditions must have been much worse in a majority of the counties. Furthermore, the emphasis was chiefly upon schools for whites. Fortunately, however, the Jeanes, Slater, Rosenwald, and General Education Board funds contributed nearly $2 million for Negro education between 1906 and 1928, and some counties

9-132 showed good faith in attempting to provide at least the minimum requirements for minority schools.

Not surprisingly, illiteracy dropped significantly; in 1910 the figure stood at 18.5 percent (31.9 for blacks, 12.3 for whites, and 8.3 for foreign born). The disparity between urban and rural schools remained a problem, but in the 1920s considerable progress was made in consolidating small substandard schools into larger, stronger ones. Ironically, it was the Great Depression that forced the General Assembly to adopt a truly statewide system of education. In 1933 the state assumed the cost of staffing and operating the schools for an eight-month term, though counties retained responsibility for providing buildings. Beginning in 1937 the state furnished basal texts for elementary students; four years later a twelfth grade was added and a retirement system for state employees and teachers was created; and in 1943 the school term was extended to nine months.

As long as each community had its own school,

9-133 students customarily walked to and from classes. Consolidation and distance created new problems. Inevitably, a few experiments were conducted in transporting students by wagon, and in 1911 the Thurman Township School in Craven County was served by three animal-drawn buses. Within six years motorized buses were in use, and by 1925 an estimated twenty-five hundred vehicles were transporting nearly ninety thousand children daily. Within fifteen years North Carolina would have the largest school bus fleet in the nation; the buses were driven by high school students, who eagerly competed for the $9.25-per-month jobs.

Fewer colleges were opened from 1900 to 1945 than were closed, and of the eleven new institutions, only eight are still in existence. Western

Carolina, Appalachian, and East Carolina were taken over by the state as teachers colleges for whites; and in 1925 the state acquired the North Carolina College for Negroes (established by James Shepard in 1910 as the National Religious Training School and Chautauqua), the first state-supported liberal arts college for blacks in the United States.

Support was regularly increased for the three flagship institutions at Greensboro, Raleigh, and Chapel Hill, and in 1931 they were consolidated into the greater University of North Carolina. By that time each of the three had attained considerable recognition, and the Chapel Hill campus was considered one of the better state universities in the South, largely because of the innovative studies of the problems of the region being undertaken there. Howard W. Odum's Institute for Research in Social Science was engaged in research which furnished articles for the institute's journal, *Social Forces*, and documentation for other publications, such as Odum's profoundly influential book *Southern Regions of the United States* (1936). Frank Porter Graham, the new president of the university, was speaking out boldly on controversial issues, despite the uproar caused by his "Industrial Bill of Rights," issued after the tragic Gastonia strikes. And Albert Coates, an indefatigable law professor, launched his quarterly *Popular Government* and two years later established the Institute of Government, which educated thousands of public officials and exerted a beneficial influence upon study commissions and legislatures for the next half-century.

Less than a dozen miles away, Gothic stone 9-134 spires reached toward the sky from a pine forest after James Buchanan Duke donated millions for the conversion of Trinity College into Duke University in 1924. At Biltmore High School near Asheville, William Henry Jones and Alonzo Carlton Reynolds started Biltmore Junior College, which, after several reincarnations, eventually became the University of North Carolina at Asheville. Not far away in 1933, John A. Rice and several unorthodox associates started the equally unor- 9-135 thodox Black Mountain College, where there were no required courses, no formal graduation, and no social distinctions between faculty and students. Intellectuals from several fields were attracted to Black Mountain, but dissension split the educational utopia and it closed shortly after mid-century.

Other unorthodox schools established during the period included the Penland School of Crafts, 9-136 founded in 1929 by Lucy Morgan, and Brasstown's John C. Campbell Folk School, established by Olive Dame Campbell on the principle of the Danish folk schools, which linked "culture of toil and culture of books in service of a better mankind." There were private schools, military schools, and other types of educational institutions, but the period from 1900 to World War II was clearly one in which public education was in the ascendancy.

In the new century the veil of modesty that had characterized North Carolina's past was at last pulled back, and literature began to flourish. The thousands of pages of colonial and state records edited and published by William L. Saunders and Walter Clark provided rich resources for scholars trained in the German, or "scientific," school of history, and monographs proliferated, many of them freed from the prejudices and misconceptions inherent in the mythical moonlight-and-magnolias 9-137 South. Historians like Robert D. W. Connor, John Spencer Bassett, William Kenneth Boyd, and Joseph Gregoire de Roulhac Hamilton preached the need for the preservation and study of manuscript as well as printed sources, and each built major collections—Connor as first secretary of the North Carolina Historical Commission, Bassett and Boyd as promoters of the Trinity College Historical Society, and Hamilton as founder of the Southern Historical Collection at Chapel Hill. This concentration of three great repositories brought national attention to North Carolina, and Connor was selected in 1934 by President Roosevelt to be the first archivist of the United States.

In 1905, Samuel A'Court Ashe published the first of eight volumes of his landmark *Biographical History of North Carolina*, and two years later he published the first volume of his *History of North Carolina* (the second volume did not appear until 1925). Though deficient when compared with later scholarship, this work—prepared with the assistance of Stephen Beauregard Weeks—was the first general history to make extensive use of primary source materials. Consequently, Ashe jarred some pet myths; because he dared question the authenticity of the alleged "Mecklenburg Declaration of Independence," some legislators sought to prevent the purchase of the book by public libraries. Several better general histories were published prior to World War II, particularly those of Connor, Boyd, Hamilton, and Archibald Henderson. Of the hundreds of more specialized studies, two of the best were Guion Griffis Johnson's *Antebellum North Carolina* (1937) and Wilbur Joseph

Cash's *The Mind of the South* (1941), the former an encyclopedic assemblage of social data, the latter an influential interpretation of the complexities of southern society.

Historical studies were accompanied by organizational activity. The membership list of the State Literary and Historical Association, founded in 1900, read like a who's who of North Carolina, and election to office in the organization was considered a high honor. Soon other cultural groups were formed—the Folklore Society, the Art Society, the Roanoke Island Historical Association, the Antiquities Society, the Society of County and Local Historians, the Archaeological Society, and others. These groups held their annual meetings on consecutive days, the unique "Culture Week," during which the Sir Walter Hotel in Raleigh sparkled with scholarship, speeches, and society. Museums, too, increased in number and popularity. The Hall of History, developed by Fred A. Olds in the previ- 9-138 ous century, was divided in 1913; part of it remained in the Department of Agriculture as the State Museum of Natural History, and the remainder went to the North Carolina Historical Commission, whose name was changed to State Department of Archives and History in 1943. A number of smaller museums also sprang up around the state.

The state produced a modest number of writers in fields other than history. Walter Hines Page's novel *The Southerner* (1909) reflected the Cary native's disrespect for prejudices of the past. Thomas 9-139 Dixon's *The Leopard's Spots* (1902) and *The Clansman* (1905), however, stirred up latent emotions by proclaiming the supremacy of the white race. The latter book by the former state legislator from Cleveland County was the basis of D. W. Griffith's *The Birth of a Nation*, generally regarded as the first successful motion picture.

John Charles McNeill was the most popular poet of his day; his verses peppered the *Charlotte Observer* and found their way into two books—*Songs, Merry and Sad* (1906) and *Lyrics from the Cotton Land* (1907). James Larkin Pearson's poetry appeared over a period of half a century, and his popular newspaper, *The Fool-Killer*, carried his 9-140 stinging but often humorous opinions on many subjects about which few poets are concerned. James E. McGirt, a black poet and short story writer from Greensboro, wrote of the aspirations of his race in *The Triumphs of Ephraim* (1907).

The mountain region was a favorite subject of authors Olive Tilford Dargan (Fielding Burke),

Margaret Warner Morley, Horace Kephart, Muriel Sheppard, and others. Two newcomers, James Boyd (*Drums*, 1925) and Inglis Fletcher (*Raleigh's Eden*, 1940, and eleven more), wrote best-selling "historical" novels. Paul Green, whose *In Abraham's Bosom* (1927) won a Pulitzer Prize, emerged as the state's leading playwright. In addition to stage and Hollywood screen scripts, he created a new art form—the outdoor symphonic drama, the first of which was *The Lost Colony* (1937).

9-141 Judging by international recognition, however, Thomas Wolfe of Asheville towered above other North Carolina literary figures of the twentieth century. A failure as a playwright, Wolfe was an instant success with his novel *Look Homeward, Angel: A Story of the Buried Life* (1929). His thinly veiled caricatures of his relatives and associates were seldom flattering, and his native city only begrudgingly forgave him after his death at the age of thirty-eight.

9-142
9-143
9-144 The proliferation of books led to a demand for more and better libraries. Large towns, and a few small ones, boasted of libraries of varying sizes and holdings. Meanwhile, the North Carolina Library Commission, established in 1909, sent traveling libraries around the state, and by the 1930s the State Library was lending books through the mail to rural residents.

9-146
9-147
9-149
9-145 Advances in the arts hardly matched those in literature, but the radio, phonograph, and motion picture opened up new uses of leisure time. Films were being shown experimentally even before the first permanent movie theater was opened in Wilmington in 1906. Two North Carolinians—Thomas Dixon, already mentioned, and Cecil B. DeMille, who grew up in "Little" Washington—made important contributions to the motion picture industry.

9-148
9-150 Although North Carolina was not distinguished in the field of music, the state did produce a number of bands and leaders, ranging from country string bands to the orchestras of Kay Kyser, Hal Kemp, and Les Brown. Classical music was introduced in many communities by the North Carolina Symphony Orchestra, founded in 1932 by Lamar Stringfield and said to be the first state-supported symphony orchestra in the country, but religious scruples retarded the development of the dance. In

9-151 social dancing, square dancing was more acceptable in rural areas than body-to-body dancing. For example, it was well after World War II before social dancing was condoned at Wake Forest College.

Increased church membership and the proliferation of sects characterized organized religion, Protestantism triumphant, in the twentieth century. Baptists, encompassing diverse elements, strengthened their numerical lead over the second-place Methodists. In the absence of strong competition from non-Protestants, denominationalism was rampant for much of the era; members of some sects openly doubted that adherents of other Christian groups qualified for heaven. Yet at the same time that the number of sects and the competition be- 9-152 tween them increased, and as tent-filling evangelists 9-153 exhorted the populace, some of the larger denomi- 9-154 nations began moving inexorably toward greater 9-155 unity. Three branches of Methodism, for instance, 9-156 separated since the Civil War, reunited in 1939. Total church membership at mid-century was 1,996,632, slightly less than half the population. Of these, there were only 42,080 Catholics, 6,000 Jews, and 510 Greek Orthodox.

Religion, education, and politics were intermingled in the complex issue of alcoholic beverages. The defeat of statewide prohibition in 1881 9-157 did not end the controversy; in fact, the legislature yielded to pressures for local determination of the issue, and by 1903 most of rural and small-town North Carolina was officially dry. Public opinion was increasingly prohibitionist, and Furnifold M. Simmons decided to make the controversy a partisan matter. He called distilleries "Hell's Kettles" and claimed that county and town dispensaries were "Republican recruiting stations." Over the intense opposition of the liquor lobby, the legislature in 1903 passed the Watts Act restricting distilleries to incorporated towns.

Some distilleries moved; some were forced out of business; but the liquor-making Williams family in Yadkin (now western Forsyth) County simply incorporated the community and continued making its famous rye and corn whiskey. To plug this loophole in the Watts Act, the next General Assembly defined an incorporated town as one having a thousand inhabitants. By 1907 about 90 percent of the state was dry, and the temperance organizations and the Democratic leaders were ready to outlaw liquor throughout the state. In a referendum held 9-158 in 1908, the citizens voted 113,612 to 69,416 for 9-159 statewide prohibition, effective the following year 9-160 with passage of the Turlington Act.

Prohibition, of course, no more solved the liquor problem than the suffrage amendment solved the race problem. Illicit distilleries operated 9-161 in nearly every county of the state, particularly in counties like Wilkes, which had voted overwhelmingly against prohibition in the referendum, and federal agents remained active. The nation joined North Carolina in 1919 when the Eighteenth Amendment was ratified, and beverages with as much as .5 percent alcohol were outlawed throughout the United States.

But the "great experiment" simply drove liquor manufacture and sale underground. Will Rogers told a Raleigh audience that North Carolinians would vote dry as long as they could "stagger to the polls." Throughout the 1920s bootlegging provided a livelihood for many North Carolinians, and tax agents fought a losing battle. Even so, the General Assembly refused to ratify the Twenty-first Amendment, and North Carolina remained officially dry until 1935 when sixteen counties were allowed local option and the first county-operated liquor store was opened at Wilson. Two years later a statewide Alcoholic Beverage Control Board was established, and local option became the policy of the state. The manufacture of alcoholic beverages was still prohibited, and the sale of liquor was restricted to county-operated stores.

Another issue brought an even nastier conflict between religion, education, and politics. During the year when the Scopes trial in Tennessee gripped national attention, antievolution forces sought legislation to prohibit the teaching of the Darwinian theory in the public schools of North Carolina. Governor Morrison had banned the use of two textbooks, and in 1925 Representative D. Scott Poole, a Hoke County editor, drew support from most Protestant groups when he introduced the bill.

9-162 During the debates, however, Harry Woodburn Chase and William Louis Poteat, presidents, respectively, of the University of North Carolina and Wake Forest College, argued that the issue was not creationism or evolution but rather the right of free inquiry. Schools, they argued, should create inquiring minds so that each student could draw his or her own conclusions based on the evidence available. When the bill came to a vote in the house, twenty of twenty-three former Wake Forest students voted in the negative, and the Poole bill was defeated 67 to 46. Ironically, the Baptists, considered the most conservative of the major sects, had made the difference.

With the educational crusade came campaigns for better health, illustrated by the war on the hookworm, a parasite whose infection reduced otherwise industrious humans to sluggish disinterestedness. As early as 1902, Dr. Charles Wardell

Stiles of the United States Public Health Service pronounced the cure, but Southerners considered it slander when the doctor claimed that hookworms were sapping the strength of the region. Beginning in 1908, however, with the support of the Rockefeller Sanitary Commission, Stiles 9-163 brought his campaign to the South, and more than a million persons were examined. Because the parasite was spread through contact with feces, Stiles urged Southerners to wear shoes and to clean up their privies. State and local health agencies continued the commission's work after 1914, and the hookworm was brought under control as sanitation was improved.

There were other good-health campaigns, in- 9-164 cluding continuing battles against flies, mosqui- 9-165 toes, and other disease-bearing insects and orga- 9-166 nisms. Chuckles resulted from what Ben Dixon McNeill called the "Tick War" on the outer banks. 9-167 In 1921 health officials ordered all livestock to be dipped in a disinfectant to kill disease-spreading ticks, but some of the independent residents became so irked by the bureaucratic trappings of the campaign that they slipped out at night and destroyed the vats and obstructed the efforts of the "outsiders."

Insects were not all harmful, and two immigrant brothers from England devoted their careers to studying and teaching about them. Clement Samuel Brimley and Herbert H. Brimley settled in 9-168 Raleigh and opened a taxidermy shop and biological supply house. Their unusual occupation led the Department of Agriculture to hire both, Clement as head of the entomology division and Herbert as director of the Museum of Natural History. Among their allies was Thomas Gilbert Pearson, a biology professor at Normal and Industrial College at Greensboro. Pearson organized the North Carolina Audubon Society, which by legislative act was given standing as a state game commission. He later served as executive secretary and president of the national Audubon Society and was credited with helping build a climate for wildlife conservation.

The line between stimulation of the mind and body was blurred in diversions and entertainment. For example, humanitarian organizations extended 9-169 their good works by providing entertainment for 9-170 the less fortunate; public ceremonies combined patriotic and recreational exercises; and country stores and corner drug stores contributed both to the transmittal of information and to an expansion of waistlines. Each social class tended to develop its own form of recreation, but organized sports crossed class lines. Horse racing did not recover after the Civil War, but the penning of wild ponies became an annual affair on the outer banks. Cockfighting lost much of its respectability, but it was still practiced in the Piedmont and west. Hunting became as much a sport as a means of acquiring meat for the table.

School and college athletics grew into businesses; by the 1930s nearly every high school fielded baseball, basketball, and sometimes football teams. Frenzied spectators followed the teams. The larger colleges competed with the nation's best and played before thousands of screaming spectators.

The coast became a magnet for summer vacationists. Wrightsville Beach developed as a mecca for both rich and poor, and even the outer banks were conquered by the automobile and ferry. Various springs of the Piedmont were popular vacation spots, and the Sandhills emerged as a resort center for high society. Pinehurst grew in the pine forests after James W. Tufts of Boston in 1895 purchased five thousand sandy acres for a health resort and sports center.

Almost within sight, blacks lived primitively, a few of them hired for menial tasks by the wealthy Yankees drawn to the moderate climate and plush hotels. For blacks there were few recreational and social opportunities except those created by themselves. Not until 1939 did the state get around to establishing Jones Lake Recreational Area in Bladen County for the use of blacks. According to a report to the governor the following year, it "achieved immediate popularity which clearly demonstrates the need for outdoor recreational facilities for Negroes."

For flatlanders the mountains have always symbolized romance, and the new century brought an era of tourist development. E. W. Grove, a wealthy manufacturer of patent medicines in St. Louis, constructed near Asheville the luxurious Grove Park Inn, which attracted countless celebrities. Scores of other accommodations were opened, and the "Land of the Sky" attracted a stream of summer residents and visitors. The construction of summer cottages boomed until the Depression, then spiraled again in the late 1930s. As in the Sandhills, the contrast between the visitors and the country folk was often stark: Most mountaineers lived much as had their pioneer ancestors. Their simple life, however, struck a responsive chord in a few of the newcomers, and the region became a favorite object of philanthropy. Religious groups also showed interest; at Presbyterian-supported

Lees-McRae and Warren Wilson junior colleges, for example, students were permitted to pay their fees in livestock, farm produce, and part-time work.

Nature periodically demonstrated its awesomeness to North Carolinians, sometimes through such disasters as hurricanes in the east and floods in the west. Among the most memorable of these visitations were destructive floods in the mountains and foothills in 1916 and 1940, both of which caused heavy losses of lives and property and left curious examples of nature's superiority over man's best designs.

There were no startling humanitarian reforms during the era. The poor, unable to care for themselves or be cared for by their relatives, were often sent to a county home, called locally the "po house." There was no great stigma attached to admission to the county home, for it was considered as a charitable institution for deserving people down on their luck, not a resting place for those too lazy to earn their own living. Tragically, however, some counties admitted mentally ill patients to the county home instead of sending them to the overcrowded asylums, where they could receive proper attention.

Treatment of offenders against society changed little. Teen-agers, for instance, were usually subject to the same penalties as adults; it was a thirteen-year-old boy's sentence to the chain gang for stealing $1.30 that started editor James P. Cook of Concord on a campaign for a school for wayward boys. Cook enlisted the aid of Confederate veterans and patriotic organizations, and in 1907 the General Assembly authorized the Stonewall Jackson Training School for juveniles. The purpose of the school, said a report of this forerunner of other juvenile treatment centers, was "to take this lazy, worthless bunch of boys, many of them steeped in the poison of nicotine from cigarettes, untrustworthy, untruthful, still more of them ignorant, dirty and neglected, and to help them catch a vision of what they can become."

Correctional policy dictated punishment for wrongdoers; rehabilitation of adult offenders was not yet a primary concern. The prisons provided much of the labor that built North Carolina's highways, and chain gangs were a familiar sight to travelers. Until 1910 hanging remained the standard means of execution of those convicted of first-degree burglary, arson, rape, or murder, and great crowds often gathered to witness the springing of the trap. The life of Henry Spivey of Bladen County was the last claimed by legal hanging, and Walter Morrison of Robeson County was the first to die in the electric chair, installed in the State Prison the same year. In all, 172 lives were taken by the electric chair before it was replaced by the gas chamber, which claimed its first victim, Allen Foster of Hoke County, in 1936. The executioner was color-blind; in 1934 a father, son, and son-in-law, all whites, were electrocuted for killing an Alexander County bank official.

At the height of a long epidemic of vigilante "justice" in the South and West, Clarence Poe described lynching as "a belated outcropping of primitive anarchy," and his father-in-law, Governor Aycock, warned that "the mob has no place in our civilization." They perhaps reflected a minority view, for occasional lynchings still blotted the name of the state; yet it was remarkable that during the period from 1888 to 1933 the number of lynching victims in the state—sixty-six—was only about one-seventh that of Georgia or Mississippi, and North Carolina ranked twentieth in lynchings among all the states.

9-195 Furthermore, men who took the law into their own hands were not always racists; in fact, nationally, until the 1880s more whites than blacks were executed extralegally. A graphic example of color blindness occurred in 1889 in Burke County when Franklin Stack, white, and David Boone, black, accused of unrelated murders, were seized and hanged together from a bridge. The coroner ruled that the prisoners died "by hanging, which was done by unknown parties." At least 115 persons certainly knew the "unknown parties," for that number took part in the gruesome act. Among those who helped turn the collective conscience of the state against lynching were women's organizations, characteristically exerting their humanizing effect upon the citizenry.

9-196
9-197 Women made their first significant progress toward full civil rights in the new century. The climate for change had been brought about less by their own advocacy of new rights than by their services to the state. The work of patriotic groups supporting prohibition and other popular causes, the remarkable work of women in the war effort, and the entry of females into the professions demonstrated the potential contributions of women in a male-dominated society. Sallie Southall Cotten, an organizer of the North Carolina Federation of Women's Clubs, reminded the public of some of the services of women: "Clean-up Day, screening foods from flies and dust, getting garbage ordinances passed, the installation of trash cans on the streets, the writing of county histories, the securing and awarding of scholarships, improving conditions in railroad stations, medical inspection in schools, drinking fountains, and other health measures carried to success, play grounds equipped, and so many things done that the retrospect is wonderful and inspiring."

That not all North Carolinians associated good works with individual rights was demonstrated in the long struggle for women suffrage. An equal-suffrage association had been formed in Asheville in 1894, but even the fusion senate three years later laughed down the first bill proposing access to the 9-198 ballot box by females. Sixteen years later the North Carolina Equal Suffrage League was formed, and soon suffragettes were marching in parades with signs reading "Votes for Women" and "Taxation without Representation Is Tyranny." Leaders of the movement emulated tactics of other special-interest groups by holding mass meetings, installing booths at fairs, and talking with legislators. A bill "to confer upon women the right to vote in all municipal elections," introduced in 1913 by Representative David McKenzie Clark of Pitt County, was treated with reasonable respect, but it, like all other equal-suffrage bills for the next several sessions, failed to pass. Even an act of 1915 authorizing the governor to appoint women as well as men as notaries public was struck down by the supreme court (over, of course, Walter Clark's dissent).

In 1920 the General Assembly refused to ratify 9-199 the Nineteenth Amendment, and a majority of the members of the house sent a telegram urging Ten- 9-200 nessee legislators not to force the "Susan B. Anthony amendment" upon the people of North Carolina. Fifteen days later the amendment was proclaimed ratified by the requisite number of states.

This development must have given satisfaction to a young representative from Buncombe County. The name was L. Exum Clement—really Lillian 9-201 Exum Clement, "Brother Exum" to her fellow representatives—the first woman to serve in the state legislature. The legal barrier against women removed, the statewide vote in 1920 nearly doubled that of four years earlier. There was no rush of women candidates, however, for the law did not eradicate bias. Nevertheless, women in small numbers began filling offices at both the state and local levels, and the dire predictions of opponents were gradually forgotten. 9-202

Of North Carolinians of Indian ancestry, only the Cherokees were officially recognized by—and 9-203 thus of special concern to—the federal government. Most of them lived in the Qualla Boundary, the largest reservation east of Wisconsin. Land was held in common under supervision of the Bureau of Indian Affairs and a popularly elected chief. Though most of the Cherokees were members of Protestant churches, some ancient customs were still evident, including several medicine men. Their isolation was relieved by military service of Cherokee men in the two wars and by an increasing flow of tourists who eagerly sought their crafts.

9-204 Meanwhile, the unorganized Indian groups of the east struggled for identity. The Croatans, later known as Lumbees, won their own school system in the 1880s, and Robeson County maintained a triracial system controlled by whites. The normal 9-205 school at Pembroke added college-level courses in the 1930s, and at one time was called the only state-supported all-Indian college in the country. The success of the Lumbees encouraged others of Indian blood to seek tribal identities, but the absence of documented history led to reluctance on the part of the legislature to differentiate between them and blacks. The Haliwa (Halifax and Warren 9-206 counties), Coharie (Sampson County), Waccamaw 9-207 (Bladen and Columbus counties), and individual Indians without collective names attended black schools, provided their own, or went without schools. In the Department of Public Instruction, Indians were the responsibility of the Division of Negro Education.

The 1900 suffrage amendment to the North Carolina Constitution accomplished its goal of banning most blacks from the ballot box (and, consequently, Republicans from elected office), but it failed in its promise to solve the "Negro problem." To be sure, some blacks—particularly those who had provided leadership for the race—left the state in disgust, but more than six hundred thousand Afro-Americans remained. They lived as neighbors of whites, often working in the same fields or factories, often cooking for whites and caring for their children and their sick, and often 9-208 sharing the vicissitudes of nature and the economy.

Yet this intimacy was bounded by an unwritten but almost universally understood line beyond which neither black nor white often ventured. 9-209 Each knew his or her "place"—and the place of 9-210 the black was a little below that of a white, regard-9-211 less of character, ability, or accomplishment. Thousands of white children shared the most intimate experiences with their black nannies, who

entered the house by the back door, ate alone in the kitchen, and never sat in the parlor when white guests were present. "Jim crow" laws enforced this 9-214 sense of place, and as a new generation came of 9-215 age, oblivious of the accomplishments of the race a few years earlier because they were not recorded in the textbooks, the rule of place increasingly appeared natural and immutable.

If the abrogation of Negro rights had been universal, southern blacks might have been less submissive during those decades. But while prejudice knew no geography and segregation was almost as evident in some northern cities as it was in the South, there were indeed better opportunities for broader citizenship above the Mason-Dixon Line, and the North became a magnet for many of the most promising blacks. Edward A. Johnson, for instance, left North Carolina and became New York's first black legislator in 1917, nearly half a century after blacks served in North Carolina's law-making body.

The depth of racial antipathy even among educated whites was sometimes exposed for all to see. In 1903, John Spencer Bassett, a white Tarboro native then teaching at Trinity College, published in the *South Atlantic Quarterly* a characterization of Booker T. Washington as "all in all the greatest man, save General Lee, born in the South in a hundred years." The outcry was instantaneous, and 9-212 howls for his dismissal were led by Josephus Daniels of the *News and Observer*, who printed the professor's name as "bASSett." The very idea of placing the name of a Negro alongside that of the idealized Lee and above those of honored Confederates! No one saw the issue more clearly than another North Carolinian, Walter Hines Page, who wrote, "The cry that has been raised is not about the truth or the folly of the remark, but wholly because it was made about a negro. It is simply the cry of prejudice—a blind howl by those who think they can rule North Carolina and do gross injustice to men who differ with them—by simply howling 'Nigger.'"

A courageous president and board of trustees refused to yield to the bigoted campaign against Bassett, but the historian gave up as lost his native state, so filled with racial intemperance, and for half a century the cry of "Nigger" continued to win or lose elections. Yet in this climate of suppression a few whites dared to speak out, and a few individual blacks began climbing toward the status that members of their race had achieved in the 1890s. They worked diligently to elevate members of their own 9-213 people; raised money for, established, and taught at schools for blacks; organized and promoted campaigns for worthy causes; served loyally during two world wars; learned new skills and entered the professions; invested in black-owned enterprises; and built pride in their communities at a time when residential segregation was generally accepted by both races. Thus, though the period between disfranchisement and World War II produced few black celebrities in North Carolina, it did produce many whose work, experiences, and activities prepared them for leadership in a postwar era when revolutionary changes would radically alter American society.

World War II provided experiences and lessons that made a societal revolution inevitable. Such a revolution, of course, was far from the minds of Americans, who in 1940 were busy putting their own country on a war footing while rushing unprecedented amounts of aid to the faltering Allies. The nation called its first peacetime draft, and over the next five years more than a million North Carolinians were registered. Many volunteered for or were drafted into the military service, while thousands of others took jobs in war industries. Vast armies of troops from all races, classes, and regions moved into the bulging military bases quickly expanded or constructed on North Carolina's soil. Not since the Civil War had virtually every citizen been so deeply affected by military conflict.

The day before the Japanese attacked Pearl Harbor in December 1941, the North Carolina Ship-

9-216 building Company of Wilmington launched the first of 126 Liberty ships that the yard would build during the war. Government agencies sprang into action to enlist industry, agriculture, and the entire population in a gigantic crusade to save the world from dictatorship. Production was immensely stimulated, and conservation was mandated. Shortages of meat, sugar, coffee, cigarettes, shoes, gasoline, rubber, and other common goods spread the sacri-

9-217 fices among civilians through rationing and price controls. Caught up in the leviathan struggle, citizens proudly planted victory gardens, signed conservation pledges, provided entertainment and food for troops stationed in the state, collected

scrap iron and rubber, pulled blackout curtains at night, organized civilian defense watches, volunteered for hundreds of causes, paid high taxes, and purchased more than a billion dollars worth of savings bonds.

Sacrifices at home were small compared with those made by 362,500 Tar Heels—including 7,000 women—who donned military uniforms. A large percentage of them served overseas; many were engaged in combat with the enemy on three continents. In the end, 4,088 were killed in battle, 9-218 about 3,000 died from other causes, and many were maimed or scarred. Some won decorations— like the Congressional Medal of Honor received by Captain Charles P. Murray of Wilmington for heroism against the Nazis and the Distinguished Service Cross awarded to Major George E. Preddy, 9-219 Jr., of Greensboro for shooting down six German planes on one mission.

North Carolinians rejoiced with other Americans when at last the war was won and those who had served began returning home. In the rejoicing and in the restoration of a peacetime society, few suspected that the war had done much more than kill millions and reorder the politics of the world. The propaganda characteristic of any war in the defense of democracy had been heard by all Americans, but it must have had a slightly ironic tone for many Americans of color. Even during the war, blacks had 9-220 generally occupied the lowest ranks—foot soldiers, orderlies, cooks aboard ship—and the rhetorical freedoms so eloquently held up for emulation by the world seemed to them more like aspirations than accomplished goals. Furthermore, the war had thrown them into company with whites from all classes and all regions, an exposure in which tensions were sometimes replaced by friendships or, at minimum, mutual tolerance. In the postwar period these young whites and blacks would question the traditions that perpetuated separate standards for Americans who had fought side by side for a government that claimed them as one nationality. The contrast between rhetoric and reality could no longer be ignored; North Carolina was on the verge of momentous social changes.

(SEC. 4.) Every person presenting himself for registration shall be able to read and write any section of the Constitution in the English language; and before he shall be entitled to vote, he shall have paid on or before the first day of May, of the year in which he proposes to vote, his poll tax for the previous year, as prescribed by Article V, Section 1, of the Constitution. But no male person, who was, on January 1, 1867, or at any time prior thereto, entitled to vote under the laws of any State in the United States wherein he then resided, and no lineal descendant of any such person shall be denied the right to register and vote at any election in this State by reason of his failure to possess the educational qualifications herein prescribed: *Provided*, he shall have registered in accordance with the terms of this section prior to December 1, 1908.

Qualifications for registration.

Proviso.

9-1
Exemption from the literacy test under the "grandfather clause" was designed to enable illiterate whites to register. Governor Aycock strongly opposed efforts to remove the deadline for registering under the exemption. (Courtesy North Carolina Collection; reprinted from *Session Laws*, 1900.)

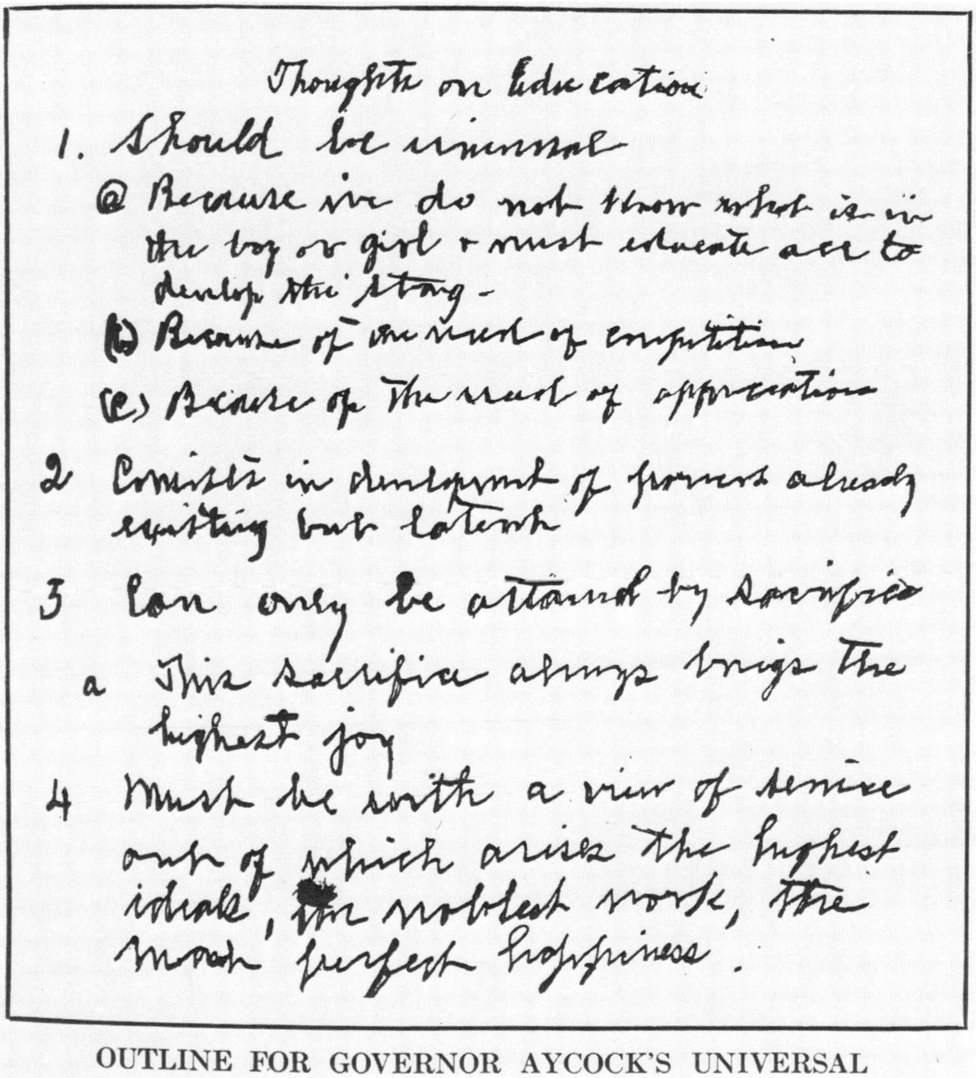

Thoughts on Education

1. Should be universal

(a) Because we do not know what is in the boy or girl & must educate all to develop the strong -

(b) Because of the need of competition

(c) Because of the need of appreciation

2 Consists in development of powers already existing but latent

3 Can only be attained by sacrifice

a This sacrifice always brings the highest joy

4 Must be with a view of service out of which arises the highest ideals, the noblest work, the most perfect happiness.

OUTLINE FOR GOVERNOR AYCOCK'S UNIVERSAL EDUCATION SPEECH

9-2
Charles Brantley Aycock (1859–1912), a product of rural Wayne County, pledged "the State, its strength, its heart, its wealth, to universal education." Nearly twelve years after he was elected governor, he used the outline pictured here for a speech on universal education in Birmingham, Alabama. His last words were "I always talked about education." At this juncture the speaker fell dead. (Reprinted from R. D. W. Connor and Clarence Poe, *The Life and Speeches of Charles Brantley Aycock* [Garden City, 1912].)

9-3 and 9-4
Neither won North Carolina's electoral votes, but both Theodore Roosevelt and William Howard Taft visited the state on several occasions, two of which are pictured here. Top, Roosevelt is speaking before twelve thousand people on the campus of Trinity College in Durham on 19 October 1905. Bottom, Taft on 9 November 1909 is driven past Wilmington school children assembled in a flag formation near the Temple of Israel (background) and St. James Church (right). (Roosevelt photo courtesy Duke University Archives; Taft photo courtesy New Hanover County Museum, Howell Collection.)

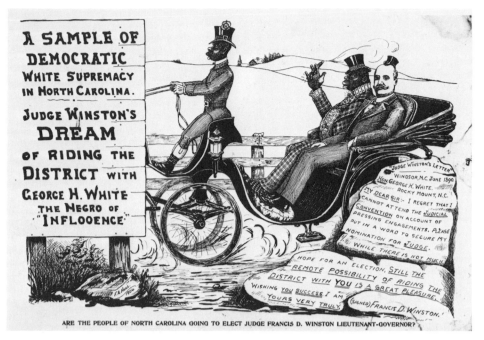

ARE THE PEOPLE OF NORTH CAROLINA GOING TO ELECT JUDGE FRANCIS D. WINSTON LIEUTENANT-GOVERNOR?

9-5
That the race issue was not dead in 1904 was indicated by this cartoon in which Francis D. Winston was ridiculed for his kind words to George H. White, the last black to serve in the Congress until modern times. Winston, a former Republican, was elected lieutenant governor on the Democratic ticket. (Courtesy North Carolina Collection.)

9-6
Furnifold M. Simmons (1854–1940), the architect of the political revolution that removed blacks and Republicans from high political office, remained in the United States Senate from 1901 to 1931. His defeat the latter year was caused partially by his refusal to support Alfred E. Smith for the presidency on the Democratic ticket in 1928. (Courtesy North Carolina Collection.)

9-7
Locke Craig's unsuccessful campaign for governor in 1908 also invoked the race issue. Craig lost the nomination to William W. Kitchin, but in 1912 he was elected Kitchin's successor. (Courtesy North Carolina Collection.)

9-8
Governor Locke Craig (1860–1924), left, stands with Edward Kidder Graham and Josephus Daniels during graduation exercises at the University of North Carolina in 1915. Graham died in the Spanish influenza pandemic three years later. (Courtesy University of North Carolina Photo Lab, Chapel Hill.)

9-9
At their meeting in Wilmington on 20 April 1906, members of the North Carolina chapter of the Society of the Cincinnati posed. Identified by numbers are 1, James Sprunt (nonmember guest); 2, Haywood Clark; 3, James Iredell McRee; 4, unidentified; 5, Marshall Delancey Haywood; 6, Junius Davis; 7, Parker Quince Moore; 8, S. Westray Battle; 9, Bennehan Cameron; 10, Joseph B. Cheshire, Jr.; 11, Samuel A'Court Ashe; 12, Walter Delyle Carstarphen; 13, William Gray Lamb; 14, Joseph Collins Daves; 15, Alfred Moore Waddell; 16, William Eve Bush; 17, Julian S. Carr (nonmember guest); 18, unidentified; 19, Pierre Mallett Holmes; and 20, unidentified. (Courtesy NCDA&H.)

9-10
The United Confederate Veterans helped keep alive the memory of North Carolina's sacrifices during the Civil War. This card was issued at one of the organization's reunions early in the twentieth century. (Courtesy Southern Historical Collection, Julius Leinbach Papers.)

9-11
Aging Cherokee veterans of Thomas's Legion attended a Confederate reunion in New Orleans early in the century. Left to right, front row: Young Deer, unidentified man, Pheasant, Chief David Reed, and Sevier Skitty; back row, the Reverend Bird Saloneta, Dickey Driver, Lt. Col. W. W. Stringfield, Lt. Suatie Owl, Jim Keg, Wesley Crow, unidentified man, and Lt. Calvin Cagle. Stringfield and Cagle were white officers of the unit. (Courtesy National Park Service, Washington.)

9-12
Claude Kitchin (1869–1923) of Halifax County, as Democratic leader in the House of Representatives, found himself out of step with most of his colleagues when he opposed the increas-ing involvement of the United States in the European war. Once war was declared, however, he loyally supported the nation's efforts. (Courtesy North Carolina Collection.)

9-13

In 1916 two North Carolinians were among the first American volunteers in the Lafayette Escadrille, a French flying unit that achieved fame during the war. James Rogers McConnell of Carthage (far left) and Kiffin Yates Rockwell of Asheville (second from left) are pictured beside one of the planes with Georges Thenault (French officer) and Norman Prince and Victor Chapman (both Americans). Within a few months all four of the Americans were dead. (Courtesy North Carolina Collection.)

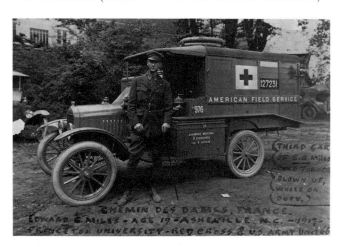

9-14
Edward G. Miles of Asheville, a driver for the American Field Service, stands with his vehicle assigned in 1917 to the Red Cross and Army Unit 66. (Courtesy NCDA&H.)

9-15
Interior view of the Raleigh Iron Works producing shells for the artillery. (Courtesy NCDA&H.)

9-16
Camp Greene at Charlotte was the first of three camps built in North Carolina during the war. The huge base of about two thousand buildings provided for fifty thousand troops. This picture was taken from atop a water tank. (Courtesy NCDA&H.)

9-19
Women performed many services for the war effort, including furnishing gifts and refreshments to military personnel aboard trains stopping in Salisbury. (Courtesy North Carolina Collection.)

9-17
North Carolina's shipyards were busy building vessels, but the war was over so quickly that none of them got into use during wartime. Shown here is the launching of the *Old North State* at the Liberty Shipbuilding Company's yard in Wilmington in 1919. (Courtesy New Hanover County Museum.)

9-20
A victory bond caravan is pictured in front of the post office in Raleigh. The truck is loaded with kaiser-style helmets. (Courtesy NCDA&H.)

9-18
With his assistant, Franklin Delano Roosevelt (left), Secretary of the Navy Josephus Daniels of North Carolina was responsible for the protection of the American troops transported to Europe. When Roosevelt became president, he appointed Daniels ambassador to Mexico. (Courtesy NCDA&H.)

9-21
To help "smoke out the kaiser," the entire production of Bull Durham roll-your-own smoking tobacco was purchased for the armed forces —two thirty-car freight trains per month. Only fourteen cars are pictured here. (Courtesy American Brands, New York.)

9-22
Victorious troops were welcomed back to Raleigh in 1919. The sign in front of the capitol reads, "Welcome Pershing Crusaders / The Flower of Carolina." (Courtesy North Carolina Collection.)

9-23

Marshal Ferdinand Foch of France toured North Carolina after the war to express thanks for American contributions to the Allied victory. He is shown here (center) with former governor Thomas W. Bickett (left) and Governor Cameron Morrison on the balcony of the Union County Courthouse on 9 December 1921. (Courtesy North Carolina Collection.)

9-24

The Ku Klux Klan and other vigilante-type organizations were revived after World War I, but they were not as active in North Carolina as they were in Indiana and several other states. Shown here in Asheville in the 1920s, robed Klansmen stand with uniformed firemen at the funeral of a city policeman. (Courtesy Ewart M. Ball Collection, Southern Highlands Research Center, University of North Carolina at Asheville.)

9-25
These four men occupied the governor's office from 1921 to 1941 with the exception of one term. Left to right: J. C. B. Ehringhaus (1933–37), O. Max Gardner (1929–33), Clyde R. Hoey (1937–41), and Cameron Morrison (1921–25). The photograph was made at the Democratic National Convention in Chicago in 1940. (Courtesy NCDA&H.)

9-26 and 9-27
"The third house of the legislature," as the Yarborough House was called, burned on 3 July 1928 (left). It was located across Fayetteville Street from the Wake County Courthouse. Most of the legislators moved to the new Sir Walter Hotel (right), diagonally across the street, where much of the state's legislation later was hammered out in "smoke-filled" rooms. The popular S & W Cafeteria is just right of center. (Yarborough House courtesy North Carolina Collection; Sir Walter Hotel courtesy NCDA&H.)

9-28
Alfred E. Smith brought his presidential campaign to Raleigh's Union Station on 11 October 1928. Left to right: E. W. G. Huffman, Willis Smith, Alfred E. Smith, Brantley Aycock, Mrs. Alfred E. Smith, Rivers Johnson, Fred Parker, O. Max Gardner, Sherwood Upchurch, E. G. Flanagan, W. W. Neal, and John Folger. (Courtesy NCDA&H.)

9-29 (top)
Under the Emergency Relief Administration, jobs were provided for men and women in a variety of productive enterprises. Shown here are workers in the First Avenue Cannery, Charlotte, canning vegetables. (Courtesy NCDA&H.)

9-30 (center)
The Emergency Relief Administration also paid adults to attend school. Here is an adult education class for blacks at Wilmington. (Courtesy NCDA&H.)

9-31 (bottom)
Black members of the Civilian Conservation Corps are shown mulching a gully on the property of a white farmer in Caswell County. The corps introduced soil and forest conservation techniques such as the construction of contour terraces and fire lanes. (Courtesy National Archives, Washington.)

9-32 (top)
A sewer system was installed by WPA workers in 1936 in Ahoskie. (Courtesy North Carolina Collection, Lee A. Wallace WPA Photo Album.)

9-33 (center)
Women were employed in this WPA sewing room in Beaufort County. (Courtesy North Carolina Collection, Lee A. Wallace WPA Photo Album.)

9-34 (bottom)
Artists were hired by the WPA to paint murals in public buildings. This one, in the Craven County courtroom, has survived. It purports to reflect the history of New Bern, but not an Indian is in view. (Courtesy *News and Observer*, Raleigh; photo by Gene Furr.)

9-35
The North Carolina Symphony Orchestra, founded in 1932 by Lamar Stringfield, was promoted by the Emergency Relief Administration.

This photograph was made about 1935. (Courtesy North Carolina Symphony, Raleigh.)

9-36
The Federal Theatre Project of the WPA employed actors and promoted drama. Here in 1937 Paul Green (seated center) is reading the script of his *Lost Colony*. Others include Frederick H. Koch (leaning against tree), Samuel Selden (right, white suit), and Howard Bailey, state director of the FTP (seated right). (Courtesy North Carolina Collection.)

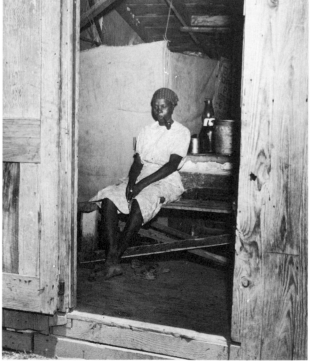

9-37 (top)
Rural medical care was extended through federal aid. Dr. Stephen A. Malloy of Yanceyville examines the child of tenant farmers on the porch of their log cabin. (Courtesy Southern Historical Collection, Howard Odum Subregional Survey.)

9-38
The improvement in the economy during the defense buildup did little to relieve the poverty of a pipe-smoking woman who in July 1940 shared this shack near Belcross, Camden County, with eleven other migrant agricultural workers. (Courtesy Library of Congress; photograph by Jack Delano, FSA.)

9-40
Early in the century a float carried the slogan, "The sun never sets on Proximity denims." A large mill village grew up around the Proximity Mills founded by the Cones. (Courtesy North Carolina Collection.)

9-39
North Carolina's congressional delegation sat for a portrait about 1937. Left to right, seated, are Senator Josiah W. Bailey, Representative Robert L. Doughton, and Senator Robert Rice Reynolds. In the back row are Congressmen William B. Umstead, Graham A. Barden, Harold D. Cooley, John H. Kerr, J. Walter Lambeth, J. Bayard Clark, Lindsay Warren, Frank Hancock, Alfred Lee Bulwinkle, and Zebulon Weaver. (Courtesy NCDA&H.)

9-41
In 1923 this wooden building just outside Burlington in the Piedmont Heights area housed the first unit of what would become Burlington Industries, the largest textile organization in the world. (Courtesy North Carolina Collection.)

9-42
A mill town depended almost solely upon the factory. After the burning of this mill in 1911, the little town of Avalon in Rockingham County gradually vanished. (Courtesy Ola Maie Foushee, Chapel Hill.)

9-43
A strange vehicle, called the "Bean Wagon," carried hot meals to workers at the mill in Roanoke Rapids in 1914 and for years afterward. Just before noon each day, William Strauther (with beard) drove past the homes of mill employees and blew a hunter's horn. The women placed hot meals on the wagon, which proceeded to the mill, arriving at the lunch hour. (Courtesy North Carolina Collection; original owned by Mrs. Cleophus Bray, Roanoke Rapids.)

Lewis Hine, representing the National Child Labor Committee, visited North Carolina in 1908–9 and photographed hundreds of scenes of textile production, of which these are but four. Hine's photographs, reflecting the exploitation of children, were influential in the passage and enforcement of additional child labor laws. (By permission of Edward L. Brafford Photography Collection, Library, University of Maryland Baltimore County.)

9-44
A mother does piecework in her home so she can take care of her children.

9-45
The day shift at a mill in Whitnel, Caldwell County. Hine noted "nearly as many small children also working on night shift."

9-46
Boy doffers in a North Carolina cotton mill. The youngster at far left has his head bandaged as if he suffered from mumps or toothache.

9-47
A girl operating heavy equipment, her hair and clothing covered with lint.

9-48
Union members gather at Loray Mill, Gastonia, for a strike meeting in 1929. As the sign in center indicates, the union led workers to believe that the "International will feed us." (By permission of Wide World Photos.)

9-49
Two women grapple with a National Guardsman during the Loray strike in 1929. (Courtesy Archives of Labor and Urban Affairs, Wayne State University, Detroit.)

9-50
Seventeen persons were arraigned for the murder of O. F. Aderholt, Gastonia's chief of police, who was killed during the violence. This is a courtroom scene during the trial, which was conducted by Judge Maurice V. Barnhill in Charlotte. (By permission of United Press International.)

9-51
Conscious of the appeal of attractive emblems on packs and in advertising, Richard J. Reynolds was inspired by this photograph to adopt the one-hump dromedary for his Camel cigarettes. The picture was made of "Old Joe" and his trainer when they came through Winston-Salem on 29 September 1913 with the Barnum and Bailey Circus. (Courtesy R. J. Reynolds Tobacco Company, Winston-Salem.)

9-52

Automation reduced the amount of labor required in cigarette making. Shown here is one of Reynolds's im- proved machines early in the century. (Courtesy R. J. Rey- nolds Tobacco Company, Winston-Salem.)

9-53

North Carolina tobacco was eagerly sought around the world. Here the Murai Com- pany in Japan advertised the Pin Head brand featuring "Old North Carolina Leaf." (Courtesy Manuscript De- partment, Duke University Library.)

Kitchen Cabinet No. 9

Base 26x50 inches, one flour bin, one meal bin with partition, ca- pacity 75 pounds, two drawers, one bread board; top, two glass doors 13x34 inches, one oak panel door 10x26 inches, three draw- ers, very convenient cabinet, height 6 feet 7 inches; weight 175 pounds. Price $9.00.

Manufactured by LAMBETH FURNITURE CO., Thomasville, N. C., U. S. A.

9-54

In 1908 this substantial oak cabinet could be purchased for only nine dollars from a North Carolina manufac- turer. (Courtesy North Caro- lina Collection.)

9-55
Panoramic view of the plant of the Champion Fibre Company at Canton just two years after it was opened in 1908. (Courtesy Library of Congress.)

9-56
Lewis Hine returned to North Carolina in 1937 for the National Research Project and made this photograph of a worker at Tomlinson Chair Company turning out eighteen identical spindles on one machine. (Courtesy National Archives, Washington.)

9-57
An ox pulled the wagon for these gatherers of rosin in the pine forests of North Carolina in 1903. (Courtesy Library of Congress.)

9-58
Mules were used to pull the ore carts in the Cumnock (or Egypt) Coal Mine on the Deep River in the early part of the century. (Courtesy North Carolina Collection; original owned by Harvey Kennedy, Sanford.)

9-61
Giant roll of seines on the waterfront at Morehead City. The vessel is the *Lynnhaven*; the Woodland Hotel is in left background. (Courtesy Library of Congress.)

9-59
An explosion in the Coal Glen Mine at Cumnock in 1925 resulted in fifty-three deaths. Here an ore cart brings out several bodies. (Courtesy North Carolina Collection.)

9-62
This picture of the interior of the Odell Hardware Company in Greensboro shows a sample of the modern conveniences available in 1908. (Courtesy North Carolina Collection; reprinted from T. E. Harvey [editor], *Commercial History of . . . North Carolina* [Charlotte, 1908].)

9-60
Clothing of the workers reflected the heat generated in the manufacturing of iron at the Charlotte Pipe and Foundry Company. (Courtesy Laney-Smith, Inc.; printed in Beth Laney Smith, *A Foundry: Being the Story of the Charlotte Pipe and Foundry Company . . .* [Charlotte, 1977], volume 1.)

9-63
Julius Schwartz, owner of the Richmond Meat Market in Raleigh, posed in 1910 with employees and customers. (Courtesy *News and Observer*, Raleigh.)

9-65
Daniel Craven and his pottery operation in the Seagrove area shortly after 1900. The mule walked in a circle to turn the pug mill which mixed the various clays. Glazing was done inside the log structure. Crocks and milk pots are arranged in the foreground. (Courtesy North Carolina Collection; reprinted from *Tar Heel Junior Historian* [Winter 1978].)

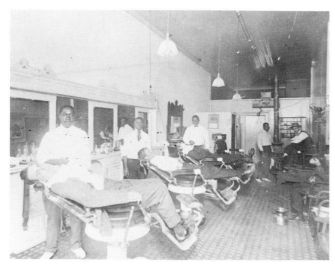

9-64
The barbers were black; the customers were white. Haywood Smith's Barber Shop, Smithfield. (Courtesy Johnston County Public Library, Smithfield.)

9-66
Caleb D. Bradham created "Brad's Drink," which became famous under the name "Pepsi-Cola." Bradham's assistant, R. F. Butler, stands in front of the pharmacy in New Bern where Pepsi-Cola was first made. (Courtesy North Carolina Collection.)

9-67
Charles Clinton Spaulding (standing) and John Merrick were among the organizers in 1898 of the North Carolina Mutual and Provident Association, which has become the oldest insurance company in continuous operation in the state and the largest Negro-owned life insurance company in the world. They are shown about 1906 with Mrs. Susan Gille Norfleet. (Courtesy North Carolina Collection.)

9-69
Women employees of Pilot Life Insurance Company in Greensboro took time out for physical exercise in the office early in the century. (Courtesy Pilot Life Insurance Company, Greensboro.)

9-68
Booker T. Washington (center, middle row) visited Durham in 1910 and praised the progress made by black businesses and the good race relations of the community. C. C. Spaulding sits fourth from left in the front row, and John Merrick is fifth from right in the middle row. (Courtesy North Carolina Collection.)

9-70

The quiet Benjamin N. Duke (left) and his more famous brother, James Buchanan Duke, were familiar figures on the boardwalk at Atlantic City around 1920. (Courtesy NCDA&H.)

9-71

Some tenants received low-interest loans from New Deal agencies, enabling them to become landowners. Nat Williamson, left, the first Negro in the United States to receive a loan under the tenant purchase program, is shown in April 1938 with E. H. Anderson, a Farm Security Administration official in Guilford County. (Courtesy Library of Congress; photograph by John Vachon, Farm Security Administration.)

9-72

This scene of tobacco harvesting in eastern North Carolina in 1926 was typical of the brightleaf belt, though the wheeled "slide" was less common than one built on runners. Whites and blacks worked side by side. Entire families participated, the men pulling ("priming") the leaves, the boys driving the slides loaded with leaves, the women and children handing leaves and stringing them. After the sticks were hoisted and placed on tiers in the barn, the tobacco was cured for two days or more by the heat from wood-fired flues. (Courtesy NCDA&H.)

9-73

A barefooted youngster removes cured leaves from a tobacco stick (which is supported by a "stringing horse"). The tobacco on the floor at right has been graded and bundled, and it is ready to be taken to the auction warehouse. (Courtesy Library of Congress; photograph by Marion Post Wolcott, FSA.)

9-75

Peddlers followed the tobacco auctions, tempting farmers to spend their once-per-year income. Here in Durham in 1939 a salesman dressed as an Indian medicine man hawks a "miracle cure." (Courtesy Library of Congress; photo by Marion Post Wolcott, FSA.)

9-74

When G. G. Viverette of the Glenview section of Halifax County arrived at a Rocky Mount warehouse in 1913 with tobacco loaded on the first automobile-drawn trailer seen in that city, a photographer was summoned to record the historic event. The axle, wheels, and pneumatic tires came from an even earlier motor vehicle. (Courtesy NCDA&H, Brimley Collection.)

9-76

These men, who loaded their tobacco on a Durham warehouse floor before daybreak, nervously await the beginnings of sales that will reward them for a year of strenuous work. (Courtesy Library of Congress; photo by Marion Post Wolcott, FSA.)

9-77
A farmer's annual income was determined in the span of a few minutes when his tobacco was auctioned off each fall. This picture in a Wilson warehouse in 1926 was posed; normally the buyers crowded around, eyeing, feeling, and smelling the bundles as they signaled their bids to the chanting auctioneer. (Courtesy North Carolina Collection.)

9-78
A metal hand-planter with two tubes (one for water and the other providing a chute for the plant) removed much of the back strain characteristic of the earlier hand-peg method of setting out tobacco, but it required three persons—one to operate the planter, one to drop the plants, and another to bring water. (Courtesy North Carolina Collection.)

9-79
Black and white cotton pickers worked side by side in
a North Carolina cotton
field about 1903. The child
tramps the cotton as it is
placed in the large basket.
(Courtesy Library of
Congress.)

9-81
Bonnets and straw hats
shielded members of the
Powell family from the hot
Johnston County sun during
berry-picking early in the
century. The building behind
them housed Hillfield Academy before the Civil War.
(Courtesy William S. Powell,
Chapel Hill.)

9-80
Bales of cotton await sale at
the market in Franklinton in
the 1920s. In the background
is the town's inn. (Courtesy
Stephen Massengill, Raleigh.)

9-82
Hog-killing time on the John Hardy Barefoot farm in Johnston County early in the century. Family and neighbors joined to butcher more than a dozen hogs in the cool fall. The carcasses were cut up and cured for use during the next year. (Courtesy Johnston County Public Library, Smithfield.)

9-83
Wheat threshing near Zionville, Watauga County, shortly after 1900. A steam engine and belt powered the primitive thresher. (Courtesy Oral History Project, Appalachian State University, Boone.)

9-84 (top)
Wheat-threshing time on the Fred Oliver Farm near Charlotte. The combine under the shed threshed the wheat and baled the hay.

(Courtesy North Carolina Collection.)

9-85
Black farmers gather for relaxation and a bottle of soda pop at a country store in Gordonton, Person County, about 1939. (Courtesy

Southern Historical Collection, Howard Odum Subregional Survey; photo by Dorothea Lange, FSA.)

9-86 and 9-87
Farm families often interrupted the monotony of chores with community gatherings around the barns. At left four washpots simmer with Brunswick stew; at right a farmer patiently barbecues two sides of meat over an open fire. The wire frame will be turned time and again for about eighteen hours, each rotation accompanied by the application of the spicy juices that give North Carolina barbecue its unique taste. (Stew scene courtesy State Travel Development Section, Raleigh; barbecue scene courtesy NCDA&H.)

9-88
Clarence Poe became editor of the *Progressive Farmer* at the age of eighteen. For more than half a century he was the state's most popular advocate of improved agricultural practices and farm life. (Courtesy NCDA&H.)

9-89
Women conduct a canning party at Jamestown in 1911. After World War I, home economics was increasingly taught in high schools, and homemakers practiced improved methods of preserving foods. (Courtesy North Carolina Collection.)

9-90
This photograph, originally owned by the historian Hugh T. Lefler, shows two hunters after a profitable day rabbit hunting. Wild game was especially welcome during the Depression. (Courtesy North Carolina Collection.)

9-91 and 9-92
Hugh MacRae acquired large tracts of land in Pender, New Hanover, and Columbus counties and established immigrant colonies: Dutch at Castle Hayne and Van Eeden; Germans at New Berlin (now Delco); and Italians, Poles, and Russians at St. Helena. Here a Dutch immigrant plows soil fourteen inches deep at Van Eeden in 1914; and at St. Helena houses are placed on adjacent corners of four farms to form a small village setting. These and other efforts, such as Mark Potter's Dutch colony at Terra Ceia in Beaufort County in the 1920s, were partially successful and introduced new peoples into a state with a miniscule foreign-born population. (Courtesy North Carolina Collection.)

9-93
Several New Deal projects assisted poverty-stricken families to move to better quarters in the 1930s, including those at Roanoke Farms, a Resettlement Administration project near Enfield. Here farmers in wagons are waiting to obtain cotton seed, which they are buying cooperatively. (Courtesy Library of Congress; photo by John Vachon.)

9-94
Trolley cars provided transportation in most cities until well into the new century. The flimsy "cowcatcher" on this Greensboro trolley was probably designed for dogs and unwary pedestrians. (Courtesy Duke Power Company, Charlotte.)

9-95
The shrewd residents of Church Island, Currituck County, in 1905 combined wind power with wooden rails. (Courtesy North Carolina Collection, Collier Cobb Collection.)

9-96
The Page family is shown on their special car of the Aberdeen and Asheboro Railroad. (Courtesy Randolph County Historical Society.)

9-97
Lumber companies sometimes built their own narrow-gauge railroads, moving them to new sites as necessary. Here the Snow Bird Valley Railroad winds up the mountain. (Courtesy North Carolina Collection.)

9-98
Early in the century in Asheville a mountaineer takes a swig from his jug as his mismatched oxen appear bored by their surroundings, which include, in the background, the White Man's Bar. (Courtesy Manuscript Department, Duke University Library.)

9-99
C. L. Hayes, who published this photograph around the turn of the century, labeled it "Sand Hill Supply Com-

pany." A pig hangs off the rear in this view made at Southern Pines. (Courtesy Library of Congress.)

9-100
Garley Hackney early in the century drives his ice wagon along a Chapel Hill or Carrboro street. The youngster carries in his tongs a twenty-five-pound block of ice. Residents wishing to buy ice hung out a five-sided cardboard wheel with the number of pounds desired at the top. (Courtesy North Carolina Collection.)

9-101
Human power was used to push little Mildred Morse (later McEwen) of Charlotte in her first baby carriage in August 1901. (Courtesy Mildred Morse McEwen, Charlotte.)

9-102
Gilbert S. Waters of New Bern built this "Buggy-mobile" in 1900—an altered buggy body with a one-cylinder, water-cooled engine and pneumatic tires. (Courtesy NCDA&H.)

9-103
Fletcher W. Waynick of Reidsville built three motor cars, of which this was the first. The five-horsepower single-cylinder gasoline engine was mounted on a buggy body. Because it was the only motor car around, the vehicle was subject to a special town ordinance. (Courtesy North Carolina Department of Transportation, Raleigh.)

9-105
A view inside the Chevrolet garage on Steele Street, Sanford, about 1917. (Courtesy NCDA&H.)

9-106
John H. Smith, shown here with customers, operated the first black-owned gas station in Wilmington at the corner of Campbell and North Sixth streets. The picture was taken about 1929. (Courtesy New Hanover County Museum; original owned by May Hubert.)

9-104
With the aid of the federal government, the Jerome Bolick Sons Company of Conover converted to the manufacture of school bus bodies in 1934. The company switched to truck bodies in 1953; twenty-five years later it closed, blaming the federal bureaucracy for hamstringing its operations. (Courtesy *Charlotte Observer.*)

9-107
P. B. Comer's red and black vehicle—a specially made body on an International truck chassis—made two round trips per day between Greensboro and Asheboro. His intercity franchise may have been the first issued by the state. (Reprinted, by permission, from the *State* [March 1976].)

9-108
Thompson Brothers garage commanded one end of the toll bridge across the Yadkin River near Salisbury. In addition to collecting the tolls, the garage offered air, oil, and repairs. The picture was taken on 11 July 1911. (Courtesy National Archives, Washington.)

9-109
Near Blowing Rock, vacationers crowded into a Buick clown with the gatekeeper before being permitted to proceed over the privately owned toll road. (Courtesy North Carolina Collection.)

9-112
At Bynum in Chatham
County a new concrete
bridge replaces a latticework
covered bridge. Odell's Mill
is seen on the opposite shore.
(Courtesy North Carolina
Collection; original owned by
Nell P. Atwater, Chapel Hill.)

9-110
Harriet Morehead Berry of
Chapel Hill (right) and
Heriot Clarkson of Charlotte
were prime supporters of the
$50 million bond issue for
roads in 1921. Harriet Berry
was secretary of the North
Carolina Good Roads Association, and Clarkson was campaign manager for Governor
Cameron Morrison. (Cour-
tesy NCDA&H.)

9-111
A child on a muddy Chapel
Hill street campaigned with a
sign reading "Object Les-
son—Vote for Good Roads."
The bond issue was approved
in a referendum. (Courtesy
North Carolina Collection.)

9-113
Not even the Morrison
bonds solved the road prob-
lems. Here in the 1920s on
Hendersonville Road near
Asheville a bus vainly tries to
keep its posted schedule.
(Courtesy University of
North Carolina Photo Lab,
Chapel Hill.)

9-114
Wilbur Wright fixes breakfast in the Kill Devil Hills shed that sheltered the brothers and their 1901 glider (right). An oil lamp bracketed on the wall at left provided light. (Courtesy Wright State University Library, Dayton, Ohio.)

9-115
Dan Tate, posing here with his family on the porch of the Kitty Hawk Post Office, and his half-brother, William, the postmaster, assisted the inventors throughout their experiments. One of the Wright brothers took the picture. (Courtesy Library of Congress.)

9-116
With Orville at the controls and Wilbur running alongside to steady the wings if necessary, the *Flyer* lifts from the starting rail. Though the first flight lasted just twelve seconds and covered only 120 feet, it marked the first time that a heavier-than-air vehicle had been lifted by mechanical power. (Courtesy Library of Congress.)

9-117
Commercial aviation was slow to develop in North Carolina, but on 14 October 1927 a crowd gathered at the Pitcairn hangar at Greensboro to welcome Charles A. Lindbergh and his *Spirit of St. Louis*, in which he crossed the Atlantic. (Courtesy Joe Knox, Newton.)

9-118
Georgia ("Tiny") Thompson Broadwicke of Henderson became the first woman to parachute from an airplane. Here on the day of her first jump at Griffith Field, Los Angeles, in 1913, she sits on a trap seat under a seaplane piloted by Glenn Martin. (Courtesy NCDA&H.)

9-119
A man sits on the wreckage of the barkentine *Priscilla*, sunk at Gull Shoal in August 1899 with the loss of four lives. (Courtesy North Carolina Collection.)

9-120
Lifesaving crews such as this one on Oak Island near the mouth of the Cape Fear River remained alert for emergency missions along the coast. The wide tires permitted the carriage to be drawn over sand. The picture was probably made about 1915. (Courtesy NCDA&H.)

9-121
Paddle-wheelers like the *Cape Fear*, shown here at its dock at Fayetteville, provided river transportation well into the twentieth century. (Courtesy Manuscript Department, Duke University Library.)

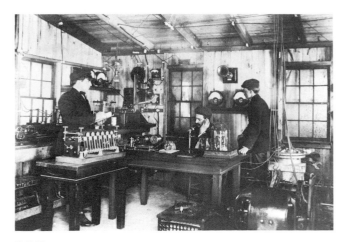

9-122
Reginald A. Fessenden in 1901–2 experimented with wireless communications in a building on Roanoke Island. (Courtesy NCDA&H.)

9-124
In this photograph, made 7 October 1932, Andrew Massey, Willard Dean, and Henry Hulick (left to right) are operating an early radio remote unit for station WPTF in Raleigh. (Courtesy North Carolina Collection.)

9-123
This unit of equipment belonging to station WBT, Charlotte, constituted the first licensed broadcast transmitter in North Carolina. Current came from a 110-volt wall fixture, but a power-line pole transformer stepped up voltage to 2,300 volts. Note the 32–Mason jar rectifier on the bottom shelf. The picture was made 4 April 1922. (Courtesy North Carolina Collection.)

9-125
Neatly coiffured women operate a telephone exchange in Randolph County early in the century. (Courtesy Randolph County Historical Society.)

9-126
Carolina Telephone and Telegraph Company's Smithfield office provided two private booths, one each for whites and "colored." (Courtesy Carolina Telephone and Telegraph Company, Tarboro.)

9-128
The Blewett Falls Dam was built near Hamlet in 1907 by the Rockingham Power Company, which in 1926 was taken over by the Carolina Power and Light Company. (Courtesy Library of Congress.)

9-127
These boys were hired to deliver the mail to remote areas near Highlands early in the century. (Courtesy Manuscript Department, Duke University Library.)

9-129
Electricity and gas, where available, brightened homes and lightened the work of housewives. Here gas appliances are demonstrated in Asheville in 1905. (Courtesy University of North Carolina Photo Lab, Chapel Hill.)

9-130
During the county commencement parade in Sampson County in 1914, the Concord community boasted that average daily attendance at its school was 70 percent. (Courtesy North Carolina Collection; reprinted from *Sampson County School Record* [November 1914].)

9-131
Most of the one-room schools built during the educational crusade were of logs; this one was of frame construction. The yardstick and blackboard may have been the only instructional equipment provided. (Courtesy North Carolina Collection.)

9-132
The Berry O'Kelly Training School at Method near Raleigh provided vocational agriculture training for all ages. In 1923 it became one of the first accredited Negro high schools in the country. (Courtesy NCDA&H.)

9-133
John Bridges of Wake County constructed a handsome tally-ho and transported his and neighboring children to Wakelon School in bad weather. Shown aboard the wagon in 1912 are his twelve children, all of whom were enrolled in the school. Second from front on the near side is Henry Lee Bridges, who served as state auditor from 1947 to 1981. (Courtesy Henry L. Bridges, Raleigh.)

9-134
A miniature Gothic city sprang from the forest as the buildings of the new Duke University were constructed in the 1920s. A special railroad was built from the campus to the rock quarry near Hillsborough. The view is toward the Medical Center. (Courtesy Duke University Archives.)

9-135
Black Mountain College was a magnet for "progressive" scholars. Pictured here at a summer institute in 1946 are, left to right, Leo Amino, Jacob Lawrence, Leo Lionni, Theodore Dreier, Bobbie Dreier, Beaumont Newhall, Gwendolyn Lawrence, Mrs. Walter Gropius, Nan Newhall, Walter Gropius, Molly Gregory, Josef Albers, and Anni Albers. In the tree is Jean Varda. (Courtesy NCDA&H.)

9-136
Lucy Morgan (1889–1981), founder of Penland School of Crafts, and Howard C. Ford are pictured as they prepared to leave for the 1933 Chicago World's Fair, where they exhibited their crafts in the small cabin. (Courtesy Penland School, Penland.)

9-137
Robert D. W. Connor (1878–1950) rode with the driver in the front seat as he conducted William Howard Taft (right) on a tour of Raleigh in 1916 when the former president was the main speaker at a meeting of the State Literary and Historical Association. Connor served as archivist of the United States, 1934–41. (Courtesy NCDA&H.)

9-138
Frederick Augustus Olds (1853–1935), a newspaperman and "father" of the Hall of History in Raleigh, became a walking legend because of his zeal in collecting historical materials and providing tours through the museum. He seldom let facts stand in the way of a good story. (Courtesy North Carolina Collection.)

9-139
Four days before he reached voting age in 1885, Thomas Dixon, Jr., of Cleveland County took his seat in the North Carolina House of Representatives. Dixon's fame, however, was earned not as a politician and Baptist minister but as the author of books that reopened the wounds of Reconstruction. (Courtesy North Carolina Collection.)

VOL. IV.   MORAVIAN FALLS, NORTH CAROLINA, JULY, 1913.   NO. 5.

9-140
James Larkin Pearson's paper, *The Fool-Killer*, declared war on all fools. Its columns were filled with his poetry and prose, much of it in mountain dialect. The longtime poet laureate of the state died in 1981. (Courtesy North Carolina Collection.)

9-141
Thomas Wolfe (1900–1938) of Asheville emerged as North Carolina's most noted novelist. He is shown here in a scene from *The Third Night*, a play that he wrote as a senior at the University of North Carolina. Left to right are Jonathan Daniels (standing), Fred Cohn, and Wolfe. (Courtesy North Carolina Collection.)

9-142 (below)
Among the cities with good libraries early in the century was Asheville. The turret of its fortresslike Pack Memorial Library—a gift of George Willis Pack (1831–1906)—is seen at far left in this photograph made by H. W. Pelton in 1910. On the crest of the hill in center background is the old Battery Park Hotel. (Courtesy Library of Congress.)

9-143
Shortly after the turn of the century, women's organizations advocated improved library service and sometimes set up small lending libraries, such as this case of books in the post office at Jamestown. (Courtesy North Carolina Collection.)

9-145
The Bijou Theatre in Wilmington opened in 1904 in a tent; this building—thought to be the first permanent movie theatre in the state— was opened two years later. Owner J. F. Howard and his dog pose with some of his patrons. The Bijou claimed to be the oldest continuously operated movie theater in the country until it closed in 1956. (Courtesy New Hanover County Museum; original owned by Leila W. Miller.)

9-144
The North Carolina Library Commission established traveling libraries in 1915. Here five large boxes (which when opened provided display cases) are carried by wagon. (Courtesy North Carolina Collection.)

9-146
One of the earliest motion pictures filmed in the state was made on Roanoke Island in 1921, sponsored by the School Extension Division. Here C. A. Rheims and Red Stephens of the Atlas Film Corporation of Chicago and Elizabeth Grimball (director) of New York prepare for filming *The Lost Colony*. (Courtesy North Carolina Collection.)

9-147
Replicas of an Indian village and a ship were constructed near Fort Raleigh for the 1921 filming, and leading citizens were given roles in the film. Sixteen years later, Paul Green adopted the same title for his outdoor symphonic drama. (Courtesy North Carolina Collection.)

9-148
Rockingham County's Charlie Poole, shown here with his group, the North Carolina Ramblers, fiddler Posey Rorer and guitar player Roy Harvey, was an early recording star of "hillbilly" records, the forerunner of modern country music. His distinctive three-finger picking style anticipated the bluegrass style later popularized by Earl Scruggs. (Courtesy Kinney Rorer.)

9-149
A converted barge, the James Adams Floating Palace Theatre, provided a seven-hundred-seat arena for theatrical performances at riverside towns in the east from 1914 to 1939. After Edna Ferber briefly worked aboard the craft and wrote her novel *Showboat*, the vessel was called the "Original Showboat." (Courtesy Mariner's Museum, Newport News.)

9-150 (above right)
Kay Kyser of Rocky Mount and his Kollege of Musical Knowledge for years played regularly on network radio. After World War II, Kyser returned to North Carolina and helped promote the state's good health campaign. (Courtesy Leo Walker, author of *The Wonderful Era of the Great Dance Bands* [New York, 1972].)

9-151
Square dancing and the Highland Fling were among the few forms of dancing acceptable to fundamentalist North Carolinians prior to World War II. Here three lasses perform at a fair at Pinehurst. (Courtesy Given Memorial Library, Pinehurst.)

9-152
Among new denominations organized around the turn of the century was the Pentecostal Holiness Church, which established headquarters, an orphanage, and a school at Falcon in Cumberland County. This scene is from the second camp meeting in 1901. (Courtesy North Carolina Collection; original owned by William Joseph Bundy, Falcon.)

9-153
Large wooden arbors provided cover for worshipers at most camp meetings in the Piedmont. This photograph was made about 1912 at a church campground in Iredell County. (Courtesy Gary L. Freeze, Statesville.)

9-154
On Wayah Bald in Macon County, Presbyterian minister Augustus E. Sample spread a cloth on a turned-up box and conducted religious services early in the century. The mountaintop, profuse with rhododendron, was a favorite campground. (Courtesy University of North Carolina Photo Lab, Chapel Hill.)

9-155
A white minister visits a barefooted black family at their
log cabin with stick chimney
near Southern Pines shortly
after 1900. The photogra-
pher found something amus-

ing about the scene; he titled
the picture, "No sir, no visitors here—just the family
home for Sunday dinner."
(Courtesy Library of Con-
gress.)

9-157
The Richard D. Long Saloon
on Tarboro Street, Rocky
Mount, was the unofficial
headquarters of the otherwise
homeless city police department at the turn of the century. Long stands in the
foreground. Most areas of

the state were dry by that
time. (Courtesy North Carolina Collection; original
owned by Mrs. O. C. Jeffcoat
[daughter of Richard Long],
Rocky Mount.)

9-156
Collier Cobb took this picture at a religious footwash-
ing service at Lake Waccamaw early in the century.
(Courtesy North Carolina
Collection.)

9-158
Carry Nation, shown here 29
July 1907 in Raleigh with
the Reverend Sylvester J.
Betts, brought her war
against liquor to North Carolina, but she had no opportunity to use her famous
hatchet on a saloon, for
Raleigh had adopted the dis-
pensary system from which
only bottled liquor could
be purchased. (Courtesy
NCDA&H.)

THE NEXT STEP IN PROHIBITION

9-159

Prior to the referendum in 1908, the *Winston-Salem Journal* predicted that prohibition would be followed by a war on tobacco. (Reprinted from *Winston-Salem Journal*, 20 May 1908.)

9-160

Among the industries put out of business by prohibition was Garrett and Company's winery, pictured here at Chockoyotte, Halifax County. The company was a successor to the famous Medoc winery. (Courtesy North Carolina Collection.)

9-161

That legal prohibition failed to end the liquor traffic is indicated by this photograph showing Sheriff J. J. Bailey of Madison County with the prizes of only three months of raids on moonshine distilleries. The picture was made 1 August 1921 in Marshall. (Courtesy North Carolina Collection.)

9-162

J. Sherwood Upchurch campaigned in 1926 against the teaching of evolution. He lost the election (though he was elected two years later). (Courtesy North Carolina Collection.)

9-163
With the aid of the Rockefeller Sanitary Commission, Dr. C. W. Stiles brought his campaign against the hookworm to North Carolina. He is shown here (in shirtsleeves to the right of tent pole) in Jacksonville, Onslow County. Citizens have come to his field clinic for examination and, if necessary, treatment. (Courtesy Rockefeller Foundation Archives, New York.)

9-165
An "antiseptic" apple tree at Crossnore, Avery County, was a favorite operating site for doctors Eustace and Mary Martin Sloop. A bush branch is used to drive away flies. Later the Sloops built a modern hospital and school in the mountain community. (Courtesy North Carolina Collection.)

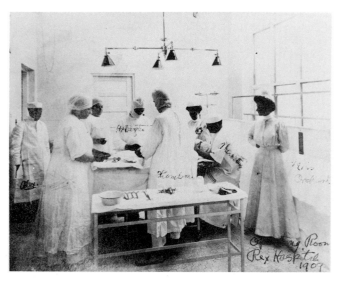

9-164
A scene in the operating room of Rex Hospital, Raleigh, in 1909 reveals the absence of sophisticated equipment invented later in the century. (Courtesy NCDA&H.)

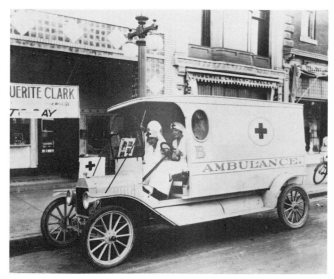

9-166
During World War I this ambulance at Goldsboro was driven by women. (Courtesy Wayne County Public Library, Goldsboro.)

9-167
Three outer bankers attempt to direct a balky wild pony to the disinfectant tank during the "Tick War" of 1921. (Courtesy North Carolina Collection.)

9-169
Fun-loving members of the Wilmington Odd Fellows Lodge also contributed to the welfare of the less fortunate. Here during a parade in 1904 they are shown with or- phans who were taken into their homes for a week. (Courtesy New Hanover County Museum; original owned by Mrs. Vivian Allen.)

9-168
Clement Samuel Brimley (left) talks with his brother, Herbert H. Brimley, about 1944. The former was an entomologist; the latter was director of the Museum of Natural History. (Courtesy NCDA&H, Brimley Collection.)

9-170
Leisure Activities took many forms prior to World War II. In Yanceyville for half a century men had gathered at the Caswell County Courthouse to play cards. When the national media publicized the tradition as the war approached, the county commissioners prohibited cardplaying in or around the courthouse. Here one of the last games is being played on the courthouse lawn. The iron fence was contributed to the scrap drive during the war. (Courtesy Library of Congress; photo by Marion Post Wolcott, FSA.)

9-171

A wagon load of Rockingham County men leave for a cockfight in 1908. Owners of fighting cocks paid farmers twenty-five cents per month to allow roosters to run with their own flocks to develop strength and wildness. (Reprinted, by permission, from Lindley S. Butler, *Our Proud Heritage: Rockingham County, North Carolina* [Bassett, Va., 1971].)

9-173

The girls' 1927 basketball team of Farmer High School, Randolph County, was typical of hundreds of such public school teams. There were few indoor courts that early; consequently, most games were played outside on dirt courts. (Courtesy North Carolina Collection; original owned by Zeb R. Denny, Roanoke Rapids.)

9-172

This was the scene from the air on 1 January 1942 when for the only time in history—owing to the danger of an air raid by the Japanese—the Rose Bowl was played away from Pasadena. In the Duke Stadium at Durham, Oregon State defeated the Blue Devils 20–16. (Courtesy Duke University Archives.)

9-174

Hundreds of spectators watched in 1926 as Jack Dempsey sparred with a partner near Indian Cave Lodge on Mt. Hebron near Hendersonville. Later that year at Philadelphia, Dempsey lost his world's heavyweight boxing championship to Gene Tunney. (By permission of the Baker-Barber Collection, Hendersonville.)

9-177
Guests relax on the broad piazzas of the Carolina Hotel at Pinehurst about 1908. The sign on the wall at left indicates a pay phone. (Courtesy North Carolina Collection.)

9-178
Not far from Pinehurst a proud black man identified only as "Ned" lived in a stick-chimney shack with his family and a few worldly possessions. The picture was made by E. C. Eddy in 1914. (Courtesy Library of Congress.)

9-175
Annie Oakley, famed markswoman of Buffalo Bill's "Wild West" show, was a familiar figure at Pinehurst, where she lived for a time, performed, and taught other women to shoot. Here she appears at a costume ball at the Carolina Hotel as "Sitting Bull, Jr." She won the prize for the best costume. (By permission of the Garst Museum, Greenville, Ohio.)

9-176
Cleveland Springs near Shelby was one of the many popular vacation spots in the Piedmont. The springs provided medicinal water, and the hotel offered comfortable accommodations and social activities. (Courtesy Stephen Massengill, Raleigh.)

9-179
The Grove Park Inn, pictured here in 1913 by H. W. Pelton, was Asheville's most luxurious showplace. (Courtesy Library of Congress.)

9-181
Grandfather Mountain provides the background for this automobile on a narrow road near Linville in 1912. (Courtesy Library of Congress.)

9-180
Among the famous persons attracted to the Grove Park Inn were, left to right, Harvey Firestone, Thomas A. Edison, Harvey Firestone, Jr., Horatio Seymour, Henry Ford, and Fred L. Seely, Sr. The photograph was made in 1918. Twelve years earlier Firestone and Ford, passing through Asheville on the way to Sylva in search of cobalt for batteries, had given many citizens their first sight of an automobile. (Courtesy Ewart M. Ball Collection, Southern Highlands Research Center, University of North Carolina at Asheville.)

9-182
"Aunt Cumi" Woody of the Deyton Bend section helped keep alive traditional mountain crafts. She grew and sheared the sheep, spun the wool, made the dyes, and wove the thread for this coverlet. (Courtesy University of North Carolina Photo Lab, Chapel Hill.)

9-183
Another mountain woman continues generations of habit by beating clothes. Bay- ard Wootten made the pic- ture about 1934. (Courtesy North Carolina Collection.)

9-185
Sam G. Brinkley (1850– 1929), a Mitchell County teacher, let his beard grow, and it eventually reached his feet. He then joined a circus and toured the country ex- hibiting the world's longest beard. (Courtesy University of North Carolina Photo Lab, Chapel Hill.)

9-186 (below)
John R. Brinkley (1885– 1942) (standing right cen- ter), who grew up in Jackson County, earned his fame after leaving the state, particularly through his practice of trans- planting the sex glands of young goats into "tired" men for a renewal of sexual viril- ity. He also sold by mail mil- lions of dollars worth of patent medicines and oper- ated several hospitals. When the Kansas State Medical So- ciety revoked his license, he ran for governor of that state and lost to Alfred M. Landon in the disputed election of 1932. He then moved to Del Rio, Texas, and built the world's most powerful radio station across the border in Mexico. (Courtesy Kansas State Historical Society, Topeka.)

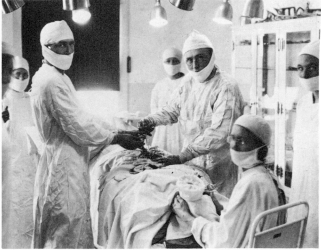

9-184
William A. Barnhill titled this touching picture "Children had few toys." The mountain boy and his pet chicken were photographed prior to 1917. (Courtesy Library of Congress.)

9-187
During the Depression, William Dudley Pelley (1890–1965), a native of New England, established in Asheville the headquarters of his Foundation for Christian Economics, which operated the short-lived Galahad College and published a flood of literature on mysticism and economics. The day following Hitler's rise to power in Germany, Pelley announced formation of the Silver Shirt Legion of America, an anti-Communist, anti-Semitic uniformed organization that grew to perhaps fifty thousand members. In 1936 he ran for president on the ticket of the Christian party, which he founded. During World War II he was sent to prison for criticism of American policies and for open sympathy for the Nazis. (Courtesy *Asheville Citizen-Times*.)

9-188
Scientists from around the world made Wadesboro something of a tent city in May 1900 during a total eclipse of the sun. At the station erected by the Smithsonian Institution, the telescope angles upward at right. (Courtesy North Carolina Collection.)

9-189
A devastating flood in July 1916 caused many deaths and millions of dollars in property losses in the mountains and foothills. Between Old Fort and Ridgecrest the fill slid down the mountain, leaving railroad tracks suspended. (Courtesy North Carolina Collection; reprinted, by permission, from Southern Railway Company, *The Floods of July, 1916* [Washington, D.C., 1917].)

9-190

The North Carolina Insane Asylum for the Colored at Goldsboro was photographed about 1915. Laundry hangs on the line in front of the building. (Courtesy Stephen Massengill, Raleigh.)

9-191

An overalled teacher and his students pose in their classroom at the Stonewall Jackson Manual Training and Industrial School near Concord prior to 1915. The school for wayward boys was established by the General Assembly of 1907. (Courtesy North Carolina Collection; reprinted from the *Uplift*, January 1915.)

9-192

Prisoners are shown clearing a railroad track in western North Carolina early in the century. Convicts sometimes were hired out to private enterprise. Armed guards stand on the flatcars. (Courtesy Manuscript Department, Duke University Library.)

9-193
J. Z. McLawhon, superintendent of chain gangs for Pitt County, stands in right center with his mobile prison camp in the fall of 1910. The sheriff leans against the tree at right near a trusty with dogs. A cook and guitar player, both trusties, stand on the steps. The horse-drawn trailers served as sleeping quarters at night and dining rooms for meals; they were moved as the road work required. (Courtesy Library of Congress.)

9-194
Dr. Frank Holmes listens for any sign of life before pronouncing dead the last man to be legally hanged in Sampson County about 1909. Beginning the following year executions were carried out by the electric chair in the State Prison in Raleigh. (Courtesy North Carolina Collection; original owned by Jim Hubbard, Clinton.)

9-195
Pictures of lynchings are rare. This extralegal hanging of a white man occurred in Iredell or Rowan County early in the century. (Courtesy North Carolina Collection.)

9-196
During World War I the state's first Red Cross Auxiliary was established at Fassifern School at Hendersonville in an effort to "humanize" the war. Here the women are knitting and sewing for the benefit of war refugees. (Courtesy North Carolina Collection; reprinted from *The Sapphire* [1918].)

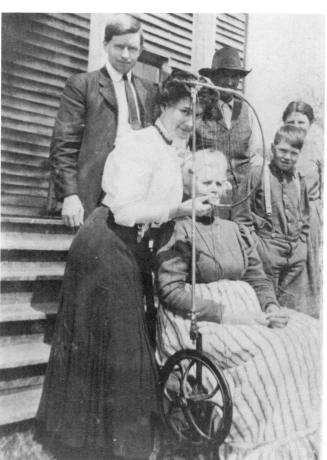

Mr. Hyatt, by unanimous consent, introduced S. B. 676, an act to provide for woman suffrage in North Carolina. Referred to Committee on Insane Asylums.

9-198
This entry in the *Senate Journal* of 1897 explains the fate of the first women's suffrage bill introduced in the General Assembly. (Courtesy North Carolina Collection.)

9-197
Dr. Daisy Zachary McGuire began practicing dentistry in 1899 and in 1912 joined practice with her husband, Dr. Wayne Patrick McGuire (standing behind the portable chair with foot pedal), in Sylva. They shared an office for sixty-five years before retiring in 1977, and their three daughters followed them into the profession. She died at age 100, he at age 94. (Courtesy Mountain Heritage Center, Western Carolina University, Cullowhee.)

9-199
Suffragettes and a lone male sympathizer holding a baby were pictured about 1920. Gertrude Weil of Goldsboro stands at far left. Parades and public meetings carried the plea for equal voting rights to all sections of the state. (Courtesy NCDA&H.)

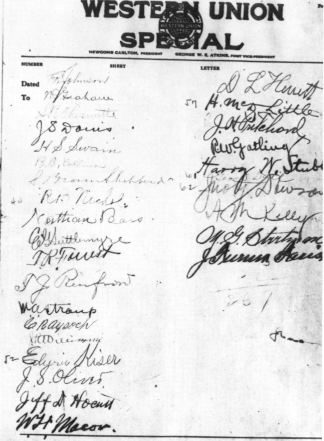

9-200
More than half of the members of the house in 1920 signed this telegram to the General Assembly of the neighboring state of Tennessee. (Courtesy North Carolina Collection.)

9-201
Lillian Exum Clement was nominated for the house of representatives by Buncombe County Democrats before she was given the right to vote and was elected in the fall following national ratification of the Nineteenth Amendment. As the first woman member of the legislature, "Brother Exum"—as colleagues called her—was well received. She married E. Eller Stafford during the session; she died in 1924. (Courtesy NCDA&H.)

9-202
Some women found their way to the professions and "public work," but most of them remained homemakers like Mrs. Mettie Macon Lowe, here removing yeast bread from her wood-burning Majestic cookstove. (Courtesy Randolph County Historical Society.)

9-204
An Indian family poses outside their stick-chimneyed log cabin in eastern North Carolina. (Courtesy NCDA&H.)

9-203
A Cherokee girl with her white doll was photographed in 1900 by James Mooney of the Smithsonian Institution. (Courtesy Smithsonian Institution National Anthropological Archives.)

9-205
The first state-supported institution for Indians grew into a college that went through several name changes; it is now Pembroke State University. (Courtesy NCDA&H.)

9-206
The Indians of Sampson County took the name Coharie and in 1911 erected this school in Herrings Township. The photograph was made about 1915, when the school was operated without government assistance. (Courtesy North Carolina Collection.)

9-207
Sylvester Chahuska Long was born of mixed blood in Winston-Salem in 1892. He assumed an Indian identity, attended Carlisle School, defeated Jim Thorpe in three footraces, and moved to Canada in whose armed forces he served during World War I. He entered journalism, claimed to be a Blackfoot Indian, acquired the name "Chief Buffalo Child Long Lance," and became something of a celebrity after playing the lead in the motion picture *The Silent Enemy*. He committed suicide in California in 1932. (Courtesy Glenbow-Alberta Institute, Calgary, Alberta.)

9-208
"Aunt Chloe" was virtually a mother to little Alice Noble, daughter of University of North Carolina professor M. C. S. Noble, and was treated much as a member of the family. But she was careful not to cross the invisible line that separated the races early in the century. (Courtesy North Carolina Collection.)

9-209, 9-210, and 9-211
Contradictions in racial segregation as practiced in
North Carolina are exhibited
in these three photographs
taken during a neighborhood
corn shucking near Stem,
Granville County, in November 1939. Blacks and whites
worked side by side, sharing
conversation and jokes. At
lunchtime ("dinnertime" on
the farm), however, they separated, and the whites ate
first. Afterward, the black
men were served at the same
table by the same Negro
cook. (Courtesy Library of
Congress; photographs by
Marion Post Wolcott, FSA.)

Teddy---Bassett---Booker T.

(Wilson News.)

Which of the three had you rather be:
Roosevelt, Bassett or Booker T.?
Teddy, the President, at Washington,
 D. C.,
Bassett, of Trinity of Durham, N. C.,
Or Washington, the negro, at Tuskegee?

Which of the three had you rather be:
Roosevelt, Bassett or Booker T.;
Teddy dined Booker, of Tuskegee,
On a social plane at Washington, D. C.,
He is lauded by Bassett, way above G
Beyond Carolina's pride—Zebulon B.

Now it is plain for every one to see
Which of the three you'd rather be,
Sink Teddy and Bassett in the deep, deep
 sea,
And be the big nigger from Tuskegee.
 —R. B. EVANS.

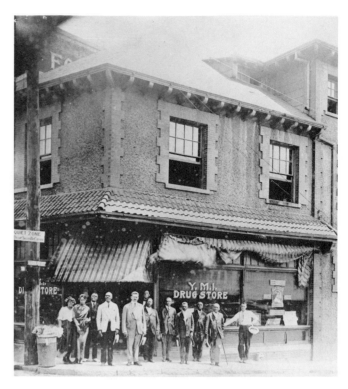

9-212
Josephus Daniels reprinted this racist poem in his *News and Observer* (18 December 1903) during his unsuccessful campaign for the dismissal of John Spencer Bassett from the Trinity College faculty. (Courtesy North Carolina Collection.)

9-214
The Young Men's Institute, constructed for them late in the nineteenth century by George Vanderbilt, provided blacks in Asheville with a community center. Barred from most publicly financed social and recreational facilities, black communities were forced to provide for their own needs. (Courtesy NCDA&H.)

9-213
A native of Henderson and granddaughter of a slave, Charlotte Hawkins Brown grew up in Massachusetts, where she was befriended by whites who assisted in her establishment of Alice Freeman Palmer Memorial Institute at Sedalia in Guilford County. Thousands of boys and girls, like the young women with her in this picture, were educated at this distinguished preparatory school for blacks. She died in 1961, and the school closed a decade later. (By permission of *Ebony* magazine.)

9-215
The Biltmore Hotel in Durham offered fine accommodations for black visitors to the "City of Negro Enterprises." Ironically, desegregation was the death knell for the once-thriving hotel. (Courtesy Stephen Massengill, Raleigh.)

9-216
The 10,500-ton Liberty ship *John Merrick*, launched 11 July 1943 by the Wilmington shipyard, was named for the cofounder of the black- owned North Carolina Mutual Life Insurance Company. (Courtesy North Carolina Mutual Life Insurance Company, Durham.)

9-217
Ration books were issued to all families, and stamps were required for the purchase of scarce items of food, clothing, and automotive products. (Courtesy NCDA&H.)

9-218
As in the earlier world war, large numbers of North Carolina troops were assigned to the Thirtieth Infantry Division. Here Tar Heels are shown picking their way— wary of snipers—through the rubble of Mortain, France. North Carolinians fought in Africa, Europe, Asia, and on dozens of Pacific islands. (Courtesy United States Army.)

9-219
Major George E. Preddy, Jr., of Greensboro holds up six fingers to signify his record-making mission—the shooting down of a half dozen Nazi planes in one day while escorting heavy bombers over Germany in 1944. On Christmas Day following, he destroyed two German planes before his own craft, *Cripes-A-Mighty*, was accidentally shot down by friendly anti-aircraft fire. Four months later, First Lieutenant William R. Preddy was also shot down on a mission and was buried beside his brother at St. Avold, France. (Courtesy United States Air Force.)

9-220
A soldier is interviewed on a battlefield by Edward R. Murrow, a native of Guilford County, whose wartime broadcasts made him the most celebrated newsman of his time. (Courtesy Edward R. Murrow Center of Public Diplomacy, Tufts University.)

10. Swept into the Mainstream, 1945–1984

During the upheaval called Reconstruction, North Carolina experienced political and social changes so alien to its customs that its usually temperate people yielded to the temptations of immoderation—even violence—at the close of the century in the attempt to arrest those changes and "redeem" the state. In the first half of the twentieth century, the state moved slowly toward an amelioration of the most glaring practices of racial repression and, in the context of the South, bleached some of the worst stains from its collective soul. In concerns other than human relations, progress also was made, and the North Carolina to which thousands of servicemen returned in 1945 exhibited, on the whole, good humor, vigor, and optimism. Veterans in great numbers took advantage of the "G.I. Bill" to attend college, setting an example for youngsters in communities never before represented in academe. They occupied a special status among a grateful people, and many of them were soon thrust into leadership roles.

The state's economy was healthy, and the administration of R. Gregg Cherry—the last governor closely associated with the "Shelby Dynasty"—was blessed with revenues ample for large increases in expenditures for education, health, mental health, and other human services. Sufficient funds were set aside to pay off the entire general fund debt.

Thus as late as 1948 there was little public perception that the state and nation faced problems beyond the obvious need for a return to normalcy and a resumption of the march toward greater prosperity and a better life for the people. Few observers sensed the degree to which the removal of external threats would encourage domestic reform movements that in less than a half century would fuel political, social, and economic revolutions comparable to the societal convulsions of the Reconstruction era. Likewise, few North Carolinians could foresee that their concerted efforts to steer their ship of state into the mainstream of American society eventually would succeed only too well: North Carolina would be swept along with that mainstream, unable to control its own rudder. In the past, change had usually come grad-

ually, if not gently; in the postwar era, it would come in torrents. North Carolina's indigenous character would be severely tested.

In retrospect, a portent of the future appeared in the elections of 1948. W. Kerr Scott, an Alamance County dairyman then serving as commissioner of agriculture, knitted together a tenuous alliance of farmers and industrial workers in his successful campaign for governor; and former governor J. Melville Broughton ousted William B. Umstead, who had been appointed by Cherry to the United States Senate to succeed Josiah W. Bailey, who died in 1946. The election of both Scott and Broughton over "machine" candidates indicated that the old political alliances were breaking down. In the presidential election, Strom Thurmond's states' rights party unfurled the flag of racial separatism, but received less than 10 percent of the vote, and Harry S Truman easily carried the state over Thomas E. Dewey.

Unorthodoxy was Scott's hallmark. Elected without obligations to what he called "special interests," he put on the cloak of populism and prodded a reluctant legislature into large appropriations for his "Go Forward" program. The General Assembly of 1949, for instance, voted more than $400 million for operation of state agencies and institutions and authorized a record-breaking capital improvements program: $75 million for state agencies and institutions, $25 million to help local governments provide school buildings, and $7.5 million in bonds to provide facilities for ocean-going vessels at the ports at Wilmington and Morehead City. More dramatic, however, was the approval by referendum of the issuance of $200 million in bonds— to be repaid by a cent-a-gallon gasoline tax increase—for road construction.

In an effort to increase efficiency and responsiveness to the public, Scott weeded out "Piddling Petes" whose bureaucratic habits slowed implementation of his policies. He prodded public utilities companies to extend their lines, and during his administration the percentage of homes with electricity rose to 87.5 percent, and those with telephones increased by more than a third. A program for improved health facilities was aided by federal funds, and more new hospitals were built during Scott's term than in any previous four-year period.

The tobacco-chewing governor's penchant for the unexpected and dramatic was illustrated following the death of Senator Broughton in March 1949. Turning aside scores of applicants and recommendations, Scott dropped a bombshell at the end of a speech in Chapel Hill, commenting, as if by afterthought, that he had persuaded Frank Porter Graham to accept appointment to the Senate seat. The announcement electrified the state and attracted national attention because Graham, president of the University of North Carolina, was perhaps the South's best-known liberal. In fact, his association with "left-wing" organizations had led to a recommendation by the Atomic Energy Commission's security review committee that Graham be denied access to atomic secrets. An attempt by Ohio Senator John Bricker to block his seating in the Senate fizzled, and as political tongues continued to wag in North Carolina, Graham was sworn in. The new senator generally supported the policies of President Truman, but his advocacy of civil rights legislation was tempered by political reality. He opposed, for instance, a strong federal equal employment practices act, though he favored its intent.

10-5

Smarting from the Graham appointment, conservatives settled on a Raleigh lawyer and former president of the American Bar Association, Willis Smith, to contest the seat in the Democratic primary of 1950. The campaign was reminiscent of those of the late 1890s: Race was the dominant issue. However, Graham was also attacked for his espousal of various liberal causes. The incumbent led in the first primary, but the votes for former senator Robert R. Reynolds and a fourth candidate denied Graham an absolute majority. Smith won in a runoff that nauseated North Carolinians to the extent that they have never since elected a statewide candidate who blatantly exploited the race issue in a campaign. In the fall, Smith and Clyde R. Hoey—the latter running for a new six-year term—were elected.

10-6

10-7

Only once before—under Woodrow Wilson—had North Carolinians been so influential in a national administration. Among the some three hundred North Carolinians holding top federal jobs in the Truman administration were Jonathan Daniels, the president's press secretary; Kenneth Royall of

Goldsboro, last secretary of war and first secretary of the army; Gordon Gray of Winston-Salem, secretary of the army; James Webb of Oxford, director of the budget and undersecretary of the Treasury; John S. Graham of Winston-Salem, assistant secretary of the Treasury; Dan Edwards of Durham, assistant secretary of defense; T. Lamar Caudle of Wadesboro, assistant attorney general; O. Max Gardner, undersecretary of the Treasury and ambassador-designate to England (he died as he prepared to sail for London); George Allen of Durham, ambassador to Iran, Yugoslavia, and India; and Capus Waynick of High Point, ambassador to Nicaragua and Colombia.

10-9

10-8

Though successful in pushing his programs through the legislature, Scott was unable to transfer his voter appeal to other candidates, such as Frank Graham in 1950 and his choice for governor, Judge Hubert E. Olive, in 1952. Former senator William B. Umstead won the Democratic nomination for governor and was elected in the fall. Scott was even denied the chairmanship of the state's delegation to the Democratic National Convention, but he and several other Tar Heels successfully supported the presidential nomination of Adlai Stevenson, some of whose forebears came from North Carolina.

Political alliances shifted dizzily in the next six years. Senator Smith died in June 1953, and Umstead appointed to the seat former state senator Alton A. Lennon, who in turn was defeated by Kerr Scott a year later. Scott, too, died in office in 1958, the seventh death or defeat of incumbents in this particular seat in twelve years (Bailey, Umstead, Broughton, Graham, Smith, Lennon, and Scott). Meanwhile, in 1954 the state's senior senator, Clyde Hoey, also died, and Governor Umstead appointed Justice Sam J. Ervin, Jr., to the vacancy. In all, five North Carolina senators served in the Eighty-third Congress. In November 1954, Umstead himself died after a long illness, and Luther H. Hodges, elected lieutenant governor in 1952 in a novel and individualistic campaign, ascended to the governor's chair with few debts to old-line politicians.

Unfettered by patronage obligations, Hodges exercised aggressive leadership in the fields of economic development and governmental administration. The "Businessman Governor" devoted special efforts to streamlining the government, and the legislature responded by creating in 1955 the nine-

10-10

member State Board of Higher Education; in 1957 the State Department of Administration, the State Prison Department, and the reorganized State Highway Commission; and in 1959 the Department of Water Resources. Hodges conducted a vigorous campaign to attract new industry to the state, and during his incumbency—despite a recession in 1957—about a billion dollars was invested in new or expanded industry. He led a foreign mission to bring investments to North Carolina, and back home he promoted plans for the development of a Research Triangle Park in the Raleigh–Durham–Chapel Hill area. The state's biennial budget went over the billion-dollar mark in 1959 for the first time.

10-11   Hodges steered the state on a moderate course during years of litigation over segregated public schools. The United States Supreme Court's decision declaring unconstitutional the "separate but equal" system of public school segregation was announced only six months prior to his succession to the governorship; consequently the issue fell directly upon his administration. A variety of policies were adopted to give the state time to adjust to the inevitable, and Hodges sought to maintain confidence in the schools without resorting to Napoleonic gestures and blatant resistance. That Hodges succeeded in avoiding the label of racist despite the fact that little mixing of the races took place during his administration was demonstrated when President John F. Kennedy appointed him secretary of commerce.

Many observers viewed the liberal administration of Kerr Scott in 1949–53 as an aberration, but the elections of 1960 demonstrated that North Carolina politics had indeed undergone complex changes. Terry Sanford, a Fayetteville attorney who cut his political teeth in the Scott organization, conducted a broad-based campaign that attracted large numbers of women, blacks, and the young. Maintaining that it was not good enough for North Carolina to hold first rank in the South, Sanford said, "I want North Carolina to move into the mainstream of America." His chief opponent, I. Beverly Lake, a law professor who, ironically, had supported Frank Graham in 1950, based his campaign upon conservative issues, particularly resistance to court-ordered desegregation. Many voters, remembering the odious campaign of 1950, recoiled from this injection of racial issues, and Sanford was nominated by a margin of 75,000 votes in a heated second primary. The election of

Sanford in the fall on a liberal platform was all the more significant because it coincided with the largest vote in the state's history for a Republican presidential candidate.

Sanford's courage—exhibited as a candidate when he broke with the "Solid South" by supporting John F. Kennedy for the Democratic presidential nomination—was quickly tested when it became clear that additional taxes would be required for the implementation of his proposal for greatly increased funds for "quality education" and human services. He persuaded a reluctant General Assembly to remove virtually all of the exemptions from the state's 3 percent sales tax, a levy that his opponents gleefully labeled "Terry's tax." Teachers' salaries were increased substantially, additional personnel was provided the school system, changes were made in the administrative structure of the educational system, and a liberalized operating budget was provided for other state agencies and institutions. The governor's legislative victory, however, was not without political costs: In the fall the voters rejected all of the ten proposed capital improvements bond issues—the first such repudiation since 1924—and in the off-year campaign of 1962, Republicans elected two congressmen, swept the legislative delegation from Guilford County, and showed surprising gains in several areas of the state. 10-12 10-13

Still, the General Assembly of 1963—meeting for the first time in the new State Legislative Building—responded to Sanford's prodding by further increasing appropriations for education and other human programs. Two-year colleges at Asheville, Charlotte, and Wilmington were elevated to state-supported four-year institutions, and machinery was established for a comprehensive system of community colleges, technical institutes, and industrial education centers, long advocated by W. Dallas Herring, chairman of the State Board of Education. Innovative institutions were established—like the Governor's School for gifted and talented students, the School of the Arts for both high school and college students, the Advancement School for eighth-grade underachievers, the Learning Institute to evaluate various teaching and learning techniques and to apply them to the schools, and the Film Board, which put the state into the business of making motion pictures.

One of the most publicized undertakings was the incorporated North Carolina Fund—financed largely by the Ford Foundation and other major 10-14 foundations—which encouraged projects to improve the economic lot of North Carolinians. Sanford appointed more blacks and women (including Susie Sharp to the North Carolina Supreme Court) than any previous governor, and he established a Good Neighbor Council and a Mayors Cooperating Committee to promote interracial peace and cooperation.

But after several administrations of aggressive gubernatorial leadership, the people in 1964 appeared ready for a return to normalcy, and the three major Democratic candidates for the governorship—federal judge Richardson Preyer, superior court judge Dan K. Moore, and attorney I. Beverly Lake—reflected that mood. Lake, still the personification of opposition to court-ordered desegregation, was eliminated in the first primary, but he threw his support in the runoff to Moore, who was nominated by a large majority. In the fall 10-15 Moore and President Lyndon Johnson carried North Carolina for the Democrats.

In keeping with the mood of the state, Moore's administration was less innovative than Sanford's, but in its own quiet way it built upon the progress of the past several years. Promoting the slogan "Total Development," Moore was interested in getting the job done rather than basking in the credit; consequently, the press showed less interest in the activities of the governor's office. Moore's administration, despite its relaxed pace, did shepherd significant measures through the legislature, including a 30 percent increase in teachers' salaries, the incorporation of Charlotte College into the state university system, the establishment of a regional university system (Agricultural and Technical, Appalachian, East Carolina, and Western Carolina), changes in the structure of state government (a new Department of Correction and a Court of Appeals, for example), traffic safety laws, a requirement for the annual inspection of motor vehicles, and an act outlawing the wearing of masks or burning of crosses for the purpose of frightening people. Extensive public attention was directed toward a law that authorized "brown bagging" (that is, permitting patrons to carry concealed alcoholic beverages into designated eating places that allowed mix-it-yourself drinks). Despite increased appropriations, income taxes were lowered, and the people approved a $300 million bond issue for highway construction and maintenance. Moore's low-key manner was evident in his handling of matters of racial controversy, and he gave strong support to an upgraded Good Neighbor Council.

In the quadrennial elections of 1968, Robert W. Scott won the Democratic nomination for governor over another son of a former governor (J. Melville Broughton, Jr.) and the first black candidate for the office (Reginald A. Hawkins). In 10-16 the lieutenant governor's race, Margaret Taylor Harper, the first woman to run for statewide office, polled nearly 150,000 votes in losing to Hoyt Patrick Taylor, Jr. Scott defeated Republican James C. Gardner, and thus exactly twenty years after Kerr Scott and Pat Taylor, Sr., had held the state's highest offices, their sons duplicated their accomplishment. Emboldened by their election of thirty-three legislators two years earlier and by increasing disaffection between southern Democrats and their national party, the Republicans waged a vigorous presidential campaign. For the first time since the Civil War, the Democratic candidate (Hubert Humphrey) came in third, with only 464,113 votes against 496,188 for George C. Wallace on the American party ticket and 627,192 for Republican Richard Nixon. The Democrats carried only twelve counties in the presidential election, but in Guilford they elected the first twentieth-century Negro delegate to the state house of representatives, Henry E. Frye.

Scott, the first of three successive young governors, bucked the conservative trend and successfully proposed tax increases to fund the largest biennial budgets to that time (reaching $4.3 million for 1971–73). Tobacco, which had remained inviolate from state excise taxes, finally fell victim to a two-cents-per-pack levy. A levy was also placed on soft drinks, and an additional two-cents-per-gallon tax was placed on gasoline. Education continued to receive the major share of general fund revenues. Public kindergartens were first placed in the public schools; career and occupational education programs were installed in the middle grades of high school; and public transportation was provided for handicapped students. Asheville-Biltmore and Wilmington colleges were elevated to university status within the Consolidated University, and five more colleges were given regional university status: Elizabeth City, Fayetteville, North Carolina Central, Pembroke, and Winston-Salem. State aid was extended to the two private medical schools; major increases were provided for human services, law enforcement, and environmental management; the Council on State Goals and Policies was established; the state was divided into seventeen multicounty planning regions; and the first appropriation was made for a state zoo.

The state constitution was amended to lower the minimum voting age to eighteen and to require the General Assembly to reduce the number of state administrative departments to not more than twenty-five. Implementation of the latter requirement was begun in 1971 with the consolidation of existing agencies into cabinet-level departments headed by secretaries appointed by the governor. Some of the predictions of opponents of reorganization appeared to come true when the new super departments developed top-heavy bureaucracies, transferred professional decision making to political employees, and exposed highly trained career employees to the patronage system. Higher education did not escape reorganization; the sixteen public colleges (excluding the community college system) were brought under a thirty-two-member board of governors elected by the General Assembly, though individual campuses retained boards of trustees with reduced powers.

10-18

In 1972 the state held its first presidential primary, and, surprisingly, former governor Terry Sanford failed to carry his own state, losing to George C. Wallace by more than 100,000 votes. Shirley Chisholm, a black congresswoman from New York, received 61,723 votes. For governor, the Democrats nominated Hargrove Bowles, Jr., over Pat Taylor, Jr. (with Reginald Hawkins and Wilbur Hobby, a white labor leader, each receiving over 50,000 votes), and the Republicans chose a quiet, young Watauga County legislator, James E. Holshouser, Jr. Nick Galifianakis ousted incumbent B. Everett Jordan for the Democratic senatorial nomination and faced Republican Jesse Helms, whose conservative "Viewpoint" television and radio editorials were familiar throughout the state. In the general election the Democratic party plunged to its nadir: It carried only two counties (Orange and Northampton) in the presidential election and lost both the governorship and the Senate seat. The Republicans also held on to four congressional seats, and their losing candidate for secretary of state, Grace J. Rohrer, received 603,226 votes—the largest total ever given a woman in North Carolina.

With Helms in Washington attracting national attention to his conservative views, the youthful Holshouser pursued a more progressive course in the state and maintained a surprisingly good working relationship with the Democratic-controlled legislature. Through the irony of politics, the reorganization of state government, begun under the Democrats, constituted a Santa's bag of gifts to the

Republicans. To head the statutory departments Holshouser chose political unknowns, several of them relative newcomers to the state. In services provided, however, the Republican administration was hardly distinguishable from preceding ones. Services were expanded and new programs were begun without additional taxes. The kindergarten program was extended throughout the state, class sizes were limited, the community college system was expanded, and the reorganization of higher education was implemented. Special attention was given to establishing rural health facilities and expanding the state parks system, and a bipartisan effort led Congress to block construction of a dam in Virginia by incorporating twenty-six miles of the New River in northwestern North Carolina into the Wild and Scenic Rivers System.

10-19

Anticipating an altered relationship between state, local, and federal governments ("New Federalism" was in his vocabulary as early as 1974), Holshouser instituted a new format for the budgeting process, and he appointed a special efficiency study commission, headed by banker Archie K. Davis, to which private businesses contributed about seventy top executives for several months. The commission submitted 676 recommendations, more than 80 percent of which were adopted at a claimed annual saving of $80 million. Holshouser also established the Governor's Commission on Community Participation to encourage volunteerism and the Office of Minority Business Enterprise to stimulate nonwhite economic development, and he installed a toll-free telephone line to the office of his "ombudsman." In his final year in office—the bicentennial of the nation's independence—the state reached a billion dollars each in industrial development, in the value of the tobacco crop, and in income from tourists.

In 1976 the gubernatorial nomination of James B. Hunt, Jr. (then lieutenant governor), without the necessity of a second primary, and his record-breaking vote (nearly 1.1 million) in the general election captured the headlines. Less noticed but nonetheless significant, Howard N. Lee received the largest vote ever given a Negro in losing to James C. Green for lieutenant governor, and Jessie Rae Scott, former first lady, and Lillian Woo, a Hawaiian native who had been in the state only six years, received the most votes ever cast for women in a primary in their unsuccessful races for commissioner of labor and state auditor, respectively. Hunt appointed Lee and two (eventually

10-21

10-20

three) women to his cabinet and placed many other blacks and women on state boards and commissions.

Hunt was elected by the efforts of the most vigorous and polished political organization of the century, his supporters covering the spectrum from liberal activists to conservative stand-patters. He moved as easily among tobacco-chewers as among afternoon tea-drinkers, and he attracted more media attention than any governor since Terry Sanford. Buoyed by his huge vote and the presence of a friendly Democrat in the White House, Hunt's office moved quickly to extend his control of the executive branch, a procedure made easier by the recent reorganization of state government and the wholesale departure of Republicans from key positions.

The General Assembly of 1977 approved practically all of the governor's proposals and adopted a biennial budget of just under $8 billion, an eightfold increase in twenty years. A graphic proof of Hunt's influence was his successful advocacy of greater power for the governorship. Previous chief executives had proposed amending the constitution to grant the governor the right of veto and of serving a second term, but only Hunt had the boldness to push for them strenuously. A shrewd negotiator, he yielded on the veto proposal, but the two-term amendment was passed by the legislature and narrowly approved by the voters in a referendum.

Universally assumed to be a candidate for a second term in 1980, the governor managed to maintain his influence during what otherwise would have been his "lame duck" legislature. Again most of his recommendations were approved, though there was a belt-tightening owing to the slowing in the growth rate of state revenues. The economy in North Carolina remained generally good, however, and the work force reached 2.6 million in 1979.

10-22 Hunt was reelected in 1980 by an even larger vote than he had received four years earlier. In his new term, the recession tempered his ambitious plans for the state, but it failed to alter his forceful style. His advocacy of a three-cents-per-gallon gasoline tax increase to fund much-needed repairs on the road system resulted in little political fallout when the oil companies lowered their prices almost simultaneously with the imposition of the tax. Most of the governor's other proposals—including the establishment of a microelectronics center, greater expenditures for teacher training in the sciences and mathematics, and stricter laws relating to drunken driving—were acted on favorably. Hunt took a special interest in promoting volunteerism

in the public schools, starting a program under which many of the schools were "adopted" by a business, civic group, or church. The tug-of-war over the balance of powers between the executive and legislative branches was at least temporarily tipped toward the governor when legislative representation on boards and commissions was challenged on constitutional grounds. Hunt was active at the national level in the Democratic party and in governors conferences, and as 1984 approached, he was widely predicted to become a candidate for the Senate seat held by Jesse Helms. Some of his supporters even proposed him for a place on the national Democratic ticket.

His popularity notwithstanding, Hunt was forced to share the political spotlight in North Carolina with Republican Senator Jesse Helms, who won reelection in 1978 with the help of a $7 million fund raised by his campaign arm, the Congressional Club. Furthermore, while Hunt was winning with ease, Helms's forces contributed to the surprising defeat of Senator Robert Morgan by Republican John East, an East Carolina University professor, and to the victory of Ronald Reagan in the presidential campaign. For the first time since 1872, both of the state's senators were Republicans. (Morgan had been elected in 1974 to succeed Senator Sam J. Ervin, Jr., the folk hero of the con- 10-23 gressional Watergate hearings that led to President Nixon's resignation. Ervin voluntarily retired to Morganton, where he continued to speak out on constitutional issues.)

This disintegration of the one-party system in North Carolina did not occur in a vacuum, of course, for marked changes were also taking place in other regions of the country. For instance, the war in Vietnam involved thousands of North Carolinians, shattered national unity, and served as a catalyst for a variety of movements that challenged traditions. Still, the most astute observer in 1949 could hardly have foreseen the revolution that would occur in North Carolina politics within a third of a century.

Of all the issues that contributed to the resurgence of the Republican party, entrance into the political arena by large numbers of blacks was the most profound. This is not to say that the issues themselves were racist but rather that the growing strength of the black vote encouraged the Democratic party to espouse policies—particularly economic policies—that increasingly alienated its historically conservative constituency. So long as the state's Democratic leaders inveighed against the liberalism of the national party—even while occasionally supporting it—they generally were tolerated by voters conditioned to party loyalty. It was when leaders of the state party appeared to *accept* the philosophy of the national organization that masses of Democrats voted Republican. Conservative Democrats who had voted for Dwight Eisenhower and Richard Nixon in presidential elections were hardly conscience-stricken, therefore, when they helped elect Jim Holshouser, Jesse Helms, John East, and several Republican congressmen. Party loyalty was no longer a virtue in the eyes of many voters. Issues replaced party labels; in 1978, for example, when Republican Jesse Helms was re-elected to the United States Senate, Democratic registrants outnumbered Republicans 1,764,126 to 567,039.

Since 1900, two generations of blacks had grown up as second-class citizens. Only a few had managed to surmount the "literacy" hurdle and gain admittance to the voter registration lists. In the Locust Hill precinct of Caswell County, for instance, the Reverend Henry Badgett was a registered voter, a "privilege" reflecting the respect with which the Baptist minister was held by local whites. A few young black men returning from the war were bold enough to appear before the registrar, a kind-hearted spinster who enrolled them because of their patriotic service. By 1950, more blacks had passed the literacy test and were voting in rural precincts like Locust Hill; in some urban districts large numbers of Negroes were registering and voting. It was not until after the courts struck down the literacy requirement, however, that blacks in great numbers were admitted to the registration lists. Soon massive campaigns were underway for the registration of minorities, and in a number of rural counties blacks came to outnumber whites on the voter lists.

Reginald A. Hawkins, a Charlotte dentist, the first candidate of his race in the twentieth century to seek statewide office, garnered 129,808 votes in the Democratic primary for governor in 1968. That fall, Henry E. Frye of Guilford County became the first black in the century to be elected to the General Assembly. The following year, Howard N. Lee of Chapel Hill was the first black to be elected mayor of a predominantly white southern town, and in 1973, Clarence Lightner won the mayorship of Raleigh. These victories reflected more than a growing black vote; they also reflected the willingness of many whites to vote for minority

candidates. Polarization appeared on the wane. In 1976, Mayor Lee received 229,195 votes in his losing race for lieutenant governor and subsequently became the first of his race to hold a cabinet appointment. Richard C. Erwin four years later was appointed a federal judge by President Carter. In 1981, Wiley Lash ran so far ahead of the ticket in the campaign for Salisbury city councillor that he would have been elected without a single Negro vote; his fellow councilmen, all white, promptly elected him mayor. In 1982 the number of blacks in the General Assembly increased to twelve following a redistricting struggle that saw the United States Department of Justice reject several proposed plans. Finally, in 1983, Henry Frye became the first black to don the robe of a state supreme court justice.

These examples of black successes in politics, nevertheless, are unimpressive in the face of statistics: Although blacks constituted over 22 percent of the population in 1981, they occupied only 255 of 5,037 elected offices in North Carolina—almost exactly 5 percent. The potential influence of black voters, therefore, lay less in electing candidates of their race than in helping choose candidates—almost invariably Democrats—favorable to political, economic, and social policies supported by much of the minority race. An unanswered question was whether the Democratic party, by catering to the burgeoning black vote, would permanently lose the conservatives, formerly its most loyal adherents. `10-24`

Firmly fixed by custom after 1900, separation of the races in social functions and public facilities continued after the ballot box was opened to blacks. Particularly in the segregated educational system, the fallacy of the "separate but equal" policy was glaring: While consolidation resulted in improved school facilities and transportation for whites, as late as the 1950s some counties retained small, unlighted, and unsanitary community schools for blacks, many of whom were required to walk several miles to and from school. State-supported colleges for blacks were doled out miserly portions of legislative appropriations for higher education, and most blacks who wanted to pursue professional studies had to leave the state.

The attack on school segregation actually began at the graduate level. In 1951 the University of North Carolina at Chapel Hill yielded to a court order and admitted a few Negroes to its law, medical, and graduate schools. Four years later the university was ordered to process applications for admission to its undergraduate school without re- `10-25`

10-26 gard to race. The barrier removed, blacks—albeit in small numbers—began taking their places in state-supported institutions, and by 1961 private colleges such as Davidson, Duke, and Mars Hill were admitting their first blacks. From that time forward, the debate at the college level centered not on whether Negroes should be admitted but on whether the institutions ought to change their academic standards in order to increase the number of minority students and on whether "disadvantaged" students, when admitted, ought to be expected to meet the same academic standards as other students.

The state was moving slowly toward integrating its public institutions of higher learning when, during the Carter administration, North Carolina was singled out with demands that, if accepted, would have transferred educational policymaking to the federal bureaucracy. The United States Department of Education, more concerned with numbers than standards, sought through the courts to set racial quotas and to transfer programs between institutions. The threat of a cutoff of federal funds not-

10-27 withstanding, President William Friday and the Board of Governors of the university system, with bipartisan political support, finally succeeded in negotiating a settlement in 1981 under which the educational integrity of the university was maintained and efforts were accelerated toward eliminating vestiges of racial separation on the sixteen campuses of the system. Ironically, by sharpening the competition for qualified minority students, the recruitment program dictated by the settlement created grave handicaps for predominantly black institutions already struggling for status or survival. It also threatened the traditional orientations of the individual institutions; for instance, whites soon outnumbered native Americans at Pembroke,

10-28 the nation's first state-supported four-year college for Indians.

Three years after the university admitted its first blacks, the dual system of secondary schools was voided. Profound shock followed the United States Supreme Court's ruling in 1954 declaring unconstitutional the "separate but equal" theory, on which the South had based its segregated school policy for more than half a century. The General Assembly of 1955 unanimously passed a resolution declaring, "The mixing of the races in the public schools within the state cannot be accomplished and if attempted would alienate public support to such an extent that they could not be operated successfully." As an immediate response to the rul-

ing, the legislature eliminated any reference to race in the school laws, delegated control over pupil assignment and transportation to local boards, and placed teachers on annual contracts.

A year later the General Assembly submitted to referendum an amendment to the constitution (referred to as the "Pearsall Plan," after Thomas J. 10-29 Pearsall, chairman of a special study commission which proposed it) which authorized the legislative body to establish by statute a means by which school units could, by popular vote, suspend the operation of their public schools. The amendment also empowered the legislature to provide for payment of educational expenses for the private education of any child "for whom no public school is available or for . . . a child who is assigned against the wishes of his parent . . . to a public school attended by a child of another race." The amendment was ratified by a decisive vote of 471,657 to 101,767, despite the opposition of a significant number of whites who rejected the notion that the state was under no obligation to maintain a free public school system.

Whatever its merit on principle or constitutional grounds, the amendment provided time during which the state could move, ever so reluctantly and slowly, toward implementation of the court's ruling. Governor Hodges and many state leaders were less concerned with resistance to integration than with maintaining public confidence in and support for the schools. The school boards of Charlotte, 10-30 Greensboro, and Winston-Salem broke precedent in 1957 by allowing the transfer of a dozen students to all-white schools. A few ugly demonstrations by whites failed to sabotage this courageous act, and several additional minority students were admitted the following year. In the fall of 1959 a few blacks entered previously all-white schools in Craven and Wayne counties.

When Terry Sanford was elected governor in 1961 on a platform of "quality education," the number of blacks in mixed schools was slightly over two hundred in eleven districts—a miniscule number, yet a considerable achievement for a people who five years before had believed integration impossible without destroying the school system. By 1965 many school districts operated on a "freedom of choice" plan; yet the Pearsall Plan's most drastic provision had not been invoked by a single school unit. By the time the plan was declared unconstitutional in 1966, it had served its purpose as a "safety valve."

Although the state adjusted to this profound

change in its traditions without the militant resistance that characterized this struggle in some southern states, desegregation was accompanied by problems both real and imagined. For instance, integration in community schools meant that the institutions were desegregated only to the extent that the school districts were racially mixed. Consequently, federal policy shifted to the busing of students outside their own communities to achieve "racial balance." In 1971 the United State Supreme Court upheld federal district judge James B. McMillan's order that the Charlotte–Mecklenburg County Board of Education utilize "any and all known ways of desegregation, including busing," and large-scale busing began in the fall. Other districts followed the controversial plan, which featured school buses passing in opposite directions, each transporting students far away from their neighborhoods.

To some who twenty years before had objected to the busing of white students past black community schools, the new plan appeared equally incongruous, and fierce opposition to busing helped account for the victories of Jesse Helms and John East. Thousands of white students left the public schools and enrolled in hastily established private schools, some of which offered no better education than that which could have been obtained in the schools from which the students had fled. Within ten years after the city of Durham began its experiment in busing, educational officials—including the city's black superintendent—voluntarily returned to the neighborhood school concept.

Meanwhile, progress was being made in eliminating other forms of racial discrimination. Less than six years after school segregation was declared unconstitutional, four students from the Agricultural and Technical College sat down at a lunch counter in Woolworth's department store in Greensboro and began a novel challenge against the separation of the races in public eating places. Their "sit-in" technique spread across the South and was instrumental in the removal of "whites only" signs from thousands of establishments. Sit-ins, protests, demonstrations, and boycotts, singly or combined, forced the opening of virtually all facilities except private clubs. Jim crow traditions fell one by one— separate drinking fountains, separate entrances to theaters, separate seating in public conveyances, separate hotels.

Victories won by dramatic confrontations were widely reported by the news media, but segrega-

tionist policies were also breached through quiet diplomacy. Raleigh's Sir Walter Hotel, for example, dropped its ban against blacks during negotiations with a committee arranging the joint meeting of the American Association for State and Local History and the Society of American Archivists during the Carolina Charter tercentenary. The registration of the first black guest went unnoticed by the press. The Good Neighbor Council and the Mayors' Cooperating Committee, established by Governor Sanford, sought to mediate disputes and to ease the trauma of changes reaching every community of the state, and the federally appointed North Carolina Advisory Committee to the United States Commission on Civil Rights monitored compliance with federal laws and decrees.

The broadening of the civil rights of blacks came neither as rapidly nor as easily as this brief recitation may suggest. The demonstrations, for instance, usually were successful only after long periods of confrontation and occasional violence between the integrationists and motley bands of counter-demonstrators. Racial tensions were heightened, and black organizations such as the National Association for the Advancement of Colored People and the Congress of Racial Equality— the latter headed by Asheville's Floyd McKissick— were countered by white supremacy groups. The Patriots of North Carolina proclaimed a goal of preserving "the purity of the white race and of Anglo-Saxon institutions," and the Ku Klux Klan went through several reincarnations as would-be grand dragons competed for power. With its chameleonic leadership and never a large membership, the Klan was a favorite subject for the news media, which gave an exaggerated impression of its strength. Even some staunch segregationists chuckled in 1958 when several hundred Lumbees, incensed by threats and cross-burnings, broke up a Klan rally near Maxton. The hooded Klansmen had to seek protection from the highway patrol, and two of them were subsequently indicted for incitement to riot.

Trials with racial and political overtones added tarnish to the image of North Carolina as a moderate state: the conviction of black Caswell County sharecropper Mack Ingram for assaulting a white woman by "leering" at her from a distance of seventy-five feet; the institutionalizing of two Negro boys from Monroe for allegedly kissing a white girl; the flight of Robert Williams to escape prosecution; the not-guilty verdict for Joan Little, accused of murdering her jailer; the conviction of

10-40 nine black men and one woman on charges of fire-bombing a white-owned business following race riots in Wilmington; the conviction of three blacks on charges of burning a stable at Charlotte; and the not-guilty verdict for four members of the Ku Klux Klan and two Nazis accused of shooting five
10-41 supporters of the Communist Workers party in
10-42 Greensboro.

The trials of the "Wilmington Ten," the "Charlotte Three," the participants in the "Greensboro Massacre," and the others, and the demonstrations they engendered, were widely and sometimes sensationally reported by the news media. Many North Carolinians felt that, regardless of the verdicts, the reporting was not always fair to the state. For instance, some of the news reports in 1982 of the conviction of two men for conspiring to enslave black migrant workers in Nash County failed to note that both of the convicted men were black and that neither was a North Carolinian.

"Women's liberation," begun modestly near the end of the previous century, made gains following extension of women's suffrage in 1920. At first a few, then more and more, women took elective or appointive positions, including legislative seats. Several women held influential positions in New Deal programs, and Ellen Black Winston headed the state's welfare program for nearly two decades before serving four years as a federal commissioner of public welfare. Eliza Jane Pratt won a special election in 1946 to serve the unexpired term of Congressman William O. Burgin. Governor Kerr
10-43 Scott broke precedent by appointing Susie Sharp to a superior court judgeship. She was elevated to the North Carolina Supreme Court by Terry Sanford and in 1974 became the first popularly elected female chief justice in the nation. In 1979 she and Chief Judge Naomi E. Morris of the court of appeals occupied high judicial posts simultaneously.
10-44 In 1977, Isabella Cannon, a 73-year-old retired librarian, won election in Raleigh as the state's first female mayor of a large city. Juanita Kreps of Duke University served as President Jimmy Carter's secretary of commerce. Grace Rohrer in 1973 occupied a seat in the Holshouser cabinet, followed in the Hunt administration by Sara Hodgkins, Sarah Morrow, and Jane Patterson. By 1979, 22 of the 170 seats in the General Assembly were held by women, 5 of them from Mecklenburg County, which regularly voted Republican in congressional races.

As leaders of the women's movement pointed out, these and other victories were statistically un-impressive, given that females constituted more than half the population. On the other hand, the influence of women on public policy was by no means limited to those holding office. Energetic and popular wives were immensely important in their husbands' political campaigns, and women were effective and highly visible lobbyists on public issues such as civil rights, abortion, and the antiwar movement. Recognizing the value of female support, both political parties designated seats for women in their organizations. Especially among the Democrats, a succession of women played key roles in the state and national parties—women such as Fay Webb Gardner, widow of the late governor; Emma Neal Morrison, wife of Governor Gardner's law partner; Bessie Bangert Ballentine, wife of the lieutenant governor; Gladys Avery Tillett, Lewellyn Williams Robinson, and Martha Clampitt McKay, national committeewomen; and Betty Ray McCain, state party chairman.

The submission of the Equal Rights Amendment to the states inaugurated a time of sharpened political activism for women. In the General Assembly of 1973 advocates of ratification, confident of legislative support but leery of a popular vote, helped defeat a referendum bill in the house, and the senate rejected ratification without the referendum provision. By the time the issue was taken up
10-45 again two years later, female opponents of ERA
10-46 had joined the fray, and both sides became in-
10-47 creasingly strident. Advocates stressed the equity of the first section of the amendment, which simply prohibited the denial or abridgement of rights "on account of sex," while opponents argued that passage would undermine the institution of marriage and clog the courts with malicious litigation. Not even personal telephone calls to some legislators from President Carter saved the amendment from repeated rejection. In 1982, in an act that illustrates the level of stridency and emotionalism of both sides in the campaign, a group of supporters sent an off-color poem and an envelope containing chicken manure to senators who voted to table the ratification bill, thus preventing a yes-or-no vote on the bill itself.

For those advocating greater involvement of women in political life, the battle over ERA was by no means a disaster, for the issue attracted tens of thousands of Tar Heel women—both supporters and opponents of the amendment—and thrust many of them into lobbying activities for the first time. Having been exposed to the political process, they were not likely to remain silent in the future.

Nor were male legislators likely to turn a deaf ear. Significantly, only days after the ERA was killed, the General Assembly amended a tenancy law to give wives equal legal rights to jointly held rental property, thus ending what sponsors exaggeratedly claimed was "the last major instance of sex discrimination in North Carolina law."

10-50
10-51 North Carolina, overwhelmingly agricultural in 1950, developed a diversified economy in the next three decades. Industry grew phenomenally; the year 1981 alone (the third best year in history) brought $2.1 billion in industrial expansion with an estimated 37,000 new jobs. Giant installations after the war included hydroelectric projects by the major power companies; P. Lorillard's new tobacco manufacturing plant at Greensboro and Philip Morris's $250 million facility at Concord; Western
10-48 Electric's installations at several locations; Texas
10-49 Gulf Sulphur's mining operations in Beaufort County; and Miller Brewing Company's high-wage operation in Eden.

In 1982 a survey of executives of the nation's 1,000 largest corporations, conducted by *Fortune* magazine, placed North Carolina second (behind Texas) as the most appealing state for companies wanting to build new plants. Contributing to the state's bright image were a friendly climate for industry, a generous labor supply, improved transportation and communication, favorable tax laws, and the growing reputation of the Research Triangle Park coupled with legislative appropriations for the establishment of a microelectronics center—the last a special project of Governor Hunt's.

Textiles produced by far the largest income among the manufactures of the state, but several other industries—including electrical equipment and chemical products, which were virtually nonexistent at the end of the war—showed even greater growth. By 1981, the estimated total value of manufactured products had reached $60 billion. Industry also underwent numerous corporate changes. Some of the famed family-owned companies, such as Cannon Mills, were bought by outsiders; and Burlington Mills, the largest textile firm in the world, grew even larger as it took over smaller companies.

The impressive figures of industrial growth masked the fact that North Carolina remained at or near the bottom of the states in wages paid to industrial workers. Nevertheless, from 1950 to 1979 the state's per-capita personal income rose from 69 to 84 percent of the national average, and

the cost of living—somewhere between 8 and 15 percent lower than the average of other states—partially made up the difference. Still, labor leaders argued that there was a direct correlation between the low percentage of Tar Heel laborers belonging to unions and the low wages. Union membership made only small gains in the state, and organized labor's membership drive, called "Operation Dixie," proved to be little more than an empty slogan. Labor relations were punctuated by only a few violent disputes, among the bitterest being a strike by the Textile Workers Union of America against the Harriet-Henderson Cotton Mills at Henderson in 1958–59. Violence flared, and Governor Hodges called out the National Guard. Eight union members, including Boyd E. Payton, TWUA's Carolinas director, were given prison terms for conspiring to blow up mill installations. Another long and angry dispute finally led in 1979 to the certification of the Amalgamated Clothing and Textile Workers Union as the bargaining agent at the Roanoke Rapids plant of the J. P. Stevens Company.

A novel social and economic experiment was launched in Warren County in 1973 when ground was broken for a black-built, black-run "new town" to be known as Soul City. With pledges of millions of dollars in assistance from the federal government, McKissick Enterprises issued a brochure pre- 10-52 dicting that by 1979 the town would have a population of 22,000, and that ten years later the number of residents would reach 50,000. As money and loan guarantees were generously dispensed by the Department of Housing and Urban Development, the General Accounting Office began investigating "unallowable expenses" and interlocking roles of members of the McKissick family. By 1978 the press was reporting "puny results" from the more than $19 million in federal grants, contracts, loans, and guarantees provided for the project; and *Time* magazine, referring to thirteen such communities receiving federal assistance, wrote that "HUD abandons a disaster." Two years later the Department of Housing and Urban Development bid $1.5 million for Soul City, thus buying back the project for which it had approved vast sums in federal grants and loan guarantees. On the property, according to the press, were 124 people, thirty-three houses, and fifteen industrial jobs. A HUD official was quoted as saying prior to the repurchase, "We've learned a very expensive lesson."

Agriculture underwent an equally phenomenal 10-53

change in the postwar decades. While the work force in manufacturing increased from 29 percent in 1950 to 33 percent in 1980, employment in agriculture fell from about one fourth of the work force to only 3.6 percent in the same thirty years.

10-54
10-56
Mechanization, which replaced scores of tasks from hand-milking of cows to hand-tying of tobacco, accounted for much of the drop in the farm population, but other contributing factors included the widespread availability of insecticides and the trend toward corporate farming. Family subsistence farms, so characteristic in 1945, were becoming subjects of folk-culture studies by the 1980s. The number of farms decreased from 288,508 in 1950 to 93,000 in 1980; the number of acres devoted to farms decreased from 19,317,937 to 11,700,000; and the average size of farms nearly doubled from 67 to 126 acres. Mules, so much a part of the farm scene fifty years before, were becoming less familiar to thousands of youngsters than camels and zebras. Wringing a chicken's neck, slopping a hog, thumping a watermelon, making a rabbit gum, cutting lightwood for kindling, drawing water from a well, and building an outdoor privy were becoming lost arts.

Despite the reduction of the number of people working on farms, agricultural production generally increased, with livestock, dairy cattle, and poultry leading the way. From 1950 to 1979, the total value of farm products rose from $804,303,000 to $3,413,439,000.

Cotton made a slight comeback in 1981 when about 80,000 acres were planted, but that was a far cry from the 1920s when 1.8 million acres were grown per year in North Carolina. Tobacco, the state's only billion-dollar crop, was threatened in the 1980s by efforts in Congress to abandon the crop quota and support system that agricultural officials credited with maintaining a high level of to-

10-55
bacco prices. A vigorous antismoking campaign, while cutting the number of new smokers, appeared to affect tobacco farmers emotionally more than economically.

Along the coast, commercial fishermen caught 355 million pounds of fish that sold for $68 million. North Carolina continued to lead the nation in the production of textiles, textile machinery, tobacco, household furniture, brick, hardwood veneer, hardwood plywood, feldspar, and mica.

The census returns of 1980 illustrated some of the results of a changing economy. With a popula-

tion of 5,874,429—a 15.5 percent increase in ten years—North Carolina displaced Massachusetts as the tenth most populous state. The trend from rural to urban living had been reversed; 55 percent of the people lived in nonmetropolitan areas, and the largest percentage increase occurred generally in counties with small populations. These figures, however, reflected not a return to agricultural pursuits but rather a return to rural living. More and more people, including many newcomers, chose to avoid the cities with their increasing problems, including higher taxes and crime. Still, the Piedmont retained the heaviest concentration of people. The mobility of the population was indicated by the fact that 24.2 percent of the residents were born outside the state, including 85,780 foreign born, triple the figure of ten years earlier. The percentage of high school graduates among the residents stood at 55.3, nearly a 50 percent increase in ten years, and the number of persons per family was 3.23, the lowest in memory. The average income per household for North Carolina was $14,876, nearly $2,000 below the national average, and 14.6 percent of the people were living below the poverty level (against 12.5 percent nationally).

By 1981 North Carolina, still the "Good Roads State," had the largest state-maintained highway system in the country—75,000 miles, every mile free from tolls—and tourism had become a $3 bil-

10-57
10-58
10-59
10-60
lion industry. The highway department, however, traditionally one of the most political of state agencies, on more than one occasion threatened the state's boast, "Good government is a habit in North Carolina." One scandal involved collusion between an employee of the department and a representative of a major producer of phosphorescent paint; another led to the conviction of several executives of construction companies on bid-rigging charges. For his inaugural address, Republican Jim Holshouser chose a site on Union Square facing the State Highway Building, promising "to plan, not plot . . . to pave, not politic." Like governors before and after him, he found the promise easier to make than to keep.

Railroad passenger service, except on through-trains, was virtually ended, though freight continued on the over four thousand miles of track, competing with truck fleets, a substantial number of them based in North Carolina. Air transporta-

10-61
tion became commonplace from the state's fifteen airports serving commercial and commuter lines. Piedmont, a Winston-Salem-based company, served

cities as distant as Dallas and Boston. The black-owned Wheeler Airlines made a promising beginning. The ports of Morehead City and Wilmington provided deep-water facilities for commercial vessels and an occasional cruise ship.

10-62 Live network television came to the state on 30 September 1950 when WBTV in Charlotte and WFMY in Greensboro, the state's first television stations, carried from South Bend the football game between the University of North Carolina and Notre Dame. For the occasion, reported the *Winston-Salem Journal*, "television parties—something you'll be hearing more of—were held in many homes whose rooftops are marked by pretzel-like television aerials." By 1982, twenty-eight television stations and more than three hundred radio stations were operating in North Carolina.

Fifty-five daily and 160 nondaily newspapers were published, plus a growing number of periodicals. The North Carolina Collection at the University of North Carolina received approximately three thousand periodical and serial titles published in North Carolina, including reports, newsletters, and popular, literary, scientific, professional, educational, political, denominational, business, and labor journals.

Each postwar administration gave high priority to public education, the recipient of a major portion of the state's budget. Since the Depression the state had provided personnel costs of the schools, and after 1949 additional aid was extended to assist in the construction or upgrading of buildings. Salaries of teachers, while lagging behind the national average, were steadily increased, and some units provided local salary supplements. Consolidation of smaller schools into larger ones was accelerated, particularly in the wake of desegregation with the closing of hundreds of formerly all-black community schools. By 1972 the number of schoolhouses was 2,054, down from 7,166 at the beginning of the century. In 1980 the 144 administrative units received 63 percent of their funds from the state, 24 percent from local sources, and 13 percent from the federal government.

Ironically, as appropriations for education mounted, public confidence in the schools waned. Grade inflation and social promotions enabled many students to be graduated from high school with inadequate basic skills, and the debate over "why Johnny can't read" became recriminatory—all this shortly after the literacy test for voting was

abolished and the age of suffrage was lowered to eighteen. The teachers' lobby defeated efforts toward a merit system under which salary increases for teachers would be based on performance rather than on longevity.

In 1977 the General Assembly decreed the introduction of competency testing of students. To graduate, students would have to pass a test certifying their abilities in basic math and language skills. Whether the tests and the accompanying appropriations reversed the decline in educational standards, they succeeded in quieting some of the more vocal proponents of the "return to basics" movement, who read press reports of improved test scores in succeeding years without questioning the base against which the scores were measured. Teachers understandably complained that informational instruction suffered because society had imposed on the schools responsibilities that traditionally had resided in homes, churches, and communities—that the schools had taken on the semblance of day-care centers. Despite these additional burdens and often with little support from their school officials, many 10-63 individual teachers resolutely attempted to maintain high standards, and thousands of students—even with diminished incentives of recognition—far surpassed the official requirements and prepared themselves for a career or for college.

Inheriting problems passed on by the high schools, colleges and universities became victims of similar leveling influences. Grade inflation was illustrated by the record of the University of North Carolina at Chapel Hill, where in 1977 more than 70 percent of the students in Afro-American studies, American studies, education, political science, sociology, and fourteen other programs were given As and Bs. The relaxation of requirements in basic subjects made it possible for a student to go through twelve grades of public school, four years of undergraduate college, and several years of professional school without ever having been exposed to a course classified as history.

Public higher educational facilities expanded phenomenally. The University of North Carolina grew from three to sixteen campuses through the consolidation of all state-supported senior institutions; 10-64 graduate programs multiplied; a four-year teaching hospital was established at East Carolina University; 10-65 the law school at North Carolina Central University was upgraded; a school of veterinary science was opened at North Carolina State University; and terms of the desegregation settlement in 1981 dictated special budgetary treatment of the historically black universities.

There were major developments also among pri-10-66 vate institutions. In the 1950s, Wake Forest College moved to its new location at Winston-Salem. In the following decade two new Methodist colleges were opened (Methodist at Fayetteville and Wesleyan at Rocky Mount), and St. Andrews Presbyterian at Laurinburg replaced Flora MacDonald, Presbyterian Junior College, and Peace (though Peace survived under new sponsorship). A number of junior colleges added two years of work, and some four-year colleges assumed the title of university. A law school was added at Campbell. North Carolina students attending in-state private colleges received tuition grants representing a fraction of the subsidy furnished by the taxpayers for students on campuses of the state university. For each North Carolinian who attended college outside the state, three non-residents entered North Carolina institutions. In 1981 the total enrollment in higher education in North Carolina was 188,178, of which 118,761 were in the public university system; in the same school year, over six hundred thousand persons took one or more courses (regardless of duration) in 10-67 the fifty-eight community and technical colleges.

One of the most controversial public issues of the postwar era involved the University of North Carolina at Chapel Hill, long a beacon of liberalism in the South. The issue itself was new, but its cause—the belief by some North Carolinians that the university corrupted the morals and minds of its students—was as old as the institution itself. Following World War II, reports out of Chapel Hill seemed—to many—to corroborate that im-10-68 pression. Junius Scales, an avowed Communist, and a small band of sympathizers operated in the community; the 1950 senatorial campaign revived charges that Frank Graham had been associated with radical causes; and student organizations, in inviting speakers to the campus, appeared almost exclusively to favor liberals and sometimes Communists or "fellow travelers." In 1963 the General Assembly enacted a law directing boards of trustees of state-supported colleges and universities to prohibit from speaking on their campuses anyone who was a member of the Communist party, who had advocated the overthrow of the constitution of the United States or of North Carolina, or who had pleaded the Fifth Amendment by refusing to answer questions concerning Communist or subversive activities.

The "speaker ban act"—or "gag law," as in-

censed academicians and civil libertarians called the new law—became a cause célèbre, and oppo- 10-69 nents whipped up protests against it on campuses 10-70 across the state. For two years the issue divided the people, damaged the state's image of moderation, weakened legislative confidence in the university, and threatened accreditation. Neither the opponents of the law, who called it an attack on academic freedom, nor its proponents, who considered it an attack on academic license, could take credit for amending the act in 1965: The victory lay with North Carolinians who recognized that the unofficial censorship of conservative viewpoints by faculties and students should not be replaced by the imposition of an official ban on radical speakers. The amendment transferred authority over campus speakers to the boards of trustees, which in turn delegated it to the chancellors. In 1968 a federal court declared the amended law too vague to be enforceable.

Churches faced increased competition from secular activities, and the religious observance of the 10-71 Sabbath waned as blue laws were repealed in most 10-72 urban areas. In 1982, over 3 million North Caro- 10-74 linians—54 percent of the population—were affiliated with one of fifty-six denominations. Baptists remained the largest sect, with over 1 million members, but in 1981 the Baptist State Convention recorded the first actual decrease in membership in its 151-year history; furthermore, Sunday school attendance was down markedly. Splintering of small sects continued, but the Methodists, the state's second largest denomination, and several others were at least partially reunited, and the Presbyterians north and south in 1983 healed a split that had existed since the Civil War era. William 10-73 Franklin (Billy) Graham of Charlotte emerged as the most famous North Carolinian of the time; his evangelistic crusades attracted enormous crowds in dozens of nations, and he was hosted by monarchs and presidents. Preachers utilized television as eagerly and successfully as did politicians, a fact that may partially help explain the decline in church attendance. The traditional doctrine of separation of church and state was challenged both by liberal ministers who equated Christianity with the welfare state and by fundamentalist preachers who placed God on the side of the free enterprise system.

Advances in the fields of journalism, literature, 10-78 and history were harbingers of increased interest in and support for other cultural activities. Millions around the world became familiar with the voices and faces of broadcasters Edward R. Murrow, who was born in Guilford County, David Brinkley, of Wilmington, and Charles Kuralt, who grew up in Charlotte. Vermont Connecticut Royster, born in Raleigh, was editor of the *Wall Street Journal*, and Tom Wicker of Hamlet, Gerald Johnson of Riverton, and Neil Morgan of the *San Diego Tribune* were widely read syndicated columnists. Jonathan Daniels, editor of the *News and Observer* (Raleigh), helped control the flow of news from the White House during the Truman administration.

Some authors born in North Carolina made their mark outside the state: Robert Ruark of Wilmington, Anne Tyler of Raleigh, Gail Godwin of Asheville, and Frank G. Slaughter of Oxford, novelists; Joseph Mitchell of Fairmont, short story writer; and A. R. Ammons of Whiteville, poet. North Carolina was not exclusively an exporter of literati, however, for several non-natives brought distinction with them to—or gained it in—their adopted state: Gerald Barrax, James Boyd, Julia Fields, Inglis Fletcher, Harry Golden, Randall Jarrell, Glen Rounds, Carl Sandburg, Betty Smith, and Manly Wade Wellman, among others.

Of greatest pride to Tar Heels, nonetheless, were writers who remained at home and brought credit to their native state: playwright Paul Green; novelists Bernice Kelly Harris, Ovid Pierce, Guy Owen, John Ehle, Reynolds Price, and Doris Betts; poets Fred Chappell, Robert Morgan, and James Applewhite; and Thad Stem, Jr., and Richard Walser, jacks-of-all-writing-trades. Three persons wore the title of poet laureate—Arthur Talmage Abernethy, James Larkin Pearson (who held it until his death at age 101), and Samuel Talmadge (Sam) Ragan. Age was no bar for Louis Round Wilson, longtime librarian at UNC–Chapel Hill, who celebrated his one hundredth birthday with a book of essays, and Charlotte Young of Black Mountain, who published a book of poetry on her centennial, then continued work on another.

History blossomed, both in literature and preservation. Hugh T. Lefler and Albert Ray Newsome's *North Carolina: The History of a Southern State* (1954) afforded the first one-volume textbook for college history courses, and for many years their grade-school text was standard. William S. Powell emerged as a productive writer of state history and compiler of historical source materials.

The State Department of Archives and History accelerated its publication of pamphlets for school students and source documents for adults. In the 1960s the department developed the largest and most comprehensive archival and records management program among the fifty states, and in 1964 it won the first Distinguished Service Award of the Society of American Archivists. In 1968 the department moved into new quarters, which included specially designed spaces for the State Archives, the Museum of History, and the State Library. The state administered a network of historic sites reaching from Fort Fisher on the coast to the Thomas Wolfe home in the west and including three battlefields, an Indian ceremonial center, an abandoned colonial town, the birthplace of the modern tobacco industry, and the site of the first documented discovery of gold in the United States. Local historical societies and a growing number of preservation groups and history museums stimulated greater interest in the heritage of their communities. All the while, history was losing ground as a course of study in the schools and colleges.

Both the rural panorama and the cityscape changed dramatically. The attrition in the built environment was accompanied by an increased concern for the preservation of historically and architecturally significant buildings. Following research and certification by the State Department (now Division) of Archives and History, hundreds of properties were placed on the National Register of Historic Places, and the rehabilitation and adaptive use of old structures became economically and socially attractive. Usually a state conservative in taste, North Carolina was introduced to more daring building designs after the war. Graduates of North Carolina State University's School of Design were particularly effective in helping to change the state's architectural tastes.

The campaign of Katherine P. Arrington and the State Art Society to provide the state with a first-class collection received a major boost when the legislature of 1947 appropriated a million dollars for the purchase of pictures on condition that a like amount be raised privately. Largely through the efforts of Robert Lee Humber of Greenville, the Samuel H. Kress Foundation offered to match the appropriation with a gift of masterpieces, and the General Assembly of 1951 authorized its acceptance. Other paintings were acquired, and in 1956 one of the first state-supported art museums in the country was opened in a renovated state office building. Despite controversy, the museum grew in holdings and stature and in 1983 moved to a new building on the western edge of Raleigh. Several additional museums—notably the

Mint Museum of Art in Charlotte and the Ackland Art Museum at the university in Chapel Hill—exhibited paintings, sculpture, pottery, crafts, and other artistic works; and the Museum of Early Southern Decorative Arts at Old Salem displayed interiors and furnishings from historic homes in North Carolina and the southern states. Several 10-92 North Carolinians—notably Romare Bearden, 10-93 Hobson Pittman, and Francis Speight—won rec- 10-94 ognition while painting beyond the borders of the state.

The North Carolina Symphony struggled along after the war with a bare subsistence appropriation from the General Assembly, and its director, Benjamin F. Swalin, spent much of his time raising the additional funds that permitted the orchestra to carry to thousands of school children their first sound of live classical music. With the awakening of corporate support for the arts, however, the symphony was able to enhance its stature among North Carolinians, and this, in turn, stimulated greater legislative funding. In the late 1970s the orchestra, under direction of John Gosling, performed at Carnegie Hall and the Kennedy Center.

One of the few North Carolinians to succeed in opera was Norman Cordon who for ten years was a member of the Metropolitan Opera Company and in 1948 returned to North Carolina to promote operatic music through the classroom and via radio. Traditional music remained popular among North Carolinians, and the mountain region produced its share of self-trained performers. Perhaps 10-95 the best known of these was Arthel (Doc) Watson, a blind guitarist and vocalist who revived ancient 10-96 ballads. The string band, often accompanied by tap or square dancers, retained its appeal as country music. Among other North Carolinians who 10-97 gained national attention in music were John Coltrane, a premier jazz saxophonist from Hamlet; Ronnie Milsap, a blind pianist and vocalist who was reared in the Governor Morehead School in Raleigh; and Charlie Daniels, a native of Wilmington and leader of one of the most popular "Southern rock" bands.

The outdoor drama—virtually fathered by Paul Green—combined music, dance, acting, history, 10-98 folklore, and fiction. *The Lost Colony* remained the foremost production of this type, and Green wrote and helped produce a dozen or more other dramas across the country. Two mountain dramas by Kermit Hunter—*Unto These Hills* at Cherokee and *Horn in the West* at Boone—retained enormous

popularity year after year. Green himself was careful to explain the difference between his stories and history: He studied history, then created out of his own mind characters to illustrate the events. The Eleanor Dare of *The Lost Colony*, he pointed out, was his, not history's.

The outdoor dramas not only provided entertainment to audiences; they also afforded stage experience for aspiring new actors, some of whom—like Andy Griffith—were successful in Hollywood and on Broadway. If the Carolina Playmakers at Chapel Hill perhaps lost some of the luster of their halcyon days, they and other theatrical groups thrived on campuses and in the larger cities. In all the performing arts, the School of the Arts at Winston-Salem—unique as a state-supported cultural school—offered training and experience.

Intercollegiate athletics grew into big business in 10-99 the postwar era. Charlie (Choo-Choo) Justice of the 1948 UNC team was one of several players to earn All-American football honors. Some, like Sonny Jurgensen of Duke and Roman Gabriel of North Carolina State, were successful in the professional ranks. Smaller colleges, such as Elon, which twice won the NAIA gridiron championship, attracted many followers.

The region became a hotbed of indoor sports after Coach Everett N. Case made William Neal Reynolds Coliseum at NCSU the sports capital of the state. The Dixie Classic drew outstanding basketball teams, but when several players were implicated in a point-shaving scheme, school administrators ended the tournament. UNC won the NCAA championship in 1957 and 1982, and North Carolina State accomplished the goal in 1974 and 1983. North Carolina State became a 10-100 powerhouse in women's basketball in the late 1970s, and UNC's women were strong in soccer. Wake Forest was a leader in golf and baseball.

In track, Dave Sime of Duke and Jim Beatty and Tony Waldrop of UNC set records. Waldrop in 1974 ran a sub-four-minute mile in nine straight indoor races, then shunned the Olympics in order to pursue graduate studies in physiology. In the 1976 Olympics, Leroy T. Walker of North Car- 10-101 olina Central coached men's track and field events, and Dean Smith was the head coach of the United States' basketball team. Jim (Catfish) Hunter of Hertford and Gaylord Perry of Williamston were but two of a string of baseball players making good 10-102 in the major leagues. Both won the Cy Young

Award as their league's outstanding pitcher, and Perry in 1982 joined the select group of pitchers with victories in more than 300 games.

10-103 Spectator sports occupied only a portion of the leisure time of Tar Heels. Lakes created by power and flood-control dams provided freshwater opportunities for swimming, boating, water skiing, and fishing; and surfing joined swimming and fishing as popular pastimes along the seacoast. Golf and tennis were played throughout the state, and jogging became almost compulsive for great numbers of men, women, and children. Hang gliding was introduced both on Grandfather Mountain and on 10-104 the sand dunes of the outer banks, and snow skiing 10-105 became a tourist attraction in the mountains. Coun- 10-106 try clubs, resorts, recreational parks, camping facilities, and hiking trails multiplied, and the highways sometimes were crowded with mobile homes and trailers carrying boats or camping equipment. All the while neighborly traditions—Saturday afternoon shopping, night visits, quiltings, corn shuckings, ice cream parties, square dances, country barbecues, and wakes—faded into memory in the hurly-burly of new times and new habits.

In 1949, V. O. Key, Jr., a native of Texas then teaching at the Johns Hopkins University, published a book that profoundly influenced the way North Carolinians viewed themselves and their state. The press and politicians carried to Tar Heels who had never heard of the political scientist his assessment of the "prevailing mood" in North Carolina: "It is energetic and ambitious. The citizens are determined and confident; they are on the move. The mood is at odds with much of the rest of the South—a tenor of attitude and of action that has set the state apart from its neighbors. Many see in North Carolina a closer approximation to national norms, or national expectations of performance, than they find elsewhere in the South. In any competition for national judgment they deem the state far more 'presentable' than its southern neighbors. It enjoys a reputation for progressive outlook and action in many phases of life, especially industrial development, education, and race relations."*

At last North Carolina's claim to the title of most progressive state in the South bore an academic stamp of respectability. It was reassuring to North Carolinians, who felt that they had made wise use of their resources, had worked hard and taxed themselves heavily for governmental services,

and had lifted themselves up by their own bootstraps. Remembering their not altogether complimentary reputation as "the vale of humility between two mountains of conceit," they found strength in measuring their progress against the twin obstacles of humble beginnings and modest resources. They had come a long way, and by 1962, when the *National Georgraphic Magazine* characterized the state as the "Dixie Dynamo," Luther Hodges was serving in the president's cabinet and Terry Sanford's liberal programs were attracting national attention.

North Carolinians judged their image as selfearned. They were especially proud that they had created this "finer Carolina" within the traditions of the state whose penchant for independence and moderation had been exhibited throughout its history. For example, the people sent to the legislature a Catholic and a Jew, both of whom were banned from officeholding under the constitution in effect at that time; they elected a woman to the legislature long before they ratified the Nineteenth Amendment; and they authorized the resumption of liquor sales without ever ratifying the Twentyfirst Amendment. These actions were characteristic of a state whose motto is *Esse Quam Videri*, for they revealed a predilection for action over talk, substance over show, change for reason rather than for the sake of change. North Carolinians have always wanted to do things their own way.

They still do. However, their confidence in hard work and self-reliance has been severely tested by revolutionary transfers of power in the past two decades, and the angry shifting of voters from one extreme to the other in recent years betrays their frustration. As North Carolinians prepare to commemorate the four hundredth anniversary of English America, they face a challenge comparable to those of the 1860s and 1890s, when their response deviated from their tradition of moderation. The new challenge requires a renewed understanding of the elements that have formed the character, the personality, the soul of the state. If North Carolinians are true to their heritage, they will find a way of purging the irrational while accepting and incorporating into their native character those changes that will be adjudged, in years to come, wise, rational, and humane. Above all, they will be 10-107 faithful to their motto, *to be rather than to seem.* 10-108

*V. O. Key, Jr., *Southern Politics in State and Nation* (New York: Knopf, 1949), p. 205

10-2
His four immediate predecessors joined Kerr Scott for his inauguration as governor in 1949. Left to right are Joseph Melville Broughton (1941–45), Robert Gregg Cherry (1945–49), Scott, Clyde Roark Hoey (1937–41), and John Christoph Blucher Ehringhaus (1933–37). (Courtesy NCDA&H.)

10-1
William Kerr Scott (1896–1958), then commissioner of agriculture, stands in 1938 with his young son, Robert Walter Scott II. Within thirty years both would be elected governor—Kerr in 1948 and Robert in 1968, only the second set of father-son governors in the history of the state. Furthermore, their lieutenant governors were also father and son—Hoyt Patrick Taylor, Sr. and Jr. (Courtesy NCDA&H.)

10-4
The Good Health Association helped stimulate support for improved health standards and facilities. Rocky Mount native Kay Kyser joined with Frank Sinatra and Dinah Shore in recording "It's All Up to You" in 1946. (Courtesy North Carolina Collection.)

10-3
By referendum the voters approved a $200 million road bond program in 1949, and in the next four years 14,810 miles of "Scott Roads" were hard-surfaced—more than had been paved in the entire history of the state prior to that time. Here a Johnston County farm family watches the "black-topping" of their country road. (Courtesy North Carolina Department of Transportation.)

WHITE PEOPLE

WAKE UP

BEFORE IT'S TOO LATE

YOU MAY NOT HAVE ANOTHER CHANCE

DO YOU WANT?

Negroes working beside you, your wife and daughters in your mills and factories?

Negroes eating beside you in all public eating places?

Negroes riding beside you, your wife and your daughters in buses, cabs and trains?

Negroes sleeping in the same hotels and rooming houses?

Negroes teaching and disciplining your children in school?

Negroes sitting with you and your family at all public meetings?

Negroes Going to white schools and white children going to Negro schools?

Negroes to occupy the same hospital rooms with you and your wife and daughters?

Negroes as your foremen and overseers in the mills?

Negroes using your toilet facilities?

Northern political labor leaders have recently ordered that all doors be opened to Negroes on union property. This will lead to whites and Negroes working and living together in the South as they do in the North. Do you want that?

FRANK GRAHAM FAVORS MINGLING OF THE RACES

HE ADMITS THAT HE FAVORS MIXING NEGROES AND WHITES — HE SAYS SO IN THE REPORT HE SIGNED. (For Proof of This, Read Page 167, Civil Rights Report.)

DO YOU FAVOR THIS -- WANT SOME MORE OF IT?

IF YOU DO, VOTE FOR FRANK GRAHAM

BUT IF YOU DON'T

VOTE FOR AND HELP ELECT

WILLIS SMITH for SENATOR

HE WILL UPHOLD THE TRADITIONS OF THE SOUTH

KNOW THE TRUTH COMMITTEE

10-7
Supporters of Smith attacked Senator Graham as a radical who was soft on Communism and an advocate of the "mingling of the races." This poster was distributed throughout eastern North Carolina. (Courtesy North Carolina Collection.)

10-5 (top)
Frank Porter Graham (1886–1972), the outspoken liberal president of the University of North Carolina, was Scott's surprise choice to succeed Senator Broughton in 1949. In this picture, made about 1940 by freshman Hugh Morton, Graham is pitching horseshoes at Chapel Hill. (Courtesy Hugh Morton.)

10-6
Raleigh attorney Willis Smith (1887–1953), second from left in this photograph made during the dedication in 1948 of the monument to the three presidents born in North Carolina, was Graham's chief opponent in the Democratic primary in 1950. He won in a runoff. From left to right are Capus Waynick, who served as ambassador to Colombia and Nicaragua; Smith; President Harry S Truman; Governor R. Gregg Cherry; Kenneth C. Royall, last secretary of war and first secretary of the army; Senator Clyde R. Hoey; and Senator William B. Umstead. (Courtesy NCDA&H.)

10-8
George V. Allen (1903–70) of Durham, here with Shah Muhhammed Reza Pahlevi, was the American ambassador to Iran, 1946–48. In addition to their official relations, Allen and the young shah were avid tennis players. Later Allen was ambassador to Yugoslavia and India. (Courtesy Duke University Manuscript Department.)

10-10
Luther Hartwell Hodges (1898–1974) was both hard-driving businessman-governor and popular participant in social activities. Here in 1959 he crowns actress Debra Paget as queen of the Azalea Festival in Wilmington. In rear are Nancy Stovall, teenage princess, and Ronald Reagan, a motion picture and television actor. (Courtesy Hugh Morton.)

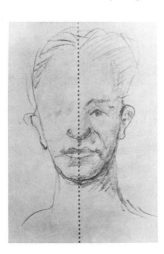

10-9
Gordon Gray (1909–82) of Winston-Salem succeeded fellow Tar Heel Kenneth C. Royall as secretary of the army in 1949. He later was president of the University of North Carolina, national security advisor to presidents, and chairman of the National Trust for Historic Preservation. This pencil sketch of Gray was made by President Dwight D. Eisenhower during a meeting of the National Security Council on 22 January 1958. (Reprinted, by permission, from Jo White Linn, *The Gray Family and Allied Lines* [Salisbury, 1976].)

10-11
The most vexing problem faced by Governor Luther H. Hodges in his more than six years as governor related to the Supreme Court's ruling against segregated schools. His dilemma was depicted by cartoonist Hugh Haynie in the *Greensboro Daily News*, 12 July 1956. (Courtesy NCDA&H.)

10-12
After winning a heated gubernatorial primary in 1960, Terry Sanford (b. 1917) broke with the majority of southern delegates to the Democratic National Convention and supported John F. Kennedy for the presidential nomination. In this photograph by Bruce Roberts, nominee Kennedy appears to be awed by the crowd outside the Charlotte Coliseum as he rides with Luther H. Hodges (left) and Sanford (right foreground). Hodges was appointed secretary of commerce in the Kennedy administration. (Courtesy Bruce Roberts.)

10-13
Governor Sanford (right) and Secretary of State Thad Eure (left) dressed in costumes for the commemoration of the three hundredth anniversary of the issuance of the Carolina Charter of 1663, but they hardly matched the headdress of Chief Osley Saunooke of the Eastern Band of the Cherokee Indians. In 1982, Eure broke Williams Hill's record for length of service of a state official, when he passed his forty-sixth year in office. (Courtesy NCDA&H.)

10-14
Controversy surrounded a highly publicized visit by President Lyndon B. Johnson to the farm home of William David Marlow near Rocky Mount on 7 May 1964. The Marlows, tenant farmers down on their luck, were selected to help demonstrate the president's "War on Poverty." Mrs. Marlow was quoted by the press after the visit: "We didn't ever feel like we were in poverty," adding, "we've been talked at, talked to, talked about, and throwed off on." She said she was instructed to have the children barefooted and a load of washing on the line when the president arrived. There was even an allegation that the White House staff thought Rocky Mount was in Appalachia. (Reprinted from Memory F. Mitchell, ed., *Messages, Addresses, and Public Papers of Terry Sanford . . .* [Raleigh, 1966].)

10-15
Governor Moore was present in Washington in March 1965 when President Johnson signed a bill establishing the Appalachian Regional Commission, which administered federal grants designed to benefit the counties of Appalachia. Standing, front row, are Senator Sam J. Ervin, Jr., Congressman Roy A. Taylor, Moore, and Senator B. Everett Jordan. (Courtesy NCDA&H.)

10-16
Reginald A. Hawkins (b. 1923), a Charlotte dentist, minister, and civil rights activist, received 129,808 votes in the Democratic gubernatorial primary in 1968. In the same race in 1972, his vote total was approximately halved, due to the competing candidacy of Wilbur Hobby, a white labor leader. (Courtesy NCDA&H.)

VOTE FOR . . .

HAWKINS

Candidate of Hope and Progress

• • • • •

GOVERNOR

10-17
Henry E. Frye (b. 1932), a Greensboro attorney and banker, was elected to the state house of representatives in 1968, the first black sent to the legislature in the twentieth century. He was a popular member of the lower house for six terms, then represented Guilford County in the state senate. In 1983, he was installed as the first black to serve as associate justice of the state supreme court. (Courtesy Shirley T. Frye, Greensboro.)

10-18
Under provisions of a constitutional amendment approved in a referendum in 1969, the General Assembly reduced the number of state administrative departments. Heads of the departments thereafter composed unofficially a "cabinet," which met for the first time in August 1972. Left to right seated in this photograph are Sam Ragan, Irvin Aldridge, Lenox Baker, Charles Bradshaw, Edwin Lanier, Henry Bridges, Governor Robert W. Scott, Edwin Gill, Frank Crane, William L. Turner, G. Andrew Jones, Fred Mills, George Randall, and John A. Lang. (Courtesy NCDA&H.)

10-19
A rare example of bipartisanship resulted in congressional action to place the New River in northwestern North Carolina in the Wild and Scenic Rivers System, thus saving it from being dammed in Virginia by a power company. The river is believed to be one of the oldest on the continent. (Courtesy Travel and Tourism Section.)

10-20
Howard N. Lee (b. 1934) of
Chapel Hill was the first
black elected in the twentieth
century as mayor of a predominantly white southern
city, and in 1976 he received,
in his losing campaign for
lieutenant governor, the
largest vote ever given a
Negro in the state's history—
229,195. He then served as
secretary of the Department
of Natural Resources and
Community Development in
the Hunt administration.
(Courtesy *News and Observer*;
photo by Karen Tam.)

10-21 (above right)
James Eubert Holshouser, Jr.
(b. 1934), a Republican attorney and legislator from
Boone, stunned political observers by winning the governorship in 1972. Four years
later the lieutenant governor,
James Baxter Hunt, Jr.
(b. 1937), regained the office
for the Democrats. Hols-
houser prepares to transfer
the great seal to his successor
(second from right) following inaugural ceremonies in
1977. Among those looking
on are Secretary of State
Thad Eure (left) and Carolyn
Leonard Hunt (right), the
new first lady. (Courtesy
NCDA&H.)

10-22
Governor Hunt poses on 17
February 1981 with his four
living predecessors at a din-
ner honoring William C.
Friday, president of the Uni-
versity of North Carolina,
and his wife, Ida H. Friday.
Left to right are Robert W.
Scott (1969–73), Terry San-
ford (1961–65), the Fridays,
Dan K. Moore (1965–69),
James E. Holshouser, Jr.
(1973–77), and Hunt.
(Courtesy *News and Observer*;
photo by Mike Sergeant.)

10-23
Senator Sam J. Ervin, Jr. (b. 1896), shown here with Senator Howard Baker of Tennessee during an informal meeting of the congressional committee whose investigation of the "Watergate" affair led to the resignation of President Richard M. Nixon, voluntarily retired to his Morganton home in 1974. (By permission of George Tames/ NYT Pictures.)

10-24
Over a caption "20 Years Ago You Wouldn't Have Seen . . . ," the *Charlotte Observer* on 14 March 1982 carried this photograph of, left to right, Phyllis Lynch, chairman of the Mecklenburg County Board of Elections; Phil Berry, chairman of the Charlotte-Mecklenburg Board of Education; F. B. Archie, captain in the Charlotte Fire Department; Robert Albright, vice-chancellor for student affairs at UNC-Charlotte; Stella M. Johnson, North Carolina National Bank branch manager; Richard T. Williams, cash management supervisor for Duke Power Company; Thebaud Jeffers, mayor of Gastonia; Clifton Johnson, first black judge of the state court of appeals; and LaFleur Paysour, music and drama critic for the *Charlotte Observer*. (By permission of the *Charlotte Observer*.)

10-25

Under federal court order, the University of North Carolina at Chapel Hill on 15 September 1955 admitted three blacks to the freshman class "with the same rights and privileges of those of other students." At the en-

trance to South Building after completing registration are, left to right, Leroy Frasier, 17, John Lewis Brandon, 18, and Ralph Frasier, 18, all of Durham. (Courtesy Roland Giduz, Chapel Hill.)

10-27

For several years before a settlement was negotiated in 1981, the United States Department of Education made repeated demands upon the University of North Carolina for program changes in an effort to accelerate integration on the various campuses. Cartoonist John Branch, a graduate of the university,

depicted President William Friday's plight in managing the system in the face of bureaucratic orders from Washington. (Reprinted, by permission, from John Branch, *Would You Buy a Used Cartoon from This Man?* [Chapel Hill, 1979]; originally published in *Chapel Hill Newspaper*.)

10-26

In 1961, Julius L. Chambers (left) was elected editor in chief of the *North Carolina Law Review* at the university's law school. He later became a prominent attorney in the

state. Other members of the staff are Francis Willett, William B. Rector, Jr., and Marlin Evans. (Courtesy North Carolina Collection.)

10-28

English E. Jones (1921–81), a Lumbee himself, administered Pembroke State University during its transformation from the nation's first state-supported all-Indian college to a fully integrated university in which whites outnumbered Lumbees. (Courtesy Bruce Roberts.)

10-29

A constitutional amendment—often referred to as the "Pearsall Plan"—was approved in a referendum in 1956. It authorized the General Assembly to provide means of delaying implementation of the Supreme Court's decision against segregated schools. Governor Luther Hodges was a strong supporter of the amendment. Hugh Haynie's cartoon appeared in the *Greensboro Daily News*. (Courtesy NCDA&H.)

10-30

A crowd of whites heckles Dorothy Geraldine Counts as the fifteen-year-old black was admitted to the eleventh grade class at Harding High School in Charlotte on 4 September 1957. She was one of a dozen Negro students admitted to formerly all-white schools in Charlotte, Greensboro, and Winston-Salem that year to begin the slow desegregation process in North Carolina. This particular student withdrew from Harding High School after several days of pressure, but others remained and were joined by more blacks in succeeding years. (By permission of the *Charlotte Observer*; photo by Jim Dumbell.)

10-32

Children often accepted integration and busing more readily than did parents. Here children of both races board a bus in Mecklenburg County in the early 1970s. (Courtesy Bruce Roberts.)

10-31

Opposition to busing children away from their neighborhood schools led to renewed protests in 1971. Here angry white mothers picket the Greensboro school board after that city adopted a system of cross-town busing to achieve racial balance. (Courtesy *Greensboro Daily News*; Nicholson photo.)

10-33

The beginnings of the "sit-ins" on 1 February 1960: Four students from North Carolina Agricultural and Technical College—Ezell Blair, Franklin McCain, David Richmond, and Joseph McNeil—are refused service at the lunch counter in F. W. Woolworth Company in Greensboro. The technique soon spread to other southern communities, and eventually color bars were lowered in public eating places. (Courtesy *Greensboro Daily News*.)

10-34

During a reunion on 1 February 1980, the four men who initiated the sit-ins twenty years before were served, amidst much media coverage, by the Woolworth store that eventually yielded to the movement. Sitting, left to right, are Joseph McNeil, David Richmond, Franklin McCain, and Jibreel Khazan (formerly Ezell Blair). Standing at left is Woolworth vice-president Aubrey Lewis. (By permission of United Press International.)

10-36

The demonstrations against segregation also drew counterdemonstrations. Pictured here during the Greensboro sit-ins is the Klan chaplain, George Dorsett, pastor of a Baptist church in Greensboro. Later accused of being an FBI informant, Dorsett was expelled from the Klan. (Courtesy *Greensboro Daily News*.)

10-35

A woman, protesting segregated theaters, leads demonstrators past the site of the last meetings of the Confederate cabinet in Charlotte in the early 1960s. (Courtesy Bruce Roberts.)

10-37

In 1982 Klan members marched around the state capitol in Raleigh to protest the imprisonment of white segregationist Lawrence R. Little, who was charged with firebombing the office of a black-owned Wilmington newspaper nine years earlier. (Courtesy *News and Observer*.)

10-38

On the night of 18 January 1958, a band of Lumbee Indians swooped down on a Ku Klux Klan rally near Maxton and with gunfire and war whoops scattered the Klansmen, who sought protection from the highway patrol. Two Lumbees—Charlie War- riax, left, and Simeon Oxen- dine, wearing his hat as district commander of the Veterans of Foreign Wars— display the KKK banner they captured during the rout. (By permission of Wide World Photos.)

10-39

Robert F. Williams jumped bail after a racial incident in Monroe and lent his name to a fiercely anti-American pub- lication, *The Crusader News- letter*, published in China, where he lived in exile before eventually returning to the United States. (Courtesy North Carolina Collection.)

10-40

After studying the evidence presented against nine black men and one white woman convicted of firebombing a white-owned grocery store during racial disturbances in Wilmington in 1971, Gover- nor Jim Hunt concluded that the trial had been a fair one, and he declined to pardon the "Wilmington Ten," though he did reduce the sentences. This photograph of the ten was made in Janu- ary 1976. The convictions were overturned on technical grounds by the federal court of appeals in 1980. (By per- mission of United Press International.)

10-41

Two supporters of the Communist Workers party, one in helmet and the other with a stick, walk past a fallen comrade following a gun battle during a "Death to the Klan" rally in Greensboro on 3 November 1979. Significantly, a television station's car is parked in the background. (By permission of Liaison Agency, New York.)

10-43

Susie Marshall Sharp (b. 1907) of Reidsville, the first woman to serve as a judge of the superior court, is shown (second from right) taking the oath of office on 1 July 1949, following her appointment by Governor W. Kerr Scott. The other judges taking the oath are, left to right, William T. Hatch, Harold Bennett, W. H. S. Burgwyn, George B. Patton, A. R. Crisp, Wilkins P. Horton, and W. I. Halstead. She was later elevated to the supreme court and finally to chief justice. (Courtesy NCDA&H; *News and Observer* photo.)

10-42

Two women supporters of the Communist Workers party arrive armed for a memorial march for the slain demonstrators on 11 November 1979. A national guardsman stands at right. (By permission of United Press International.)

10-44

Isabella Cannon, the first female mayor of a major North Carolina city, is pictured at a pro-ERA rally on 21 January 1979 with actor Alan Alda. She was defeated for reelection. (Courtesy *News and Observer*.)

10-45
The battle for ratification of the Equal Rights Amendment became more heated as it was repeatedly rejected by the General Assembly. This cartoon ran in the *Charlotte Observer* on 13 March 1975. (Courtesy *Charlotte Observer*.)

10-46
The vote board in the state senate tells the story of the rejection of the ratification bill in 1977. A light in the left column represented a vote for the bill. Some persons in the gallery appear stunned, some elated. (Courtesy United Press International.)

10-47
Anti-ERA forces, learning from their opponents, mastered the techniques of mass demonstrations. Here a little girl is enlisted in the cause. (Courtesy *News and Observer*.)

10-48
Among the companies expanding into North Carolina after the war was Western Electric. Here job-seekers wait in line at the company's Winston-Salem plant on 29 April 1946. (Courtesy Bill East Collection.)

10-49
Originally a tobacco company, R. J. Reynolds Industries branched out into a variety of products and built this modernistic world headquarters in Winston-Salem. (Courtesy R. J. Reynolds Industries.)

10-50
Skilled artisans continued in demand after industrialization. George Black started his brick company in Winston in 1900; at age 92 he was sent to Guyana to teach brick-making to the people of that newly independent country. (Courtesy Agency for International Development.)

10-51
Arthur Ray Cole (1893–1974) continued his work as a master potter at Sanford until his pottery fell victim to a new highway. He was one of a half dozen or so master potters who worked in Moore, Lee, and bordering counties. (Courtesy North Carolina Collection; photo by Diana Caplow.)

10-52
With large amounts of federal aid, Floyd McKissick (one of the first four blacks to be admitted to the University of North Carolina and later director of the Congress of Racial Equality) planned a model black "Soul City" in Warren County with a predicted population of 22,000 people by 1979. In 1979, as the Department of Housing and Urban Development prepared to foreclose on the project, the community had only 124 residents. This air view was taken in 1975. (Reprinted from *Information on the New Community of Soul City . . .* [Washington, 1975].)

10-53
W. Kerr Scott, the first farmer to attain the governorship in the twentieth century, is greeted during his inaugural in 1949 by Margaret Hood Caldwell. They had much in common: Scott had served as master of the State Grange, and both Mrs. Caldwell and her husband later held the position. (Reprinted from Stuart Noblin, *The Grange in North Carolina, 1929–1954* [Greensboro, 1954].)

10-55
Joseph Califano, secretary of the Department of Health, Education, and Welfare during the Carter administration, spearheaded an anti-smoking campaign. Dana Summers's cartoon depicts the joy of farmers when Califano left office in 1979. (By permission of *Fayetteville Times*.)

10-54
The grimy, back-tiring job of pulling or priming tobacco leaves from the stalks was largely replaced in the postwar period by automated tobacco harvesters. This one is at work near Garner. (Courtesy *News and Observer*.)

10-56
Hundreds of farmers, unhappy with low prices of their produce and high prices of their purchases, paraded in a tractorcade during President Carter's visit to Fayetteville in 1977. (Courtesy *Fayetteville Observer*; photo by Ken Cooke.)

10-57
Skiing became a popular pastime in the mountains. When natural snow was lacking, artificial snow was manufactured. Bruce Roberts captured this view of the first production of artificial snow at Hound Ears in the 1960s. (Courtesy Bruce Roberts.)

10-58
A new tourist attraction at Wilmington was the decommissioned battleship USS *North Carolina*, shown here being towed into the harbor on 2 October 1961 after Hugh Morton led a campaign for funds to provide for its preservation as a museum. (Courtesy Hugh Morton.)

10-61
This sleek new airport for Greensboro–High Point opened in 1982 only a few months after Charlotte's modern facility had begun operation. Raleigh–Durham constructed a second terminal. (Courtesy Greensboro–High Point Airport Authority.)

10-59
Oil companies developed their own distinctive logos, and the Shell Oil Company provided a unique design for this station at Peachtree and Sprague streets in Winston-Salem. (Courtesy NCDA&H.)

10-62
The camera at left, which cost more than $20,000, was used by television station WFMY-TV, one of the two first stations to go on the air in North Carolina in 1949 (the other was WBTV, Charlotte). Here, on 23 No-vember, the station telecasts the swearing-in ceremony as (left to right) Darrell Smith, Douglas Beesen, Muncie Wall, and Franklin Thomas are inducted into the army. (Courtesy WFMY-TV.)

10-60
Environmentalists lost their battle to block a mammoth open cut through Beau-catcher Mountain at Asheville. Here work is in progress; in the center is the entrance to Beaucatcher Tunnel, which had become a bottleneck as tourists streamed through the city. (Courtesy *Asheville Citizen-Times*.)

10-65
The legislature approved a second state-supported four-year medical school in 1974. Here after the opening of the East Carolina University School of Medicine, faculty members perform a kidney transplant on a patient at Pitt Memorial Hospital. (Courtesy East Carolina University School of Medicine.)

10-63
The quality of education offered to students depended heavily upon the competence and commitment of local school officials and teachers. For example, in 1981 students in Sunbury Elementary School in tiny Gates County regularly scored above the national average in reading, math, spelling, and language. This is a scene in the fourth grade; the teacher is Jane Rountree. (Courtesy *Greensboro Daily News.*)

Bookends

10-64
The intense competition for funds among supporters of the various state-supported colleges and universities led the General Assembly to bring the sixteen campuses under one board of governors. This cartoon appeared in the *News and Observer*, 23 February 1971. (Courtesy NCDA&H.)

10-66
President Harry S Truman, here accompanied by Secretary of the Army Gordon Gray (right) and greeted by Governor Kerr Scott, delivered the address at ground-breaking ceremonies for the new campus of Wake Forest College in Winston-Salem on 15 October 1951. (Courtesy *Winston-Salem Journal*; photo by Frank Jones.)

10-67
The Archie K. Davis Building housing the National Humanities Center in Research Triangle Park provides virtually a monastic setting for fellows chosen from various scholarly disciplines around the world. The Research Triangle claimed the highest percentage of Ph.D.s in the country. (Courtesy Kent Mullikin.)

10-69
The "speaker ban" act passed in 1963, which forbade the use of the facilities of state-supported colleges or universities by a Communist or anyone who had pleaded the Fifth Amendment in regard to subversive activities, was viewed by many academicians as interfering with the teaching of the social sciences. (Courtesy *Durham Morning Herald*.)

10-68
Junius Irving Scales, chairman of the Communist party in the Carolinas from 1947 to 1956, carried on some of his operations in Chapel Hill. In 1958 he was convicted in federal court a second time and sentenced to six years in prison for violating the Smith Act for advocating the violent overthrow of the government. He is shown here in October 1961 as he left the courthouse in New York to begin his sentence. (By permission of Wide World Photos.)

10-70
When, under provisions of the amended "speaker ban," the chancellor of the University of North Carolina at Chapel Hill for the second time rejected student requests for permission for Herbert Aptheker to speak on university property, an estimated two thousand persons gathered on the northern edge of the campus on 9 March 1966 as the Communist (extreme left) spoke from the Franklin Street right-of-way. (By permission of Wide World Photos, New York.)

10-71

Religious faith was demonstrated in an unusual way when, during an interstate convention of snakehandlers in Durham in October 1948, a woman lifts a huge serpent. At extreme right, partially cut off by the picture, the Reverend Colonel Hartman Bunn, pastor of Zion Tabernacle in Durham, wears one snake on his head and holds in his hands several wriggling copperheads and rattlesnakes whose venom sacs and teeth, laboratory tests revealed, were indeed in place. Bunn was sentenced to thirty days in jail for violating a municipal ordinance against handling poisonous reptiles. (Courtesy NCDA&H; photo by *News and Observer*.)

10-72

A weakening of the influence of Protestant churches was measured in 1978 when the General Assembly, by shrewd parliamentary maneuvers, revived and passed a bill authorizing local-option referendums on the sale of mixed drinks. Happy cartoonist John Branch graphically reported the results of the referendum in Orange County. (Reprinted, by permission, from John Branch, *Would You Buy a Used Cartoon from This Man?* [Chapel Hill, 1979]; originally published in *Chapel Hill Newspaper*.)

10-73

Billy Graham (b. 1918), a native of Charlotte and a resident of Montreat, drew millions to his sermons around the world. Here, with Grandfather Mountain in the background, he preaches to nearly 100,000 persons at the annual "Singing on the Mountain." (Courtesy Bruce Roberts.)

10-74
A few families on Hatteras Island maintain the tradition of celebrating Old Christmas with "Old Buck" as a central figure. The January date is a legacy of the Julian calendar, which was discarded in England in 1752. (Courtesy Travel and Promotion Section.)

10-76
Inglis Clark Fletcher (1879–1969) spent her early career exploring the wilds of Africa, then settled near Edenton and wrote a series of novels with settings in eastern North Carolina. In 1950 she helped organize the North Carolina Writers Conference. Here she poses (second from left) at the 1955 conference at Pisgah View Ranch with Jonathan Daniels (1902–81), left, and Bernice Kelly Harris (1894–1973) and Richard Gaither Walser (b. 1908), all prolific Tar Heel writers. (Courtesy Bernadette Hoyle, Raleigh.)

10-77
The most famous newcomer among the literati was Carl Sandburg, who lived in a historic house at Flat Rock and raised goats while continuing his writing. Here (left) he works with his biographer, Harry Golden, an adopted Tar Heel who, with tongue in cheek, coined the term "vertical integration," noting that desegregation was not objectionable to whites so long as members of both races were standing. (By permission of Tom Walters, Charlotte.)

10-75
Vermont Royster (b. 1914), who grew up in Raleigh, was the longtime editor of the *Wall Street Journal* before returning to Chapel Hill to teach in the School of Journalism and to write a syndicated column. (Courtesy North Carolina Collection.)

10-78

The most prestigious award for nonfiction given in North Carolina is the Mayflower Society Cup. In 1970, James H. Brewer (1920–74) became the second black to receive the award. Here he accepts the award from Mrs. William Thomas Powell, governor of the society, for his book, *The Confederate Negro*.

Other top literary prizes include the Sir Walter Raleigh award for fiction, the Roanoke-Chowan award for poetry, and the American Association of University Women award for juvenile literature. (Courtesy NCDA&H.)

10-79

As a young man, Paul Green (1894–1981), second from right, won a Pulitzer Prize for *In Abraham's Bosom*, then pioneered in writing outdoor dramas. He also spent several years in Hollywood writing screen plays. He and his wife, Elizabeth Lay Green, are shown here with United States Senator Robert Mor-

gan (from his home county of Harnett) on Green's eighty-fourth birthday (17 March 1978), when he received the North Caroliniana Society Award for outstanding contributions to North Carolina literature. (Courtesy Durham *Herald-Sun* Papers; photo by Jim Sparks.)

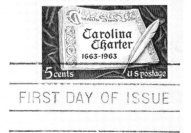

10-80

The Department of Archives and History in 1959 inaugurated the most comprehensive state-financed local records program in the nation. Unfortunately, some county and municipal records

had already been lost through fire, decay, neglect, or theft, but the surviving records provided rich sources for local history and genealogy. (Courtesy NCDA&H.)

10-81

The tercentenary of the Carolina Charter, commemorated nationally by a colorful postage stamp, was marked in the state by a low-keyed but dignified observance, including the beginning of a new Archives and History–State Library Building and a new series of the *Colo-*

nial Records of North Carolina. Simultaneously, the Confederate Centennial Commission conducted a commemoration of the state's role in the Civil War, the most lasting project of which was the beginning of a new roster of North Carolina troops in the Civil War. (Author's collection.)

10-84

The Town Creek Indian Mound in Montgomery County, dating back at least to the sixteenth century, was excavated and the ceremonial buildings reconstructed. In the background atop a mound is the major temple; the circular building in the foreground is a burial hut. (Courtesy NCDA&H.)

10-82

The workshop of David Marshall (Carbine) Williams was acquired by the State Department of Archives and History and reassembled in its Museum of History. Here in 1951 General Douglas MacArthur signs one of the rifles invented by the Cumberland County native, who appears in the foreground. MacArthur called the carbine "one of the strongest contributing factors in our victory in the Pacific." (Courtesy NCDA&H.)

10-83

Somerset, the Josiah Collins II house on Lake Phelps, was restored, furnished, and opened to the public by the State Department of Archives and History as one of approximately two dozen state historic sites. One of the canals that drained the land is seen in foreground. (Courtesy Bill Edwards, NCDA&H.)

10-85

Charlotte's first skyscraper, the Independence Building, was reduced to rubble in 1982. Interest in historic preservation and liberalized tax incentives, however, led to the adaptive use of many serviceable structures. The Sir Walter Hotel in Raleigh, for example, was converted to apartments. (By permission of *Charlotte Observer*.)

10-86
Even the state government joined the preservation movement by saving and moving the Capehart-Crocker House from the path of new public buildings near the State Legislative Building. The Archdale Building is at right. (Courtesy Ken Cooke, *Fayetteville Observer*.)

10-87 (middle)
Dorton Arena on the State Fairgrounds in Raleigh helped usher in a new era in architectural style. Critics ridiculed the building as the "Cow Palace" until it was acclaimed nationally for its engineering and stylistic innovations. (Courtesy NCDA&H.)

10-88 (bottom)
The pyramid-domed State Legislative Building, designed by Edward Durrell Stone in association with Holloway-Reeves and opened in 1963, was followed by other public buildings of modern design. Left to right in left background are the Administration Building and the Albemarle Building, and in the right foreground the Archives and History–State Library Building and the Bath Building. The historic headquarters of the Raleigh and Gaston Railroad to the right of the Albemarle Building was moved to make way for an additional series of structures. (Courtesy NCDA&H.)

10-89
In the Research Triangle Park the Burroughs Wellcome Building, designed by Paul Rudolph, provides a striking landscape from Interstate 40. Many of the other buildings in the park also were innovatively designed. (Courtesy Burroughs Wellcome Company.)

10-90
Affluent North Carolinians built summer homes by the thousands along the Atlantic coast. Two air views—the one at left made in 1964, the one at right made in 1971—show the rapid development of Pine Knoll Shores on Bogue Banks. (Reprinted from Simon Baker, *Aerial Photography for Planning and Development in Eastern North Carolina* [Raleigh, 1976].)

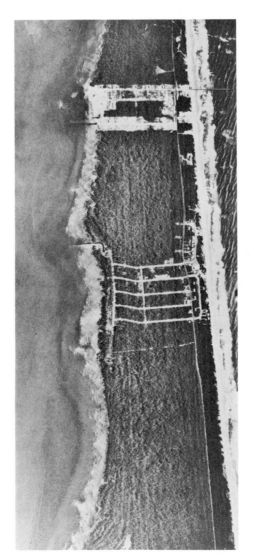

10-91
The awesome force of nature took its toll as periodic hurricanes and storms swept the coast. Here is the result of the Ash Wednesday Storm that hit Nags Head Beach in March 1962. (Courtesy David Stick; photo by Aycock Brown.)

10-92
Romare Bearden was born in Charlotte in 1914, and he visited that city often while growing up in the North. With a degree in mathematics, he turned to art, and he became one of the nation's best-known black artists. This is his collage on board titled *Carolina Shout*, 1974. (Courtesy Mint Museum of Art, Charlotte; photo by Geoffrey Clements, Staten Island.)

10-93
Francis Speight (b. 1896) of Bertie County taught art in the North before returning to North Carolina. His favorite subjects included scenes in his native state, like this oil painting (1965) of the Sans Souci ferry. (Courtesy North Carolina Museum of Art.)

10-94

Many North Carolinians painted for pleasure rather than profit. One was professional musician and historian Lillian Parker Wallace (1890–1971), professor at Meredith College, who painted this watercolor, "Sunday Morning in Milton, N.C.," in 1951. (Author's collection.)

10-96

Frank Proffitt (1913–65) was another popular mountain musician. Here in 1959 he and his wife's great aunt, Buna Hicks, play on the porch of a Beech Mountain home as Ray Hicks dances. (Courtesy Anne Warner; photo by Frank Warner.)

10-95

Arthel (Doc) Watson (b. 1923), a blind musician from Watauga County, began his musical career with a five-string banjo made by his father. He also mastered the guitar and became a popular vocalist. (Courtesy Bruce Roberts.)

10-97

John Coltrane (1926–67) was born in Hamlet and grew up in High Point. In 1965 he was *Down Beat*'s tenor saxophonist of the year. He died two years later. (By permission of Music Division, The New York Public Library at Lincoln Center, Astor, Lenox, and Tilden Foundations.)

10-98
William Samuel (Andy) Griffith (b. 1926), at right in this scene during the early 1950s, started his professional acting career in *The Lost Colony*, Paul Green's pioneering outdoor symphonic drama at Fort Raleigh. Lillian Prince plays the part of Queen Elizabeth I; Sylvia Cox is the female page. (Courtesy David Stick; photo by Aycock Brown.)

10-99
The earnestness of intercollegiate athletics is illustrated by these two youngsters cheering on the Tar Heels in Kenan Stadium, Chapel Hill. (Courtesy North Carolina Collection.)

10-100
North Carolina State University's basketball team ended UCLA's long NCAA reign in 1974 and then defeated Marquette 76–64 for the national championship. Members of the team and staff are, left to right: front row—Coach Norman Sloan, Monte Towe, Morris Rivers, Bruce Dayhuff, Coach Art Musselman; second row—Coach Eddie Biedenbach, All-American David Thompson, Greg Hawkins, Dwight Johnson, Craig Kuszmaul, Coach Sam Exposito; back row—Steve Nuce, Tommy Burleson, Tim Stoddard, Mike Burrma, Mark Moeller, Phil Spence, Bill Lake, Manager Biff Nichols. (Courtesy NCSU Sports Information Office.)

10-101
Leroy T. Walker's remarkable record in developing outstanding sprinters and hurdlers at North Carolina Central University was recognized in 1976 when he was picked as head coach for the men's track and field events for the United States Olympic team. In 1983, Walker was appointed acting chancellor of the university. (Courtesy Durham Chamber of Commerce.)

10-102
Jackie Robinson, who broke the color barrier in the major leagues in 1947, played one of his first games with Brooklyn against the Dodgers' farm team in Asheville. The mountain city was chosen when exhibition games were canceled in Jacksonville and Atlanta for fear of racial violence. Here in McCormick Field the young player joins his manager, Chuck Dressen (left), in objecting to an umpire's call. (Courtesy *Asheville Citizen-Times*; photo by June Glenn, Jr.)

10-103
"King Richard," as Richard Petty of Level Cross was sometimes called, followed in the path of his father as a stock car racing star; his son Kyle also carried on the family tradition. Here Petty leads cheers of fellow Republicans in Randolph County, where he was elected county commissioner in 1978. (Reprinted, with permission, from *Randolph County 1779–1979* [Asheboro, 1980].)

10-104
The popular sand dune, Jockey's Ridge near Kitty Hawk, was a favorite launching place for adventuresome hang gliders in the 1970s. (Courtesy J. Foster Scott, Manteo.)

10-105 and 10-106

Aycock Brown of Manteo devoted his career of more than a half century to observing and photographing North Carolina people, scenes, and events. On the night of 20 July 1969, he set up his camera, framed in the lens the quarter-moon and the Wright Brothers Memorial, turned on his portable radio, and waited. At the precise moment when astronaut Neil Armstrong stepped upon the moon, Brown snapped this picture commemorating the first powered flight and the first human contact with the moon. (Left, reprinted, with permission, from David Stick [editor], *Aycock Brown's Outer Banks* [Norfolk, 1976]; photo by Emory Kristoff. Right, courtesy Aycock Brown.)

10-107
The old saying that politics stops at water's edge was demonstrated—literally—by Senator Jesse Helms, left, and Governor James B. Hunt, Jr., who joined in efforts to save the historic Cape Hatteras Lighthouse from the encroaching Atlantic Ocean. Leaders, respectively, of the Republican and Democratic parties in the state, Helms and Hunt appeared headed for an epic race in 1984 for the seat held for a dozen years by Helms, the first Republican senator elected from North Carolina in this century. (Courtesy Hugh Morton.)

10-108
The quintessence and the innocence of the North Carolina character are captured by four youngsters gaily walking along a rocky country lane near Winston-Salem in the mid-1970s, toting their fishing rods, a can of worms, and a chain of fish. The leader, the only one with shoes, whistles contentedly, oblivious to—or unbothered by—the symbol of the Confederate flag worn on the cap of a companion. By the year 2000, North Carolina will be governed by the generation represented by this quartet of black and white youths sharing an outdoor experience. (Courtesy Jane Corey, author of *North Carolina: a Camera Profile* [Chapel Hill, 1976]; photo by and with permission of Charles Buchanan, *Winston-Salem Journal*.)

Index